PAUL'S EARLY PERIOD

PAUL'S EARLY PERIOD

Chronology, Mission Strategy, Theology

by

Rainer Riesner

translated by

Doug Stott

WILLIAM B. EERDMANS PUBLISHING COMPANY
GRAND RAPIDS, MICHIGAN / CAMBRIDGE, U.K.

© 1998 Wm. B. Eerdmans Publishing Co.
255 Jefferson Ave. S.E., Grand Rapids, Michigan 49503 /
P.O. Box 163, Cambridge CB3 9PU U.K.

Printed in the United States of America

02 01 00 99 98   7 6 5 4 3 2 1

Translated from the German edition,
Die Frühzeit des Apostels Paulus,
© 1994 J. C. B. Mohr (Paul Siebeck), Tübingen

Library of Congress Cataloging-in-Publication Data

Riesner, Rainer, 1950-
Paul's early period: chronology, mission strategy, theology / Rainer Riesner.
p.   cm.
A revision of the author's thesis (doctoral — Eberhard Karl University, 1991)
presented under title: Die Frühzeit des Apostels Paulus.
Includes bibliographical references and indexes.
ISBN 0-8028-4166-X (alk. paper)
1. Paul, the Apostle, Saint.
2. Bible. N.T. Acts — Chronology.
3. Bible. N.T. Epistles of Paul — Chronology.
4. Bible. N.T. Thessalonians, 1st — Theology.
I. Title.
BS2506.R57   1998
225.9′2
[B] — DC21   96-53634
                                      CIP

To my wife Cornelia
for our first seven years
(Eph. 3:17)

Contents

Foreword

Chronology is the backbone of history, including that of the early Church. In the last fifteen years there has been not only much discussion but even confusion regarding the chronology of the apostle Paul. The present study was accepted as my *Habilitationsschrift* in the Winter Semester of 1990/91 by the *evangelisch-theologische Fakultät* of the Eberhard Karl University in Tübingen. A revised form was published in 1994 under the title *Die Frühzeit des Apostels Paulus. Studien zur Chronologie, Missionsstrategie und Theologie* in the series *Wissenschaftliche Untersuchungen zum Neuen Testament.* Through the considerable kindness of Professor Peter Stuhlmacher (Tübingen) I was able to begin this work already during the time I served as his assistant. The *Deutsche Forschungsgemeinschaft* then supported me with a two-year stipend from 1987 to 1989, during which period the leadership of the Lutheran Württemberg *Landeskirche* granted me a generous sabbatical. Professor Martin Hengel offered much encouragement and many valuable suggestions, and Professor Earle E. Ellis promoted this American edition.

Besides some corrections this edition contains only some minor additions to the German version. Among other things I refer to literature that was published since the German original was completed at the end of 1993. To interact with all the work done, especially in the last two years, could have delayed the book far too long. Here I would like to single out four works to which I was not able to do justice. Marie-Émile Boismard, Arnaud Lamouille, and Justin Taylor's *Les actes des deux apôtres* (Paris, 1990ff.) is a challenging example of subtle literary criticism. But with the majority of scholars I am not convinced of its most important presupposition, namely, the originality of one version of the so-called Western text in the Acts of the Apostles (see P. Head, "Acts and the Problem of Its Text," in Bruce W. Winter and Andrew D. Clarke, eds., *The Book of Acts in Its Literary Setting* [Grand Rapids and Carlisle, 1993] 415-44). Two new contributions strongly support my general view of Pauline chronology. Martin Hengel and Anna Maria

Schwemer's *Paul between Damascus and Antioch* (London, 1997) is extremely rich in information. And Helga Botermann's *Das Judenedikt des Kaisers Claudius* (Stuttgart, 1966) is by far not limited to the problem in its title. Theologians have much to learn from this professor of ancient history at the University of Göttingen, who treats Luke-Acts as a rather reliable source. The series The Book of Acts in Its First Century Setting (Grand Rapids and Carlisle, 1993ff.), edited by Bruce W. Winter (Tyndale House, Cambridge), will prove to be a landmark in research on Acts. One would like to see a similar work on the question of the so-called "historical Jesus."

This book would not have been possible without the support of our "extended family." My brothers-in-law Andreas, Johannes, and Christoph Schilling, as well as my wife Cornelia, assisted on the computer. Their invaluable help saved me an enormous amount of time, which I was then able to devote to actual research. Vicars Paul-Gerhard Roller and Ernst Nestele and his wife Mag. Theol. Maria Nestele, as well as university students Stefan Bischoff and Christian Grewing, also provided important support. Doug Stott has done a tremendous job of translating this book. I had to correct only one sentence, and this because the German original was unclear! My gratitude also goes to the staffs of Mohr-Siebeck in Tübingen and Eerdmans in Grand Rapids. Among others I would like to mention Jill Sopper, who made many friendly contacts across the Atlantic.

It was a great privilege to do research in Thessalonica from September to November 1988. My contact with Albertos Nar of the Center of Historical Studies of the Judaism of Thessaloniki was of great value. It is sad to recall that until the Second World War Thessalonica had one of the strongest Sephardic congregations in the area of the Mediterrannean. Professors Joannis Karavidopoulos and Joannis A. Galanis of the Greek Orthodox faculty helped me greatly. Above all, however, my wife and I will never forget the hospitality of the Evangelical congregation of Thessalonica and its pastoral husband-and-wife team, Stelios and Tassoula Kaloterakis. They reminded us of the words of the apostle concerning his own Macedonian congregations (2 Cor. 8:11ff.).

RAINER RIESNER

Abbreviations

Abbreviations follow S. Schwertner's *Internationales Abkürzungsverzeichnis für Theologie und Grenzgebiete* (Berlin/New York, 1974). Additional abbreviations include:

AAA	Ἀρχαιολογικὰ Ἀνάλεκτα ἐξ Ἀθηνῶν (Athens)
ABD	*Anchor Bible Dictionary*
A1CS	The Book of Acts in Its First Century Setting, ed. Bruce W. Winter (Grand Rapids and Carlisle)
AncMac	*Ancient Macedonia* (Thessalonica)
ANRW	*Aufstieg und Niedergang der römischen Welt* (Berlin/New York)
AW	*Antike Welt* (Feldmeilen)
Beginnings	*The Beginnings of Christianity,* ed. F. J. Foakes-Jackson and K. Lake; London, 1920-33)
BCR	*Biblioteca di cultura religiosa* (Brescia)
BMC	*British Museum Catalogue* (London)
BN	*Biblische Notizen* (Munich)
Compendia	Compendia Rerum Judaicarum ad Novum Testamentum (Assen)
DaM	*Damaszener Mitteilungen* (Mainz)
EDNT	*Exegetical Dictionary of the New Testament* (Grand Rapids)
FEUNTK	*Forschungen zur Entstehung des Urchristentums, des Neuen Testaments und der Kirche* (Kiel)
FGNKAL	T. Zahn, *Forschungen zur Geschichte des neutestamentlichen Kanons und der altkirchlichen Literatur* (Leipzig)
GBL	*Das Große Bibellexikon* (Wuppertal)
GNS	*Good News Studies* (Wilmington)

IBD	*Illustrated Bible Dictionary* (Leicester)
IGRR	Inscriptiones Graecae ad Res Romanas pertinentes
ISBE	*International Standard Bible Encyclopedia* (Grand Rapids)
JET	*Jahrbuch für evangelikale Theologie* (Wuppertal)
JRA	*Journal of Roman Archeology* (London)
JSHRZ	*Jüdische Schriften aus hellenistisch-römischer Zeit* (Gütersloh)
JSNT	*Journal for the Study of the New Testament* (Sheffield)
JSNTSup	*Journal for the Study of the New Testament (Supplement Series)* (Sheffield)
JSOTSup	*Journal for the Study of the Old Testament (Supplement Series)* (Sheffield)
JSPSS	*Journal for the Study of the Pseudepigrapha (Supplement Series)* (Sheffield)
Mak	Μακεδονικά (Thessalonica)
MAMA	*Monumenta Asiae Minoris Antiqua* (London)
MBib	*Le Monde de la Bible* (Paris)
NEB	*Neue Echter Bibel* (Würzburg)
NewDoc	*New Documents Illustrating Early Christianity* (Macquarie University)
NIGTC	*New International Greek Testament Commentary* (Grand Rapids)
NTOA	*Novum Testamentum et Orbis Antiquus* (Freiburg [Switzerland]/Göttingen)
OBO	Orbis Biblicus et Orientalis (Freiburg [Switzerland]/Göttingen)
SBAB	Stuttgarter Biblische Aufsatzbände (Stuttgart)
SBLDS	Society of Biblical Literature Dissertation Series (Chicago)
Schuerer	E. Schuerer, *The History of the Jewish People in the Age of Jesus Christ* I-III/1-2 (revised and ed. G. Vermes, F. Millar, and M. Black; Edinburgh, 1973-87)
SEG	Supplementum Epigraphicum Graecum (Leiden)
SIMA	Studies in Mediterranean Archaeology (Göteborg)
SJLA	Studies in Judaism in Late Antiquity (Leiden)
TANZ	*Texte und Arbeiten für neutestamentlicher Zeitgeschichte* (Tübingen and Basel)
TB	Theologische Beiträge (Wuppertal)
TSAJ	Texte und Studien zum antiken Judentum (Tübingen)
WBC	Word Biblical Commentary (Waco)

INTRODUCTION
Chronologies and Theologies

Any history of the early church without access to a sufficient number of fixed chronological points will lack the necessary supporting framework, and any attempt to reconstruct the edifice of the history of primitive Christianity without taking into consideration this framework easily ends up building castles in the air. A description of the first thirty years of the primitive church is largely a description of the course of Paul's life. But the apostle's biography deserves more than merely our historical attention. The doctrinal convictions of the New Testament emerged from that which human beings received from God in quite specific situations in history, and which through crises and other struggles they sought to preserve as basic insights. This applies in a special way to Paul, who shaped his own theology within those particular challenges that confronted him as a missionary and founder of congregations. The apostle's theological insights were also subject to historic development, though Paul would have challenged the notion that the insights he received from God simply lost their validity amid changing circumstances. To view the Pauline statements within their historical context does not necessarily mean to relativize them. It is precisely the person seeking binding answers from the apostle who will gratefully acknowledge any historical aids to understanding.

If, however, Pauline theology and chronology are indeed interrelated, then the words of A. Suhl are applicable: "Anyone who from the outset is unwilling to forgo a genuinely historic understanding of Paul's letters is directed to an overall view of the Pauline corpus. If in so doing one is satisfied merely with a relative chronology, the danger arises that although the sequence of individual letters is fixed, their actual temporal separation from one another is left undetermined, and in the final analysis one does, after all, end up explaining the individual letters in and for themselves merely on the basis of their various situations."[1] Outlines that explain the apostle's theological development in part on the basis of the length of certain time spans show that various chronologies

1. *Paulus und seine Briefe* (1975) 338.

1

can indeed give rise to various Pauline theologies. Such explanations are especially dependent on a persuasive chronological framework. Because the history of early Christianity and the development of its theological convictions are inseparably connected, Pauline chronology belongs to the prolegomena of New Testament theology.

§1

Status of Scholarship: A Survey

1.1. From Multiplicity to Relative Consensus

1.1.1. The Early Critical Period

A glance at the chronologies advocated by well-known scholars during the early critical period of scriptural exegesis shows just how significant was the finding of that particular inscription dating the administration of the Achaian proconsul Gallio (Acts 18:12; §11). As representatives of the period from the beginning of the seventeenth to the middle of the nineteenth centuries, we will mention the views of the Catholic C. Baronius (1538-1607), the Anglican J. Ussher (1581-1656), the Reformed thinker S. Basnage (1638-1721), the Pietist J. A. Bengel (1687-1752), the rationalist J. G. Eichhorn (1752-1827), and K. Wieseler (1813-83), the author of what is even today an interesting chronological study.[1] This schema follows the framework of five journeys to Jerusalem as provided by Acts (Acts 9:26; 11:29f.[12:25]; 15:2-4; 18:22; 21:15):

	Baronius	Ussher	Basnage	Bengel	Eichhorn	Wieseler
Crucifixion	32	33	33	30	32	30
Conversion	34	35	37	31	37/38	40
Jerusalem I	37	38	40	33	40/41	43
Jerusalem II	42	44	42	41/44	44	45
Jerusalem III	49	52	50	47	52	50
Corinth	50	54	51	48	54	52
Jerusalem IV	52	56	53	49	56	54
Ephesus	53-55	56-59	53-55	50-52	57-59	54-57
Jerusalem V	56	60	56	53	60	58
Festus	56	62	59	55	62	60

1. The following dates are taken from his "Chronologically Comparative Table of the Apostolic Church of the New Testament," *Chronologie des apostolischen Zeitalters* (1848) after 606. Cf. also K. Wieseler, *Brief Pauli an die Galater* (1859) 553-600 (Excursus

All these attempts were hindered by the lack of any absolute date for anchoring Pauline chronology. Even the crucifixion of Jesus ranged from 30 to 33 B.C. depending on the different determinations for the Passover date (§3). The differing information provided by ancient church tradition regarding Paul's conversion (one to two or seven years after the crucifixion of Jesus [§4]) led to additional divergence. The apostle's conversion was assumed to have taken place variously between A.D. 31 and 40. The connection between the second Jerusalem journey (Antiochene collection [Acts 11:29f.; 12:25]) and the year of the death of Herod Agrippa I (Acts 12:20-23), which earlier scholars were already able to determine with some approximation (§7.2), also helped in determining this more closely. Dates for the second journey to the holy city differed by at most five years (between A.D. 41 and 45). The various interpretative possibilities (§17.1.3) allowed by the time spans mentioned in Acts and Galatians (Gal. 1:18 [in Jerusalem three years after his conversion]; 2:1 [again in Jerusalem fourteen or seventeen years after his conversion]) then raised the maximal difference between dates to seven years. According to Bengel, Paul came to Jerusalem for the last time in A.D. 53, whereas Ussher and Eichhorn dated this visit no earlier than A.D. 60. Because of contradictions in the ancient sources (§12.4), the secular-historical date of the Judean transfer of power from Felix to Festus (Acts 24:27) was also unable to ameliorate the differences here.

1.1.2. The Situation at the Turn of the Century

Let us look first at the period immediately preceding the publication of the Gallio-inscription by E. Bourguet in the year 1905.[2] Again, six scholars can serve as representatives[3]: the liberal Protestant A. von Harnack,[4] the conservative T. Zahn,[5] the mediating G. Hoennicke,[6] the American B. W. Bacon,[7] the conservative Englishman W. M. Ramsay,[8] and the Catholic J. E. Belser.[9]

---

on Chronology). Additional surveys of the chronological outlines of early scholars can be found in G. Wandel, *ZKWKL* 9 (1888) 176; C. Clemen, *Die Chronologie der paulinischen Briefe* (1893) 292; D. Plooij, *De chronologie van het leven van Paulus* (1919) table II after 174.

2. *De rebus delphicis imperatoriae aetatis capp.* II (1905) 63.

3. Additional bibliographical information from this period can be found in A. J. and M. B. Mattill, *A Classified Bibliography on the Acts of the Apostles* (1966) 220-32; B. M. Metzger, *Index to Periodical Literature on the Apostle Paul* (²1970) 4f.

4. *Chronologie der altchristlichen Litteratur* I (1897) 236f.

5. *Einleitung in das Neue Testament* II (1900) 644-47; cf. translation of third edition, *Introduction to the New Testament* (Eng. trans., 1909) 3.450-80.

6. *Chronologie des Lebens des Apostels Paulus* (1903) 70f.

7. *Exp* V/10 (1899) 412-30.

8. *St. Paul the Traveller and the Roman Citizen* (1897) 395f.

9. *Einleitung in das Neue Testament* (²1905) 399-407; 426-30; 444f.; 518f.

Here, too, the basis is the outline in Acts with the five Jerusalem journeys, and the beginning of what is known as the first missionary journey is also given (Acts 13–14):

	Harnack 1897	Ramsay 1897	Bacon 1899	Zahn 1900	Hoennicke 1903	Belser 1905
Crucifixion	29(30)	30	30	30	30 (33)	30
Conversion	30	33	31(34)	35	33 (35)	33
Jerusalem I	33	35	33(36)	38	36 (38)	36
Jerusalem II	(44)	45/46	—	44	45 (46)	46
Mission I	45	47	44-46	50	49	46
Jerusalem III	47	49/50	47	52	50 (52)	49/50
Corinth	48	51	50	52	52	51
Jerusalem IV	50	53	(51/52)	54	54	53
Jerusalem V	54	57	55	58	57 (59)	58
Festus	56	59	57	60	59 (61)	60

Things had become clearer insofar as most scholars, as a result of improved astronomical calculations, advocated A.D. 30 as the year of Jesus' death, though dates of A.D. 29 and 33 were also introduced into the discussion. One additional factor contributing to this more unified dating was the fact that ancient church tradition concerning Paul's conversion was now accorded little attention, attempts being made instead to determine Paul's chronology primarily on the basis of the information given in Acts and Galatians. Commensurate with the various interpretative possibilities and the uncertainty attaching to the point of departure (Paul's conversion), the dates now diverge up to five years. As before, the date of Festus' accession to power offered no help, since ancient historians similarly advocated different datings. Occasionally, even the framework of Acts itself was abandoned, for example, when B. W. Bacon deleted as unhistorical Paul's second visit, that is, the Antiochene collection journey (Acts 11:29f.; 12:25).

1.1.3. From 1905 to 1980

The following overview shows how much the discovery of the Gallio-inscription contributed to a mitigation of differences regarding the middle phase of Pauline chronology. This overview encompasses the schemata of ten scholars as different as D. Plooij,[10] K. Lake,[11] A. Wikenhauser,[12] F. Hahn,[13]

10. *De chronologie van het leven van Paulus* (1919) table II after 174.
11. In *BC* V (1933) 467-74.
12. *New Testament Introduction* (Eng. trans., 1958) 351-61.
13. *Das Verständnis der Mission im Neuen Testament* (1963) 74-79.

D. Georgi,[14] G. Ogg,[15] W. G. Kümmel,[16] E. Haenchen,[17] F. F. Bruce,[18] and M. Hengel.[19] This selection is centered in the 1960s and 1970s for the sake of clearly demonstrating a relative consensus[20] for this period.

	Plooij	Lake	Wiken.	Hahn	Georgi	Ogg	Küm.	Hae.	Bruce	Hengel
Crucifixion	29	29	(30)	27	30	33	(30)	30	30	
Conversion	30/33	32/33	34	28/31	35	35	31/32	35	33	32/34
Jerusalem I	32/33	37	(37)	38	34/35	37/38	35	34/36		
Jerusalem II	45/46	—	45	46/48	—	45/46	—	—	46	—
Mission I	46		46			46			47	
Jerusalem III	48	46	49	43/44	48	48	48	48/49	49	48
Corinth	50	49/50	51	49/50	49/50	50	49	49/50	50	49/50
Jerusalem IV	52	51/52	54	(51)	(52)	53	51/52	(51/52)	52	(51/52)
Jerusalem V	57	55	58	56	56	59	55/56	55	57	56/57
Festus	59	56	60	58	58	61		55	59	58

Discounting for a moment F. Hahn's divergent early dating of the Apostolic Council (see below, p. 121), the datings have come noticeably closer together. The most frequently assumed year for the crucifixion is A.D. 30, and the apostle's conversion is usually dated relatively early. As a rule, Paul's second visit to Jerusalem mentioned in Acts is regarded as unhistorical. Regarding the middle phase around the first visit to Corinth, dates differ at most by three years. As before, the accession to power of Festus is given widely differing dates (maximum six years). Regarding the methodological concurrence of these scholars, W. G. Kümmel noted in a pregnant formulation "that the sequence of Paul's missionary activities that can be inferred from his letters is so remarkably compatible with the information from Acts that we have good grounds for deriving the relative chronology of Paul's activity from a critical combination of the information from Paul's letters with the account in Acts."[21] Since the 1970s, however, chronologies differing from this relative consensus are increasingly finding favor, chronologies which in part appropriate the suggestions of somewhat eccentric scholars of the past.[22] Even if

14. *Die Geschichte der Kollekte des Paulus für Jerusalem* (1995) 91-96.

15. *The Chronology of the Life of Paul* (1968) 200.

16. *Introduction to the New Testament* (Eng. trans., 1975) 252-55.

17. E. Haenchen, *Acts* (Eng. trans., 1971) 66f.

18. *Paul* (1977) 475.

19. *Zur urchristlichen Geschichtsschreibung* (1979) 8.

20. Just how W. R. Farmer, *JBL* 101 (1982) 296, can speak of a "German consensus" is a complete mystery.

21. *Introduction to the New Testament* (Eng. trans., 1975) 254. Similarly also P. Vielhauer, *Geschichte der urchristlichen Literatur* (1985) 71f.

22. In my opinion, the history of scholarship shows (§1.4.1-3) that J. Knox, *Chapters in a Life of Paul*, rev. ed. (1987) 42, note 11, underestimates the significance of these predecessors.

overlapping transitions are evident, recently suggested chronological outlines can be divided into three categories according to their treatment of the framework of Acts.

1.2. Preservation of the Framework of Acts

There has always been a minority of scholars who consider all of Paul's visits to Jerusalem as portrayed in Acts to be historical. The problems generated here can be seen in the fact that the framework of Acts is harmonized in extremely varied ways with the information in the letter to the Galatians. After 1970, such attempts were made in more extensive studies especially by J. J. Gunther,[23] J. van Bruggen,[24] D. Moody,[25] and C. J. Hemer:[26]

	Gunther (1972)	Bruggen (1973)	Moody (1981)	Hemer (1989)
Crucifixion	30	33	30	
Conversion	31	35/37	36	32/33
Jerusalem I	33/34	(37/38)	39	35/36
Jerusalem II	44		46	46/47
Mission I	46/47	48/48	47/48	
Jerusalem III	48/49	47/48	49	49
Corinth	50/51	49/50	49	50
Jerusalem IV	52/53	51	51	52
Jerusalem V	57		55	57
Festus	59		57	59

At first glance, these four chronologies seem to deviate only slightly from the variations customary within the relative consensus discussed earlier. In reality, however, three completely different reconstructions of events underlie these outlines. As perhaps already John Chrysostom (*Ad Gal* 2.1 [MPG 61:633])[27] and Martin Luther in his commentary on Galatians (*WA* 40/I, 151-55), and then especially K. Wieseler,[28] J. van Bruggen equates Gal. 2:1-

---

23. *Paul: Messenger and Exile* (1972) 15f. (Chronological Table).

24. *"Na veertien jaren"* (1973) 233-39 (English Summary).

25. In *Festschrift J. Finegan* (1989) 223-40. This volume appeared six years late (*ibid.*, VII), which probably explains why D. Moody does not yet take into account the work of G. Lüdemann. The most recent title is dated 1981 (*ibid.*, 266, note 10). The *Festschrift* is called *Chronos, Kairos, Christos*; in view of the utterly divergent positions represented there, however, *Chronos and Chaos* would also have been a fitting title.

26. *The Book of Acts in the Setting of Hellenistic History* (1989) 251-70.

27. Challenged by V. Weber, *Die antiochenische Kollekte* (1917) 79f.

28. *Chronologie des apostolischen Zeitalters* (1848) 201-8.

10 with Acts 18:22, and in so doing even displays a measure of sympathy with a scholar otherwise utterly different from him, namely, J. Knox (§1.4.4).[29] As first of all apparently John Calvin,[30] and then especially W. M. Ramsay,[31] so also J. J. Gunther and C. J. Hemer equate Gal. 2:1-10 with Acts 11:29f. and Acts 12:25.[32] By contrast, D. Moody's identification of Gal. 2:1-10 with Acts 15 follows the majority opinion.

1.3. Corrective to the Framework of Acts

The three chronologies worked out by A. Suhl,[33] R. Jewett,[34] and S. Dockx[35] go beyond the largely accepted elimination of Paul's second Jerusalem visit as described in Acts. The sequence of their outlines is oriented toward the dates their own main works appeared. The preliminary studies[36] and various editions of their comprehensive presentations were published over such a long span of time that the three authors were able mutually to criticize one another.[37] Although they all reckon only with those three visits to Jerusalem specified in Paul's letters (Gal. 1:18; 2:1; Rom. 15:26-28),[38] for the rest they differ considerably from one another. In the following table, Jerusalem I-III stands for these three visits to Jerusalem,

29. Other advocates of this identification can be found in J. van Bruggen, *"Na veertien jaren"* (1973) 166-99; R. K. Jewett, *A Chronology of Paul's Life,* 78-87.

30. *Commentarius in Epistolam ad Galatas, CR* 78, 182.

31. So, e.g., in *A Historical Commentary on St. Paul's Epistle to the Galatians* (²1900).

32. Concerning other representatives of this view, see R. K. Jewett, *A Chronology of Paul's Life,* 69-75; R. Y. K. Fung, *The Epistle to the Galatians* (1988) 16-22.

33. *Paulus und seine Briefe,* 314-38 (Summary). A. Suhl strengthens his case in *NTS* 38 (1992) 430-47 and in *ANRW* II, 26.2 (1995) 939-1188 (without reference to my work).

34. *A Chronology of Paul's Life,* diagram after 160. R. Jewett would classify himself among those advocating outlines that depart from the framework in Acts in the lineage of J. Knox (§1.4) and not among the "compromise chronologies" he himself decisively rejects (in B. C. Corley, *Colloquy on New Testament Studies* [1983], 271-84). With some justification, however, J. Knox (*ibid.,* 361-64) and his student J. C. Hurd (*ibid.,* 266-69) dispute that this relationship is indeed one of affinity.

35. *Chronologies néotestamentaires et Vie de l'Église primitive* (²1984) 399-403 (Table chronologique générale, Synopse chronologique).

36. E.g., R. Jewett, *Paul's Anthropological Terms* (1971) 11-48; S. Dockx, *NT* 13 (1971) 261-304; *RB* 81 (1974) 183-95.

37. Cf. A. Suhl, *Paulus und seine Briefe,* 305-14; R. Jewett, *A Chronology of Paul's Life,* 73-75; S. Dockx, *Chronologies néotestamentaires* (²1984) 391-97.

38. S. Zeitlin, *JQR* 57 (1966/67) 171-78, deserves credit for having made do with only two trips to Jerusalem (Gal. 1:18; 2:1).

M I-III for the three Lukan missionary journeys (Acts 13–14; 16–18; 19–20):

Suhl		Jewett		Dockx	
30	Crucifixion (27) Conversion			30	Crucifixion
32/33	Jerusalem I	33	Crucifixion		
		34	Conversion		
				35	Conversion
				36/37	Martyrdom of Stephen
		37	Damascus Jerusalem I	37	Damascus Jerusalem I
		37-43	Syria Cilicia	37-47	Syria Cilicia
43/44	Jerusalem II	43	Antioch		
		43-45	Cyprus Galatia (M I)		
		46	Antioch		
		46-49	Galatia Macedonia (M II)		
47/48	Antioch		Jerusalem II	47/48	Antioch
				48	Jerusalem II
48/49	Galatia Macedonia (M II)			48/49	Antioch Macedonia (M II)
49	Corinth			49	Corinth
		50	Corinth		
51	Gallio	51	Gallio	51	Gallio
				51-54	Ephesus (M III)
52-54	Ephesus (M III)				
54-55	Corinth	53-55	Ephesus (M III)	54-55	Corinth
55	Jerusalem III Festus	55	Jerusalem III		Festus
		56-57	Corinth		
		57	Jerusalem III		
		59	Festus		

Here, too, the fundamental importance of the Gallio-incident is evident, where we encounter the greatest degree of chronological agreement. The considerable deviations in the periods before and after derive from two factors:

1. Different individual dates possess special significance. For R. Jewett and S. Dockx, this is the apostle's flight from Damascus under the ethnarch of Aretas (2 Cor. 11:32f.), which they date at A.D. 37 (§5). A. Suhl and S. Dockx assert that a change of office in the Judean procuratorship from Felix to Festus (Acts 24:27) can be securely dated at A.D. 55 (§12.4). For both of them, a Sabbatical year figured at A.D. 54/55 (§5.5.2) also plays an important

9

role in determining the date of the final journey to Jerusalem to deliver the collection.

2. Each of the three scholars ascribes a different value to Acts as a source. Although R. Jewett does repeatedly emphasize the methodological priority of Paul's letters as primary sources over the secondary witness of Acts, he does consider their we-accounts to be the recollections of eyewitnesses (albeit redactionally reworked).[39] Thus Jewett, too, follows the framework of Acts most closely by maintaining the three missionary journeys, though he does believe that because of time constraints the Apostolic Council mentioned in Gal. 2:1-10 must be arranged in place of the third Lukan visit to Jerusalem (Acts 18:22) (§16.2.2). By contrast, he appraises the value of the chronological information in Acts 20–28 as extremely high (§12.2-5), and arrives from that point of departure at his own reconstruction of Paul's final period. S. Dockx, too, reckons with a reworking of authentic travel notes, though at the same time also with even more extensive redactional activity, activity which in keeping with French tradition he attempts to disclose with the utmost literary-critical care. A. Suhl appraises Acts most highly as a secondary source. Thus he feels free to date the apostolic assembly of Gal. 2:1-10 as early as the time immediately preceding the death of Agrippa I (Acts 12) (§7.2.2). Between the Apostolic Council (Gal. 2:1) and the Antiochene incident, Suhl assumes a span of about five years, while Paul travels from Antioch to Corinth in less than a year (§16.2.2). Suhl's chronology provides the transition to outlines that become completely independent of the framework of Acts and use only individual dates from that source.

1.4. Abandonment of the Framework of Acts

1.4.1. Gustav Volkmar

Two factors played a role in the emancipation from the historical portrayal of Acts: the assumption of a framework largely artificially constructed by Luke, and the application of an evolutionary schema to Paul's own letters. The first aspect was still extremely prominent in the work of G. Volkmar, who used a

---

39. *A Chronology of Paul's Life,* 7-24. R. Jewett has been accused of inconsistency in the use of his own premise regarding the absolute priority of Paul's letters; see esp. J. Knox, in B. C. Corley, *Colloquy on New Testament Studies* (1983) 361-64, though also G. Lüdemann, *JBL* 103 (1984) 118-21. Reservations prompted by different factors have also been expressed by, among others, G. B. Caird, *JTS* 31 (1980) 170-72; J. W. Drane, *JSNT* 9 (1980) 70-75; A. J. M. Wedderburn, *ET* 92 (1981) 105-7; H. Paulsen, *ThZ* 40 (1984) 85-57. J. R. Armogathe, *Paul* (1980) 207-9, largely follows Jewett.

sharp literary-critical eye in analyzing Luke's portrayal.[40] He viewed both Acts 11:29f. and Acts 15:2ff. as doublets to a Jerusalem trip that allegedly took place in a completely different period. But what Volkmar takes from Luke with one hand he then takes beyond him with the other. After the Apostolic Council, he maintains, the apostle allegedly undertook yet two collection journeys to the holy city! Volkmar came up with the following equations:

Gal. 1:18	=	Acts 9:26
Gal. 2:1	=	Acts 21
Gal. 2:10	=	Acts 24:17
1 Cor. 1:6-9	=	Acts 20:4ff.

Volkmar's recreation of Pauline chronology has (as yet) found no followers. His outline, however, might serve as a warning against putting too much faith into one's own constructions as opposed to preserving a certain skepticism toward Luke.

1.4.2. Carl Clemen

This scholar was the first to establish a consistent connection between the literary-critical dissolution of the framework of Acts and a reconstruction of Pauline chronology on the basis of the doctrinal developments evidenced in the letters. A certain conservative element attaches to Clemen's reconstruction by way of his assumption that some sections of the Pastoral Epistles represent genuine fragments of Paul. Here his outline demonstrates a certain similarity to the attempt of J. J. Gunther (§1.2), who despite his basically conservative posture does not shy away from dividing certain letters internally.[41] Thorough investigations led Clemen in 1893 to the following pattern of Pauline activity:[42]

---

40. *Paulus von Damaskus bis zum Galaterbrief* (1887) 22-79. The chapter heading reads "A Walk through Both Acts, Paul's and Luke's in Connection with the Apostolic Dispute." A thorough critique of this can be found in A. Hilgenfeld, *ZWTh* 31 (1888) 1-29.

41. *Paul: Messenger and Exile* (1972) 16 (Chronological Table). Despite the proximity of such argumentation, C. Clemen is not mentioned in J. J. Gunther. F. J. Badcock followed a similar method in *The Pauline Epistles and the Epistle to the Hebrews in Their Historical Setting* (1937). It was probably the ensuing world war that caused this perspicaciously and interestingly presented chronology of Paul to remain completely ignored.

42. *Die Chronologie der paulinischen Briefe* (1893) 285f. (Survey of Paul's Apostolic Activity).

11

37	Conversion	
40	Jerusalem I	
40-*ca.* 45	Galatia (M I)	
ca. 45-50	Greece, Antioch, Galatia, Ephesus (M II)	
47/48	Corinth	1 Thess.
48		2 Thess.
49 (?50)	lost Cor.	
50-52	Ephesus	
50		1 Cor.
51		2 Cor. 9
		2 Cor. 10–13
52-54	Greece	
52		2 Cor. 1–8
52/53	Nicopolis	Titus 3:12-14
53/54	Corinth	Rom.
54	Jerusalem II (Council)	
	Antioch	
after 54		Gal.
ca. 56	Asia Minor	2 Tim. 4:9-18
58	Jerusalem III	Phil. I, Col., Phlm.
		2 Tim. 4:9-18
61	Rome	2 Tim. 1:15-18
63/64 (?)		Phil. II
64	Martyrdom	

Although Clemen anticipated at least two essential elements of unconventional contemporary chronologies (European mission before the Apostolic Council, Galatians after Romans), he is hardly mentioned in recent works.[43] His attempt, too, might represent a warning against trusting too much in an evolutionary reconstruction of Pauline theology, since later (1904), in an extensive monograph on Paul, Clemen retracted in every form essential parts of his own undertaking ("in certain passages I had to polemicize against myself here"[44]), and presented a rather conservative chronology for the apostle:[45]

43. Exceptions include J. Knox, *JBL* 58 (1939) 18, note 6; G. Lüdemann, *Paulus, der Heidenapostel I* (1980) 21f., note 11; R. Jewett, *A Chronology of Paul's Life,* 131, 141.

44. *Paulus: Sein Leben und Wirken* I (1904) VII. This fulfilled the hope that J. Weiss, *ThStKr* 68 (1895) 296, had already expressed in the following words: "May it please the author to rein in his great gifts and knowledge, as well as his unusual powers of association, and to place them in the service of strict and simple exegesis and criticism that restricts itself to what is actually possible."

45. *Ibid.,* 349-410 (411: Chronological Survey of Paul's Life).

31	Conversion	
34	Jerusalem I	
42/43	Antioch	
43-47	South Galatia (M I)	
48	Jerusalem II (Council)	
49-52	Asia Minor	
	Greece (M II)	
50		Gal.
51		1/2 Thess.
53-59	Ephesus, Greece (M III)	
56		1 Cor.
57		2 Tim. 4:19-22; 2 Cor. 10–11; 1–9;
		Titus 3:12-15
59		Rom.
59-61	Jerusalem III, Caesarea	
59/60		Col., Phlm.
61		2 Tim. 4:9-18
62-64	Rome	
62		2 Tim. 1:15-18
63		Phil.
64	Martyrdom	

Whatever one may think of the details of this reconstruction, Clemen in any case provided us with a noteworthy example of how a renowned scholar is able to change his views on the basis of new insights. Furthermore, Clemen's change of heart is also an indication that the trend away from the framework of Acts may not necessarily be irreversible.

1.4.3. Ernst Barnikol

Using similarly extensive literary-critical techniques not only with regard to Acts, but also in Paul's letters themselves, this scholar developed a new chronological schema in a series of treatises that are, unfortunately, extremely difficult to read.[46] His procedure of exploiting Acts as a quarry for the raw material of a completely unconventional chronology was made easier by the assumption that Acts was not composed until about A.D. 135. Barnikol deduced the following series of events:[47]

46. *Die vorchristliche und frühchristliche Zeit des Paulus* (1929); *Die drei Jeru-salemreisen des Paulus* (1929); *Personen-Probleme der Apostelgeschichte: Johannes Markus, Silas und Titus* (1931); *Römer 15 — Letzte Reiseziele des Paulus: Jerusalem, Rom und Antiochien* (1931); *Die Christwerdung des Paulus in Galiläa und die Apostelberufung vor Damaskus und im Tempel* (1935).

47. Summaries: *Die drei Jerusalemreisen des Paulus* (1929) 62f. (Tabular Overview); *ThJb(H)* 1 (1956) 16-20.

Crucifixion of Jesus	36
Paul's Conversion in Galilee	38
Jerusalem I	40
"Pentecost," Emergence of the Hellenist Church	41
Martyrdom of Stephen	43
Paul in Antioch	45/46
Cyprus, South Galatia with Barnabas	46/47
Galatia, Macedonia, Corinth	48/51
Jerusalem II	51
Persecution of the Hebrews-Church, Death of the Zebedees, Peter's Flight	51/52
Jerusalem III	57

Barnikol, whose methodological rigor is especially emphasized by R. Jewett[48] and N. Hyldahl,[49] was more radical than almost every other critic of Acts insofar as he not only challenged the connection between Paul's conversion and the persecution of the Hellenists (§4.3.1), but also eliminated any connection between the martyrdom of the Zebedee James and the reign of Agrippa I (§7).

1.4.4. John Knox and His Students

A whole section of the history of research into Pauline chronology as well as its problematic was embodied in the person of this scholar (1900-1990). Knox's original point of departure was the view that the "revelation fourteen years ago" (2 Cor. 12:2) refers to the Damascus event. Thus the same period would be at issue as in Gal. 2:1 ("after fourteen years" [i.e., after his conversion]).[50] In this case, Knox's teacher, D. W. Riddle, allowed his own pupil to persuade him. On the basis of Knox's chronological premises and assuming that developments did take place in Pauline theology, Riddle[51] then came up with a sequence for the apostle's letters. Other modern scholars[52] influenced by Knox, such as C. H. Buck and G. R. Taylor,[53] as well as J. C. Hurd,[54] tried

48. *A Chronology of Paul's Life,* 80f.
49. *Die paulinische Chronologie* (1986) 2.
50. *JR* 16 (1936) 341-49; *JBL* 58 (1939) 15-29.
51. *Paul — Man of Conflict* (1940).
52. Concerning the influence exerted by his writings, cf. J. C. Hurd, *FS J. Knox* (1967) 225-34; J. Knox, in B. C. Corley, *Colloquy on New Testament Studies* (1983) 341-45; D. R. A. Hare, in J. Knox, *Chapters in a Life of Paul,* rev. ed. (1987) IX-XIX. Individual studies influenced by J. Knox include P. S. Minear, *AThR* 25 (1943) 389-96; C. H. Buck, *JBL* 70 (1951) 113-22; R. W. Funk, *JBL* 75 (1956) 130-36; M. J. Suggs, *NT* 4 (1960) 60-68.
53. *Saint Paul: A Study in the Development of His Thought* (1969) 21-175.
54. *CJT* 14 (1968) 189-200; *IDB Supplement* (1976) 166f.

the same thing. Compared with the final version of the hypothesis of Knox,[55] their results appear as follows:

Riddle	Buck-Taylor	Hurd	Knox
Jerusalem I	Jerusalem I	Jerusalem I	Jerusalem I
1 Thess.	2 Thess.	1 Thess.	1 Thess.
2 Thess.	1 Thess.	2 Thess.	2 Thess.?
1 Cor.		Lost Cor.	
Col., Phlm.			Col.?, Phlm.?
Phil. (1–2; 4)			
Jerusalem II	Jerusalem II	Jerusalem II	Jerusalem II
2 Cor. 10–13	1 Cor.	1 Cor.	Phil. ?
Gal.	2 Cor. 10–13		1 Cor.
Phil. (3:2-16)	Phil.	Phil.	
	2 Cor. 1–9	2 Cor. 1–9	2 Cor.
	Gal.	Gal.	
Rom.	Rom.	Rom.	Rom.
		2 Cor. 10–13	
Jerusalem III	Jerusalem III	Jerusalem III	Jerusalem III
	Col., Phlm.	Col., Phlm.	Gal.
	Jerusalem IV		

Picking up on the title of the book by D. W. Riddle, one is tempted, in the face of this overview, to use the formulation "chronologies in conflict." It is quite obvious that a considerable element of subjectivity is involved in the evaluation of developments within the corpus of Pauline letters.[56] The relatively strong agreement between Buck and Taylor as well as Hurd derives also from that fact that Hurd worked out his own sequence simply according to the majority principle (within the Knox school). By contrast, Hurd had in an earlier study expended considerable effort supporting the assertion that the lost letter to the Corinthians (cf. 1 Cor. 5:9) was composed immediately after the Apostolic Council.[57] According to Knox, the absence of any reference to the collection even allows Colossians and Philemon (as well as Phil. 1–2; 4) to be dated before the Apostolic Council, though he considers equally possible the imprisonment in Caesarea or Rome — if the letter to the Colossians is not simply inauthentic in the first place.

Knox weighs the possibility that the letter to the Galatians was composed after that to the Romans, perhaps even during the imprisonment in Caesarea,

55. *Chapters in a Life of Paul,* rev. ed. (1987) 71-73.
56. Cf. V. P. Furnish, *JAAR* 38 (1970) 289-303; J. W. Drane, *TynBul* 27 (1976) 3-26.
57. *The Origin of I Corinthians* (1969) 240-74.

15

since the dispute with the Judaizers allegedly came to a climax after the last visit to Jerusalem.[58] It is not clear just how this is related to his thesis that Gal. 2:10 (μόνον τῶν πτωχῶν ἵνα μνημονεύωμεν, ὃ καὶ ἐσπούδασα αὐτὸ τοῦτο ποιῆσαι) is referring to the one-time collection of 1 Cor. 16:4 and Rom. 15:25-32,[59] which would already have been delivered if one assumes a late date for the letter to the Galatians.[60] Considering that the letter to the Galatians, because of its abrupt treatment of the question of the law, has recently been viewed as Paul's oldest letter and dated before the Apostolic Council (see p. 290 below), the relativity of the evolutionary argument once again becomes quite evident.

The only really stable sequence is that involving 1 Thessalonians — 1 Corinthians — 2 Corinthians (with variations of division within the letter) — Romans, a sequence that does, however, emerge from information contained in the letters themselves and without any developmental schema (see pp. 231-34 below). Yet even this sequence has been called into question by a developmental argument. According to J. R. Richards, the stronger expectation of the parousia in the first letter to the Corinthians shows, among other things, that it is to be dated *after* the letter to the Romans.[61] Hence it is difficult to see the reasoning behind the emphatic assertion of J. C. Hurd: "The suggestions which scholars have made about the sequence of the letters from internal evidence all agree with one another."[62]

Subsequent to his initial attempts, Knox revised his own chronological arguments and suggestions regarding several essential issues. His doubts concerning previous chronologies had been aroused by the equation of the two periods of fourteen years in Gal. 2:1 and 2 Cor. 12:2 (see p. 14 above), though Knox later abandoned this identification.[63] Whereas he originally figured the two periods of three (Gal. 1:18) and fourteen years (Gal. 2:1) taking the conversion as the point of departure,[64] Knox now considered it possible to understand these only as ongoing calculations (together approximately seventeen years).[65] Since Knox elsewhere reckons with the fact that scholars seek out interpretative

---

58. *JBL* 58 (1939) 27f.; *IDB* II (1962) 338-43; *Chapters in a Life of Paul,* rev. ed. (1987) 62.

59. *Chapters in a Life of Paul* (1987) 36-40.

60. Here J. Knox could have drawn on the work of D. R. Hall, *ET* 82 (1970/71) 309-11, who understands ἐσπούδασα as a past perfect, though at the same time he identifies the collection — which has already been concluded — with Acts. 11:29f.; 12:15.

61. *NTS* 13 (1966/67) 14-30 (esp. 27f.).

62. In B. C. Corley, *Colloquy on New Testament Studies* (1983) 331. J. C. Hurd refers in this context to his own article in *CJT* 14 (1968) 189-200.

63. *Chapters in a Life of Paul* (1987) 34f., note 1. This was yet only a possibility in *Chapters in a Life of Paul* (1950) 78, note 3.

64. *JBL* 58 (1939) 15.

65. *Chapters in a Life of Paul* (1987) 34, note 1.

possibilities commensurate with their own finished chronological schemata, one might pose the question whether he was bound to remain with this consecutive understanding for the sake of regaining the three years he surrendered elsewhere (namely, at Paul's conversion) (see below on this page). As the following overview shows, Knox also modified other dates in his schema over the years:[66]

	1939	1950	1987
Crucifixion			30
Conversion	37	34 (37)	34
Jerusalem I	40	37 (40)	37
Macedonia, after			40
Corinth, after			43
Ephesus, after			46
Jerusalem II	51	51	51
Corinth			53/54
Jerusalem III	53	53 (54)	54 (55)

Knox's methodological rigor is impressive. His argumentation becomes thin when specific dates are at issue, while that is the pronounced strength of the work of R. Jewett, whom Knox criticizes as inconsistent. When Knox[67] considers even G. Lüdemann's treatment of Acts to be too conservative, one must emphasize that Knox himself draws at least the absolute dates of his own chronology from Acts alone, although he understood them to be a response to Marcion and thus dates them in the third quarter of the second century.[68] The evaluation of Acts takes place in a more apodictic fashion strongly contrasting the otherwise customary methodological skepticism ("third, to establish the probability of the dates 34 and 54 [or dates in their close neighborhood] for the beginning and the end, respectively, of Paul's career").[69] For the first date, Knox presupposes without further discussion a crucifixion date of A.D. 30 (§3), and then concludes further from the spread of Christianity at the apostle's conversion as far as Damascus (and according to Knox also as far as Antioch): "Time must be allowed for the development of that phase of the movement. Thus, A.D. 34 is a more probable date for Paul's conversion than any earlier year."[70]

---

66. Cf. the tables in J. Knox, *JBL* 58 (1939) 23; *Chapters in a Life of Paul* (1950) 85; *Chapters in a Life of Paul* (1987) 68.

67. In B. C. Corley, *Colloquy on New Testament Studies* (1983) 359-61.

68. *Marcion and the New Testament* (1942; ²1980). Concerning J. Knox's treatment of Acts, cf. J. B. Tyson, in M. C. Parsons and J. B. Tyson, *Cadbury, Knox, and Talbert* (1992) 55-80; J. T. Townsend, *ibid.*, 81-89.

69. *Chapters in a Life of Paul* (1987) 53.

70. *Ibid.*, 46.

Really? Why, given the close connection between the two Jewish groups (see p. 88 below), should the new messianic faith not have spread faster from Jerusalem to Damascus? Elsewhere, *ca.* three years are sufficient in Knox's opinion for Christianity to spread across approximately twice the distance from Antioch to Galatia.[71]

Knox derives his date for Paul's final journey directly from Acts, which associates Paul's imprisonment in Caesarea with the change in Judean procuratorship from Felix to Festus (Acts 24:27). The rationale Knox offers here should be kept in mind during the following investigation: "Although there is no corroborative evidence for this statement in the letters, there is no contradictory evidence, and there seems to be no adequate reason for distrusting it."[72] Among the dates discussed in connection with the change in procurators, Knox prefers A.D. 55, since later dates are allegedly dictated only by an effort to balance out this date with the rest of Pauline chronology. This assertion can be shown to be false (§12.4). On the other hand, A.D. 55 is the only date possible within Knox's own outline. In order to defuse the Gallio-date as a criterion for his chronology, Knox[73] is quite generous in determining the proconsul's administrative tenure between A.D. 50-54 (§11), though he also considers it possible that Luke invented the incident in the first place.[74] If commensurate with his own principle one then asks just which statement within Paul's letters contradicts this information in Acts, one must answer: the chronology Knox himself has stipulated for the apostle, a chronology to which the latter must kindly adhere.

1.4.5. Charles H. Buck and Greer Taylor

Whereas Riddle and Hurd do without any absolute chronology, Buck and Taylor depend on an unusual combination of dates.[75] They identify the "man of lawlessness" (ὁ ἄνθρωπος τῆς ἀνομίας) of 2 Thess. 2:3 with Caligula, the "one who restrains" him (ὁ κατέχων) in 2 Thess. 2:7 with Claudius, and the divine chastisement of the Jews (1 Thess. 2:16) with the famine that occurred in Judea in A.D. 46 (§8). Hypotheses such as these are piled one on top of another in such a way that the emerging chronological schema[76] seems a less than stable edifice:

71. Cf. *ibid.,* 59.
72. *Chapters in a Life of Paul* (1987) 46.
73. *Ibid.,* 68f.
74. *Ibid.,* 69.
75. *Saint Paul* (1969) 145-62.
76. *Ibid.,* 214f.

18

32	Conversion	
35	Jerusalem I	
40/41	Galatia, Macedonia	
44		2 Thess.
46	Corinth	1 Thess.
	Jerusalem II (Council)	
	Antioch	Lost Cor.
47	Galatia	
	Ephesus	1 Cor., 2 Cor. 10–13, Phil.
	Macedonia	2 Cor. 1–9, Gal.
	Corinth	Rom.
48	Jerusalem III (Collection)	
49-52	Ephesus	Col., Phlm., Eph.
52/53	Corinth (Gallio)	
53	Jerusalem IV	
55	Festus	

R. Jewett justifiably asks why, according to this reconstruction, Paul, quite contrary to his own plans in Rom. 15:22-24 (§15.5), turned his attention once again to the east (Jerusalem IV).[77] It is also doubtful whether this additional journey is sufficient to rescue the Gallio-date (§11). Furthermore, in view of the distances involved one wonders whether the apostle did not overextend himself in the years A.D. 46/47 (§16.2.2-3). Finally, Buck and Taylor do not address the dating — one advocated by many scholars — of the crucifixion in A.D. 33, which would render their own chronology impossible at its very point of departure.

1.4.6. Gerd Lüdemann

The most thorough attempt at a chronology for the most part not dependent on the framework of Acts is that presented by Gerd Lüdemann.[78] Because of its thorough and multidimensional treatment of the problems, this outline has prompted not only much criticism,[79] but also unequivocal concur-

77. *A Chronology of Paul's Life,* 78.
78. *Paulus, der Heidenapostel I: Studien zur Chronologie* (1980). *Paul: Apostle to the Gentiles: Studies in Chronology* (Philadelphia, 1984) (with a foreword by J. Knox, xiiif.).
79. Cf. A. Lindemann, *ZKG* 92 (1981) 344-49; A. J. M. Wedderburn, *ET* 92 (1981) 105f.; *SJTh* 20 (1981) 87-91; H. Hübner, *ThLZ* 107 (1982) 741-44; M. Rese, *ThZ* 38 (1982) 104-9; R. Jewett, *A Chronology of Paul's Life,* 81-85; R. A. Wild, *Bibl* 65 (1984) 423-26; K. Grayston, *JTS* 37 (1986) 180-82; K. W. Niebuhr, *ZdZ* 41 (1987) 299f.; I. H. Marshall, *The Acts of the Apostles* (1992) 87-95.

rence.[80] The particulars of Lüdemann's outline can be demonstrated clearly in a simplified overview of his results.[81]

27 (30)	Crucifixion of Jesus	
30 (33)	Return to Damascus	
33 (36)	Jerusalem I	
34 (37)	Syria and Cilicia	
	South Galatia (together with Barnabas)	
ca. 36 (39)	Independent Pauline Mission	
	Philippi, Thessalonica	
41	*Edict of Claudius concerning the Jews*	
41	Paul in Corinth	1 Thess.
	before or afterward in Galatia	
	Incident in Antioch	
47 (50)	Jerusalem II (Council)	
48-50 (51-53)	Ephesus	
48 (51)		Lost Cor.
49 (52)		1 Cor.
		Letter of Tears
49/50 (52/53)	Imprisonment in Ephesus?	
50 (53)	Macedonia	2 Cor. 1–9
		2 Cor. 10–13
		Gal.
51/52	*Gallio as Proconsul of Achaia*	
51/52 (54/55)	Corinth	Rom.
52 (55)	Jerusalem III (Collection)	

Lüdemann's reserved posture regarding hypotheses of divisions within letters is noteworthy, a posture contrary to current trends. It is striking that he offers two chronologies deviating by two or three years; only in the case of the earlier one is he able to maintain the Gallio-date. This early variant forces him to accept the problematical crucifixion date of A.D. 27 (§3.5.2). To be sure, Lüdemann does believe that in Acts 18:1-17 Luke has fused the traditions of an earlier and a later

---

80. So especially (though naturally not in every detail) K. Rudolph, *Gnosis* (Eng. trans., 1984) 300f.; J. Gnilka, *BZ* 25 (1981) 148-50; W. Schneemelcher, *Das Urchristentum* (1981) 46-53; J. Murphy-O'Connor, *RB* 89 (1982) 71-91 (see also n. 112 below); H. H. Schade, *Apokalyptische Christologie bei Paulus* ([2]1984) 173-75, 290-92; C. Andresen, *Handbuch der Dogmen- und Theologiegeschichte* I (1984) 4f.; J. C. Hurd, *Interpretation* 40 (1986) 323f.; U. Schnelle, *NTS* 32 (1986) 207-9; E. Richard, *Jesus, One and Many* (1988) 239-62; concerning additional positive reaction, cf. G. Lüdemann, *Paul: Apostle to the Gentiles* (1984) 293.

81. Cf. G. Lüdemann, *Paul: Apostle to the Gentiles* (1984) 262f. (Chronological Chart).

visit by the apostle in Corinth (§11.2.2), so that at most only the second visit can be dated by the Gallio-incident. Lüdemann finds support for an early commencement of the Pauline mission to Europe in a dating of the Roman Jewish Edict of Claudius, mentioned in Acts 18:2, to A.D. 41 (§10). This absolute date, however, does not provide any help in creating an absolute chronology for Paul, since the Pauline letters alone do not enable us to figure any time spans either before or after the sojourn in Thessalonica, which Lüdemann assumes took place during this year. How does Lüdemann, quite independent of Luke, come to attempt these absolute dates? This remains utterly unclear in his investigations.

In one discussion, Lüdemann explains: "So I end up with the relative chronology. And then I come to the evidence of Acts and the only absolute date which I accept is the date for the crucifixion of Jesus, 30 or 27, and I just guess that the conversion of Paul must have happened around 32. From that I start and then try to fit the thirteen years, not fourteen years [Gal. 2:1], and the two years [Gal. 1:18] into this scheme."[82] In reality, this is pure guesswork. Lüdemann insists that "after three years" in Gal. 1:18 refers to the return to Damascus,[83] and that we thus cannot know how long Paul was in "Arabia" after his conversion (§17.1.3). A.D. 32 as a conversion date leaves behind the early chronological variant (including the Gallio-date). Lüdemann arrives at a dating for the Apostolic Council in A.D. 47 or 50 apparently by adding seventeen (not fifteen!) years to a date (which he simply postulates) of 30 or 33 for the return to Damascus. In view of the obvious difficulties involved in moving from this kind of stipulation to an absolute chronology for Paul, one understands the brittle opinion of J. Knox, who obviously would rather have seen this sort of attempt never undertaken in the first place.[84] Lüdemann himself, in contradistinction to R. Jewett (§5.2.3), does admit with regard to Paul's letters: "Here the evidence for absolute dates is just ambiguous and cannot be used."[85]

One further peculiarity of Lüdemann's outline is that on the basis of the formal classification of the letter to the Galatians as an "apologetic letter" he considers himself empowered to date the Antiochene incident (Gal. 2:11ff.) before the Apostolic Council (Gal. 2:1-10) (see p. 232 below). A worrisome question arises for us in view of the end of this chronology: regarding the early Pauline mission to Europe, the new outlines argue that the apostle could not have lingered for years in Tarsus or its vicinity without our learning something more specific about this. But how can one then explain that Paul disappears from the history of primitive Christianity possibly as early as A.D.

82. In B. C. Corley, *Colloquy on New Testament Studies* (1983) 316.
83. *Paul: Apostle to the Gentiles* (1984) 61-64.
84. *Chapters in a Life of Paul*, rev. ed. (1987) 68.
85. In B. C. Corley, *Colloquy on New Testament Studies* (1983) 327.

52 (§12.5.2)? Even in the subsequent volume of his chronology, Lüdemann offers no direct answer to this question.[86]

The potential theological relevance of chronological considerations becomes particularly evident in the work of G. Lüdemann. With regard to the earlier, relative consensus, he writes: "I wish to emphasize at this point that if this view were correct, then all of Paul's letters would have been composed within about five years of one another. They would have been written by a man who had already been a Christian for about nineteen years and who was a veteran missionary. Accordingly, one should expect the letters to be quite homogenous; little room would be left for any theory regarding a development in Paul's thought reflected in the letters. The historian's exposition of the letters could rather proceed from the old theological principle *scriptura ipsius interpres*."[87] To be sure, these statements are immediately subject to qualification. In the first place, Lüdemann considerably oversimplifies the preceding situation in scholarship. Even in conventional chronologies, over twelve years can separate the first letter to the Thessalonians from that to the Philippians (assuming Roman provenience). For scholars who date the letter to the Galatians before the Apostolic Council (§17.1.3; §21.1.1), this writing is separated by up to ten years from the letter to the Romans. When Lüdemann assumes the presence of fundamental eschatological differences between the first letter to the Thessalonians and the first to the Corinthians (§20), is it then of such considerable significance whether one assumes an intervening period of around five years (conventional opinion) or eight (Lüdemann's tightest allowance)? Radical changes in theological thinking are as little guaranteed by longer periods as they are prevented by shorter ones. Each of us is acquainted with theologians who even in secondary matters persist in their positions for decades, and others who alter their entire system of coordinates every five years. Lüdemann's reflections do, however, remain relatively justified: fundamental new developments are sooner to be expected over longer periods of time than within extremely short ones.

1.4.7. Niels Hyldahl

At the moment, the second most recent attempt to develop a chronology for Paul entirely independently of the framework in Acts has been presented by the

---

86. *Opposition to Paul in Jewish Christianity* ((Eng. trans., 1989). This book presents other problems as well. Cf. R. A. Wild, *Bibl* 65 (1984) 426-28. Thus for me the general anti-Paulinism of the relatives of the Lord (δεσπόσυνοι) asserted by G. Lüdemann, *ibid.*, 119-28, does not seem commensurate with the sources. Cf. R. A. Pritz, *Nazarene Jewish Christianity* (1988). Contra the elimination of the Pella-tradition (Eus. *HE* iii.5.3; Epiph. *Pan.* xxix.7.7) cf. C. Koester, *CBQ* 51 (1989) 90-106.

87. In B. C. Corley, *Colloquy on New Testament Studies* (1983) 291.

Danish scholar N. Hyldahl.[88] His chronological schema can be traced back to three considerations: (1) Three years separate the conversion from the first visit to Jerusalem (Gal. 1:18), and fourteen years separate the same point of departure from the second journey to the holy city. (2) The revelation "fourteen years ago" (2 Cor. 12:2) is to be associated directly with the flight from Damascus mentioned shortly before (2 Cor. 11:32f.). (3) An absolute chronological fixed point is provided by the Sabbatical Year in A.D. 54/55, in which the collection for Jerusalem was to be delivered. Since "the — albeit confusing — indications of time regarding Paul's Ephesian sojourn in Acts 19:8, 10 and 20:31 . . . somehow involve a period of altogether three years,"[89] one arrives at a date of A.D. 51 for the beginning of this (first) sojourn. This accords well with the proconsulate of Gallio (A.D. 51-52), and the following schema then emerges:

1			39/40
	Conversion		
2			40/41
3		14	41/42
	Jerusalem I		
4	Syria-Cilicia	13	42/43
5		12	43/44
6		11	44/45
7		10	45/46
8		9	46/47
9		8	47/48
10		7	48/49
	Corinth		
11		6	49/50
12		5	50/51
	Gallio, Ephesus		1/2 Thess.
13		4	51/52
14		3	52/53
	Jerusalem II,		
	Ephesus		
		2	53/54
			Phil., Col.,
			Phlm., Gal.,
			1 Cor.
		1	54/55
	Macedonia, Corinth		2 Cor., Rom.
	Jerusalem III		55

88. *Die paulinische Chronologie* (1986). I would like to thank the author for making this book available to me at the earliest possible time.
89. *Ibid.,* 120.

As striking as these coincidences seem at first glance, at second glance we immediately encounter questions: (1) Does 2 Cor. 11:32f. really constitute a chronologically intended nexus with 2 Cor. 12:2 (§13.3.3)? (2) How secure is a Sabbatical Year in A.D. 54/55 as an absolute date (§15.5.2)? (3) Is it conceivable that the writings to the Philippians, Colossians, Philemon, and Galatians, the first and second letters to the Corinthians, and finally even that to the Romans came about in little more than a year? Hyldahl also accommodates a sidetrip from Ephesus to Colossae and the journey to Corinth within the same period (§16.2.3). The outline of N. Hyldahl marks the preliminary end of the development put into motion by J. Knox. Hyldahl really does get along almost completely without any reference to Acts. In the process, however, the systematic restrictions into which one enters become evident in a special way: Paul's letters must now be chronologically squeezed out. The results which Hyldahl presents with such great assurance, however, have been criticized sharply precisely by those who share his adherence to an absolute chronological priority of Paul's own letters.[90] In view of the two requirements presented by G. Lüdemann (absolute priority of Paul's letters, situational and genre-appropriate interpretation of the information they contain), M. Rese has not without reason issued the warning: "What Lüdemann's first principle provides in the way of speculative freedom, his second principle takes back again."[91]

1.4.8. Karl P. Donfried

In his article "Chronology," which appeared in the *Anchor Bible Dictionary,* a work that in six massive volumes ambitiously seeks to summarize contemporary biblical studies,[92] Donfried attempts a synthesis of the new chronologies that do not depend on the framework in Acts. The unpolemical and more cautious approach he takes might well exert a measure of influence in the future. Although on the one hand Donfried insists "on the radical priority of the Pauline letters,"[93] on the other he willingly concedes: "For when all is said and done, Paul gives us not one specific date. Inevitably, if one is to establish a possible chronology of this period, there will have to be some dependence on Acts."[94] Donfried is even inclined to view the sequence of

---

90. The recensions of R. Jewett, *JBL* 107 (1988) 549f.; J. Murphy-O'Connor, *RB* 95 (1988) 309f., and of A. Suhl, *ThLZ* 113 (1988) 186-191, are devastating critiques.

91. *ThZ* 38 (1982) 105.

92. *ABD* I (1992) 1011-22. The essentials of this article were apparently already finished in 1988. Cf. K. P. Donfried, in R. F. Collins, *The Thessalonian Correspondence* (1990) 4, note 8.

93. *Ibid.,* 1021.

94. *Ibid.,* 1017.

events in Acts 21–28 and their secular-historic connection as provided by Luke as generally correct,[95] though in so doing he does entangle himself in self-contradiction. That is, he believes that Luke, as a member of the Antiochene congregation,[96] knew the early Paul himself, and then was able to use especially Barnabas as an informant; by contrast, we owe the we-accounts to Luke's own literary creativity.[97] But then why did the author of Acts create such a hopeless chronological mess precisely in the middle portion, for which he had access to direct information, while in the fictionalized concluding part, of all places, he followed the correct historical sequence? Here, too, we see that anyone seeking a coherent Pauline chronology cannot so easily get rid of Luke. Donfried clearly underscores the theological relevance of the chronological questions: "It has been precisely my rethinking of Paul's chronology which has been a major factor in my willingness to posit an early and a late Paul."[98]

1.5. New Clarity?

1.5.1. Radical Attempts

As unified as these latter outlines are in their skepticism toward the reliability of the historical framework of Acts, they have yielded little in the way of even moderately unified results. This applies both to the sequence itself of Paul's letters as well as to the actual course of his mission and any absolute dating. The following comparative lists make this clear. Jerusalem I-III again represent the apostle's three trips to Jerusalem as attested in the letters, and Corinth I and Ephesus I his respective initial stays in these cities:

	Buck-Taylor	Knox	Lüdemann	Hyldahl
Crucifixion		30	27 (30)	
Conversion	32	34	32 (?)	40
Jerusalem I	35	37	33 (36)	42
Corinth I	41	43	41	49
Jerusalem II	46	51	47 (50)	53
Ephesus I	47	46	48 (52)	51
Jerusalem III	48	54/55	52 (55)	55

95. *Ibid.*, 1021.
96. K. P. Donfried is here following J. A. Fitzmyer, *The Gospel According to Luke*, vol. I (1982) 47-51.
97. In R. F. Collins, *The Thessalonian Correspondence* (1990) 24.
98. *Ibid.*, 4f.

According to Knox and Hyldahl, then, Paul arrived at Ephesus already before his second visit to Jerusalem; according to Lüdemann, he did not arrive until after that second visit. The datings regarding the period prior to the Apostolic Council differ between ten and five years, those regarding the third Jerusalem visit up to nine years. Hence in this respect we have progressed as far as we did 150 years ago, when K. Wieseler wrote his *Chronology of the Apostolic Age* in 1848 (§1.1.1).

A look at the sequence of Paul's letters as assumed in these four chronologies is also sobering:

Buck-Taylor	Knox	Lüdemann	Hyldahl
2 Thess.	1 Thess.	1 Thess.	1 Thess.
1 Thess.	2 Thess.	1 Cor.	2 Thess.
1 Cor.	Col./Phlm.?	2 Cor. 1–9	Phil.
2 Cor. 10–13	Phil.?	2 Cor. 10–13	Col./Phlm.
Phil.	1 Cor.	Gal.	Gal.
2 Cor. 1–9	2 Cor.	Rom.	1 Cor.
Gal.	Rom.		2 Cor.
Rom.	Gal.		Rom.
Col./Phlm.			

The only sequence of two (!) letters that all four chronologies share is the sequence 1 Corinthians/2 Corinthians. Yet opinions immediately diverge again when the question is raised whether the second Corinthian letter should itself be divided, whereby 2 Corinthians 10–13 would follow 2 Cor. 1–9 or vice versa.

1.5.2. Recent Publications

A similarly confusing picture emerges from the chronological summaries presented during the last years. Our examples here include the five books on Paul by M. A. Hubaut,[99] J. Becker,[100] H. D. Saffrey,[101] M. F. Baslez,[102] and S. Légasse,[103] the three commentaries on Acts by F. L. Arrington,[104] F. F. Bruce,[105] and S. J. Kistemaker,[106] an account of the history of primitive

---

99. *Paul de Tarse* (1989) 29-57 (47: Table chronologique).
100. *Paulus* (1989) 17-33 (32: Dates of Paul's Life) (Eng. trans., *Paul: Apostle to the Gentiles* [1993]).
101. *Histoire de l'apôtre Paul* (1991) 175-84.
102. *Saint Paul* (1991) 401-5 (Essai de chronologie paulinienne).
103. *Paul apôtre* (1991). The missing chronological table was appended by M. Trimaille, *MBib* 81 (1993) 9.
104. *The Acts of the Apostles* (1988) 275.
105. *The Acts of the Apostles* (³1990) 92f. (List of Approximate Dates).
106. *Acts* (1990) 19f. (Chronology).

Christianity by E. Dassmann,[107] and the most recent comprehensive introductory work by D. A. Carson, D. J. Moo, and L. Morris:[108]

	Arr. 1988	Hub. 1989	Beck 1989	Bru. 1990	Kist. 1990	Dass. 1991	Saf. 1991	Bas. 1991	Lég. 1991	Car. 1992
Conv.	33	34	32	33	35	32/33	36	34	34	34/35
J I	36	37	34/35	35	37	35	38	37	37	37
J II	44/45	—	—	46	46		—	40/41	—	45/47
J III	49	51	48/49	49	49	48/49	49	51	52	48/49
M II	49/52	46/51	49/51	49/52	49/52		49/51	49/51	52	49/51
J IV	52	—	—	52	52			—	—	52
J V	58	57	57/58	57	57	55	58	55	58	57
Death		62	62	65	67/68	60		67/68	65/67	64/65

Here, almost everything is open to question. Although the majority of
scholars reduce the Jerusalem trips to those three attested in Paul's letters,
Luke, too, continues to find adherents for the five journeys he presents.
The historian M. F. Baslez mediates between the two by deleting the fourth
(Acts 18:22) while yet defending the second Lukan Jerusalem trip (Acts
11:29f.; 12:25). She does, however, agree with M. A. Hubaut and S. Légasse that the second missionary journey (Acts 16–18) is to be placed before
the Apostolic Council (Acts 15). By contrast, a scholar such as J. Becker
— one not exactly uncritical toward Luke to begin with — maintains Luke's
sequence, and H. D. Saffrey even considers this order of events to be
"certain."[109] As before, just as little agreement obtains regarding the
Aretas-incident (§5) as regarding the transition in procuratorship from Felix
to Festus (§12.4).

   In view of such utterly divergent tendencies within the most recent
publications, one can still — or now especially — understand the heartfelt
sigh of H. Paulsen: "Anyone who critically examines chronological investigations is easily tempted to juxtapose their divergent results and then play
them off against one another. In so doing, however, one easily overlooks the
objective necessity for such studies. Nevertheless, perplexity and a certain
element of resignation remain in view of the present difficulties attaching to
any chronology."[110] Paulsen asks "whether one ought not forswear in a more
sustained fashion the use of information from Acts in reconstructing a
chronology."[111] The history of scholarship, however, seems rather to confront
us with two alternatives: either we can be certain regarding at least the relative

107. *Kirchengeschichte* I (1991) 6 (Chronological Table), 48-52.
108. *An Introduction to the New Testament* (1992) 223-31 (231: Chronology of
Paul's Missionary Career).
109. *Histoire de l'apôtre Paul* (1991) 175.
110. *ThZ* 40 (1984) 87.
111. *Ibid.*

reliability not only of isolated dates but also of the overall framework of Acts, or we must give up the notion of ever attaining again any broader consensus concerning Pauline chronology.[112]

112. This assertion is strongly contested by J. Murphy-O'Connor, *Paul: A Critical Biography* (1966) 1-31. His chronological outline is very similar to that of R. Jewett (§1.3), whose presentation he calls "the best . . . in terms of both prudence and ingenuity" (ibid. 8). Murphy-O'Connor nowhere discusses my arguments against his reconstruction in *Die Frühzeit des Paulus* (1994). However, he wrote a review in *RB* 103 (1996) 141-43. I am grateful for some valuable criticisms; unfortunately, however, Murphy-O'Connor misrepresents my views at important points. The reader may compare the review of my book by professor of ancient history H. Botermann, *Gnomon* 69 (1997) 235-39.

§2

Further Procedure

2.1. Methodological Considerations

Our presentation of the most recent outlines of Pauline chronology has shown how far we presently are from results that enjoy even moderately general acceptance. The overview of the history of scholarship clearly revealed two opposing movements. After the discovery of the Gallio-inscription, there was a definite trend toward more agreement in respect to Pauline chronology. By contrast, attempts to free the chronology from the framework of Acts, attempts that have moved more prominently into the foreground during the past ten years, have resulted in a new level of confusion rather than in any more precise specification. Hence a new examination of the attendant problems seems to be called for, even if hardly any new sources can be adduced. As long as no new epigraphic material becomes accessible and no unexpected discoveries are made in the libraries of the former Soviet Union, we must interrogate as attentively as possible the sources already familiar to us.

This presentation of the history of scholarship prompts several conclusions and cautionary guidelines:[1]

1. A threefold *caveat* applies to the thesis of the absolute priority of statements by Paul himself before those of the writer of Acts:

(a) One cannot exclude the possibility that even autobiographical ac-

---

1. R. Jewett, *A Chronology of Paul's Life* (1979) 1-6, offers an ambitious methodological reflection. Although it is perhaps too harsh to speak here of "pretentious scientific mumbo-jumbo" (E. Best, *SJT* 33 [1980] 488), Jewett's assertion in B. C. Corley, *Colloquy on New Testament Studies* (1983) 275, does perhaps go too far: "Luedemann's work and mine . . . provides a basis for testability. Whereas the compromise chronologies resisted refinement, their internal tensions causing infinite variations that defied falsification, there is now a possibility of objective evaluation." The history of scholarship shows that chronologies oriented toward the framework of Acts are quite capable of fundamental modifications. At the same time, doubts arise whether the variations will ever diminish between the various outlines that do not draw on the Lukan schema.

counts might have gaps or be biased; the historian cannot therefore *a priori* exempt Paul from this possibility.[2]

(b) Acts claims to be offering firsthand information in its "we-accounts." This claim may be false. If, however, upon closer examination this claim proves to be possible or even probable, then in a certain sense we would have access to two primary sources.[3] All the scholars participating in the current discussion reckon in some way with having access to usable material in Acts.[4] This is justified, however, only if its author either directly or indirectly had access to eyewitness recollections (cf. Lk. 1:1-4). This simple consideration is sometimes obscured a bit too much by references to "valuable traditions."

(c) One needs to clarify when one is dealing with a clear contradiction between Luke and a Pauline assertion, and when one is dealing merely with a contradiction to a possible or probable interpretation of the apostle's statements. In view of these considerations, it seems justified to speak merely about a "relative" priority of Paul's letters before the chronological information contained in Acts.

2. As is shown especially by the radically inconsistent dating of the letter to the Galatians, turning considerations of Paul's own development into primary chronological arguments is a precarious undertaking. Rather, such evolutionary schemata should be acquired if at all possible from independently determined dates. Ideas develop in a consistent and uninterrupted fashion in one's study; they may not always do so in reality.

3. It does not seem possible to arrive at any absolute dates for Paul's chronology without drawing on information from Acts. The outline of C. H. Buck and G. R. Taylor, the most rigorous attempt to do this, has justifiably attracted almost no adherents.

4. Greater variations in these outlines emerge especially because scholars tie their reconstructions to one or two individual events. Given the uncertain or limited character of most of the material at our disposal, this is a risky undertaking. The more we can relate independently determined dates to one another meaningfully, the more we may hope to acquire firmer ground under our feet.

---

2. To this extent, the attempt of J. T. Sanders (*JBL* 85 [1966] 335-43) to question critically Galatians 1–2 regarding its historical consistency possesses at least experimental value. G. Lüdemann, in B. C. Corley, *Colloquy on New Testament Studies* (1983) 294, also remarks that "Paul did not write as a historian, either. His statements require critical consideration, due weight being given to the circumstances in which he wrote and to the literary genre of his statements." See also pp. 236, 261, and 271f. below.

3. Cf. J. W. Drane, *JSNT* 9 (1980) 73f.

4. This applies even to C. H. Buck and G. R. Taylor, *Saint Paul* (1969) 179-215, and to J. Knox, *Chapters in a Life of Paul,* rev. ed. (1987) 50f., indeed even to N. Hyldahl, *Die paulinische Chronologie* (1986) 118-20.

5. Regarding the Pauline literature itself, the present study takes as its point of departure the almost unanimous consensus in scholarship regarding the authenticity (albeit not necessarily the unity) of the letters to the Romans, Corinthians, Galatians, and Philippians, the first letter to the Thessalonians, and the writing to Philemon. We will not address the question whether additional parts of the *corpus Paulinum* might be authentic after all,[5] contain Pauline fragments,[6] or at least derive from the school of Paul[7] such that chronological information might be gleaned from them. Here, too, one should proceed from the certain to the more disputed.

6. No *a priori* judgments should be made regarding the reliability of the chronological material in Acts; rather, it is precisely the analysis of such nontheological evidence that can aid us in arriving at a more independent judgment regarding the historical value of Acts. As we have seen, none of the chronological outlines worked out until now has been able to emancipate itself completely from Luke.

2.2. Division

The first main part of our investigation, "Early Pauline Chronology: From Jerusalem to Achaia," attempts to determine absolute or relative dates for the apostle's activity by relating information from Paul's letters and Acts to extratestamental evidence. The question regarding the date of Jesus' crucifixion has been accorded relatively broad treatment in relationship to a framework for Paul's chronology. This date can under certain circumstances present

5. The authenticity of the second letter to the Thessalonians is again being advocated quite strongly by R. Jewett, *The Thessalonian Correspondence* (1986). Cf. also T. Holtz, *Der erste Brief an die Thessalonicher* (1986) 277f.; L. T. Johnson, *The Writings of the New Testament* (1986) 266-71; J. Murphy-O'Connor, *RB* 95 (1988) 311; M. Bockmuehl, *Themelios* 14 (1989) 71f., and recently esp. C. A. Wanamaker, *The Epistles to the Thessalonians* 1990) 17-63. The majority of scholars, however, do apparently opt for its pseudonymity. Cf. R. F. Collins, in *The Thessalonian Correspondence* (1990) xiv.

6. J. D. Quinn, *The Letter to Titus* (1990) 9 *et passim*, again argues this for the Pastoral Epistles.

7. Concerning this possibility, cf. P. Stuhlmacher, in J. D. G. Dunn, *Jews and Christians* (1992) 159-75. One especially interesting assumption is that the letter to the Colossians was written by the apostle's co-worker Timothy during an Ephesian incarceration of the apostle (§12.1.1) (W. H. Ollrog, *Paulus und seine Mitarbeiter* [1979] 219-33, 236-42) whereby the concluding greeting (Col. 4:7-18) might even come from Paul himself (E. Schweizer, *Der Brief an die Kolosser* [³1989] 26). These considerations involve a particular understanding of the secretary hypothesis, earlier considered to be the domain of conservative scholars but at the moment seeming to gain adherents beyond that sphere as well (see p. 409 below).

insuperable difficulties already at the outset for the chronological outlines of C. H. Buck and G. R. Taylor, though also for the attempt of G. Lüdemann.[8] Since this variously involves important cornerstone dates in the reconstructions of R. Jewett and S. Dockx or G. Lüdemann, particular attention was given to Paul's flight from Damascus under the ethnarch of the Nabatean king Aretas (§5) and to the Roman edict concerning the Jews issued by Claudius (§10), something also attested by the scope of these studies. By contrast, and commensurate with the limited goal of the work, the chronology of Paul after the Gallio-incident (§12) is presented only cursorily. The primary goal here is to acquire dates from the final part of Acts to use as comparative material for an evaluation of information in the first part. Chronological questions going beyond Acts 28 are not addressed as specific themes.

The second main section, "Stages in Pauline Missionary Strategy," tries to establish a correlation between the chronological data thus gained, the stages of Paul's ministry that become visible in his letters, and the framework of Acts. The attempt at making a specific contribution to the disputed problem regarding the extent to which the Lukan outline can be reconciled with Paul's own statements resides in the question of the apostle's missionary strategy. Do the theological and historical statements of these letters offer any information concerning the historic-geographical course of his mission that might verify or refute the Lukan picture (§§13-15)? Finally, we will pay special attention to the question of traveling in antiquity in order to evaluate the unusually long duration of the journeys assumed by R. Jewett as well as what for some periods are the extremely compressed chronologies of S. Dockx and N. Hyldahl (§16). The chronological results of the entire investigation are then summarized under the subtitle "Attempt at a Chronological Synthesis" (§17), a synthesis most easily viewed in the table on p. 322.

The third main section, "Early Pauline Theology: The First Letter to the Thessalonians," focuses on that particular Pauline writing which G. Lüdemann — assuming an early dating — posits as an almost irreconcilable theological antithesis to the apostle's later letters. First, 1 Thessalonians is classified within our chronological reconstruction (§18). Then the question is addressed regarding the extent to which this writing has been shaped not only by Paul's particular biographical situation but also by the specific circumstances and problems of the young Christian congregation in the Hellenistic metropolis of Thessalonica (§19). The letter's only explicated theological theme, namely, the problem of the parousia, is used as the basis for discussing its reconcilability with Paul's other eschatological statements (§20). Finally, we must discuss why the doctrine of justification seems to play no role in the first letter to the Thessalonians (§21).

8. R. Jewett justifiably emphasizes this point in B. C. Corley, *Colloquy on New Testament Studies* (1983) 285.

I. Early Pauline Chronology: From Jerusalem to Achaia

§3

The Crucifixion of Jesus

Amid all the divergent opinions regarding Pauline chronology, at least one view has not yet been advocated, namely, that he was a pre-Easter follower of Jesus. Hence the crucifixion remains the fixed *terminus post quem* for the apostle's conversion. As far as the dating of Jesus' death itself is concerned, however, an account merely of the history of scholarship would require a separate monograph.[1] The following discussion will therefore only present what, in my opinion, are the most important dating arguments, address several more recent suggestions relevant to the present context, and evaluate critically the datings of the crucifixion presented by G. Lüdemann and R. Jewett.

3.1. The Possible Time Frame

Extremely different New Testament writings — such as the Gospels of Matthew (Mt. 27:2ff.) and Mark (Mk. 15:1ff.), the Lukan double work (Lk. 23:1ff.; Acts 3:13; 4:27; 13:28), and the Pastoral Epistles (1 Tim. 6:13), though also the Gospel of John (Jn. 18:29ff.; 19:1ff.) — agree with Tacitus (*Ann.* xv.44)[2] and Josephus (*Ant.* xviii.63f.)[3] that Jesus was crucified when Pontius Pilate

---

1. Cf. U. Holzmeister, *Chronologia Vitae Christi* (1933) 156-222; G. Ogg, *The Chronology of the Public Ministry of Jesus* (1940) 203-77; J. Finegan, *Handbook of Biblical Chronology* (1964) 285-98; J. Blinzler, *Der Prozeß Jesu* (⁴1969) 101-8; A. Strobel, *Ursprung und Geschichte des frühchristlichen Osterkalenders* (1977) 70-121; W. P. Armstrong and J. Finegan, *ISBE* I (1979) 688f.; H. W. Hoehner, *Chronological Aspects of the Life of Christ* (⁵1981) 95-114; R. Jewett, *A Chronology of Paul's Life* (1979) 26-29.

2. For the text, see pp. 164f. below. Concerning the possible sources from which Tacitus might have drawn for his remark about Jesus, cf. M. J. Harris, in D. Wenham, *Gospel Perspectives* V (1985) 347-52.

3. For bibliographical information concerning the substantive authenticity of the *testimonium Flavianum,* see L. H. Feldman, *Josephus and Modern Scholarship* (1984) 680-84, 957f.; R. Riesner, *Jesus als Lehrer* (³1988) 264f. Concerning the recent skepticism of P. Bilde, *DTT* 44 (1981) 99-135, and J. N. Birdsall, *BJRL* 67 (1985) 609-22, cf. the detailed philological-historical analysis by G. Vermes, *JJS* 38 (1987) 2-10, as well as G. H.

35

was prefect of the "special territory" of Judea, subject to the governor of Syria. The tenure of his prefecture[4] thus provides the possible time frame for the execution of Jesus. The beginning and end of Pilate's time in office are subject to more vehement discussion than the simple reference to the years "A.D. 26-36," as also found in scholarly encyclopedias, might suggest. For example, even A. N. Sherwin-White, in a more recent lexicon article on Pontius Pilate,[5] does not discuss these chronological questions. The dating of Paul's conversion takes A.D. 26 as the utterly self-evident beginning of the prefecture of Pilate.[6]

3.1.1. The Dismissal of Pilate

Regarding the dismissal of the governor, most scholars[7] probably follow Josephus in accepting the following sequence of events: (1) Lucius Vitellius, governor of Syria, dismisses Pilate (Josephus, *Ant.* xviii.89). (2) Afterward, Vitellius visits Jerusalem at the occasion of a Passover festival (Josephus, *Ant.* xviii.90-95). (3) During an additional visit to the holy city at a Jewish festival, similarly identified as the Passover, Vitellius hears the news of the death of Tiberius on March 16, A.D. 37 (Josephus, *Ant.* xviii.122-26). Hence Pilate would already have left Judea before the Passover in the year A.D. 36. This does admittedly create a problem insofar as despite the considerable haste (cf. Josephus, *Ant.* xviii.89) to which he was obliged (Dio, liii.15.6), he would have arrived in Rome only after the death of the emperor. The average duration of a trip between Jerusalem and the capital of the empire is assumed to have been two months (except during winter, November 11 until March 10).[8] Yet another factor militating against the usual reconstruction is that the mention of an otherwise unknown Marcellus (Μαρχέλλος) as Pilate's successor (Josephus, *Ant.* xviii.89) might involve a misspelling

---

Twelftree, in D. Wenham, *Gospel Perspectives* V (1984) 290-310; L. H. Feldman and G. Hata, *Josephus, the Bible and History* (1989) 430-34. There is little of substance in S. Mason, *Josephus and the New Testament* (1992) 163-75.

4. The Pilate-inscription, discovered in 1961 in Caesarea Maritima (A. Frova, *RIL.L* 95 [1961], 419-34), confirmed what previously was already thought likely (A. N. Sherwin-White, *PBSR* 2 [1939] 12; A. H. M. Jones, *Studies in Roman Government and Law* [1960] 117-25), namely, that the official title of the governor of Judea prior to Claudius was actually *praefectus Iudaeae.* Cf. J. P. Lemonon, *Pilate et le gouvernement de la Judée* (1981) 23-32, 43-58; *ANRW* II, 26.1 (1992) 748-52.

5. *ISBE* III (1986) 867-69.

6. Cf. among many others A. J. M. Wedderburn, *ET* 92 (1981) 107; H. W. Hoehner, in *Dictionary of Jesus and the Gospels* (1992) 615f.

7. Cf. Schuerer, I, 386-88.

8. So also Schuerer, I, 397, note 180. Individual examples are provided by J. Blinzler, *Der Prozeß Jesu* (⁴1969) 272f. Cf. also §16.3.

of Μαρούλλος.[9] It is expressly said that at the accession of Caligula, that is, probably A.D. 37, the latter immediately appointed Marullus as governor of Judea (Josephus, *Ant.* xviii.237).

D. R. Schwartz,[10] following a reference by W. Otto,[11] tries to resolve the chronological problem through source criticism. Schwartz understands Josephus, *Ant.* xviii.90-95 and *Ant.* xviii.120-26, as parallel accounts of a priestly or courtly source regarding the visit to the same Passover festival by Vitellius. Schwartz finds additional references to this event in Josephus, *Ant.* xv.403-9 as well as *Ant.* xx.6-14, which in his opinion belong to the lost ending to Philo's *Legatio ad Gaium*. J. Blinzler,[12] following J. Jeremias,[13] counters Otto's source criticism with the argument that "Josephus so convincingly explains the motivation for Vitellius' visits to Jerusalem that the assumption of a doublet is not at all suggested, and is certainly not required."[14] During the first visit (to the Passover festival), Vitellius allegedly would have put things in order after the dismissal of Pilate (Josephus, *Ant.* xviii.90); during the second visit he, together with Herod Antipas, would have prepared for the military campaign against the Nabatean king Aretas IV (Josephus, *Ant.* xviii.120-22).[15] The strongest evidence militating against the assumption of doublets is that according to Josephus, Joseph Caiaphas, the high priest at the trial of Jesus (Mt. 26:3, 57; Jn. 18:13f., 24, 28) was dismissed during the first visit (Josephus, *Ant.* xviii.95), while his successor Jonathan, son of Ananus, was dismissed during the second visit (Josephus, *Ant.* xviii.123). According to Blinzler, the Passover is referring to the festival of A.D. 37, while the second festival — not identified more specifically — is referring to the following Pentecost festival. Accordingly, Pilate would have been dismissed from office toward the end of A.D. 36 or the beginning of A.D. 37. In a fashion different from reconstructions that, while similarly assuming a dismissal after Passover A.D. 36, identify the second but not the first festival with a Passover,[16] Blinz-

---

9. Cf. U. Holzmeister, *Bibl* 13 (1932) 232; S. J. de Laet, *AnCl* 8 (1939) 418f. As a possibility also Schuerer I, 383.

10. In *Studies in the Jewish Background of Christianity* (1992) 182-201. My thanks to the author, Professor Daniel R. Schwartz (Hebrew University, Jerusalem), for having made both this article (originally published in Modern Hebrew, *Tarb* 51 [1982], 383-98) and the one cited in note 18 available to me in an English translation before their actual publication. K. S. Krieger, *BN* 61 (1992) 27-32; 68 (1993) 18-23, argues similarly.

11. *Herodes* (1913) 192-94; *PRE Suppl.* I/2 (1913) 185-87.

12. *Der Prozeß Jesu* (⁴1969) 271-73.

13. *Jerusalem zur Zeit Jesu*, II/B (1929) 55, note 8.

14. *Der Prozeß Jesu* (⁴1969) 271.

15. Concerning the problematic attaching to this campaign, however, see p. 42 below.

16. U. Holzmeister, *Chronologia Vitae Christi* (1933) 52-55; E. M. Smallwood, *JJS* 5 (1954) 12-21; *JTS* 14 (1962) 22f.

ler's resolution attempt is able to maintain Josephus' wording. Regardless of whether one follows Blinzler or the source-critical analysis of Schwartz, the chronological difficulties just discussed do militate for a dismissal of Pilate only after Passover in A.D. 36.[17]

3.1.2. Pilate's Accession to Office

Regarding the beginning of the governor's tenure in office, too, D. R. Schwartz[18] contradicts the consensus, which in this case almost unanimously[19] takes the year A.D. 26 as its point of departure. Here Schwartz picks up anew the dating of R. Eisler.[20] On the basis of (1) the extremely brief portrayal of the tenure of Pilate's predecessor Valerius Gratus (Josephus, *Ant.* xviii.33-35), (2) the date A.D. 21 as that of the trial of Jesus, as mentioned in the pagan Acts of Pilate (Eus. *HE* i.9.3f.), and (3) the mention of an expulsion of Jews from Rome in the year A.D. 19 (see p. 174 below) in the middle of the account of Pilate (Josephus, *Ant.* xviii.81-84), Eisler decided on the date of A.D. 19, possibly even the end of A.D. 18.[21] Schwartz attempts to support this dating by pointing out that both the annual installation of high priests and the casting of procuratorial coins seem to have ceased after A.D. 18, though his main argument is a structural analysis of Josephus, *Ant.* xviii-xx, which in his opinion militates for an appointment date of A.D. 19.

Schwartz admits that the numismatic evidence is ambivalent in this case.[22] The appearance of Judean coins from the years 15/16, 16/17, 17/18, 18/19, and 24/25 is remarkably the same, while it differs markedly from that of the years 28/29-31/32. From this, P. L. Hedley was the first to conclude that a change in procuratorship occurred around A.D. 26/27,[23] and many concurred with him in this point.[24] By contrast, Schwartz associates the cessation of annual coinage with the change from Gratus to Pilate. The impression of Josephus' account of Gratus (*Ant.* xviii.33-35) seems to favor

---

17. So also J. P. Lemonon, *Pilate et le gouvernement de la Judée* (1981) 241-45, who does admittedly go beyond J. Blinzler in reckoning with yet a third visit to Jerusalem by Vitellius already in A.D. 36 (cf. Josephus, *Ant.* xv.405).

18. In *Studies in the Jewish Background of Christianity* (1992) 202-17 (previously published in Modern Hebrew in *Zion* 48 [1983] 325-45). Cf. also D. R. Schwartz, *ABD* V (1992) 396f.

19. Regarding the exception, J. Vardaman, see p. 52 below, note 107.

20. ΙΗΣΟΥΣ ΒΑΣΙΛΕΥΣ ΟΥ ΒΑΣΙΛΕΥΣΑΣ I (1929) 125-30.

21. A thorough critique of the Gospel chronology of R. Eisler can be found in G. Ogg, *The Chronology of the Public Ministry of Jesus* (1940) 277-85.

22. In *Studies in the Jewish Background of Christianity* (1992) 183.

23. *JTS* 35 (1934) 56-58.

24. E.g., E. Stauffer, *NC* 1/2 (1949/50) 496, 501; J. Blinzler, *Der Prozeß Jesu* ([4]1969) 40, note 6; H. W. Hoehner, *Herod Antipas* ([2]1980) 172, note 2.

Eisler and Schwartz: We hear merely about the dismissal of three high priests after a year or an even shorter period. If Gratus' departure for Rome followed immediately upon the appointment of Joseph Caiaphas (A.D. 18), as one might conclude from Josephus' succinct manner of expression (*Ant.* xviii.35), then the governor would have served only about four years in this post after his appointment. But Josephus' own time frame regarding the period between the installation of Caiaphas and the departure of Gratus is extremely imprecise (καὶ Γρᾶτος μὲν ταῦτα πράξας . . .).

By contrast, the immediately following determination is quite precise. Gratus allegedly occupied this office for eleven years. Since Josephus does not provide simply a rounded-off number, his indication of ten years for Pilate in Judea (*Ant.* xviii.89) should probably also be taken as credible,[25] and, indeed, this provides the strongest argument for the usual chronology. Schwartz must assume that the text of Josephus has been subjected to Christian redaction.[26] He tries to counter the absence of corresponding variants by pointing out that the pagan Acts of Pilate, which in his eyes, too, was forged in the fourth century, read either no numbers at all or different numbers in Josephus. Further discussion will have to show whether the structural analysis of the Pilate account in Josephus suggested by Schwartz can adequately support the assumption of such textual corruption.[27] If one does reckon with the chronology of Schwartz as one possibility, then the potential time frame for the trial of Jesus expands from Passover A.D. 19 to Passover A.D. 36. Information in the Gospels, however, allows this time frame to be narrowed down further.

3.2. References in the Gospels

3.2.1. The Emergence of John the Baptist

According to the famous synchronism in Lk. 3:1, which the third evangelist probably drew from a Jewish-Christian source,[28] John the Baptist appeared on the scene "in the fifteenth year of the reign of Emperor Tiberius (ἐν ἔτει δὲ πεντεκαιδεκάτῳ τῆς ἡγεμονίας Τιβερίου Καίσαρος)." A. Strobel[29] has provided additional arguments for the view — established earlier especially

---

25. Cf. J. P. Lemonon, *Pilate et le gouvernement de la Judée* (1981) 126f.

26. In *Studies in the Jewish Background of Christianity* (1992) 184.

27. K. S. Krieger, *BN* 68 (1993) 22, assumes that Joseph has made a simple mistake in dating the Roman expulsion of Jews under Tiberius (Josephus, *Ant.* xviii.65-84).

28. Cf. R. Riesner, in K. Bockmühl, *Die Aktualität der Theologie Adolf Schlatters* (1988) 64f.

29. *Ursprung und Geschichte des frühchristlichen Osterkalenders* (1977) 84-92.

by A. W. Zumpt[30] and continued by T. Zahn[31] — that the term ἡγεμονία here refers to what for the provinces was the determinative coregency of Tiberius.[32] The third evangelist, whose origin in Antioch seems to be relatively well attested,[33] is writing from the standpoint of the provinces, in which a distinction was made between the actual exercise of rule (ἡγεμονία) and titular rule (βασιλεία). The decision concerning the coregency of Tiberius (Tacitus, *Ann.* i.3; *Mon. Anc.* ii.8) was made according to Velleius (*Hist. Rom.* ii.121, 123) shortly before, and according to Suetonius (*Tib.* 21) shortly after the triumph at Illyricum, which can now be dated inscriptionally to October 23, A.D. 12 by what are known as the *fasti Praenestini*.[34] Numismatic evidence also attests the rise of Tiberius to coregent after A.D. 13.[35] The fifteenth year of the coregency of Tiberius would accordingly have been A.D. 26/27.

If according to Luke's chronology the activity of John the Baptist began around A.D. 26, this also explains why according to the evangelist's understanding Jesus' own work began when he was "about thirty years old (καὶ ἦν Ἰησοῦς ἀρχόμενος ὡσεὶ ἐτῶν τριάκοντα)" (Lk. 3:23). John the Baptist and thus also Jesus were born before the death of Herod the Great (Lk. 1:5; cf. Mt. 2:1, 19), the dating of which to 4 B.C.[36] Luke might have

30. *Das Geburtsjahr Christi* (1869) 281-301.

31. *Das Evangelium des Lucas* ($^{3/4}$1920) 182-89. In this way, T. Zahn is able to explain how in a remark concerning Lk. 3:1 Tertullian can speak about the "*anno XII Tiberii Caesaris*" (Tertullian, *Adv. Marc.* 1.15).

32. Cf. also the overview in J. Finegan, *Handbook of Biblical Chronology* (1964) 259-73.

33. Cf. J. A. Fitzmyer, *The Gospel According to Luke* I (1982) 47-51; R. Riesner, *Jesus als Lehrer* (^{3}1988) 24f.; K. P. Donfried, in R. F. Collins, *The Thessalonian Correspondence* (1990) 24. Still worthy of consideration is A. von Harnack, *Luke the Physician* (Eng. trans., 1907) 4f.

34. Cf. V. Ehrenberg and A. H. M. Jones, *Documents Illustrating the Reigns of Augustus and Tiberius* (1949) 53.

35. Cf. *BMC Roman Empire* (1923), plate 13 (nos. 1-5), plate 22 (nos. 1-3).

36. W. E. Filmer, *JTS* 17 (1966) 283-98; E. L. Martin, *The Birth of Christ Recalculated* (^{2}1980) 106-31; in *Festschrift J. Finegan* (1989) 85-92; J. Thorley, *GaR* 28 (1981) 81-89; O. Edwards, *PEQ* 114 (1982) 29-42 (summarized in *Chronologie des Lebens Jesu* [1978] 27-32), and P. Keresztes, in *Imperial Rome and the Christians* I (1989) 1-43, all advocate in works of varying seriousness 1 B.C. as the year of death. T. D. Barnes, *JTS* 19 (1968) 204-9, is inclined to accept B.C. 5. J. van Bruggen, *NTSuppl* 48 (1978) 1-17, and P. M. Bernegger, *JTS* 34 (1983) 526-31, demonstrate that the decisive presupposition for a late dating is erroneous. Josephus by no means always reckons in actual years, but rather quite often also inclusively. Now as before, most of the evidence militates for 4 B.C. as the year of death. Cf. Schuerer, I, 326-28; D. Johnson, in *Festschrift J. Finegan* (1989) 93-100; H. W. Hoehner, *loc. cit.,* 101-12; P. L. Maier, *loc. cit.,* 115-18; D. R. Schwartz, in *Studies in the Jewish Background of Christianity* (1992) 157-68.

known.[37] Factors militating against the identification of the ἡγεμονία with the actual successorship of Augustus (who died 19 August A.D. 14) by Tiberius (elected 17 September A.D. 14) and a resulting dating of the calling of John the Baptist in A.D. 28/29[38] also include the most likely dates for the arrest of John the Baptist and the beginning of the ministry of Jesus.

3.2.2. The Death of John the Baptist

The impression given by the first two Gospels is that Jesus began his public ministry in Galilee shortly after the arrest of John (Mt. 4:12-17/Mk. 1:14f.). According to all three Synoptics, John's execution occurred during Jesus' own ministry (Mt. 14:1f./Mk. 6:14-16/Lk. 9:7-9; cf. Mt. 14:12; Mt. 17:9-13/Mk. 9:9-13). The fourth Gospel offers a different picture. According to its version, John the Baptist is active when Jesus is gathering his first disciples (Jn. 1:35-51) in the northern part of the holy land, in the Batanaea (cf. Jn. 1:28 [ἐν Βηθανίᾳ πέραν τοῦ Ἰορδάνου])[39] and in Galilee (Jn. 1:43), performs his first miracle in Cana (Jn. 2:1-12), and goes up to the Passover in Jerusalem for the first time with his followers (Jn. 2:13ff.). The fourth evangelist expressly states that "[at that time] John, of course, had not yet been thrown into prison" (Jn. 3:24; cf. Jn. 4:1f.). Although the death of the Baptist is perhaps alluded to in Jn. 3:30 ("he must increase, but I must decrease"), the Gospel of John nowhere indicates just when this took place.

W. Schenk assumes that in this case the fourth Gospel is drawing its chronological information from groups associated with the Baptist, groups

37. This reckoning also makes the suggestion of K. Haacker, *BN* 38/39 (1987) 39-43, problematical, namely, that one translate Lk. 2:1f. (ἐγένετο δὲ ἐν ταῖς ἡμέραις ἐκείναις ἐξῆλθεν δόγμα παρὰ Καίσαρος Αὐγούστου ἀπογράφεσθαι πᾶσαν τὴν οἰκουμένην. αὕτη ἀπογραφὴ πρώτη ἐγένετο ἡγεμονεύοντος τῆς Συρίας Κυρηνίου) as follows: " 'In those days' [i.e., when John the Baptist was a child] 'a decree went out from Emperor Augustus that all the world should be registered. This registration was *not* taken *until* [was *first* taken when] Quirinius was governor of Syria" (*loc. cit.*, 42). If one takes the dating of a census under Quirinius as recounted by Josephus (*Ant.* xviii.1-5), then Jesus would have been born around A.D. 6. Even if Luke were to date Jesus' appearance from 28/29 onward, the reckoning behind the thirty years would remain incomprehensible. The historical problems with the census in Luke are well known (Schuerer I, 399-427), though his error is not as completely obvious as it appears according to G. Lüdemann, *Paul. Apostle to the Gentiles* (1984) 9. Josephus' account also has its problems. Cf. Excursus II (pp. 330f.).

38. C. Cichorius, *ZNW* 22 (1923) 16-20, taking into account the Antiochene origin of the evangelist, accordingly dates the first year of the reign of Tiberius commensurate with the reckoning of the Syrian New Year festival as 1 October A.D. 27 to 1 October A.D. 28. But even if it is highly unlikely that fourteen days (17 September to 1 October) were actually reckoned as one year, still it is especially the numismatic evidence that militates against this assumption. Cf. J. K. Fotheringham, *JTS* 35 (1934) 153.

39. Cf. R. Riesner, *TynBul* 38 (1987) 29-63.

with which it had to come to terms.[40] From the information in Josephus (*Ant.* xviii.109-25) Schenk concludes further that the execution of the Baptist immediately preceded the defeat of Herod Antipas in the Nabatean campaign against Aretas IV, and thus is to be dated between A.D. 34 and 36, though probably around A.D. 35.[41] The historian C. Saulnier has vehemently rejected this reconstruction by pointing out the chronological problems attaching to the portrayal of Josephus.[42] According to Ms. Saulnier, the preparation of a campaign of vengeance by Vitellius in A.D. 36/37 is extremely improbable, and she, like other scholars (§3.1.1), views the accounts of the governor's two Jerusalem visits as doublets. In her view, Josephus falsely portrayed accounts of an anticipated campaign against the Parthians, whose mercenary troops were in part recruited from Arabians (Nabateans?) (Tacitus, *Ann.* vi.50.7) as a vengeance measure undertaken against Aretas IV.[43] Following the Gospel chronology (!), she assumes the year A.D. 29 for the victory of Aretas against Antipas.

But even if one grants Josephus more credibility here than does Ms. Saulnier, the assumption of a close chronological relationship between the defeat of Antipas and the execution of John the Baptist is not compelling. Although Josephus' portrayal can indeed evoke such an impression,[44] the excursus on John the Baptist (Josephus, *Ant.* xviii.116-19) might also have been inserted here for thematic reasons. Why should not a few Jews, around ten years after the execution of John the Baptist, still view this lost battle as God's judgment on Herod Antipas (Josephus, *Ant.* xviii.116)?[45] According to the Gospels (Mt. 14:3f./Mk. 6:17f./Lk. 3:19f.) — and the context in Josephus supports this portrayal — the illegitimate marriage (Lev. 18:16) between Antipas and Herodias, the wife of his half-brother,[46] occasioned the Baptist's

---

40. *NTS* 29 (1983) 456-59.

41. *Ibid.,* 459-64. So also N. Kokkinos, in *Festschrift J. Finegan* (1989) 131-37.

42. *RB* 92 (1984) 362-76; *Histoire d'Israël* (1985) 239-41.

43. *Ibid.,* 92 (1984) 371-75.

44. E. M. Smallwood, *The Jews under Roman Rule* ([2]1981) 185, note 20, speaks about a "misleading impression," since she similarly considers the Gospel chronology to be dependable.

45. So also G. Hölscher, *SHAW* 1939/40 III (1940) 28-30.

46. Josephus calls him Herod (*Ant.* xviii.110), though under certain circumstances he might also have borne the distinguishing surname Philip, which Mk. 6:17 provides for him. This possibility, pointed out by H. W. Hoehner, *Herod Antipas* ([2]1981) 131-36, and followed by R. Pesch, *Markusevangelium* I ([4]1984) 340, cannot be refuted simply by apodictic judgments such as that of D. Lührmann, *Markusevangelium* (1987) 114 ("attempts at harmonization"). Cf. nonetheless E. Haenchen, *Der Weg Jesu* ([2]1968) 238, note 1. In other ways, too, Mk. 6:17-29 is not necessarily as hopelessly unhistorical as asserted by W. Schenk, *NTS* 29 (1983) 466-68. Mark might very well presuppose the execution of John the Baptist at the fortress Machaerus in eastern Transjordan (Josephus, *Ant.* xviii.119)

words of chastisement and constituted at least one of the reasons for his arrest.[47] If one follows E. M. Smallwood's dating of the marriage to *ca.* A.D. 25,[48] an assumption W. Schenk also approximates,[49] then an interesting congruency emerges with our own dating of the beginning of John the Baptist's ministry: in the year A.D. 26/27, indignation on the part of believers concerning this breach of the law was still quite fresh. Fear of unrest may have caused a quick elimination of this impressive penitential preacher to seem advisable to Antipas. Antipas might have had an additional reason for arresting John the Baptist in the year A.D. 27/28.

3.2.3. John the Baptist, Jesus, and the Year of Release

In several publications, A. Strobel has pointed out the significance that the anticipation of a messianic Year of Release possesses for the chronology of Jesus' ministry,[50] though commensurate with recent calculations of the Sabbatical Years by B. Z. Wacholder[51] his dating must be increased by one year. In this calculation, a Sabbatical Year did not occur until A.D. 27/28. Both Strobel and Wacholder emphasize how seriously many Jewish groups took the reckoning of the messianic time by trying to combine the prophecy in Dan. 9:24-29 with the cycle of Sabbatical Years in circulation. Wacholder coined the term "chronomessianism" for these efforts.[52] Of course, the various

---

(F. Manns, *SBFLA* 21 [1981] 287-90; R. Riesner, *BiKi* 39 [1984] 176), and even the designation of Herodias' daughter as κοράσιον may be correct (Schuerer, I, 348f., note 28). On this entire complex, cf. R. H. Gundry, *Mark* (1993) 311-21.

47. N. Kokkinos, *PEQ* 118 (1986) 39-42, suggests a new solution to these problems, namely, that the husband of Herodias before her marriage with Antipas was actually the tetrarch Philip. Since Herodias allegedly remarried only after the death of Philip (A.D. 33/34), the execution of John the Baptist would be dated at A.D. 35 and the death of Jesus at A.D. 36. In addition to other difficulties (§3.5.1), N. Kokkinos must draw support from the version of the Slavonic Josephus (textual expansion according to Josephus, *B.J.* ii.168 [ed. Thackeray III, 646f.]) and assume that the Baptist's reprimand was prompted by Jesus' prohibition against remarriage (Mk. 10:11)!

48. *The Jews under Roman Rule* (²1981) 185; similarly also A. Barrett, *Caligula* (1989) 183. The illegitimate marriage with Herodias was associated with a trip to Rome to Tiberius (Josephus, *Ant.* xviii.110f.). Since the emperor left the city in A.D. 26 for good (W. Otto, *PRE Suppl* I/2 [1913] 182), this year constitutes a *terminus ad quem*.

49. *NTS* 29 (1983) 465: "probable from 20/25 on."

50. *ThLZ* 92 (1967) 251-54; in E. Grässer and W. Eltester, *Jesus in Nazareth* (1972) 38-51; *Ursprung und Geschichte des frühchristlichen Osterkalenders* (1977) 92-97; *NTS* 41 (1995) 466-69. Cf. already the brief references in J. van Goudoever, *Biblical Calendars* (²1961) 268f.

51. *HUCA* 44 (1973) 153-96. In my opinion, B. Z. Wacholder, *HUCA* 54 (1983) 123-33, persuasively refuted the objections presented by D. Blosser, *HUCA* 52 (1981) 129-39.

52. *HUCA* 46 (1975) 201-18.

circles differed in their dating.[53] According to one possible calculation, with the year A.D. 27/28 ten Jubilee-Year periods had passed since the reestablishment of the observation of Sabbatical Years by Ezra from 457/56 B.C. on (Ezra 7:8), or the decisive and final year of weeks (A.D. 27/28-34/35) had commenced according to Dan. 9:26.[55] If an explosive apocalyptic mood has to be assumed for many circles around the year A.D. 27/28, then an arrest of John the Baptist around this same period seems especially understandable. Josephus explicitly mentions the fear Herod Antipas had of a potential rebellion (*Ant.* xviii.118: δείσας Ἡρώδης τὸ ἐπὶ τοσόνδε πιθανὸν αὐτοῦ τοῖς ἀνθρώποις μὴ ἐπὶ στάσει τινὶ φέροι, πάντα γὰρ ἐῴκεσαν συμβουλῇ τῇ ἐκείνου πράξαντες . . .). John the Baptist's public criticism of the ruler's illegitimate marriage might have been one of the decisive factors prompting action. The account of Josephus on the one hand, and the portrayals in the Synoptics on the other, do not necessarily stand irreconcilably opposed here, but rather can complement one another at least partially.[56]

Was it fortuitous that according to our reckoning John the Baptist appeared publicly one year before the beginning of what was possibly an eschatologically significant Sabbatical Year, or were the corresponding apocalyptic expectations also of significance for him? One must reckon seriously with this possibility. If John originally came from a milieu close to that of the Essenes,[57] then one must recall the preeminent significance the tenth Jubilee according to Dan. 9:24f. possesses in the apocalyptic Melchizedek Fragment from Cave 11.[58] According to the proclamation of the Year of Release (Isa. 61:1), the eschatological atonement (Lev. 25:9) by Melchizedek (11QMelch 2:7) will come at the end of the tenth Jubilee (הֹן[וא]ה ס[וף הֹיוֹ[בל העשירי). According to a probable reconstruction, 11QMelch 2:18 anticipates that the coming of an anointed one, identified with the messenger of joy in Isa. 52:7 (והמבשר הוֹ[אה] מֹשֹיח הרוֹן[ח]), and commensurate with Daniel (Dan. 9:25), will be preceded by seven sabbatical cycles, whereby because of the fragmen-

---

53. Cf. B. Z. Wacholder, *HUCA* 46 (1975) 209-13; R. T. Beckwith, *RQ* 10 (1980/81) 167-202, 521-42.

54. Cf. B. Z. Wacholder, *HUCA* 52 (1973) 157f., 185.

55. Cf. A. Strobel, *Ursprung und Geschichte des frühchristlichen Osterkalenders* (1977) 94-96.

56. Cf. also Excursus II (pp. 328ff.).

57. Cf. the bibliography in R. Riesner, *Jesus als Lehrer* ([3]1988) 292f., and in S. L. Davies, *NTS* 29 (1983) 569-71; O. Betz, in B. Mayer, *Christen und Christliches in Qumran?* (1992) 159-64; O. Betz and R. Riesner, *Jesus, Qumran, and the Vatican* (1994) 143-45.

58. Cf. B. Z. Wacholder, *HUCA* 54 (1975) 210f. Concerning textual reconstruction see M. de Jonge and A. S. van der Woude, *NTS* 12 (1965/66) 301-26; J. T. Milik, *JJS* 23 (1972) 95-144, and now especially É. Puech, *RQ* 12 (1987) 483-514, according to which our columnization is given.

tary condition of the Pesher the point of departure of these calculations remains unclear, and the relationship between the messianic figure and the heavenly Melchizedek is also difficult to determine. John the Baptist anticipated the "one who is to come" (Mt. 11:3/Lk. 7:19: ὁ ἐρχόμενος), that is, the "Son of Man coming on the clouds of heaven" (הוה אתה, LXX Theodotion ἐρχόμενος ἦν) of Dan. 7:13[59] — and not, for example, "God's coming" as such, as has repeatedly been asserted. It would, after all, have been quite peculiar had John the Baptist given thought to the thongs of God's sandals (Mk. 1:7/Lk. 3:16).

John's doubts regarding Jesus' sending would be especially understandable if the Sabbatical Year A.D. 27/28 concluded without his having heard, in prison, of the release of prisoners and of God's vengeance, as could be anticipated for the messianic Year of Release according to Isa. 61:1f. It is in any case striking that Jesus' response, with its reference to the good news to the poor, picks up precisely on Isa. 61:1 (לבשׂר ענוים) (Mt. 11:5/Lk. 7:22 [πτωχοὶ εὐαγγελίζονται]). The so-called inaugural sermon in Nazareth also militates for a connection between Jesus' own emergence and the Sabbatical Year A.D. 27/28. The Sabbatical Year provides the thematic background both in the version of the separate Lukan tradition (Lk. 4:17-21 [Lk. 4:18f. = Isa. 61:1f.]) and, independent of that version, in the Markan version (Mk. 6:1 [καὶ ἔρχεται εἰς τὴν πατρίδα αὐτοῦ] cf. Lev. 25:10).[60] This concurrence of independent strands of tradition suggests that this is an accurate recollection. One further possible reference to the beginning of Jesus' ministry in the Sabbatical Year A.D. 27/28 can be found in the Johannine tradition.

3.2.4. John 2:20

To Jesus' announcement at his first public Passover festival (Jn. 2:19): "Destroy this temple, and in three days I will raise it up (λύσατε τὸν ναὸν τοῦτον καὶ ἐν τρισὶν ἡμέραις ἐγερῶ αὐτόν)," his Jewish adversaries respond: τεσσεράκοντα καὶ ἓξ ἔτεσιν οἰκοδομήθη ὁ ναὸς οὗτος, καὶ σὺ ἐν τρισὶν ἡμέραις ἐγερεῖς αὐτόν; (Jn. 2:20). It is extremely unlikely that the Johannine intention is to provide a symbolic interpretation of the year number (gematria value of the Greek word ΑΔΑΜ), as provided later, for example, by Augustine[61] (In Joh. tr. X [CC 36, 107f.]).[62] Any reference to the (second) temple of Zerub-

---

59. Concerning the historicity of the pericope of John the Baptist's query, cf. W. G. Kümmel, *Jesu Antwort an Johannes den Täufer* (1974); R. Riesner, *Jesus als Lehrer* (³1988) 299-301 (with bibliography).

60. Cf. A. Strobel, in E. Grässer and W. Eltester, *Jesus in Nazareth* (1976) 38-51; O. Betz, in *Der Messias Israels* (1987) 311f.

61. Cf. H. J. Vogels, *BZ* 6 (1962) 102-7.

62. Cf. R. Schnackenburg, *The Gospel According to St. John* I (Eng. trans., New York, 1990) 351f.

babel, as advocated again now by R. Jewett[63] drawing on earlier scholars,[64] must be rejected because of the demonstrative οὖτος. The reference is to the holy site existing at the time of the dialogue,[65] that is, to the (third) temple constructed by Herod the Great.[66] For the beginning of the construction work, Josephus offers the two competing dates of the fifteenth (23/22 B.C. [Josephus, *B.J.* i.401]) and the eighteenth year (20/19 B.C. [Josephus, *Ant.* xv.380]) of Herod. A newly discovered founder-inscription from the area south of the temple wall, which mentions the twentieth year of a king (namely, of Herod, 18/17 B.C.),[67] is unable to resolve this question. However, since the eighteenth year of Herod coincides with the journey of Augustus to Syria in the spring or early summer of 20 B.C. (Dio, *Hist.* liv.7), almost all modern scholars date the beginning of the temple construction around this time.[68]

Following the lead of J. Finegan,[69] H. W. Hoehner[70] differentiates between the overall (ἱερόν) and inner sanctuary (ναός).[71] He relates Jn. 2:20 to the finishing of the actual temple edifice (ναός), which, according to Josephus, took place one-and-a-half years after the beginning of construction (Josephus, *Ant.* xv.421), and translates: "The temple has stood as a completed building for forty-six years."[72] The Passover in question would then be dated in A.D. 29/30. The *tertium comparationis* for the response of Jesus' Jewish dialogue partners, however, is his prediction that he will need a construction time of only three days for the new temple (Jn. 2:19). The sense of Jn. 2:20 can thus hardly be any other than "this temple was built in forty-six years."[73] Since the construction of the external sanctuary (ἱερόν) similarly began immediately, the evaluation of the suggested terminological distinction changes nothing in the calculations. Depending on whether one assumes that Herod did not begin the temple construc-

63. *A Chronology of Paul's Life* (1979) 28, 119, note 25.

64. E. A. Abbott, *ClR* 8 (1895) 89-93; H. W. Husband, *TARA* 46 (1915) 14f. Similarly E. Schwartz, *AGWG.PH* VII/5 (1904) 7f.

65. Cf. T. Zahn, *Das Evangelium des Johannes* ([5/6]1921) 176.

66. This is also assumed, e.g., by a modern Jewish scholar such as B. Mazar, in H. Shanks, *Recent Archaeology in the Land of the Bible* (1985) 143, who reckons quite self-evidently with having access to useful chronological information in John.

67. B. Isaac, *IEJ* 33 (1983) 86-92.

68. Cf. the bibliography in Schuerer, I, 292, note 12; E. M. Smallwood, *The Jews under Roman Rule* ([2]1981) 92, note 112. So also, e.g., K. P. Donfried, *ABD* I (1992) 1014.

69. *Handbook of Biblical Chronology* (1964) 278-80.

70. *Chronological Aspects of the Life of Christ* ([5]1981) 40-43.

71. The same differentiation was already made by J. van Bebber, *Zur Chronologie des Lebens Jesu* (1898) 123-30. E. Power, *Bibl* 9 (1928) 257-88, provided probably the most thorough argumentation for this distinction. For further representatives, see A. Strobel, *Ursprung und Geschichte des frühchristlichen Osterkalenders* (1977) 97, note 2.

72. *Loc. cit.,* 42.

73. Cf. C. K. Barrett, *The Gospel According to St. John* ([2]1978) 200.

tion until the second half of the year 20/19 B.C., and then calculates either inclusively or conclusively, the possibilities that emerge for the Johannine dating of the temple cleansing are Passover A.D. 27[74] or A.D. 28.[75]

Even if calculations involving these individual references from the Gospels do yet contain elements of uncertainty, our own dating does have the advantage that a historically meaningful sequence emerges even though the information is drawn from mutually independent sources: (1) The emergence of John the Baptist in the fifteenth year of the coregency (A.D. 26/27) of Tiberius (separate Lukan tradition); (2) the emergence of Jesus in an apoca-lyptically significant (A.D. 27/28) Sabbatical Year (Mark, separate Lukan tradition); (3) Jesus' first public Passover in A.D. 27 or 28 (John).

3.2.5. The Duration of Jesus' Ministry

References to a longer ministry found in the first Gospels militate for the Johannine outline of Jesus engaging in a ministry lasting several years, and against the impression of barely a single year as portrayed in the Synoptics.[76] We will mention only three of the most important observations[77]: (1) The oracle of judgment on Jerusalem found in Mt. 23:37/Lk. 13:34 ("How often [ποσάκις] have I desired to gather your children together . . .") presupposes in the understanding of the original listeners — who had to associate this logion first of all with Jesus' own ministry (and not immediately with that of preexistent wisdom) — at least one, and more likely several previous visits to the holy city prior to the Passover of the crucifixion.[78] (2) The mention of "green grass" in Mk. 6:39 suggests an additional Easter period beyond the Passover of his death (cf. Jn. 6:4, 10).[79] (3) The parable of the sparing of the fig tree (Lk. 13:6-9) can, taken together with the symbolical cursing of the fig tree at the final Passover (Mt. 21:18f./Mk. 11:12-14), quite easily have in mind an approximately three-year ministry to Israel[80] for Jesus.[81] Depending

74. So, e.g., A. Strobel, *Ursprung und Geschichte des frühchristlichen Osterka-lenders* (1977) 97f.

75. Cf. among others J. Blinzler, *Der Prozeß Jesu* (⁴1969) 103.

76. The older (also patristic) discussion is summarized by W. Homanner, *Die Dauer der öffentlichen Wirksamkeit Jesu* (1908).

77. Cf. further A. Strobel, *Ursprung und Geschichte des frühchristlichen Oster-kalenders* (1977) 78-81; J. A. T. Robinson, *The Priority of John* (1985) 124-27, and also H. Windisch, *ZNW* 12 (1911) 141-75.

78. Cf. R. Riesner, *Jesus als Lehrer* (³1988) 327f. (with bibliography).

79. Cf. J. A. T. Robinson, *The Priority of John* (1985) 126f.

80. Concerning the fig tree as a metaphor for the people of God, cf. Hos. 9:10; Jer. 8:13; Jer. 24:1-10.

81. Cf. E. Klostermann, *Das Lukasevangelium* (²1929) 143; J. J. Gunther, *Paul: Messenger and Exile* (1972) 23.

on whether one finds reference to yet another Easter in Jn. 5:1 beyond the Passover festivals John mentions expressly (Jn. 2:13; 6:4; 12:1ff.), from the fourth Gospel one might then conclude that Jesus' ministry lasted a bit longer than two[82] or three years.[83] From the perspective of our calculations to this point (first Passover in A.D. 27 or 28), the possible time frame for the Passover of the crucifixion would thus be the years A.D. 29-31.

3.3. The Day of the Crucifixion

3.3.1. John and the Synoptics

According to all four Gospels, the day of Jesus' execution was the day of preparation (παρασκευή) for a sabbath (Mt. 27:62/Mk. 15:42/Lk. 23:54-56/Jn. 19:31, 42), and thus a Friday. Since the Synoptics speak of a Passover meal taking place the night before the crucifixion (Mt. 26:17-19/Mk. 14:12-16/Lk. 22:7-13, 15), they seem to assume that the day of death was the fifteenth of Nisan. By contrast, John clearly assumes that the crucifixion took place on the day of preparation for the Passover festival (cf. Jn. 18:28; 19:14 [παρα-σκευὴ τοῦ πάσχα]).[84] But even if John had a theological interest in the Passover symbolism (cf. Jn. 19:33-36), his dating is also supported on historical grounds, of which we will mention only a few:[85]

(1) Paul might already be presupposing the fourteenth of Nisan as the day of death[86] by calling Jesus the Passover lamb slaughtered for the believers (καὶ γὰρ τὸ πάσχα ἡμῶν ἐτύθη Χριστός; 1 Cor. 5:7). In the same letter, the apostle refers to the resurrected one as the "the first fruits (ἀπαρχή) of those who have died [fallen asleep]" (1 Cor. 15:20). This comparison might have been prompted by the fact that the firstling sheaf of the grain harvest (Lev. 23:10f., LXX ἀπαρχή) was consecrated to God in the temple on the sixteenth of Nisan,[87] and in the same context Paul mentions the resurrection "on the third day" (ἐγήγερται τῇ ἡμέρᾳ τῇ τρίτῃ; 1 Cor. 15:4).

(2) The Passover amnesty also mentioned by the Synoptics (Mt. 27:15-

---

82. Thus the reconstructions of, among others, S. Dockx, *Chronologies néotestamentaires* (²1984) 3-11; J. A. T. Robinson, *The Priority of John* (1985) 123-57.

83. Thus the assessment of, e.g., A. Strobel, *Ursprung und Geschichte des frühchristlichen Osterkalenders* (1977) 98-100.

84. Cf. E. Ruckstuhl, *Die Chronologie des Letzten Mahles und des Leidens Jesu* (1963) 20f.; *Jesus im Horizont der Evangelien* (1988) 121f.; in B. Mayer, *Christen und Christliches in Qumran?* (1992) 131f.

85. Cf. further J. Blinzler, *Der Prozeß Jesu* (⁴1969) 101-9.

86. Cf. J. Blinzler, *loc. cit.* 106.

87. So already E. Preuschen, *ZNW* 5 (1904) 15f.

26/Mk. 15:6-15/Lk. 23:17-25) was meaningful as a political appeasement measure only before the festival.[88] Here the Mishna (*mPesaḥ.* 8:6) supports the dating of the amnesty on the fourteenth of Nisan as presupposed by John (Jn. 18:39f.).[89]

(3) If, as is probable, Pilate's visit in Jerusalem was a normal court journey *(conventus, iurisdictio),* then the trial had to be concluded before the beginning of the Passover festival,[90] since no trials were conducted on indigenous *dies nefasti* either.[91]

(4) A Baraita of the Babylonian Talmud (*b. Sanh.* 43a), one that can hardly be dependent on either the fourth Gospel or any other Christian tradition, preserves a tradition of the second century[92] and dates the execution of Jesus clearly on the day prior to the Passover festival (בערב הפסח).[93]

(5) Although the Gospel of Peter from the middle of the second century[94] does presuppose the canonical Gospels and to that extent does not represent an independent source,[95] it retains interest as the oldest interpretation. It formulates unmistakably: "And he [Herod Antipas? Pilate?] gave him over to the people on the day before their Festival of Unleavened Bread (πρὸ μιᾶς τῶν ἀζύμων)" (*PtEv* 5 [SC 201,42]). Hence even scholars[96] who do not grant to John the value of a historical source[97] do decide in favor of his dating of the crucifixion on the fourteenth of Nisan.[98]

---

88. Cf. E. Ruckstuhl, *Jesus im Horizont der Evangelien* (1988) 148f., 182f.

89. Cf. B. Chavel, *JBL* 60 (1941) 273-78; J. Blinzler, *Der Prozeß Jesu* (⁴1969) 106, 317-20; A. Strobel, *Die Stunde der Wahrheit* (1980) 120-24; R. H. Gundry, *Mark* (1993) 934-36.

90. Cf. B. Kinman, *TynBul* 42 (1991) 282-95.

91. A good example is the decree of Marcus Agrippa, which, *ca.* 14 B.C., freed the Jews from trial obligations on the sabbath (Josephus, *Ant.* xvi.168).

92. Cf. J. Blinzler, *Der Prozeß Jesu* (⁴1969) 41-45. Contra J. Maier, *Jesus von Nazareth in der talmudischen Überlieferung* (1978) 219-32, who doubts the connection between the Talmud passage and Jesus, cf. O. Betz, *ANRW* II 25.1 (1982) 570-80. The objections of O. Betz also apply to G. H. Twelftree, in D. Wenham, *Gospel Perspectives* V (1984) 319-21.

93. The Hebrew term does not refer to the evening of the Passover (15 Nisan), but rather, like its Greek equivalent in Jn. 19:14, to the preceding day or day of Preparation of the festival, and can virtually be used as a reference to a specific day of the month (14 Nisan). Cf. Bill. II 812, note 1; 834f.

94. Cf. W. Schneemelcher, *NTApo* II (⁵1987) 182-85.

95. Cf. M. G. Mara, *Évangile de Pierre* (1973) 213f. A different view is taken by H. Koester, *Ancient Christian Gospels* (1990) 216-30, who does not, however, consider the implications of the dating.

96. H. Braun, *Jesus* (1984) 41; G. Bornkamm, *Jesus of Nazareth* (Eng. trans., 1995 [copyright 1960]) 160; K. P. Donfried, *ABD* I (1992) 1015f.

97. For the Passion story (including its chronology), the ancient historian F. Millar prefers John over the Synoptics, in *Festschrift G. Vermes* (1990) 355-81.

98. The question thus arises whether the Synoptics are simply in error, are

3.3.2. The Contribution of Astronomy

Advances during recent years enable astronomers to determine to a high degree of probability the possible dates of the Jewish Passover festivals during the New Testament period.[99] Let us choose cautiously first the longer time frame from A.D. 26 (according to Lk. 3:1 the first possible public Passover for Jesus) until A.D. 36 (last Easter festival under the prefecture of Pilate), which also corresponds to the majority opinion concerning the duration of this prefect's time in office. The dates emerging then for a fourteenth or fifteenth of Nisan on Friday are:

Jewish Day	Julian Date
14 Nisan	11 April 27
	7 April 30
	3 April 33
15 Nisan	11 April 27
	23 April 34

In the year A.D. 27, it was possible under poor viewing conditions that the new moon could not be observed until the following day, and thus the fourteenth of Nisan could be either a Thursday or a Friday. In the year A.D. 34, the fifteenth of Nisan could fall on a Friday only if because of extraordinarily bad weather conditions an additional month was inserted; we have no information regarding any such intercalation in the years A.D. 26 to A.D. 36. However, the two years A.D. 27 and 34 can also be excluded on the basis of other references in the Gospels (§3.2). A substantive aid in deciding which of the astronomically possible dates in the years A.D. 30 and 33 represents the actual date of Jesus' crucifixion is provided by the extensive material available in the early Christian calendar tradition.

---

consciously narrating in an abbreviated manner, or whether at least the sources or traditions from which they drew still betray any knowledge of the historically correct chronology. E. Ruckstuhl, *Jesus im Horizont der Evangelien* (1988) 101-84, recently tried again to demonstrate a combination of the last two possibilities. A useful overview of harmonizing and nonharmonizing suggestions for solutions can be found in R. T. France, *VE* 16 (1986) 43-59; D. L. Bock, *Luke* II (1996) 1951-60.

99. Cf. now esp. C. J. Humphreys and W. G. Waddington, *Nature* 306 (1983) 743f.; *JASA* 37 (1985) 2-4. R. T. Beckwith, in *Festschrift J. Finegan* (1989) 183-98, correctly points out possible elements of uncertainty in the ancient Jewish calculations. But cf. K. Ferrari D'Occhieppo, *Der Stern der Weisen* (^{2}1977) 152-60.

3.4. The Early Christian Tradition

3.4.1. The Day of the Crucifixion

If one eliminates those dates mentioned in the ancient church that were calculated on the basis of symbolism (e.g., the association of equinoxes with Jesus' act of redemption) or are obviously chronologically erroneous (as are all dates in March because of the grain harvest), then 7 April acquires unequivocal primacy.[100] Clement of Alexandria already mentions 7 April as one of the three dates calculated by "careful researchers" (Clement of Alexandria, *Stromateis* i.21.146). In contrast to the larger Church, the Montanists, whose traditions extend back at least into the middle of the second century A.D., always celebrated the remembrance of the death of Jesus on the same day of the month, earlier probably on 7 April, and then later on 6 April. W. Huber[101] has correctly pointed out contra B. Lohse[102] that this group accepted the Johannine Passion chronology because it was already older than the composition of the fourth Gospel. Huber's attempt to explain the origin of this chronology on the basis of purely typological considerations, however, is inadequate.[103]

3.4.2. The Year of the Crucifixion

Early Christian writings mention years almost exclusively between 28 and 33, and as a rule the information in the Gospels we discussed earlier (§3.2) constitutes the point of departure for the calculations. With some degree of certainty, however, two strands of tradition are independent of this information. Within what is always the extremely conservative liturgical tradition, the sixteen-year Easter cycle of Hippolytus, preserving traditions passed down from the second century, probably presupposes A.D. 30 as the year of Jesus' death. The same applies to the ancient Christian Easter cycle of eighty-four years with its interesting connections to the Essene solar calendar, and to the similarly ancient Alexandrian cycle.[104] A dating of the crucifixion in the "year of the Gemini" (i.e., of the consuls Rubellius and Fufius Geminus, A.D. 29) was widespread, and here Tertullian is our first witness (Tertullian, *Adv. Jud.* 8 [PL 2.615f.]). But because this calculation presumably stems from Egypt,

---

100. Cf. A. Strobel, *ZNW* 51 (1960) 69-101; *Ursprung und Geschichte des frühchristlichen Osterkalenders* (1977) 122-456.

101. *Passa und Ostern* (1969) 21-25.

102. *Das Passahfest der Quartadecimaner* (1953) 89-112.

103. Cf. A. Strobel, *Ursprung und Geschichte des frühchristlichen Osterkalenders* (1977) 167-224.

104. Cf. *ibid.*, 122-66, 281-324.

where years began on August 29, this tradition, too, can originally be referring to the Passover of the year A.D. 30.[105] Thus a critical evaluation of the ancient Christian tradition clearly points to 7 April A.D. 30 as the date of Jesus' death.

3.5. The Most Probable Date

Whereas earlier every conceivable year between A.D. 26 and 36 was advocated as that of the crucifixion of Jesus,[106] in the publications of the past decade only four datings have attracted more than one advocate.[107] From the two preceding decades I am familiar with only a few exceptions advocating A.D. 29.[108] The soundness of the current dates can now be examined also on the basis of the previous discussion.

3.5.1. The Year A.D. 36

This particular date, advocated in the nineteenth century by K. T. Keim in his influential *Life of Jesus,*[109] has been defended in the twentieth century only

---

105. Cf. U. Holzmeister, *Chronologia Vitae Christi* (1933) 169-72.

106. Overviews can be found in K. Wieseler, *Chronologie des apostolischen Zeitalters* (1848), tables after 606; D. Plooij, *De chronologie van het leven van Paulus* (1919), comparative table after 174; J. Blinzler, *Der Prozeß Jesu* (⁴1969) 101f.

107. J. P. Lemonon, *Pilate et le gouvernement de la Judée* (1981) 133, does mention 27 April A.D. 31 as a possibility, but offers no further justification for this date. He is probably alluding to J. Jeremias (see note 4). W. Hinz, *ZDMG* 139 (1989) 303-6, taking erroneous assumptions as a point of departure (e.g., A.D. 11: Tiberius coregent, Jn. 2:13-20: Passover of the crucifixion), arrives at the date A.D. 28. An utterly unconventional chronology is offered by J. Vardaman, in *Festschrift J. Finegan* (1989) 55-82, esp. 66-77 (printing errors involving the dates amplify the confusion). In this view, A.D. 14/15 was the beginning, and 25/26 the end of Pilate's time in office. Jesus began his ministry in A.D. 15. Vardaman concludes this from previously unseen "micro-letters" on a coin cast in Damascus which designates A.D. 16 as the "first year of Jesus' reign." Because a census took place in A.D. 21, Jesus was crucified in this year. The relationship between the two events remains just as obscure as does the possibility of reconciling a ministry of six years for Jesus with the information in the Gospels. Vardaman assumes the presence of a scribal error in Lk. 3:1 (second instead of fifteenth year of Tiberius). I am grateful to Dr. Jerry Vardaman (Mississippi State University) for having made his hypothesis available to me in an early form (*Biblical Illustrator* [4/1985] 12-18). Here he also comes to terms with Lk. 3:1 by assuming that the fifteenth year of Tiberius is to be reckoned from the latter's proconsular *imperium* in the year A.D. 4 (cf. Suetonius, *Tib.* 21.3) onward, which would, to be sure, then yield a date of A.D. 18/19 for the emergence of John the Baptist.

108. L. Dupraz, *De l'association de Tibère au principat à la naissance du Christ* (1966) 236f.; H. C. Snape, *Numen* 17 (1970) 195.

109. *Jesu von Nazara* III (1872) 489-93.

by outsiders such as H. J. Schonfield[110] and E. Barnikol (§1.4.3). Because he dates the execution of John the Baptist around A.D. 35 (§3.2.2), N. Kokkinos has now again expressed support for this year,[111] and has even found support from F. Millar.[112] This date, however, though still falling within the prefecture of Pilate (§3.1.1), fails not least because of astronomical considerations. In A.D. 36, the fourteenth and fifteenth of Nisan fell on Saturday/Sunday.[113] Kokkinos also gets into difficulties with Pauline chronology by dating the conversion of Paul to A.D. 37, since according to the tightest possible calculation (cf. Gal. 2:1ff.), the Apostolic Council would then have taken place in A.D. 50/51. Kokkinos finds that a fourteen-year period in the life of the apostle about which we know almost nothing is hard to accept. He shares this unwillingness with advocates of the new chronologies,[114] but finds himself forced to embrace even more radical measures in order to eliminate this problem: "It therefore seems *compulsory* to adopt the variant reading [for Gal. 2:1] of τέσσαρον found in the twelfth-century manuscript 1241ˢ (Sinai, Gr. 260), instead of δεκατέσσαρον."[115] Kokkinos seeks help here in the history of scholarship: "My conclusion on this point is in agreement with past research. For example, K. Wieseler wrote: 'Because of chronological embarrassment, not a few scholars . . . have wanted to write *tessáron* for *decatessáron,* though contra all manuscript evidence.' "[116] With that, Kokkinos himself (despite the one minuscule now known) cites the judgment on his own hypothesis.

3.5.2 The Year A.D. 27

G. Lüdemann is convinced that one "should also take the 27 into consideration, for G. Hölscher has presented arguments for this date that as yet have not been thoroughly refuted."[117] The greater part of Hölscher's work is actu-

---

110. *The Lost Book of the Nativity of John* (1929) 27f.

111. In *Festschrift J. Finegan* (1989) 133-63. N. Kokkinos, *PEQ* 118 (1986) 45f., falsely ascribes this dating also to K. Lake, who actually advocated A.D. 29 (*BC* V [1933] 467).

112. In *Festschrift G. Vermes* (1990) 380, note 1.

113. Cf. C. J. Humphreys and W. G. Waddington, *Nature* 306 (1983) 744.

114. K. P. Donfried, *ABD* I (1992) 1021: The new chronology "eliminates the long and problematic 'silent period' early in Paul's career. . . ."

115. In *Festschrift J. Finegan* (1989) 145; my emphasis.

116. In *Festschrift J. Finegan* (1989) 145. The quotation comes from K. Wieseler, *Commentar über den Brief Pauli an die Galater* (1859) 91.

117. G. Lüdemann, *Paul: Apostle to the Gentiles,* 171. A similar position was taken, albeit more cautiously ("weighty if not completely compelling reasons support A.D. 27") by P. Vielhauer, *Geschichte der urchristlichen Literatur* (1975) 78, and previously already by F. Hahn, *Das Verständnis der Mission im Neuen Testament* (1963) 76, who with respect to the astronomical dates draws support from the outdated studies of J. Jeremias,

ally an investigation into the sequence of high priests in Josephus without any direct relevance for the chronology of the Gospels.[118] For the dating of the crucifixion, Hölscher briefly mentions only two and one-half arguments:[119]

(1) Since Peter allegedly never returned to Jerusalem after his flight from the persecution of Herod Agrippa I as recounted in Acts 12:17, one must date the Apostolic Council at which Peter did participate (Gal. 2:9) to A.D. 43/44, and the conversion of Paul according to Gal. 1:18; 2:1 fifteen to sixteen years earlier, that is, A.D. 27/28 or 28/29. Lüdemann does not really follow this calculation, since he dates Paul's second Jerusalem visit and the Apostolic Council to A.D. 47 or 50![120]

(2) Hölscher calculated the beginning of Jesus'.ministry in A.D. 27 by drawing on the synchronism in Lk. 3:1, which Lüdemann, however, considers to be an unhistorical, redactional construction of Luke himself.[121]

(3) Finally, one uncertain dating argument Hölscher also mentioned is the dating of the first Passover festival of Jesus according to Jn. 2:20 in A.D. 27. It is difficult to imagine that Lüdemann considers precisely this Johannine piece of information to be "[a significant argument] that as yet [has] not been thoroughly refuted." One thus wonders whether really anything militates for dating the crucifixion in A.D. 27 other than the fact that a *terminus post quem* this early would be particularly favorable for Lüdemann's own schema of Pauline chronology. Besides the astronomical uncertainty (§3.2.2), one must object historically that this particular year of death would necessitate abandoning the Johannine multiple-year chronology as well as the ancient church tradition of A.D. 30.

3.5.3. The Year A.D. 33

This year is astronomically possible and is advocated by a whole series of scholars.[122] R. Jewett arrived at this crucifixion year from his decisive chrono-

---

The Eucharistic Words of Jesus (Eng. trans., 1966) 36-41. A. Schmidt, *ZNW* 81 (1990) 122-31, arrives at a crucifixion date of A.D. 27 through an accumulation of postulates. In this regard see p. 73, note 86 below.

118. *Die Hohenpriesterliste bei Josephus und die evangelische Chronologie* (1940) 3-22.

119. *Ibid.,* 25-28.

120. G. Lüdemann, *Paul: Apostle to the Gentiles,* 262.

121. *Ibid.,* 34, note 28.

122. So esp. H. E. W. Turner, in *Historicity and Chronology* (1965) 67-74; H. W. Hoehner, *Chronological Aspects of the Life of Christ* (1981) 95-114; in *Dictionary of Jesus and the Gospels* (1992) 119-22; B. Reicke, *The New Testament Era* (Eng. trans., 1968) 176-84; P. Keresztes, in *Imperial Rome and the Christians* I (1989) 36-43. Further representatives can be found in J. Blinzler, *Der Prozeß Jesu* (⁴1969) 101; R. Jewett, *A Chronology of Paul's Life* (1979) 28, 119, note 28.

logical fixed point, namely, Paul's flight from Damascus and his first visit to the early church in Jerusalem in A.D. 37 (§5.2), as well as the assumption of a conversion around 1½ years after the crucifixion of Jesus (§4.1).[123] In order to maintain this date, however, he must insist on other problematical assumptions. He associates Jn. 2:20 with the temple of Zerubbabel (§3.2.4) and only allows A.D. 28/29 to be considered as the "fifteenth year of Tiberius" (Lk. 3:1) (§3.2.1). Although Jewett is indeed familiar with the earlier version of the work of A. Strobel concerning the early Christian Easter calendar,[124] he does not indicate why he apparently considers the evidence militating for A.D. 30 to be irrelevant.

As an argument for the year A.D. 33, Jewett also points out that Pilate's accommodating posture toward the Sanhedrin as portrayed in the Gospels competes with the picture Philo and Josephus give of this governor's emphatically anti-Jewish attitude.[125] Pilate's behavior at the trial of Jesus allegedly is comprehensible only after the fall of his protector, the Roman Prefect of the Praetorian Guard and notorious Jew-hater (Philo, *Flacc.* 1; *Leg. ad Gaium* 159-61) Lucius Aelius Sejanus in the year A.D. 31.[126] But the extent to which the picture of Pilate presented by the Jewish sources is one-sidedly slanted is a matter of dispute.[127] J. P. Lemonon, who has undertaken the most extensive recent investigations regarding the prefect, concludes: "The Pilate of the Gospel sources is not noticeably different from that of the secular texts. . . . All the Gospels, like Josephus, suggest a measure of relative cooperation between Pilate and the high priests."[128]

In any event, the prefect's concern would become comprehensible at latest from that particular moment when the representatives of the Sanhedrin threatened to denounce him to the emperor on the basis of a *crimen laesae maiestatis,* as presupposed by the fourth Gospel (Jn. 19:12).[129] We possess more than merely general witnesses to the sensitivity with which Tiberius reacted to such suspicions (Tacitus, *Ann.* iii.38; Suetonius, *Tib.* 58). For this very reason, he even banished Agrippina, the granddaughter of Augustus, to the island of Pandateria in the year A.D. 29, where she subsequently starved to death (Tacitus, *Ann.* v.3f.; vi.25; xiv.63; Suetonius, *Tib.* 53). Reference to

123. *Loc. cit.,* 26-29.

124. A. Strobel, *ZNW* 51 (1960) 69-101.

125. *A Chronology of Paul's Life* (1979) 28.

126. So esp. A. D. Doyle, *JTS* 42 (1941) 190-93; E. Bammel, *ThLZ* 77 (1952) 205-10; P. L. Maier, *CH* 37 (1968) 3-13; H. W. Hoehner, *Chronological Aspects of the Life of Christ* (1981) 105-11; R. H. Gundry, *Mark* (1993) 931.

127. Cf. A. Strobel, *Die Stunde der Wahrheit* (1980) 99-105; B. C. McGing, *CBQ* 53 (1991) 416-38.

128. *ANRW* II 26.1 (1992) 776.

129. Cf. J. Blinzler, *Der Prozeß Jesu* (⁴1969) 337f.

the fall of Sejanus might thus be adduced at most as an additional argument if A.D. 33 were probable for other reasons as a date for the crucifixion. But Pilate as the mere executor of the antisemitic policies of Sejanus — this hardly holds up to the witness of all extant sources.[130]

New, unequivocal evidence for a crucifixion date of A.D. 33 was claimed by C. J. Humphreys and W. G. Waddington,[131] whose work enjoyed an unusual measure of publicity.[132] These two scholars deserve credit for having confirmed even further the astronomical possibilities already familiar regarding the crucifixion date (§3.3.2), though their assumption is erroneous that the lunar eclipse ascertainable for 3 April A.D. 33 has never been adduced in dating the crucifixion.[133] Ever since the reference by J. J. Scaliger in his work on the "improvement of the times"[134] from the year 1598, scholars have repeatedly associated this event in one way or another with the death of Jesus.[135] Humphreys and Waddington adduce for this association (missing in the Gospels) the sermon of Peter in Acts 2:20 ("the sun shall be turned to darkness and the moon to blood [= Joel 3:4 (Eng. 2:31)]"). That is, after Peter considers this passage from the prophecy of Joel concerning the pouring out of the spirit in the end time to be fulfilled through the Pentecost event (Acts 2:15f.), one must ask whether this does not also apply to other parts of the oracle. Moreover, the Acts of Pilate explicitly mentions that on the day of Jesus' death the moon turned the color of blood (*Acts Pil.* [ed. James] 154). At this point, however, the apocalyptic language is taken all too concretely,

130. Cf. D. Hennig, *L. Aelius Seianus* (1975) 174-79. Contra the assumption of a consciously anti-Jewish coinage by Pilate, cf. J. P. Lemonon, *ANRW* II 26.1 (1992) 757.

131. *Nature* 306 (1983) 743-46; *JASA* 37 (1985) 2-10, and now also in *Festschrift J. Finegan* (1989) 165-81.

132. Referential articles appeared in publications as different as the *Frankfurter Allgemeine Zeitung* (298 [Dec. 23, 1983] 7) and *Der Spiegel* (38/1 [Jan. 2, 1984] 126f.), the latter of which did, to be sure, falsely impute the following conclusion to the authors: "The two Oxford scientists believe that the unusual play of colors in the night sky must have moved the observers profoundly indeed, lending to the Messiah — still hanging on the cross — a kind of supranatural aura in the eyes of the spectators without which his message quite possibly might not have survived" (*loc. cit.,* 127).

133. *Nature* 306 (1983) 745: "We now consider further evidence that has not, to the best of our knowledge, been used in helping to date the crucifixion — the subsequent occurrence of a lunar eclipse." And even more strongly in *JASA* 37 (1985) 6: "We now consider the new evidence . . . , which provides the first positive dating of the crucifixion."

134. *De emendatione temporum* (1598) 561. Cf. U. Holzmeister, *Bibl* 13 (1932) 100, note 4.

135. E.g., A. Calmet, *Commentaire littéral sur S. Matthieu* (1725) 622; G. B. von Scharberg, *Die Chronologie des Lebens Jesu* II (1929) 86; R. Hennig, *Astronomische Nachrichten* 242 (1931) 110-13; J. K. Fotheringham, *JTS* 35 (1934) 160f. (this article is even cited by C. J. Humphreys and W. G. Waddington, *Nature* 306 [1983] 746, note 9; *JASA* 37 [1985] 10, note 12!); A. Strobel, *BHH* III (1966) 2224.

and the historical value of this apocryphal writing from the third/fourth century A.D. is considerably overestimated.[136] Even Humphreys and Waddington themselves must admit that the lunar eclipse in question here was not all that impressive: at the rising of the moon in Jerusalem it covered barely twenty percent of the lunar surface.[137] This "new" consideration, too, might be adduced at most only supplementally if A.D. 33 were otherwise the most likely date.

3.5.4. The Year A.D. 30

In arguing against this particular year, H. W. Hoehner[138] and R. Jewett[139] both adduce the evidence of a computer study by H. H. Goldstine[140] according to which in A.D. 30 the fourteenth of Nisan allegedly fell on a Thursday. But here they precipitately identify the date of the full moon (6 April 30), which was also known prior to Goldstine, with the fourteenth of Nisan. On 6 April 30, however, the full moon became visible only during the late afternoon, and accordingly could not be observed during the preceding night, but rather only in the night from the sixth to the seventh of April, during which, according to the Jewish manner of reckoning, April 7 began. Furthermore, consideration was not given to the fact that Goldstine makes his own calculations in "Greenwich mean time," whereas for the reckoning of local time in Jerusalem one must add two hours and twenty minutes.[141] In the year A.D. 30, the night of the actually visible full moon was thus 7 April = 14 Nisan. This equivalency is secured yet again by its attestation in the astronomical calendar of the Babylonians.[142]

Even C. J. Humphreys and W. G. Waddington, despite their own preference for A.D. 33, consider it "highly improbable" that in A.D. 30 the fourteenth of Nisan fell on a Thursday.[143] But the year A.D. 30 is not only astronomically possible. In contrast to A.D. 27 and 33, the year A.D. 30 can be reconciled without significant difficulties with the other information in the Gospels as well (§3.2), and this date is the only one that has a serious early

---

136. Cf. also H. Riesenfeld, *SEÅ* 51/52 (1986/87) 198-202.

137. *Nature* 306 (1983) 746; *JASA* 37 (1985) 8. U. Holzmeister already drew attention to this in *Bibl* 13 (1932) 100.

138. *Chronological Aspects of the Life of Christ* (1981) 100.

139. *A Chronology of Paul's Life* (1979) 117f., note 12.

140. *New and Full Moons 1001 B.C. to A.D. 1651* (1973) 86.

141. I would like to thank the former Professor of Theoretical Astronomy at the University of Vienna, Professor Konradin Ferrari d'Occhieppo (Innsbruck) for an epistolary discussion of the questions relating to this complex.

142. Cf. R. A. Parker and W. H. Dubberstein, *Babylonian Chronology* (1956) 46.

143. *Nature* 306 (1983) 744.

Christian tradition (§3.4) on its side. Therefore, the fourteenth of Nisan (7 April) of the year A.D. 30 is, apparently in the opinion of the majority of contemporary scholars as well,[144] far and away the most likely date of the crucifixion of Jesus.

144. So, among others, M. Hengel, in *Festschrift O. Cullmann* (1972) 44; in M. Hengel and U. Heckel, *Paulus und das antike Judentum* (1991) 265f.; J. J. Gunther, *Paul* (1972) 19-24; R. H. Mellersh, *Chronology of the Ancient World* (1976) 287; A. Strobel, *Ursprung und Geschichte des frühchristlichen Osterkalenders* (1977) 70-121; W. P. Armstrong and J. Finegan, *ISBE* I (1979) 688f.; C. J. Hemer, in *Festschrift F. F. Bruce* (1980) 13; S. Dockx, *Chronologies néotestamentaires* ([2]1984) 21-29; E. Ruckstuhl, *Jesus im Horizont der Evangelien* (1988) 121f.; K. F. Doig, *New Testament Chronology* (1991) 237-324; K. P. Donfried, *ABD* I (1992) 1016; J. Gnilka, *Paulus von Tarsus* (1996) 310; B. Wander, *Trennungsprozesse zwischen frühem Christentum und Judentum* ([2]1997) 54, 277. Further representatives can be found in J. Blinzler, *Der Prozeß Jesu* ([4]1969) 101.

§4

Persecution of Stephen and Conversion

4.1. The Time of the Persecution of Stephen

4.1.1. The Seven-Year Tradition

In the fourteenth century, Nicephorus Callistus claims in his church history to have learned from "Evodius the follower of the apostles" that "the period from the suffering . . . and the resurrection and assumption . . . into heaven till the stoning . . . of Stephen was seven years" (Nicephorus, *HE* ii.3 [PG 145.757]). The reference is probably to that particular Evodius whom Eusebius mentions as the first bishop of Antioch (Eusebius, *HE* iii.22). An addendum in a Milanese manuscript of the apocryphal Martyrdom of Stephen (*AnBoll* 72 [1954] 330) is presumably citing the same tradition as does Nicephorus.[1] This seven-year period is firmly attested in the *World Chronicle* of Hippolytus of Thebes from the seventh/eighth centuries A.D., who also understands the conversion of Paul as following six months upon the martyrdom of Stephen (iii.1f. [ed. Diekamp 3f.]). In the ninth century, Epiphanius Monachus also accepted this date, which otherwise attracted few explicit advocates.[2]

    A. Strobel, however, draws attention to two additional chronological traditions of this sort.[3] Manuscript B of the *Chronographer of A.D. 354* dates the martyrdom of Stephen to the sixth year after what the chronographer has accepted as a crucifixion date of A.D. 29, that is, A.D. 34 (*ASGW* I [1850] 659). According to the *Syrian Chronicon ad A.D. 846 p. Chr. pertinens* (*CSCO* III/4 137,25f.), Peter's founding of the Antiochene church took place in the year 350 of the Alexandrian era, and thus in A.D. 38. If the prior persecution is referring to the expulsion of the Hellenists from Jerusalem (Acts 11:27), the latter might

---

    1. Cf. S. Giet, *TU* 63 (1957) 607f.

    2. Cf. F. Diekamp, *Hippolytos von Theben* (1898) 86f. Perhaps the singular dating of the *Chronicon Paschale* in the ninth year after the Passion (ed. Dindorf, I 433) is also dependent on this tradition.

    3. *Ursprung und Geschichte des frühchristlichen Osterkalenders* (1977) 116.

59

be presupposed for A.D. 37/38. By contrast, Elijah Nisibenus, in his *Opus chronologicum* (*CSCO* III/7 38,4f.), dates the founding of this church to the year 353 (A.D. 41), though in this context the reference seems to be to Peter's flight from Jerusalem (Acts 12:17) (§7.2.2). The *Chronicon miscellaneum ad A.D. 724 pertinens* has Peter's founding of the Antiochene church preceding the stoning of Stephen, and dates both to the year 343 or 344 (A.D. 31/32) of the Alexandrian era (*CSCO* III/7 89,20f.; 114,23ff.). Either the chronological information here has been corrupted,[4] or this still represents what is already a somewhat disrupted recollection of an early date for the persecution of Stephen (see p. 71 below).

Hence the information concerning the absolute date of the persecution of Stephen varies, while the period of six to seven years from the crucifixion appears in more than one tradition. This prompts the question whether at the beginning of the tradition some speculation concerning the symbolic number seven played a role. Indeed, the writer of the *Pseudo-Clementine Recognitions* asserts in the second century A.D. that the primitive Jerusalem church was able to expand during a week of years: *Septimana iam una ex passione domini complebatur annorum et ecclesia dei in Hierusalem constituta copiosissime multiplicata crescebat* (*Ps.-Clem. Rec.* I 43,3 [GCS 51,33]). A later formulation reads similarly: *Ecce enim ex adventu iusti et veri prophetae vixdum septem anni sunt, in quibus ex omnibus gentibus convenientes homines ad Iudaeam* (*Ps.-Clem. Rec.* IX 29,1 [GCS 51,312]). This assertion of a seven-year period of peaceful growth might have provided the point of departure for the various absolute calculations of the martyrdom of Stephen, though one cannot, of course, exclude the possibility that an actual period of approximately seven years between the crucifixion and the initial persecutions was not retrospectively given a symbolic interpretation. As a matter of fact, several scholars do draw attention to a fact of contemporary history that might support this dating of the persecution of Stephen.

4.1.2. Trial Procedure[5]

The consensus of more recent scholarship is correctly inclined to assert that during the time of Roman rule the Sanhedrin did not possess the *ius gladii*.[6] This does, to be sure, create a problem for the portrayal of Acts, according to which the death sentence against Stephen was the result of a trial before the

---

4. So A. Strobel, *Ursprung und Geschichte des frühchristlichen Osterkalenders* (1977) 116.

5. Concerning the history of scholarship, see H. W. Neudorfer, *Der Stephanuskreis* (1983) 183-218.

6. Cf. esp. A. Strobel, *Die Stunde der Wahrheit* (1980) 6-45; J. P. Lemonon, *Pilate et le gouvernement de la Judée* (1981) 74-97; *ANRW* II 26.1 (1992) 752-56.

Jerusalem συνέδριον (Acts 6:12; 7:1). As we have seen, however, the transition from A.D. 36 to 37 was a time of procuratorial vacancy due to Pilate's having been recalled (§3.1.1). In the year A.D. 62, the high priest Ananus son of Ananus used such an interim to have James the brother of Jesus executed, though he was then relieved of his office for just that reason (Josephus, *Ant.* xx.200-203). One might similarly explain the dismissal of the high priest Jonathan, which occurred immediately after the recall of Pilate (Josephus, *Ant.* xviii.95, 123; cf. xix.313), as a reaction of the Romans to an illegal trial in the Stephen affair. Although A. Hausrath[7] did develop such a solution, his assertion that tradition contains no indication Jesus and Stephen died under the same high priest is untenable, since according to the *Pseudo-Clementine Recognitions*, Caiaphas was still in office at the beginning of the persecution of Stephen (*Ps.-Clem. Rec.* I 53,3 [GCS 51,38]). The dating of the martyrdom of Stephen during the procuratorial interim was earlier more widespread especially among Catholic exegetes.[8] In more recent years, it has again been advocated by S. Dockx,[9] though also by Protestant exegetes[10] and in a somewhat altered form by the Jewish scholar D. R. Schwartz.[11]

To be sure, this solution is possible only if the trial against Stephen really was a regular trial before the high council. The majority of contemporary exegetes reject this presupposition, ascribing instead the portrayal of a deliberation of the συνέδριον to Luke,[12] who allegedly altered an account of

7. *Neutestamentliche Zeitgeschichte* II (1872) 318.

8. Bibliography in V. Weber, *Die Abfassung des Galaterbriefs* (1900) 358-60; F. Prat, *DBS* I (1928) 1283; A. Vitti, *CivCatt* 88 (1937) 385-94.

9. *Chronologies néotestamentaires* (²1984) 223-29.

10. B. Reicke, *The New Testament Era* (Eng. trans., 1968) 191f.; N. Kokkinos, in *Festschrift J. Finegan* (1989) 145-47; D. Moody, *loc. cit.*, 224.

11. *Agrippa I* (1990) 71-73. D. R. Schwartz considers the tumultuous features in Acts 7:54ff. to be a secondarily inserted, anti-Jewish prejudice, and thus assumes a normal trial before the Sanhedrin. In the years A.D. 39-41, Judea was without any Roman governor, since Gaius Caligula kept it in "cold storage" during this period for the released Agrippa (I) (*loc. cit.*, 62-76). During this period, the high priest Simon Cantheras carried through the persecution of Stephen, and was then allegedly deposed by the newly appointed king Agrippa I for this legal presumption (cf. Josephus, *Ant.* xix.313). But this reconstruction encounters several problems: (1) Even according to Schwartz, *loc. cit.*, 63f., Judea was not without Roman supervision between A.D. 39 and 41. Why did it not intervene? (2) Why did Agrippa use a persecution of Christians as the occasion to depose a high priest? After all, ultimately the king himself became a persecutor of the primitive Jerusalem church (Acts. 12:1ff.), something Schwartz, *loc. cit.*, 153-57, does not contest. (3) Schwartz, *loc. cit.*, 72, note 21, resolves the problems with Pauline chronology (the earliest possible date for the Apostolic Council [Gal. 2:1ff.] in A.D. 52) by suspending the relationship between the martyrdom of Stephen and the conversion of Paul. But cf. §4.3.1.

12. Cf. G. Schneider, *Die Apostelgeschichte* I (1980) 433f.; J. Roloff, *Die Apostelgeschichte* (1981) 111f.; A. Weiser, *Die Apostelgeschichte* (1981) 181f.; G. Schille, *Die*

a case of lynch justice in this way in order to attain greater parallelism with the trial of Jesus. It is not difficult to imagine how an event taking place before the leadership of a synagogal congregation (cf. Acts 6:9) could be displaced by means of the catchword συνέδριον (Acts 6:12; cf. Mk. 13:9) to the high council.[13]

Following the lead of A. Schlatter,[14] J. Jeremias has suggested a different solution to these problems,[15] and has drawn support from G. Stählin.[16] From Josephus' remark that the Jews were forbidden to carry out executions without the concurrence of the governor (χωρὶς τῆς ἐκείνου γνώμης) (Josephus, *Ant.* xx.202), Schlatter concluded that such executions were indeed permitted with his agreement.[17] According to Jeremias, such authorization by Pilate to proceed against the Christians is supported not only by the good relationship between Caiaphas and the governor, a relationship also emphasized in more recent scholarship,[18] but also by the expansion of this persecution beyond Judea itself (Acts 9:2).[19] The sugges-

---

Apostelgeschichte (1983) 185f.; R. Pesch, *Die Apostelgeschichte* I (1986) 235f.; S. Légasse, *Stephanos* (1992) 207-10. Earlier representatives can be found in H. W. Neudorfer, *Der Stephanuskreis* (1983) 197-99. Almost everyone assumes that the basic framework of the martyrdom itself derives from a tradition handed down from the circle of Hellenists. Cf. most recently again P. Dschulnigg, *Jud* 44 (1988) 195-213.

13. Cf. M. Hengel, *ZThK* 72 (1975) 188-90.

14. *Geschichte der ersten Christenheit* (1926) 98-100.

15. In *Abba* (1966) 141f. With reference to K. Bornhäuser, *Studien zur Apostelgeschichte* (1934) 73f., J. Jeremias considers the shouts and rushing toward Stephen (Acts 7:57) to be a legal prevention of any further blasphemy; moreover, the laying of clothes at the feet of the court member who was leading the execution (Acts 7:58; cf. 8:1) underscores its normal course.

16. *Die Apostelgeschichte* ([6]1978) 115. G. Stählin drew attention to the following difficulty: "A tumultuous execution outside the city, which after all presupposes transport of the victim through a portion of the excited city, is hardly conceivable given the attentive supervision of the Romans over the Jews and especially over the high council (cf. [Acts] 21:27–23:22, esp. 23:15)." This doubt would gain further support if the oldest local tradition handed down in the pre-Constantine Jewish-Christian church of Jerusalem is correct (B. Bagatti, *Ant* 49 [1974] 527-32), according to which Stephen was stoned at the foot of the stairs (extant today only in traces) leading from what is known as the "Golden Gate" into the Kidron Valley (B. Bagatti, *Recherches sur le site du Temple* [1979] 14f.6* and plate X).

17. *Der Evangelist Johannes* (1930) 338.

18. Cf. E. M. Smallwood, *JTS* 13 (1962) 22; *The Jews under Roman Rule* ([2]1981) 172; J. P. Lemonon, *Pilate et le gouvernement de la Judée* (1981) 274f.; D. Flusser, *Jerusalem Perspective* 4 (1991) 23-28.

19. By contrast, F. F. Bruce's reference, *The Book of Acts* (1988) 159, to the Jewish right to kill transgressors of the temple boundaries immediately is insufficient (Philo, *Leg. ad Gaium* 212; Josephus, *B.J.* v.194; vi.124f.; *Ant.* xv.417; *Ap.* ii.103f.), since according to Acts 7:58 Stephen was pushed outside the city.

tion of A. Strobel is similar, according to which the Jewish authorities considered themselves authorized by the precedent of the trial of Jesus to act against Stephen because of the similarity of these two cases (seduction of the people).[20]

The ancient historian M. Sordi takes a similar path, though her admittedly fairly daring hypothesis is completely independent of the previously mentioned explicative attempts.[21] Ms. Sordi views as essentially accurate the accounts according to which Pilate sent to Tiberius a report on the newly arisen messianic faith (Justin, *Apol.* i.35, 48; Tertullian, *Apol.* 5.2; 21.24). According to Eusebius, this document would have arrived in Rome in A.D. 35 (Eusebius, *Chron.* [ed. Helm 178]). In the same year, the emperor dispatched Vitellius as his special envoy to Syria in order to clarify the Oriental affairs (Tacitus, *Ann.* vi.38.5). The recall of Pilate and the dismissal of Caiaphas immediately thereafter were allegedly also connected with the persecutory measures against the followers of Jesus which the governor had authorized for the Jewish high council. Thereafter, nascent Christianity allegedly enjoyed Roman tolerance (cf. Acts 9:31: ἡ μὲν οὖν ἐκκλησία καθ' ὅλης τῆς Ἰουδαίας καὶ Γαλιλαίας καὶ Σαμαρείας εἶχεν εἰρήνην) until this policy changed under Nero. According to Ms. Sordi's evaluation of Gal. 1:15-24, the martyrdom of Stephen and the conversion of Paul took place *ca.* A.D. 34. The main part of her hypothesis, however, is not dependent on this chronology.

A. Strobel considers it "far more likely that the criminal procedure against Stephen was already carried out during the very first years of the early church, approximately around A.D. 31/32. This explains the duplicity of cases, which by no means is merely a literary one."[22] It would be conceivable that Pilate's even more accommodating posture toward the Sanhedrin in comparison to the trial of Jesus would have been occasioned by the fall of Sejanus in the year A.D. 31 (see p. 55 above).[23] Hence the dating of the martyrdom of Stephen to the procuratorial interim of A.D. 36/37 is not chronologically compelling even if one presupposes a convocation of the συνέδριον, and it is completely unnecessary in the case of an act of tumultuous lynch justice.

---

20. *Die Stunde der Wahrheit* (1980) 22f., note 65.

21. *StRo* 8 (1960) 393-409; *The Christians and the Roman Empire* (1986) 12-22. She is followed by, among others, V. Monachino, *Le persecuzioni e la polemica pagano-cristiana* (1974) 21-41; S. Bacchiocchi, *AUSS* 21 (1983) 5-12.

22. *Die Stunde der Wahrheit* (1980) 88.

23. So already C. F. Nösgen, *Commentar über die Apostelgeschichte* (1882) 69.

4.2. The Year of the Conversion

4.2.1. The Gnostic Tradition

A. von Harnack associated the tradition of the year-and-a-half during which the resurrected Jesus continued to appear among the circle of his disciples on the one hand, with that of the conversion of the apostle Paul on the other,[24] and several contemporary scholars follow Harnack in this assumption.[25] The period of eighteen months is attested in two gnostic groups of the second century. Irenaeus reports concerning the Ophites: *"remoratum Jesum post resurrectionem XVIII mensibus et sensibilitate in eum descendente didicisse, quod liquidum est, et paucos ex discipulis suis, quos sciebat capaces tantorum mysteriorum, docuit haec et sic receptus est in coelem"* (Irenaeus, *Haer.* i.30.14). The pupils of the Valentinian Ptolemaeus advocated the following view according to the church father: Τοὺς δεκαοκτὼ Αἰῶνας φανεροῦσθαι διὰ τοῦ μετὰ τὴν ἐκ νεκρῶν ἀνάστασιν δεκαοκτὼ μησὶ λέγειν διατετριφέναι αὐτὸν ['Ιησοῦν] σὺν τοῖς μαθηταῖς (Irenaeus, *Haer.* i.3.2). No mystical significance to this number is immediately apparent, though neither can it be excluded. Harnack draws attention to one possible path of tradition along which a historical date from the life of Paul might have found its way into the writings of the Valentinian gnosis[26]: Ptolemaeus referred in his letter to Flora to apostolic tradition (*Ad Floram* 5.10; 6.6 [SC 24.64, 68]), and Clement of Alexandria mentions an otherwise unknown pupil of Paul, Theodas, as tradent before Valentinus (Clement of Alexandria, *Strom.* vii.17.106).

4.2.2. Ascension of Isaiah 9:16

Independently of one another, F. Westberg[27] and A. von Harnack[28] associated this passage with the conversion of Paul: "And when he [Christus] has made spoil of the angel of death, he will arise on the third day (and will remain in that world 545 days)" (*NTApo* II[5] 558). Because the words in parentheses are not found in the Old Slavonic versions and in one of the two Latin manuscripts of the *Ascension of Isaiah,* M. A. Knibb considers them to be a secondary

---

24. *SPAW.PH* (1912) 673-82.

25. E.g., A. Strobel, *Ursprung und Geschichte des frühchristlichen Osterkalenders* (1977) 120; R. Jewett, *A Chronology of Paul's Life* (1979) 29f. Cautiously also M. Hengel, in M. Hengel and U. Heckel, *Paulus und das antike Judentum* (1991) 266.

26. *SPAW.PH* (1912) 680, note 2.

27. *Zur Neutestamentlichen Chronologie und Golgathas Ortslage* (1911) 50f. R. Jewett, *A Chronology of Paul's Life* (1979) 120, note 40, erroneously also ascribes to F. Westberg a reference to the gnostic dates.

28. *SPAW.PH* (1912) 678.

insertion from gnostic tradition.[29] However, this is contradicted by the fact that the activity of the antichrist is also given in days, namely, 1332, in what is text-critically an undisputed passage (*Asc. Isa.* 4:14). This number corresponds approximately to the other indication of three years, seven months, and twenty-seven days (*Asc. Isa.* 4:12), together 1335 days, during which Beliar, in the figure of a matricidal king (Nero Redivivus), will persecute the plant (the Christian church) (*Asc. Isa.* 4:2f.). Perhaps the author has even included here a concealed reference to the date of the martyrdom of Peter in Rome (13 October A.D. 64),[30] which would document an interest in historical dates relating to apostles, albeit in encoded form. One is thus permitted to keep *Asc. Isa.* 9:16 as a witness for a period of approximately a year-and-a-half during which the resurrected Jesus appeared.

Harnack pointed out that the attestation of this tradition not only in gnostic but also in orthodox writings suggests that it is extremely old.[31] Although the *Ascension of Isaiah* is normally dated to the second century A.D., several factors suggest going back even further, namely, to the end of the first century: (1) For E. Hammershaimb, "considering the development of the relationship between the Christian church and the Jews, it is hardly credible that a Christian author in the second century would have adopted a Jewish legend such as the *Martyrdom of Isaiah* into his writing."[32] (2) *Asc. Isa.* 4:13 presupposes that eyewitnesses of Jesus will still be alive at the coming of the antichrist.[33] In that case, however, one must reckon with a composition before *ca.* A.D. 110. (3) Perhaps Ignatius of Antioch (*Eph.* 19) is already referring to *Asc. Isa.* 11:16 around A.D. 110.[34] In any event, the notion of the hidden quality of the birth of Christ occurs in the *Ascension* in an apparently earlier form than in Ignatius, just as in general the entire work is sooner characterized by archaic than heretical theology.[35]

P. Riessler already advocated the position that the basic Jewish account of the *Martyrdom of Isaiah* as adopted into the *Ascension of Isaiah* (*Asc. Isa.* 1–5) derives from Essenic circles.[36] Subsequent to the findings in Qumran,

---

29. In J. H. Charlesworth, *The Old Testament Pseudepigrapha* II (1985) 170, note v.

30. So M. Guarducci, *ParPass* 23 (1968) 81-117; *The Tomb of St. Peter* (Eng. trans., 1960) 25-43.

31. *SPAW.PH* (1912) 679: "Something that is found in the gnostics, the Valentinians, and in the *Ascension of Isaiah* must be traced back at least into the earliest post-apostolic age."

32. *JSHRZ* II/1 (²1977) 19.

33. Cf. M. A. Knibb, in J. H. Charlesworth, *The Old Testament Pseudepigrapha* II (1985) 162, note 1.

34. Cf. R. H. Charles, *The Ascension of Isaiah* (1900) xiv.

35. Cf. J. Daniélou, *The Theology of Jewish Christianity* (1964) 12-14.

36. *Altjüdisches Schrifttum außerhalb der Bibel* (1928) 1300f.

there is even more reason to assume this,[37] even if no fragments of this writing have been discovered among them. The final Christian redactor's parallels with an Essenicizing language are quite noticeable when he calls the antichrist Beliar (*Asc. Isa.* 4:2, 4, 14, 16, 18)[38] and the Christian church a plant (*Asc. Isa.* 4:3).[39] If one asks just where Essenicizing Jewish Christians lived who might have had an interest in traditions concerning Paul, the most likely region is that around Damascus (§13.1), and, indeed, D. Flusser has found in the author of the *Martyrdom of Isaiah* an Essene with this geographical background.[40] Such hypothetical observations cannot, of course, be regarded as more than suggestive of possibilities worthy of consideration.

4.2.3. The Connection with Paul

The hardly contestable extreme antiquity of the tradition of the resurrection appearances having occurred within a period of one-and-a-half years might support this as an accurate recollection. On the other hand, Paul emphasized with unmistakable clarity that the final appearance was bequeathed to him (1 Cor. 15:8: ἔσχατον δὲ πάντων ὡσπερεὶ τῷ ἐκτρώματι ὤφθη κἀμοί).[41] Regarding the relationship between these two matters, the judgment of A. von Harnack still deserves our consideration: "Here and — as far as I can see — only here we have the key to explaining the eighteen months; for if we now hear from an extremely old tradition that Jesus yet visited with his disciples eighteen months after the resurrection, this will be precisely that period of time between the resurrection itself and that day in Damascus, after which he no longer appeared to his disciples in this manner and thus a new period began. But the fact that here a tradition was indeed extant is nothing less than striking; for Paul must frequently enough have had and taken the opportunity to speak about the time or year of his own conversion, and such an account could not easily have been lost within the circles of his

---

37. Cf. R. Meyer, *RGG*³ III (1959) 336; M. Philonenko, in *Pseudépigraphes de l'Ancien Testament et manuscrits de la mer Morte* I (1967) 1-10; L. Rost, *Einleitung in die alttestamentlichen Apokryphen und Pseudepigraphen* (²1979) 114; C. D. G. Müller, *NTApo* II (⁵1989) 548f.

38. Outside the Qumran texts, this expression is found only in writings close to the Essenes such as the book of *Jubilees, the Testaments of the Twelve Patriarchs,* and the *Damascus Document,* as well as in the similarly Essene-like section 2 Cor. 6:14–7:1 (2 Cor. 6:15). Cf. the citations in J. A. Fitzmyer, in K. E. Grözinger *et al., Qumran* (1981) 120f.

39. After Isa. 60:21 cf. only 1QS 8:5; 11:8; CD 1:7; *1 Enoch* 84:6. Additional passages in K. G. Kuhn, *Konkordanz zu den Qumrantexten* (1960) 120f.; J. H. Charlesworth, *Graphic Concordance to the Dead Sea Scrolls* (1991) 393.

40. *IEJ* 3 (1953) 34-47.

41. In this regard, cf. esp. P. R. Jones, *TynBul* 36 (1985) 3-34.

pupils, particularly since there were quite soon also Pauline Christians who would have viewed this particular date as a fundamental fact of salvation history.''[42] Harnack's confidence in this tradition was strengthened further by the fact that the combination of the Gallio-inscription and the information in Galatians 1–2 also led him to this early a date for the conversion of Paul (§17.1.3).

4.2.4. The Apocryphon of James

According to the investigations of A. von Harnack, the *Apocryphon of James,* which mentions resurrection appearances during 550 days (*NHC* I 2:19-24), represents yet another witness for the tradition of one-and-a-half years.[43] According to a probable textual emendation, this period of time is summarized in a later passage as eighteen months (*NHC* I 8:3).[44] Just why eighteen months is figured as 550 days is as obscure as the background of the number 545 days in *Asc. Isa.* 9:16.[45] There are widely varying assumptions regarding the geographical, temporal, and theological origin of the *Apocryphon of James.*[46] W. C. van Unnik has fundamentally disputed any gnostic character for this writing.[47] Even if one does not deny a certain gnostic element,[48] this represents rather an early stage of gnosis. One cannot exclude the Syrian-Palestinian region as its place of origin, nor even a date of composition toward the end of the first century A.D.,[49] but in any case one can hardly date it any later than the first half of the second century. The *Apocryphon of James* thus represents what is sooner a complementary argument for accepting the antiquity of the tradition of one-and-a-half years.

At the same time, however, a problem arises in connection with Harnack's view, one which R. Jewett[50] does not discuss. Whereas the other passages offer no information concerning the witnesses to the resurrection

---

42. *SPAW.PH* (1912) 679f.

43. Translation by F. E. Williams, in J. M. Robinson, *The Nag Hammadi Library* (New York, 1977) 30; D. Kirchner, *NTApo* I[5] (1987) 239.

44. *NHC* I 8:1-4: "For after the [suffering] you have compelled me to stay with you [beyond this] another eighteen [years (instead of days)] for the sake of the parables." Cf. D. Kirchner, *NTApo* I[5] (1987) 241, note 35.

45. Three calendary systems were in use among gnostic groups (B. Przybylski, *VigChr* 34 [1980] 56-70): a year of 365 days, a year of 360 + 5 intercalated days, and a year of 360 days. The duration of eighteen months would accordingly involve 547/48 or 540 days. Assuming a solar calendar of 364 days, it would be 546 days.

46. Cf. K. Rudolph, *ThR* 34 (1969) 169-75.

47. *VigChr* 10 (1956) 149-56.

48. Cf. D. Kirchner, *NTApo* I[5] (1987) 237f.

49. Cf. *ibid.,* 235f.

50. *A Chronology of Paul's Life* (1979) 29.

appearances, in the *Apocryphon of James* it is the Twelve (*NHC* I 2:7ff.) and then especially James and Peter (*NHC* I 2:33ff.) who witness the last appearance (*NHC* I 15:5ff.). In view of the extreme antiquity of the *Ascension of Isaiah,* however, the possibility remains that the numerical information concerning days or months was already available to the gnostics standing behind the *Apocryphon of James,* "since they play on it like on the numbers in the N[ew] T[estament]."[51] Can one conceive of any reason why the *Apocryphon of James* displaces Paul as the last resurrection witness? The emphasized role of James and Peter may already contain an anti-Pauline barb. According to the reconstructed beginning of the *Apocryphon* ("[James wr]ites to [the son Kerin]thos"),[52] a connection with Cerinthian gnosis seems possible.[53] Cerinthus, with his unique synthesis of gnosis, docetism, libertinism, and Judaistic millenarianism,[54] had no place in his own system for Paul and the latter's emphasis on corporeal resurrection.[55] An original connection between the one-and-a-half years and the conversion of Paul thus remains at least a possibility. However, a certain liturgical tradition might additionally support this suspicion.

4.2.5. The Second Year after the Ascension

To my knowledge, the tradition of the one-and-a-half years has never yet been associated with that of other ancient church tradition dating the conversion of Paul to the second year after the ascension. This may reflect the fact that this definitive dating is only accessible in an extremely late liturgical work. The edition of the *Martyrologium Romanum* put together under Pope Gregory XIII notes for 25 January: *"Conversio sancti Pauli Apostoli, quae fuit anno secundo ab Ascensione Domini."*[56] The *Martyrologium Romanum vetus* put together by Ado of Vienne in the mid-ninth century does not contain this information; it comes from the *Martyrologium* of Usuard of St. Germain

51. W. C. van Unnik, *VigChr* 10 (1956) 153.

52. *NHC* I 1.1 (*NTApo* I⁵, 238).

53. Cf. D. Kirchner, *NTApo* I⁵ (1987) 236f. The relationship between the *Apocryphon of James* and Johannine tradition (P. Perkins, *JBL* 101 [1982] 403-14) might support this assumption, since there was a connection — albeit only polemical — between Cerinthus and the Johannine circle. Cf. F. Neugebauer, *Die Entstehung des Johannesevangeliums* (1969) 28-39.

54. T. Wurm, *ThQ* 86 (1904) 20-38, and G. Bardy, *RB* 30 (1921) 344-73, have correctly drawn attention to these strongly Judaizing features, while at the same time overly neglecting the gnostic inclination. The person of Cerinthus is a clear indication of the importance of Jewish groups in the development of gnosis.

55. Cf. J. Daniélou, *The Theology of Jewish Christianity* (1964) 68f.

56. *Martyrologium Romanum Gregorii Papae XIII* (1930) 20.

(around A.D. 875).[57] From the textual tradition of the *Martyrologium Hiero-nymianum* (fifth century A.D.)[58] one can conclude that in Gaul a festival of the *conversio Pauli* was already being celebrated in the fifth century and was influenced perhaps by Greek traditions.[59] To be sure, the text of the *Martyrologium Hieronymianum* lacks any specification of year, though the conversion of the apostle was apparently accorded special remembrance in Gaul.

The *Martyrologium* of Usuard owes its specification of year as well as other details to Isidore of Seville.[60] The specific assertion in his writing *De ortu et obitu patrum* (between 586 and 615)[61] that Paul was "baptized in the second year after the ascension of the Lord *(Illic secundo post Ascensionem Domini anno baptizatus)*" (120 [PL 83.150; ed. C. Chaparro Gómez, 199]) was doubtless not introduced by Isidore himself, since one cannot see how he could have calculated this from New Testament information. The writings of this "last occidental church father" (*ca.* A.D. 560-636), who comes from the Byzantine sphere of power (Cartagena),[62] are "usually merely excerpts assembled in the fashion of a mosaic from other works," though they did "save many treasures of the knowledge of antiquity for future generations."[63] Hence we must assume that, as at other places in his biographical work, he owes his information to some other source.[64]

Indeed, this remark is also found in what is known as the *Breviarium Apostolorum*: "*Paulus qui interpretatur pius, ortus ex tribu Beniamin, apos-*

---

57. *Propylaeum ad ActaSS. Dec*, ed. H. Delehaye *et al.* (1940) 34.

58. Cf. H. Delehaye, in *ActaSS. Nov* II/2 (1931) 61f.

59. Cf. J. P. Kirsch, *RivAC* 2 (1925) 71-79; *JLW* 5 (1925) 48-67. In the Syrian *Martyrologium* of A.D. 411, which can be traced back to a Greek source of the second half of the fourth century (R. Stieger, *LThK* VII [1962] 138), the martyrdom of Stephen (26 December) is exactly a month earlier (MartSyr [ed. H. Lietzmann, *KlT* 2 [1903] 9]). However, the Roman date 25 January probably did not originally refer to the conversion of the apostle, but rather to the translation of his remains. Cf. R. A. Lipsius, *Die apokryphen Apostelgeschichten und Apostellegenden* II/1 (1887) 414; K. Erbes, *ZKG* 43 (1925) 61f.; H. Delehaye, *AnalBoll* 45 (1927) 306f.

60. Cf. J. Dubois, *Le martyrologe d'Usuard* (1965) 66, 168.

61. Concerning this dating, cf. J. A. de Aldama, in *Miscellanea Isidoriana* (1936) 57-89. The authenticity of the writing in its first recension is generally accepted today. Cf. R. E. McNally, in *Festschrift M. C. Díaz y Díaz* (1961) 315f.; H. J. Diesner, *Isidor von Sevilla* (1973) 19; B. Altaner and A. Stuiber, *Patrologie* (1980) 495, and esp. C. Chaparro Gomez, *Isidoro de Sevilla: De ortu et obitu patrum* (1985) 4-19.

62. Cf. K. Baus, *LThK* V (1960) 186.

63. B. Altaner and A. Stuiber, *Patrologie* (1980) 494.

64. Concerning the sources used by Isidore in general, cf. J. N. Hillgarth, in *Festschrift M. C. Díaz y Díaz* (1961) 32-38; U. Dominguéz Del Val, *loc. cit.,* 211-21; concerning *De ortu et obitum patrum* specifically, cf. C. Chaparro Gomez, *Isidoro de Sevilla* (1985) 47-52.

tolus gentium, hic secundo post ascensionem Domini anno baptizatus est . . ." (ed. Schermann, 207).[65] This list of apostle-celebrations precedes in many manuscripts the *Martyrologium Hieronymianum,* though also the Greek apostle catalogs and Pseudo-Abdias.[66] Since the *Breviarium* must already have been known around A.D. 600, Isidore could have used it. More likely, however, both works are referring back to a common but unknown source[67] whose age and significance we are unfortunately unable to evaluate. Without a doubt, Isidore had access to extremely old traditions, and was familiar, for example, with the writings of Julius Africanus;[68] similarly, it should be recalled that sources such as the complete works of Papias were still extant in the medieval West.[69]

Perhaps the source of both Isidore and the *Breviarium* also stands behind a corresponding remark made by John Malalas, according to whom Paul apparently left Antioch in the fourth year after the Passion, and was there replaced by Peter: Μετὰ δὲ ἔτη τέσσαρα τῆς ἀναστάσεως καὶ ἀναλήψεως τοῦ σωτῆρος ἡμῶν Ἰησοῦ Χριστοῦ, ἐπὶ τῆς βασιλείας τοῦ αὐτοῦ Τιβερίου Καίσαρος, μετὰ τὸ ἐξελθεῖν τὸν ἅγιον Παῦλον ἀπὸ Ἀντιοχείας τῆς μεγάλης (John Malalas, 242.8-11 [ed. von Stauffenberg, 21]). In accordance with Gal. 1:18, the conversion of the apostle would have to be dated to either the first or second year after the ascension. One can also refer to Solomon of Bassorah (first half of the thirteenth century), who often used older sources and according to whom Paul died thirty-six years after the Passion after having worked for thirty-five years as an apostle.[70] The same chronological tradition includes an apostle list incorrectly attributed to Hippolytus of Thebes (though perhaps older),[71] as well as — if the corresponding remark is authentic — even

---

65. Peculiarly, T. Schermann, *Propheten- und Apostellegenden* (1907), 290, asserts that the *Breviarium* dates the conversion of Paul "not until sixteen years after the resurrection of the Lord." This is not the only contradiction between his own edition of the text on the one hand, and the accompanying investigation on the other. Pseudo-Epiphanius, whom Schermann dates at the beginning of the eighth century (*loc. cit.,* 349-51), recounts — according to Schermann — that the conversion of the apostle took place one year after ascension (*loc. cit.,* 390). The text itself, however, only says: Παῦλος ὁ ἀπόστολος μετὰ τὴν εἰς οὐρανοὺς τοῦ κυρίου ἀνάληψιν ἤρξατο κηρύσσειν (ed. Schermann, 114). By contrast, the assertion of one year is correct in the case of Pseudo-Hippolytus (ed. Schermann, 167: Παῦλος δὲ μετ' ἐνιαυτὸν ἕνα τῆς τοῦ Χριστοῦ ἀναλήψεως εἰσῆλθεν εἰς τὴν ἀποστολήν), whom Schermann dates in the middle of the ninth century (*loc. cit.,* 353f.).

66. Cf. B. de Gaiffier, *AnBoll* 81 (1973) 89-116.

67. Cf. *ibid.,* 113.

68. Cf. K. Baus, *LTK* V (1960) 787.

69. Cf. F. Siegert, *NTS* 27 (1980/81) 610.

70. Cf. R. A. Lipsius, *Die apokryphen Apostelgeschichten und Apostellegenden,* Ergänzungsheft (1890) 21.

71. Cf. F. Diekamp, *Hippolytos von Theben* (1898) LX.

Euthalius[72] (PG 85.708BC: τὸ ἔτος ἐκεῖνο) in the fourth century, according to which one year separated the Passion of Jesus on the one hand, and Paul's baptism on the other.[73] With extreme caution we might also adduce one final witness to the conversion of the apostle in the second year after the crucifixion. In the introduction of the Codex Brixianus to the Acts of Paul, we read: *"N[a]mque anno secundo post ascensionem [domini b]eatus Paulus apostolus conversus est ad . . . fidem"* (*TU NF* 7,2 130). To be sure, the age of this introduction is variously evaluated. P. Corssen[74] viewed it as original, O. von Gebhardt[75] as secondary. Since the beginning of the Acts is not found in any of the previously known manuscripts, we have no point of comparison. If Corssen is correct, one might possibly date this chronology of the date of Paul's conversion back to the end of the second century, since the apocryphal Acts (before Tertullian, *De Bapt.* 17) were composed between 185 and 195 in Asia Minor.[76]

With similarly great caution we might further mention one absolute date deriving from ancient church tradition. As we have seen (see p. 60 above), the *Chronicon miscellaneum ad* A.D. *724 pertinens* dates the stoning of Stephen to the year 344 of the Alexandrian era (*CSCO* III/7 114,23ff.), and thus to A.D. 32. One cannot completely exclude the possibility that this particular date derives from the tradition of an early martyrdom of Stephen. Admittedly, this source is compromised at least by its assertion that Peter founded the Antiochene church during the previous year (*CSCO* III/7 89,20f.). This might, however, represent a secondary insertion, since the development of tradition does exhibit the inclination to make the premier apostle into the real founder of the various churches, despite the mention of Hellenistic proclamation activity in Acts 11:27 (see p. 121, note 86 below).

Even if the tradition-history of the assertion "in the second year after the ascension" is difficult to illuminate in its details, it remains striking that this particular date agrees extremely well with the date of Paul's conversion as deduced hypothetically from the *Ascension of Isaiah* and the gnostic sources. According to our own dating of the crucifixion of Jesus on 7 April A.D. 30, these assertions — even considering the reservations prompted by the sources themselves — would lead to the years A.D. 31/32.

---

72. Cf. B. Kraft, *LTK* III (1959) 1206f.

73. It is unclear how Georgios Synkellos arrived at a figure of three years (ed. Dindorf, I 623).

74. *ZNW* 4 (1903) 46f.

75. *TU NF* 7,2 (1902) CVIf.

76. Cf. W. Schneemelcher, *NTApo* II (³1964) 241.

4.3. The Chronological Nexus

4.3.1. Persecution and Conversion

For S. Dockx,[77] it is possible to preserve the seven-year tradition for Stephen's martyrdom while dating the apostle's conversion earlier (A.D. 35), since this Belgian scholar, following E. Haenchen,[78] considers the connection between Paul's own persecutory activity and Stephen's death to be a Lukan construct. Objections can be made against this view, however, based on Paul's own statements. The apostle's assertion in Gal. 1:13, namely, that he "persecuted the church of God and destroyed it (ἐδίωκον τὴν ἐκκλησίαν τοῦ θεοῦ καὶ ἐπόρθουν αὐτήν)," refers to violent persecution,[79] and there is no evidence for any other persecution during this particular period except that against the Hellenists. Any earlier connection between Paul and Jerusalem has repeatedly been countered by reference to his own statement in Gal. 1:22, namely, "I was still unknown by sight to the churches of Judea that are in Christ."[80] Then, however, one might actually call into question the apostle's preceding assertion as well concerning his brief visit to Jerusalem (Gal. 1:18-20). The statement concerning the lack of familiarity with the churches of Judea is referring to Paul as a Christian,[81] and stems from his intention of proving his independence from the apostolic authorities in the holy city.[82] When the apostle speaks of those who praise God that their former persecutor is now proclaiming the gospel (Gal. 1:23f.), then according to the preceding sentence this can only be referring to the churches of Judea (ἐκκλησίαι τῆς Ἰουδαίας) (Gal. 1:22).[83] There seems to be no cogent reason why one should exclude precisely the Jerusalem church from this group. That Paul received a scribal education in Jerusalem is not only asserted by

77. *Chronologies néotestamentaires* ([2]1984) 223-30.
78. *Acts* (Eng. trans. 1971) 297-99. Cf. among the earlier advocates of this view, e.g., M. S. Enslin, *JR* 7 (1927) 370-74.
79. P. H. Menoud, *Festschrift E. Haenchen* (1964) 178-86, incorrectly restricts the meaning of πορθεῖν to verbal opposition. Cf. by contrast M. Hengel, in M. Hengel and U. Heckel, *Paulus und das antike Judentum* (1991) 274f.; K. W. Niebuhr, *Heidenapostel aus Israel* (1992) 35-43.
80. So, e.g., by E. Haenchen, *Acts* (Eng. trans. 1971) 335, and H. Conzelmann, *History of Primitive Christianity* (Eng. trans., 1973) 80. Cf. by contrast J. Blank, *Paulus und Jesus* (1968) 238-48; H. Kasting, *Die Anfänge der urchristlichen Mission* (1969) 64f.; M. Hengel, *loc. cit.,* 276-83; K. W. Niebuhr, *loc. cit.,* 58-60, and among earlier scholars H. E. Dana, *AThR* 20 (1938) 16-26.
81. Cf. also A. Oepke, *ThStKr* 105 (1933) 422.
82. A. J. Hultgren, *JBL* 95 (1976) 105-7, correctly emphasizes this.
83. Cf. C. Burchard, *Der dreizehnte Zeuge* (1970) 50, note 37.

Luke (Acts 22:3),[84] but also suggested by Gal. 1:13f. against its contemporary background.[85]

4.3.2. The Chronological Alternative

Hence if one must hold to the historical connection between the persecution of Stephen and the conversion of the apostle, there is no possibility of accepting both strands of dating from church tradition, and we find ourselves before the alternative of A.D. 31/32 or 36/37. To me, the tradition suggesting dating Paul's conversion to the second year after the crucifixion of Jesus seems somewhat better grounded. This tradition is found in a larger number of older and in part mutually independent sources, and a derivation from early Christian numerical speculation is less easy to explain than in the case of the seven-year tradition, which is evident only later. Also, that only a short span of time passed between the crucifixion of Jesus and the persecution of Stephen is historically quite conceivable.[86] The formation of this group of Hellenists (Acts 6:1: Ἑλληνισταί) should not be posited too late; it "might very well go back to the beginnings of this 'founding period' [of the early church], perhaps to the Festival of Weeks after the Passover of Jesus' death, when the disciples apparently appeared publicly in Jerusalem for the first time."[87] The crucifixion of Jesus might have represented the precedent case for Jewish

84. Cf. in this regard W. C. van Unnik, *Sparsa Collecta* I (1973) 259-320, 321-27.

85. Cf. M. Hengel, *Zur urchristlichen Geschichtsschreibung* ([2]1984) 71f.; in M. Hengel and U. Heckel, *Paulus und das antike Judentum* (1991) 212-56. Concerning Paul's education, see Excursus I/4 below, pp. 154f.).

86. With respect to the conversion of the apostle, A. Schmidt, *ZNW* 81 (1990) 130, objects (contra A. Suhl, *Paulus und seine Briefe* [1975] 314) that "a later dating is more likely because a church already existed in Damascus, also because the problems of the primitive church in *puncto* the dispute between Hebrews/Hellenists (Acts 6) had already taken place, and finally because a development of tradition must be presupposed (cf. 1 Cor. 15). Hence the theory of Paul's conversion in the year of the crucifixion of Jesus proves to be untenable." These postulates, which in part seem quite remote from real-life considerations and which do not become more persuasive through their number of three, need but one response: Why?

87. M. Hengel, *ZThK* 72 (1975) 172. The assertion has repeatedly been made (e.g., also by J. Knox, *Chapters in a Life of Paul,* rev. ed. [1987] 46) that the events portrayed in Acts 1–8 required a period of several years. In this case, however, it is precisely the more skeptical scholars who peculiarly have allowed themselves to be impressed by the quantity of material offered by Luke, material that by no means, however, must imply a longer period of time. Although the model calculations of earlier scholars such as V. Weber, *Die Abfassung des Galaterbriefs* (1900) 356-58 (at most two years), or C. Clemen, *Paulus* I (1904) 349f. (a few months), are naturally completely hypothetical, they do nonetheless demonstrate the possibilities that should be considered on the basis of the early church accounts concerning an early date for Paul's conversion.

73

persecution measures against the Hellenistic portion of the congregation. However, neither is the dating of Stephen's persecution to A.D. 31/32 able to stand on its own.[88] Its credibility is dependent on its correlation with other dates from Pauline chronology (§17.1.3).

88. J. Gnilka, *Paulus von Tarsus* (1996) 310-12, now also opts for this date.

§5

Flight from Damascus

5.1. 2 Corinthians 11:32-33

At the end of his famous catalog of peristases toward the end of the second letter to the Corinthians (2 Cor. 11:23-31), Paul adds an example of a "weakness"[1] "of which I will boast" (2 Cor. 11:30): "In Damascus, the ethnarch under King Aretas guarded the city of Damascus in order to seize me, but I was let down in a basket through a window in the wall, and escaped from his hands (ἐν Δαμασκῷ ὁ ἐθνάρχης Ἀρέτα τοῦ βασιλέως ἐφρούρει τὴν πόλιν Δαμασκηνῶν πιάσαι με,[2] καὶ διὰ θυρίδος ἐν σαργάνῃ ἐχαλάσθην διὰ τοῦ τείχους καὶ ἐξέφυγον τὰς χεῖρας αὐτοῦ)" (2 Cor. 11:32f.). Aretas is the only name of a person from contemporary history mentioned in an undisputed letter of Paul, and for that reason 2 Cor. 11:32f. possesses potentially great significance for any chronological outline seeking to extricate itself from the framework of Acts.

5.2. The Nabatean King Aretas IV

5.2.1. Chronology of Aretas IV

The ruler mentioned by Paul is the king of the Nabateans,[3] Aretas IV Philopatris.[4] He came to power in the year 9/8 B.C. (Josephus, *Ant.* xvi.294),[5]

---

1. Concerning the relationship of this passage within the context, see §13.3.3.

2. The insertion of θέλων (ℵ, D[2] etc.) represents a later stylistic correction that changes nothing in the meaning of the sentence. Cf. B. M. Metzger, *Textual Commentary* ([2]1975) 584.

3. Concerning the history of this people, cf. J. Starcky, *BA* 18 (1955) 84-106; *DBS* VII (1966) 886-1017; A. Negev, *PEQ* 101 (1969) 5-14; *Die Nabatäer* (1976); *ANRW* II 8 (1978) 520-686; *BARev* 14/6 (1988) 26-45; P. C. Hammond, *The Nabataeans* (1973); J. I. Lawlor, *The Nabataeans in Historical Perspective* (1974); M. Lindner, in *Petra und das Königreich der Nabatäer* ([3]1980) 38-103; H. P. Roschinski, in G. Hellenkemper-Salies,

but was not confirmed by Augustus until two years later (Josephus, *Ant.* xvi.353-55). The splendor of his regency, which lasted almost five decades, is impressively illustrated by the quality of contemporary ceramics and architecture.[6] "The development of all the branches of Nabatean art takes place during this half century under the reign of Aretas," according to the judgment of A. Negev, one of the most learned scholars of this proto-Arabian kingdom.[7] One particularly vivid example of the development of such splendor under Aretas IV is the lion-griffin temple in Petra, excavated from 1973 to 1983.[8] Most of the dateable Nabatean inscriptions come from the epoch of Aretas IV.[9]

Coinage also reached a high point under Aretas, though the clear diminution in quality of materials (silver-bronze-alloys) and execution since A.D. 18 does suggest economic problems during the second half of his reign.[10] The fact that between A.D. 18 and 40 apparently more coins were produced than in all the rest of the Nabatean period[11] suggests an inflationary development deriving possibly from the ruler's expensive construction activities. The sharp break in the silver content of coins probably resulted from the fact that the Nabateans lost control over the northern route of Indo-Arabian trade in their battle against the incursion of Arabian tribes from the desert.[12] Since both coins and inscriptions attest Aretas' forty-eighth year of rule as his last known,[13] the clear majority of modern scholars date his death in A.D. 40.[14] The date of A.D. 39, occasionally still assumed by some scholars without

---

Die Nabatäer (1981) 1-26; G. W. Bowersock, *Roman Arabia* (1983); R. Wenning, *Die Nabatäer — Denkmäler und Geschichte* (1987); D. F. Graf, *ABD* IV (1992) 970-73.

4. The title "friend of the fatherland," corresponding to the inscriptionally attested expression "who loves his people (רחם עמה)," probably represents a concealed delimitation over against the obedience to Rome exhibited by other clientele rulers. Cf. Schuerer I, 582f.

5. Cf. A. Schalit, *König Herodes* (1969) 613-16.

6. This is clearly demonstrated by the catalog of Nabatean monuments by R. Wenning, *Die Nabatäer* (1987). Cf. further A. Negev, *ANRW* II 8 (1978) 570-634.

7. *Die Nabatäer* (1976) 7.

8. Cf. P. C. Hammond, in M. Lindner, *Petra. Neue Ausgrabungen und Entdeckungen* (1986) 16-30.

9. A fine overview, if no longer completely up to date, can be found in Y. Meshorer, *Nabataean Coins,* 46f. Cf. also G. L. Harding, *An Index and Concordance of Pre-Islamic Names and Inscriptions* (1971).

10. Cf. Y. Meshorer, *loc. cit.,* 41-81.

11. Cf. *ibid.,* 81.

12. Cf. A. Negev, *PEQ* 114 (1982) 119-28.

13. Concerning the numismatic evidence, cf. Y. Meshorer, *Nabataean Coins,* 46f.; Schuerer I, 583. *CIS* II 214 (251f.) lines 3f.: *"Mense Nisan anni quadrogenti octavi Heretat."*

14. J. Starcky, *DBS* VII (1966) 916 (A.D. 40/41); J. I. Lawlor, *The Nabataeans* (1974) 109; Y. Meshorer, *Nabataean Coins,* 87; A. Negev, *ANRW* II 8 (1978) 567;

any further justification,[15] is now advocated with extensive argumentation by J. van Bruggen.[16] R. Jewett[17] has also adopted this dating, which circumscribes a bit more tightly what for him is the important period of Paul's flight from Damascus (§5.2.3), though he does draw support from a study from the nineteenth century by A. von Gutschmid.[18] But van Bruggen himself must admit that even if one applies rigorous standards, the death of Aretas may have occurred in January or February of the year A.D. 40.[19]

5.2.2. Niels Hyldahl

This Danish scholar writes: "For any determination of absolute chronology, Acts *doubtless* possesses much less significance than earlier assumed; it is precisely the contemporary remark that Paul himself makes about Aretas (2 Cor. 11:32) that then *perhaps* acquires all the greater significance."[20] The element of caution coming to expression in the second sentence is all too justified. Any attempt to arrive at an absolute chronological fixed-point from this Pauline allusion encounters considerable difficulties, as already emphasized by T. Mommsen: "We will probably have to renounce the possibility of finding a chronological fixed-point for Paul's life history in the activity of the Nabatean king in Damascus."[21]

It is extremely likely that the flight from Damascus occurred shortly before the apostle's first visit to Jerusalem (Gal. 1:17f.) (§13.3.1), and this is also the conclusion of Hyldahl.[22] According to his outline, however, this particular trip by Paul to the holy city took place in A.D. 42,[23] and the Damascus incident accordingly at earliest in A.D. 41, that is, one year after what is far and away the most probable date of Aretas' death! Concerning this newly emerging problem, Hyldahl merely remarks: "As far as Aretas is concerned (2 Cor. 11:32f.), the chronology presented above does, to be sure, force us to admit that the only thing that can be said with any certainty

---

K. Schmitt-Korte, in M. Lindner, *Petra und das Königreich der Nabatäer* ([3]1980) 104; R. Wenning, *Die Nabatäer* (1987) 13; D. F. Graf, *ABD* I (1992) 374f. More recent scholarship has almost completely confirmed the chronology of Nabatean kings deduced from the numismatic evidence by R. Dussaud, *JA* 3 (1904) 189-238.

15. So, e.g., C. Colpe, *KP* I (1964) 529.
16. *"Na veertien jaren"* (1973) 13-19.
17. *A Chronology of Paul's Life* (1979) 30.
18. In J. Euting, *Nabatäische Inschriften aus Arabian* (1885) 84-89.
19. *"Na veertien jaren"* (1973) 19.
20. *Die Paulinische Chronologie* (1986) 17 (emphases as in the original).
21. *Römische Geschichte* V ([5]1904) 477, note 26.
22. In *Die Paulinische Chronologie,* 17, note 38, he cites as agreeing in this sense A. Suhl, *Paulus und seine Briefe* (1975) 314f.
23. *Ibid.,* 121.

about Paul's flight from Damascus — if indeed it was such — is that Paul came to Jerusalem before the death not of the king in the year 40, but rather of his ethnarch."[24]

Previously, scholars at least generally agreed that Paul's remark presupposes that Aretas IV was still living at the time of the incident. Hyldahl defends his divergent view by pointing out that "it is usually overlooked that Damascus was not guarded by Aretas himself, but rather by his ethnarch; as an analogy I would refer to Syllaeus, the *epitropos* of Aretas' predecessor."[25] This argumentation, however, is questionable for several reasons. As we will demonstrate later, the ethnarch in Damascus did not have the function of a governor (§7.4). Furthermore, the position of Syllaeus was in every respect unique.[26] He was not merely a Nabatean sheik, but rather the vice-regent (ἐπίτροπος) designated as "brother of the king (ἀδελφὸς βασιλέως)."[27] In actuality, Syllaeus exercised power in place of the weak Obodas III (or, according to a different numbering, Obodas II) (Josephus, *Ant.* xvi.220, 280). H. P. Roschinski calls Syllaeus an "almost omnipotent vizier."[28] In A.D. 9, Obodas was then poisoned, apparently at the instigation of Syllaeus (Josephus, *Ant.* xvi.296), who at just that time — probably not coincidentally — was on his way to Rome, where he intrigued without success to attain the recognition of Augustus (Josephus, *Ant.* xvi.282-97). Above all, however, this reference to Syllaeus does not explain why Paul yet spoke of the "ethnarch of *Aretas*" (2 Cor. 11:32), whereas according to Hyldahl's chronology Aretas' by no means insignificant son Malichus II[29] was already in power. Peculiarly, Hyldahl also places a question mark after the apostle's flight from Damascus, itself genuinely and unequivocally attested by 2 Cor. 11:32f. The feeling of methodological coercion cannot quite be shaken: because A.D. 40 — specifically the beginning of this year — disrupts as *terminus ad quem* the chronology deduced along a different path, this particular date is played down as much as possible.

24. *Ibid.*, 123.
25. *Ibid.*, 123, note 21.
26. Cf. J. Starcky, *DBS* VII (1966) 911-13; Schuerer I, 580f.; M. Lindner, in *Petra und das Königreich der Nabatäer* (³1980) 65-69.
27. Cf. Strabo, xvi.4.23f. and the consecration inscription of Syllaeus for Obodas in Miletus (*CRAI* [1907] 389-91). A similar inscription, one that to my knowledge is still unpublished, comes from Delos. Cf. J. Starcky, *DBS* VII (1966) 913.
28. In G. Hellenkemper-Salies, *Die Nabatäer* (1981) 913.
29. Concerning him, cf. J. Starcky, *DBS* VII (1966) 916-19; Schuerer I, 583; A. Negev, *ANRW* II 8 (1978) 569f.; M. Lindner, in *Petra und das Königreich der Nabatäer* (³1980) 78-80.

5.2.3. Robert Jewett

In an earlier chronological outline, Hyldahl[30] assumed Paul's flight from Damascus took place in the summer of the year A.D. 36, in which he dated the victory of Aretas IV over Herod Antipas (Josephus, *Ant.* xviii.113-16).[31] The new reconstruction forces Hyldahl to declare that a more exact determination of the historical circumstances of this flight is impossible.[32] R. Jewett evaluates things quite differently here; he is certain that "the transfer of Damascus to Nabataean control indicated by 2 Cor. 11:32f. probably also occurred during the early years of Caligula's administration."[33] Jewett is even convinced that the time of the flight can be determined fairly accurately: "Since the negotiations about the transfer could scarcely have been completed before the summer of A.D. 37, this provides a *terminus a quo* for Paul's escape from the ethnarch of Aretas. Paul's escape occurred sometime within the two-year span until the death of Aretas in A.D. 39. This is a datum whose historical solidity is capable of anchoring a chronology."[34] This last sentence is more emphatic in the original English edition than in the German translation, which reads in effect: "One can thus construct a chronology on this historically reliable basis."[35] Jewett later referred to this date as "the cornerstone of my hypothesis."[36] This temporal determination, so acquired, is one essential reason that Jewett dates the Apostolic Council after the second missionary journey (see pp. 9f. above). To be sure, attention has justifiably been drawn to the fact that the Aretas-date, too, can be localized more precisely within a biography of Paul only with the aid of Acts.[37] The letter itself does not indicate whether the incident ended the apostle's first or second stay in Damascus (cf. Gal. 1:17).

---

30. In *Festschrift B. Noack* (1975) 102-7.

31. Concerning the question of this dating, see §3.2.2 above.

32. *Die Paulinische Chronologie,* 123.

33. *A Chronology of Paul's Life,* 32; the most recent treatment by J. Taylor, *RB* 99 (1992) 719-28, hardly goes beyond R. Jewett.

34. *Loc. cit.,* 33.

35. *A Chronology of Paul's Life,* 33; German edition: *Paulus-Chronologie. Ein Versuch* (Munich, 1982) 62f.

36. In B. C. Corley, *Colloquy on New Testament Studies* (1983) 279. C. S. Voulgaris, Χρονολογία τῶν γεγονότων τοῦ βίου τοῦ Ἀποστόλου Παύλου (1980) 283-88, employs similar argumentation in taking this point of departure for his own chronology of Paul. Cf. the chronological table in *Theol(A)* 53 (1982) 488f. My thanks to Dr. Chrys Caragounis (University of Lund) for making these articles, which are difficult to obtain, available to me.

37. Cf. G. B. Caird, *JTS* 31 (1980) 171; A. J. M. Wedderburn, *ET* 92 (1981) 105.

5.3. Damascus and the Nabateans

Before we entrust ourselves to this anchor which Jewett has cast, these two assertions must be examined, namely, that (1) 2 Cor. 11:32f. presupposes the direct rule of the Nabateans over Damascus, and (2) the surrender of the city occurred at the beginning of the rule of Caligula around approximately A.D. 37.

5.3.1. Numismatic Evidence

The assumption of Nabatean sovereignty over Damascus during Paul's time became the long predominant view within Protestant circles through the authority of E. Schürer,[38] and in Catholic exegesis on the basis of a monograph by A. Steinmann.[39] For both scholars, one particular peculiarity in the numismatic evidence was, along with 2 Cor. 11:32f., the main argument.[40] M. de Vogüé had already pointed out in 1868 that coins of Caligula and Claudius were not attested in Damascus.[41] Unfortunately, we do not know substantively more about this matter now than at that time. The complaint of H. Seyrig still applies: "The coins of Damascus are widely dispersed. . . . There are many unpublished ones in several different collections."[42] The great posthumous work of A. Spijkerman, *Coins of the Decapolis and Provincia Arabia,*[43] unfortunately excludes Damascus, as is also the case in the shorter catalog of Y. Meshorer.[44]

In his standard work on the coins of the Nabateans, Y. Meshorer, too, assumes the latter's sovereignty over Damascus during the days of Paul,[45] and in this regard tries to evaluate further, in addition to 2 Cor. 11:32f., the numismatic evidence. Meshorer explains the complete absence of coins of the Nabatean king Malichus II from the final years of his rule (twenty-fourth to thirty-first years = A.D. 63-70) as a result of a lack of silver, itself the result of a political crisis, which Meshorer associates with the Damascus problem: "As we have seen, minting [in Damascus] was interrupted during the days

---

38. *ThStKr* 72 (1899) 93-99; *Geschichte des jüdischen Volkes* I (³/⁴1901) 737; II (⁴1907) 108, 153f.

39. *Aretas IV. König der Nabatäer* (1909). Cf. earlier J. Aberle, *BZ* 1 (1903) 257-66.

40. Cf. E. Schürer, *Geschichte des jüdischen Volkes* II (⁴1907) 153; A. Steinmann, *Aretas* (1909) 33f.

41. *Mélanges d'archéologie Orientale* (1868) 33.

42. *Syr* 27 (1950) 34, note 4.

43. *The Coins of the Decapolis and Provincia Arabia* (1978).

44. *City-Coins of Eretz-Israel and the Decapolis* (1985).

45. *Nabataean Coins* (1975) 63f.

of Aretas IV when the city once more came into the possession of the Nabataeans. From numismatic evidence we learn that 'city coins' were once again issued in Damascus under the emperor Nero, most of whose coins bear the date ZOT = 377. This era of Damascus is according to the Seleucid era, which began in 312 B.C.E., and hence these coins are of the year 64/65 C.E. [In a footnote Meshorer mentions a coin dating possibly from the year A.D. 63/64 (COT).] Here we have an interesting numismatic circumstance. Damascus minting was renewed shortly after the cessation of Nabataean minting. . . . In 63 C.E., a political change apparently took place in the Nabataean kingdom, perhaps chiefly in its relations with, or in its obligations to Rome her [sic!]. This political change must have been detrimental to the Nabataeans, for in that year they were deprived of the city of Damascus — which had until then been under their rule, and the Nabataean mint also probably ceased to operate, ownce [sic!] to the crisis which led to the loss of the city and which appears to have had economic implications."[46]

This internationally recognized expert has nonetheless made several errors here. According to his catalog, minting of coins by Malichus II did not end until during the latter's twenty-fifth year.[47] Furthermore, in the case of official counting, the Seleucid era must be reckoned according to the Macedonian calendar.[48] Accordingly, the final coins of Malichus must be dated in A.D. 65/66. The first known Damascus city-coin under Nero already dates from the year 374 (ΔOT) of the Seleucid era,[49] and thus comes from A.D. 62/63. These two numismatic peculiarities thus by no means coincide so strikingly in the same year as Meshorer's portrayal maintains. Moreover, the period in which coins of Malichus are absent is reduced to around four years, and that might, after all, be merely accidental. Of course, it is possible to assume that the loss of Damascus before A.D. 62/63 resulted in the cessation of Nabatean minting after A.D. 65/66, though any elevation of this conclusion above the status of a mere suspicion would depend on determining in and of itself just what change occurred in the possession of Damascus.

In my opinion, the gap in the numismatic evidence between the years A.D. 33/34 and 62/63 must for two reasons be eliminated as an argument regarding the status of sovereignty in Damascus: (1) Coins from the early Roman period are extremely rare in the city in any case.[50] In addition to

---

46. *Ibid.,* 67. R. Jewett does not discuss this argument, though he is familiar with the work of Y. Meshorer (*A Chronology of Paul's Life,* 121, note 51).

47. *Loc. cit.,* 108 (no. H8).

48. Cf. T. Fischer, *OLZ* 74 (1979) 244.

49. T. Mionnet, *Description de médailles antiques* V (1811) 286.

50. Cf. *ibid.,* 285-87; F. de Saulcy, *Numismatique de la Terre-Sainte* (1874) 35f.; *BMC Syria,* 283.

several bronze pieces of Augustus, we can variously confirm numismatically three years of Tiberius (A.D. 33/34 as the last) and of Nero (A.D. 62/63 as the first). There is no known numismatic evidence for either Caligula and Claudius or for Vespasian and Titus, indeed not even for Nerva and Trajan. (2) A different picture, of course, would emerge through findings of Nabatean coins from the period between A.D. 37 and 62/63. Even if such coins are as yet completely absent, this is all the more noteworthy in view of the high minting activity in the second half of the rule of Aretas IV (§5.2.1). Even though the argument would be extremely useful to him, R. Jewett also openly admits that at this time the numismatic evidence does not permit any persuasive conclusions.[51]

5.3.2. The Reorganization of the East by Caligula

The only argument remaining for Jewett is the general reference that, "reversing the policies of his predecessor, Gaius reestablished a system of client kings in the east and parceled out substantial sections of the province of Syria to various princes."[52] But this confirms nothing more than the possibility of an investiture of Damascus to Aretas. Although rational reasoning was not always at work in the measures undertaken by Caligula, Aretas had demonstrated friendship to the Romans neither in his epithet (see note 4 above) nor in his earlier behavior (see p. 42 above). In his report about the reorganization of circumstances in the eastern part of the empire, Dio Cassius is silent regarding Damascus (Dio Cassius, *Hist.* lix.12.2). It seems even more noteworthy that in the consistently rich epigraphic and numismatic documentation from the rule of Aretas IV (§7.2.1) we possess not a single reference to any event that might have elevated the king to the same status as his predecessor in name, Aretas III, who exercised sovereignty over Damascus after his victory over Antiochus XII in the year A.D. 85 (Josephus, *Ant.* xiii.387-92; *B.J.* i.99-103).[53] Coins minted in Damascus are also attested for Aretas III.[54] In the realm of ancient history, one is permitted to adduce negative evidence only with the greatest caution. But Jewett's view concerning the status of sovereignty in Damascus also lacks any positive evidence outside the New Testament.

Although Jewett does maintain that "these considerations have led most specialists to assume that Aretas IV gained some supervisory control over

---

51. *A Chronology of Paul's Life,* 32; R. Jewett (*loc. cit.,* 122f., note 71) only mentions the work of T. Mionnet (see note 50 above).

52. *Ibid.,* 32.

53. Cf. Schuerer II, 128.

54. Cf. Y. Meshorer, *Nabataean Coins,* 12-15.

Damascus itself,"[55] he enumerates almost exclusively earlier scholars.[56] More recently, it seems as if this question is either left open[57] or answered in the negative,[58] even if the view preferred by Jewett still finds new advocates, who usually do not, however, support their position.[59] Ultimately, of course, such statistics of opinion do not constitute an argument. The history of scholarship makes it clear, however, that the main reason for assuming renewed Nabatean sovereignty over Damascus after its inclusion in the Roman province of Syria in the year A.D. 66 (Josephus, *Ant.* xiv.29; *B.J.* i.127) was not actually evidence from outside the New Testament,[60] but rather a certain understanding of 2 Cor.

55. *A Chronology of Paul's Life,* 31.

56. *Ibid.,* 122, note 61. With supporting arguments: E. Schürer, *Geschichte des jüdischen Volkes* II ([4]1907) 153f.; A. Steinmann, *Aretas IV. König der Nabatäer* (1909) 33-37; H. Bietenhard, *ZDPV* 79 (1963) 55-58. As a mere assertion: P. Ewald, *RE*[3] I (1896) 797; H. Leclerq, *DACL* XIII (1938) 2579; E. Barnikol, *ThJb(H)* 1 (1933) 93f.; F. M. Abel, *Géographie de la Palestine* II (1938) 302; R. Janin, *DHGE* XIV (1960) 43.

57. Cf. Schuerer I, 582; J. I. Lawlor, *The Nabataeans* (1974) 115-18; A. Suhl, *Paulus und seine Briefe* (1975) 314f.; A. Negev, *ANRW* II 8 (1978) 569; M. Lindner, in *Petra und das Königreich der Nabatäer* ([3]1980) 74 (though still differently in the second edition [1974] 130f.!); C. J. Hemer, *Festschrift F. F. Bruce* (1980) 4f.; G. Schneider, *Die Apostelgeschichte* II (1982) 36, note 30; A. Barrett, *Caligula* (1989) 183; D. F. Graf, *ABD* I (1992) 375.

58. Cf. the bibliography in note 72.

59. G. L. Harding, *The Antiquities of Jordan* (1960) 123; C. Colpe, *KP* I (1964) 530; N. Glueck, *Deities and Dolphins* (1966) 40; G. Ogg, *The Chronology of the Life of Paul* (1968) 16-23; M. Gawlikowski, *Le temple Palmyrénien* (1973) 45; Y. Meshorer, *Nabataean Coins,* 63f.; H. Bietenhard, *ANRW* II 8 (1978) 256-58; W. P. Armstrong and J. Finegan, *ISBE* I (1979) 689f.; J. Murphy-O'Connor, *RB* 89 (1982) 74f.; D. Sack, in *Im Land des Baal* (1982) 362 (later abandoned, see note 72 below); S. Dockx, *Chronologies néotestamentaires* ([2]1984) 81; N. Kokkinos, in *Festschrift J. Finegan* (1989) 145; J. McRay, *ABD* II (1992) 8; J. Taylor, *RB* 99 (1992) 724-27.

60. Only in exceptional instances (G. W. Bowersock, *Roman Arabia* [1983] 68f., similarly M. F. Baslez, *Saint Paul* [1991] 104f.) is the view defended — one frequently expressed earlier (e.g., E. H. Plumptre, *The Acts of the Apostles* [no date] 56) — that Aretas IV also occupied Damascus during the course of his campaign against Herod Antipas, at the end of A.D. 36 or the beginning of 37 (Josephus, *Ant.* xviii.113-15). But the risk of unavoidably provoking thereby a Roman counterreaction in what was already a problematic situation for him already militates against this view. Josephus says nothing of any such significant incident. The assumption is also problematic according to which Aretas occupied Damascus in preparation for the attack of the Syrian governor Vitellius. If one considers the chastising expedition of Vitellius to be historical (but cf. §3.2.2), then its route over Ptolemais and Galilee to Petra (Josephus, *Ant.* xviii.120-22) — without taking back Damascus — seems strategically incomprehensible. Contra the conquest hypothesis, consider the still persuasive work of V. Weber, *Die Abfassung des Galaterbriefs* (1900) 365-67. Nabatean sovereignty over Damascus by permission of Tiberius, of all people, is utterly incredible. Cf. A. Steinmann, *Aretas IV. König der Nabatäer* (1909) 26-28. R. Jewett, *A Chronology of Paul's Life,* 31f., also justifiably takes issue with this thesis.

11:32f. But does the ethnarch of Aretas whom Paul mentions here really constitute a compelling argument for Nabatean sovereignty over Damascus?

5.4. The Ethnarch of Aretas

The judgment of a specialist in Nabatean history such as A. Negev already shows that things are more complicated than Jewett would have us believe: "The transference of the territory of Philippus to Agrippa I (37 C.E.) and the gradual enlargement of his kingdom did not affect the Nabateans. Just about this time, in the last year[s ?] of Aretas' life, as we learn from the epistles [sic!], an *ethnarchos* [sic!] of king Aretas, responsible for keeping the city of Damascus under observation, arrested [sic!] Paul (II Cor. 11:32-33, and cf. Gal. 1:15-17). The existence of a Nabatean ruler at Damascus at this time has never been satisfactorily explained."[61] What is interesting here is not the oversights and obvious misunderstanding of the passage in the letter itself, but rather the indication of a problem in the final sentence.

5.4.1. The Title Ethnarch

It contradicts the use of the word familiar to us[62] to understand the ethnarch of Aretas in 2 Cor. 11:32 as representative or governor of the Nabatean king in Damascus. Nabatean governors bore the title στρατηγός or אסרתגה, as Josephus (*Ant.* xviii.112) and the inscriptional evidence[63] unanimously attest. T. Zahn already pointed out that one should not underestimate the significance of ἔθνος as a constituent part of the title ἐθνάρχης.[64] The designation implies rule over a specific people. The expression ἐθνάρχης can thus also refer to a tribal leader,[65] and the thesis has thus been suggested that this ethnarch was a Bedouin sheik who was supposed to apprehend Paul outside the city.[66] This

---

61. *ANRW* II 8 (1978) 569.

62. The information in *EDNT* I (1990) 381, is disappointing. The difficulty attaching to this expression has even led to the assumption of a gloss (G. A. Simcox, *JTS* 2 [1901] 589f.).

63. *CIS* II 160, 169, 195, 196, 213. Cf. J. Cantineau, *Le Nabatéen* II (1932) 66; Schuerer, II, 97, note 50; M. Sartre, *Trois études sur l'Arabie romaine et byzantine* (1982) 122-28; E. A. Knauf, *ZNW* 74 (1983) 145, note 6; H. I. Macadam, *Studies in the History of the Roman Province of Arabia* (1986) 154f.; J. Taylor, *RB* 99 (1992) 720-24.

64. *NKZ* 15 (1904) 36-38.

65. Cf. E. A. Knauf, *ZNW* 74 (1983) 145f.

66. T. Zahn, *NKZ* (1904) 38-41; *Die Apostelgeschichte* (1919) 329, note 16; P. Bachmann, *Der zweite Brief des Paulus an die Korinther* (³1918) 387f., note 1; D. Plooij, *De chronologie van het leven van Paulus* (1919) 3-9; K. Lake, *BC* V (1933) 193; R. C. H. Lenski, *The Interpretation of I and II Corinthians* (1937) 1289.

view, rarely supported today,[67] falters on the circumstances presupposed for Paul's flight.[68] The notion of lowering Paul over the city wall in a basket (2 Cor. 11:33) makes sense only if danger threatened from inside the city or at least in the immediate vicinity of the city gates. Yet Acts also presupposes that the city gates were guarded (Acts 9:24). If a Nabatean patrol really was supposed to lie in wait for Paul in the extended area outside the city, then he would have been safer in the city itself. The whole notion of the ethnarch as a Bedouin sheik, however, is problematical not least because the Nabateans had already ceased being nomads in the second century b.c., and were now the Hellenized ruling class of an empire with a thoroughly mixed population.[69]

By contrast, no terminological problems arise if the ethnarch of Aretas was the "head of the Nabatean trade colony in Damascus, who at the same time probably also represented the interests of the Nabatean state, and was thus a kind of consul."[70] A corresponding use of ἐθνάρχης is attested in Josephus (*Ant.* xiv.117; cf. xix.283) and Strabo (xvii.798) in reference to the head of the Jewish population group in Alexandria. This solution, favored by both earlier[71] and more recent scholars,[72] is supported by the existence of

67. Exceptions include B. Rigaux, *The Letters of St. Paul* (Eng. trans., 1968) 71; H. P. Roschinski, in G. Hellenkemper-Salies, *Die Nabatäer* (1981) 24; F. Lang, *Die Briefe an die Korinther* (1986) 345.

68. Cf. H. Bietenhard, *ANRW* II 8 (1978) 257f.

69. Cf. E. A. Knauf, in M. Lindner, *Petra. Neue Ausgrabungen und Entdeckungen* (1986) 74-86.

70. E. A. Knauf, *ZNW* 74 (1983) 147.

71. There are considerably more than one might surmise from E. A. Knauf, *loc. cit.*, 146, note 10, who mentions only E. Schwartz, *NGWG.PH* (1906) 367-69, and U. Kahrstedt, *Syrische Territorien in hellenistischer Zeit* (1926) 55, note 2. But cf., e.g., also C. F. Nösgen, *Commentar über die Apostelgeschichte* (1882) 205; O. Holtzmann, *Neutestamentliche Zeitgeschichte* (1895) 97; V. Weber, *Die Abfassung des Galaterbriefs* (1900) 364-70; E. W. Burton, *Galatians* (1921) 57; E. Meyer, *Ursprung und Anfänge des Christentums* III (1923) 346, note 1; A. Schlatter, *Paulus, der Bote Jesu* (1934) 658 (as a possibility). Even earlier advocates can be found in G. Wandel, *ZKWKL* 8 (1887) 435.

72. A. D. Nock, *St. Paul* (1938) 83; J. Klausner, *Von Jesus zu Paulus* (1950) 314, note 5; J. Starcky, *DBS* VII (1966) 915; F. F. Bruce, *1 and 2 Corinthians* (1971) 244f.; *BJRL* 69 (1986) 275f.; P. C. Hammond (1973) 37f., 109; J. Rey-Coquais, *JRS* 68 (1978) 50; M. Lindner, in *Petra und das Königreich der Nabatäer* (³1980) 74 (as a possibility); E. A. Knauf, *ZNW* 74 (1983) 146f.; D. C. Braund, *Rome and the Friendly King* (1984) 89, note 86; H. J. Klauck, *2. Korintherbrief* (1986) 90f.; R. P. Martin, *2 Corinthians* (1986) 385f.; R. Wenning, *Die Nabatäer* (1987) 25; P. Trummer, in *Aufsätze zum NT* (1987) 217f.; D. Sack, *Damaskus* (1989) 14; K. F. Doig, *New Testament Chronology* (1991) 331-35; S. Légasse, *Paul apôtre* (1991) 73-76; K. P. Donfried, *ABD* I (1992) 1020f.; M. Harding, *NTS* 39 (1993) 531f. A mediating solution is advocated by A. Kasher, *Jews, Idumaeans, and Ancient Arabs* (1988) 184-86. He similarly sees in the ethnarch the head of the Nabatean colony, but at the same time believes that he was appointed — by the Roman governor of Syria and in consultation with Aretas — as governor of Damascus in order to compensate the Nabateans after the

Nabatean trade colonies at least in Gerasa,[73] and presumably also in other cities of the Decapolis such as Capitolias, Philadelphia, and Hippos.[74] Damascus, too, as we shall see, had a Nabatean quarter.

5.4.2. The Circumstances of Paul's Flight

In their groundbreaking study of ancient Damascus, C. Watzinger and C. Wulzinger drew attention to the fact that "the ancient name of one city quarter, namely, en-Naibatûn, yet attests Nabatean sovereignty in the first century B.C. [i.e., under Aretas III]."[75] According to Ibn Shākir (fourteenth century), it was "so named because it was inhabited exclusively by Nabateans."[76] Except for one instance of metathesis, the Arabic name exactly renders the Greek genitive Ναβαταίων, and the designation thus derives from the pre-Islamic period.[77] Information from medieval Arabic geographers[78] clearly points to the northeast quarter (see illustration 2 [p. 417]) between the Roman East Gate (Bāb Sharki) and the St. Thomas Gate (Bāb Tūmā).[79] The reliability of local tradition can be additionally supported by archeological evidence. In his pioneering study of the development of the city of Damascus, J. Sauvaget pointed out that the streets of this northeast quarter do not quite fit into the original plan of the Seleucid city of the third and second centuries B.C.[80] His explanation that a Nabatean settlement originally situated outside the city walls was subsequently integrated into walls during the period of their sovereignty in the first century B.C. has been confirmed by comparative research, above all in Antioch on the Orontes and in Bozrah.[81] In her new, extensive study on the topography of Damascus, D. Sack also claims that the former Nabatean quarter has now been positively located.[82]

In the middle of the former Nabatean quarter today stands the Ananias Chapel, whose local tradition goes back at least to the pre-Arabic period.[83]

---

accession of Caligula for the demonstrations of favor to other rulers. A. Kasher refers again to the alleged numismatic evidence. He does not discuss the problem of Pauline chronology.

73. Cf. R. Wenning, *Die Nabatäer* (1987) 54-56.

74. Cf. E. A. Knauf, *ZNW* 74 (1983) 146f.; R. Wenning, *ZDPV* 110 (1994) 1-35.

75. *Damaskus* (1921) 65, note 112.

76. The Arabic text can be found in H. Sauvaire, *JA* 4 (1895) 379.

77. Cf. J. Sauvaget, *Syr* 26 (1949) 344.

78. Cf. *loc. cit.*, 344f., note 5; J. Starcky, *DBS* VII (1966) 915f.

79. Maps can be found in D. Sack, in *Land des Baal* (1982) 361, illustration 73; *DaM* 2 (1985) 215, illustration 2.

80. *Syr* 26 (1949) 344f.

81. Cf. F. E. Peters, *DaM* 1 (1983) 272-76.

82. *Damaskus* (1989) 10-14.

83. Cf. J. Nasrallah, *Souvenirs de St. Paul* (1944) 35-40; *MBib* 31 (1983) 35-37; *POC* 35 (1985) 266f.

This local tradition was strengthened by excavations in 1921, during which on the west wall of the contemporary crypt the remains of a Byzantine church from the fifth/sixth centuries were exposed.[84] Investigations in Jerusalem[85] and Rome[86] suggest that the local traditions attaching to title-churches of the early Byzantine period should be taken more seriously than was long the case. Reference to Ananias (Acts 22:12) as ἀνὴρ εὐλαβής (חסיד) might suggest that he belonged to a Jewish-Christian-ascetic splinter group with an Essenic background.[87] In that case, it would be possible that, as in Jerusalem,[88] this group had its own small, circumscribed residential quarter in Damascus as well.[89] This, too, could have contributed to the stability of local tradition. Although any considerations here must be cautious, J. Starcky has nonetheless tentatively posed the question whether the location of the house of Ananias in the precinct of the Nabatean quarter might help clarify the situation of 2 Cor. 11:32f.[90] Starcky does not mention that according to the supposed map of the Hellenistic-Roman city the house of Ananias might have been located, unlike today, directly next to the wall (cf. 2 Cor. 11:33).[91]

As an objection to a possible connection between the topographical circumstances and Paul's flight, Starcky suggests that 2 Cor. 11:32 gives the impression that the ethnarch was guarding the entire city (ἐφρούρει τὴν πόλιν) rather than merely one quarter.[92] But did the apostle have any interest in portraying to the Corinthians the exact local circumstances? Nonetheless, the expression πόλις Δαμασκηνῶν (2 Cor. 11:32), attested on coins (see note 50 above) as a designation of the Roman free city, might contain a reference to the political situation of the time.[93] When in his letter to the Galatians (Gal. 1:17) Paul says he returned to Damascus from "Arabia" (ἀλλὰ ἀπῆλθον εἰς Ἀραβίαν, καὶ πάλιν ὑπέστρεψα εἰς Δαμασκόν), this more readily militates against than

84. Cf. M. E. Pottier, *Syr* 4 (1923) 319; G. Contenau, *Syr* 5 (1924) 205, and plate XLVIII; J. Sauvaget, *Les monuments historiques de Damas* (1932) 10f. Bibliography can be found in D. Sack, *Damaskus* (1989) 89.

85. Cf. the overview in R. Riesner, *GBL* II (1988) 668-73.

86. Cf. P. Lampe, *Die stadtrömischen Christen in den ersten beiden Jahrhunderten* (²1989) 10-35.

87. Cf. R. Riesner, *ANRW* II 26.2 (1995) 1862f.

88. Concerning the Essene quarter in Jerusalem, cf. R. Riesner, *BiKi* 40 (1985) 64-76; in *Festschrift J. T. Milik* (1992) 179-86; B. Pixner, *ZDPV* 105 (1989) 96-104.

89. H. Stegemann, in J. Trebolle Barrera and L. Vegas Montaner, *The Madrid Qumran Congress* I (1992) 146-48, assumes Essenes to have been in Damascus since the middle of the second century B.C. See also pp. 238-40 below.

90. *DBS* VII (1966) 915f.

91. This becomes especially clear in the maps in *MBib* 28 (1983) 26 and 31 (1983) 33; D. Sack, *Damaskus* (1989) 17. See illustration 2 (p. 417 below).

92. *DBS* VII (1966) 916.

93. Cf. T. Zahn, *NKZ* 15 (1904) 40.

for the city belonging to the Nabatean kingdom.[94] To be sure, the geographical meaning of Ἀραβία is disputed (§13.3.1). The verb φρουρέω can refer just as well to guarding something from the outside as from the inside,[95] though in both the LXX (Jdt. 3:6; 1 Esdr. 4:56) and the New Testament (Gal. 3:23; Phil. 4:7; 1 Pet. 1:5) the second meaning seems to predominate,[96] fitting well with the solution suggested here (cf. Josephus, *Vita* 53). By contrast, πιάσαι must not necessarily mean that this was an official arrest. The expression can also mean merely that the ethnarch wanted to seize Paul in order to get rid of him.[97]

What reasons did the ethnarch have for such measures? If one assumes that Paul had become undesirable because of his mission activity among the Nabateans,[98] then this militates both against Nabatean possession of Damascus and against his stay in the vicinity precisely of the Nabatean quarter of the city. The apostle likely would not have exposed himself voluntarily to such danger. But the assumption of a mission among the pagan Nabateans at such an early time seems rather problematical (§13.3). Hence the topographical explanation considered here (Nabatean quarter) remains one possibility, and the information in Acts, too, should not be dismissed from the outset, namely, that Jewish adversaries were behind the plot (Acts 9:23f.). As much as this latter account may seem to correspond to Luke's agenda of mentioning only Jews as persecutors, it is unlikely that he simply invented it.[99] Damascus had a strong Jewish community (Josephus, *B.J.* ii.560; vii.368) which obviously stayed in close contact with Jerusalem (Acts 9:2, 28f.; 22:5; 26:12). Perhaps the Damascene Jews had not only their own quarter,[100] but also, as in Alexandria, even their own ethnic-religious leader.[101] In that case, they themselves

94. Cf. V. Weber, *Die Abfassung des Galaterbriefs* (1900) 369; A. Kasher, *Jews, Idumaeans, and Ancient Arabs* (1988) 185, note 142.

95. Cf. T. Zahn, *Die Apostelgeschichte* (1919) 329.

96. Cf. E. L. Hicks, *ClR* 1 (1887) 7f.; G. Ogg, *The Chronology of the Life of Paul* (1968) 17f.

97. Cf. Jn. 10:39 with Jn. 10:31.

98. So, e.g., K. P. Donfried, *ABD* I (1992) 1020f.

99. The fact that certain details might betray Luke's familiarity with a Pauline story also militates against this. See §13.3.3 below.

100. If this is to be sought in the area of the Jewish quarter of the Islamic period, then it was situated south of the "Street Called Straight" (Acts 9:11: ἡ ῥύμη ἡ καλουμένη Εὐθεῖα), today the considerably more narrow Derb el-Mustaqīm between the Little Gate (Bāb al-Ṣaghīr) and St. Paul Gate (Bāb Kaysān). Cf. B. Meistermann, *Durch's Heilige Land* (1913), map after p. 560. It is doubtful whether the "house of Judas" (cf. Acts 9:11) attested first at the beginning of the seventeenth century by Quaresimus at the northwest end of this quarter actually goes back to an older local tradition. Cf. J. Nasrallah, *Souvenirs de St. Paul* (1940) 25-29.

101. This is the suspicion of F. F. Bruce, *1 and 2 Corinthians* (1971) 245, and apparently also J. Starcky, *MBib* 28 (1983) 28.

could have searched for Paul in their own quarter, as Luke portrays it in an oversimplified narrative. When the apostle's adversaries noticed that he had found refuge in the area under the influence of the Nabatean ethnarch, they tried to resolve the issue through him in the way they thought fit. Unfortunately, almost anything can be had for the right price, then as today. Perhaps Aretas was concerned with cultivating good relationships with Jewish circles during his conflict with Herod Antipas (§3.2.2).[102] In any event, at the decisive battle against Antipas, Jews did go over to the Nabatean army (Josephus, *Ant.* xviii.114). Perhaps Paul also wanted to spare his own countrymen by not mentioning their participation in the persecution in Damascus.[103] Mention of the ethnarch might by contrast derive from the fact that this flight from Damascus, as the end of the very first stage of his missionary activity, was of decisive significance for the apostle (§13.3).

5.5. Chronological Findings

Although much in our reconstruction remains hypothetical, it at least seems possible to make both the Pauline and the Lukan accounts historically comprehensible. The negative results should be kept in mind: neither from archeological evidence, secular-historical sources, nor New Testament texts can Nabatean sovereignty over Damascus in the first century A.D. be proven. Our own investigation thus confirms the judgment of A. Suhl: "2 Cor. 11:32f. allows us to conclude only that Paul must have fled Damascus before the death of Aretas."[104] We can also agree with G. Lüdemann that "trying to extract more information from 2 Cor. 11:32f. ends up yielding less."[105] This passage in 2 Corinthians has proven to be unsuitable, contra R. Jewett (§5.2.3), as the cornerstone for an absolute chronology.[106] The death of Aretas IV in A.D. 40, however, remains a *terminus ante quem* for Paul's flight from Damascus, which occurred immediately before his first Jerusalem visit. This determination is not completely without value, however, since in one important point it raises doubts regarding the chronology outlined by N. Hyldahl (§5.2.2).

---

102. Cf. J. Dupont, *Les actes des apôtres* (1954) 94, note b.
103. So F. F. Bruce, *1 and 2 Corinthians* (1971) 245.
104. *Paulus und seine Briefe* (1975) 315.
105. *Paulus, der Heidenapostel* I (1980) 21, note 10.
106. To be sure, J. Murphy-O'Connor, *RB* 89 (1982) 75, is correct here with his criticism that G. Lüdemann too quickly dismisses the calculation of R. Jewett, although the latter's argumentation recalls his own dating of the edict of Claudius in A.D. 41 (§10). If Paul fled Damascus between A.D. 37 and 39, Lüdemann's own chronology (Pauline mission in Syria, Asia Minor, and Greece before A.D. 41) would encounter considerable difficulties.

§6

The Religious Policies of Claudius

The following chronologically problematic events — the beginning of the mission to the Gentiles, an allegedly empire-wide famine, the Cyprian proconsulate of Sergius Paulus, a Roman edict concerning the Jews, and the governorship of Gallio in Achaia (§§7-11) — all took place during the rule of Claudius (A.D. 41-54). Before we turn our attention to these individual questions, it seems wise to consider the relationship between this emperor and the Jews (and Christians) against the background of his administration in general, though especially in connection with his religious policies. This undertaking will also delimit the historical framework for an essential phase of the history of primitive Christianity.

6.1. The Personality and Work of the Emperor

6.1.1. Earlier Scholarship

Hardly any ancient emperor has undergone so fundamental a reevaluation by modern scholarship as has Emperor Claudius (10 B.C.-A.D. 54).[1] Prior to the great T. Mommsen, earlier historical writing depended almost exclusively on the literary tradition. The task of rendering an account of Claudius consisted largely in writing out and, where necessary, harmonizing the main sources, namely, Tacitus (*Ann.* xi-xii), Suetonius (*Claudius* 1-46), and Dio Cassius (*Hist.* lx). In evaluating the emperor, judgments such as the following as formulated by Suetonius were determinative: "Wholly under the control of these [the freedmen Pallas and Narcissus] and of his wives, as I have said, he played the part, not of a prince, but of a servant, lavishing honours, the command of armies, pardons or punishments, according to the interests of

---

1. An overview of the changes in the understanding of Claudius can be found in T. F. Carney, *ACl* 3 (1960) 99-104; E. Manni, *ANRW* II 2 (1975) 131-37; B. Levick, *Claudius* (1990) 195-97.

each of them, or even their wish and whim; and that too for the most part in ignorance and blindly" (Suetonius, *Claudius* 29.1). If one follows the explicit evaluations of the literary sources, a picture emerges of a sickly,[2] spiritually unbalanced,[3] and morally corrupt[4] ruler without any really independent accomplishments.[5] The great portrayals of Claudius by A. von Domaszewski[6] and H. Dessau[7] from the first quarter of the twentieth century still follow this pattern.

Isolated positive estimations, however, have also come down from antiquity. The legate of Gaul, Julius Vindex, who was the first to rebel against Nero, remarked in a speech in A.D. 68 that next to Augustus, only Claudius really had the right to bear the honorific names Caesar and Princeps (Dio Cassius, *Hist.* lxiii.22.2-6). Vespasian showed his admiration by rebuilding the temple begun in honor of Claudius by Nero but then torn down under the same emperor (Suetonius, *Claudius* 45; *Vespasian* 9.1). Admittedly, this renaissance did not come about free of ulterior political motives. Like Claudius, Vespasian was a usurper whose rule depended on the power of the legions.[8] Pliny the Elder (A.D. 23-79), whose lost *Histories* probably provided one of the sources for Tacitus, Suetonius, and Dio Cassius, likely gave the emperor a fairly positive portrayal.[9] Hence even earlier scholarship did not completely lack a more benevolent estimation of Claudius. H. Willenbücher sketched a picture of Claudius in 1914 coinciding strikingly with the most recent developments (§6.1.3). However, since the article appeared in the year the First World War broke out, and was published in the program of a *Gymnasium* (secondary school),[10] Willenbücher's view seems hardly to have attracted any attention.

2. Cf., e.g., Seneca, *Apocolocyntosis* 1.5-7; Juvenal, *Sat.* vi.622f.; Suetonius, *Claudius* 2.2; 30-31; Dio Cassius, *Hist.* lx.2.1.

3. Cf., e.g., Seneca, *Apocolocyntosis* 6; Josephus, *Ant.* xix.258; Tacitus, *Ann.* xi.28, 31; xii.1; Suetonius, *Claudius* 6; 10; 15.1; 16.1; 26.2-3; 35.1; 39; Dio Cassius, *Hist.* lx.2.6; 11.8; 14.2.

4. Cf., e.g., Tacitus, *Ann.* xii.59; Suetonius, *Claudius* 5; 34; Dio Cassius, *Hist.* lx.2.6; 18.2-3.

5. Cf., e.g., Tacitus, *Ann.* xii.7; Suetonius, *Claudius* 25.5; Dio Cassius, *Hist.* lx.2.4; 8.4; 14.1; 28.2.

6. *Geschichte der römischen Kaiser* II ([2/3]1921) 21-46.

7. *Geschichte der römischen Kaiser* II/1 (1926) 137-73.

8. Cf. B. Levick, *Claudius* (1990) 190f.

9. Cf. V. M. Scramuzza, *Claudius* (1940) 34; E. Huzar, *ANRW* II 32.1 (1984) 615f. (note 22 containing further bibiliography); B. Levick, *loc. cit.,* 192.

10. *Neues Gymnasium Mainz,* Program No. 917 (1914) 3-14.

6.1.2. The New Understanding

Two factors are largely responsible for the changing estimation of Claudius. First, new epigraphic evidence provided original documents with which to compare the literary sources.[11] Second, inquiries directed now more strongly toward social and economic history resulted in greater independence over against the biographically restricted view of the ancient authors. Thus the great article on Claudius by E. Groag in *Pauly's Realencyclopädie der classischen Altertumswissenschaft* from the year 1899 is already characterized by an obvious element of tension. Because Groag was already able to draw on a great deal of inscriptional material, he arrived at an extremely positive judgment concerning the results of Claudius' reign. But in the spirit of earlier tradition, he denied that the emperor himself had any real responsibility for this positive rule: "One must admit that the rule of the freedmen of C[laudius] was one of the best ever bestowed upon the Roman Empire."[12] Hence Groag's evaluation of the emperor's personality adhered completely to the traditional schema.[13] By contrast, a pioneer in research into the economic history of antiquity such as M. Rostovtzeff also suggested that Claudius himself played a more positive role, though his evaluation was inconsistent.[15]

The biography of A. Momigliano, appearing in 1932 in Italian[16] and then in 1943 in English as well,[17] led to a radical revision of our understanding of Claudius. Momigliano showed that the enormous accomplishment in centralizing the Roman world empire under Claudius can only be explained on the basis of the Princeps himself having assumed an extremely active role.[18] In this undertaking, the emperor was aided by his own thorough knowledge of Roman history and legal tradition,[19] which not even Suetonius contests (Suetonius, *Claudius* 40-41). In 1940, V. M. Scramuzza then further bolstered this new view with his great biography of Claudius. Above all, he was also able to show that many of the ancient biographers' judgments can be explained in terms of the *ressentiments* they harbored as representatives of the increasingly powerless senatorial and courtly class over against the emperor and his efficient adminis-

11. A handy collection can be found in E. M. Smallwood, *Documents Illustrating the Principates of Gaius, Claudius and Nero* (1967).
12. *PRE* 6 (1899) 2817.
13. *Loc. cit.,* 2832-36.
14. *Gesellschaft und Wirtschaft im römischen Kaiserreich* I (1931) 67f. *et passim.*
15. *Geschichte der alten Welt (Rom)* (1942) 304f.
16. *L'opere dell'imperatore Claudio* (1932).
17. *Claudius: The Emperor and His Achievement* (1943; ²1961).
18. *Claudius* (²1961) 39-73.
19. *Loc. cit.,* 1-19. Concerning Claudius' education, cf. also H. Bardon, *Les empereurs et les lettres latines* (1940) 125-61; B. Levick, *AJPh* 99 (1978) 79-105; *Claudius* (1990) 11-20.

trative apparatus.[20] To this one can add the inclination to overemphasize Roman court gossip, whereas the governing style in the provinces was of little interest. If one eliminates this "tendentious inclination," then the actual successes of Claudius' reign become evident even in Tacitus and Suetonius, and especially in Dio Cassius (*Hist.* lx.8.4). G. May gave what one might even call an enthusiastic evaluation especially of Claudius' legal and religious policies.[21]

This new picture of Claudius has not, to be sure, been completely free of opposition. W. Steidle has objected that one cannot portray the emperor in complete contradiction to the extant literary tradition.[22] The portrayals of Suetonius invited one to engage in psychoanalytical investigations whose results were less than advantageous for Claudius.[23] Finally, R. Syme explained A. Momigliano's positive Claudius-portrayal as the result of the sympathy of a modern pedant for an ancient one, and in his great work on Tacitus attempted to rehabilitate the older image of the emperor.[24] Furthermore, the image of the great centralizer, as Momigliano portrayed it in the days of Mussolini's rule and Roosevelt's "New Deal," was not without its anachronistic elements.[25] Nonetheless, the salient feature of the reevaluation initiated by Momigliano and Scramuzza have been able to assert themselves, as demonstrated by the most recent portrayals by A. Garzetti,[26] E. Huzar,[27] and B. Levick.[28] Hence H. Bengtson's appraisal of Claudius can be taken as representative of the present status of scholarship: "On the whole, his reign was one of the best of the entire early Principate as far as the capital and the empire were concerned. The style of many of his edicts and decrees shows that he did indeed participate in his government. . . . The picture of the emperor outlined in the ancient sources, though especially in Suetonius and then certainly in Seneca's *Apocolocyntosis,* is in need of strong correctives."[29]

6.1.3. The Current Understanding of Claudius

To be sure, recent scholarship is also characterized by the inclination to draw at least some distinctions within this unrestrictedly positive picture of

20. *The Emperor Claudius* (1940) 5-34. Cf. also D. Flach, *Tacitus* (1973) 160-73.
21. *RHDFE* 15 (1936) 55-97, 213-54; 17 (1938) 1-46.
22. *Sueton und die antike Biographie* ([2]1963) (= 1951) 85.
23. Cf. esp. E. F. Leon, *TAPA* 79 (1948) 79-86. Earlier bibliography in V. M. Scramuzza, *Claudius,* 238, note 3.
24. *Tacitus* I (1958) 436f.
25. Cf. T. F. Carney, *ACl* 3 (1960) 99; B. Levick, *Claudius* (1990) 195.
26. *From Tiberius to the Antonines* (1974) 106-45, 586-605.
27. *ANRW* II 32.1 (1984) 611-50.
28. *Claudius* (1990) 196f.
29. *Römische Geschichte* ([2]1976) 247.

Claudius. Even if we are better able today to see through the "tendentious inclination" of the ancient biographers, we are not exempt from the question regarding just which phenomena provided points of departure for their colored portrayal.[30] The warning against writing portrayals of the emperors completely contra the literary sources is underscored by the almost exclusively positive estimation of Caligula (A.D. 37-41) by J. W. Humphrey,[31] an estimation to which not only Gaius' successor Claudius would have objected,[32] but which is also provoking the criticism of the most recent biographer.[33] Even V. M. Scramuzza admitted with respect to Claudius: "There was no doubt a basis for some of the tales about him,"[34] and the American scholar suggested that toward the end of Claudius' reign the ruler's energy, especially as regards policy along the eastern frontiers of the empire, was declining.[35] Even A. Momigliano could occasionally admit weaknesses in the emperor's personality.[36] Momigliano and Scramuzza also concluded somewhat too precipitately that Claudius' effective administration of the provinces attested his strength of character in all other matters as well.[37] Seneca's *Apocolocyntosis,*[38] one of the most malicious and influential satires in world history, could not have been published immediately after the death of Claudius (Dio Cassius, *Hist.* lx.35.3) had not genuine weaknesses been exploitable. A reading of an original document such as Claudius' speech of A.D. 48 on the *ius honorum* of the Gauls[39] leaves a completely ambiguous impression. The broad visions of a statesman[40] stand next to meanderings and pedantic and self-satisfied erudition.[41]

30. Cf. A. Garzetti, *Tiberius* (1974) 106f.

31. *Cassius Dio's Roman History (Book 59)* (1976).

32. Cf. *CIL* VI 1252; Josephus, *Ant.* xix.284f. (see p. 99 below) and also Dio Cassius, *Hist.* lx.4.5; 22.3f.

33. A. Barrett, *Caligula* (1989), with the telling subtitle "The Corruption of Power."

34. *Claudius* (1940) 44.

35. *Ibid.,* 192.

36. *Claudius* (^{2}1961) 70.

37. Concerning this criticism, cf. S. I. Oost, *AJP* 79 (1958) 124f.; K. von Fritz, *CP* 52 (1957) 80; T. F. Carney, *ACl* 3 (1960) 100f., 104, and also already M. P. Charlesworth, *CAH* X (1934) 697-701.

38. The authenticity of this writing is accepted today by the large majority of scholars. Cf. K. Bringmann, *ANRW* II 32/2 (1985) 885-89.

39. *CIL* XIII 1668 = *ILS* 212; E. M. Smallwood, *Documents* (1967) 97-99. A redacted version can be found in Tacitus, *Ann.* xi.24.

40. Cf. A. Momigliano, *Claudius* (^{2}1961) 11-18; E. Huzar, *ANRW* II 32.1 (1984) 627, 632.

41. Cf. A. Gaheis, *PRE* 6 (1899) 2838f.; H. Bengtson, *Römische Geschichte* (^{2}1976) 247.

The new portrayal by E. Huzar attempts to integrate the various, contradictory aspects into a comprehensive picture of Claudius. She summarizes her view as follows: "The evidence is too much and too consistent about his mind wandering, his digressions, his inconsistencies, his quick fears and violent reactions to deny his mental as well as his physical disabilities. . . . Normally, he was fair, generous, and deeply committed to legal traditions. Normally, he was conscientious and able. But under pressure he could become erratic, careless, even foolish. . . . In all the major aspects of the empire Claudius was personally involved: and his concern was for Rome's well-being, not his own. Some of his concerns were trivial, even foolish. But it is in the larger responsibilities of government and expansion of the empire that the breadth of his historical vision is valued. He relished tradition, but did not let it stagnate change. He had a long view of Rome's role, and justified innovation by historical precedents. His policies of evolving change, increasing centralization of power, and empire-wide equality stand as tributes to Claudius' wisdom."[42] The author of the most recent Claudius-biography, B. Levick, is extremely reserved with any overall evaluation,[43] though she does not allow the emperor's problematical personality simply to disappear behind his incontestable accomplishments. Ms. Levick ascertains after approximately A.D. 48 a clearly diminishing capacity for judgment and achievement, resulting in striking political mistakes. Nero mentioned several of them in his inaugural speech (composed by Seneca) before the senate (Tacitus, *Ann.* xiv.11.2), and in so doing could count on the concurrence of the senators.

The enormously amplified position of power occupied by the Princeps resulted in Claudius being much more dependent on the counsel of his closest associates than were his predecessors.[44] Although he was never simply the prisoner of any one person among them, as tradition asserted (see pp. 90f. above), several of them nonetheless did come to exercise unusually strong influence for a time.[45] Thus even H. Bengtson considers "unknown the extent to which individual decisions are to be traced back to Claudius himself or to his counsels."[46] The freedman Marcus Antonius Pallas acquired particular influence[47] and played an important role in Claudius' final marriage — one violating current Roman law (Tacitus, *Ann.* xii.7.2; Suetonius, *Claudius* 26.3) — with his niece Julia Agrippina in the year A.D. 48.

The appearance of this woman does at least make it somewhat understandable why earlier scholarship, following tradition (Tacitus, *Ann.* xii.1;

---

42. *ANRW* II 32.1 (1984) 619, 647, 650.
43. *Claudius* (1990) 187-97.
44. Cf. already V. M. Scramuzza, *Claudius,* 49.
45. Cf. T. A. Dorey, *Altertum* 12 (1966) 144-55; A. Garzetti, *Tiberius* (1974) 114.
46. *Römische Geschichte* (²1976) 245.
47. Cf. S. I. Oost, *AJP* 79 (1958) 113-39; T. A. Dorey, *Altertum* 12 (1966) 152.

Suetonius, *Claudius* 29.1; Dio Cassius, *Hist.* lx.2.4, *et passim*), was able to speak of a "regiment of women" in connection with the final phase of the emperor's reign.[48] Even if this particular characterization is not entirely accurate, one should not by contrast play down Agrippina's role the way A. Momigliano does, dismissing her influence with a single sentence.[49] As a modern biographer, A. Garzetti attributes this particular element of deterioration in Claudius' rule during the final years in part also to the intrigues of Agrippina,[50] who was the first to bestow upon herself the title *Augusta* (Tacitus, *Ann.* xii.26). Her influence becomes evident, among other ways, in the fact that one of the most capable and successful soldiers in the empire, the later emperor Galba, withdrew into private life because of her hostilities (Suetonius, *Claudius* 17.3).[51] The swift rise of the *praefectus praetorio* Afranius Burrus was her work.[52] Finally, with the help and the intrigues of her lover Pallas, she was able to assert her son Nero as successor against Britannicus, whom Claudius favored.[53] She apparently also exercised an influence on the emperor in religious policies (§6.3.3).

6.2. Measures Taken upon Assuming Power

6.2.1. The Model of Augustus

"He adopted as his most sacred and frequent oath, 'By Augustus!' " This occasional remark by Suetonius (*Claudius* 11.2) points to a fundamental feature in the reign of Claudius. In architecture,[54] the minting of coins,[55] and in imperial edicts (see pp. 99f. below) — Augustus is evident everywhere as the model for structuring the Principate.[56] In addition to his historical acquain-

---

48. E. Kornemann, *Römische Geschichte* II ([7]1977 [1939]) 192.

49. *Claudius* ([2]1961) 76: "Agrippina holds a place in the history of Claudius' reign only in virtue of her share in certain isolated events, such as the substitution of Nero for Britannicus, which had no influence upon the general character of Claudius' government." At the very least, the choice of successor did decide concerning the continuation of Claudius' own work!

50. *Tiberius* (1974) 117, 126, 141f. Similarly also B. W. Jones, *ABD* I (1992) 1054f.

51. Cf. T. A. Dorey, *Altertum* 12 (1966) 148.

52. Cf. M. P. Charlesworth, *CAH* X (1934) 672f.

53. Cf. T. F. Carney, *ACl* 3 (1960) 104f.; A. Garzetti, *Tiberius* (1974) 142; H. Bengtson, *Römische Geschichte* ([2]1976) 245f.

54. Cf. E. Huzar, *ANRW* II 32.1 (1984) 613.

55. Cf. R. Hanslik, *KP* I (1964) 1216.

56. Cf. Pliny the Elder, *HN* xxxv.94; Suetonius, *Claudius* 11, and further E. Huzar, *ANRW* II 32.1 (1984) 646.

tance with the accomplishments of his great-uncle, psychological factors may also have contributed to Claudius' estimation of Augustus. In contrast to other members of the family, Augustus had demonstrated at least a modicum of interest in Claudius (Suetonius, *Claudius* 4). Claudius also formulated the principles of his own religious policies completely along the lines of his greatest predecessor.[57] Efforts at reviving the ancient Roman cult were accompanied by attempts at fostering tolerance among the varied religions of the world empire, though also by decisive action in cases involving the interests of the state. From the perspective of Augustus' own behavior,[58] one could have expected basically benevolent accommodation in Claudius' policies toward the Jews.[59] Claudius was further encouraged in this disposition by the circumstances of his own accession.

6.2.2. Claudius and Agrippa I

Agrippa I played what in scholarship is still a disputed role in the dramatic events of 24 January A.D. 41, events which on the following day resulted in the accession of Claudius. Josephus has provided two accounts of the events differing not inconsiderably from one another. Over against the older account (between A.D. 75 and 79) in *De Bello Judaico* (Josephus, *B.J.* ii.206-13), the later one (A.D. 93/94) in the *Antiquitates Judaicae* (Josephus, *Ant.* xix.236-66) amplifies the role of Agrippa. Without a doubt, Josephus wanted in this way to accommodate what in the meantime was the regnant anti-Claudius mood in later Flavian Rome,[60] and to speak favorably to Agrippa II. But even in the later account (Josephus, *Ant.* xix.62-66; cf. Tacitus, *Ann.* xi.29.1f.), the Jewish historian did not conceal the preeminent role of the freedman Callistus. The portrayals of some modern accounts that degrade Agrippa to a mere courier of Claudius[61] probably do not reflect the historical reality.[62] The suggestion of an

---

57. Cf. A. D. Nock, *CAH* X (1934) 498-501; V. M. Scramuzza, *Claudius,* 145-56; A. Momigliano, *Claudius* (²1961) 20-38; A. Garzetti, *Tiberius* (1974) 139-41, 601-5; E. Huzar, *ANRW* II 32.1 (1984) 648f.

58. The most important sources are Philo, *Leg. ad Gaium* 154-58 (encomium to Augustus); Josephus, *Ant.* xvi.162-65. Cf. E. M. Smallwood, *The Jews under Roman Rule* (²1981), esp. 136-43, 246-49.

59. Cf. T. Reinach, *RÉJ* 79 (1924) 113-44; T. Zielinski, *RUB* 32 (1926/27) 128-48; V. M. Scramuzza, *Claudius,* 64-79, 151f.; A. Momigliano, *Claudius* (²1961) 29-38; M. Grant, *The Jews in the Roman World,* 132-46; E. M. Smallwood, *The Jews under Roman Rule* (²1981) 210-16.

60. Cf. V. M. Scramuzza, *Claudius,* 11-18; E. Huzar, *ANRW* II 32.1 (1984) 616; and C. Saulnier, *RB* 96 (1989) 545-62.

61. So, e.g., A. Garzetti, *Tiberius* (1974) 107f. Similarly also D. R. Schwartz, *Agrippa I* (1990) 91.

62. Cf. M. Grant, *The Jews in the Roman World,* 133.

important role as negotiator in Josephus (*B.J.* ii.206, 213) is confirmed by Dio Cassius (*Hist.* lx.8.2). The codeterminative function of Agrippa in the transition of power can also be surmised from the fact that the emperor was very grateful for this show of loyalty in what was still an extremely equivocal situation.

Judea ceased being a province and was assigned to the territory of Agrippa such that he received the entire area over which his grandfather Herod the Great had ruled as well as the kingdom of Lysanias (Josephus, *B.J.* ii.215/*Ant.* xix.274f.). This investiture was announced by an edict engraved on bronze tablets and kept at the Capitol (Josephus, *B.J.* ii.216). The Roman people even concluded a formal contract with the Jewish king, something not only recounted by Josephus (*Ant.* xix.275), but also attested by numismatic evidence.[63] Herod, Agrippa's brother, received the kingdom of Chalcis (Josephus, *B.J.* ii.216/*Ant.* xix.277). The favor of Claudius for Agrippa might also have been strengthened by the fact that the Jewish prince had been his companion during the difficult years of his youth (Josephus, *Ant.* xviii.165f.). Moreover, at the beginning of his reign the emperor trusted especially men who, like Vitellius (Tacitus, *Ann.* xi.3.1), Valerius Asiaticus, or Agrippa (Josephus, *Ant.* xviii.164-66), enjoyed the support of the imperial mother Antonia,[64] whose wealth in Alexandria was administered by Philo's brother Julius Alexander (Josephus, *Ant.* xix.276).

Agrippa probably did in fact play an important part in the emperor's initial measures favorable to the Jews, as Josephus asserts (*Ant.* xix.279, 287).[65] In the *Antiquitates,* the Jewish historian reproduces two edicts from the first year of Claudius' reign (A.D. 25 January 41–25 January 42). Despite some opposition,[66] the majority of more recent scholarship is inclined to view these decrees as essentially authentic, though one cannot exclude the possibility that in his Greek rendering of what were probably Latin originals Josephus may have exercised a certain measure of freedom.[67] According to Josephus, one of the two edicts was to be publicized throughout the entire empire (Josephus, *Ant.* xix.286-91). It is not only the reference back to the example of Augustus (Josephus, *Ant.* xix.289) that is typical of Claudius; in immediate proximity to the expansion of the religious freedoms of the Jews (Josephus, *Ant.* xix.290) stands the admonition to exercise tolerance: "I there-

63. Cf. Y. Meshorer, *Jewish Coins* (1966) 140 (no. 93).

64. Cf. T. A. Dorey, *Altertum* 12 (1966) 145.

65. Cf. *ibid.,* 147; M. Grant, *The Jews in the Roman World,* 136; E. Huzar, *ANRW* II 32.1 (1984) 638-40.

66. E.g., H. R. Moehring, *Festschrift M. Smith* III (1975) 124-58; D. Hennig, *Chiron* 5 (1975) 328-35.

67. Cf. A. Momigliano, *Claudius* (²1961) 30f., 98; V. Tcherikover, *Hellenistic Civilization and the Jews* (1959) 409-15; E. Huzar, *ANRW* II 32.1 (1984) 638; A. Kasher, *The Jews in Hellenistic and Roman Egypt,* 262-89. Bibliography in *CPJ* II 70f.

fore consider it fit to permit the Jews, who are in all the empire under us, to keep their ancient customs without being hindered so to do. And I do charge them also to use this my kindness to them with more tolerance (ἐπιεικέστερον χρῆσθαι) and not to show contempt of the superstitious observances of other nations, but to keep their own laws."

6.2.3. The Alexandrian Unrest

The other edict (Josephus, *Ant.* xix.279-85) addresses the controversies that had arisen in Alexandria at the end of the reign of Caligula between the Jewish and other Hellenistic inhabitants of the city. Here, too, Claudius adduces the example of Augustus (Josephus, *Ant.* xix.282f.). The decree grants to the Jews their old privileges, but also exhorts both parties to moderation in its concluding part: "I wish, therefore, that the nation of the Jews be not deprived of their rights and privileges on account of the madness (παραφροσύνη) of Caius; but that those rights and privileges, which they formerly enjoyed, be preserved to them, and that they may continue in their own customs. And I charge both parties to take very great care that no troubles (ταραχή) may arise after the promulgation of this edict" (Josephus, *Ant.* xix.285).

The general contents of this edict are confirmed by a letter (Pap. London 1912 = *CPJ* I 153)[68] preserved as a copy[69] which Claudius addressed to all the inhabitants of Alexandria shortly thereafter, still in the year A.D. 41.[70] This document, which completely reflects the emperor's personal style, played an important role in the modern revision of the understanding of Claudius.[71] The final part of the letter again addresses the relationship between the Jews and the other Alexandrians (ll. 73-104), since in the meantime new unrest (τῶν πάλειν ἀρξαμένων) had broken out (l. 78). Claudius again mentions Augustus (l. 87), and the reference to a preceding confirmation of Jewish privileges (l. 88) might be alluding to the edict

---

68. *Editio princeps*: H. I. Bell, *Jews and Christians in Egypt* (1924) 23-29 (our line numbering follows this edition).

69. A. Kasher, *The Jews in Hellenistic and Roman Egypt*, 133-326, shows that statements in Philo, *Flacc.* 47, 78-80; Josephus, *Ant.* xix.281; and *PLond* 1912 (line 81) concerning the legal status of Alexandrian Jews are not contradictory. Similarly already V. M. Scramuzza, *Claudius*, 74-77.

70. Cf. in this regard T. Reinach, *RÉJ* 79 (1924) 113-32; V. M. Scramuzza, *loc. cit.*, 64-79; H. I. Bell, *Jews and Christians* (1924) 1-37; E. Huzar, *ANRW* II 32.1 (1984) 641-44; A. Kasher, *loc. cit.*, 312-26.

71. A. Momigliano, *Claudius* (1943) xiii: "The discovery, in particular, of one of the most interesting historical papyri ever brought to light, Claudius' letter to the Alexandrians, has made a new and important contribution to the materials for any judgement on the Emperor."

reproduced by Josephus.[72] Here, too, the admonition to non-Jewish Alexandrians (ll. 82-88) is accompanied by a warning to the Jews, one whose tone seems even more stringent:[73] "The Jews, on the other hand, I order not to aim at more than they have previously had and not in the future to send two embassies as if they lived in two cities, a thing which has never been done before, and not to intrude themselves into the games presided over by the gymnasiarchs and cosmetes,[74] since they enjoy what is their own, and in a city which is not their own possess an abundance of good things. Nor are they to bring in or invite Jews coming from Syria or Egypt, or I shall be forced to conceive graver suspicions. If they disobey, I shall proceed against them in every way as fomenting a common plague for the whole world" (lines 88-100).

Although this reference to Jews immigrating from Syria prompted some earlier scholars to think of itinerant Christian missionaries,[75] the expression regarding the contagious disease affecting the world empire (lines 99f.: κοινήν τινα τῆς οἰκουμένης νόσον), which does indeed recall the complaint against the Christians in Acts 24:5 (λοιμὸν . . . κατὰ τὴν οἰκουμένην), actually reflects a universally familiar topos from antiquity (e.g., Plato, *Prt.* 322D) for political unrest.[76] Moreover, the suggestion of Jewish Christians is not accompanied by any explanation of just how at such an early period these might already have moved from inner Egypt to Alexandria.[77] The letter's manner of expression also seems to be referring to larger groups of people rather than merely to a few itinerant missionaries. Hence this interpretation was generally abandoned,[78] resurfacing at most only in portrayals that in other respects as well still depended on an earlier status of scholarship.[79] However,

---

72. This alone disproves the assumption of T. Zielinski, *RUB* 32 (1926/27) 125f., that the edict reproduced in Josephus, *Ant.* xix.279-85, actually represents a completely distorted version of the letter. One wonders already upon reading the title of his essay, "The Emperor Claudius and the Idea of the World Domination of the Jews," whether the Warsaw professor was able to escape completely the antisemitic spirit of the times.

73. A. Kasher, *The Jews in Hellenistic and Roman Egypt,* 326, downplays the harshness of the letter's tone by paying too little attention to the differing length and character of the emperor's admonitions to the Jewish and other Alexandrians.

74. So A. Kasher, *loc. cit.,* 310-21.

75. So esp. S. Reinach, *RHR* 90 (1924) 108-22. Additional advocates and opponents can be found in V. M. Scramuzza, *Claudius,* 286; H. Gülzow, *Christentum und Sklaverei* (1969) 11, note 1.

76. Cf. S. Lösch, *Epistula Claudiana* (1930) 24-33.

77. Cf. F. F. Bruce, *BJRL* 44 (1961/62) 313.

78. Additional counterarguments can be found in S. Lösch, *Epistula Claudiana* (1930) 12-24; F. F. Bruce, *Jesus and Christian Origins outside the New Testament* (1974) 196-98.

79. So in M. C. Tenney, *New Testament Times* (1965) 222f.

because it fits his own reconstruction of the events surrounding the Jewish edict in Rome, G. Lüdemann has now again expressed support for this earlier interpretation,[80] though without providing any further justification.

The unequivocal warning at the conclusion to the letter demonstrates in a pregnant fashion the third principle attaching to Claudius' religious policies, next to restoration of the Roman religion and empire-wide tolerance. Whenever political peace was at stake, his patience and even his benevolence toward the Jews had their limits. But the emperor's posture of being generally friendly toward the Jews during the first year of his reign becomes evident in the trial against the two Alexandrian anti-Semites Isidor and Lampon (cf. Philo, *Leg. ad Gaium* 355; *Flacc.* 125-27, 135-50), whose martyrdom (*Acta Isidori),* preserved in four papyrus fragments (*CPJ* I 154-59), in part contains historical information.[81] Claudius' friendliness toward the Jews was perceived in Alexandrian-pagan circles as being so great that he was even accused of being the illegitimate son of a Jewish woman by the name of Salome (ed. Musurillo, 19), a probable reference to the sister of Herod the Great.[82] In all likelihood, this trial took place during A.D. 41.[83] This particular dating is now also supported by a Strasbourg Papyrus (to my knowledge as yet unedited) which also demonstrates that the unrest emanated out as far as Philadelphia in Fayûm.[84]

6.3. Subsequent Developments

6.3.1. Reestablishment of the Province of Judea

Even Agrippa, who had never failed to demonstrate his loyalty,[85] came to understand how the good of the state was more important to Claudius even than old friendships. When the new governor of Syria, Gaius Vibius Marsus (A.D. 42-45), generated suspicion, the Jewish king had to discontinue con-

---

80. G. Lüdemann, *Paul: Apostle to the Gentiles* (1984) 168.

81. Cf. H. Musurillo, *The Acts of the Pagan Martyrs* (1954) 236-77; *Acta Alexandrinorum* (1961) 11-17; E. M. Smallwood, *The Jews under Roman Rule* ([2]1981) 250-55. Additional bibliography in E. Huzar, *ANRW* II 32.1 (1984) 645, note 159.

82. Cf. H. Musurillo, *The Acts of the Pagan Martyrs,* 282.

83. Contra the date of A.D. 53, advocated esp. by H. Musurillo, *loc. cit.,* 118-24, cf. V. Tcherikover, *CPJ* I (1957) 70; M. Stern, CRINT I/1 (1974) 129; E. M. Smallwood, *loc. cit.,* 250-55; A. Kasher, *The Jews in Hellenistic and Roman Egypt,* 271f.; D. R. Schwartz, *Agrippa I* (1990) 96-98.

84. Cf. J. D. Butin and J. Schwartz, *RHPhR* 65 (1985) 127-29.

85. This is especially evident in his minting of coins. Cf. Y. Meshorer, *Jewish Coins* (1966) 139f.

struction of the third north wall of Jerusalem (Josephus, *Ant.* xix.326f.; cf. Tacitus, *Hist.* v.12). If one identifies this wall with the Mayer-Sukenik line,[86] then this was indeed an edifice of threatening dimensions (cf. Josephus, *B.J.* ii.218; v.152). Claudius reacted even more decisively when in A.D. 43 Agrippa invited his brother Herod of Chalcis together with five other vassal kings to Tiberias, a conference that had to be ended prematurely due to orders from the emperor (Josephus, *Ant.* xix.338-42). Events such as these might have prompted the emperor, after the sudden death of Agrippa and against his early intentions, to divide Agrippa's territory again (Josephus, *B.J.* ii.219f./*Ant.* xix.343-52, 360-63; Tacitus, *Hist.* v.9). The decision to place Judea under direct Roman rule again as a province, however, was to prove fateful for the relationship with the Palestinian Jews.[87]

6.3.2. From Fadus to Cumanus

Tacitus' statement, with certain qualifications, still applied to Palestine under Tiberius: *"sub Tiberio quies"* (Tacitus, *Hist.* v.10).[88] The first escalation was provoked by Caligula's attempt in A.D. 40 to erect his own likeness in the temple (§7.1.4). The loss of Jewish independence and the incompetence of the procurators then led to increasingly intense Zealot activities, and finally to the catastrophe of the Jewish War of A.D. 66-70. It was under the first procurator Cuspius Fadus (A.D. 44-?46)[89] that Theudas appeared, whom Josephus mentions as the first pseudo-prophet in Judea (Josephus, *Ant.* xx.97f.; cf. Acts 5:36).[90] Claudius' decision in the conflict regarding the keeping of the high-priestly vestments shows how he tried to adhere to his policy of accommodation to the Jews despite the substantially more tense situation. At the bidding of the younger Agrippa, a son of King Agrippa I, the emperor ordered — against the regulation enacted by Fadus — that the insignia be returned to Jewish guardianship (Josephus, *Ant.* xx.6-10). Josephus has reproduced in full the emperor's rescript, translated perhaps from the Latin[91] (Josephus, *Ant.* xx.11-14). The first justification he gives for his decision is typical for Claudius: "I have complied with your desire in the first place out

86. Cf. G. Schmitt, *ZDPV* 97 (1981) 153-70; A. Kloner, *Levant* 18 (1986) 121-29; J. P. Price, *Jerusalem under Siege* (1992) 290-92.
87. Cf. M. Hengel, *Die Zeloten* (²1976) 349-65 (Eng. trans., *The Zealots* [1989]); E. M. Smallwood, *The Jews under Roman Rule* (²1981) 256-92.
88. Cf. P. W. Garnett, *NTS* 21 (1975) 564-71.
89. Concerning the chronological problem here, cf. E. M. Smallwood, *The Jews under Roman Rule* (²1981) 257f., note 6.
90. Concerning the question of identifying the persons mentioned in the two passages, see Excursus II, section 8 (pp. 331f.).
91. Cf. E. Huzar, *ANRW* II 32.1 (1984) 644f.

of regard for that piety which I profess, and because I would have everyone worship God according to the [religious] laws of their fathers" (Josephus, *Ant.* xx.13).

The emperor's tolerant posture, however, could not solve the country's problems in any abiding fashion, especially since he committed the tactless blunder of appointing the Jewish apostate Tiberius Alexander (Josephus, *Ant.* xx.100) as procurator. During earlier food crises, Herod the Great had ameliorated the consequences through state intervention. During the famine under the procuratorship of Alexander (A.D. ?46-48), which had already begun while Cuspius Fadus was in office (§8.2.4), only private aid seems to have been undertaken.[92] In the wake of this crisis, apocalyptic expectation swelled and armed incidents increased; this mood apparently even seized the Jews of Antioch (see p. 196 below). The harsh intervention of Tiberius Alexander brought only temporary respite, and the procuratorship of Ventidius Cumanus (A.D. 48-49) then brought the final turn for the worse.[93] Again, Claudius intervened in favor of the Jews — presumably already in A.D. 49 (§12.4.1) — by dismissing Cumanus because of his handling of a bloody clash between Jews and Samaritans (Josephus, *B.J.* ii.232-46/*Ant.* xx.118-36). This time, too, the emperor acted at the initiative of the younger Agrippa, who in A.D. 50 then received instead of Chalcis the more important territories of Trachonitis, Batanaea, Gaulanitis (i.e., the tetrarchy of Philip) and Abilene as his kingdom (Josephus, *B.J.* ii.247/*Ant.* xx.138). Agrippa II energetically represented the interests of the Jews, albeit apparently no longer with the same effectiveness as his father Agrippa I.[94]

Perhaps this same political context also includes an inscription sent to Paris from Nazareth in 1878; it contains an imperial rescript against graverobbing, and was first published only in 1930, at the initiative of M. Rostovtzeff, by F. Cumont.[95] A. Momigliano originally believed that because of the disturbances after the death of Agrippa I, Claudius now also became aware of Christianity, and reacted with his measures against this faith in the resurrection of Jesus.[96] Later, however, Momigliano expressly recanted this interpretation.[97] By contrast, E. M. Smallwood maintains

---

92. Cf. G. Theissen, *Soziologie der Jesusbewegung* ([4]1985) 41f. (Eng. trans., *Sociology of Early Palestinian Christianity* [1978]).

93. Cf. E. M. Smallwood, *The Jews under Roman Rule* ([2]1981) 263.

94. Cf. A. Momigliano, *Claudius* ([2]1961) 32.

95. *RH* 48 (1930) 241-66.

96. *Claudius* (1934) 35-37.

97. *Claudius* ([2]1961) IX. G. Lüdemann, *Paul: Apostle to the Gentiles,* 168f., note 89, has apparently overlooked this. Lüdemann's argument that the inscription allegedly cannot be associated with narratives such as Mt. 28:12-15 not least because the empty tomb actually represents a theologumenon of only isolated Christian groups, one that was

Momigliano's earlier view,[98] and A. Garzetti considers it at least possible.[99] The questions attaching to the Nazareth Inscription need to be addressed once again.[100]

6.3.3. The Procuratorship of Felix

In connection with the dismissal of the procurator Cumanus, the Jewish king was successful in winning Agrippina as his intercessor with the emperor (Josephus, *Ant.* xx.135). This had hardly anything to do with any particular pro-Semitic inclinations on the part of the empress; rather, it provided her with a welcome opportunity to advance the career of Antonius Felix. He replaced Cumanus (Josephus, *B.J.* ii.245f./*Ant.* xx.134-36), and under his rule the situation in Judea worsened (Josephus, *Ant.* xx.160). Although Felix "contributed considerably to the decline of Roman rule in Palestine,"[101] he retained his position even after the murder of Claudius (13 October A.D. 54) until the year A.D. 59 (§12.4). Antonius Felix was a brother of that Pallas who after the marriage between the emperor and Agrippina (see pp. 95f. above) had risen to a position of extraordinary power. Soon after the appointment of Felix, Pallas attained the high point of his influence when in the year A.D. 52 he received the *ornamenta praetoria* and a large sum of money from the senate (Pliny the Elder, *HN* vii.9.2; viii.16.3; Suetonius, *Claudius* 28). One is probably not wrong in seeing a connection between the rise of Pallas and the appointment of his brother. Apparently, Agrippina's influence on the emperor also increased in Jewish matters.

Shortly before the death of Claudius, Felix received permission to marry Drusilla, the sister of Agrippa I (Josephus, *Ant.* xx.148). This step of leaving her husband, King Azizus of Emesa, who had just converted to Judaism and whom she had just married (A.D. 53) (Josephus, *Ant.* xx.139-41) in order to marry an uncircumcised man was perceived as a serious violation of the law by all pious Jews (cf. Acts 24:24f.). The illegal cir-

---

"not yet reflected in Paul's letters," is extremely questionable. Cf. W. L. Craig, in R. T. France and D. Wenham, *Gospel Perspectives* I (1980) 47-74.

98. *The Jews under Roman Rule* (²1981) 213.

99. *Tiberius* (1974) 140, 604.

100. B. M. Metzger, "The Nazareth Inscription Once Again," in E. E. Ellis and E. Grässer, ed., *Jesus und Paulus. Festschrift Werner Georg Kümmel* (Göttingen, ²1978) 221-38, gives an instructive overview of the problems, though his assumption (*loc. cit.,* 233) that the inscription comes from the Decapolis is not supported, and the bibliography is by no means complete. Cf. J. Schmitt, *DBS* VI (1960) 361-63; A. Garzetti, *loc. cit.,* 361-63; R. Riesner, *GBL* II (1988) 1037; B. Levick, *Claudius* (1990) 222, note 20; C. K. Barrett and C. J. Thornton, *Texte zur Umwelt des Neuen Testaments* (1991) 15.

101. M. Hengel, *Die Zeloten* (²1976) 355 (Eng. trans., *The Zealots* [1989]).

cumstances of his own marriage to Agrippina probably did not make it any easier for the emperor to avoid this capital political mistake.[102] Still in the first year of his marriage with Agrippina (A.D. 49) and at the instigation of his wife, Claudius allowed Seneca, who hated the emperor, to return from exile, entrusting him with the education of Agrippina's son Nero, whom she had brought into the marriage. In the year A.D. 50, Agrippina secured for Seneca the Praetor (Tacitus, *Ann.* xii.8.2), for she had extensive political plans with him as her close adviser.[103] These measures also attest Agrippina's increasing influence on the emperor, who himself had sent Seneca into exile on Corsica at the beginning of his reign (41/42) because of an intrigue, and who as late as A.D. 43/44 had not been moved by the flattery of the *Consolatio ad Polybium,*[104] with which Seneca had tried to gain permission to return. Based on his extant, biased statements concerning the Jewish religion, one could not expect Seneca to exercise any pro-Semitic influence on the ruling couple.[105]

6.4. Restoration of Roman Religion

6.4.1. The Religious-Political Measures of A.D. *47-49*

During the second part of Claudius' reign, one can clearly observe an intensification of his efforts at reviving the ancient Roman religion.[106] Just as in his reservations concerning any deification of the emperor, here, too, he followed the example of Augustus.[107] In the year A.D. 47, Claudius initiated a solemn celebration of the eight-hundredth anniversary (21 April) of the founding of Rome with *ludi saeculares* (Pliny the Elder, *HN* vii.159; Tacitus, *Ann.* xi.11; Suetonius, *Claudius* 21; *Nero* 7; *Vit.* 2). Probably immediately after these festival celebrations, the emperor, commensurate with the model of Augustus,[108] took up the office of Censor (Pliny the Elder, *HN* vii.159; Tacitus, *Ann.* xi.13; xii.4; *Hist.* iii.66; Suetonius, *Claudius* 16; *Vit.* 2), which

---

102. Even A. Momigliano, *Claudius* (²1961) 69, speaks here of an "elementary error in judgement."

103. Cf. K. Abel, *ANRW* II 32.2 (1985) 670.

104. Concerning this dating, cf. K. Abel, *loc. cit.,* 707, 715-17; J. E. Atkinson, *loc. cit.,* 864-66.

105. Seneca, *Ep. Mor.* 95.47; *De superstitione* (in Augustine, *CivD* vi.11: "*sceleratissima gens*"). Cf. M. Stern, *Greek and Latin Authors on Jews and Judaism* I (1976) 429-34.

106. Cf. V. M. Scramuzza, *Claudius,* 145-56.

107. Cf. E. Huzar, *ANRW* II 32.1 (1984) 649.

108. Cf. R. Hanslik, *KP* I (1964) 1217.

had not been discharged in the traditional way for sixty-eight years.[109] In the same year, A.D. 47, Claudius proposed to the senate a law that would check the demise of the orders of the *haruspices* and would revive ancient Roman oracular practice. The speech Claudius gave before the senate on this occasion, reproduced — unfortunately only summarily — by Tacitus (*Ann.* xi.5), seems to have exhibited programmatic character.[110] In the next year (A.D. 48),[111] the emperor elevated several families to the status of patrician so that he might refill the vacant priestly positions (Tacitus, *Ann.* xi.25).

Finally, in the year A.D. 49 the emperor ordered two important religio-political measures for the imperial capital. The *pomerium*, that is, the boundary within which only Roman gods could be worshipped, was expanded to include the area of the Aventine and a portion of the Campus Martius (Tacitus, *Ann.* xii.23f.).[112] Besides this, Claudius also reintroduced the *augurium salutis (ibid.)*. The emperor's restorative religious intentions also manifested themselves when in the same year the incestuous union of Silanus with his sister Calvina in the sacred grove of Diana prompted Claudius to have an atonement ritual performed according to the prescriptions of King Servius Tullius (Seneca, *Apocolocyntosis* 8.2; Tacitus, *Ann.* xii.4.8), the legendary sixth king of Rome.

6.4.2. Claudius and Oriental Cults

Sources do not support the assertion that the emperor also favored several oriental cults in Italy.[113] In this case, the emperor's restorative tendencies led, on the contrary, to a kind of "anti-oriental policy," to borrow an expression from K. Lake.[114] In his programmatic speech to the senate committee concerning the *haruspices,* the emperor had already complained that foreign superstition was taking over *"quia externae superstitiones valescant"* (Tacitus, *Ann.* xi.15). Measures against non-Roman cults in Italy were a quite consistent result of Claudius' positive program.[115] Contact especially with oriental astrologers now became politically dangerous. Commensurate denunciations had a good chance of success probably also because the emperor himself now lived in fear of prophecies that might bring disaster (Tacitus, *Ann.* xi.4). In A.D. 49,

109. Cf. E. Groag, *PRE* 6 (1899) 2802f.

110. Cf. V. M. Scramuzza, *Claudius,* 147.

111. V. M. Scramuzza, *loc. cit.,* 148, mistakenly dates this in A.D. 47. This measure, however, was undertaken during the consular period of Aulus Vitellius and Lucius Vipstanus (Tacitus, *Ann.* xi.23).

112. Cf. *loc. cit.,* 149.

113. Cf. *loc. cit.,* 152-55.

114. *BC* V (1933) 460.

115. Cf. A. Garzetti, *Tiberius* (1974) 140.

Agrippina succeeded in securing the banishment of her rival Lollia Paulina, whose father had at any rate been *consul suffectus* under Augustus (Tacitus, *Ann.* xii.1.2). The charge was that she queried Chaldeans, magicians, and the statue of Claros Apollo concerning the emperor's marriage: *"Chaldaeos magos interrogatumque Apollonis Clarii simulacrum super nuptiis imperatoris"* (Tacitus, *Ann.* xii.22). In A.D. 52, Furius Scribonianus was then sent into exile because he allegedly inquired of Chaldeans concerning the end of the Princeps: *"quasi finem principis per Chaldaeos scrutaretur"* (Tacitus, *Ann.* xii.52). Again at the initiative of Agrippina, Statilius Taurus was accused in the following year (A.D. 53) primarily of *"magicae superstitiones,"* whereupon he committed suicide (Tacitus, *Ann.* xii.59). The charge of foreign or magical superstition was thus still quite effective and relevant, even though Claudius had already had the astrologers banned from Italy following the trial of Furius Scribonianus (Tacitus, *Ann.* xii.52; cf. Dio Cassius, *Hist.* lxi.33.3). The emperor's fear of astrological and magical practices should also be kept in mind when considering the attitude of Roman officials toward the young Christian faith.

§7

Mission to the Gentiles and Persecution

7.1. The Beginnings of the Mission to the Gentiles

7.1.1. The Mission of the Hellenists

In the broad portrayal of the story of Cornelius, Luke emphasizes Peter's conversion of the Roman *centurio* in Caesarea as a special breakthrough for the mission to the Gentiles, underscoring in this way the fundamental unanimity of Peter and Paul in this question that was so decisive for primitive Christianity. Despite his theological agenda, however, Luke did not suppress the historical circumstance that the initiative for preaching to Gentiles did not come from Peter.[1] In Acts 11:19ff., his portrayal goes back to the dispersion of the Jerusalem Hellenists (cf. Acts 8:4) and adds an important piece of information:[2] "Now those who were scattered because of the persecution that took place over Stephen traveled as far as Phoenicia, Cyprus, and Antioch, and they spoke the word to no one except Jews. But among them were some men of Cyprus and Cyrene who, on coming to Antioch, spoke to the Greeks also, proclaiming the gospel (καὶ πρὸς τοὺς Ἕλληνας[3] εὐαγγελιζόμενοι) of the Lord Jesus" (Acts 11:19f.).

---

1. P. Gaechter, in *Petrus und seine Zeit* (1958) 168-74, overlooks this in his efforts to secure the theological and jurisdictional priority of Peter over against the Antiochene church as well. His construction acquires chronological plausibility because he dates the persecution of Stephen in A.D. 36/37 (*loc. cit.,* 175). Earlier scholars argued similarly, e.g., W. L. Knox, *St. Paul and the Church of Jerusalem* (1925) 156-65. Cf. by contrast §4.1.

2. A consideration of, e.g., Sallust shows just how widespread the literary device of prolepsis was in the literature of antiquity. Cf. K. Bringmann, *RMP* 114 (1971) 98-113.

3. This reading, attested by P[74] ℵ[c] A D*, though also by Eusebius and Chrysostom, is to be preferred to Ἑλληνιστάς in B D[c] E Ψ etc. because of the contrast with Ἰουδαίους (Acts 11:19). Cf. M. Hengel, *ZThK* 72 (1975) 164f.; G. Schneider, *Die Apostelgeschichte* II (1982) 89, note 22; F. F. Bruce, *The Book of the Acts* (1988) 223, note 16. The view of D. R. Fotheringham, *ET* 45 (1933/34) 430, namely, that with the expression Ἑλληνισταί Luke wanted here to draw attention to the beginning of the mission among Greek-speaking peoples, is untenable in view of the use of the word already in Acts 6:1; 9:29.

This transition from a pure mission to the Jews to a mission to the Gentiles conducted by Hellenists should be understood not as a one-time event, but rather as a process.[4] First, they turned their attention to Greek-speaking fellow Jews (Acts 6:9). The first more organized mission outside Judaism in the narrower sense occurred among the Samaritans (Acts 8:4-25), who could, however, still be viewed as members — albeit partially apostate — of the holy people Israel. From these Greek-speaking synagogues, the Hellenists then reached the circles of "God-fearers" (cf. Acts 8:26-39), that is, those Gentiles standing in variously intensive connections with Judaism.[5] A special role in this transition to the Gentile mission was played by the Palestinian coastal plain — inhabited largely by Gentiles — with the cities of Gaza (Acts 8:26), Azotus/Ashdod, and Caesarea (Acts 8:40).[6] With M. Hengel we may consider it "highly likely that Philip and other 'Hellenists' in this area made the transition gradually and by steps to a mission to the Gentiles free of the law, whereby the expression 'free of the law' initially meant foregoing the demands of circumcision and the observation of ritual law."[7]

4. Cf. M. Hengel, *Zur urchristlichen Geschichtsschreibung* ([2]1984) 63-70; B. F. Meyer, *The Early Christians* (1986) 67-83; K. Löning, in J. Becker, *Die Anfänge des Christentums* (1987) 80-101; R. Pesch, *ThJb(L)* (1987) 347-67; L. Schenke, *Die Urgemeinde* (1990) 186-97. W. Michaelis, *ZNW* 30 (1931) 83-89, argued that before the European mission of Barnabas and Paul (Acts 13:4ff.) there was no Gentile mission that was free from the law. Yet this view is based on surface impressions from Acts and overlooks the historical differentiations discernible even in Luke's simplified portrayal.

5. From the problems attaching to any clearly fixed terminology (cf. M. Wilcox, *JSNT* 13 [1981] 102-22), one should not conclude that this group did not actually exist or did so only in a completely marginal fashion. Thus variously A. T. Kraabel, *Numen* 28 (1981) 113-26; *JJS* 33 (1982) 445-64; T. M. Finn, *CBQ* 47 (1985) 75-84; R. S. MacLennan and A. T. Kraabel, *BARev* 12/5 (1986) 46-53. But the literary and archaeological evidence leaves no doubt concerning the existence of a larger number of Gentiles who were drawn to Judaism. Cf. F. Siegert, *JSJ* 4 (1973) 109-64; J. G. Gager, *HThR* 79 (1986) 91-99; S. J. D. Cohen, *HThR* 80 (1987) 409-30; J. A. Overman, *JSNT* 32 (1988) 17-26; C. H. Gempf, in C. J. Hemer, *The Book of Acts in the Setting of Hellenistic History* (1989) 444-47; P. Fredriksen, *JTS* 42 (1991) 540-43. L. H. Feldman, *BARev* 12/5 (1986) 58-63, can even speak of the "omnipresence of God-fearers." Of the greatest importance is the finding of a synagogue inscription from the third century in Aphrodisias/Asia Minor (J. M. Reynolds and R. Tannenbaum, *Jews and God-fearers at Aphrodisias* [1987]). Cf. also P. W. van der Horst, in *Essays on the Jewish World of Early Christianity* (1990) 166-81; P. Trebilco, *Jewish Communities in Asia Minor* (1991) 145-66, 246-55. The discussion concerning terminology continues. While J. Murphy-O'Connor, *RB* 99 (1992) 418-24, considers θεοσεβής to be ambivalent even in the Aphrodisias-inscription, I. Levinskaya, *TynBul* 41(1990) 312-18, concludes from this perspective the presence of technical terminology for the Lukan φοβούμενος (σεβόμενος) τὸν θεόν. See now I. Levinskaya, ed., *The Book of Acts in Its Diaspora Setting* (1996) 1-126.

6. Cf. M. Hengel, *ZDPV* 99 (1983) 164-69.

7. *Zur urchristlichen Geschichtsschreibung* ([2]1984) 70.

Because this transition to the Gentile mission actually involved a process taking place in different places and in several different stages, it can be circumscribed chronologically only approximately within the period between the martyrdom of Stephen possibly in the year A.D. 31/32 (§4.1) and the persecution of the Jerusalem church under Herod Agrippa I probably already at the beginning of A.D. 41 (§7.2). To that extent, Luke is probably oversimplifying things when he explicitly mentions only Antioch as the locus of this new stage (Acts 11:20), though he is no doubt correct in referring to the virtually inestimable significance of this particular metropolis for primitive Christianity and for the development of its mission. It was there that the first larger or largely Gentile-Christian church emerged. The existence of a church also encompassing Gentile Christians can possibly be determined with even more temporal exactitude.

7.1.2. Antioch and the Designation "Christian"

The association in ancient church writings between the founding of the Antiochene church in the years between A.D. 35 and 39 on the one hand, and the role of Peter on the other, probably represents an abbreviated way of referring to his assumption of a leading position in this city (see note 86 below). The bearers of this tradition were probably aware that the Antiochene church had already been founded by Jerusalem Hellenists (Acts 11:19-21). We do not know exactly when the mission of the Hellenists who were driven from Jerusalem reached Antioch. The close ties between the Jewish inhabitants of the two cities are also evident in the fact that the Jerusalem Hellenist Nicolaus was a proselyte born in Antioch (Acts 6:5).[8] It may be that both Nicolaus[9] and Lucius of Cyrene (Acts 13:1)[10] belonged to the Hellenists from the holy city (cf. Acts 11:20) who fled to Antioch.[11] After their expulsion from Jerusalem, some Hellenists probably settled immediately in the metropolis, whose prosperous economy[12] offered various opportunities for newcomers. It is equally possible, however, that other Jewish Christians (more faithful to the law) were already there even before the expelled Hellenists (cf. Gal. 2:11-14).

According to strongly varying estimates, Antioch on the Orontes had

8. An ossuary inscription found in 1990 in the Kidron Valley probably attests a proselyte by the name of Ariston/Judah who immigrated from Apamea in Syria to Jerusalem (T. Ilan, *Scripta Classica Israelica* 11 [1991/92] 149-55).

9. Cf. K. Bauer, *Antiochia in der ältesten Kirchengeschichte* (1919) 19f.; G. Downey, *Ancient Antioch* (1963) 121

10. Cf. K. Pieper, *ThGl* 22 (1930) 713, note 13.

11. Cf. also J. P. Meier, in *Antioch and Rome* (1983) 33.

12. Cf. G. Haddad, *Aspects of Social Life in Antioch* (1949) 20-30; J. Lassus, *ANRW* II/8 (1978) 83-87.

between 150,000 and 600,000 inhabitants in the first century A.D.,[13] making it the third- (Josephus, *B.J.* iii.29) or fourth-largest city in the empire (Libanius, *Or.* 20) after Rome, Alexandria, and perhaps also Seleucia on the Tigris.[14] The strong contingent of Jews in the metropolis (Josephus, *B.J.* vii.43) is estimated to have included between 20,000 and 60,000 persons,[15] and thus included over 10 percent of the population. Although some of these were quite wealthy (cf. Josephus, *Ant.* xvii.24), the majority probably belonged to the lower middle class and the lower classes.[16] Josephus explicitly mentions an extremely large number of Greek-speaking Gentiles who were attracted to Judaism (Josephus, *B.J.* vii.45). Since such "God-fearers" (see note 5 above) were also quite open to the mission of primitive Christianity, reports of significant missionary successes among non-Jews seem credible (Acts 11:21). The Antiochene church included, along with Manaen, the σύντροφος of the tetrarch Herod Antipas (Acts 13:1), also a member of the upper class whose origin was in Palestine.[17] Although Luke's assertion that even in Antioch the Hellenists originally turned their attention only to Jews (Acts 11:19) does sound somewhat schematic, it is not necessarily without value.[18] At the beginning of their activity the Hellenists probably did address primarily their fellow Jews. Although we do not know when the transition to a Gentile mission took place, we can perhaps provide a *terminus ante quem*.

Luke's assertion (Acts 11:26) that "it was in Antioch that the disciples were first called 'Christians' (χρηματίσαι τε πρώτως ἐν Ἀντιοχείᾳ τοὺς μαθητὰς Χριστιανούς)" is today generally considered to be correct.[19] The

13. For a larger number, cf. C. H. Kraeling, *JBL* 51 (1932) 135f.; G. Haddad, *loc. cit.*, 67-73; G. Downey, *TAPA* 89 (1958) 84-91; *A History of Antioch* (1961) 582f.; F. W. Norris, *TRE* III (1978) 99; for a lower number, cf. J. H. W. G. Liebeschütz, *Antioch* (1972) 40f., 92-96; W. A. Meeks and R. L. Wilken, *Jews and Christians in Antioch* (1978) 8.

14. Cf. I. Benzinger, *PRE* 1 (1894) 2443; J. Kollwitz, *RAC* I (1950) 461.

15. Cf. C. H. Kraeling, *JBL* 51 (1932) 136; W. S. McCullough, *A Short History of Syriac Christianity* (1982) 15.

16. Cf. W. A. Meeks and R. L. Wilken, *Jews and Christians in Antioch* (1978) 12.

17. Cf. M. Hengel, *Zur urchristlichen Geschichtsschreibung* (²1984) 63f.; W. A. Meeks and R. L. Wilken, *loc. cit.*, 15.

18. Cf. also M. Hengel, *loc. cit.*, 84f.

19. Cf., e.g., J. Roloff, *Die Apostelgeschichte* (1981) 177; G. Schneider, *Die Apostelgeschichte* I (1981) 274; J. P. Meier, in *Antioch and Rome* (1983) 35; G. Lüdemann, *Das frühe Christentum nach den Traditionen der Apostelgeschichte* (1987) 143 (Eng. trans., *Early Christianity according to the Traditions in Acts* [1989]). P. Zingg, *Das Wachsen der Kirche* (1974) 226f., e.g., reckons with an already extant written tradition for Acts 11:26b. By contrast, M. Pasinya, *RATh* 1 (1977) 31-66, criticizes all previous attempts at distinguishing sources in Acts 11:19-26, and assumes the presence of a thoroughgoing formulation by Luke himself with the simultaneous employment of extant information. The Antiochene origin of the designation "Christian" is also supported by the fact that its first Christian mention outside the New Testament is found in the writings of Ignatius of Antioch (Ignatius, *Magn.* 10.1.3; *Rom.* 3.2; *Philad.* 6.1). Cf. V. Corwin, *St. Ignatius and Christianity in Antioch* (1960) 189.

development of a larger church composed of Jews and Gentiles would itself already make it comprehensible that outsiders would coin this new, distinguishing name Χριστιανοί.[20] At the same time, this does not exclude the possibility that Christians themselves also soon adopted this particular appellation, since it would have corresponded to their own new self-consciousness as a third entity over against Jews and Gentiles;[21] especially in the social environment of the metropolis Antioch, this self-consciousness probably acquired clear contours.[22] These two assumptions do not necessarily contradict yet another suggestion.

Following R. Paribeni,[23] it was especially E. Peterson[24] who presented noteworthy evidence that in Acts 11:26 Luke is introducing an official designation used by the Roman authorities to refer to the new religious group.[25] That is, the verb χρηματίσαι occurs in official contexts just as does πρώτως (not πρῶτον as in the D-text!) in legal documents, and, finally, the construction Χριστιανός corresponds to other party names with a Latin ending.[26] The objection has been raised that χρηματίσαι here cannot be understood passively.[27] But in the only comparable New Testament passage (Rom. 7:3), the verb has "passive meaning in the sense of a popular designation for foreigners."[28] The element of reservation in some Christians' acceptance of the word militates against its being an original self-designation,[29] reservation still coming to expression, for example, in an Egyptian papyrus of the third century (*NewDoc* II.172f.).[30] One consideration prompting this reservation may also have been the fear of losing the privileges of a *religio licita* through a name distinguishing them from Judaism.[31]

An official expression is also suggested by the various contexts involving state measures emerging in the two remaining New Testament pas-

20. Cf. W. A. Meeks and R. L. Wilken, *Jews and Christians in Antioch* (1978) 15f.

21. Malalas, 246.20ff., asserts that Bishop Evodius was the first to coin this name (*ca.* A.D. 41; see note 34 below).

22. Cf. D. W. Riddle, *JR* 7 (1927) 146-63; L. Schenke, *Die Urgemeinde* (1990) 318f.; C. K. Barrett, *The Acts of the Apostles* (1994) 555-57.

23. *NBAC* 19 (1913) 37-41.

24. In *Frühkirche, Judentum und Gnosis* (1959) 64-87.

25. He is followed by, among others, G. B. Downey, *A History of Antioch in Syria* (1961) 275f.; M. Sordi, *The Christians and the Roman Empire* (1986) 15, 22, note 27; cautiously also by J. P. Meier, in *Antioch and Rome* (1983) 35, note 81.

26. So also, with additional examples, C. Spicq, *StTh* 15 (1961) 68-70.

27. E. Bickerman, *HThR* 42 (1949) 112f. (in *Studies in Jewish and Christian History* III [1986] 140f.); J. Moreau, *NC* 1/2 (1949/50) 190f.; C. Spicq, *loc. cit.,* 70-72.

28. A. Weiser, *Die Apostelgeschichte* I (1981) 279. Cf. Bauer-Aland, *Wb* 1766.

29. Cf. E. Peterson, in *Frühkirche, Judentum und Gnosis* (1959) 86f.

30. Cf. E. A. Judge and S. R. Pickering, *JAC* 20 (1977) 66-69.

31. Cf. E. Haenchen, *Acts* (Eng. trans. 1971) 367f.

sages (Acts 26:28; 1 Pet. 4:16) and in the oldest extra-Christian attestations (Tacitus, *Ann.* xv.44; Pliny the Younger, *Ep.* x.96).[32] If Luke had viewed the name "Christian" as a self-designation, it would be difficult to explain why except in the mouth of Agrippa II (Acts 26:28) the name does not occur again in the entire book of Acts.[33] By contrast, it would fit the character of his work if the *auctor ad Theophilum* in Acts 11:26 would as an aside introduce the origin of an official designation that later played a role in the measures undertaken by the state against the Christians. At a dramatic juncture in the trial against Paul, the Jewish king then uses a name in reference to himself that at latest since Nero had a connection with trial procedure: *quos per flagitia invisos vulgus Chrestianos appellabat"* (Tacitus, *Ann.* xv.44).

Peterson associated the designation of these believers as "Christians" by the Roman authorities with the period of persecution under Agrippa I.[34] But at least two earlier occasions are also conceivable as having prompted this designation. G. Downey[35] and, following him, F. W. Norris,[36] associate the emergence of this name with disturbances which, according to Malalas, broke out between Jews and Gentiles in Antioch in the third year of Caligula (A.D. 39-40)[37] (Malalas, 244.15–245.20 [ed. von Stauffenberg, 23f.]).[38] The account of Malalas has strong elements of legend, but it is apparently not without a historical core.[39] In the winter of A.D. 39/40, Caligula had ordered that his statue be set up in the Jerusalem temple (Philo, *Leg. ad Gaium* 185-90).[40] After antisemitic unrest in Alexandria in A.D. 40/41 (§6.2.3),

32. Cf. E. Peterson, in *Frühkirche, Judentum und Gnosis* (1959) 78-81. Concerning Suetonius, *Claudius* 25.4, cf. §10.2.2.

33. Cf. M. Pasinya, *RATh* 1 (1977) 52.

34. According to Malalas, 246.20ff., in the tenth year after the ascension, which the Syrian chronicler dated in A.D. 31, Evodius became Bishop of Antioch and gave to these believers the designation "Christians." This would indeed lead to the beginning of the reign of Claudius after A.D. 41. But other sources date the episcopate of Evodius in A.D. 44 (Jerome, *Chron.* [ed. Helm 179]) or A.D. 45/46 (Eusebius, *Chron.* [ed. Schöne II 152]), and his activity as a leading member of the church may have begun even later. Hence one should not build too much on the date given by Malalas. Cf. G. B. Downey, *A History of Antioch in Syria* (1961) 285f.

35. *A History of Antioch in Syria,* 194f.

36. *TRE* III (1978) 102.

37. Concerning the role of Gentiles in Antioch, cf. F. W. Norris, *ANRW* II 18.4 (1990) 2322-79.

38. H. Grégoire, *Byz* 1 (1924) 644-46, even considered the Christian proclamation to have been the catalyst.

39. Cf. C. H. Kraeling, *JBL* 51 (1932) 148-50; G. Downey, *A History of Antioch* (1961) 192-95; D. R. Schwartz, *Agrippa I* (1990) 93, note 15.

40. Our main sources contradict one another regarding the exact chronological sequence of events: Philo, *Leg. ad Gaium* 184-348, and Josephus, *Ant.* xviii.261-309. Cf. Schuerer, I 394-98, esp. note 180; M. Stern, CRINT I/1 (1974) 70-74.

Claudius, at the request of Agrippa I, also sent to Antioch an edict confirming the privileges of the Jews there (Josephus, *Ant.* xix.279). This suggests the presence of earlier difficulties as in Alexandria. In connection with this newly emerging anti-Semitism, especially the Gentile Christians in Antioch probably saw the value in not being viewed as a Jewish group, a circumstance which then might have led to their special designation as Χριστιανοί. Such political circumstances, resulting in a distancing from Judaism, were probably also a factor in the transition to a Gentile mission free of the law.[41] One might with M. Sordi[42] date an official Roman designation even earlier, namely, to the intervention of Vitellius in Syria in A.D. 36/37, if one follows her thesis that the intervention of the governor was also connected with the illegal persecution of Christians under Pilate (§4.1.2).[43]

7.1.3. Peter and Cornelius

K. Haacker[44] has shown that the influential essay of M. Dibelius, "Die Bekehrung des Cornelius,"[45] hardly represents the last word in the form-critical analysis of this pericope (Acts 10:1–11:18). This account exhibits several archaic features and might well preserve recollections of the momentous conversion of a highly placed Gentile by Peter.[46] G. Lüdemann, too, despite assuming the presence of strong Lukan redaction, maintains that the author of Acts owes the story of the conversion of the Gentile Cornelius in Caesarea by Peter to a tradition with a historical core.[47] The assertion that Cornelius belonged to the Italian Cohort (ἐκ σπείρης τῆς καλουμένης Ἰταλικῆς, Acts 10:1), however, Lüdemann considers "historically incorrect," since "the Italian Cohort existed only from 69 C.E. into the second century, and in Syria."[48] One of the two studies he cites, however, figures on the basis of an inscription from Carnuntum/Kärnten (*ILS* 9168) that the *cohors II Italica Civium Romanorum* providing the possible reference here was already stationed in Syria

---

41. Cf. also M. Hengel, *Zur urchristlichen Geschichtsschreibung* (^{2}1984) 87.

42. *The Christians and the Roman Empire* (1986) 15.

43. The historical possibilities here render the assumption of H. B. Mattingley, *JTS* 9 (1958) 26-37, superfluous; Mattingley, writing contra Luke's chronological classification of Acts 11:26, assumes a construction analogous to the name of the *Augustiani,* which are attested as a group only after A.D. 59 (Tacitus, *Ann.* xiv.15).

44. *BZ* 24 (1980) 234-51.

45. In *Aufsätze zur Apostelgeschichte* (^{5}1968) 96-107.

46. Cf. further M. Hengel, *Zur urchristlichen Geschichtsschreibung* (^{2}1984) 79-84.

47. G. Lüdemann, *Early Christianity according to the Traditions in Acts* (Eng. trans., 1989) 124-33.

48. *Ibid.,* 126.

before A.D. 69.[49] Although the objections against the stationing of an auxiliary cohort in Caesarea around A.D. 40 should be taken seriously,[50] they are — especially in view of the frequent troop movements (cf. Josephus, *Ant.* xix.364-66) — not insuperable.[51] For the moment, our own lack of evidence renders certainty in one direction or another impossible. We do not even know whether at the time of the reported event Cornelius was still on active duty or had only settled in Caesarea as a veteran.[52] Hence no more exact dating of the Cornelius-episode based on evidence outside the New Testament is possible at this time.[53] The general chronological impression of Acts suggests a time around the accession of Agrippa I (§§7.2.2-3). If the incident took place under the reign of Caligula, this would also ameliorate somewhat the problem of the Lukan reference to the cohort.

7.1.4. Caligula, Near Expectation, and the Gentile Mission

Although not the first to do so,[54] G. Theissen has now drawn attention with particular intensity to the fact that the Markan apocalypse (Mk. 13) was probably first committed to written form during the reign of Caligula (A.D. 37-41).[55] Although Theissen does consider the clear insertion (Mk. 13:10) "and the gospel must first be proclaimed to all nations (καὶ εἰς πάντα τὰ ἔθνη πρῶτον δεῖ κηρυχθῆναι τὸ εὐαγγέλιον)" to be Markan redaction from around A.D. 70,[56] G. Dautzenberg believes that the concept of the εὐαγγέλιον τοῦ θεοῦ already goes back to an extra-Palestinian missionary movement of Hellenistic Jewish Christians antedating the composition of the Gospel of

49. T. R. S. Broughton, *BC* V (1933) 441f. W. M. Ramsay, *Exp* V/4 (1896) 194-201; V/5 (1897) 69-72, had already drawn attention to the significance of the inscription even before its publication in the accessible collection of H. Dessau (*ILS* 9168) contra E. Schürer, *Exp.* V/4 (1896) 469-72.

50. Cf. Schuerer I, 361-65.

51. Cf. M. Hengel, *ZDPV* 99 (1983) 171, note 109; C. P. Thiede, *GBL* II (1988) 822f.; C. J. Hemer, *The Book of Acts in the Setting of Hellenistic History* (1989) 164. Several considerations from earlier scholarship are similarly by no means resolved. Cf. A. Bludau, *ThPM* 17 (1907) 139f.; T. Zahn, *Introduction to the New Testament* (Eng. trans., 1909) 59f.; A. Wikenhauser, *Die Apostelgeschichte und ihr Geschichtswert* (1921) 314f.

52. Cf. T. R. S. Broughton, *BC* V (1933) 443.

53. L. M. Hopfe, *ANRW* II 18.4 (1990) 2400, mentions A.D. 44/45, though without any justification.

54. Cf., e.g., W. L. Knox, *St. Paul and the Church of Jerusalem* (1925) 172, note 6; 187, note 9; *The Sources of the Synoptic Gospels* I (1953) 103-14; F. F. Bruce, *Neutestamentliche Zeitgeschichte* II (1976) 56; R. Riesner, *Jesus als Lehrer* (³1988) 494f., and esp. G. Zuntz, in H. Cancik, *Marcus-Philologie* (1984) 47-50.

55. *Lokalkolorit und Zeitgeschichte in den Evangelien* (1989) 133-76.

56. *Ibid.,* 250.

Mark itself.[57] However, one might also think of the Jerusalem Hellenists, who perhaps were able to tie in terminologically to Jesus' own use of language (cf. Mk. 1:15; 14:9).[58] Occasionally, Mk. 13:10 is even viewed as an "originally free-floating," pre-Markan "slogan."[59]

If one assumes a more conservative transmission of the Jesus tradition, then one must try to explain on the basis of which authority and circumstances an addendum like Mk. 13:10 could be inserted into a discourse of Jesus. K. Bauer suggested that the apocalyptic mood of the Caligula-period[60] also generated prophecies on the necessity of an eschatological world mission.[61] The question of just which hour of God had now tolled had to awaken especially in the moment when Caligula's own death prevented his statue from being set up in the temple (cf. Mk. 13:14). What had looked like the end proved to be merely "but the beginning of the birth pangs" (Mk. 13:8). What was the meaning of the "time of refreshing" (cf. Acts 3:20) that had apparently yet been granted? The words of a prophet could provide guidance: the task of the mission to the nations is yet before us! With Peter's vision (Acts 10:9-13), this sort of prophetic element does in any event reside within the context of the Cornelius-story, which according to our chronological considerations is to be dated around the beginning of the reign of Agrippa I and thus in immediate proximity to the death of Caligula in January A.D. 41 (§§7.2.2-3). A visionary experience associated with Paul's transition to the Antiochene mission might point to a slightly later time (§14.3). The emigration of apostles such as Peter out of the holy land itself, prompted by the persecution of Agrippa I, was able to strengthen the conviction that a new redemptive-historical age had begun. The twelve-year tradition we will shortly examine (see pp. 119f. below) represents a late reflex of this notion. Prophetic instructions, the experience of history, and reference to a genuine Jesus-tradition (Mk. 14:9) may, after the surprising end of Caligula on 24 January A.D. 41 (Suetonius, *Gaius* 60.1; Josephus, *Ant.* xix.105-14), have led to an interpretative insertion such as Mk. 13:10.[62]

---

57. In *Zur Geschichte des Urchristentums* (1979) 19-24.

58. Cf. P. Stuhlmacher, in *The Gospel and the Gospels* (Eng. trans., 1983) 21f.

59. R. Pesch, *Das Markusevangelium* II ([3]1984) 285.

60. Concerning the Jewish policies of Gaius, cf. A. Barrett, *Caligula* (1989) 182-91.

61. *Antiochia in der ältesten Kirchengeschichte* (1919) 35f.

62. It is clear enough that we are dealing here with a different process from an indistinct admixture of words of the earthly and of the exalted Jesus. Concerning criticism of this view, cf. esp. D. E. Aune, *Prophecy in Early Christianity* (1983) 233-45, and the bibliography in R. Riesner, *Jesus als Lehrer* ([3]1988) 8-11, 515.

7.2. Persecution under Agrippa I

7.2.1. The Death of Agrippa I

Josephus dates the death of Herod Agrippa I three full years (Josephus, *Ant.* xix.343: τρίτον δὲ ἔτος αὐτῷ βασιλεύοντι τῆς ὅλης ᾽Ιουδαίας πεπλήρωτο) after the accession of Claudius (cf. Josephus, *Ant.* xix.351; *B.J.* ii.219). Coins extending to the eighth year of the reign of Agrippa (as tetrarch since A.D. 37) also confirm A.D. 44 as the year of death.[63] Older datings, which also reckoned with A.D. 43,[64] must thus be abandoned. There is no unanimity concerning which festival games in Caesarea in honor of the emperor (Josephus, *Ant.* xix.343: συνετέλει δ᾽ἐνταῦθα θεωρίας εἰς τὴν Καίσαρος τιμὴν ὑπὲρ τῆς ἐκείνου σωτηρίας ἑορτήν τινα ταύτην ἐπισάμενος) are to be associated with the death of Agrippa.[65] K. Wieseler[66] suggested the athletic games founded by Herod the Great in his twenty-eighth year (10/9 B.C.), held regularly every four years (Josephus, *Ant.* xvi.136-41). According to Wieseler, these began on 1 August, Claudius' birthday (cf. Suetonius, *Claudius* 2.1).[67] We otherwise have no information concerning special celebrations on the emperor's *dies natalis*. Above all, the quinquennials were celebrated on the founding day of Caesarea (Josephus, *Ant.* xvi.136f.), that is, on 5 March (Eusebius, *Mart. Pal.* xi.30). Hence E. Schwartz decided in favor of a date of death in March.[68] Reckoning from the twenty-eighth year of Herod the Great, however, rather suggests the games were held in A.D. 43.[69] Another possibility would be competitions held on the occasion of Claudius' triumph in Britain (Dio Cassius, *Hist.* lx.23.4f.) in the spring of A.D. 44.[70]

The question can be left in abeyance here, since the frequent presup-

63. Cf. J. Meyshan, *IEJ* 4 (1954) 186-200; W. Wirgin, *Herod Agrippa 1* (1968) 102-51; A. Stein, *Israel Numismatic Journal* 5 (1981) 22-26.

64. Cf. K. Lake, *BC* V (1933) 452. Cf. N. L. Collins, *NT* 34 (1992) 99-101, contra D. R. Schwartz (*Agrippa I* [1990] 108-11, 203; in *Studies in the Jewish Background of Christianity* [1992] 173-80), who cites Josephus incorrectly and thus arrives at the end of A.D. 43.

65. Cf. G. Ogg, *The Chronology of the Life of Paul* (1968) 39-42.

66. *Chronologie des apostolischen Zeitalters* (1848) 129-36.

67. C. J. Hemer, *The Book of Acts in the Setting of Hellenistic History* (1989) 166, also is inclined to accept this date, though without determining the actual character of the games.

68. *NGWG.PH* (1907) 263-66. So also E. Meyer, *Ursprung und Anfänge des Christentums* III (1923) 167.

69. Cf. Schuerer I, 453, note 43.

70. So D. Plooij, *De chronologie van het leven van Paulus* (1919) 10-15; Schuerer, *ibid.*; G. Ogg, *The Chronology of the Life of Paul* (1968) 41f.; M. Stern, CRINT I/1 (1974) 299, note 3.

position is incorrect that the account of Acts forces one to assume that Agrippa left Jerusalem for Caesarea Maritima (Acts 12:19) immediately after the Passover festival[71] before which Peter was arrested (Acts 12:3). Luke associates only an indefinite period of time with Agrippa's stay (διέτριβεν), and he relates the death of the Jewish king immediately after the persecution in order to make clear the connection between this action and the divine punishment (Acts 12:22f.). The Lukan portrayal itself does not allow us to determine how much time really separated the two events.[72] The death of Agrippa I thus provides us only with a *terminus ante quem* for the persecution related by Acts, though its more exact chronological determination is possible in a different way.

7.2.2. The Beginning of the Persecution

After his installation by the new emperor Claudius on 25 January A.D. 41 (§6.2.2), Agrippa I returned to his country — probably immediately after the reopening of shipping on 10 March, or perhaps even earlier, given the official nature of his journey (§16.1) — because it was in a religious-revolutionary uproar as a result of the temple sacrilege intended by Caligula (§7.1.4). Just how far-seeing and skillful Agrippa's emphatically Torah-loyal policies were[73] is attested with abundant clarity by the Zealot resistance movements that started to develop after his death (§6.3). At this time of the year, the king could reckon with a sea journey of at most three weeks (see pp. 314-17 below). Immediately upon arriving in Jerusalem, the king implemented measures demonstrating the new policy. To the temple he donated the golden chain which he had received from Caligula on the occasion of his release, presented thanksgiving offerings, and covered the costs for a large number of Nazirites (Josephus, *Ant.* xix.294). This makes it probable that Agrippa began his actions against the original Jerusalem church "to please the Jews" immediately during his first Passover festival (cf. Acts 12:3), which in A.D. 41 fell on 5 April.[74] In any case, there is no reason to go beyond A.D. 42. When he had James the

71. In A.D. 44, the Passover festival probably did not occur until 1 May because of an intercalary Adar. Cf. R. A. Parker and W. H. Dubberstein, *Babylonian Chronology* (1956) 46.

72. R. Jewett, *A Chronology of Paul's Life* (1979) 34, does not acknowledge this difficulty when he writes that "Agrippa's persecution of the church the year before his death in A.D. 44 is a well-established date in the history of the early church." He similarly presupposes without further questioning the death of the Jewish king in March A.D. 44.

73. Cf. Schuerer I, 445-51.

74. So also G. B. Caird, *IBD* I (1962) 603f.; R. Pesch, *Simon-Petrus* (1980) 61f.; *Die Apostelgeschichte* I (1986) 368.

son of Zebedee executed by the sword rather than through stoning (Acts 12:2), even though it was actually a religious matter, he may have been emphatically demonstrating his own possession of the *ius gladii*.[75]

A dating of the persecution and, with it, Peter's departure from Jerusalem (Acts 12:17) in the year A.D. 41 or 42 is supported by yet another chronological complex. According to the *Acts of Peter* (*Acts Pet.* 5:22) from the second century A.D., the apostle remained in Jerusalem for twelve years before going to Rome as the result of a vision (*"adimpletis XII annis, quod [quot?] illi praeceperat, dominus Christus ostendit illi visionem talem"* [ed. Lipsius I 49]). Taking the death of Jesus in the year A.D. 30 as the point of departure, one would arrive at A.D. 41/42. A Syrian tradition in Elijah Nisibenus (*CSCO* III/7 38.4f.) seems to presuppose the same dating (see p. 60 above). According to Eusebius (*HE* ii.14.6; cf. Eusebius, *Chron.* [ed. Helm 179]) and Jerome (*De Vir. Ill.* 5), Peter reached Rome in the second year of Claudius (25 January A.D. 42–24 January A.D. 43) and, according to the legendary *Teaching of Cephas,* in the third year.[76] The complicated tradition concerning the date of the martyrdom of Peter also suggests this sort of twelve-year period.[77] Regardless of whether one considers this early a sojourn in Rome to be possible for the apostle,[78] the consistent date of twelve years after the crucifixion for his leaving the holy city does in any case have a counterpart in a different chronological tradition, one whose value was accepted by no less a scholar than A. von Harnack.[79]

Clement of Alexandria read in the *Kerygma Petri,* dating probably

75. Cf. S. Dockx, *Chronologies néotestamentaires* ([2]1984) 166. J. Blinzler, *NT* 5 (1962) 191-206, argued that the Sanhedrin condemned James and that the execution by the sword can be explained on the basis of the normal Sadducean punishment for the preacher of apostasy (מדיח) according to Dt. 13:16. However, it is problematical to presuppose that Sadducean criminal law was the only applicable law in the period prior to A.D. 66. Cf. A. Strobel, *Die Stunde der Wahrheit* (1980) 46-61.

76. W. Cureton, *Ancient Syriac Documents* (1864) 35.

77. Cf. C. Erbes, *TU* 4 (1899) 1-16.

78. So among more recent authors G. Downey, *Ancient Antioch* (1963) 127; J. W. Wenham, *TynBul* 23 (1972) 94-102; K. Buchheim, *Der historische Christus* (1974) 110-46; S. Dockx, *Chronologies néotestamentaires* ([2]1984) 166-71; J. A. T. Robinson, *Redating the New Testament* (1976) 111-17; A. Feuillet, *DBS* X (1985) 757; C. P. Thiede, *Simon Peter* (1986) 153-55; in *Das Petrusbild in der neueren Forschung* (1987) 221-29; H. Botermann, *Das Judenedikt des Kaisers Claudius* (1996) 136-40. An especially decisive non-Catholic representative of this view in the older generation was G. Edmundson, *The Church in Rome in the First Century* (1913) 59-75. Older Catholic bibliography can be found in S. Lyonnet, *VD* 33 (1955) 143f.

79. *Geschichte der altchristlichen Litteratur* II/1 (1897) 243f. Cf. also J. Wagenmann, *Die Stellung des Apostels Paulus neben den Zwölf* (1926) 15. By contrast, the very conservative Catholic F. Spadafora, *VD* 21 (1941) 310, assumes that this tradition is a mere extrapolation from Acts 12.

from the first quarter of the second century A.D., that the apostles, according to the instructions of the resurrected Jesus, offered Israel penance for twelve years before going out to the world of nations: Διὰ τοῦτό φησιν ὁ Πέτρος εἰρηκέναι τὸν κύριον τοῖς ἀποστόλοις . . . μετὰ [δὲ] δώδεκα ἔτη ἐξέλθετε εἰς τὸν κόσμον (Clement of Alexandria, *Strom.* vi.43.3 [ed. Stählin II 453.22ff.]). Eusebius recounts a similar tradition, one going back at least to the anti-Montanist Apollonius at the end of the second century A.D. (ὡς ἐκ παραδόσεως): "The Saviour ordered his apostles not to leave Jerusalem for twelve years (τὸν σωτῆρά φησι προστεταχέναι τοῖς αὐτοῦ ἀποστόλοις, ἐπὶ δώδεκα ἔτεσι μὴ χωρισθῆναι τῆς Ἰερουσαλήμ)" [Eusebius, *HE* v.18.14]. The combination of two further accounts leads to the same period.[80] In his popular, unfortunately only partially preserved *World Chronicle* (between A.D. 650 and 750),[81] Hippolytus of Thebes claims that Mary lived eleven years after the death of Jesus,[82] that is, until about A.D. 41 (Hippolytus of Thebes 3.3f. [ed. Diekamp 27f.]). In the *Acts of John* of Prochorus, the disciples' mission begins after her death (ed. Zahn 4.4f.). Contrary to the older view (at least fourth century A.D.), which understands Mary's death as following a short time (usually two years) after the ascension,[83] Hippolytus associated the *dormitio* with the end of the disciples' stay in Jerusalem. A reflex of this latter tradition is quite obviously found also in the gnostic theory of a period of special instruction to the disciples by the resurrected Jesus lasting twelve years, as recounted in the *Pistis Sophia* 1 (*GCS* 45.1) and in the second *Book of Jeu* 44 (*GCS* 45.306f.). This notion is found in a slightly different form within the orthodox-ecclesiastical tradition.[84]

Yet another consideration suggests that the death of James the son of Zebedee did indeed take place on the threshold of the period of a conscious mission to the Gentiles. Whereas the betrayer Judas was replaced in the circle of twelve (Acts 1:15-26), we hear nothing of this in connection with the martyrdom of James. Jesus had already brought to expression with this number

---

80. Cf. F. Diekamp, *Hippolytos von Theben* (1898) 92-94; A. Strobel, *Ursprung und Geschichte des frühchristlichen Osterkalenders* (1977) 117.

81. This work is viewed by some as largely a product of the imagination (so J. Kraus, *LThK* V [1960] 380), though the question remains here concerning the value of individual older accounts which Hippolytus is known to have used. Cf. F. Diekamp, *loc. cit.,* 160-62.

82. A. von Harnack's assertion, *Geschichte der altchristlichen Litteratur* II/1 (1897) 243, that the *Acts of John* of Prochorus already mentions this date is incorrect. This text provides only the indefinite reference μετὰ χρόνον τινά (ed. Zahn 3f.).

83. Cf. F. Diekamp, *Hippolytos von Theben* (1898) 91f.

84. Concerning the Milan manuscript Ambrosiana H 150 inf, cf. A. Strobel, *Ursprung und Geschichte des frühchristlichen Osterkalenders* (1977) 290-93; concerning the Venerable Bede, *In Acta Apostolorum* 13 (*PL* 92.973C), cf. F. Diekamp, *loc. cit.,* 93, note 2.

twelve his own eschatological claim and his mission to Israel, the people of twelve tribes (cf. Mt. 19:28/Lk. 22:29f.).[85] When Peter, as the leader among the twelve, now left the holy city and the holy land itself,[86] now completely under the rule of Agrippa I, this marked a clear cut in the activity on behalf of Israel itself. This absence of any reestablishment of the circle of twelve to its entirety betrays a consciousness of living in a new age, one in which missionary efforts on behalf of the older people of God in Jerusalem and in the holy land no longer constituted the only task.

If the persecution under Agrippa I did indeed occur during the first period of his reign in A.D. 41 or at the latest 42, then this dating also militates against a dating of what is known as the Apostolic Council in A.D. 43/44, since James the son of Zebedee, whose alleged participation in the assembly serves as a justification for its early dating, would at that time already have died. The earlier dating, following E. Schwartz[87] and also advocated by several modern scholars,[88] however, is to be rejected for other reasons as well:[89] (1) The resulting necessity of dating Paul's conversion in A.D. 30 at the latest requires the hardly possible dating of the crucifixion of Jesus in A.D. 27 (§3). (2) The readers of the letter to the Galatians would not have been able to understand that the James in Gal. 2:9 is actually a different one from James the brother of Jesus mentioned in the immediate context (Gal. 1:19; 2:12).[90] (3) The assumption of

85. Cf. J. Jeremias, *New Testament Theology* (Eng. trans., 1971) 233f.

86. At the least, Antioch may at that time have been a possibility for Peter (cf. R. Pesch, *Simon-Petrus* [1980] 78). This in any event is the assertion of Eusebius (*Chron.* [ed. Helm 179]) and Jerome (*De Vir. Ill.* 5). The Armenian version of the *Chronicon* (ed. Schöne ii.151) names as founding year the third year of Caligula (A.D. 39/40). Malalas, 242.8-22, even dates Peter's first visit as early as A.D. 35. A similarly early date is also suggested by *Ps.-Clem. Rec.* x.68-71 (*GCS* 51.368-71) and *Ps.-Clem. Hom.* xx.23 (*GCS* 42.281) by having Peter arrive in Antioch already after his encounter with Simon Magus (Acts 8:9-24). Presumably the tradition that the apostle visited Antioch at an early period was distorted by the agenda of making him the first bishop and thus the real founder of the church there. The contradictory accounts in tradition regarding whether Evodius or Ignatius was the first monarchic bishop (after Peter) are probably to be interpreted in favor of the former. Cf. G. B. Downey, *A History of Antioch in Syria* (1961) 281-84, 583-86 (sources).

87. *NGWG.PH* (1907) 263-84.

88. F. Hahn, *Das Verständnis der Mission im Neuen Testament* (1963) 76-78; J. J. Gunther, *Paul: Messenger and Exile* (1972) 36-44; A. Suhl, *Paulus und seine Briefe* (1975) 69; P. Vielhauer, *Geschichte der urchristlichen Literatur* (1978) 78; P. Klein, *ZNW* 70 (1979) 250f.; W. Pratscher, *Der Herrenbruder Jakobus und die Jakobustradition* (1987) 50-55 (*ibid.*, 51f., note 14 providing further bibliography).

89. Cf. further D. Georgi, *Die Geschichte der Kollekte des Paulus für Jerusalem* (1965) 91-94 (Eng. trans., *Remembering the Poor* [1992]); R. K. Jewett, *A Chronology of Paul's Life*, 33f.

90. Cf. D. Georgi, *loc. cit.*, 92; A. J. M. Wedderburn, *ET* 92 (1981) 107; F. F. Bruce, *The Epistle of Paul to the Galatians* (1982) 121.

a simultaneous martyrdom of the Zebedees John (cf. Gal. 2:9) and his brother under Agrippa I, which E. Schwartz[91] so energetically advocates, is based on isolated late accounts in Philip Sidetes (fifth century) and George Harmartolos (ninth century).[92] These accounts, however, can be interpreted as misunderstood Papias-fragments which do not necessarily contradict the rest of ancient church tradition.[93]

7.2.3. Reasons for the Persecution

Agrippa's measures were possibly prompted not only by political reasoning but also an attempt to bolster his aspirations of being acknowledged as a messiah-like ruler. In any event, in his monograph on the Jewish king, W. Wirgin does interpret several of Agrippa's activities in this sense.[94] The per-

91. *AGWG.PH* VII/5 (1904); *ZNW* 11 (1912) 89-104.

92. These texts are easily accessible in J. Kürzinger, *Papias von Hierapolis und die Evangelien des Neuen Testaments* (1983), Fragments 16 and 17 (116-19).

93. Cf. F. M. Braun, *Jean le Théologien et son évangile dans l'église ancienne* (1959) 375-85, 407-11; J. H. Bernard, in K. H. Rengstorf, *Johannes und sein Evangelium* (1973) 273-90; R. Schnackenburg, *The Gospel According to St. John* (Eng. trans., New York, 1968) 86-88; R. Riesner, in K. Bockmuehl, *Die Aktualität der Theologie Adolf Schlatters* (1988) 57-60 (bibliography); D. R. Schwartz, *Agrippa I* (1990) 208-12. A different view is taken by M. Hengel, *Die johanneische Frage* (1993) 88-92 (Eng. trans., *The Johannine Question* [1990]).

94. *Herod Agrippa 1* (1968) 68-101. Perhaps this also explains why Acts 12:1, 6, 19, 21 calls Agrippa I "Herod," for which no other contemporary source provides a parallel. Numismatic evidence which was for a time believed to attest the name "Herod Agrippa" (Y. Meshorer, *Ancient Jewish Coinage* II [1982] 57 and 248 [no. 5]), is to be interpreted as a commemorative coin at the common crowning of the brothers Agrippa and Herod (of Chalcis) in A.D. 41 (A. Burnett, in *Festschrift P. Bastien* [1987] 33-37). D. R. Schwartz, *Agrippa I* (1990) 120, note 51, assumes that Luke confused the two kings on the basis of information he read in Josephus (Josephus, *Ant.* xx.104) (*loc. cit.,* 215f.). Now, the assertion that Luke used the *Antiquitates Judaicae* (A.D. 93) is already thoroughly problematical in and of itself (C. J. Hemer, *The Book of Acts* [1989] 94-96; F. F. Bruce, *The Acts of the Apostles* [³1990] 43f.; earlier bibliography can be found in G. Schneider, *Die Apostelgeschichte* I [1980] 88, note 36); here, however, such presupposed acquaintance accompanied by this sort of confusion would be even more astounding. The judgment of E. Schürer, *ZWTh* 19 (1876) 582, also applies to the assumption of Schwartz: "Either Luke took absolutely no notice of Josephus in the first place, or he subsequently forgot everything he read. The former assumption is the simpler of the two, and in my opinion is to be preferred." As a rule, the assumption is that a popular use of language is the case: Luke "no doubt reflects popular usage, in which Herod had become a dynastic name" (A. H. M. Jones, *The Herods of Judaea* [1938] 211, note 1; similarly E. M. Smallwood, *Philonis Alexandrini Legatio ad Gaium* [²1970] 251; U. Kellermann, *EDNT* II [1991] 123). Herod the Great had already harbored messianic hopes for his family (on the basis of astrological speculations) (cf. A. Strobel, *ANRW* II 20.2 [1987] 1063-77). W. Horbury, in *Festschrift*

secutory measures of Agrippa I against the new messianic faith were doubtless also to the liking of the Sadducees, as becomes clear in the latter's behavior regarding the persecution of Stephen (§4.1.2) and later at the execution of James the brother of Jesus (Josephus, *Ant.* xx.200). Luke recounts that Agrippa "laid violent hands upon some who belonged to the church (ἐπέβαλεν Ἡρῴδης ὁ βασιλεὺς τὰς χεῖρας κακῶσαί τινας τῶν ἀπὸ τῆς ἐκκλησίας)" (Acts 12:1). Perhaps this particular manner of expression is consciously alluding to the fact that the king's repressive measures, similar to the persecution of Stephen, were aimed only at part of the church. The most likely group was the one that, with Peter (and perhaps James the son of Zebedee), was open to the mission to the Gentiles.[95] In that case, Agrippa's actions could impress not only the party of the Sadducees but also believers sympathetic to the Zealots, for whom without a doubt the first-known examples of a Jewish-Christian mission to the Gentiles were perceived as signs of apostasy. Several considerations suggest that those particular Jewish Christians who urged Paul to impose circumcision on Gentile Christians were influenced not only by theological motives, but also by the swelling mood of Zealotism (§6.3). At the very least, the fears of Palestinian Jewish Christians do seem comprehensible. Association with fellow believers who because of their contacts with Gentiles were suspected of apostasy made the position of Jewish Christians in the holy land problematical or even wholly untenable.[96]

7.3. Chronological Sequence

After their expulsion from Jerusalem (presumably A.D. 31/32), the Hellenists made the transition to a Gentile mission in various stages. The origin of the designation "Christian" suggests that a larger Jewish-Christian group existed

---

E. *Bammel* (1991) 103-49, speaks about "Herodian messianism" (*loc. cit.,* 147) with reference to the Jewish king and his descendants especially in connection with the construction of the temple. Perhaps Luke in Acts 12 is following a Jewish-Christian source that alludes here to the messianic aspirations of the son (Agrippa I) with the catchword "Herod." The Ἡρῳδιανοί of the Gospels (Mt. 22:16/Mk. 12:13; Mk. 3:6), however, might be referring to adherents of a messianic claim of the Herodians, as suggested by Tertullian, *De praescr. haeret.* 45; Epiphanius, *Pan.* 20.1, and other patristic witnesses (U. Holzmeister, *Historia Aetatis Novi Testamenti* [1938] 265, note 6).

95. Cf. F. F. Bruce, *Men and Movements in the Primitive Church* (1979) 26-28.

96. D. R. Schwartz, *Agrippa I* (1990) 122-24, argues against any connection between the persecution and the incipient Gentile mission; instead, he assumes the presence of purely political reasons. But the references adduced to Zealotist tendencies on the part of James the Zebedee and Peter (Mt. 16:17; Mk. 3:17; Lk. 9:54; Jn. 18:10) involve exclusively pre-Easter situations. Concerning Schwartz's assumption of Jewish-Christian unrest in A.D. 41 in Rome as the occasion for measures by Agrippa I, cf. §10.

in the metropolis Antioch on the Orontes. This designation may perhaps have been used by the Roman authorities for the first time in A.D. 36/37 at the occasion of the dispatch of Vitellius to Syria or a bit later (A.D. 39/40) as a result of the disturbances in Antioch. Prophetic oracles for an active mission to the Gentiles were apparently issued in Palestine as well in connection with the end of the rule of Caligula in January A.D. 41. Initial missionary attempts in the Jewish motherland as well as in its immediate environs may have been one motive prompting Herod Agrippa I to undertake persecutory measures at the beginning of his reign, probably in the year A.D. 41 or at the latest A.D. 42. The persecution, including even martyrdom, as well as the flight of leading members of the original church from the holy city, was perceived by many Palestinian Jewish-Christians (in analogy to the fate of the Hellenists) as a sign of the progression of salvation history: God really does want the mission to move out into the world of nations. The gradual path to an evangelization of Gentiles and especially the emergence of the Petrine-Palestinian mission out of a situation of persecution hindered any fundamental theological resolution of outstanding questions that might have met general approval, and this is one of the roots of the conflicts with which Paul found himself confronted.

§8

Famine and Apocalyptic Prophecy

8.1. Acts 11:27-28

After the founding of the church in Antioch by Jerusalem Hellenists (Acts 11:19-24) and Paul's move to this city (Acts 11:25f.), Luke adds yet another individual story bringing Barnabas and Paul into contact with the events in the holy city broadly portrayed in Acts 12: "(27) At that time prophets came down from Jerusalem to Antioch. (28) One of them named Agabus stood up and predicted by the Spirit that there would be a severe famine over all the empire;[1] and this took place during the reign of Claudius (λιμὸν μεγάλην μέλλειν ἔσεσθαι ἐφ' ὅλην τὴν οἰκουμένην, ἥτις ἐγένετο ἐπὶ Κλαυδίου)" (Acts 11:27f.). Afterward, the Antiochene Christians undertook a collection of money and sent it to the churches in Judea by Barnabas and Paul (Acts 11:29f.; 12:25). It is not yet our intention here to address the question of just how the collection journey portrayed by Luke is to be understood within the parameters of Paul's biography (§17.1), but rather only to determine the general chronological implications of this narrative, which are independent of any participation by the apostle.[2] It will thus suffice to refer to the virtually unanimous consensus of more recent commentaries that Luke owes to an older tradition at least Agabus' prediction of famine.[3]

---

1. Luke is thus using οἰκουμένη (cf. Lk. 2:1) according to the context (Acts 11:28b: mention of the emperor) and the otherwise attested hyperbolic manner of expression (cf. merely Rom. 10:18).

2. Several scholars assume that Luke has constructed an erroneous connection here. Cf. among others E. Haenchen, *Acts* (Eng. trans., 1971) 376f.; M. Hengel, *Zur urchristlichen Geschichtsschreibung* (²1984) 94; R. Pesch, *Die Apostelgeschichte* I (1986) 356. M. F. Baslez, *Saint Paul* (1991) 113-15, 337f., defends Paul's participation (A.D. 41/42).

3. H. Conzelmann, *Acts.* (Eng. trans. 1987) 90; E. Haenchen, *Acts* (Eng. trans., 1971) 375-77; I. H. Marshall, *The Acts of the Apostles* (1980) 203f.; A. Weiser, *Die Apostelgeschichte* II (1981) 275; J. Roloff, *Die Apostelgeschichte* (1981) 182; G. Schneider, *Die Apostelgeschichte* II (1982) 94; G. Schille, *Die Apostelgeschichte* (1983) 365-67;

We must still address the assertion, however, that the prophecy of Agabus belongs not in Antioch, but rather in Jerusalem. Arguments presented in support of this view include:[4] (1) Luke speaks of a group of prophets from the holy city. But itinerant prophets, according to the argument, always appeared only as individuals, not in groups, and for that reason the entire scene belongs in Jerusalem. But can we, given our narrow base of sources, so apodictically assert that an extant source thereby becomes worthless? Moreover, in Acts 13:1 Barnabas and Paul are identified as prophets, and then journey together as a missionary pair. The language of Acts 15:32 allows that one may also view the Jerusalem emissaries Judas and Silas as prophets.[5] (2) Reference to Acts 21:10 accompanies the objection that Agabus was not an itinerant prophet at all, but rather lived in Jerusalem. But this same passage also says that he "came down (κατῆλθεν)" from Judea (i.e., from the holy city) to Caesarea (cf. Acts 21:8). One must thus immediately eliminate two remarks that do not fit the picture. (3) Since the church in Antioch itself had several prophets in its ranks (Acts 13:1), it would not have needed commensurate reinforcement from Jerusalem. If one may judge from the analogy of charismatic groups today, prophets do not always do exactly what one expects them to do. If they are convinced that they possess a divinely inspired message, they are usually driven to deliver this message to other circles as well. If with R. Pesch one assumes the presence of a causal connection between prophecy and collection,[6] one has a plausible reason for Agabus' inclination to travel: with his prediction he did not merely want to provide information concerning the future, but also to issue an exhortation to support Jerusalem.

F. Mussner, *Apostelgeschichte* (1984) 72; D. J. Williams, *Acts* (1985) 194; G. A. Krodel, *Acts* (1986) 211; G. Lüdemann, *Das frühe Christentum nach den Traditionen der Apostelgeschichte* (1987) 143-45 (Eng. trans., *Early Christianity according to the Traditions in Acts* [1989]); C. K. Barrett, *The Acts of the Apostles* (1994) 559. One exception is W. Schmithals, *Die Apostelgeschichte* (1982) 113, who considers Luke's information here to be "artificially constructed" and influenced by the latter's "devotion to the poor" and his intention of bringing Paul into close contact with the original Jerusalem church. By contrast, H. Patsch, *ThZ* 28 (1972) 232, also considers it possible that a historical core can be found here.

4. Most completely in J. Roloff, *loc. cit.,* 181f.

5. Cf. E. E. Ellis, in *Prophecy and Hermeneutic* (1978) 131f., and J. Lindblom, *Gesichte und Offenbarungen* (1968) 179.

6. R. Pesch, *Die Apostelgeschichte* I (1986) 356, assumes that the connection between all the information in Acts 11:27-30; 12:25 derives from a pre-Lukan tradition.

8.2. Famine under Claudius

8.2.1. Definition of Famine in Antiquity

Especially in antiquity, periods of famine were characterized not so much by absolute lack of foodstuffs as by the inability of individual locales or social groups to make use of the food resources already available.[7] In Hellenistic-Roman antiquity, hunger was in fact primarily a problem of distribution and class. Anyone with access to sufficient financial resources almost always had access also to the available, albeit sparse, stores. In the case of famine, Josephus (*Ant.* iii.320) and Tacitus (*Ann.* xii.43) thus also provide concrete information concerning the price of grain. In times of distress, price speculation reached record levels (cf. Rev. 6:6), so that the authorities often had to intervene by confiscating grain stores.[8] One can render the expression λιμός in Acts 11:28 not only by "hunger, famine," but also by "dearth."[9] These circumstances are not addressed by the objection that in Luke's introduction of a worldwide famine, "Luke did not note the inconsistency that Antioch would also have been involved in such a famine."[10] Moreover, Acts speaks not of simultaneity, but rather of a prediction of future distress; and the original Jerusalem church, given its special situation (arrival of Galileans, partial communal circumstances, boycott by fellow Jewish citizens), was economically extremely vulnerable.[11] The rural churches in Judea, Galilee, and southern Syria similarly seem not to have had access to any great wealth. By contrast, from the very outset an extremely large church community apparently developed in Antioch, and it included members of the upper class as well (see p. 110 above). We hear that the Jewish community in Antioch was able to send quite expensive consecratory gifts to the temple (Josephus, *B.J.* vii.45). If the prophecy of Agabus really was supposed to constitute an exhortation to provide help, then Antioch was not the worst place to give his address.

---

7. So P. Garnsey, in *Trade and Famine in Classical Antiquity* (1983) 5, following A. Sen, *Poverty and Famines* (1981); and B. Winter in A1CS 2 (1994) 60-75.

8. Cf. M. Rostovtzeff, *Economic History of the Roman Empire* II ([2]1957) 599f., note 9. Whereas an export surplus was often the case with oil and wine, the emperors had to force the cultivation of grain. Cf. M. Rostovtzeff, *Gesellschaft und Wirtschaft im römischen Kaiserreich* I (1931) 85, 123-25, 165f., 277-79, note 9.

9. Cf. F. F. Bruce, *The Acts of the Apostles* ([2]1952) 239.

10. H. Conzelmann, *Die Apostelgeschichte* ([2]1972) 90. Cited in agreement by G. Lüdemann, *Paul: Apostle to the Gentiles* (1984) 11.

11. Cf. M. Hengel, *Property and Riches in the Early Church* (Eng. trans., 1974) 31-34; R. Riesner, *Formen gemeinsamen Lebens* ([2]1984) 30f. The economic circumstances in Jerusalem at that time were unstable in general. Cf. M. Goodman, *The Ruling Class of Judaea* (1987) 51-54.

Josephus' account of the circumstances during the visit of Queen Helena of Adiabene in Jerusalem shows the considerable extent to which access to greater financial resources could be of help in the case of famine in antiquity: "A famine did oppress them at that time, and many people died for want of money to procure the necessary food (καὶ πολλῶν ὑπ᾽ ἐνδείας ἀναλωμάτων φθειρομένων)" (Josephus, *Ant.* xx.51).

8.2.2. A Series of Local Famines

Considerable problems accompany any attempt to write a history of famines in the Roman world empire. Ancient authors did not mention crises in food provisioning only when they were genuinely catastrophic. "Famine" references also serve a variety of rhetorical purposes: they may function as premonitory signs to broad portions of the population, mark the beginning of important events, or illustrate the capabilities or weaknesses of rulers.[12] The one-sided nature of the literary sources can be balanced only in part by inscriptions and papyri. The most thorough historical portrayal of famines in the Roman empire is still a dissertation by K. S. Gapp (1934).[13] Although more recent studies do illuminate excellently the economic and political background of provisioning crises,[14] they provide no historical overview.[15] Hence it is not easy to evaluate with any historical acccuracy the empire-wide famine asserted in Acts 11:28.[16]

12. Cf. P. Garnsey, in *Trade and Famine in Classical Antiquity* (1983) 57.

13. *Famine in the Roman World from the Founding of Rome to the Time of Trajan* (1934). I would like to thank Professor James H. Charlesworth (Princeton) and his assistant, Loren Stukenbrock, for their cordial assistance in securing this work for me.

14. Cf. esp. G. E. Rickman, *The Corn Supply of Ancient Rome* (1980); P. Garnsey, *Famine and Food Supply in the Graeco-Roman World* (1988).

15. The closest to such an overview is R. MacMullen, *Enemies of the Roman Order* (1966) 249-54.

16. Cf. W. M. Ramsay, *Paulus in der Apostelgeschichte* (1898) 40-43; V. Weber, *Die Abfassung des Galaterbriefs* (1900) 371-74; *Die antiochenische Kollekte* (1917) 38-41; D. Plooij, *De Chronologie van het Leven van Paulus* (1919) 15-20; A. Wikenhauser, *Die Apostelgeschichte und ihr Geschichtswert* (1921) 407-9; T. Zahn, *Introduction to the New Testament* (Eng. trans., 1909) 3.130f., 458-63; J. Felten, *Neutestamentliche Zeitgeschichte* I (2/31925) 217f.; K. Lake, *BC* V (1933) 452-55; K. S. Gapp, *Famine in the Roman World* (1934) 87-96, 163-67; *HThR* 28 (1935) 258-65; F. F. Bruce, *The Acts of the Apostles* (²1952) 429f.; A. M. Tornos, *EstEccl* 33 (1959) 303-16; B. Rigaux, *The Letters of St. Paul* (Eng. trans., 1968) 73f.; J. Jeremias, in *Abba* (1966) 233-37; J. Dupont, *Études sur les Actes des Apôtres* (1967) 163-65; G. Ogg, *The Chronology of the Life of Paul* (1968) 49-55; J. J. Gunther, *Paul: Messenger and Exile* (1972) 37-42; Schuerer I, 457; A. Suhl, *Paulus und seine Briefe* (1975) 57-62; E. Haenchen, *Acts* (Eng. trans., 1971) 61-64; R. Pesch, *Simon-Petrus* (1980) 79; C. J. Hemer, *The Book of Acts* (1989) 164f.; B. W. Winter, *TynBul* 40 (1989) 88-91; B. Levick, *Claudius* (1990) 109; 218f., note 14.

For the reign of Claudius, the following famines are either securely attested or possible: (1) In the winter of A.D. 40/41, Rome experienced a scarcity of foodstufs (Dio Cassius, *Hist.* lix.17.2; cf. Suetonius, *Gaius* 39.1).[17] On the day Caligula died (24 January A.D. 41), allegedly only enough stores were available for six or seven days (Seneca, *Brev. vit.* xviii.5). (2) The crisis in food provisioning lasted at least into the second year of Claudius (A.D. 42/43) (Dio Cassius, *Hist.* lx.11.1-4; cf. Aurelius Victor, *De Caes.* iv.3). The account of Dio Cassius suggests that problems accompanied the production of grain in the main agricultural area of Egypt (see below).[18] (3) Judea was plagued by food problems for several years, probably between A.D. 44 and 49 (§8.2.4). (4) This crisis of provisions affected all of Syria beginning in the fourth year of Claudius (A.D. 44/45) (Orosius, *Adv. Pag.* vii.6.12). (5) From papyri found in Tebtunis (PMichigan 123, 127), K. S. Gapp[19] concluded that Egypt experienced famine in the years between A.D. 45 and 47 as a result of excessively high (cf. Pliny the Elder, *HN* v.10.58) or low water levels in the Nile,[20] a conclusion subsequently strengthened by additional papyrus-publications (PMichigan 238-40).[21] Harvest problems in Egypt of necessity had far-reaching effects, since this country was one of the most important grain exporters in the Mediterranean basin beginning with the period of the Ptolemies.[22] Failed harvests in Egypt during the time before Trajan threatened especially the provisioning of Rome (cf. Acts 27:6ff.) (Pliny the Younger, *Paneg.* 31).[23]

(6) K. S. Gapp suspected that Galba's campaign against the Moors in the year A.D. 45 might also have affected shipments from the other great grain export region, Mauretania.[24] (7) M. Rostovtzeff already considered the report of Eusebius (Eusebius, *Chron.* [ed. Helm 181]; cf. also George Syncellus, *Chronogr.* [ed. Dindorf I 332D-335D]) concerning a famine in Greece in the eighth or ninth year of Claudius (A.D. 48-50) to be supported by inscriptional evidence in Corinth,[25] at least generally as this applies to the reign of

17. Cf. K. S. Gapp, *Famine in the Roman World* (1934) 87-89; P. Garnsey, *Famine and Food Supply* (1980) 222f.

18. Cf. J. Mottershead, *Suetonius: Claudius* (1986) 73.

19. *HThR* 28 (1935) 238-40. Already suspected by T. Zahn, *Introduction to the New Testament* (Eng. trans., 1909) 3.130f.

20. Concerning the connection between the level of the Nile and famine in Hellenistic antiquity, cf. G. E. Rickman, *The Corn Supply of Rome* (1980) 113-18.

21. Cf. C. J. Hemer, *The Book of Acts* (1989) 165, note 10.

22. Cf. D. Rathbone, in P. Garnsey and C. R. Whittaker, *Trade and Famine* (1983) 50-53.

23. Concerning the particular provisioning problems of the imperial capital, cf. P. Garnsey and R. Saller, *The Roman Empire* (1984) 83-88.

24. *HThR* 28 (1935) 263.

25. *Corinth* VIII/2 (1931) nos. 83, 86.

Claudius.[26] A later source (George Syncellus, *Chronogr.* [ed. Dindorf I 630D]) mentions for this period the unusually high[27] grain price of forty-eight *sestertii.* A new study by B. M. Winter has considerably refined this picture.[28] The Corinthian citizen Dinippos is the only Corinthian known to us who occupied the office of *curator annonae* three times.[29] Taken in analogy to an inscription from Samos (*SEG* II 336), this suggests obstinate problems in food provisioning. Two separate crises in provisioning can be dated to the time of Claudius, namely in A.D. 51 and between the end of 52 and 54. Paul may be alluding to the latter in 1 Cor. 7:26 (§15.4.1).

(8) Tacitus (*Ann.* xii.43) attests an additional crisis in provisioning for Rome in the eleventh year of Claudius (A.D. 51) (see p. 187 below).[30] The dating of the tenth year by Orosius (*Adv. Pag.* vii.6.17) deviates only slightly, while the textual tradition in the chronicle of Eusebius varies between the ninth and tenth year (*Chron.* [ed. Helm 181]). Hence in her biography of Claudius, B. Levick argues that the problems in provisioning possibly lasted from A.D. 49 to 51.[31] (9) One can also mention in this context the problems in provisioning the military in Armenia in the year A.D. 51 (Tacitus, *Ann.* xii.50.3). (10) There was speculation regarding the price of grain at this time in Phrygian Kibyra.[32] (11) If the *Epitome* of Zonaras is correctly citing Dio Cassius, then in A.D. 53 Agrippina exploited a scarcity of bread in Rome to incite unrest against Claudius (Dio Cassius, *Hist.* lx.33.10).[33] (12) A metrical inscription (*CIG* I 3973) from Apollonia in Galatia, which W. M. Ramsay dates in the year A.D. 57,[34] mentions a famine in Asia Minor in the not too distant past, though today this is as a rule dated to the time of Marcus Aurelius (A.D. 161-80).[35] Because of its universal terminology (κόσμον ἐπέχεσθε πάντα), however, this inscription does retain interest as a parallel to Luke's own manner of expression. Several other crises in food provisioning can as yet be dated only generally during the first century A.D.[36]

26. *Economic History of the Roman Empire* II (²1957) 599.

27. Cf. G. E. Rickmann, *The Corn Supply of Ancient Rome* (1980) 148f.

28. *TynBul* 40 (1989) 86-106. Cf. earlier J. Wiseman, *ANRW* II 7.1 (1979) 505.

29. *Corinth* VIII/2 (1931) nos. 86-90; VIII/3 (1966) nos. 158-63.

30. Cf. K. S. Gapp, *Famine in the Roman World* (1934) 94-96.

31. *Claudius* (1990) 219, note 14.

32. Cf. M. Rostovtzeff, *Gesellschaft und Wirtschaft im Römischen Kaiserreich* II (1931) 322f., note 20.

33. J. Mottershead, *Suetonius: Claudius* (1986) 74, argues the reference is rather to the famine of A.D. 51, and that the Epitomator has made a mistake in this instance.

34. *Studia Oxonensia* 4 (1896) 52ff. (*non vidi*).

35. Cf. R. MacMullen, *Enemies of the Roman Order* (1966) 252.

36. So for Thuburnica/North Africa (*CIL* VIII 25703f.), Perga (*IGRR* III 796), and Teus in Asia Minor (*IGRR* IV 1572).

8.2.3. Famine throughout the Empire?

If one understands here a famine that in the same year afflicted every part of the *imperium Romanum,* then Luke's assertion is without a doubt exaggerated.[37] It is an altogether different question, however, whether the Jewish-Christian contemporaries, the author as well as the readers of Acts, could not view the series of local famines during the reign of Claudius as a fulfillment of the prophecy of Agabus. In any event, Luke himself was convinced of this; otherwise he would not have appropriated or written the particular remark confirming fulfillment. Regardless of whether one follows the usual dating of his work (*ca.* A.D. 80) or an earlier one (before A.D. 70), his readers still included a sufficient number of eyewitnesses from the time of Claudius. K. S. Gapp, like E. Meyer before him[38] and based on his own studies of famines in antiquity, even defended the manner of expression of the *auctor ad Theophilum* as being essentially on the mark.[39] Gapp figured that the problems in the main agricultural regions of Egypt and North Africa after A.D. 45, not least because of speculation, resulted in a general rise in the price of grain in both the East and the West, and subsequently in widespread crises in food provisioning.

At any rate, Claudius himself took these threats to the stability of his own rule quite seriously. Coins in Rome from the first and second years of his reign *(ceres Augusta)* thematize the provisioning of grain (*BMC* I, nos. 183f., 191).[40] Famine at the beginning of his reign prompted him to plan the new provisioning harbor of Ostia (Dio Cassius, *Hist.* lx.11.3), and in other ways, too, the emperor implemented energetic measures for securing the provisioning of Rome (Suetonius, *Claudius* 18-19). The *communis opinio* of earlier scholarship[41] remains essentially correct,[42] even if the objection of G. E. Rickmann[43] proves to be accurate that Claudius did not

37. So also the conclusion of P. Garnsey, *Famine and Food Supply* (1988) 21.

38. *Ursprünge und Anfänge des Christentums* III (1923) 165f. G. Lüdemann, *Das frühe Christentum nach den Traditionen der Apostelgeschichte* (1987) 141 (with a minimal list): "Meyer . . . peculiarly considers the aforementioned famines to be a confirmation of Luke's assertions." Cf. in contrast the much more positive remarks of the Claudius-biographer B. Levick, *Claudius* (1990) 74, 109, 179, and the judgment of the Jewish scholar D. R. Schwartz, in *Studies in the Jewish Background of Christianity* (1992) 237: "Various literary and archaeological data from the Mediterranean basin testify to a general famine in the late forties, until as late as 51 C.E.."

39. *HThR* 28 (1935) 261-63. Similarly B. W. Winter, *TynBul* 40 (1989) 89f.

40. Cf. G. E. Rickman, *The Corn Supply of Ancient Rome* (1980) 260.

41. A good summary can be found in T. F. Carney, *Festschrift H. L. Gonin* (1971) 39-57.

42. So also, e.g., M. Le Glay, *MBib* 51 (1987) 11.

43. *The Corn Supply of Ancient Rome* (1980) 73-79.

transfer the provisioning of grain from the *aerarium* to the *fiscus*.[44] Claudius' measures were apparently quite successful, at least later, since after his reign and except for Nero's later period (Suetonius, *Nero* 45.1; cf. Dio Cassius, *Hist.* lxii.18.5)[45] we hear nothing of famine in the imperial capital for three hundred years.[46] The end of Claudius' reign, to be sure, was overshadowed yet one more time by the serious crisis in food provisioning of A.D. (49? until) 51 (see p. 131 above), a crisis which might have been a late result of the provisioning crisis that began spreading from Egypt in A.D. 45.[47] B. Levick considers it possible that the clear increase in festivals and circus events offered in Rome after A.D. 48 was intended to distract the population from the continuing provisioning constrictions.[48] The significance this crisis in provisioning had for the last years of Claudius is shown by the fact that the granting of the *imperium* for Nero (A.D. 53) might be related to it (Dio Cassius, *Hist.* lxi.33.10 [Zonaras]). Thus the rule of the emperor was remembered as an uninterrupted time of failed harvests (*assiduae sterilitates,* Suetonius, *Claudius* 18.2). If one is inclined to criticize Luke for his manner of expression (Acts 11:28), then one can hardly criticize Suetonius any less.

8.2.4. The Famine in Judea

In the dating of this famine by Josephus, manuscript evidence suggests reading the plural ἐπὶ τούτοις rather than the singular ἐπὶ τούτου, which the *Epitome* attests exclusively as *lectio facilior* (Josephus, *Ant.* xx.101).[49] One can hardly refer this to anything other than the time of the two procurators[50] Cuspius Fadus (A.D. 44-?46) and Tiberius Alexander (A.D. ?46-48),[51] just as the Old Latin tradition *(horum temporibus)* in fact does. With this remark, Josephus refers back to the time in which Queen Helena of Adiabene provided support for the starving Jerusalemites (Josephus, *Ant.* xx.51-53). This action, however, had already begun under Fadus (cf. Josephus, *Ant.* xx.2), and the famine might thus have begun already in A.D. 44, the year Herod

---

44. Cf. also P. Garnsey, *Famine and Food Supply* (1988) 230-34.
45. Cf. M. Hengel, in H. Cancik, *Markus-Philologie* (1984) 34, note 129.
46. Cf. R. MacMullen, *Enemies of the Roman Order* (1966) 250f.
47. Cf. C. J. Hemer, *The Book of Acts* (1989) 165.
48. *Claudius* (1990) 73f.
49. Cf. K. Lake, *BC* V (1933) 454; A. M. Tornos, *EstEccl* 33 (1959) 307; B. Rigaux, *The Letters of St. Paul* (Eng. trans., 1968) 207, note 22.
50. Concerning the problems of this dating, cf. §6.3.2.
51. Cf. Schuerer I, 457, note 8. A. Suhl, *Paulus und seine Briefe* (1975) 60, justifiably objects to the translation of ἐπὶ τούτοις as "then, next" by E. Haenchen, *Acts* (Eng. trans., 1971) 62f., note 6.

Agrippa I died.[52] Indeed, Eusebius (*Chron.* [ed. Helm 181]) and Orosius (*Adv. Pag.* vii.6.12)[53] expressly mention the fourth year of Claudius (A.D. 44/45) as the beginning of the famine. Furthermore, the development of relationships between the kingdom Adiabene, the Parthians, and the Roman empire seems to suggest that the visit of Queen Helena (Josephus, *Ant.* xx.51-53) is to be dated in A.D. 44.[54] If the queen did indeed set out this early, it would be easier to understand how she was still able to purchase grain in Alexandria for the inhabitants of Jerusalem (Josephus, *Ant.* xx.51) before the onset of the poor harvest there (see p. 131 above), though the possibility cannot be excluded that even after a poor harvest in Egypt, Helena was still able to purchase grain if she was able to pay the inflated prices to the wholesalers.[55]

A rabbinic remark regarding Rabbi Eleazar Ben Zadok seems to assume that the famine lasted several years (*b. Yebam.* 15b).[56] Josephus, too, suggests that the crisis in provisioning, during which many people died (Josephus, *Ant.* xx.51), continued in Judea even beyond A.D. 48.[57] That is, in a different passage (Josephus, *Ant.* iii.320) the Jewish historian refers to a famine during the time of Emperor Claudius and the high priest Ishmael ben Phiabi (Κλαυδίου Ῥωμαίων ἄρχοντος Ἰσμαήλου δὲ παρ' ἡμῖν ἀρχιερέως ὄντος, καὶ λιμοῦ τὴν χώραν ἡμῶν καταλαβόντος). If D. R. Schwartz[58] has indeed solved

52. So also B. Levick, *Claudius* (1990) 219, note 14. V. Weber, *Die Abfassung des Galaterbriefs* (1900) 377, objected against this early a dating that, according to Acts 12:20, immediately before the death of the ruler emissaries from Tyre and Sidon turned to Agrippa I in order to secure grain provisioning from his region (cf. 1 Kgs. 5:9, 11; Ezk. 27:17; Josephus, *Ant.* xiv.203): "Hence at that time, A.D. 44, there were still no failed harvests in Palestine." But if one considers the character of ancient famines (§8.2.1), then this remark can also suggest that signs of a crisis in provisioning had already begun manifesting themselves. The wealthy harbor cities were in a position to pay inflated prices even in the case of failed harvests in the neighboring kingdom of Agrippa.

53. J. Wellhausen, *Kritische Analyse der Apostelgeschichte* (1914) 21f., argued that Orosius deduced this date from Acts. However, this seems less likely given the fact that in the same context, the church historian mentions other dates that he could not possibly have derived from Acts. Cf. §10.4.2.

54. The winter of A.D. 43/44 is the most probable date for the attempt of the Parthian king Vardanes to win over Izates of Adiabene for a coalition against Rome. At that time, his mother Helena had already set out for Jerusalem (Josephus, *Ant.* xx.69-71). These chronological considerations have not yet been discussed seriously because they were presented in a Spanish publication. J. J. Gunther, *Paul: Messenger and Exile* (1972) 37-39, however, agrees with A. M. Tornos, *EstEccl* 33 (1959) 311-14.

55. Cf. K. S. Gapp, *HThR* 28 (1935) 262f.

56. Cf. A. Schlatter, *Synagoge und Kirche bis zum Barkochba-Aufstand* (1966) 80f.

57. Concerning the great impression these events had on the historian, cf. T. Rajak, *Josephus* (1983) 123-25.

58. In *Studies in the Jewish Background of Christianity* (1992) 218-39 (esp. 237f.).

the riddle of this particular high priest's tenure, namely, that Ishmael assumed office in A.D. 49, then the famine had not yet ended at that time either. J. Jeremias[59] already referred earlier to the significance the Sabbatical Year at that time had in further exacerbating the conditions of food provisioning, though he still advocated the old dating of A.D. 47/48 instead of A.D. 48/49.[60] The effects of the Sabbatical Year would not have been overcome until the new harvest was gathered in the spring of A.D. 50,[61] though one must not assume that the years between A.D. 44 and 49 represent years of consistently or equally severe famine. The situation could, however, have been unstable as a result of overpopulation.[62] The strongest attestations for a time of severe stress in Judea point to the years A.D. 44-46.

J. Jeremias adduced evidence only for famine around the year A.D. 48, and for that reason assumed that Luke incorrectly repeated Paul and Barnabas' journey to the Apostolic Council (A.D. 48/49), placing it before this assembly and identifying it as a collection journey, since he — Luke — had access to two different reports from different sources.[63] There are, however, no compelling chronological reasons for this hypothesis; indications of a Palestinian famine between A.D. 44 and 46 suggest rather that the Lukan account of an Antiochene collection for Jerusalem around the death of Agrippa in some way goes back to reliable information.[64]

8.3. Chronological Implications

8.3.1. The Prophecy of Agabus

According to the outline of Acts, this particular prophecy came before the death of Herod Agrippa I (§9.2.2) in the year A.D. 44. By contrast, it is uncertain whether Luke intends to say here that the Jerusalem prophets appeared publicly in the city only after Paul's own arrival in Antioch (Acts 11:25f.). The temporal reference ἐν ταύταις δὲ ταῖς ἡμέραις is extremely general (Acts 11:27), and Luke can actually only now mention the prophecy so as to provide a transition to the collection journey to Jerusalem (Acts 11:29;

59. In *Abba* (1966) 233-35.
60. Cf. B. Z. Wacholder, *HUCA* 44 (1973) 191.
61. Concerning the climatic conditions prompting poor harvests (esp. insufficient rainfall during the winter), cf. G. Dalman, *Arbeit und Sitte in Palästina* I/1 (1928) 194-99.
62. G. Theissen refers to this factor in *Studien zur Soziologie des Urchristentums* (²1983) 138. Cf. also M. Goodman, *The Ruling Class of Judaea* (1987) 61f.
63. In *Abba* (1966) 235-37.
64. Contra the thesis of J. Jeremias, cf. also A. Suhl, *Paulus und seine Briefe* (1975) 59-62; A. Schmidt, *ZNW* 81 (1990) 126.

12:25).[65] Ever since J. A. Bengel,[66] exegetes have repeatedly concluded from the identifying remark "that took place during the reign of Claudius" (Acts 11:28b) that the prophecy of Agabus was delivered already under his predecessor.[67] The last two years of Caligula (A.D. 40-41) were a time of apocalyptic distress for both Jews and Jewish-Christians because of his plans to erect his own statue in the temple (§7.1.4). The cessation of agriculture by the excited Jewish population of Palestine in the year A.D. 40 (Josephus, *B.J.* ii.200/*Ant.* xviii.272) threatened food provisioning. Unfortunately, we do not know when during the reign of Claudius that particular earthquake occurred in Antioch that affected even cities in Asia Minor (Malalas 246.9-19)[68] and could have been interpreted in connection with famine as a portent of the end (cf. Mt. 24:7/Mk. 13:8/Lk. 21:11). In any event, the Sabbatical Year commencing in A.D. 41/42[69] offered occasion enough to anticipate eschatological convulsions. The question is legitimate whether Jewish disturbances in Antioch in the third year of Caligula (A.D. 39/40) (Malalas 244.15–246.2) also represented an anticipation of heightened apocalyptic tension (see pp. 113f. above). The prediction of worldwide famine seems especially comprehensible at this time.[70]

8.3.2. The Antiochene Collection for Jerusalem

The willingness of the Antiochene church to heed the prophetic word and to prepare financial help for the Jerusalem Christians might have been strengthened by reports of the difficulties Rome itself was experiencing in providing food (and by reports of agricultural problems in Egypt) in the years A.D. 41-42 (see p. 129 above). We do not know whether the faith of the Antiochenes extended so far that they sent the gifts to the holy city even before the effects of the distress were felt (after A.D. 44). Reference to the elders (πρεσβύτεροι) as recipients of the collection (Acts 11:30) suggests that this occurred during the period after the execution of James the son of Zebedee and after Peter's flight from Jerusalem, when the leadership of the church there passed to a committee of elders under the leadership of James the brother of Jesus,[71] though this does admittedly provide only an approximate dating to the period

65. Cf. T. Zahn, *Introduction to the New Testament* (Eng. trans., 1909) 460f.

66. *Ordo temporum* (²1770) 247.

67. Cf. E. Preuschen *Die Apostelgeschichte* (1912) 74; F. J. Badcock, *The Pauline Epistles* (1937) 16; W. L. Knox, *The Acts of the Apostles* (1948) 35; K. F. Nickle, *The Collection* (1966) 25; G. Schneider, *Die Apostelgeschichte* II (1982) 95.

68. Cf. G. Downey, *A History of Antioch* (1961) 196.

69. Cf. B. Z. Wacholder, *HUCA* 44 (1973) 190.

70. B. Z. Wacholder, *HUCA* 46 (1975) 216, sees the apocalyptic context, but assumes the reference is to the Sabbatical Year A.D. 48/49.

71. Cf. R. Pesch, *Simon-Petrus* (1980) 71-77.

after A.D. 41/42 (§7.2.1). We can probably not improve on Luke's own vague remark that the collection took place around the time (κατ' ἐκεῖνον δὲ τὸν καιρόν) of the persecution of the primitive church by Herod Agrippa I and of the latter's death. Given the dating of the Judean famine (§8.2.4), however, the last conceivable year seems to be A.D. 45.

§9

The Cypriot Proconsul Sergius Paullus

9.1. Acts 13:6-12

At the beginning of the first missionary journey of Barnabas and Paul, Luke presents the encounter between the two missionaries and the Cypriot proconsul Sergius Paulus (after the Latin more correctly: Paullus). Acts (Acts 13:7, 8, 12) accurately gives him the title of proconsul (ἀνθύπατος), for since 22 B.C., Cyprus was a senatorial province. Since Sergius Paullus allowed a Jewish magician to practice at his court (Acts 13:7), this proconsul apparently belonged to the wide and open circle of sympathizers attracted by Judaism (§7.1.1). An interesting parallel is found in Josephus' account according to which a Jewish magician from Cyprus by the name of Atomos was active in the surroundings of the procurator Felix (Josephus, *Ant.* xx.142).[1] In his own more recent commentary on Acts, R. Pesch enumerates a number of reasons why this report may be assumed to derive from what is basically an accurate tradition.[2] By contrast, his assertion that "the name of this proconsul . . . is probably inscriptionally attested," is presented without any more extensive proof.[3] Other commentaries[4] similarly deal

---

1. Although T. Zahn, *NKZ* 15 (1904) 195-200, even wanted to identify the two, his assumption that the alternative name attributed to Bar Jesus was actually Ἕτοιμος (cf. Acts 13:8D) contradicts the textual evidence. Cf. B. M. Metzger, *A Textual Commentary of the Greek New Testament* (²1975) 402f. Neither is the textual tradition of the name in Josephus without its own problems (ed. L. H. Feldman, x.76). One quite plausible solution is to understand Ἐλύμας as the Grecized rendering of the Aramaic חַלְמָא, "dreamer, magician (Acts 13:8: μάγος)." Cf. L. Yaure, *JBL* 79 (1960) 297-314. R. Pesch, *Die Apostelgeschichte* II (1986) 24: "The explanation (8b) thus asserts that 'Elymas' is to be translated by 'the magician' (and not 'Bar-Jesus' by 'Elymas,' which would be meaningless)."

2. *Die Apostelgeschichte* II (1986) 20-26.

3. *Ibid.*, 24.

4. So, e.g., G. Schille, *Die Apostelgeschichte* (1983) 287f. The source of his epigraphic information is still D. G. Hogarth, *Devia Cypria* (1889) 114! A. Weiser, *Die Apostelgeschichte* II (1985) 316, similarly relies on outdated material.

somewhat too hastily with this complicated question.[5] Since Luke mentions only the proconsul's *nomen gentile* and *cognomen,* but not the *praenomen* as well, any identification from outside the New Testament evidence itself is made difficult from the very outset. Three inscriptions have been associated with Sergius Paullus.

9.2. Extrabiblical Evidence for Sergius Paullus?

9.2.1. An Inscription from Soloi in North Cyprus

This Greek inscription (*IGRR* III, 930) offers the following dating (albeit appended at a later time): ΕΠΙ ΠΑΥΛΟΥ [ΑΝΘΥ]ΠΑΤΟΥ (lines 9f.), and in the original text an obscure numerical sign (line 7). D. G. Hogarth, who was the first to publish the inscription in full, read this as "thirteen,"[6] T. B. Mitford later as "ten."[7] Assuming a dating of the inscription under Claudius, one would thus arrive at the years A.D. 50 or 53. Because the chronological implications of the Gallio-inscription require us to date Paul's arrival in Corinth within the time frame of Acts in A.D. 50 at the latest (§11), a serious problem in dating would arise here. It is thus somewhat puzzling that according to M. F. Unger the inscription is to be associated "without any reasonable doubt" with the New Testament Sergius, offering thus a brilliant confirmation of Luke's own historical accuracy, and this is even more puzzling considering that Unger himself dates the inscription in A.D. 52/53.[8] R. Jewett's own dating of Sergius Paullus peculiarly also adduces only the Soloi-inscription.[9] This problem has been resolved, however, insofar as the inscription itself must be dated much later than the time of Paul. After a new reading, T. B. Mitford[10] identified in line 6 of the inscription (ΔΕΚΑΠΡΩΤΕ[Υ]Σ[ΑΣ]) the office of the δεκάπρωτος, one known only since Hadrian, and thus dated the proconsul Paulus conjecturally in A.D. 126.[11]

---

5. Cf. esp. K. Lake, *BC* V (1933) 455-59; B. Van Elderen, in *Festschrift F. F. Bruce* (1970) 151-56; J. J. Hughes, *ISBE* III (1986) 729f.; C. J. Hemer, *The Book of Acts* (1989) 109, 166f.; R. Riesner, *GBL* III (1989) 1431; F. F. Bruce, *The Acts of the Apostles* (³1990) 297; C. Breytenbach, *Paulus und Barnabas in Galatien* (1996) 180-87. Helga Botermann, professor of ancient history at the University of Göttingen, is preparing a very important prosopographical study on the Sergeii Paulli.

6. *Devia Cypria* (1889) 114.

7. *ABSA* 42 (1947) 203.

8. *Archaeology and the New Testament* (1962) 185f.

9. *A Chronology of Paul's Life* (1979) 36.

10. *ABSA* 42 (1947) 202.

11. *ANRW* II 7.2 (1980) 1302f., note 62. Cf. already T. B. Mitford, *ABSA* 42 (1947) 205f.

9.2.2. An Inscription from Kytheria in Cyprus

This inscription (*IGRR* III, 935) contains an imperial decree concerning sacrificial regulations and derives according to paleographical evidence from the first century A.D.[12] Although the dating at the end of the inscription is unfortunately only fragmentary, it does point clearly to an emperor in the Julio-Claudian family. For a long time, the last three lines were reconstructed as follows (*SEG* 20 [1964] 302.9-11):

9 . . . ΚΛΑΥΔ]ΙΟΥ ΚΑΙΣΑΡΟΣ ΣΕΒΑΣΤΟΥ ΚΑΙ
10 [— ΕΠΙ Κ]ΟΙΝΤΟΥ ΣΕΡΓ
11 [ΙΟΥ ΠΑΥΛΟΥ ΑΝΘΥΠΑΤΟΥ —]

A whole series of scholars was thus more or less strongly inclined to identify this Quintus Sergius with the Sergius Paulus of Acts.[13] According to a new decipherment of the inscription (a fragmentary A instead of Δ) by T. B. Mitford, however, the emperor's name would have to be read as Γ]αίου and not Κλαυ]δίου.[14] The reference would then be to an official from the reign of Caligula between A.D. 37 and 41 whose *cognomen* has not been preserved and must be surmised (see p. 140). To be sure, this particular correction can only be tested against the original.

9.2.3. An Inscription from Rome

An obelisk *(cippus urbanus)* mentions as one of the five Curators of the Tiber *(curatores riparum et alvei Tiberis)* under Claudius (A.D. 41-54) one Lucius Sergius Paullus (*CIL* VI 31545, line 3 = *ILS* 5926). Unfortunately, the inscription does not identify the year of his term of office. Because the emperor does not bear the title of the *censor,* E. Groag concluded a dating prior to the year A.D. 47.[15] Several factors still suggest that at this time Claudius did take over the office of censor (§6.4.1), though the inscription's silence in this regard might also be accidental. Since in any event the *nomen gentile* and the *cognomen* fit, this Curator is identified by some as the person mentioned in the New Testament; many earlier scholars accepted this iden-

---

12. Cf. B. Van Elderen, in *Festschrift F. F. Bruce* (1970) 155.
13. Completely persuaded scholars include E. Gabba, *Iscrizione Greche e Latine* (1958) 71-73; H. Halfmann, *Die Senatoren aus dem östlichen Teil des Imperium Romanum* (1979) 101f., in *Tituli* 5 (1982) 645 (but see n. 17 below). More cautious are B. Van Elderen, *Festschrift F. F. Bruce* (1970) 155f.; F. F. Bruce, *The Acts of the Apostles* ([3]1990) 297; T. W. Martin, *ABD* V (1992) 205 (on the whole extremely unsatisfactory).
14. *ANRW* II 7.2 (1980) 1300, note 54.
15. *PRE* II/4 (1923) 1717.

tification,[16] and it is still considered a possibility by several contemporary scholars.[17] The position of the name on the stone suggests that L. Sergius Paullus was at that time probably a member of the praetorian rank,[18] of which there were about a hundred.[19] Since Sergius Paullus is an extremely rare name, the probability of the identification is significantly increased. The Sergii originated in Italy and went as colonists to Asia Minor (see pp. 275-76). Possibly already under Tiberius they came from the equestrian rank to the senate.[20]

T. B. Mitford, in his reconstructed list of Cypriot proconsuls,[21] also takes as his point of departure this identification of the Roman Curator of the Tiber and the Sergius Paul(l)us of Acts, although because Luke did not mention the *praenomen,* and because the inscription itself offers no more specific dating, absolute certainty cannot be attained. There is, however, another consideration militating in favor of this identification: Whereas one can only conjecture that Quintus Sergius (Paullus) is referring to a brother of Lucius Sergius Paullus,[22] we can identify (family tree of the *gens Sergia* in Illustration 1 [p. 416]) a descendant, probably a grandson, L. Sergius L. f. Paullus, through an inscription from Pisidian Antioch.[23] The Sergii owned large landed estates in the province Galatia, and this connection may help explain why the apostle Paul went directly from Cyprus to Galatia (§14.5.2).

We are not on solid ground with other reconstructions. W. M. Ramsay had assumed that Christian influence came into the family of the Sergii through the Cypriot proconsul Lucius Sergius Paullus, who had been impressed by the apostle, and through the further activity of the missionaries in Galatia.[24] Ramsay found little support,[25] and even fairly conservative exegetes rejected

16. Considered self-evident by, e.g., P. von Rohden and H. Dessau, *Prosopographia Imperii Romani (Saec. I.II.III.)* III (1898) 221, and similarly, e.g., T. Mommsen, *ZNW* 2 (1901) 83, note 3; T. Zahn, *NKZ* 15 (1904) 190; E. Groag, *PRE* II 4 (1923) 1715-18.

17. E.g., K. Lake, *BC* V (1933) 458; F. F. Bruce, *The Acts of the Apostles* (²1952) 256; G. Winkler, *KP* V (1975) 137; H. Halfmann, in *Tituli* 5 (1982) 649 [self-correction!]; J. Devreker, *Festschrift G. Sanders* (1991) 109f.; S. Mitchell, *Anatolia* II (1993) 7; H. Botermann, "Die Sergii Paulli und das Christentum" (forthcoming).

18. Cf. T. Mommsen, *ZNW* 2 (1901) 83, note 3.

19. Cf. F. Jacques, in *Tituli* 4 (1982) 137ff.

20. Cf. H. Halfmann, in *Tituli* 5 (1982) 606.

21. *ANRW* II 7.2 (1980) 1301 (no. 20).

22. Cf. H. Halfmann, *Die Senatoren aus dem östlichen Teil des Imperium Romanum* (1979) 101f.

23. Cf. J. Devreker, *Festschrift G. Sanders* (1991) 110-19, and B. M. Levick, *Roman Colonies in Southern Roman Asia Minor* (1967) 112; S. Mitchell, *ANRW* II 7.2 (1980) 1074.

24. *ET* 29 (1917/18) 324-28; *The Bearing of Recent Discovery* (⁴1920) 150-72.

25. So, e.g., in E. C. Hudson, *JNES* 15 (1956) 103-7.

his theses.[26] Indeed, much was based on speculation, for example, the reflections concerning Christianity of Sergia L. f. Paulla, the granddaughter of the proconsul, who married the consul of A.D. 90, C. Caristanius Fronto, and of her eldest son. More recently, Italian scholars have asserted that a *collegium* attested in twenty-three Roman inscriptions,[27] one usually appearing as *collegium quod est in domo Sergiae Paullinae* (*CIL* VI 9148f., 10260-10264), actually represents a Christian house church[28] whose founder is named L. Sergius L. f. Paullus. This grandson of the Cypriot proconsul is probably not identical with the Lucius Sergius Paullus of a Roman founder's inscription (*CIL* VI 253),[29] who was presumably consul in the year A.D. 72 (or 78).[30] Sergia Paullina, who was married to the consul of the year A.D. 112, Cornelius Severus, carried on the *collegium*. A daughter from this marriage herself married M. Acilius Glabrio, the consul of the year A.D. 124 and son of that Acilius Glabrio who was executed under Domitian perhaps because of Christian inclinations (cf. Dio Cassius, *Hist.* lxvii.14.1-3).[31] Although other Italian scholars have opposed this interpretation[32] M. Sordi has defended it anew.[33]

9.2.4. Mentioned in Pliny the Elder?

The view that the Cypriot consul is also mentioned twice by Pliny the Elder in the table of contents to Books ii and xviii of his *Historia Naturalis* was earlier advocated not only by a conservative such as J. B. Lightfoot,[34] but also by scholars such as A. Hausrath[35] and C. Clemen.[36] Following

26. Cf. B. Van Elderen, in *Festschrift F. F. Bruce* (1970) 153f.

27. An overview of the material can be found in M. Bonfioli and S. Panciera, *RPARA* 44 (1971/72) 186-99; 45 (1972/73) 133-38.

28. M. Sordi and M. L. Cavigiolo, *RSCI* 25 (1971) 269-374.

29. Cf. J. Devreker, *Festschrift G. Sanders* (1991) 112-19 (see also SEG 41 [1991] 1822).

30. Different views are taken in R. Syme, in *Roman Papers* III (1984) 1328, note 95; V (1988) 473, note 189; 551, note 26; 677, note 37; and S. Mitchell, *Anatolia* II (1993) 6 [identical with the Cyriote proconsul]; E. Groag, *PRE* II 4 (1923) 171f. [identical with his presumed son, L. Sergius L. f. Paullus]; H. Halfmann, *Die Senatoren aus dem östlichen Teil des Imperium Romanum* (1979) 163f. [identical with a proconsul of A.D. 168, but the inscription is clearly Flavian].

31. Cf. M. Sordi, *The Christians and the Roman Empire* (1986) 44-50, 185f., 189. Contra any connection between the Acilii and Christianity, cf. M. Stern, *Greek and Latin Authors on Jews and Judaism* II (1980) 380-84.

32. M. Bonfioli and S. Panciera, *RPARA* 44 (1971/72) 185-201; 45 (1972/73) 138.

33. *RIL.L* 113 (1979) 14-20; *The Christians and the Roman Empire* (1986) 185f.

34. *Essays on the Work Entitled Supernatural Religion* (1889) 295.

35. *Neutestamentliche Zeitgeschichte* II (1872) 525.

36. *Paulus* I (1904) 221.

K. Lake's[37] treatment of the question, however, this conjecture has generally
been viewed as disproved.[38] Lake did not, however, address the essentially
expanded and revised form of the hypothesis as presented by T. Zahn.[39] Above
all, Lake has inaccurately rendered the text-critical evidence regarding the
two passages.[40] The manuscript tradition of the table of contents to Pliny the
Elder, *HN* ii, by no means unanimously attests Sergius Plautus, whom one
might identify with the well-known Stoic philosopher Lucius Sergius Plautus.[41] As shown by the critical apparatus in the edition of D. Detlefsen,[42]
which Lake mentions (!), most of the manuscripts read *Platone,* and only a
single emendation reads *Plauto,* the latter of which apparently represents an
emendation of the meaningless Plato. Contrary to Lake's assertion, the textual
tradition of the table of contents to Pliny the Elder, *HN* xviii, is not split
between Sergius Plautus and Sergius Paulus, but rather unanimously attests
the latter (ed. Detlefsen I, 42, line 37), and it seems at least possible to read
this name as a conjecture in the first passage as well.[43]

Beyond this text-critical reconstruction, a compositional consideration
also supports the assumption that Pliny is indeed referring to the Cypriot
proconsul Sergius Paullus. The two books in question here variously also
contain interesting information about Cyprus (esp. Pliny the Elder, *HN* ii.210;
xviii.68), concerning which Zahn remarks that "since Pliny consistently lists
the writers in the same order in these registers in which he treats of the excerpts
from them, one expects something of Sergius toward the end of the second
book and in an earlier part of the eighteenth book. This does indeed correspond
to the passages occupied by the aforementioned remarks about Cyprus."[44]
Although the identification of the source of Pliny with the Sergius Paul(l)us
of Acts does not possess as high a degree of probability as Zahn believes, it
does seem to remain a possibility, though we still do not by this means acquire
any new fixed chronological point.

37. *BC* V (1933) 457f.
38. One exception is M. F. Unger, *Archaeology of the New Testament* (1962) 186, albeit
not on the basis of any independent investigation into the question. On the whole, M. F. Unger's
work is extremely limited in its familiarity with the more recent discussion since W. M. Ramsay.
39. *NKZ* 15 (1904) 190-92.
40. *BC* V (1933) 458.
41. Cf. V. Fadinger, *KP* V (1975) 137.
42. *C. Plinii Secundi Naturalis Historia* I (1866) 22, note 9.
43. So already D. Detlefsen, *ibid.,* 22, line 9, and H. Rackham, *Pliny: Natural
History* I ([2]1949) 28. Cf. further T. Zahn, *NKZ* 15 (1904) 190f.
44. *NKZ* 15 (1904) 191f.

9.2.5. Cypriot Proconsuls under Claudius

Neither are we able to circumscribe more closely the time in office of the Sergius Paul(l)us of Acts by referring to the identifiable years of service of other Cypriot proconsuls. One coin (*BMC Cyprus* no. 17 [CXXI]) and one inscription (*SEG* VI 834) allow us to determine with certainty only the time in office of T. Cominius Proculus in the years A.D. 43/44.[45] If J. Devreker's reading[46] of an inscription from Paphos (*SEG* XVIII 587, line 4: Κλαυδ]ίου Καίσαρος Σεβαστοῦ instead of Γα]ίου Κ.Σ.) is correct, then with T. Clodius Eprius Marcellus we would know one further Cypriot proconsul under Claudius, albeit without being able to specify exactly when he held office.[47] By contrast, T. B. Mitford stands by his earlier restitution and dates the proconsulship of Marcellus commensurate with the date of the inscription in A.D. 58/59,[48] though any decision here depends on how one reconstructs the *cursus honorum* of Marcellus from the remaining sources. L. Annius Bassus (twelfth year) and his immediate predecessor Q. Julius Cordus almost certainly belong in the time of Nero (i.e., after A.D. 64/65 or 65/66) rather than in that of Claudius.[49]

9.3. Sergius Paullus and Paul

9.3.1. The Name Change from Saul to Paul

In connection with the encounter with the Cypriot proconsul Sergius Paullus, Luke mentions for the first time (Acts 13:9) the apostle's Roman name: Paul (Παῦλος). Interpreters even before Origen believed that the apostle took this name in place of his previous Jewish one (שָׁאוּל, Σαούλ) only after his encounter with the Cypriot proconsul (Origen, *Comm. ad Rom. praef* [*PG* 14.836]), and Jerome later became an ardent subscriber to this understanding as well (Jerome, *De Vir. Ill.* 5; *Comm. in Phlm.* 1). In the first quarter of the twentieth century, this view was promoted especially by H. Dessau,[50] and still attracted advocates.[51] However, Luke's own manner of expression (ὁ καί) is frequently attested in papyri, and serves to introduce a double name ("who

---

45. Cf. T. B. Mitford, *ANRW* II 7.2 (1980) 1300.

46. *Epigraphica* 38 (1976) 180. J. Devreker refers mistakenly to line 3.

47. Cf. G. H. R. Horsley, *NewDoc* I (1981) 45.

48. *ANRW* II 7.2 (1980) 1301.

49. Cf. T. B. Mitford, *ibid.*; C. J. Hemer, *The Book of Acts in the Setting of Hellenistic History* (1989) 166f., note 16.

50. *Hermes* 45 (1910) 347-68.

51. E.g., E. Meyer, *Ursprünge und Anfänge des Christentums* III (1923) 196f.; E. Groag, *PRE* II/4 (1923) 1716.

is also called''), in which case one can virtually translate it with the term *alias*.[52] Roman inscriptions (e.g., *ILS* 2839) also attest a corresponding expression *(qui et)*. Hence Luke is clearly presupposing that Paul already had this name previously,[53] and the general assumption today is justifiably that this mention of a name change at precisely this juncture has something to do with the redactional intentions of the *auctor ad Theophilum:*[54] through this spectacular conversion of a Gentile from the upper classes,[55] Paul proves himself as the apostle to the nations who now moves to the center of the story. The fact that this was the same name as that of the proconsul may have supplied an additional literary motif prompting Luke to insert the name at just this point, though one should not completely exclude the possibility that this reflects a historical recollection: after such a dramatic experience, the apostle may well have used his Roman name when dealing with the Gentile world.[56]

9.3.2. The Apostle's Roman Name

If, however, the apostle did indeed bear the name Paul even before his encounter with the Cypriot proconsul, then how did he acquire this Roman name, one that was otherwise apparently extremely rare[57] among Jews? This might

52. Cf. further A. Deissmann, *Bibelstudien* (1895) 181-85; M. Lambertz, *Glotta* 4 (1913) 78-143; 5 (1914) 99-170; E. Preuschen, *Die Apostelgeschichte* (1912) 81f.; F. F. Bruce, *The Acts of the Apostles* (^{3}1990) 298; G. H. R. Horsley, *NewDoc* I (1981) 89-96; *ABD* IV (1992) 1012f.

53. Cf. H. Conzelmann, *Acts.* (Eng. trans., 1987) 100; G. Schneider, *Die Apostelgeschichte* II (1982) 122, note 37. Concerning tomb inscriptions of children with double names, cf. G. H. R. Horsley, *NewDoc* I (1981) 90, 92; *Numen* 34 (1987) 7, 15 (note 36).

54. Cf. A. Weiser, *Die Apostelgeschichte* II (1985) 317f.; R. Pesch, *Die Apostelgeschichte* II (1986) 25; G. H. R. Horsley, *Numen* 34 (1987) 7f.

55. Concerning the role of such persons of respect in the Lukan double work, cf. M. Hengel, *Festschrift O. Michel* (1963) 243-56. One of Luke's agenda is obviously also to elicit in the Christian churches a certain understanding for the Roman Empire. Cf. P. W. Walaskay, *"And so we came to Rome"* (1983), who does, however, unnecessarily deny Luke's other literary intention, namely, that Luke was also concerned with presenting an apology for Christianity to the Roman state.

56. Cf. G. A. Harrer, *HThR* 33 (1940) 32, and now also T. J. Leary, *NTS* 38 (1992) 467-69, who follows the lead of E. B. Howell, *GaR* 11 (1964) 10, in pointing out a possible negative connotation evoked by σαῦλος in Greek ears.

57. Although the numerous Jewish inscriptions from Cyrenaica do attest isolated instances of Jews with Roman citizenship (J. M. Reynolds, in G. Lüderitz, *Corpus jüdischer Zeugnisse aus der Cyrenaika* [1983] 193, 197 [variously from the first century A.D.]), in not a single instance does the name Paul or anything similar appear. The same findings emerge from a survey of the indices to the works of Josephus (A. Schalit, *Namenwörterbuch zu Flavius Josephus* [1968]), the European Jewish inscriptions in the *Corpus Inscriptionum Judaicarum* (J. B. Frey, *CIJ* I^2 [1975] 614, 624), and in the three

represent the substitution of a name of similar sound for his Hebrew name Saul as attested by Acts[58] (Grecized Σαῦλος or Σαοῦλος),[59] though the Greek name that literally translates "Saul" would actually have been Ἔτητος ("the entreated one"),[60] and it is by no means certain whether "Paul" was perceived as the phonetic transcription of "Saul."[61] Hence it is more likely that one of the two names is actually an alternative name *(supernomen* or *signum).* P[46], which mentions the apostle exclusively by his Semitic name Σαούλ during his pre-Christian period, goes back at least to the beginning of the third century A.D. and may even be considerably older (see pp. 404f. below), and in any case is to be classified within the first category of texts.[62] Thus the form with the Greek ending might be simply a Christian construction analogous to Παῦλος.[63] Paul(l)us is attested in only very few instances as a *praenomen,* and in those instances can be explained easily as an earlier *cognomen* having been appropriated from family tradition as a first name.[64] Paullus was apparently a relatively common *cognomen,*[65] and in that case may indicate that the apostle possessed the *civitas Romana,*[66] since every Roman citizen also had to have a Roman name.[67] G. H. R. Horsley calls Paullus "an upper-class

---

volumes of the *Corpus Papyrorum Judaicarum* published thus far. Cf. also M. Hengel, in M. Hengel and U. Heckel, *Paulus und das antike Judentum* (1991) 197f. A (cautiously) different view was taken by A. Deissmann, *Bibelstudien* (1895) 185. Only in later (second-fourth centuries A.D.) Jewish tomb inscriptions (N. Avigad, *Beth Sheʿarim* III [1971] 29f. and plate XII) does one encounter the name *Paulinus.*

58. Cf. Acts 7:58; 8:1, 3; 9:1, 4, 8, 11, 17, 22, 24; 11:25, 30; 12:25; 13:1, 2, 7, 9; 22:13.

59. So, e.g., A. N. Sherwin-White, *Roman Society and Roman Law* (1963) 153f.; G. Mussies, *NTS* 29 (1985) 361.

60. Cf. G. Mussies, CRINT II (1976) 1052.

61. Cf. G. Lüdemann, *Das frühe Christentum* (1987) 249.

62. Cf. K. Aland and B. Aland, *The Text of the New Testament* (Eng. trans.; rev. ed., 1989) 99.

63. So G. A. Harrer, *HThR* 33 (1940) 24-26.

64. Cf. *ibid.,* 27, note 24.

65. Cf. C. J. Hemer, *TynBul* 36 (1985) 183 contra A. N. Sherwin-White, *Roman Society and Roman Law* (1963) 153f.

66. So also, e.g., J. P. V. D. Balsdon, *The Early Roman Empire and the Rise of Christianity* (1980) 87; H. Balz, *EDNT* III (1993) 59.

67. Concerning the possibilities and difficulties of concluding on the basis of a change from the peregrine to the Roman name form that citizenship was bestowed, cf. H. Wolff, *Festschrift F. Vittinghoff* (1980) 229-55. Many Roman citizens from the eastern provinces did not know Latin. Cf. J. P. V. D. Balsdon, *Romans and Aliens* (1979) 132. For Claudius this was reason enough to cancel their citizenship in the case of conflict (Dio Cassius, *Hist.* lx.17.4). Perhaps Paul spoke a bit of Latin (A. Souter, *Exp* VIII/1 [1911] 337-42). See also p. 301, note 113 below.

name in the Roman onomasticon.''[68] If Paul's ancestors acquired citizenship through *manumissio,* then this particular *cognomen* might have come from their patron. Although the apostle's Roman citizenship is currently being disputed, the reasons for doing so are inadequate (Excursus I). In dealing with Gentile-Christian churches in which at most a minority possessed Roman citizenship, the apostle did not use his full name, probably for reasons of modesty.[69] He used only the last of the *tria nomina* of the Roman citizen because the *cognomen* functioned best for distinguishing a person.[70]

9.4. Chronological Conclusions

The possible existence of a Cypriot proconsul by the name of Quintus Sergius under the emperor Caligula (§9.2.2) would be of potential interest for G. Lüdemann's assumption of an extremely early Pauline mission to the Gentiles (§14.2). Lüdemann, however, considers the Cyprus mission Barnabas and Paul undertook together to be a Lukan construct.[71] As we have seen, the connection between the account of Acts and this particular Roman official is very unlikely. Even if one identifies Sergius Paulus in Luke with Quintus' presumed brother, the Tiber Curator Lucius Sergius Paullus under Claudius — as his family connection with Galatia strongly suggests — still, at the present time no more specific dating from outside the New Testament can be attained. Indeed, in his own list of the proconsuls of Cyprus, the ancient historian T. B. Mitford[72] dates the administration of Lucius Sergius Paullus between the years A.D. 46 and 48 based on the chronology of Acts itself (!).

---

68. *NewDoc* I (1981) 94.
69. Cf. also 1 Cor. 15:9, based perhaps on a wordplay with *paulus/*ἐλάχιστος.
70. Cf. C. E. B. Cranfield, *The Epistle to the Romans* I (³1980) 49f.
71. G. Lüdemann, *Early Christianity according to the Traditions in Acts* (Eng. trans., 1989) 148f.
72. *ANRW* II 7.2 (1980) 1301.

Excursus I: Paul's Roman Citizenship

W. Stegemann adduces especially socio-historical evidence in disputing the apostle's Roman citizenship asserted by Luke (Acts 16:37f.; 22:25ff.; 23:27; cf. 21:39; 25:10f.; 28:19).[1] K. Wengst presents an argument similar to that of Stegemann, though without passing any concluding judgment on the issue;[2] his work, however, generally gives occasion for strong critical counterqueries.[3] It is noteworthy that G. Lüdemann does defend Acts as regards this particular detail, and does so with good reasons even if his own explications might be augmented.[4] This effort to move Paul closer to the urban proletariat corresponds without a doubt to a widespread stream in contemporary theology; however, social empathy and historical acumen are not the same thing. Although it is not possible to discuss the complex problem of Paul's citizenship in all its aspects here, the following remarks may demonstrate that the question has by no means been decided negatively.

1. *EvErz* 37 (1985) 482-86; *ZNW* 78 (1987) 200-229. Other scholars who take this position include M. A. Hubaut, *Paul de Tarse* (1989) 7f.; J. C. Lentz, *Luke's Portrait of Paul* (1993) 43-56. E. W. Stegemann and W. Stegemann, *Urchristliche Sozialgeschichte* (1995) 256-60, is not of much help.

2. *Pax Romana* (1986) 94f.

3. Cf. U. Victor, *BThZ* 4 (1987) 95-106; S. Fowl, *JSNT* 35 (1989) 127. Concerning the significance of the *Pax Augusta* for primitive Christianity, cf. esp. H. E. Stier, *Paderborner Studien* 3/4 (1983) 76-87. The ancient historian H. Botermann, *ThR* 56 (1991) 301, remarks critically that "for generations, it has been generally customary among New Testament scholars to view the Roman Empire through the eyes of the Jewish Zealots."

4. G. Lüdemann, *Early Christianity according to the Traditions in Acts* (Eng. trans., 1989) 240f. Cf. now also H. W. Tajra, *The Trial of St. Paul* (1989) 76-89; J. Mélèze-Modrzejewski, in *Festschrift J. Imbert* (1989) 397-412; M. F. Baslez, *Saint Paul* (1991) 19-25, 307-9; S. R. Llewelyn, *NewDoc* VI (1992) 152-55; M. Hengel, in *idem;* U. Heckel, *Paulus und das antike Judentum* (1991) 193-208; K. Haacker, *ANRW* II 26.2 (1995) 831-47; B. Rapske, *Paul in Roman Custody* (1994) 83-90; S. Légasse in A1CS 4 (1995) 368-72.

(1) The Apostle's Class Membership

Does Paul's manual trade betray his origin in the lower classes, necessarily excluding thereby any possibility of Roman citizenship? The discussion concerning just what σκηνοποιός exactly means has not yet been concluded. The meaning suggested by R. F. Hock,[5] namely, "leather worker," is not the only possible one, and the traditional understanding "tentmaker" continues to be supported by certain arguments.[6] If one follows the assumption of P. Lampe that Paul made tents from linen and precious materials for private citizens,[7] then at least his Tarsan citizenship encounters no insuperable social difficulties (Acts 21:39: Ταρσεὺς τῆς Κιλικίας, οὐκ ἀσήμου πόλεως πολίτης). His ancestors might have acquired such a business through legitimate purchase.[8] To be sure, citizenship in a Greek *polis* did present considerable problems for any practicing Jew, since civil and religious life were inseparable from one another.[9] Individual arrangements, however, do not seem to have been entirely excluded, especially when extremely wealthy Jews were involved.[10] The possession of city citizenships by Jews in Asia Minor cannot be proven from the extant evidence, even though powerful indicators do point in this direction.[11] It is also possible that Luke is using the term πολίτης here commensurate with its use in the Septuagint (e.g., Prov. 11:9, 24, 28), that is, merely as a general designation of origin and not implying any legal assertion about Paul's status.[12] In any event, during the Julio-Claudian period, the *civitas Romana* and citizenship in a different city were no longer necessarily mutually exclusive,[13] and, indeed, in Alexandria such citizenship in the city itself was the prerequisite for Roman citizenship (*KP* I [1964] 244). Philostratus seems to presuppose that several Jews enjoyed Tarsan citizenship during the time of Titus (Philostratus, *VA* 6.34).[14]

---

5. *JBL* 97 (1978) 555-64.

6. Cf. C. J. Hemer, *The Book of Acts* (1989) 119, note 46; 233.

7. *BZ* 31 (1987) 256-61.

8. Cf. M. Hengel, in *idem,* and U. Heckel, *Paulus und das antike Judentum* (1991) 188-93. B. Doer, *Helikon* 8 (1968) 49-69, presents a thorough defense of Paul's Tarsan citizenship.

9. Cf. E. M. Smallwood, *Philo Alexandrini Legatio ad Gaium* ([2]1970) 13f.

10. Cf. A. D. Nock, *GRBS* 4 (1963) 50f., and P. Trebilco, *Jewish Communities in Asia Minor* (1991) 173-83, 258-62.

11. Cf. P. Trebilco, *Jewish Communities in Asia Minor* (1991) 167-72, 255-58.

12. Thus the query of M. Hengel, in *idem,* and U. Heckel, *Paulus und das antike Judentum* (1991) 191.

13. Cf. A. N. Sherwin-White, *Roman Society and Roman Law in the New Testament* (1963) 182. Concerning the complex question of dual citizenship, cf. esp. D. Nörr, *TRG* 31 (1963) 525-600; E. Ferenczy, *ANRW* II 14 (1982) 1046-53.

14. Cf. C. J. Hemer, *The Book of Acts* (1989) 127, note 75.

It is by no means certain that Paul had received his vocational education already during his pre-Christian period. W. Stegemann cannot imagine that the apostle would have given up his high social status and taken up a manual trade.[15] But why not? Quite apart from the fact that we do not know what conversion to the new messianic faith meant for his portion of family property,[16] the renunciation of possessions was certainly not something unusual in early Christianity.[17] And if Paul had contact in Damascus and Arabia with a strand of early Christianity that itself was connected with Essenism (§13.2), then voluntary poverty would be even less remarkable. Be that as it may, the apostle had before him the example of Christ himself as regards voluntary poverty (2 Cor. 8:9; cf. 2 Cor. 11:7). It is also possible that Paul developed a Jewish-Christian ethos regarding manual vocations in conscious contrast to the societal ideas of his time (§19.3.1).

E. A. Judge, a specialist in ancient history, prompts us to consider whether in the Greek cities of the first century A.D. Roman citizenship really was as decisive a factor for one's social status as is usually assumed.[18] A study of the names from the apostle's milieu suggests that several were actually Roman citizens,[19] so at least as a Christian the apostle did have access to such circles. It is striking how strongly oriented his later missionary activity was toward the metropolitan areas and provincial capitals (Antioch on the Orontes, Thessalonica, Ephesus, Rome) and Roman colonies (Pisidian Antioch, Iconium, Lystra, Troas, Philippi, Corinth). It is hardly likely that the communities awaiting Paul in Spain were Jewish (cf. Rom. 15:24, 28) (§15.5.3); on the contrary, this population was one of the most strongly Romanized in the Empire, and one that spoke Latin almost exclusively.[20]

(2) Mistreatment and Roman Citizenship

Do the apostle's tribulations — which according to 2 Cor. 11:24f. included synagogal punishment by beating on at least five occasions and civil scourging on at least three — contradict his Roman citizenship? W. Stegemann himself mentions that infringements might occur,[21] just as Luke does indeed presup-

15. *EvErz* 37 (1985) 483.

16. Disinheritance cannot be excluded. Cf. N. A. Dahl, *Studies in Paul* (1977) 36.

17. Cf. M. Hengel, *Property and Riches in the Early Church* (Eng. trans., 1974) 31-34; R. Riesner, *Formen gemeinsamen Lebens* (²1984) 30f.

18. *JAC* 15 (1972) 25. Cf. now also S. M. Baugh, *Paul and Ephesus* (1990).

19. Cf. E. A. Judge, *Rank and Status in the World of the Caesars and St. Paul* (1982) 12f.; in *NewDoc* II (1982) 106-8.

20. Cf. E. C. Polomé, *ANRW* II 29.2 (1983) 523-25.

21. *EvErz* 37 (1985) 485; *ZNW* 78 (1987) 223f.

pose for Philippi (Acts 16:29-39). Neither was it all that easy to prove one's Roman citizenship in any given encounter,[22] assuming Paul did not always carry a birth certificate with him.[23] Yet even such a certificate could have been lost through various adverse circumstances (cf. 2 Cor. 11:25).[24] E. A. Judge points out further that apparently there was more flexibility in the legal treatment of Roman citizens in the first century A.D. than is usually assumed.[25] With good reason, reference is repeatedly made to the fact that in A.D. 66 the Judean procurator Gessius Florus had Jews whipped and crucified even though they were members of the Roman equestrian order (Josephus, *B.J.* ii.306-8). Such crucifixion of Roman citizens is also mentioned under Galba (Suetonius, *Galba* 9.1), and additional examples of executions and chastisement might also be adduced.[26]

W. Stegemann objects that "Paul would be . . . the only case known to us that a Roman citizen was subject to chastisement in the synagogue (and five times at that!). All this could admittedly only have occurred voluntarily and accompanied by an inclination to masochism."[27] But should one not suppose that the apostle, from the perspective of his own understanding of the suffering Christ, consciously took such mistreatments upon himself? He was evidently proud of his "marks of Jesus" (Gal. 6:17; cf. Phil. 3:10; 2 Cor. 4:10f.; 6:4f.). We should be cautious about precipitately classifying as psychopathological a phenomenon alien to modern, secularized Christianity. If the apostle also understood himself to be called to Israel, then the judgment of T. Mommsen should be recalled as regards the synagogal chastisements especially in the early period of his mission (§14.1.3): "The correct Jew — and it is very much as such that Paul encounters the Jews — took leave from his people by appealing to his own acceptance among the Romans."[28] After the *provocatio ad Caesarem*, Paul expressly assures the Roman Jews in Acts that this did not take place "in order to bring any charge against my people" (οὐχ ὡς τοῦ ἔθνους μου ἔχων τι κατηγορεῖν)" (Acts 28:19). Even if the formulation comes from Luke, it presumably reproduces accurately Paul's own attitude.

22. Cf. H. J. Cadbury, *BC* V (1933) 316, note 5; A. N. Sherwin-White, *Roman Society and Roman Law* (1963) 148f.

23. So F. Schulz, *JRS* 33 (1943) 63f., and as a possibility J. P. V. D. Balsdon, *Romans and Aliens* (1979) 95.

24. Cf. F. F. Bruce, *Paul* (1979) 39f.

25. *JAC* 15 (1972) 26, esp. note 32.

26. Cf. P. Garnsey, *JRS* 56 (1966) 174-76; H. Conzelmann, *Acts* (Eng. trans., 1987) 133; M. Hengel, *Crucifixion* (1977) 39-45; M. Black, *RestQ* 24 (1981) 215f.

27. *EvErz* 37 (1985) 485.

28. *ZNW* 2 (1901) 90, note 2.

(3) Roman Citizenship and Jewish Religiosity

It seems to me that the most weighty critical question is whether the granting of Roman citizenship must not betray a somewhat lax engagement in Judaism on the part of the apostle's ancestors, which would then contradict Paul's own testimony (Phil. 3:5). Even if during the New Testament period Jews were clearly striving to attain the rights of citizens, it is nonetheless hardly likely that all those interested in this were potential apostates. It is more likely that multiple possibilities were available, ranging from complete assimilation to the full preservation of one's identity with the aid of regulations that allowed exceptions. Certainly, the danger of deviation and apostasy did indeed reside in the duties expected of the normal Roman citizen.[29] Circumstances in Rome itself, however, show that the acquisition of Roman citizenship by no means automatically resulted in a renunciation of Judaism. In this context, it is worth citing Philo, *Legatio ad Gaium* 155: "He was aware that the great section of Rome on the other side of the Tiber is occupied and inhabited by Jews, most of whom were Roman citizens emancipated. For having been brought as captives to Italy they were liberated by their owners and were not forced to violate any of their native institutions (οὐδὲν τῶν πατρίων παραχαράξαι βιασθέντες)." The Jewish philosopher then mentions Augustus' respect for the synagogues, the sabbath commandment, and the collections for Jerusalem (Philo, *Leg. ad Gaium* 156f.), and he concludes with the following statement about the Jews of the imperial capital: The emperor "nevertheless neither ejected them from Rome nor deprived them of their Roman citizenship because they were careful to preserve their Jewish citizenship also (οὔτε τὴν Ῥωμαϊκὴν αὐτῶν ἀφείλετο πολιτείαν, ὅτι καὶ τῆς Ἰουδαϊκῆς ἐφρόντιζον)." There is no reason to doubt Philo's statements here,[30] statements supported by Tacitus (Tacitus, *Ann.* ii.85.4).[31] This probably addresses W. Stegemann's objection "that Roman citizenship also included the obligation to sacrifice Roman gods [sic!]. To my knowledge, Jews with Roman citizenship were not freed from this obligation."[32]

We do not know how Paul's ancestors acquired Roman citizenship. Were they already settled in Tarsus by the Seleucids, as suggested by W. M. Ramsay[33] and often assumed since?[34] Did they begin to follow the direction of the

29. Cf. M. Stern, CRINT I/1 (1974) 420-63.

30. Cf. E. M. Smallwood, *Philonis Alexandrini Legatio ad Gaium* (²1970) 234-36. J. Schwartz, in *Festschrift I. Lévy* (1955) 591-604, considered Philo himself to be a *civis Romanus*; M. F. Baslez, *Saint Paul* (1991) 32, follows him in this assumption.

31. Cf. M. Stern, *Greek and Latin Authors on Jews and Judaism* II (1980) 69-73; G. Fuks, *JJS* 36 (1985) 26.

32. *ZNW* 78 (1987) 224.

33. *The Cities of St. Paul* (1907) 161-86.

34. Cf., e.g., C. J. Hemer, *ISBE* IV (1988) 735.

Pharisees (Phil. 3:5) only in a later generation, after the acquisition of Tarsan or Roman citizenship (under Caesar?)?[35] But a person did not become a Pharisee outside Palestine.[36] Paul's father, however, might also have acquired citizenship only after having been freed as an enslaved prisoner of war,[37] which is indeed asserted by Jerome (*Comm. in Phlm.* 23; *De Vir. Ill.* 5)[38] and, apparently independent of him, the patriarch Photius (*Quaest. Amphil.* 116 [*PG* 101.687-90]).[39] T. Zahn presented a thorough defense of this tradition.[40] Several more recent scholars also take seriously the assertion that Paul's parents came from Galilee,[41] and G. Kehnscherper is convinced that the enslavement took place on the occasion of Varus' Galilean campaign in 4 B.C. (Josephus, *B.J.* ii.68/*Ant.* xvii.288f.).[42] If Luke's own assertion is correct, namely, that the apostle had citizenship by birth (Acts 22:26-29), then this connection with Varus might prove questionable because of Paul's presumed date of birth around the turn of the century (§12.1.1), though after Pompey's conquest of Palestine in the year 63 B.C. there were other disturbances as well during which Galilean Jews might have become Roman slaves.[43] In both earlier and more recent scholarship, treatment of this Gischala-tradition is often unsatisfactory.[44] As the son of a

35. Cf. C. B. Welles, *MUSJ* 38 (1962) 61f.

36. Cf. M. Hengel, in *idem,* and U. Heckel, *Paulus und das antike Judentum* (1991) 225-32. Among earlier scholars, H. E. Dana, *AThR* 20 (1938) 18, emphasized this.

37. Concerning the emergence of this legal possibility, cf. H. Chantraine, *ANRW* I 2 (1972) 59-67; concerning its legal foundations, cf. E. Weiss, *PRE* II 14.2 (1930) 1366-77.

38. Contrary to the translation of T. Mommsen, *ZNW* 2 (1901) 82, the commentary to Philemon does presuppose the apostle's birth in Tarsus. Cf. T. Zahn, *NKZ* 15 (1904) 26-28. Even if Jerome's formulation in the second passage could suggest that Paul was born in Galilean Gischala (concerning this locale, cf. R. Riesner, *GBL* I [1987] 468; concerning the possibility of a Jewish-Christian tradition, cf. B. Bagatti, *Antichi villaggi cristiani di Galilea* [1971] 228-36), this one oversight is not sufficient to render the entire tradition worthless.

39. The common source might have been the commentary on Philemon by Origen. Cf. A. von Harnack, *TU* 42/4 (1919) 145f.

40. *NKZ* 15 (1904) 23-34; *Introduction to the New Testament* (Eng. trans., 1909) 1.47-51, 67-70.

41. E.g., H. Lietzmann, *An die Korinther* I/II ([5]1969) 150; M. Adinolfi, *Ant* 41 (1966) 366-73; K. Haacker, *ThBeitr* 6 (1977) 5; W. Grundmann, *Die frühe Christenheit und ihre Schriften* (1983) 33; W. Feneberg, *Paulus der Weltenbürger* (1992) 13-15. A certain sympathy for this thesis is also evident in E. A. Judge, *JAC* 15 (1972) 25f., note 30; S. Kim, *The Origin of Paul's Gospel* ([2]1984) 35, note 6. Earlier advocates can be found in K. W. Niebuhr, *Heidenapostel aus Israel* (1992) 108, note 137. Among them, one should also mention A. von Harnack, *Die Mission und Ausbreitung des Christentums* ([4]1924) 63f., note 1.

42. *TU* 87 (1964) 419-21. His assertion that the first advocate of this view was W. Hartke, *Vier urchristliche Parteien* II (1961) 415f., peculiarly overlooks T. Zahn, *NKZ* 15 (1904) 30.

43. An overview can be found in G. Fuks, *JJS* 36 (1985) 26-28. Concerning bestowal under Augustus, cf. M. Woloch, *Helikon* 11/12 (1971/72) 452-54.

44. This applies, e.g., to T. Mommsen, *ZNW* 2 (1901) 82f., note 4; E. Fascher,

freedman *(libertus/libertinus),* Paul would have been considered a fully recognized citizen *(ingenuus).*[45]

T. Zahn already drew attention to the importance of *manumissio* in connection with Paul's citizenship,[46] while W. Stegemann peculiarly addresses the possibility only of "bestowal [variously because of meritorious service to Rome] by a Roman emperor [Augustus?] or after many years of service in the Roman military."[47] The far-reaching legal act of *manumissio* required only the willingness of the slaveholder, but no additional permission from the state itself. This is probably not an early indication of some new, universal *humanitas,* but rather merely evidence of the preservation of an archaic privilege.[48] If Paul's immediate ancestors did indeed come from Palestine, then it is easier to understand that he could describe himself as Ἑβραῖος ἐξ Ἑβραίων (Phil. 3:5), and that his sister apparently lived as a married woman in Jerusalem (Acts 23:16).[49] Acts mentions that Jerusalem had a synagogue of freedmen which included Cilicians among its members (Acts 6:9: τινες τῶν ἐκ τῆς συναγωγῆς τῆς λεγομένης Λιβερτίνων καὶ Κυρηναίων καὶ Ἀλεξανδρέων καὶ τῶν ἀπὸ Κιλικίας καὶ Ἀσίας).[50] Luke might

---

PRE Suppl VIII (1958) 435; A. N. Sherwin-White, *Roman Society and Roman Law* (1963) 152; C. Burchard, *Der dreizehnte Zeuge* (1970) 34, note 42; H. D. Betz, *ABD* V (1992) 187; J. Murphy-O'Connor, *RB* 99 (1992) 440. Although W. Stegemann, *ZNW* 78 (1987) 224, note 89, does mention G. Kehnscherper, he does not address his thesis.

45. The sons of *libertini* were considered *ingenui* since the late Republic. Cf. A. Steinwenter, *PRE* II 13.1 (1927) 106. To my knowledge, the restrictions applicable at various times to the descendants of freedmen (e.g., the assumption of office) referred to the right of *provocatio* or *appellatio.* Cf. also J. Bleicken, *PRE* I 23.2 (1959) 2458; *Die Verfassung der römischen Republik* (1975) 15.

46. *NKZ* 15 (1904) 31.

47. *ZNW* 78 (1987) 224, despite *ibid.,* 214.

48. E. Meyer, *Römischer Staat und Staatsgedanke* (²1961) 186, remarks in this regard: "This peculiarly liberal situation, namely, that every Roman citizen, at his own initiative and without any previous queries to the state, could exercise independently such an important right of sovereignty as bestowing citizenship, can probably be explained as one of several relics from the murky past that conservative Rome dragged along amid completely altered circumstances; for originally such release no doubt involved merely a transition into the status of client to the liberating master, i.e., into continued dependence on the master in a different form and without political rights. And when then these clients became free and, as plebes of a new form, acquired more and more political rights, the old principle, unchanged, remained in place."

49. Cf. also J. Jeremias, *Der Schlüssel zur Theologie des Apostels Paulus* (1971) 10.

50. The reference is most likely to but a single synagogue (F. W. Danker, *ISBE* II [1982] 360f.), which may have been identical with the one mentioned in the Theodotos-inscription (*CIJ* II 1404) (L. H. Vincent, *RB* 30 [1921] 247-77). Cf. M. Hengel, *ZThK* 72 (1975) 184f. See now R. Riesner in A1CS 4 (1995) 179-212.

assume that Paul belonged to this particular synagogue.[51] If Paul's father acquired citizenship as a freedman apart from his own efforts, then both he and, of course, Paul himself could decide the extent to which they would make further use of this. In this context, it is interesting that in the tomb inscriptions of Rome's Jewish catacombs, references to the *manumissio* are consciously omitted, apparently for religious reasons (cf. Josephus, *Ant.* xviii.23).[52] By contrast, an ossuary from the monumental tomb of a presumably priestly family in Jericho notes with a certain element of pride that here the remains of a freedman of the Empress Agrippina are interred (ΘΕΟΔΟΤΟΥ ΑΠΕΛΕΥ-ΘΕΡΟΥ ΒΑΣΙΛΙΣΣΗΣ ΑΓΡΙΠΠΕΙΝΗΣ ΣΟΡΟΣ).[53]

(4) Paul's Education

W. Stegemann does not specifically address this question. In my opinion, the apostle's interpretation of the Old Testament[54] betrays an extremely high degree of scholarly training. The strong parallels with rabbinic exegesis that become evident in methodological and thematic respects demonstrate that Paul could not have acquired this knowledge and proficiency only after having become a Christian missionary. The judgment of A. Oepke also continues to apply, namely, that "a diaspora Jew who consistently cites the LXX while doubtless also having a familiarity with the original text is not an everyday phenomenon."[55] This at least indirectly confirms the Lukan assertion that Paul studied under Gamaliel the Elder (Acts 22:3) (see p. 268 below). The question of importance for our own problem is just how the young Saul was able to finance his education. Either he was wealthy, which would support the assumption of his noble origin, or he had to support himself by working at a trade. W. Stegemann,[56] with reference to R. F. Hock,[57] assumes that such a connection between scholarly proficiency and the exercise of a vocation was allegedly not required until the second century A.D. But a tradition probably correctly ascribed to Shemaiah and Abtalion

---

51. Cf. H. J. Cadbury, *The Book of Acts in History* (1955) 73.
52. Cf. G. Fuks, *JJS* 36 (1985) 30-32.
53. Cf. R. Hachlili, *BASOR* 235 (1979) 33, 45-49, 70; *idem* and A. Killebrew, *BARev* 9/1 (1983) 52f.
54. Cf. E. E. Ellis, *Paul's Use of the Old Testament* (1957); in *Prophecy and Hermeneutics in Early Christianity* (1978) 173-81, 213-20; CRINT II/2 (1988) 691-725; O. Michel, *Paulus und seine Bibel* (²1972); R. N. Longenecker, *Biblical Exegesis in the Apostolic Period* (1975) 104-32.
55. *ThStKr* 105 (1933) 443.
56. *EvErz* 37 (1985) 483.
57. *The Social Context of Paul's Ministry* (1980) 22-25.

(*ca.* 47-20 B.C.)[58] already demands that the scholar "love labor and hate mastery" (*m 'Abot.* 1:10). Moreover, Pharisees, who for the most part came from the middle class,[59] found that vocational work was a pure necessity if they had to earn their keep themselves as scholars. It is also quite possible that in certain houses of learning some form of compensation still had to be paid in the first century A.D.[60]

(5) Paul's Trial

The objections W. Stegemann[61] presents, following E. Haenchen,[62] in connection with the *provocatio ad Caesarem* due Paul as *civis Romanus* (Acts 25:9ff.) can in my opinion be refuted.[63] It is precisely with regard to the *civitas Romana* that Acts does clearly reflect the circumstances of the first half of the first century A.D., circumstances considerably different in many respects from those of the later period.[64] Although W. Stegemann does indeed allow that Luke had a general knowledge in these matters,[65] he nonetheless still

---

58. Cf. C. Schedl, *Talmud — Evangelium — Synagoge* (1969) 38f.; W. Wiefel, *NovT* 11 (1969) 114f.

59. Cf. R. Riesner, *Jesus als Lehrer* ([3]1988) 174 (bibliography).

60. Cf. *ibid.,* 185.

61. *ZNW* 78 (1987) 207-13.

62. *Acts* (Eng. trans., 1971) 667f.

63. Cf. A. W. Lintott, *ANRW* I 2 (1972) 226f.; C. J. Hemer, *The Book of Acts in the Setting of Hellenistic History* (1989) 130f., 180, 214; A. Moda, *BeO* 35 (1993) 22-35. This still applies even if the distinction between the earlier legal institution of the *provocatio* and a later *appellatio* does not hold as presented by A. H. M. Jones, *Studies in Roman Government and Law* (1960) 53-65, 69-98, and A. N. Sherwin-White, *Roman Society and Roman Law* (1963) 57-70 (following the lead of T. Mommsen). So, e.g., J. Bleicken, *PRE* XXIII/2 (1959) 2444-63; P. Garnsey, *JRS* 56 (1966) 167-89; *Social Status and Legal Privilege in the Roman Empire* (1970) 75f., 267. Cf. the discussion in A. W. Lintott, *ANRW* I 2 (1972) 226-67. The more recent debate is apparently unknown to C. J. Hemer, *The Book of Acts* (1989) 214, and to W. W. Gasque, *TynBul* 40 (1989) 152.

64. Cf. A. N. Sherwin-White, *Roman Society and Roman Law* (1963) 144-62, 172-85; J. J. Nicholls, *JRH* 3 (1964) 92-95; M. Stahl, *Imperiale Herrschaft und provinziale Stadt* (1978) 151-56; E. A. Judge, *JRH* 11 (1980/81) 208; C. J. Hemer, *The Book of Acts* (1989) 127, 170; H. W. Tajra, *The Trial of St. Paul* (1989) 63-196.

65. *ZNW* 78 (1987) 205f. The legal expert O. Eger, mentioned approvingly by W. Stegemann, even concluded in his Basel *Rektorat* address for 1918 that "in view of the fact that the portrayal of these proceedings [before Festus] against Paul, as just presented, exhibits a close affinity with administrative terminology, one must ask whether the official minutes of the Pauline trial might not perhaps in some way have provided the basis for this account (or at least for some parts of it)" (*Rechtsgeschichtliches zum Neuen Testament* [1919] 17).

considers the portrayal of the proceedings before Festus to be fiction. So one is left to assume that in one and the same act Luke both freely invented this account and reconstructed it with historical accuracy. Although W. Stegemann is unable to explain convincingly the apostle's transport to Rome,[66] as the result of a procedure *extra ordinem*[67] it is easily comprehensible,[68] even in the case of a Roman citizen without high social status.[69] The entire circumstances of the trial as portrayed, however, show that at least at that time Paul was viewed as a person of higher status.[70]

Hence W. Stegemann's treatment of this problem is doubtless not the last word. Although he drew attention to several long-familiar difficulties in connection with the Lukan assertions, none of these problems is so insuperable as to require us to eliminate Paul's Roman citizenship as a historically impossible, apologetic invention by Luke.[71] No even moderately convincing reason can be adduced regarding why Paul would have had to mention his citizenship in one of the extant letters. Not one of these writings is addressed to a Roman authority or official. Compared with the heavenly πολίτευμα (Phil. 3:20), Roman citizenship was of tertiary significance, and the apostle preferred to portray for his churches his sufferings in Christ rather than some privileges of status. By contrast, it is commensurate with the narrative genre of Acts to inform us how in certain situations Paul did make use of the privileges of the *civitas Romana* for the sake of furthering his work.

66. W. Stegemann, *EvErz* 37 (1985) 486, even indirectly admits as much himself: "One can . . . naturally only surmise, and beyond this only speculate, whether these reasons [for the transport to Rome] had something to do with the noteworthy disturbances in the Jewish country against Roman hegemony and its Jewish collaborators." Cf. by contrast justifiably J. Becker, *Paulus* (1989) 56 (Eng. trans., *Paul* [1993]).

67. Cf. A. W. Lintott, *ANRW* I 2 (1972) 264f., contra the assumption of P. Garnsey, *JRS* 56 (1966) 182-89, that the case of Paul's intervention did not involve a form of *appellatio* at all, but rather a *reiectio iudicii*.

68. Cf. A. H. M. Jones, *Studies in Roman Government and Law* (1960) 59-63; M. Black, *RestQ* 24 (1981) 216f.

69. Cf. A. N. Sherwin-White, *ANRW* I 2 (1972) 54, who remarks elsewhere that "it is, however, possible that the right of appeal was more lively in the East, where the citizenship spread only by individual grants, than in the West, where wholesale extension of it must have led to some practical limitation of a right, which would have become a nuisance when universalized" (*The Roman Citizenship* [²1973] 273).

70. Cf. B. Reese, *EQ* 47 (1975) 138-45; G. Clark, *ET* 96 (1985) 110f.

71. We know that the following Jews of Asia Minor were Roman citizens in the first century A.D.: Tyrronius Kladus (Acmonia [*MAMA* VI 264]), almost certainly the family of Titus Flavius Alexander (Acmonia [*CIJ* II 770]), and from the second century A.D. M(arkus) Ar(elius) Moussius (Ephesus [L. Robert, *Hellenica* 11/12 [1960] 381-84]). Concerning Roman citizenship before A.D. 212 among Jews in Carthage, Cyrenaica, and Alexandria, cf. P. Trebilco, *Jewish Communities in Asia Minor* (1991) 258, note 22 (bibliography).

§10

Claudius' Roman Edict
concerning the Jews

10.1. Sources and Problems

When Paul reached Corinth from Athens, according to the account in Acts he met there "a Jew named Aquila, a native of Pontus, who had recently come from Italy with his wife Priscilla, because Claudius had ordered all Jews to leave Rome" (Acts 18:2). At least three other ancient sources mention this emperor's implementation of an anti-Jewish measure in the imperial capital. In the second decade of the second century, Suetonius wrote in his biography of Claudius that "since the Jews constantly made disturbances at the instigation of Chrestus, he [Claudius] expelled them from Rome"[1] (*Claudius* 25.4). In his *Roman History,* whose sixtieth book was probably completed in A.D. 216,[2] Dio Cassius remarks in connection with his portrayal of the initial period of Claudius' reign that "the Jews had once again increased so greatly that because of their great numbers it would have been difficult to bar them from the city without creating a tumult. So he did not drive them out, and even allowed them to continue their traditional manner of life, but forbade them to hold meetings"[3] (*Hist.* lx.6.6). Finally, in his *Historia Adversus Paganos,* which appeared in A.D. 417/18, Paulus Orosius, before citing the passage from Suetonius just mentioned, remarks that "in the ninth year of the same reign, Josephus reports that the Jews were expelled from the city by Claudius"[4] (*Adv. Pag.* vii.6.15).

It is a consolation of sorts for New Testament exegesis that the his-

1. Translation according to H. Conzelmann, *Acts* (Eng. trans., 1987) 151.
2. Cf. F. Millar, *A Study of Cassius Dio* (1964) 194.
3. Translation according to H. Conzelmann, *History of Primitive Christianity* (Eng. trans., 1973) 164.
4. Translation according Roy J. Deferrari, *Paulus Orosius: The Seven Books of History against the Pagans* (1964) 297.

torical problems do not commence only with Christian sources. The interpretation and evaluation of the remarks made by the two Roman writers are also highly disputed.[5] Are they referring to the same thing? Can their accounts

5. Older bibliography can be found in H. H. Wendt, *Apostelgeschichte* (1888) 394f.; E. Schürer, *Geschichte des jüdischen Volkes* III (⁴1909) 63, note 92. A bibliographical selection from 1872 to 1975 can be found in M. Stern, *Greek and Latin Authors on Jews and Judaism* II (1980) 114, which complements Stern's bibliography in CRINT I/1 (1974) 182f., which G. Lüdemann, *Paul: Apostle to the Gentiles* (1984) 186, note 63, incorrectly ascribes to S. Safrai. The same mistake recurs in R. Penna, *NTS* 28 (1982) 343, note 78, who apparently is dependent on Lüdemann. Since M. Stern includes an inordinate number of older titles that are in part also of little value, while omitting many more recent noteworthy contributions, I am providing here a comprehensive bibliography: F. Huidekoper, *Judaism at Rome* (1880) 222; K. T. Keim, *Rom und das Christenthum* (1881) 171-73; J. E. Hild, *RÉJ* 11 (1885) 58f., note 3; T. Mommsen, *HZ* 64 (1890) 408; O. Holtzmann, *Neutestamentliche Zeitgeschichte* (1895) 125-27; T. Reinach, *Textes d'auteurs Grecs et Romains relatifs au Judaïsme* (1895) 188, 329; H. Smilda, *C. Suetonii Vita Divi Claudii* (1896) 123-25; H. Vogelstein and P. Rieger, *Geschichte der Juden in Rom* I 1896) 19f.; J. E. Belser, *ThQ* 80 (1898) 367-72; A. Gaheis, *PRE* I 3 (1899) 2810; E. Groag, *PRE* I 9 (1899) 2790; V. Weber, *Die Abfassung des Galaterbriefs* (1900) 389; G. Hoennicke, *NKZ* 13 (1902) 596-98; W. Sanday and A. C. Headlam, *Epistle to the Romans* (⁵1902) xxif.; C. Weizsäcker, *The Apostolic Age* (Eng. trans., 1907-1912) 1.78f.; A. Bludau, *Kath* 83 (1903) 125-28; T. Mommsen, *Römische Geschichte* V (⁵1904) 222f.; E. G. Hardy, *Studies in Roman Law* (1906) 43; E. Schürer, *Geschichte* II (⁴1909) 61-63; A. von Harnack, *SPAW.PH* (1912) 673-76; E. Preuschen, *Apostelgeschichte* (1912) 111; G. Edmundson, *The Church in Rome* (1913) 9-11; K. Linck, *De antiquissimis veterum quae ad Iesum Nazarenum spectant testimoniis* (1913) 104-7; J. Juster, *Les Juifs dans l'empire Romain* II (1914) 171; E. Preuschen, *ZNW* 15 (1914) 96; M. Radin, *The Jews among the Greeks and Romans* (1915) 313-15; D. Plooij, *Chronologie van het leven van Paulus* (1918) 45-48; A. Wikenhauser, *Der Geschichtswert der Apostelgeschichte* (1921) 323f.; H. Graetz, *History of the Jews,* vol. II (Eng. trans., 1893) 202; E. Meyer, *Ursprung und Anfänge des Christentums* III (1923) 37f., 462f.; A. von Harnack, *Die Mission und Ausbreitung des Christentums* (⁴1924) 10; E. T. Merrill, *Essays in Early Christian History* (1924) 102-5; T. Reinach, *RÉJ* 79 (1924) 131; T. Zahn, *Introduction to the New Testament* (Eng. trans., 1909) 3.466f.; G. A. Deissmann, *Paulus* (²1925) 222f. (Eng. trans., Paul [²1926]); J. Felten, *Neutestamentliche Zeitgeschichte* I (²/³1925) 286f.; E. Jacquier, *Les Actes des Apôtres* (²1926) 543; H. S. Jones, *JRS* 16 (1926) 31; T. Zielinski, *RUB* 32 (1926/7) 143f.; G. La Piana, *HThR* 20 (1927) 376; T. Zahn, *Die Apostelgeschichte* II (³/⁴1927) 635f.; J. B. Frey, *RSR* 20 (1930) 278f.; W. M. Ramsay, *St. Paul* (¹⁷1930) 254; W. Seston, *RHPhR* 11 (1931) 299-301; K. Lake, *BC* V (1933) 459f.; M. Goguel, *Das Leben Jesu* (1934) 37; H. Janne, *AIPh* 2 (1934) 531-53; P. de Labriolle, *Le reaction païenne* (1934) 42f.; A. Momigliano, *Claudius* (1934) 31-35, 98f.; A. D. Nock, *CAH* X (1934) 500f.; A. Steinmann, *Die Apostelgeschichte* (1934) 214f.; P. Styger, *Juden und Christen im alten Rom* (1934) 10; F. J. Badcock, *The Pauline Epistles* (1937) 41f.; H. Last, *JRS* 27 (1937) 88; A. S. Barnes, *Christianity at Rome* (1938) 26f.; G. May, *RHDFE* 17 (1938) 37-45; V. M. Scramuzza, *The Emperor Claudius* (1940) 151, 286f., note 20; M. Dibelius, *SHAW* 32 (1941/2) 30f.; J. Moreau, *Les plus anciens témoignages profanes sur Jésus* (1944) 49-53; J. W. Swain, *HThR* 37 (1944) 348f.; H. Fuchs, *VigChr* 4 (1950) 71f.; S. L. Guterman, *Religious Tolera-*

be harmonized? Does one (or do perhaps both of them) give an erroneous account? In order to answer such questions, we must also become familiar with the peculiarities of the two authors and their works.

tion and Persecution (1951) 149f.; J. Klausner, *Jesus* (Eng. trans., 1943) 60f.; F. F. Bruce, *The Book of Acts* (1954) 368f.; L. Goppelt, *Christentum und Judentum* (1954) 222f.; H. J. Cadbury, *The Book of Acts in History* (1955) 115f.; C. Cecchelli, *RivAC* 31 (1955) 71-73; W. Den Boer, *RAC* III (1957) 180f.; E. Gabba, *Iscrizione greche e latine* (1958) 77; C. K. Barrett, *Die Umwelt des Neuen Testaments* (1959) 24f.; E. Peterson, in *Frühkirche, Judentum und Gnosis* (1959) 77; E. Bammel, *ZThK* 56 (1959) 295-301; M. Gough, *The Early Christians* (1960) 41; R. O. Hoerber, *CThM* 31 (1960) 690-94; H. J. Leon, *The Jews of Ancient Rome* (1960) 23-27; G. B. Caird, *IDB* I (1961) 604a; F. F. Bruce, *BJRL* 44 (1961/62) 313-18; B. Rigaux, *The Letters of St. Paul* (Eng. trans., 1968) 87f.; W. H. C. Frend, *Martyrdom and Persecution* (1965) 160f.; H. W. Hoehner, *Chronology of the Apostolic Age* (1965) 80-87; J. L. Moreau, *BS* 10 (1965) 36; E. M. Smallwood, *HT* 15 (1965) 236; M. Sordi, *Il Cristianesimo e Roma* (1965) 62-69; E. A. Judge, *RThR* 25 (1966) 84-88; A. Jaubert, *Les premiers chrétiens* (1967) 65-67; E. Koestermann, *Hist* 16 (1967) 457-60; T. D. Barnes, *JRS* 25 (1968) 43f.; G. Ogg, *The Chronology of the Life of Paul* (1968) 99-103; S. Benko, *ThZ* 25 (1969) 406-18; A. Feuillet, in *Petrus et Paulus Martyres* (1969) 94-96; B. Boulvert, *Esclaves et affranchis impériaux* (1970) 358; L. Herrmann, *Chrestos* (1970) 165-67; W. Wiefel, *Jud* 26 (1970) 75-78; S. Benko, in *idem* and J. J. O'Rourke, *The Catacombs and the Colosseum* (1971) 54; J. Moreau, *Christenverfolgung* (²1971) 32f.; M. Hengel, *NTS* 18 (1971/2) 16f.; H. Conzelmann, *Acts. Hermeneia* (Eng. trans., 1987) 151; M. Grant, *The Jews in the Roman World* (1973) 146; F. F. Bruce, *Jesus and Christian Origins* (1974) 20f.; A. Garzetti, *From Tiberius to the Antonines* (1974) 140; M. Stern, *CRINT* I/1 (1974) 180-83; A. Hamman, *Festschrift M. Pellegrino* (1975) 92-96; A. Suhl, *Paulus und seine Briefe* (1975) 326f.; J. Friedrich, W. Pöhlmann, and P. Stuhlmacher, *ZThK* 73 (1976) 58f., note 111; F. F. Bruce, *Zeitgeschichte des NT* II (1976) 96-101; I. M. Tronskij, in *Mel. Petrovski* (1976) 34-42 (*non vidi*) F. F. Bruce, *Paul* (1977) 381-83; E. Haenchen, *Acts* (Eng. trans., 1971) 65; O. Michel, *Der Brief an die Römer* (⁵1978) 34f.; H. M. Schenke and K. M. Fischer, *Einleitung in die Schriften des Neuen Testaments* I (1978) 134f.; J. P. V. D. Balsdon, *Romans and Aliens* (1979) 106; O. Montevecchi, *Festschrift G. Lazzati* (1979) 500; M. Stern, *Zion* 44 (1979) 18-23; J. W. Drane, *Festschrift F. F. Bruce* (1980) 216-18; S. Freyne, *The World of the New Testament* (1980) 74f.; E. A. Judge, *IBD* I (1980) 298; G. Lüdemann, *Paul: Apostle to the Gentiles* (1984) 164-71; M. Stern, *Greek and Latin Authors* II (1980) 113-17; J. Bleicken, *Verfassungs- und Sozialgeschichte des Römischen Kaiserreiches* (1981) 159; G. Howards, *RestQ* 24 (1981) 175-77; W. Schneemelcher, *Das Urchristentum* (1981) 24f., 47f.; M. Simon, in *Religion et culture dans la cité Italienne* (1981) 42-44; E. M. Smallwood, *The Jews under Roman Rule* (²1981) 210-16; R. K. Jewett, *A Chronology of Paul's Life* (1979) 36-38; R. Penna, *NTS* 28 (1982) 325, 331; B. Reicke, *The New Testament Era* (Eng. trans., 1968) 205, 226, 239; H. H. Scullard, *From the Gracchi to Nero* (⁵1982) 295, 472; J. Murphy-O'Connor, *RB* 89 (1982) 84-86; *St. Paul's Corinth* (1983) 130-40; S. Bacchiocchi, *AUSS* 21 (1983) 12f.; B. Baldwin, *Suetonius* (1983) 356; R. E. Brown and J. P. Meier, *Antioch and Rome* (1983) 100-102; G. Lüdemann, in B. C. Corley, *Colloquy on New Testament Studies* (1983) 302f.; H. Solin, *ANRW* II 29.2 (1983) 688-90; R. Pesch, *Die Apostelgeschichte* II (1986) 152, note 22; J. Gascou, *Suétone historien* (1984) 731, note 114; M. Hengel, *Urchristliche Geschichtsschreibung* (²1984) 91; E. Huzar, *ANRW* II 32.1

10.2. Suetonius

10.2.1. The Biographer

Gaius Suetonius Tranquillus was probably born around A.D. 70 (perhaps in Hippo, North Africa).[6] After an education in the rhetorical arts, as was commensurate with his lineage in the equestrian class, he was active at the bar. Through his friendship with the Younger Pliny, he received after approximately A.D. 114, probably still under Trajan, the offices *a studiis* and *a bibliothecis,* and was thus entrusted with the imperial archives. In A.D. 119, probably through the influence of the later praetorian prefect Septicius Clarus, Hadrian awarded him the most important court office,[7] appointing him secretary of his chancellery *(ab epistulis).* With the fall of Clarus in the year A.D. 122, with whom he had become too familiar, Suetonius, too, lost his office. He nevertheless dedicated the first volume of his *De vita*

(1984) 638; M. Whittaker, *Jews and Christians* (1984) 104; C. Saulnier, *DBS* X (1985) 963f.; C. Andresen, in *Orosius* (1985) 41f.; G. Barbaglio, *Paolo di Tarso* (1985) 25f.; A. Feuillet, *DBS* X (1985) 757f.; K. M. Fischer, *Das Urchristentum* (1985) 99f.; M. J. Harris, in D. Wenham, *Gospel Perspectives* V (1985) 353-56, 364-66; S. Benko, *Pagan Rome and the Early Christians* (1986) 18-20; J. Mottershead, *Suetonius: Claudius* (1986) 149-57; T. Holtz, *Der erste Brief an die Thessalonicher* (1986) 18; J. A. T. Robinson, *Redating the New Testament* (Philadelphia, 1976) 35f.; U. Schnelle, *NTS* 32 (1986) 208f.; E. Schuerer, *The History of the Jewish People,* ed. G. Vermes, F. Millar, and M. Goodman; III/1 (1986) 77f.; M. Sordi, *The Christians and the Roman Empire* (1986) 24-26; F. Watson, *Paul, Judaism and the Gentiles* (1986) 91-94, 207f.; P. Lampe, *Die stadtrömischen Christen* (1987) 4-8; E. Larsson, in *Festschrift P. J. Borgen* (1987) 112-19; C. Saulnier, *MBib* 51 (1987) 8f.; F. F. Bruce, *The Book of Acts* (1988) 347f.; T. A. Robinson, *The Bauer Thesis Examined* (1988) 78-81; C. J. Hemer, *The Book of Acts* (1989) 167f.; D. Slingerland, in J. Avery-Peck, *New Perspectives on Ancient Judaism* IV (1989) 133-44; *JQR* 79 (1989) 305-22; P. Stuhlmacher, *Paul's Letter to the Romans* (Eng. trans., 1994) 6-8; H. W. Tajra, *The Trial of St. Paul* (1989) 52-54; F. F. Bruce, *The Acts of the Apostles* (³1990) 390f.; K. P. Donfried, in R. F. Collins, *The Thessalonian Correspondence* (1990) 7f.; B. Levick, *Claudius* (1990) 121f.; D. R. Schwartz, *Agrippa I* (1990) 94-96; D. Slingerland, *JBL* 109 (1990) 687-90; C. P. Thiede, *Jesus* (1990) 114-17; C. K. Barrett and C. J. Thornton, *Texte zur Umwelt des Neuen Testaments* (²1991) 14f.; E. Dassmann, *Kirchengeschichte* I (1991) 96f.; K. F. Doig, *New Testament Chronology* (1991) 343f.; G. Lüdemann, in *Festschrift G. Schneider* (1991) 289-98; S. Légasse, *Paul apôtre* (1991) 138f.; J. Molthagen, *Hist* 40 (1991) 58; C. J. Thornton, *Der Zeuge des Zeugen* (1991) 201f., note 3; M. Sordi, *Humanistica e Teologia* 13 (1992) 64; D. A. Carson, D. J. Moo, and L. Morris, *An Introduction to the New Testament* (1992) 229; D. Slingerland, *JQR* 88 (1992) 127-44; H. Lichtenberger, in *Festschrift H. Schreckenberg* (1993) 249; W. Reinbold, *Der älteste Bericht über den Tod Jesu* (1994) 212. Additional bibliography can be found in n. 256 below.

    6. Concerning his life and work, cf. G. Funaioli, *PRE* II/7 (1931) 593-641; M. Fuhrmann, *KP* V (1975) 411-13; A. Wallace-Hadrill, *Suetonius* (1983) 1-96.

    7. Cf. G. B. Townend, *Hist* 10 (1961) 375-81.

Caesarum to this praetorian prefect, and seems to have worked on the overall piece until sometime after A.D. 130.[8] The Claudius-biography of interest to us here was presumably written during the A.D. 120s, and Suetonius was able to draw information for his work from his acquaintance with the imperial archives.[9]

Suetonius' *De vita Caesarum* was an extremely influential work,[10] though more recent scholarship offers widely varying opinions concerning the quality of this biography.[11] K. Bringmann especially has presented strong objections to the generally positive estimation of W. Steidle.[12] In his analysis of the Tiberius-*vita,* Bringmann critically alleges that Suetonius did not compose it according to any perspective suggested by the material itself, but rather rigidly imposed a preconceived dispositional schema. Bringmann concludes that "from a literary perspective, considerable caution should thus be exercised with regard to the writer Suetonius, and similar reservations are in order from the historical perspective as well."[13] One can hardly avoid the conclusion that Suetonius also wrote his biographies of the Caesars as popular literature,[14] often virtually "from the perspective of the personal servant."[15] It is noteworthy that the biography of Caligula is almost twice as long as that of Claudius, even though the latter reigned approximately three times as long as his predecessor. Apparently the biography of Claudius, despite diligent research, yielded fewer scandals and gossip items. Nonetheless, recent years have seen an increasingly more positive estimation of the accomplishments of Suetonius, and to her bibliography to *De vita Caesarum,* which includes the years 1950 to 1988, P. Galland-Hallyn even gives the subtitle "Vers une réhabilitation."[16] The historiographical qualities of Suetonius are as a rule given an especially positive evaluation. Thus J. Gascou attributes to the writer a preference for primary sources, a critical sensibility, and an inclination to use verbatim citations.[17]

8. Cf. G. B. Townend, *CQ* 9 (1959) 285-93.

9. Cf. A. Wallace-Hadrill, *Suetonius* (1983) 78-96; A. Dihle, *Greek and Latin Literature of the Roman Empire* (Eng. trans., 1994) 258-62, and esp. L. de Conninck, *ANRW* II 33.5 (1991) 3675-3700.

10. Cf. G. B. Townend, in T. A. Dorey, *Latin Biography* (1967) 96-108.

11. A survey of this discussion extending to the death of the author (1973) can be found in H. Gugel, *Studien zur biographischen Technik Suetons* (1977) 11-22. Cf. recently G. Lewis, *ANRW* II 33.5 (1991) 3623-74; P. Galland-Hallyn, *ibid.,* 3576-3622.

12. *Sueton und die antike Biographie* (²1963).

13. *RhM* 116 (1972) 285.

14. Cf. M. Fuhrmann, *KP* V (1975) 412; D. Flach, *Gymn* 79 (1972) 288.

15. O. Hiltbrunner, in *Kleines Lexikon der Antike* (⁴1975) 528.

16. *ANRW* II 33.5 (1991) 3576.

17. *Suétone historien* (1984), esp. 458-567. A more critical view is taken by B. Baldwin, *Suetonius* (1983) 101-213 (esp. 193f.).

In one sense, Suetonius' portrayal of Claudius is two-faced.[18] The intention of the critic from the equestrian class (§6.1) is quite evident, namely, that of having the emperor appear in an unfavorable light by recounting true or merely circulated scandals in the literary tradition of Seneca's *Apocolocyntosis*.[19] The biographer also, however, offers a wealth of information concerning administration policies whose justification and efficacy are at odds with his simultaneous character portrayal. Here Suetonius had access to excellent sources, sources which probably included the emperor's own autobiography,[20] from which this biographer alone cites a fragment (Suetonius, *Claudius* 2). To be sure, as a rule Suetonius offers such historically valuable material only in an extremely abbreviated form, and precisely the passage of interest to us prompts the groan of G. B. Townend regarding "all too many pieces of information which modern historians would like to be able to place in a satisfactory context. . . . From this point of view Suetonius can be infuriating. Again and again he passes over some interesting topic with an oblique reference, as the expulsion of the Jews under 'Chrestus' in *Cl.* 25.4."[21]

10.2.2. Vita Claudii 25.4

The famous passage reads: *"Iudaeos impulsore Chresto assidue tumultuantis* [sic!] *Roma expulit."*[22] This brief remark is part of a whole series of religious, civil, and military-legal measures undertaken by Claudius which Suetonius basically evaluates positively,[23] though he makes reference to the initiative of his wives and freedmen in denying that the emperor himself was their author (Suetonius, *Claudius* 25.5). Since this information thus does not accord with Suetonius' "agenda" as an author, there is no reason to assume Suetonius himself invented it. The biographer was probably simply passing on information he found in the imperial archives.[24] Even D. Flach, who on the whole offers a negative evaluation of Suetonius' biographical accomplishments,

---

18. Cf. V. M. Scramuzza, *Claudius* (1940) 27; T. F. Carnery, *ACl* 3 (1960) 104; A. Momigliano, *Claudius* (²1961) 76.

19. Cf. V. M. Scramuzza, *loc. cit.*, 26-32.

20. Cf. A. Momigliano, *Claudius* (²1961) 8; E. Huzar, *ANRW* II 32.1 (1984) 617.

21. In T. A. Dorey, *Latin Biography* (1967) 83f.

22. Text according to J. C. Rolfe, *Suetonius* II (1979) 52. The word *tumultuantis* represents not a typographical error, but rather an older special form.

23. Suetonius, *Claudius* 22: *"Quedam circa caerimonias civilemque et militarem morem, item circa omnium ordinem statum domi forisque aut correxit aut, exoleta revocavit aut etiam nova instituit"* (ed. Rolfe II, 44). Suetonius remarks positively concerning the measures undertaken against the Jews by Augustus (*Aug.* 93.2) and Tiberius (*Tib.* 36.1f.).

24. Cf. H. Janne, *AIPh* 2 (1934) 546; P. de Labriolle, *La réaction païenne* (1934) 42; J. Moreau, *NC* 1/2 (1949/50) 192; A. Hamman, *Festschrift M. Pellegrino* (1975) 92.

speaks with regard to such isolated bits of information about the "diligence Suetonius exercises in tracking down and using historiographically undisclosed material."[25] Perhaps Suetonius saw the imperial edict of expulsion himself. In any event, H. Fuchs is convinced of this, namely, "that, given the character of the information Suetonius has collected together in the chapter in question, it is highly probable that either Suetonius himself or the person from whom this information derives read the actual imperial order of expulsion, and perhaps merely misunderstood the situation that prompted it."[26]

Specifically, this remark stands in an enumeration of measures concerning Claudius' policies toward the non-Roman peoples of the empire (Suetonius, *Claudius* 25.3: *"peregrinae condicionis homines . . ."), something J. Mottershead[27] overlooks, whose division into merely political (Suetonius, *Claudius* 25.3f.) and purely religious measures (*Claudius* 25.5) is artificial and thus cannot serve as an argument against the religious background (what other would have been possible?) of the Jewish disturbances in Rome. Since Suetonius is using this information concerning Rome's Jews apparently to illustrate something that was typical of the emperor's policies, one would sooner view this as a measure of wider scope,[28] though the actual wording, because of the missing article in the Latin, leaves open the question of just how large was the circle of those who were expelled. One can also understand the participial expression as limiting,[29] and translate: "From Rome he expelled [such] Jews as were continually restive because of the instigator Chrestus." Of course, Suetonius could have expressed this sense with an indefinite pronoun such as *nonnulli* or a substantive such as *pars*.[30] Moreover, among the altogether five occurrences[31] of *Iudaeus* in Suetonius, the definite article should, given the sense of the passages, definitely be added in translation in three instances (*Tib.* 36; *Vesp.* 4.5; 8.1) and should probably be added in another (*Jul.* 84.5); only one passage (*Aug.* 76.2) is unclear.[32]

Broad controversies have surrounded the expression *"Chresto impulsore."*[33] This particular wording excludes the possibility that the expression

25. *Gymn* 79 (1972) 289.

26. In V. Pöschl, *Tacitus* (1969) 567, note 10.

27. Suetonius, *Claudius* (1986) 154, note 5.

28. Concerning the Roman policy of expulsion in general, cf. J. P. V. D. Balsdon, *Romans and Aliens* (1979) 97-115, 275-77.

29. So, among others, G. Lüdemann, *Paul: Apostle to the Gentiles* (1984) 164; E. M. Smallwood, *The Jews under Roman Rule* ([2]1981) 216; P. Lampe, *Die stadtrömischen Christen* ([2]1989) 6.

30. Cf. M. Simon, in *Religion et culture dans la cité Italienne* (1981) 42.

31. Cf. A. A. Howard and C. N. Jackson, *Index verborum C. Suetonii Tranquili* (1922) 127.

32. Cf. D. Slingerland, *JQR* 58 (1992) 134.

33. The earlier discussion is summarized in H. Janne, *AIPh* 2 (1934) 537-46.

is alluding in a completely general fashion to messianic disturbances among the Jews of Rome.[34] The word *impulsor* always refers to a specific person,[35] and *Chrestus/Christus* was incomprehensible in the Greco-Roman linguistic sphere as a designation for the anointed king.[36] Earlier, the view was frequently advocated that Suetonius is speaking here about an otherwise unknown Jewish agitator.[37] Especially E. A. Judge and G. S. R. Thomas, E. Koestermann, as well as S. Benko, though also M. Sordi[38] and D. Slingerland,[39] have recently tried to revive this thesis. Judge and Thomas believe that prior to Paul, there was in Rome as yet no public proclamation of the gospel, nor any Christian assemblies apart from the synagogues.[40] To maintain this thesis, however, they must play down all those passages in the Letter to the Romans that make it clear that Paul is writing to concrete house congregations with specific problems.[41] According to Koestermann,[42] Rome, too, experienced Jewish-messianic unrest in A.D. 49, when Judea was transformed into a Roman province. Here, however, the philologist of ancient languages is following the erroneous dating (§12.4.1) of Tacitus (Tacitus, *Ann.* xii.23.1). Benko's assumption[43] that Tacitus uses consistent orthography with *"i"* for *Christus/Christiani,* and that as a result Suetonius cannot be referring to (Jesus) Christ, is erroneous. The oldest text (Codex Mediceus 68 II) of Tacitus, *Ann.* xv.44.3, reads[44]: *"Nero subdidit reos et quaesitissimis poenis adfecit, quos*

34. This has now again been advocated by M. Borg, *NTS* 19 (1972/73) 212f.

35. Cf., e.g., Cicero, *In Vatinium* 24; Tacitus, *Hist.* iv.68.3. Suetonius uses the word only in this one passage. Cf. A. A. Howard and C. N. Jackson, *Index verborum C. Suetonii* (1922) 112.

36. Cf. M. Hengel, *Festschrift C. K. Barrett* (1982) 143; M. J. Harris, in *Gospel Perspectives* V (1985) 353f., 364f., note 42.

37. So, among others, T. Reinach, *Textes d'auteurs Grecs et Romains relatifs au Judaïsme* (1895) 329, note 2; M. Radin, *The Jews among the Greeks and Romans* (1915) 313; K. Linck, *De antiquissimis veterum quae ad Iesum Nazarenum spectant testimoniis* (1913) 104-7; E. T. Merrill, *Essays in Early Christian History* (1924) 102-8; earlier bibliography can be found in A. Hilgenfeld, *Historisch-kritische Einleitung in das Neue Testament* (1875) 303, note 4.

38. *The Christians and the Roman Empire* (1986) 24-26; *Humanistica e Teologia* 13 (1992) 64.

39. In A. J. Avery-Peck, *New Perspectives on Ancient Judaism* IV (1989) 133-44.

40. *RThR* 25 (1966) 81-94.

41. Cf. P. Stuhlmacher, *ZNW* 77 (1986) 180-93.

42. *Hist* 16 (1967) 459f.

43. *ThZ* 25 (1969) 411f. S. Benko summarizes his view in *ANRW* II 23.2 (1980) 1056-62, without picking up the ensuing discussion at all! It is not quite clear whether H. Solin, *ANRW* II 29.2 (1983) 689f., is following Benko.

44. Cf. E. Koestermann, *Hist* 16 (1967) 457; H. Fuchs, in V. Pöschl, *Tacitus* (1969) 563-69. Additional bibliography in P. Keresztes, *ANRW* II 32.1 (1979) 250, note 12; H. Hommel, in *Sebasmata* II (1984) 196.

per flagitia invisos vulgus Chrestianos appellabat. Auctor nominis eius Christus Tiberio imperitante per procuratorem Pontium Pilatum supplicio adfectus erat." The reading *"Chrestianos"* is additionally supported by the observation that we are apparently dealing here with the ironic play on words "worthies, philistines."[45] On balance, Benko inappropriately plays down the vacillation of the name forms (prompted by, among other things, itacism[46]) in the second and third, and indeed even in the fourth[47] century A.D.[48] Neither is his additionally necessary assumption tenable, namely, that Aquila and Priscilla (Acts 18:2) were not yet Christians when they were in Rome[49] (see pp. 190f. below).

Evidence militating against the hypothesis that by "Chrestus" Suetonius is referring to an otherwise unknown Jew includes especially the fact that this particular name form, while certainly occurring in abundance in Rome,[50] nowhere refers to a Jew (including outside the imperial capital).[51] If Suetonius had been referring to a person who was unknown in the Rome of his own time,[52] he would probably have written *"Chresto impulsore quodam/aliquo."*[53] This also eliminates the desperate assumption of H. Graetz,

45. Cf. A. Wlosok, *Rom und die Christen* (1970) 8-10. The suggestion of a wordplay goes back to H. Hommel, *ThV* 3 (1951) 17. Cf. H. Hommel, in *Sebasmata* II (1984) 196.
46. Cf. F. Blass, *Hermes* 30 (1895) 468-70; H. Hommel, *Sebasmata* II (1984) 179f.
47. Cf. Tertullian, *Apol.* 3.5; *Ad Nat.* 1.3; Lactantius, *Div. Inst.* iv.7.5; Lebaba-Inscription (southeast from Damascus, Marcionite, A.D. 318/19 [*OGIS* 608]), and Acts 11:26; 26:28; 1 Pet. 4:16 in א.
48. Documentation can be found in H. Fuchs, in V. Pöschl, *Tacitus* (1969) 565f., note 7; E. Gibson, *The "Christians for Christians" Inscriptions of Phrygia* (1978) 15-17; O. Montevecchi, in *Festschrift G. Lazzati* (1979) 485-500; G. H. R. Horsley, *NewDoc* III (1983) 128-36; M. J. Harris, in *Gospel Perspectives* V (1985) 354.
49. *ThZ* 25 (1969) 413.
50. The name occurs over one hundred times in *CIL* VI (e.g., *CIL* VI 7.5.6324-26). Cf. also Liddell-Scott-Jones, 1741f.
51. Cf. M. Hengel, *NTS* 18 (1971/72) 16, note 9; M. Stern, *Greek and Latin Authors on Jews and Judaism* II (1980) 116; R. E. Brown and J. P. Meier, *Antioch and Rome* (1983) 100. The woman's name ΧΡΕΣΤΕ in reference to a Jewish woman is attested once on an inscription from A.D. 80 in Panticapaeum (*CIJ* I, no. 683, line 5 [495f.]). Hence only the first part of the sentence of M. Sordi is correct (*The Christians and the Roman Empire* [1986] 25): "The use of the name 'Chrestus' was widespread in antiquity and, given its meaning ('chrestós' means 'good' in Greek), it was undoubtedly very popular among the Jews, who liked to use names of this kind (e.g., Justus)."
52. S. Benko, *ThZ* 25 (1969) 409f., suggests this: Suetonius "says simply that in A.D. 49 the Jews of Rome were incited to riotous actions by *someone* called Chrestus" (my emphasis).
53. Cf. M. Goguel, *Das Leben Jesu* (1934) 37; M. J. Harris, in *Gospel Perspectives* V (1985) 353 (who refers to Suetonius, *Claudius* 42.1: *"cuidam barbaro"*), and already K. T. Keim, *Rom und das Christenthum* (1881) 171f. One might also mention that in his Claudius-biography Suetonius otherwise mentions only significant names in connection with the imperial household. Cf. J. Mottershead, *Suetonius: Claudius* (1986) 150.

namely, that Chrestus was an otherwise unknown Christian apostle.[54] The suspicion of R. Eisler is not much better, according to whom this represents an allusion to the activity of Simon Magus in Rome (§10.5.3),[55] a view for which E. Bammel shows a certain sympathy.[56] Our sources, however, nowhere say that Simon bore the title Christ.[57] Neither does Acts 8:10, to which Bammel refers,[58] say anything of this sort.

The most obvious assumption is thus still that with *Chrestus* Suetonius is referring to the founder of the group of *Christiani,* a group he does indeed mention later (Suetonius, *Nero* 16.2).[59] His contemporary Tacitus proves that as an educated Roman at the beginning of the second century, one could indeed be familiar with these circumstances. It is entirely possible that Suetonius belonged to the entourage of Pliny the Younger when the latter, during his governorship in Bithynia, had to deal with the Christian question (Pliny the Younger, *Ep.* x.96-97).[60] Whether Suetonius was thinking of "Chrestus" as being actually present in Rome is, given the brevity of his expression, not at all as unequivocal as is often asserted.[61] The meaning can also be that the movement emanating out from Christ (in Palestine) had created disturbances as far as Rome. Unfortunately, Suetonius does not provide any more precise information concerning the reasons for the turmoil, though his manner of expression *(tumultuare/i)*[62] does show that these were not mere disputations; rather, the situation must have resulted in incidents that the Roman authorities viewed as disturbances of public order. The designation "Christian," which was applied to the new movement apparently by outsiders, possibly even by the Roman authorities, initially occurs above all in connection with state measures (§7.1.2). Hence E. Peterson re-

---

54. *History of the Jews,* vol. II (Eng. trans., 1893) 202.

55. ΙΗΣΟΥΣ ΒΑΣΙΛΕΥΣ ΟΥ ΒΑΣΙΛΕΥΣΑΣ I (1929) 132f.

56. *ZThK* 56 (1959) 299.

57. Cf. F. F. Bruce, *Paul* (1977) 381.

58. *ZThK* 56 (1959) 299, note 9.

59. It is incomprehensible why the — again, extremely brief — remark *"afflicti suppliciis Christiani, genus hominum superstitionis novae ac maleficae"* (Suetonius, *Nero* 16.2) should exclude any earlier mention of "Chrestus (= Christus)" (so D. Slingerland, in A. J. Avery-Peck, *New Perspectives on Ancient Judaism* IV [1989] 136, following B. Baldwin, *Suetonius* [1983] 355). One should rather not underestimate Suetonius' familiarity with early Christianity. Perhaps the birth legends mentioned in connection with Augustus (Suetonius, *Aug.* 9.3f.) are consciously anti-Christian. Cf. J. Gascou, *Suétone historien* (1984) 461, note 15.

60. Cf. J. Mottershead, *Suetonius: Claudius* (1986) 149.

61. So, e.g., E. Preuschen, *ZNW* 15 (1914) 96; E. Meyer, *Ursprung und Anfänge des Christentums* III (1923) 463; M. Dibelius, *SHAW* 32 (1941/2) 30; M. Grant, *The Jews in the Roman World* (1973) 146; B. Reicke, *The New Testament Era* (Eng. trans., 1968) 205, 226, 239.

62. Otherwise found also in Suetonius, *Jul.* 69; *Gaius* 9; 17.1; 51.3; 55.1; *Galba* 9.2; 19.2.

marked concerning this passage: "One can say perhaps that *Iudaei impulsore Chresto tumultuantes* is the exact rendering of what the Roman authorities in Antioch wanted to identify with the word Χριστιανός."[63]

10.2.3. Chronology

H. J. Cadbury considers the dating of the measure in the first year of Claudius' reign (A.D. 41) to be "a natural inference from the reference in Suetonius."[64] Perhaps there is merely a typographical error in the case of Dio Cassius (§10.3.3), who, however, is otherwise not mentioned by Cadbury in this context. In any event, the sequence of measures mentioned in the context of the Jewish edict in Suetonius shows that *Vita Claudii* 25.4 contains a thematic enumeration (see p. 163 above), something demonstrated by a glance at some of the events mentioned previously. Dio Cassius first mentions the withdrawal of the *civitas Romana* from unworthy foreigners for the year A.D. 43 (*Hist.* lx.17.5). In A.D. 44, Claudius elevated Achaia and Macedonia to senatorial provinces again (Tacitus, *Ann.* i.76; Dio Cassius, *Hist.* lx.24). By contrast, Lycia already became an imperial province in A.D. 43 (Dio Cassius, *Hist.* lx.17.3f.), while Rhodes did not reacquire its freedom, lost in A.D. 44, until A.D. 53, as did Ilion its freedom from taxation.[65] The attempt at introducing the Eleusinian mysteries in Rome, mentioned after the expulsion of the Jews, might have occurred in the years A.D. 47-49.[66] Hence if at all, one would have to find a later date for the edict concerning the Jews. G. Lüdemann, however, is quite correct in rejecting any chronological classification here,[67] although A.D. 41 would indeed fit well with his own outline (see pp. 177f. below).

10.3. Dio Cassius

10.3.1. The Historian

Dio Cassius was born in Bithynian Nicaea in A.D. 163 or 164 as a member of a senatorial family.[68] He entered the senate under Emperor Commodus

63. In *Frühkirche, Judentum und Gnosis* (1959) 77.
64. *The Book of Acts in History* (1955) 134, note 13.
65. Cf. B. Levick, *Claudius* (1990) 74.
66. Cf. *loc. cit.*, 87.
67. In *Festschrift G. Schneider* (1991) 291.
68. Concerning his life and work, cf. E. Schwartz, *PRE* I 3 (1899) 1684-1722; F. Millar, *A Study of Cassius Dio* (1964) 5-27; G. Wirth, in *Cassius Dio* I (1985) 7-60. The birth date of A.D. 155, advocated again now by G. Wirth (*loc. cit.*, 7), is untenable. Cf. F. Millar, *loc. cit.*, 13, esp. note 4.

around A.D. 189. After a respectable but unremarkable career, Dio was entrusted with high offices under Severus Alexander (emperor after A.D. 222). He served as proconsul in Africa (A.D. 223) and as legate for Dalmatia (A.D. 224-26) and Pannonia (A.D. 226-28). Because his strictness made him unpopular among the praetorians, he could exercise his second consulate (A.D. 229) only outside Rome itself, and thus returned to his home in Bithynia. The swift rise of Dio under Severus Alexander was connected with a renewed strengthening of the senate following a considerable weakening of the monarchy after the reign of Elagabalus (A.D. 218-22) and after the initial, representative regency of the imperial mother for Severus Alexander, who was only thirteen years old at his accession (Herodian vi.1.2; Dio Cassius, *Hist.* lxxx.1).

Dio's *Roman History* was composed between A.D. 207 and 229, and the book of interest to us (the sixtieth) in A.D. 216.[69] Because Dio was writing from the senatorial perspective, he appropriated part of the venomous criticism of Claudius passed down by tradition and was thus not quite just in his portrayal of the emperor.[70] Dio, too, portrays Claudius as a weak character dependent on the schemes and moods of his wives and freedmen (Dio Cassius, *Hist.* lx.2.4; 14.1f.; 17.8; 28.2, *et passim*). Even more strongly than in Suetonius, however, this evaluation is contrasted with flattering information concerning measures from the emperor's reign, and Dio even attributes a whole series of these to Claudius himself when the latter was able to free himself from the influence of others (Dio Cassius, *Hist.* lx.3.1; 8.4).

As a portrayal of the time of the emperors, Dio's *Roman History* is of inestimable value to us, even if one must classify the work as the kind of "semi-popular history"[71] favored among the more educated classes during the entire history of the Roman empire. In addition, its historical value is also sometimes impaired by his manner of literary composition. Although the general structure of the work is "annalistic, there are also more thematic organizational principles at work that lead to chronological ambiguity."[72] This manner of composition shows that Dio was indebted to the historiographical theories of Greek tradition.[73] The author had at his disposal for this work a wealth of sources, including apparently such important ones as the *Histories*

---

69. Cf. F. Millar, *A Study of Cassius Dio* (1964) 193f. The general considerations of M. M. Eisman, *Latomus* 36 (1977) 658f., can in my opinion not call into question the detailed analysis of F. Millar, *loc. cit.,* 28-72.

70. Cf. V. M. Scramuzza, *Claudius* (1940) 32-34. Concerning the political convictions of Dio that influenced his historiography, cf. R. Bering-Staschewski, *Römische Zeitgeschichte bei Cassius Dio* (1981). The senatorial position becomes especially evident in Dio Cassius, *Hist.* liii.17.1-9. Cf. *loc. cit.,* 131f.

71. M. M. Eisman, *Latomus* 36 (1977) 659.

72. K. Stiewe, *KP* I (1964) 1077.

73. Cf. C. Questa, *SUSF* 31 (1957) 37-53.

of Pliny the Elder and imperial annals and edicts.[74] The account of Claudius
has been preserved for us not only in Byzantine excerpts, but in part also in
the original version. Unfortunately, however, the conclusion to the sixtieth
book is truncated, so that the portrayal extends only to the year A.D. 46, and
the time after this is only insufficiently covered by the Byzantine excerpts.

10.3.2. Historia Romana lx.6.6

Here Dio Cassius writes: Τούς τε ᾿Ιουδαίους πλεονάσαντας αὖθις ὥστε
χαλεπῶς ἂν ἄνευ ταραχῆς ὑπὸ τοῦ ὄχλου σφῶν τῆς πόλεως εἰρχθῆναι, οὐκ
ἐξήλασε μέν, τῷ δὲ δὴ πατρίῳ βίῳ χρωμένους ἐκέλευσε μὴ συναθροίζεσθαι.[75] The historian presents this remark within an enumeration of measures
undertaken by Claudius which are cast in a positive light by framing remarks
in *Hist.* lx.3.1 (οὐκ ὀλίγα καὶ δεόντως ἔπραττεν) and *Hist.* lx.8.4 (ταῦτα μὲν
οὖν αὐτοῦ τε τοῦ Κλαυδίου ἔργα ἦν καὶ ὑφ᾽ ἁπάντων ἐπηνεῖντο). Hence
there is no reason to attribute this information to Dio's anti-Claudian agenda.
Like all Roman historians, Dio was extremely anti-Jewish, as demonstrated
by his numerous remarks concerning the Jews.[76] He remained silent about the
Christians because the latter simply were not permitted even though they had
long become numerous, and though he did at least indirectly polemicize
against them in Maecenas' speech.

The measure Dio portrays here also concurs completely with two of
the basic principles of Claudius' religious policies (§6.2.3). Although if at all
possible the traditional religions were to be tolerated and supported, they were
not permitted to threaten public order. The strong increase of Jews in Rome
was probably caused primarily by the influx of fellow countrymen from other
parts of the empire, something Claudius was not glad to see in the case of
Alexandria (§6.2.3). One further reason may have been the considerable
success in in attracting proselytes, which under Tiberius resulted in an expulsion of Jews from Rome (see p. 174 below). According to Dio, however,
Claudius allegedly did not enact such a measure precisely because he feared
such steps would provoke public unrest.

It was typical of Claudius to allow the Jews to structure their lives
commensurate with their patriarchal traditions (τῷ πατρίῳ βίῳ χρεῖν), concerning which T. Zahn remarks that "since the observation of the Sabbath
and the religious services in the synagogue on the Sabbath were a prime
feature of their ancestral customs, the decree against συναθροίζεσθαι cannot

---

74. Cf. E. Huzar, *ANRW* II 32.1 (1984) 618; A. Dihle, *Greek and Latin Literature
of the Roman Empire* (Eng. trans., 1994) 348f.

75. Text according to E. Carey, *Dio's Roman History* VIII (1968) 382.

76. Cf. M. Stern, *Greek and Latin Authors on Jews and Judaism* II (1980) 347-407.

refer to the religious services."[77] Hence Zahn translated the Greek expression as "tumultuous gatherings,"[78] and this verb can indeed be used to refer to the mustering of soldiers (e.g., Xenophon, *An.* vii.2.8)[79] and occasionally to a rebellious assembly of the people (Acts 19:25). In other passages, however, συναθροίζεσθαι[80] unequivocally refers to an assembly for religious purposes, and indeed with respect both to synagogal (Josephus, *B.J.* ii.289: συναθροί-ζεσθαι εἰς συναγωγήν) and Christian worship services (Ignatius, *Magn.* 4; cf. Acts 12:12). The context in Dio sooner suggests that this prohibition against assembly involved more than politically motivated, conspiratory assemblies. Immediately following (Dio Cassius, *Hist.* lx.6.6b), Dio speaks about the prohibition of political clubs (ἑταιρεῖαι) and taverns (καπηλεῖα) (*Hist.* lx.6.7). Perhaps, however, one should translate this remark concerning the anti-Jewish measure as openly as it sounded in the original: "When the Jews had again so increased in number that it would have been difficult, given the great crowd, to expel them from the city without causing an uproar, he [Claudius] did not drive them out, but rather ordered that they not assemble, even though they [otherwise] were able to carry on their traditional way of life." Prior to A.D. 70, synagogal worship services were for many Jews not yet as indispensable a part of Jewish life as Zahn believed. From a later period we even learn that some Jews concealed their lifestyle in Rome externally so as to escape payment of the temple tax (see p. 200 below). For devoted Jews, however, such a prohibition of synagogal assembly certainly would have constituted a strong impetus to emigrate.

10.3.3. Chronology

Dio reports these anti-Jewish actions in Rome within his portrayal of the first year (cf. Dio Cassius, *Hist.* lx.9.1; 10.1) of Claudius (A.D. 25 January 41–25 January 42), and many earlier scholars considered this to be the only possible dating of these measures.[81] Their main representative, H. Janne,[82] was encouraged in this position especially by his assumption, one that today has been virtually abandoned (see p. 100 above), that Claudius' letter to the

---

77. *Introduction to the New Testament* (Eng. trans., 1909) 3.466. Similarly also M. Simon, in *Religion et culture dans la cité Italienne* (1981) 43.

78. *Ibid.*

79. Cf. further Liddell-Scott-Jones, 1692b.

80. The verb occurs in the middle form only in this passage in Dio. The active form occurs in *Hist.* vii.10.12; 21.4; ix.23.5; xlvi.41.5; lxiii.22.2. Cf. W. Nawijn, *Cassii Dionis Historiarum Romanorum Quae Supersunt* V (1931) 757.

81. So T. Zielinski, *RUB* 32 (1926/27) 143; P. de Labriolle, *La réaction païenne* (1934) 42; J. W. Swain, *HThR* 37 (1944) 348f.

82. *AIPh* 2 (1934) 550-53.

Alexandrians from the year A.D. 41 was referring to Jewish Christians who, coming from Palestine, caused unrest there because of their missionary activities.[83] More recently, this particular dating of Claudius' measure has been advocated especially by H. J. Leon,[84] M. Stern,[85] D. Slingerland[86] and D. R. Schwartz,[87] as well as G. Lüdemann,[88] the latter of whom finds here one of his main points of departure for a complete revision of Pauline chronology.

The Tiberius-biographer A. Garzetti, however, assumes that Dio incorrectly dated Claudius' measure in this instance.[89] As demonstrated by his account of Claudius' campaign in Britain, Dio is by no means free of incorrect chronological assumptions with regard to the reign of this emperor.[90] Garzetti, like other scholars before him,[91] draws support for his criticism from Claudius' initially benevolent policies toward the Jews, which would not have allowed this hostile an action as early as the first year of his reign. But even if one does not downplay the emperor's original benevolence and especially the influence of Agrippa I (§6.2.1-2) as strongly as does D. Slingerland,[92] this argument is still not persuasive. As demonstrated by the events in Alexandria (§6.2.3), Claudius was fully capable of intervening decisively even at the beginning of his reign if this was in the interest of public order. One might even assume that it was out of consideration for the Jewish king that Claudius did not in fact expel the Jews from Rome.[93]

Anyone who identifies the events reported by Dio with the expulsion measure attested by Suetonius (§10.4) must plausibly explain how the emergence of the Christian faith in Rome had already caused disturbances by A.D. 41. There may very well have been Christians in the imperial capital at this early date. The relationship between the Jews of Rome and those of Jerusalem was close,[94] and the new messianic faith presumably had already reached the

---

83. *RA* 35 (1932) 268-81; *AIPh* 4 (1936) 273-95.

84. *The Jews of Ancient Rome* (1960) 27.

85. CRINT I/1 (1974) 182; *Zion* 44 (1979) 18-23; *Greek and Latin Authors on Jews and Judaism* I (1980) 116.

86. *JQR* 79 (1989) 307-16.

87. *Agrippa I* (1990) 94-96.

88. *Paul: Apostle to the Gentiles* (1984) 165-71; *Festschrift G. Schneider* (1991) 289-98.

89. *Tiberius* (1974) 140.

90. Cf. A. Barrett, *Britannica* 11 (1980) 31-35.

91. H. Vogelstein and P. Rieger, *Geschichte der Juden in Rom* I (1896) 19; E. Schürer, *Geschichte des jüdischen Volkes* II (⁴1909) 62; R. O. Hoerber, *CThM* 31 (1960) 691; S. Benko, *ThZ* 25 (1969) 407; W. Wiefel, *Jud* 26 (1970) 78.

92. *JQR* 79 (1989) 308-13; 88 (1992) 129-31.

93. So also H. Solin, *ANRW* II 29.2 (1983) 689.

94. Consider merely the significance of pilgrimages (Acts 2:10). Cf. in this regard A. Causse, *RHPhR* 20 (1940) 120-41. The "synagogue of *Libertines*" mentioned in Acts

imperial capital through returning festival pilgrims quite soon after the crucifixion and resurrection of Jesus.[95] Other information, however, introduces
certain problems into the assumption that an expulsion took place in the first
year of Claudius. An account found in Augustine (Augustine, *Ep.* 102.8),
passed on under the name of Porphyrius (A.D. 243-301/5), one that quite
obviously is erroneously referring to Jews, apparently dates the beginning of
Roman (Jewish-)Christianity either in the last years of Caligula or in the first
years of Claudius.[96] This accords strikingly with yet another ancient church
tradition. Eusebius (*HE* ii.14.6; *Chron.* [ed. Helm 179]) and Jerome (*De Vir.
Ill.* 5) concur in their assertion that Peter was in Rome during the second year
of Claudius (A.D. 42/43). Whatever the truth may be concerning this tradition
(§7.2.2), those who passed it on were in any event not familiar with any
prohibition preventing foreign Jews from staying in Rome during this period.
According to Orosius, too, who probably follows Jerome here, Peter was
active in Rome at the beginning of Claudius' reign (Orosius, *Adv. Pag.*
vii.6.1f.).

J. Murphy-O'Connor,[97] following E. M. Smallwood,[98] claims to have
found in Philo a clear reference to anticipated anti-Jewish measures by
Claudius during the first year of his reign (A.D. 41). The Jewish philosopher's
praise of Augustus for having ordered neither an expulsion from Rome nor
any prohibition of worship (Philo, *Leg. ad Gaium* 157) seeks to ward off
Claudius' own threatening action. But another advocate of the early dating,
H. Janne, did consider it certain that "on ne peut donc admettre que Philon
eût écrit le §23 de son ouvrage, conçut tout entier pour flatter le nouvel
Empereur judéophile, si Claude venait d'interdire, à Rome, les réunions juives:
c'eût une allusion blessante, une critique maladroite et dangereuse."[99] Hence
one should not make too much of this section in Philo, particularly since the
Jewish philosopher does in fact seem to expect a turn for the better.

6:9 "is probably that of the Roman contingent in which according to both Philo and
Tacitus the freed Jewish prisoners of war played a decisive role" (M. Hengel, *ZThK* 72
[1975] 183).

95. Cf. J. Munck, *The Acts of the Apostles* (1967) 176. Among others, M. J.
Lagrange, *Saint Paul: Épître aux Romains* (²1922) XXI, and O. Michel, *Der Brief an die
Römer* [⁵1978] 34), suggest that this might have taken place already after the first Pentecost
(cf. Acts 2:10). An account in Ambrosiaster (*Ep. ad Rom.,* Prologue [*CSEL* 81/1.5f.]),
which may derive from an older tradition (F. Watson, *Paul, Judaism and the Gentiles*
[1986] 93f.), ascribes the founding of the church to conservative Jewish Christians without
any participation of the apostles.

96. Cf. T. Zahn, *Der Brief des Paulus an die Römer* (²1910) 8f., note 16.

97. *St. Paul's Corinth* (1983) 136f.

98. *The Jews under Roman Rule* (²1981) 214.

99. *AIPh* 2 (1934) 535, note 1. Similarly already W. Seston, *RHPhR* 11 (1931)
300.

Several scholars have asked whether in the context of interest to us here Dio has in fact proceeded in a strictly chronological fashion or rather composed thematically.[100] F. Millar has ascertained that basically "even in the supposedly chronological sections, . . . he does not keep strictly to the annalistic structure."[101] This can be demonstrated especially in the portrayals of the reigns of Hadrian[102] and Caracalla.[103] But for the time of Claudius, too, there is at least one sure indication of such compositional technique. What Dio (*Hist.* lx.11.8) remarks concerning the acceptance of equestrians among the tribunes "has been included in the history of the year 42 probably only because of the nature of this summarizing account,"[104] even though it in fact belongs after A.D. 48. G. Lüdemann[105] refers to the earlier opinion of F. Millar,[106] namely, that in his *Hist.* lx.3.1, Dio switches from a more general characterization of Claudius to a chronological narrative. Yet in his revision of the corresponding section in the historical work of E. Schürer, Millar now retains the sentence: "With the words λέξω δὲ καθ' ἕκαστον ὧν ἐποίησε in chapter 3, Dio does not switch to chronological narrative, but to a description of Claudius' good features."[107] Such a division into positive (Dio Cassius, *Hist.* lx.3.1) and negative actions (*Hist.* lx.8.4) thus occurs in this form only at the beginning of the reign, and this might betray the presence of an at least partially thematic organizational principle.

Some scholars have thus considered whether the more strictly chronological narrative technique begins only with Dio Cassius, *Hist.* lx.8, in the first place.[108] However, G. Lüdemann[109] and D. Slingerland[110] are correct in asserting that Dio, *Hist.* lx.3.2–8.7, given the chronological information supplied there, intends to speak generally about the first year of Claudius' reign: He reports sequentially the execution of the murderers of Caligula (*Hist.* lx.3.4), the repeal of the laws passed by him (*Hist.* lx.4.1f.), and "ἐν τῷ ἔτει τούτῳ" the marriage of one of Claudius' daughters to Lucius Junius Silanus (*Hist.* lx.5.7). He speaks about the anti-Jewish measure (*Hist.* lx.6.6) prior to a more recent elimination of laws of Gaius (*Hist.* lx.6.8), and thereafter (μετὰ

100. So, e.g., K. Lake, *BC* V (1933) 459; R. O. Hoerber, *CThM* 31 (1960) 692; H. Solin, *ANRW* II 29.2 (1983) 689, note 221.

101. *A Study of Cassius Dio* (1964) 40. See also p. 171 above.

102. Cf. F. Millar, *loc. cit.,* 66f.

103. Cf. F. Millar, *JEA* 48 (1962) 124f.

104. E. Groag, *PRE* I 3 (1899) 2805.

105. *Paul: Apostle to the Gentiles* (Philadelphia: Fortress, 1984) 187, note 67.

106. *A Study of Cassius Dio* (1964) 40.

107. Schuerer III/1 (1986) 77, note 91; cf. *ibid.,* V.

108. Cf. G. Hoennicke, *NKZ* 13 (1902) 597; A. Bludau, *Kath* 83 (1903) 127f.

109. *Festschrift G. Schneider* (1991) 292.

110. *JQR* 79 (1989) 307f.

τοῦτο) about the return of Commagene to Antiochus IV (*Hist.* lx.8.1). Immediately thereafter, we hear of the bestowal of territories to Agrippa I (§6.2.2) and his brother Herod of Chalcis (*Hist.* lx.8.2f.), which Josephus securely dates in the year A.D. 41 (Josephus, *Ant.* xix.274-77). In "the same year" (καὶ τούτῳ τῷ ἔτει) he dates victories against the Chatti and Cauchi as well as the Imperator-title for Claudius (*Hist.* lx.8.7). A renewed campaign against the Moors is then dated in the next year (τῷ δὲ ἐχομένῳ) (*Hist.* lx.9.1). For the reasons cited above, however, this does not yet resolve the dating of every event mentioned. Here one must point out that especially *Hist.* lx.6.1–7.4 largely portrays measures and events of an extremely general kind. To mention but three examples: that the anecdote about Claudius' politeness toward the consuls in the Senate (*Hist.* lx.6.1) took place precisely in A.D. 41 seems just as uncertain as does the assumption that it was only in this year that the emperor lived in Neapolis (*Hist.* lx.6.2). Immediately prior to the anti-Jewish measures, we hear about behavior that was quite typical of the emperor during his entire reign: he normally prevented any repetition of the equestrian competitions (*Hist.* lx.6.5). Hence although a dating of the Roman measures concerning the Jews in A.D. 41 is indeed possible, it is by no means certain. As we have seen, other sources neither eliminate as impossible nor confirm as probable this particular chronological placement.

10.4. The Relationship between the Accounts

10.4.1. The Sources

Josephus (*Ant.* xviii.81-84), Tacitus (*Ann.* ii.85.4), Suetonius (*Tib.* 36), and Dio Cassius (*Hist.* lvii.18.5) all report in various ways a banning of Jews from Rome under Tiberius. Based on Tacitus, this measure is as a rule dated in the year A.D. 19. Because of Philo's silence (cf. Philo, *Leg. ad Gaium* 160f.), and because Josephus reports the incident in the middle of his portrayal of the procuratorship of Pontius Pilate (A.D. 26-36) (Josephus, *Ant.* xviii.84), L. Herrmann has advocated the time around A.D. 30.[111] However, the chronological placement in the Jewish historian is vague, and the position of the fragment Dio Cassius, *Hist.* lvii.18.5a in John of Antioch seems rather to favor A.D. 19.[112] Both Josephus and Tacitus, in those extant parts of his *Annales* dealing

---

111. *Chrestos* (1970) 10-12. L. Herrmann also finds an allusion to this expulsion in Acts 2:10 (οἱ ἐπιδημοῦντες Ῥωμαῖοι).

112. Cf. E. M. Smallwood, *The Jews under Roman Rule* ([2]1981) 209, and 202f., note 6. Concerning the problems of dating in Josephus, cf. §3.1.2.

with the reign of the emperor (Tacitus, *Ann.* xi-xii regarding A.D. 47-54), are silent regarding any expulsory actions directed against the Jews under Claudius. This situation makes it extremely difficult to determine the relationship between the measures mentioned in Suetonius and Dio Cassius.

10.4.2. Two Temporally Distinct Events?

The differences between these remarks have prompted many scholars to assume that we are dealing here with two distinct measures undertaken by Claudius.[113] Dio's remark might suggest a police action following the unrest at the end of the reign of Caligula.[114] The edict reported by Suetonius would then represent a more stringent measure. Because the later reign of Claudius (after A.D. 46/47) is only insufficiently documented in the Byzantine excerpts, A. Momigliano has suspected that Dio reported the second, more stringent measure as well.[115] Of course, one wonders why Xiphilinus would have omitted precisely such an event affecting the Jews. One of the examples mentioned briefly above can show clearly just how precarious such an *argumentum e silentio* can be. For A.D. 53, Zonaras mentions an otherwise unattested shortage of bread in Rome (Dio Cassius, *Hist.* lx.33.10); by contrast, the Byzantine excerpts make no mention of the Roman famine of A.D. 51, which is indeed attested elsewhere (see p. 132 above). With regard to the Jewish edict, T. Zahn was of the opinion that "Dio Cassius alludes through the first negative sentence (οὐκ ἐξήλασε μέν) that he is indeed familiar with the later expulsion of Jews from Rome, even though we have no evidence of

---

113. So H. Smilda, *C. Suetonii Vita Divi Claudii* (1896) 123f.; E. Groag, *PRE* I 6 (1899) 2790, 2810; A. Gaheis, *ibid.,* 2829; G. Hoennicke, *NKZ* 13 (1902) 597; E. Preuschen, *Die Apostelgeschichte* (1912) 111; T. Zahn, *Introduction to the New Testament* (Eng. trans., 1909) 466f.; E. Meyer, *Ursprung und Anfänge des Christentums* III (1923) 463; H. S. Jones, *JRS* 16 (1926) 31; A. D. Nock, *CAH* X (1934) 500; E. Bammel, *ZThK* 56 (1959) 296; A. Momigliano, *Claudius* (²1961) 31-33; W. Wiefel, *Jud* 26 (1970) 78; F. F. Bruce, *Paul* (1977) 381f.; E. M. Smallwood, *The Jews under Roman Rule* (²1981) 211-15; R. K. Jewett, *A Chronology of Paul's Life* (1979) 36-38; H. Solin, *ANRW* II 29.2 (1983) 688-90; F. Watson, *Paul, Judaism and the Gentiles* (1986) 91-94; E. Larsson, in *Festschrift P. J. Borgen* (1987) 111-19; D. Slingerland, *JQR* 79 (1989) 305-22; in A. J. Avery-Peck, *New Perspectives on Ancient Judaism* IV (1989) 143f.; *JBL* 109 (1991) 687-90; and now H. Botermann, *Das Judenedikt des Kaisers Claudius* (1996) 44-140.

114. So E. Preuschen, *Apostelgeschichte* (1912) 111; J. W. Swain, *HThR* 37 (1944) 348f., who even assumes that Agrippa I, by letter, prompted Claudius to undertake measures against the Jewish-Christians after his own example (Acts 12). Similarly also F. F. Bruce, *BJRL* 44 (1961/2) 321. J. Mottershead, *Suetonius: Claudius* (1986) 152f., argues the possibility that in the year A.D. 41 the Alexandrians Isidor and Lampon (see p. 101 above) engaged in antisemitic agitation in Rome as well.

115. *Claudius* (²1961) 31f.

this from his own hand."[116] It is certain only that Dio's remark (*Hist.* lx.6.6) contains a clear allusion to the expulsory action under Tiberius ('Ιουδαίους πλεονάσαντας αὖθις),[117] about which he had earlier reported (*Hist.* lvii.18.5). If in the *"assidue tumultuantis"* (Suetonius, *Claudius* 25.4) one finds a direct connection between the two measures, then the remark in Dio (*Hist.* lx.6.6) would constitute a witness to an extremely early beginning for Christianity in Rome.[118]

10.4.3. Different Accounts of the Same Event?

E. Schürer wondered whether it would not be extremely remarkable if from the two anti-Jewish measures in Rome under Claudius, Suetonius and Dio Cassius had each chosen a different one.[119] Hence a larger number of scholars consider that the two events thus portrayed are actually identical, though the details of their arguments deviate widely.[120] T. Zielinski was the first to assume that Dio was consciously correcting the account of Suetonius which he had before him by disputing that Claudius enacted a ban.[121] H. Janne[122] and J. Moreau[123] followed his suggestion. Problems attending this interpretation,

116. *Die Apostelgeschichte* II ([3]1924) 635, note 14.
117. Cf. T. Mommsen, *HZ* 64 (1890) 408, note 2; E. Meyer, *Ursprung und Anfänge des Christentums* III (1923) 463; H. Janne, *AIPh* 2 (1934) 533; F. F. Bruce, *Neutestamentliche Zeitgeschichte* II (1976) 97; P. Lampe, *Die stadtrömischen Christen* ([2]1989) 8. D. Slingerland, *JBL* 109 (1990) 689, writes as if he were the first to discover this.
118. So F. Watson, *Paul, Judaism and the Gentiles* (1986) 93.
119. Cf. E. Schürer (here edited by F. Millar) III/1 (1986) 77, note 91.
120. E. Schürer, *Geschichte des jüdischen Volkes* III ([4]1909) 62, note 91; A. von Harnack, *Die Mission und Ausbreitung des Christentums* ([4]1924) 10; W. M. Ramsay, *St. Paul* ([17]1930) 254; A. Steinmann, *Apostelgeschichte* ([4]1934) 214f.; J. Felten, *Neutestamentliche Zeitgeschichte* I ([2/3]1925) 286; K. Lake, *BC* V (1933) 459; P. de Labriolle, *La réaction païenne* (1934) 42; J. W. Swain, *HThR* 37 (1944) 348f.; H. J. Leon, *The Jews of Ancient Rome* (1960) 27; R. O. Hoerber, *CThM* 31 (1960) 691; S. Benko, *ThZ* 25 (1969) 406f.; M. Stern, CRINT I/2 (1974) 182; O. Michel, *Der Brief an die Römer* ([5]1977) 34f., note 1; G. Lüdemann, *Paul: Apostle to the Gentiles* (1984) 164-71; in *Festschrift G. Schneider* (1991) 289-93; R. Penna, *NTS* 28 (1982) 331; M. Stern, *Greek and Latin Authors on Jews and Judaism* II (1980) 116; J. Murphy-O'Connor, *RB* 89 (1982) 84-86; *St. Paul's Corinth* (1983) 134-39; B. Baldwin, *Suetonius* (1983) 356; J. Mottershead, *Suetonius: Claudius* (1986) 152f.; E. Schuerer (ed. F. Millar), III/1 (1986) 77, note 91; H. W. Tajra, *The Trial of St. Paul* (1989) 52-54; D. R. Schwartz, *Agrippa I* (1990) 94-96. Earlier representatives can be found in H. Janne, *AIPh* 2 (1934) 533, note 7; D. Slingerland, *JQR* 79 (1989) 306, note 4.
121. *RUB* 32 (1926/27) 143f., note 2. An allusion in this direction can already be found in H. Willenbücher, *Vergangenheit und Gegenwart* 3 (1913) 364, note 1.
122. *AIPh* 2 (1934) 534f.
123. *Témoignages profanes sur Jésus* (1944) 50.

however, are already demonstrated by the fact that Janne made the error of viewing the rejection of the expulsory edict as a merely inaccurate suspicion on the part of Dio, while at the same time accepting the date suggested by him. Janne did not explain why Dio would have falsely corrected Suetonius and then provided correct information beyond him. Without naming his predecessor,[124] G. Lüdemann[125] formulated a similar hypothesis, one which especially J. Murphy-O'Connor[126] picked up. "The solid historical kernel of the reports about Claudius's edict concerning the Jews in the year 41 C.E.," according to Lüdemann, is that "the emperor expelled the people who were directly involved in the disturbances involving Chrestus in a Roman Jewish synagogue. Fearing political implications, he denied the other members of the synagogue the right to meet together and thus retracted the right of association."[127] Suetonius and Dio allegedly drew from a common source for this incident, one Suetonius embellished such that one could understand him at least in the sense of a summary expulsion of all Jews. To avoid this misunderstanding, Dio questioned any expulsion and mentioned only the withdrawal of the right to assembly. To be sure, Dio "seems to have generalized unhistorically when he spoke of *the* Jews in his account."[128]

Significant objections and questions can be raised with regard to this reconstruction: (1) The shared features between the accounts of Suetonius and Dio Cassius are at the same time those between Dio's report of the expulsion under Tiberius (*Hist.* lvii.18.5) and the decree passed down involving Claudius. Thus the agreements are to be explained on the basis of the material in the works themselves, and cannot be evaluated as they concern the actual source situation. (2) Why did Suetonius and Dio stylize an event as insignificant as the closing of *one* synagogue into a event allegedly typical of Claudius' policy toward the Jews? Inscriptions mention at least twelve synagogal communities. (3) The assumed measure does not exactly concur with the new estimation of the historian Suetonius to the extent he recounts Claudius' political measures (see p. 162 above). When one sees how quickly, on the other hand, the information in Orosius (§10.4.2) concerning the anti-Jewish measure is put aside,[129] one is astonished at the unbroken faith in the contents

---

124. Two earlier advocates are mentioned with their thesis at least in the material used by G. Lüdemann: T. Zielinski in V. M. Scramuzza, *Claudius* (1940) 286, note 19, and A. Momigliano, *Claudius* (²1961) 99, note 30, as well as H. Janne in W. den Boer, *RAC* III (1957) 180.

125. *Paul: Apostle to the Gentiles* (1984) 164-67.

126. *RB* 89 (1982) 85f.; *St. Paul's Corinth* (1983) 134-36; *Paul* (1996) 9-15.

127. *Paul: Apostle to the Gentiles* (1984) 166.

128. *Ibid.,* emphasis in the original.

129. G. Lüdemann, *Paul: Apostle to the Gentiles* (1984) 164; J. Murphy O'Connor, *RB* 89 (1982) 84f.; *St. Paul's Corinth* (1983) 131f.

of sources one does not see. Even U. Schnelle, who otherwise follows Lüdemann's chronology, admits: "This is the weak link in Lüdemann's argumentation, for he naturally interprets the (actually non-extant!) common source in the sense of his own thesis."[130]

Can one harmonize the two Roman authors such that a somewhat plausible scenario emerges without having to adduce hypothetically constructed, undemonstrable sources? A number of ancient historians are undertaking such an attempt (one usually scorned in connection with the Gospels). For example, one has suggested that the prohibition against assembly (Dio) immediately preceded the expulsion (Suetonius).[131] This, however, leaves unexplained why Dio finds such a measure to be problematical. An expulsion of some sort was indeed enacted, and this is supported not only by the possibilities in Suetonius (§10.2.1), but also by his agreement with Acts (§10.6). The divergence between the statements of Suetonius and Dio would sooner be comprehensible if, after a time, what was perhaps in any event a merely limited expulsory edict (Suetonius) was ameliorated into a general prohibition against assembly (Dio).[132] Then it would remain possible that Dio, too, was familiar with the expulsory edict, and was pointing out that it did not develop into an expulsion in the style of Tiberius.

10.4.4. The Least Problematical Solution

The virtually equal distribution of scholars holding to these two different interpretations shows how difficult is a decision regarding the relationship between the accounts of Suetonius and Dio Cassius. At present, the suggestion of G. Lüdemann has found advocates especially among theologians.[133] His solution can explain relatively well the evidence in Tacitus (§10.4.1) and Dio Cassius (see pp. 174f. above), though auxiliary constructions are possible here even if one assumes we are dealing with two different events: for A.D. 49, Dio's work is preserved only incompletely in the Byzantine excerpts, so that we cannot say with any certainty whether he reported there concerning a Jewish edict. If Tacitus wrote something in the lost portion of his *Annales* about Claudius' first anti-Jewish measure in Rome, then he might also have

130. *NTS* 32 (1986) 222, note 20.

131. So A. Bludau, *Kath* 83 (1903) 128.

132. So, variously, most of the authors mentioned in note 76, excepting those following T. Zielinski and G. Lüdemann.

133. G. Lüdemann, *Paul: Apostle to the Gentiles* (1984) 290, expresses the expectation: "It is therefore to be hoped that the dating of Claudius' edict agianst the Jews to the year 41 C.E. will soon become part of common knowledge in New Testament scholarship." G. Lüdemann, *Festschrift G. Schneider* (1991) 289-98, does not address the criticism of E. Larsson and D. Slingerland (see note 113).

mentioned there the later expulsion, commensurate with the thematic context of the passage, especially if that expulsion was not as extensive as that under Tiberius. Josephus' silence regarding a measure hostile to the Jews not only in the year A.D. 49 but also in A.D. 41 remains an embarrassment for Lüdemann, particularly in light of the fact that the Jewish historian reports in considerably more detail about Claudius' beginnings than about his later years. This shows how precarious the *argumentum e silentio* is here as well. In view of the *testimonium Flavianum* (Josephus, *Ant.* xviii.63f.), it is unlikely that Josephus would have refrained from mentioning the measure(s) so as to avoid speaking about the Christians (see p. 35 above).

The confusing plethora of attempted scenario variations leads one to view skeptically the assumption that we are dealing here with accounts of ultimately one and the same event. D. Slingerland mentions no fewer than ten scenarios, and then only those that are more characteristic.[134] One notices that today, too, ancient historians are more inclined to prefer the assumption of two different events.[135] Despite all its attendant problems, this seems to be the most economical hypothesis,[136] since it avoids literary-critical operations with merely postulated sources and violent attempts at harmonization of what are actually mutually exclusive statements (concerning the implementation of an expulsion). The assumption of two different events would be significantly strengthened if one could establish a date different from A.D. 41 for the measure mentioned by Suetonius.

---

134. *JQR* 79 (1989) 321.

135. In addition to A. D. Nock, A. Momigliano, E. M. Smallwood, and H. Solin (mentioned in note 113), cf. also W. H. C. Frend, *Martyrdom and Persecution* (1965) 160; J. P. V. D. Balsdon, *Romans and Aliens* (1979) 106; D. Kienast (cf. H. Hübner, *ThLZ* 107 [1982] 743); E. Huzar, *ANRW* II 32.1 (1984) 638; C. J. Hemer, *The Book of Acts* (1989) 167f.; B. Levick, *Claudius* (1990) 121; J. Molthagen, *Hist* 40 (1991) 58; and especially forcefully H. Botermann, *Das Judenedikt des Kaisers Claudius* (1996) 44-140.

136. In the final version of my *Habilitationsschrift* (*Die Frühzeit des Paulus* [1990] 146-53), I still assumed (albeit with some reluctance) that these were partially complementary accounts of the same event. This change of opinion, which I share with F. F. Bruce (*The Acts of the Apostles* [²1952] 368; differently in ³1990, p. 391), represents an (extremely small) additional element of relief for the chronology I advocate. Probably because of E. M. Smallwood's extremely concise manner of expression (*HT* 15 [1965] 236), D. Slingerland, *JQR* 79 (1989) 321, note 70, falsely attributes the same change of opinion to Smallwood, *The Jews under Roman Rule* (²1981) 215. Apparently, modern historians, too, are sometimes not so easy to interpret.

10.5. Paulus Orosius

10.5.1. The Universal Historian

In A.D. 417/18, Paulus Orosius, a presbyter from Braga in what is today Portugal, published at the request of Augustine his *Historia adversus Paganos,* a work divided into seven books[137] which established him as the "founder of Christian universal historical writing."[138] Indeed, one can even say that in the larger sense this represents "the first self-enclosed and literarily sophisticated world or universal history."[139] In a complement to Augustine's *De civitate Dei,* Orosius wanted to show that despite the conquest of Rome by the West Goths, even the external circumstances of humankind had changed for the better since the advent of Christ.[140]

Orosius drew from a larger number of sources for his work,[141] sources which were accessible to him among other places also in the bishop's library of Hippo Regius (cf. Augustine, *Civ. Dei* iv.6). The estimation of Orosius' historiographical accomplishments is also quite divided. The objection of "hastiness in the use of sources"[142] is countered by the assertion that "apart from this one-sided inclination [namely, Orosius' concentration on wars and other catastrophes] and several instances of exaggeration, especially in providing numbers, his use of sources is quite precise."[143] Orosius was already remarkably aware of the fundamental difficulties of writing history (e.g., Orosius, *Adv. Pag.* iii praef 1f.; 2.9f.). Judged against the standard of ancient historians, he should probably be counted among those of higher quality.[144]

---

137. Concerning his life and work, cf. W. S. Teuffel, *History of Roman Literature* (Eng. trans., 1900) 2.454-57; F. Wotke, *PRE* II 35 (1939) 1185-95; E. Corsini, *Introduzione alle "Storie" di Orosio* (1968) 9-33; B. Lacroix, *Orose et ses idées* (1965) 29-39; C. Andresen, in *Orosius* I (1985) 5-57.

138. B. R. Voss, *KP* IV (1972) 350.

139. F. Wotke, *PRE* II 35 (1939) 1189.

140. Concerning Orosius' theology of history, cf. esp. B. Lacroix, *Orose* (1965) 87-110; F. Paschoud, *Roma Aeterna* (1967) 276-92; E. Corsini, *Introduzione alle "Storie" di Orosio* (1968) 35-215.

141. Cf. in this regard W. S. Teuffel, *Geschichte der römischen Literatur* III (1913) 407f. (Eng. trans., *Teuffel's History of Roman Literature* [1900]); B. Lacroix, *Orose* (1965) 58-62; C. Andresen, in *Orosius* I (1985) 36-41.

142. W. S. Teuffel, *loc. cit.,* 407.

143. F. Wotke, *PRE* II 35 (1939) 1192. H. W. Goetz, *Die Geschichtstheologie des Orosius* (1980) 18, comes to a similar conclusion.

144. Cf. esp. B. Lacroix, *Orose* (1965) 51-69. G. Lüdemann, in *Festschrift G. Schneider* (1991) 295, draws support for his own negative conclusion one-sidedly from C. Andresen, in *Orosius* I (1985) 36.

10.5.2. Adversus Paganos vii.6.15

This passage reads: *"Anno eiusdem nono expulsos per Claudium Vrbe Iudaeos Iosephus refert. sed me magis Suetonius mouet, quit ait hoc modo: Claudius Iudaeos impulsore Christo adsidue tumultuantes Roma expulit; quod, utrum contra Christum tumultuantes Iudaeos coherceri et conprimi iusserit, an etiam Christianos simul uelut cognatae religionis homines uolerit expelli, nequaquam discernitur"* (Orosius, *Adv. Pag.* vii.6.15f.).[145] "In the ninth year of the same reign, Josephus reports that the Jews were expelled from the city by Claudius. But Suetonius impresses me more,[146] who speaks in the following manner: 'Claudius expelled the Jews from Rome, who at the instigation of Christ were continually causing disturbances.' But it is by no means discernible whether he ordered that [only] the Jews causing disturbances against Christ were to be checked and repressed, or whether he simultaneously wanted to expel the Christians as well, as adherents of a related religion."

Whereas one accepts the fact that Orosius accurately identified Chrestus with Christ, his description of Christianity as *cognata religio* has been severely criticized.[147] Apart from the fact that he leaves the question undecided, and that he would have the support of several modern scholars in answering the question positively (see p. 63 above), this objection does not affect the sources he names here. He cites Suetonius (Suetonius, *Claudius* 25.4) verbatim except for the substantively appropriate addition of the subject Claudius, suggesting that he also found the preceding sentence in a source. One much-discussed difficulty emerges from the fact that the extant writings of Josephus do not contain the kind of dating which Orosius provides. One cannot exclude the possibility that Orosius is referring to a writing under the name of the Jewish historian which we no longer possess,[148] but since he seems to have known Josephus only by way of the *Chronicle* of Eusebius,[149]

145. Ed. C. Zangmeister, *CSEL* V (1882) 451.

146. The assertion of G. Lüdemann, in *Festschrift G. Schneider* (1991) 293, that Orosius is "correcting" "Josephus" here is too strong.

147. Cf. J. Murphy-O'Connor, *St. Paul's Corinth* (1983) 131.

148. Thus the query of A. Deissmann, *Paulus* ([2]1925) 223 (Eng. trans., *Paul* [[2]1926]; M. Goguel, *Das Leben Jesu* (1934) 421, note 49. Nothing of this sort is found in the so-called Pseudo-Hegesippus, a Latin paraphrase of Josephus' *De Bello Judaico* from *ca.* 370 (H. Schreckenberg, in *Jewish Historiography and Iconography in Early and Medieval Christianity* [1991] 71-73) (*PL* 15.2061-2326).

149. Cf. A. von Harnack, *SPAW.PH* (1912) 675; G. Bardy, *RHE* 43 (1948) 185f.; H. Schreckenberg, *Die Flavius-Josephus-Tradition* (1972) 95. The assumption of R. Eisler, ΙΗΣΟΥΣ ΒΑΣΙΛΕΥΣ ΟΥ ΒΑΣΙΛΕΥΣΑΣ I (1929) 134, that a corresponding remark in Josephus, *B.J.* ii, or Josephus, *Ant.* xx, allegedly fell victim to the Christian censor is untenable. Cf. by contrast D. Slingerland, *JQR* 88 (1992) 137f.

and since in its extant form (*GCS* 47) the latter contains nothing of this sort, this assumption is highly unlikely.

Orosius apparently also seems to have used sources other than Eusebius for the reign of Claudius. Orosius' relatively favorable portrayal of the initial reign of the emperor is no cause for objection,[150] and has rather prompted praise from modern scholars.[151] This estimation probably also has something to do with the sources he had before him. As far as one of Claudius' positive measures is concerned, namely, the amnesty he issued at his accession, A. Mehl has shown that the *Annales* of Tacitus were the most likely source (Orosius, *Adv. Pag.* vii.6.1-5).[152] But the ecclesiastical writer cannot have gotten the date in Orosius, *Adv. Pag.* vii.6.15 from Tacitus, since the latter's work for the year A.D. 49/50, though extant, contains nothing of this sort.

B. Rigaux has considered the possibility that Orosius calculated his date from Acts,[153] and J. Murphy-O'Connor is certain of this: "Since Orosius was a priest, he certainly knew *Acts,* and he might have worked out his date for the edict by simply subtracting 18 months (*Acts,* XVIII,11) from the date of Gallio's term of office which may have been reflected in his Roman sources!"[154] Hence Orosius allegedly proceeded no differently than the majority of contemporary New Testament scholars (§11). But why did he then refer to Josephus? Had he in the meantime forgotten his own calculations, or is he consciously and deceptively adducing an authority whom he, on the other hand, did not value all that much? Such suspicions should be considered only when all other explicative possibilities have been exhausted. Above all, however, Murphy-O'Connor does not address the decisive question: How, at the beginning of the fifth century in Spain, did Orosius have access to the *fasti consulares* for the province of Achaia in the first century A.D.? Although Byzantine chronographers such as Sulpicius Severus and Julius Hilario, as well as the *Chronicon Paschale,* did use *fasti* of the consuls of Rome, these contain only extremely sparse information concerning the pre-Diocletian period.[155]

Without referring to Murphy-O'Connor, G. Lüdemann is now also supporting the view that "the ninth year of Claudius" was calculated from

---

150. So G. Lüdemann, *Paul: Apostle to the Gentiles* (Philadelphia: Fortress, 1984) 186f., note 64 (cited below).

151. Cf. V. M. Scramuzza, *Claudius* (1940) 34; T. F. Carney, *ACl* 3 (1960) 104.

152. *RhM* 121 (1978) 185-94.

153. *The Letters of St. Paul* (Eng. trans., 1968) 88.

154. *RB* 89 (1982) 85 (without referring to B. Rigaux); so also J. Mottershead, *Suetonius: Claudius* (1986) 151.

155. Cf. H. Gelzer, *Sextus Julius Africanus und die byzantinische Chronographie* II (1885) 119f., 128, 156-67.

Acts.[156] He argues that Eusebius could refer his readers to the documents of the proconsul Aemilius Frontinus concerning the Montanist Alexander (second century) in the archives of Ephesus (Eusebius, *HE* v.18.9). But the bibliographical resources of the imperial court historian, who in the first half of the fourth century traveled back and forth between Caesarea and Byzantium, are not without further qualification comparable to those of the Spanish presbyter at the beginning of the fifth century. If Orosius had initiated research in the archives of Corinth, why did he mention neither the source nor his efforts to his readers, falsely naming Josephus instead? D. Slingerland goes even further and considers the information concerning the year to be an apologetic invention of Orosius himself,[157] who allegedly wanted to explain the difficulties that Claudius encountered in his tenth year[158] as the divine response to the emperor's anti-Christian actions during the previous year. Slingerland does, to be sure, forget to ask just why the clever forger put himself at risk by adducing for his invention precisely a source that was quite well known, relatively widespread, and hence could be checked. As an example for such data manipulation, Slingerland observes[159] that Orosius (*Adv. Pag.* vii.6.1f.) dates Peter's arrival in Rome in the first year of Claudius, while the *Chronicle of Eusebius*, one of his sources, speaks of the second year (Eusebius, *Chron.* [ed. Helm 179]). To be sure, Orosius does date this only generally at the beginning of the emperor's reign *"exordio regni eius Petrus . . . Romam uenit"* (ed. Zangemeister 447). One can, but must not necessarily, understand this as the first year. A shift of one year would also be something different from the complete invention of a date, particularly since tradition did indeed offer various dates for Peter's arrival in Rome (see p. 119 above). Apart from information concerning the year, G. Lüdemann also assumes the presence of information concerning an expulsion of Roman Jews which Orosius acquired from hearsay, as its rendering in indirect discourse allegedly shows.[160] Lüdemann observes insightfully that Orosius' slight criticism of this information does suggest the presence of an extant tradition.

Based on his dating of the Claudius-measure in A.D. 41, Lüdemann critically remarks: "According to Orosius, Christianity first appeared in Rome at the beginning of the reign of Claudius — as a result of the proclamation by Peter (7.6.1-2). Orosius was sure, on the basis of the report of Suetonius (and Acts 18:2), that Claudius's decree concerning the Jews was related to Christ's impact in Rome. For chronological reasons he could hardly follow a

---

156. In *Festschrift G. Schneider* (1991) 296.
157. *JQR* 88 (1992) 139-42.
158. Concerning the problems with this date, see p. 187 below.
159. *JQR* 88 (1992) 140, note 58.
160. In *Festschrift G. Schneider* (1991) 294f.

tradition that reported an act by Claudius against the Jews (Jewish Christians) in the first year of his reign. Further, Orosius presents a very favorable picture of the first years of this emperor."[161] As we have seen, however, one *can* understand Orosius as saying that Peter came to the imperial capital already in the first year of Claudius' reign.[162] But would it not have enhanced the apostle's fame if on the basis of his proclamation such an uproar had arisen among the Jews? Orosius also reckons with the possibility that only Jews were expelled. Would it not have accorded with the "very favorable picture" if the emperor had "checked and repressed the riotous Jews" (Orosius, *Adv. Pag.* vii.6.16)? If one is going to engage in hypothetical considerations concerning Orosius' literary technique, then why not this one as well? T. Holtz justifiably protests "the attempt to eliminate Orosius at the very outset," and insists that "sources of a secondary character must and may also constitute the point of departure for conclusions if sources of a primary character are absent; both the latter and the former must be critically secured in any event."[163]

One of the sources Orosius uses most frequently is the *Chronicle* of Eusebius in the version edited by Jerome. No less than 286 references can be demonstrated,[164] and Orosius follows the guide of the *Chronicle* for his portrayal of the reign of Claudius as well. A. von Harnack pointed out that the information which in this section begins with *"anno eius,"* as does the present notice, "has come *completely* and almost verbatim from the Chronicle."[165] This passage is indeed not found in the *Chronicle* (see above); elsewhere as well, however, Orosius has quite obviously used an edition with addenda that are otherwise unknown to us,[166] one apparently enriched above all from the earlier historical work of Julius Africanus.[167] Harnack thus considered it possible that the interpolator read the indication of year in a context in which Josephus was also mentioned, and a mixup occurred.[168] Julius

161. G. Lüdemann, *Paul: Apostle to the Gentiles* (1984) 187, note 64.

162. Cf. also A. Mehl, *RhM* 121 (1978) 188.

163. *Der erste Brief an die Thessalonicher* (1986) 18, note 48. Compare how B. Levick, *Claudius* (1990) 218f., note 14, adduces dates from Orosius for her biography of the emperor.

164. Cf. B. Lacroix, *Orose* (1965) 62 (bibliography).

165. *SPAW.PH* (1912) 675. The occurrences are Orosius, *Adv. Pag.* vii.6.2 = Jerome, *Chron.* 2085; Orosius, *Adv. Pag.* vii.6.9 = Jerome, *Chron.* 2061; Orosius, *Adv. Pag.* vii.6.12 = Jerome, *Chron.* 2061; Orosius, *Adv. Pag.* vii.6.13 = Jerome, *Chron.* 2064; Orosius, *Adv. Pag.* vii.6.14 = Jerome, *Chron.* 2064; Orosius, *Adv. Pag.* vii.6.17 = Jerome, *Chron* 2065. Hence this is by no means a discovery of G. Lüdemann, as it might appear in *Festschrift G. Schneider* (1991) 293f.

166. Cf. C. Andresen, in *Orosius* I (1985) 38f.

167. Cf. C. Zangemeister, *CSEL* V (1882) XXIV.

168. *SPAW.PH* (1912) 676.

Africanus himself also seems to have used Josephus.[169] A more remote possibility Harnack considers is "whether the remark does not derive from Justus of Tiberias, whom Africanus demonstrably did use in his chronicle . . . and who could easily be confused with Josephus."[170]

Once alerted to this possibility of a confusion of names, one can then inquire further which other Jewish or early Christian historian known to us possessed a similar name. The Jewish Christian (Eusebius, *HE* iv.22.8) Hegesippus (Ἡγήσιππος) was called after the Old Testament "Joseph" (יוֹסֶף; יוֹסֵפוֹס). Julius Africanus concluded his *Chronography* in A.D. 217,[171] while Hegesippus wrote his *Memoirs* (cf. Eusebius, *HE* iv.8.17) around A.D. 180.[172] The extant fragments of the *Chronography*[173] do not allow us to decide whether Africanus used the work of Hegesippus. However, Africanus' considerable chronological interest becomes evident from the fragment on the suffering of Jesus.[174] He apparently also demonstrated a similar considerable personal interest in the history of the family of Jesus (Eusebius, *HE* i.7), about which the Jewish-Christian historian provided much information (Eusebius, *HE* ii.23.3-19; iii.11; 19-20.6; 32.1-16; iv.22.4-6). Hegesippus' search for elements of genuine apostolic tradition also took him to Corinth (Eusebius, *HE* iv.22.1-3) and Rome (Eusebius, *HE* iv.11.7; 22.1f.), where he might have learned more about the edict of Claudius.

Given our knowledge at present, any considerations regarding the possible source from which Orosius acquired this date must remain conjectural. G. Lüdemann counters such attempts by suggesting that "the problem is simply shoved from one place to another, and nothing much has been gained as regards the question of the reliability of the indication of year."[175] But from the fact that Lüdemann himself incorrectly ascribes to the series editor S. Safrai a bibliography concerning the remark in Suetonius, instead of to the author M. Stern (see p. 158, note 5 above), one may not also then conclude that the dates of publication given in that bibliography are without exception false. Moreover, Julius Africanus and Hegesippus are at least as real as the nonextant common source(s) of Suetonius and Dio Cassius from which Lüdemann reconstructs the events. A parallel to the difficulty in Orosius can be found in Origen. Three times this church

169. Cf. H. Gelzer, *Sextus Julius Africanus und die byzantinische Chronographie* I (1898) 254, 265.

170. *SPAW.PH* (1912) 676, note 2. Concerning Julius Africanus' use of Josephus, cf. H. Gelzer, *loc. cit.,* 255-65.

171. Cf. J. Sickenberger, *PRE* I 19 (1918) 116.

172. Cf. B. Altaner and A. Stuiber, *Patrologie* (1980) 109.

173. M. J. Routh, *Reliquiae Sacrae* II (²1846) 238-308; *PG* 10, 63-94.

174. M. J. Routh, *loc. cit.,* 297-306. In this regard, cf. H. Gelzer, *Sextus Julius Africanus* I (1898) 46-50.

175. G. Lüdemann, *Paul: Apostle to the Gentiles* (1984) 164.

father adduces the authority of Josephus (Origen, *Cels.* i.47 ["in the eighteenth book of the *Antiquities*"]; ii.13; *In Mt.* x.17 [on 13:55 (*GCS* 10.22)]) in support of the statement that Jerusalem was destroyed in requital for the death of James the brother of Jesus, even though nothing of the sort can be found in Josephus. T. Zahn believes this to be a Christian interpolation of Josephus,[176] though then it is difficult to explain how this particular variant — one of interest to Christians — disappeared so completely from the textual tradition that has come down to us. Zahn also admitted that Eusebius had acquired the same statement (Eusebius, *HE* ii.23.20) neither from Origen nor from an interpolated version of the *Antiquities*.[177] A. Schlatter[178] surmised that Origen acquired the information from a now lost chronicle of the relative of Jesus and Jewish-Christian bishop Judah of Jerusalem[179] from the period around A.D. 140. This chronicle allegedly combined information from Josephus with Christian interpretation in such a way that Origen arrived at his erroneous statement. Hence this chronicle of Judah Kyriakos would also be a potential candidate as the source of Orosius.

It is also interesting to point out that in Eusebius, the alleged citation from Josephus (Eusebius, *HE* ii.23.20) follows closely on a passage from the *Memoirs* of Hegesippus (Eusebius, *HE* ii.23.3-19) that concludes with a similar statement about the connection between the martyrdom of James and the destruction of Jerusalem (Eusebius, *HE* ii.23.18). J. Klausner thus assumed that both Origen and the author of the *Chronicon Paschale* (*Chron. Pasch.* [ed. Dindorf, I 463]) confused Hegesippus and Josephus.[180] The remark in the *Chronicon Paschale* as well as Hegesippus agrees more strongly, and this is why E. Schürer[181] assumes that at least here such confusion of names did occur. At present we can only hypothesize about the character of Orosius' source; but there are as few persuasive reasons supporting the assertion that the presbyter simply invented the reference to the "ninth year of Claudius" as there are in the case of the problematical Josephus-citation of Origen. Both Origen and Orosius are ancient church scholars to be taken seriously, and not simply frivolous fabricators.[182] The fact that they were also subject to errors in citation merely makes them more like us.

176. *FGNKAL* VI (1900) 301-5.

177. *Ibid.,* 304.

178. *Der Chronograph aus dem zehnten Jahre Antonins* (1894) 66-75.

179. Concerning him, cf. also R. Riesner, in K. Bockmühl, *Die Aktualität der Theologie Adolf Schlatters* (1989) 60-65.

180. *Jesus* (Eng. trans., 1943) 59f. So also now Schuerer I, 430, note 1.

181. *Geschichte des jüdischen Volkes* I (⁴1901) 582, note 45.

182. The devaluation of Orosius is not the domain only of skeptical scholars. A conservative Protestant such as G. Wohlenberg, *ThLBl* 33 (1912) 510, found only "historical error," because he thought the ninth year of Claudius did not fit the overall chronological concept; a similar view was held by the Catholic G. H. Guyot, *CBQ* 6 (1944) 29.

10.5.3. The Chronological Information

The dating in the "ninth year of Claudius" (Orosius, *Adv. Pag.* vii.6.15) takes us to the time from A.D. 25 January 49 to 25 January 50. W. M. Ramsay believed that Orosius was always one year behind in his portrayal of the reign of Claudius because he allegedly confused years of the calendar with those of the reign.[183] Ramsay adduced two examples of this.[184] A famine in Syria, which Orosius shifts to the fourth year of Claudius (A.D. 44/45) (Orosius, *Adv. Pag.* vii.6.12), allegedly did not take place until A.D. 45/46, since Josephus dates it under Tiberius Alexander (Josephus, *Ant.* xx.101). However, a failed harvest may also already have led to famine under Cuspius Fadus in the year A.D. 44 (§8.2.1). A more serious example is that Orosius dates a famine in Rome in the tenth year of Claudius (A.D. 50/51) (Orosius, *Adv. Pag.* vii.6.17), while Tacitus definitively places it in the eleventh (A.D. 51/52) (Tacitus, *Ann.* xii.43). Apart from the fact that Orosius even finds a certain measure of understanding in this regard from the modern Claudius-biographer B. Levick,[185] the remark of K. Lake does apply here: "Because Orosius once made this error it does not follow that he always did so."[186] However, Ramsay's argument is weakened especially by the fact that in this case Orosius is not passing on his own calculations, but rather the dating of some source.[187] Orosius' date remains a possibility even after critical evaluation, though it can acquire probability only through correlation with other independent evidence.

10.6. Additional Sources?

10.6.1. Eusebius, Ecclesiastical History ii.18.9

Here we read: "At this time (κατὰ δὲ τούσδε τοὺς χρόνους), while Paul was finishing his journey from Jerusalem and round about unto Illyricum, Claudius banished the Jews from Rome, and Aquila and Priscilla, with the other Jews, left Rome and came into Asia, and lived there with Paul the Apostle, while he was strengthening the foundations of the churches there which had recently been laid by him. The sacred Scripture of the Acts teaches this also."[188] Prior

---

183. *St. Paul the Traveller and the Roman Citizen* ([17]1930) 254. W. M. Ramsay followed J. E. Belser, *ThQ* 80 (1898) 369f.

184. *Loc. cit.,* 68.

185. *Claudius* (1990) 219, note 18.

186. In *BC* V (1933) 459. Similarly also R. O. Hoerber, *CThM* 31 (1960) 691, note 4.

187. A. Deissmann, *Paulus* ([2]1925) 222 (Eng. trans., *Paul* [[2]1926]).

188. Translation according to Kirsopp Lake, *Eusebius: The Ecclesiastical History* I (1949) 161.

to this, the church historian reports concerning the Jewish legation to Caligula (A.D. 41), which included Philo (Eusebius, *HE* ii.18.8). Hence one might ask whether Eusebius is thinking of an early date for the expulsion of Jews from Rome. Yet immediately thereafter, he reports (Eusebius, *HE* ii.19.1), following Josephus (Josephus, *B.J.* ii.227), an event during the procuratorship of Cumanus, and then with a direct reference to the Jewish historian (Josephus, *B.J.* ii.247f.) the installation of Felix, which is traditionally dated A.D. 48-52 or 52.[189] P. Schmidt thus believed (prior to the discovery of the Gallio-inscription) that from the perspective of the rest of Pauline chronology he could date the expulsory edict to the years A.D. 52/53.[190] But the Greek reference is so general that it says no more than that the measure was implemented under Claudius. Just how sweepingly Eusebius is reporting can also be seen from the fact that he does not mention Aquila and Priscilla's stay in Corinth at all, but rather has them travel immediately to Asia Minor (Eusebius, *HE* ii.18.9). One might in any case ask whether the church historian here did not possess some independent information about a plan Paul already had for pushing on to Rome then by way of Illyricum (§18.4.2). But perhaps this only represents his own, albeit questionable combination drawing on Rom. 15:19. Nothing suggests compellingly that Eusebius used anything except Acts in his account of the expulsory edict,[191] a source which he does, after all, explicitly adduce (Eusebius, *HE* ii.18.9). His formulation, strongly resembling that of Acts 18:2, also suggests that this was his direct source.

10.6.2. Doctrina Addai

This Syriac version of the legend of Abgar (cf. Eusebius, *HE* i.13) is usually dated around A.D. 400.[192] The *Doctrina Addai* views the expulsion of Jews from Rome under Claudius as punishment for the fact that the Jerusalem Jews denied Christians there access to Golgotha and to the tomb of Jesus.[193] The emperor was informed of this by his wife "Protonike," who had undertaken a pilgrimage to the holy city after Peter converted her in Rome to faith in the Messiah Jesus.[194] This information is of no use in reconstructing historically the events surrounding the Roman edict concerning the Jews. G. Howard does at least want to view as accurate the assertion that even before the expulsory

189. Concerning a divergent dating in A.D. 48-49 and 49, cf. §12.4.1.
190. *Der erste Thessalonicherbrief* (1885) 87-90.
191. So, among others, also E. Schürer, *Geschichte des jüdischen Volkes* III (⁴1909) 63, note 92; H. J. Leon, *The Jews of Ancient Rome* (1960) 24; A. Suhl, *Paulus und seine Briefe* (1975) 326.
192. Cf. B. Altaner and A. Stuiber, *Patrologie* (1980) 139.
193. *The Teaching of Addai*, ed. G. Howard (1981) 32f.
194. *Ibid.,* 21f.

edict there were disturbances between the Jews and Christians in Jerusalem, too.[195] Perhaps disturbances genuinely did occur at that time (§15.1), but their main cause was the fanatical opposition to the Jewish-Christian mission to the Gentiles. By contrast, we have no supporting source for the assertion that property rights to Golgotha also played a role at that time. The narrative of the *Doctrina* presumably represents a free combination of information from Acts (Acts 18:2), the tradition that Peter visited Rome early (§7.2.2), and the most recent form of the legend of the finding of the cross.[196]

10.6.3. Scholium to Juvenal iv.117

The *CL Scholia in Iuvenalem* were composed around A.D. 400. The only independent information about the Jews from an unknown source reads: " '*Dignus Aricinos qui mendicaret ad axes*': *Qui ad portam Aricinam sive ad clivum mendicaret inter Iudaeos, qui ad Ariciam transiereant ex urbe missi.*"[197] "Well-fitted to beg at the wheels of Arician chariots: Who should go a-begging at the Arician gate or at the hill among the Jews, who passed over to Aricia after they had been expelled from Rome." According to Martial (Martial ii.19.3), a large colony of beggars lived near the much-frequented pilgrimage locale Aricia.[198] Scholars variously identify — without justification — the expulsion mentioned in the scholion with that under Tiberius (A.D. 19),[199] Claudius,[200] or with some other unknown police action.[201] A connection between this expulsion and Claudius might be supported by the fact that Aricia is also mentioned as the place where Simon Magus stayed and to which he withdrew (*Act. Verc.* 32). Given the witness of Justin (Justin, *Apol.* i.26f.; cf. Irenaeus, *Haer.* i.23.1), one can hardly dispute historically that Simon did stay in Rome during the reign of Claudius. Hence one cannot completely exclude the possibility that with this scholion we possess, along with Acts

195. *RestQ* 24 (1981) 177.

196. Cf. J. Jeremias, *Golgotha* (1926) 30f.

197. Text according to M. Stern, *Greek and Latin Authors on Jews and Judaism* II (1980) 655. It seems doubtful that the Acts of Vercelli (see below) associated Simon Magus with Aricia because of this passage (so R. A. Lipsius, *Die apokryphen Apostelgeschichten* II/1 [1887] 274).

198. Cf. L. Friedländer, *D. Junii Juvenalis Saturarum Libri V* (1895) I 252. T. Zahn, in *Altes und Neues* (1927) 114-23, 131-36, identified the "mountain of Arcadia" (*Herm. Sim.* ix.1.4) with the Monte Gentile in Aricia.

199. E. Schürer, *Geschichte des jüdischen Volkes* III (⁴1909) 63; J. Juster, *Les Juifs dans l'empire Romain* I (1914) 180, note 9.

200. A. Momigliano, *Claudius* (²1961) 30, 96.

201. So, as a possibility, M. Stern, *Greek and Latin Authors on Jews and Judaism* II (1980) 655.

and Suetonius, yet a third independent source regarding the expulsion of Jews from Rome under Claudius.

10.7. Acts

10.7.1. Acts 18:2

Acts represents our oldest source concerning a measure hostile to the Jews under Claudius in Rome, regardless of whether one accepts the date of composition suggested by the majority (around A.D. 80) or minority opinion (prior to A.D. 70). Luke mentions the imperial expulsory edict with extreme brevity: "(1) After this Paul left Athens and went to Corinth. (2) There he found a Jew named Aquila, a native of Pontus, who had recently (προσφάτως) come from Italy with his wife Priscilla, because Claudius had ordered all Jews to leave Rome (διὰ τὸ διατεταχέναι Κλαύδιον χωρίζεσθαι πάντας τοὺς Ἰουδαίους ἀπὸ τῆς Ῥώμης). Paul went to see them, (3) and, because he was of the same trade, he stayed with them, and they worked together — by trade they were tentmakers" (Acts 18:1-3).[202]

It is altogether remarkable that Luke mentions the edict of Claudius at all since, given the structure and direction of his work, he would have had reason enough to pass over it in complete silence. One can see how inopportune the decree was for him by the fact that he does not expressly mention any connection with disturbances also affecting Roman Christianity. Upon Paul's arrival in Rome, the Jewish elders talk as if they themselves have not yet had any closer acquaintance with the new messianic faith (Acts 28:21f.).[203] Although Luke does realize that Christians were already living in Rome long before the apostle arrived (Acts 28:14f.), he structures his narrative such that Paul's arrival in the imperial capital has the effect of a new beginning.

This is also why Luke does not expressly state that Aquila and Priscilla were Jewish Christians,[204] although this is, despite occasional doubts to the contrary, obvious: "That a Jewish couple expelled because of the conflict with Christians in Rome deliberately gave a Christian missionary work and shelter is far more improbable than that Paul found lodgings with Christians who had fled from Rome."[205] Aquila and Priscilla are not mentioned among those

202. For the secondary character of the so-called Western text of Acts 18:2-4, cf. B. M. Metzger, *Textual Commentary* (²1975) 460f.
203. An attempt at a historical explanation can be found in T. A. Robinson, *The Bauer-Thesis Examined* (1988) 80f.
204. Cf. concerning this whole question J. Roloff, *Die Apostelgeschichte* (1981) 270; G. Schneider, *Die Apostelgeschichte* II (1982) 248f.
205. E. Haenchen, *Acts* (Eng. trans., 1971) 533, note 4.

whom the apostle baptized in Corinth (1 Cor. 1:14-16), and Stephanas is mentioned as the first convert in Achaia (1 Cor. 16:15). "The most obvious conclusion is that the married couple was already baptized when Paul arrived in Corinth as the first Christian missionary."[206] Though both are referred to as "Jews," one should keep in mind that in Acts the term Ἰουδαῖος first refers to the ethnic group, and thus can also include Jewish Christians (Acts 16:1, 20; 21:39; 22:3, 12).[207] Hence one must not with G. Schille assume that Luke intentionally but incorrectly portrayed Aquila and Priscilla as "pure Jews."[208] Rather, as in other contexts, the author of Acts passes over substantive matter he considers inappropriate for the intentions of his overall portrayal. The historiographical problem seems to reside less in the fact that Luke is inventing material than that he is passing over it in silence.

Especially as regards the Claudian edict concerning the Jews, there is no reason to assume Luke invented what for him was an awkward measure. The agreement with an independent source such as Suetonius makes it certain that under Claudius the situation really did result in an expulsion of Jews from Rome.[209] Although T. Mommsen surmised that the edict was directed only against Jews with Roman citizenship,[210] his legal reflections are questionable,[211] and the origin of Aquila in Pontus (Acts 18:2) is at the very least not a particularly supportive argument for this view. One further, indirect witness for the expulsion of Jews (Jewish Christians) from the imperial capital is the list of greetings at the end of the letter to the Romans.[212] The long enumeration of Roman Christians whom Paul already knows (Rom. 16:3-15) is most easily comprehensible if the apostle encountered the majority of them as exiles during his travels, something we do, after all, know explicitly about Aquila and Priscilla (Rom. 16:3; cf. Acts 18:2f.).

206. P. Lampe, *Die stadtrömischen Christen* (²1989) 4.

207. Although Acts 18:7 D it^h do presuppose that Aquila was still a Jew while in Corinth, here, too, the D-text proves to a secondary, albeit interesting redaction. Cf. G. Stählin, *Die Apostelgeschichte* (⁶1978) 243.

208. *Die Apostelgeschichte* (1983) 362f.

209. Cf. A. Momigliano, *Claudius* (²1961) 31: "We cannot dismiss . . . the evidence of two such independent authorities as Suetonius and Acts." Theologians should not blithely pass by the judgment of this renowned historian of ancient history. Cf. also G. Boulvert, *Esclaves et affranchis impériaux* (1980) 358.

210. *HZ* 64 (1890) 407f.

211. Cf. A. N. Sherwin-White, *Roman Society and Roman Law in the New Testament* (1963) 81f.

212. Concerning the original relationship of chapter 16 to the letter to the Romans, cf. H. A. Gamble, *The Textual History of the Letter to the Romans* (1977); U. Wilckens, *Der Brief an die Römer* I (1978) 24-27; W. H. Ollrog, *Festschrift G. Bornkamm* (1980) 221-44; P. Stuhlmacher, *ZNW* 77 (1986) 187f.; *Paul's Letter to the Romans* (Eng. trans., 1994) 254-56; P. Lampe, *Die stadtrömischen Christen* (²1989) 124-35.

10.7.2. Expulsion of All Jews?

This married couple stood in an extremely independent relationship with Paul as fellow workers,[213] and we can therefore assume that they played an important and active role already in Rome's pre-Pauline Christian church. From this scholars have concluded further that their expulsion suggests that Claudius' measure was directed primarily or even exclusively at the "ringleaders."[214] This assumption seems to be contradicted by Luke's explicit assertion that "all Jews" were expelled. Luke exhibits a relative preference for the word πᾶς,[215] and the *auctor ad Theophilum* often uses it plerophorically (Acts 2:5; 3:18; 8:1; 9:35; 19:10).[216] This passage, too, may represent an exaggeration. Neither, to be sure, is there a scarcity of attempts to explain πᾶς differently. Thus R. O. Hoerber considers whether the difficulty cannot be resolved grammatically: "An attributive position of πάντας in Acts 18:2 . . . would stress totality, but the predicate position appears to permit the interpretation that only the 'ringleaders' suffered banishment."[217] G. Ogg considers it possible that both Luke and Suetonius, whose text (see pp. 162f. above) presents a similar problem,[218] were familiar with an edict of Claudius that, while originally intending the expulsion of all Jews, was then ameliorated because it could not be implemented.[219] The Lukan "all" is thus not as unequivocally clear as might seem at first glance, and in comparison with Suetonius also not as impossible as is usually assumed. The scope of this expulsion[220] can

---

213. Cf. W. H. Ollrog, *Paulus und seine Mitarbeiter* (1979) 24-27.

214. So, among others, G. May, *RHDFE* 17 (1938) 43; P. de Labriolle, *La réaction païenne* (1934) 42; E. Haenchen, *Acts* (Eng. trans., 1971) 65; R. E. Brown and J. P. Meier, *Antioch and Rome* (1983) 102; G. Lüdemann, in B. C. Corley, *Colloquy on New Testament Studies* (1983) 302f.; C. Saulnier, *DBS* X (1985) 963f.; P. Lampe, *Die stadtrömischen Christen* (²1989) 6. Further bibliography in D. Slingerland, *JQR* 79 (1989) 321.

215. The numbers are Matthew (129), Mark (68), Luke (157), John (65), Acts (172), Romans (71), 1 Corinthians (112), 2 Corinthians (52), Ephesians (52), Hebrews (53). Cf. K. Aland, *Vollständige Konkordanz* II (1978) 214f. If one considers the various lengths of the writings, Luke's preference is admittedly no longer quite so unusual.

216. Cf. R. O. Hoerber, *CThM* 31 (1960) 692f.

217. *Ibid.,* 693.

218. D. Slingerland, *JQR* 88 (1992) 134, is convinced: "Both texts mention an expulsion including the entire Jewish population, so that no distinction may be made on this basis between them." It then seems all the more like tormented skepticism, however, when Slingerland, for no real reason, does after all consider it possible that Luke and Suetonius are mentioning two different expulsions.

219. *The Chronology of the Life of Paul* (1968) 100. See also p. 178 above.

220. Hardly any exegete reckons so clearly with a total expulsion as does E. Bammel, *ZThK* 56 (1959) 299f. C. J. Hemer, *The Book of Acts in the Setting of Hellenistic History* (1989) 167f., also seems to understand the Lukan information in this way. In any event, he does not discuss the problems at all.

perhaps be determined with the aid of other sources and additional considerations (§10.8.2).

10.7.3. Lukan Chronology

The chronological implications of the Gallio-incident (Acts 18:12-17) suggest that Paul probably came to Corinth in the spring of A.D. 50 (§11). This placement concurs best with the date Orosius mentions in connection with the expulsion, namely, the "ninth year of Claudius" (A.D. 25 January 49–25 January 50),[221] which thus receives a certain confirmation. This calculation also allows one to take προσφάτως in Acts 18:2 in its most immediate sense: Aquila and Priscilla met Paul in Corinth because they had a short time before been expelled from Rome. Attempts have been made to refute this conclusion by pointing out that we are not told how long the couple stayed in Italy before departing for Greece.[222] Until now, admittedly only those scholars arrived at this interpretation who needed an early date for the edict of Claudius. But if eight years had already passed since the expulsion from Rome, then Luke had even less reason to mention an event which for him was inopportune. In that case one must agree with G. Lüdemann's conclusion that he "is probably not even aware of the chronological relationship between the two [the expulsion and Paul's arrival]."[223] If based on a different overall view of Lukan historical writing one does not share this view without further qualification (§12.2.2), then a different explanation is also possible regarding why the author of Acts mentions the edict of Claudius at all: in this way the beginning of the Pauline mission in Europe acquires a reference point from contemporary history.[224]

The edict issued at that time can perhaps also help us understand better the path upon which the apostle embarked on his first journey to Europe. Apparently he already intended to travel to Rome at that time. But when in Macedonia at the turn of A.D. 49/50 he heard about Claudius' Roman measure, he had to give up this plan for the time being, and missioned instead in Athens and Corinth (§18.4.2-3).

---

221. The first to suggest this were A. Deissmann, *Paulus* (1911) 175f.; A. von Harnack, *SPAW.PH* (1912) 676.

222. So already T. Zielinski, *RUB* 32 (1926/27) 144, note 2; H. Janne, *AIPh* 2 (1934) 552f., note 5; H. J. Leon, *The Jews of Ancient Rome* (1960) 25, and now N. Hyldahl, *Die paulinische Chronologie* (1986) 124.

223. *Paul: Apostle to the Gentiles* (1984) 170.

224. Neither can one object here that Luke "*does not date* the expulsion of the Jews" (G. Lüdemann, *ibid.*). The *auctor ad Theophilum*, after all, provides an absolute date only once, namely, the famous synchronism in Lk. 3:1.

10.8. Circumstances and Time of the Anti-Jewish Edict

10.8.1. Reasons for the Edict

With respect to the question whether the expulsory measure belongs in the year A.D. 41 or 49, R. Jewett has insisted that "this question should be addressed within the larger context of Claudius' policies towards the Jews and his sensitivity about religious propaganda."[225] Our portrayal of the emperor's religious policies (§8) has probably made it clear enough that the year A.D. 49 was a particularly critical time for Roman Jews. Seneca returned from exile at that time, and this meant that an influential advisor was now present at the imperial court who was characterized by an unequivocally anti-Jewish attitude (see p. 105 above). Claudius had intensified his program of restoring ancient Roman religion, and in the same year had extended the *pomerium* of the imperial capital to the Aventine (§6.4.1). In her Claudius-biography, B. Levick remarks concerning the emperor's religio-political measures that "the clustering of relevant material round the years 47-49 reflects political anxiety: Claudius' fear for his own position and general fear for Rome's security."[226]

H. W. Hoehner has even surmised that the extension of the *pomerium*, which meant the closing of synagogues within the expanded sacred precinct, itself caused the Jewish disturbances about which Suetonius reports (Suetonius, *Claudius* 25.4).[227] C. Saulnier argues this view in even more detail:[228] The closed synagogue on the Aventine, to which Aquila and Priscilla also belonged, allegedly reconstituted itself not far from there in the area around the Porta Capuana (cf. Juvenal, *Sat.* iii.13f.). However, Ms. Saulnier does not say how she conceives the connection between the closing of the synagogue and the Christian-Jewish disturbances which she, too, considers to have been the main cause of the expulsion. It is difficult to see how the closing of a single house synagogue should have led to a direct confrontation between the Jewish synagogue members and the Roman authorities. Even though such a measure by the emperor doubtless did not improve the mood of the Roman Jews, his actions attest above all the state attempts at restoring Roman religion. The expansion of the *pomerium* was a result of the triumph in Britain, which had demonstrated not only Rome's own superiority, but also that of its gods. Nationalistic-religious feelings soared in this year, a situation that could become dangerous for every foreign group upon whom any suspicion might fall.

Rome was also a magnet for itinerant religious preachers of Jewish

---

225. In B. C. Corley, *Colloquy on New Testament Studies* (1983) 285.
226. *Claudius* (1990) 87.
227. *Chronology of the Apostolic Age* (1965) 85f.
228. *MBib* 51 (1987) 9.

origin. From the time of Claudius we know at least about Simon Magus, Aquila and Priscilla, Paul, and perhaps Peter. As the emperor's letter to the Alexandrians shows, he was in general no great friend of Jewish influx into the large cities (see p. 100 above). Because Aquila and Priscilla, though not Pauline converts themselves, immediately entered into a trusting working relationship with the apostle, one suspects that they were connected with the circle of "Hellenists," which was open to the mission to the Gentiles (cf. Acts 6:1).[229] Under Tiberius, however, the conversion of Gentiles to Judaism had been the reason for the expulsion (Josephus, *Ant.* xviii.81-84; Dio Cassius, *Hist.* lvii.18.5a; cf. Tacitus, *Ann.* ii.85.4). Dio associates Claudius' measure (Dio Cassius, *Hist.* lx.6.6) with that of Tiberius (see p. 176 above), and one can thus ask whether the reasons prompting these two measures were not also comparable. The mission to the Gentiles of the new Jewish-messianic sect, free from the law, might have generated greater interest than the traditional solicitations of Judaism, which although reaching a great many "God-fearers" (see p. 109 above), made only few proselytes. A variation of Judaism capable of eliciting the interest of even more Romans for this foreign *superstitio* must have aroused the mistrust of the authorities and the Princeps to an even greater degree.

Acts sketches a vivid picture of how in the synagogue communities of Asia Minor and Europe the Christian mission repeatedly provoked disputes capable of leading even to violence. Such incidents are reported for Pisidian Antioch (Acts 13:45, 50), Iconium (Acts 14:2, 5), Lystra (Acts 14:19), Thessalonica (Acts 17:4-8), Beroea (Acts 17:13), and Corinth (Acts 18:12-17). The credibility of the historical details can be left in abeyance, since the overall picture has on its side not only historic probability, but also the self-witness of Paul (cf. 1 Thess. 2:15f. [§18.3.1]; 2 Cor. 11:24).[230] In connection with the disturbances in Thessalonica, Acts uses the two verbs θορυβεῖν and ὀχλοποιεῖν (Acts 17:5), which represent good equivalents of the word used by Suetonius, namely, *tumultuare/i* (Suetonius, *Claudius* 25.4). One can thus conclude that the main cause of Claudius' measure included incidents in one or several Roman synagogues prompted by the appearance of Christian missionaries.[231] The tumults can actually "be connected with

229. So already C. Weizsäcker, *The Apostolic Age* (Eng. trans., 1907-12) 1.78. Cf. more recently U. Wilckens, *Der Brief an die Römer* I (1978) 35-39.

230. So more recently the scholars of ancient history J. Molthagen, *Hist* 40 (1991) 46-63; H. Botermann, *ThBeitr* 24 (1993) 75-84.

231. So, among others, M. Dibelius, *SHA* 32 (1941/2) 30; V. M. Scramuzza, *Claudius* (1940) 151; J. Klausner, *Jesus* (Eng. trans., 1943) 61; L. Herrmann, *Chrestus* (1970) 165f.; F. F. Bruce, *Jesus and Christian Origins* (1974) 21; M. Stern, CRINT I/1 (1974) 180; E. M. Smallwood, *The Jews under Roman Rule* (²1981) 211; U. Wilckens, *Der Brief an die Römer* I (1978) 35f.

the attempt of Jewish Christians there to make the transition in Rome, too, to a Gentile mission free of the law."[232] Through what is known as the "Apostolic Council" in the year A.D. 48 (§17.1.3), this mission had indeed acquired new impetus, and was able to flourish also in communities which, as was probably still the case in Rome at that time, consisted largely of Jewish Christians.

A bit of information preserved in the chronicle of John Malalas concerning Antioch might show how critical things had become in the year A.D. 48 even outside of Palestine: Τῷ δὲ ὀγδόῳ ἔτει τῆς βασιλείας τοῦ Κλαυδίου Καίσαρος διωγμὸν μέγαν ἐποίησαν οἱ Ἰουδαῖοι κατὰ τῶν ἀποστόλων καὶ τῶν μαθητῶν αὐτῶν καὶ τυραννίδα κατὰ Ῥωμαίων ἐμελέτων. Ὅθεν πρῶτος ἐπέμφθη κατ᾽ αὐτῶν χιλίαρχος Φῆστος (Malalas 247.5-10 [ed. Stauffenberg 25]). Because the disturbances in Palestine began after A.D. 48 under Ventidius Cumanus (§6.3.2), A. von Stauffenberg remarked concerning this information that "the date provided by Malalas, namely, the eighth year of Claudius' reign, is thus remarkably accurate."[233] Stauffenberg sees here a genuine recollection of disturbances in which Jews participated as instigators and/or victims. To be sure, Malalas misunderstood a lemma in another chronicle and incorrectly introduced Festus into these events,[234] and Stauffenberg similarly considers the reference to a Jewish persecution of Christians to be an anachronistic misunderstanding. However, the demand for the circumcision of Gentile Christians propagated by Jewish Christians around the year A.D. 48 in Antioch as well (Acts 15:1-5) might have had a connection with the revival of pressures exerted by the Zealots (§15.1). Violent attacks on Christians, perhaps as the by-product of Jewish-Gentile conflicts that actually had a different origin, by no means seem out of the question. In view of the serious disturbances that had broken out in such a context a short time before in the empire's third-largest city (see pp. 113f. above), Antioch, the beginnings of Jewish unrest in Rome itself must have seemed like a red flag to authorities, prompting their decisive intervention. The conscious omission of references to liberation by Roman masters in grave inscriptions of Rome's Jewish catacombs prior to A.D. 70 (see p. 154 above) may suggest that Zealotism enjoyed a certain sympathy there as well.[235]

Nascent Christianity could no doubt cause Judaism itself to appear even more suspect in the eyes of the Roman leadership, and thus provoke these authorities to undertake drastic measures. A previous outbreak of famine prompted a powerful revivification of apocalyptic sentiment in Palestine under

---

232. M. Hengel, *Urchristliche Geschichtsschreibung* ([2]1984) 91.
233. *Die Römische Kaisergeschichte bei Malalas* (1931) 200.
234. Cf. *ibid.*, 200-202.
235. Cf. G. Fuks, *JJS* 36 (1985) 32.

the procurator Tiberius Alexander (A.D. ?46-48) (§6.3.2). The anticipation of famines was also part of primitive Christianity's apocalyptic proclamation (Mt. 24:7/Mk. 13:8/Lk. 21:11; Rev. 6:8); for the time of Claudius, Acts (Acts 11:27f.) even reports a concrete prophecy regarding an impending, empire-wide famine (§8). Because of the perpetually precarious conditions of food provisioning in the imperial capital (Dio Cassius, *Hist.* lx.11.1f.), the circulation of such apocalyptic prophecies in Rome itself was politically explosive. Two events illustrate this. In the year A.D. 47, a Roman equestrian by the name of Petra was executed because he retold a dream which one might interpret as foretelling impending inflation (Tacitus, *Ann.* xi.4.1f.). Tacitus reports the following concerning another occurrence from the year A.D. 51, one which Suetonius also found worthy of mention (Suetonius, *Claudius* 18.2): "Many prodigies occurred during the year. Ominous birds took their seat on the Capitol; houses were overturned by repeated shocks of earthquake, and, as panic spread, the weak were trampled underfoot in the trepidation of the crowd. A shortage of corn, again, and the famine which resulted, were construed as a supernatural warning. Nor were the complaints always whispered. Claudius, sitting in judgment, was surrounded by a wildly clamorous mob, and, driven into the farthest corner of the Forum, was there subjected to violent pressure, until, with the help of a body of troops, he forced a way through the hostile throng" (Tacitus, *Ann.* xii.43).

Trafficking with apocalyptic prophecies could easily cast suspicion on Jewish Christians of having engaged in futuristic prophecies in the style of the Chaldeans or *mathematici*. Jewish magicians were a quite familiar phenomenon in the Roman empire.[236] Seneca even viewed Judaism in the larger sense as *superstitio* (Augustine, *Civ. Dei* vi.11). Apparently it was especially the attraction of proselytes which prompted the Roman educated class to view Judaism, along with Egyptian religion, as the absolute *superstitio*.[237] Although this objection did not render religions at large liable to punishment,[238] it could in concrete instances prompt official measures. The trial against Lollia Paulina for alleged contacts with magicians (§6.4.2) took place in the year A.D. 49. Indeed, even into the upper classes, the Romans were extremely receptive to all sorts of magic.[239] In A.D. 52, Claudius ordered (the?) magicians banned from Rome (§6.4.2), a coercive measure which some have even incorrectly

236. Cf. Acts 13:8; Josephus, *Ant.* xx.142; Juvenal, *Sat.* iii.13; vi.542-47; Lucian, *Trag.* 173f.; Origen, *Cels.* i.26. Additional documentation can be found in A. Hamman, *Festschrift M. Pellegrino* (1975) 95, note 28.

237. Cf. M. Hengel, *NTS* 18 (1971/72) 16.

238. Cf. the important Excursus V: Superstitio, in R. Freudenberger, *Das Verhalten der römischen Behörden gegen die Christen* (1967) 189-99, and also M. Hengel, *Crucifixion* (1977) 2-5.

239. Cf. A. Hamman, *Festschrift M. Pellegrino* (1975) 95.

identified with Claudius' anti-Jewish edict.[240] Shortly before his death (13 October A.D. 54), the emperor, at the instigation of Agrippina, had executed his former mother-in-law, Domitia Lepida — in any event a granddaughter of Augustus' sister Octavia (Tacitus, *Ann.* xii.6) — because she allegedly was resorting to magic *("devotionibus petivisset")* in order to take the life of the empress (Tacitus, *Ann.* xii.65).[241] In a way, magicians, astrologers, diviners, and prophets were more feared in Rome than were external enemies.[242]

Tacitus (*Ann.* xii.43) and Suetonius (*Nero* 16.2), like Pliny the Younger before them (*Ep.* x.96.9), counted Christianity among the *superstitiones externae*. Suetonius' formulation *"superstitio malefica"* (*Nero* 16.2) almost certainly contains the direct accusation of magic.[243] The writings of Justin (*Apol.* i.14.1f.) suffice to show how strong was this suspicion in the environment of primitive Christianity,[244] and it was not easy for the inhabitants of Rome, nor even for the state officials, to distinguish among many obscure groups the Christian congregations that had broken with magic (cf. Acts 19:18f.).[245] Yet even in these congregations, apocalyptic prophecies were passed on, and this may have become known even among those around the emperor.[246] In this connection, the observation of R. Freudenberger is significant: "More recent research again emphasizes more the continuity of the persecution of Christians under the Principate with the police actions of the Republic and of the first

240. So also the query of E. Jacquier, *Les Actes des Apôtres* ([2]1926) 543. Cf. by contrast G. Ogg, *The Chronology of the Life of Paul* (1968) 101f. (older bibliography); D. Slingerland, *JQR* 88 (1992) 143f.

241. H. Willenbücher, *Vergangenheit und Gegenwart* 3 (1913) 367-69, even believed that she was converted to Christianity. But this does not accord well with Tacitus' other characterization of her (Tacitus, *Ann.* xii.64).

242. Cf. R. MacMullen, *Enemies of the Roman Order* (1966) 95-161, 316-35.

243. Cf. A. Hamman, *Festschrift M. Pellegrino* (1975) 94-96; L. F. Janssen, *VigChr* 33 (1979) 153-57.

244. Cf. further the material in M. Smith, *Jesus the Magician* (1978).

245. A. Hamman, *loc. cit.,* 96: "How could one ask the pagans, or the Roman authorities, to distinguish the tares from the wheat? How could this not arouse the suspicion in the spirit of those for whom the clandestine, nocturnal meetings were at first suspected of magic?"

246. This possibility is supported by the fact that a freedman of Tiberius (cf. Josephus, *Ant.* xviii.167), the Samaritan historian Thallus (E. Schürer, *Geschichte des jüdischen Volkes* III [[4]1909] 494f.), was according to Julius Africanus (*George Syncellus* [ed. Dindorf I 610]) familiar with the supernatural signs at the death of Jesus. Cf. S. Bacchiocchi, *AUSS* 21 (1983) 14f. Now as before it is also worth considering whether the wife of the conqueror of Britain, Aulus Plautius, namely, Pomponia Graecina, was a Christian. According to Tacitus, she was in A.D. 57 accused of a *superstitio externa* to which she had belonged since A.D. 43 (Tacitus, *Ann.* xiii.32). Cf. G. Scarpat, *Il pensiero religioso di Seneca* (1977) 130-32; S. Bacchiochi, *loc. cit.,* 15f.; and esp. M. Sordi, *The Christians and the Roman Empire* (1986) 26f., 36, note 9.

two *principes,* though also with those of Claudius (Suetonius, *Vita Claudii* 25.4!) against certain *superstitiones externae* that had been introduced into Rome or Italy."[247]

10.8.2. The Scope of the Expulsion

The size of the Jewish population, which has been estimated at up to fifty thousand in an overall population of around one million,[248] could have been one reason militating against any summary expulsion of all Jews for a ruler with a humanitarian sensibility such as Claudius. In any case, such a measure could be carried out legally only against the *peregrini.*[249] All Jews who possessed Roman citizenship to any degree had, according to the law, to be brought first individually before the court. Under Claudius, their number was probably considerably higher than earlier,[250] since in the meantime many Jews who had come to Rome as slaves had been freed (see p. 151 above). One can adduce two possible parallels to such an expulsory edict not quite implemented in its totality. According to Josephus (Josephus, *Ant.* xviii.83), Tacitus (Tacitus, *Ann.* ii.85.4), and Suetonius (Suetonius, *Tiberius* 36), the expulsion of Jews under Tiberius was total. By contrast, Dio Cassius (*Hist.* lvii.18.5a) states that the emperor "banned most of them" (τοὺς πλείονας ἐξήλασεν). There was in fact a whole series of affected groups for whom special regulations seem possible.[251] Even Tacitus might be referring to rules of exception with his not quite unequivocal remark *"ceteri cederunt Italia nisi certam ante diem pro-fanos ritus exuissent"* (Tacitus, *Ann.* ii.85.4). Though we have nothing attesting an official repeal of the edict, Tiberius seems already to have ameliorated or annulled it after the fall of Sejanus (A.D. 31) (cf. Philo, *Leg. ad Gaium* 160f.). The opposite relationship of sources is involved in the edict of banishment against magicians from the year A.D. 52 (§6.4.2). Here Dio (*Hist.* lx.33.3b), who is admittedly accessible in this instance only in a Byzantine excerpt (Zonaras 11.10), speaks about a total expulsion. According to Tacitus, however, this involved a "drastic but ineffectual *(atrox et inritum)"* senatus con-sultum (Tacitus, *Ann.* xii.52). Perhaps such astrologers who foreswore their activities were pardoned after the example of a Tiberian measure (cf. Sue-

---

247. *Das Verhalten der römischen Behörden* (1967) 13.

248. Cf. J. Juster, *Les juifs dans l'empire Romain* I (1914) 209f.

249. Cf. E. Bammel, *ZThK* 56 (1959) 297; E. M. Smallwood, *The Jews under Roman Rule* (²1981) 215f. The sending of four thousand Jews capable of bearing arms, *"liberti generis"* (Tacitus, *Ann.* ii.85.5), to Sardinia under Tiberius apparently involved a repeal of exemption from military service. Cf. H. Solin, *ANRW* II 29.2 (1983) 686f.

250. Cf. E. M. Smallwood, *The Jews under Roman Rule* (²1981) 215.

251. *Ibid.,* 208.

tonius, *Tib.* 36). Many astrologers were possibly also out of reach because members of upper classes protected them (and some Christians?).

Another possibility for escaping the expulsion consisted in concealing one's affiliation with Judaism. From the time of Domitian we hear that Jews concealed their ritual lifestyles in order to escape the collection of the *fiscus Judaicus* (Suetonius, *Dom.* 12.2). By contrast, for pious Jews any general prohibition against assembly (Dio Cassius, *Hist.* lx.6.6) rendering synagogue services impossible represented a powerful reason to leave the imperial capital, even if they were Roman citizens.[252] To be sure, one can assume that all restrictions were lifted at the beginning of the reign of Nero (A.D. 54-68),[253] since at the beginning this emperor was extremely accommodating to the Jews (Josephus, *Vita* 13-16; *Ant.* xx.189-96).[254] In any event, when at the beginning of A.D. 57 (§15.5.2) Paul wrote to Rome, Jews were again living there (see p. 191 above), as Acts also presupposes at his arrival there (Acts 28:17-28). This confirms once more Dio's observation that "this class exists even among the Romans, and though often repressed has increased to a very great extent and has won its way to the right of freedom in its observances" (*Hist.* xxxvii.17).

The scope of the expulsion of Jews from Rome is given extremely varied interpretations in contemporary scholarship;[255] although only exceptionally do scholars assume the expulsion to have been total (§10.7.2), something against which the preceding considerations do in fact militate, one should reckon with a greater number of expulsions than is presently customary. Although one need not necessarily understand the remark in Suetonius (*Claudius* 25.4) in a general fashion (§10.2.2), it must be referring to a measure that was typical for the emperor; this is also supported by the context, which is concerned paradigmaticaly with the treatment of various peoples and religions (Suetonius, *Claudius* 25.3-5). Hence one should not underestimate the circle of persons actually expelled; otherwise it is difficult to explain why Suetonius mentions the measure at all, why Luke could write (either hyperbolically or predicatively) πάντες Ἰουδαῖοι at the latest thirty or forty years afterward, and how perhaps Paul, too, saw in this edict a decisive event (1 Thess. 2:16b) (§18.3.1).

252. Cf. E. Schürer, *Geschichte des jüdischen Volkes* III (⁴1909) 62; J. Felten, *Neutestamentliche Zeitgeschichte* I (²/³1925) 286.

253. It is, however, unclear how J. W. Drane, *Festschrift F. F. Bruce* (1980) 217, arrives at the assertion "that according to Dio the Jews were not allowed back until the beginning of Nero's reign." As we have seen, Dio does not mention any expulsion, and Suetonius is silent concerning the length of the measure.

254. Concerning *clementia* as a cardinal virtue of the initial years of his reign, cf. M. T. Griffin, *Nero* (1984) 64f.

255. An overview can be found in D. Slingerland, *JQR* 79 (1989) 321.

10.8.3. Chronological Conclusions

Claudius' Roman edict concerning the Jews confirms a rule also applicable in other instances for broad stretches of ancient history: we can arrive at a relatively satisfying reconstruction of events only through the most comprehensive combination of sources, each of which is both incomplete and one-sided when taken alone. In the present case, the following picture emerges:[256] the punitive measure was precipitated by the proclamation of the messiah Jesus in Roman synagogues. Perhaps especially because of the forced proclamation of a gospel free of the law, this provoked violent incidents. The transmission of apocalyptic prophecies by Jewish Christians may have strengthened the suspicion already present among the authorities that Jews were especially open to magic, futuristic prophecies, and revolutionary ideas. Suetonius and Acts attest unanimously that this resulted in expulsions possibly affecting a larger circle of persons. It is less certain what connection this had with the prohibition of assembly mentioned by Dio Cassius. It was most likely a preventative measure separate from the actual expulsory edict. If the actual implementation of this edict involved an expulsion on a smaller scale, then the silence of Josephus, Tacitus, and Dio would be easier to understand. But here, too, any dependence on the *argumentum e silentio* remains extremely precarious. A dating of the prohibitive measure in Dio to A.D. 41 is, because of the literary context, not completely certain, and for this reason alone it cannot without further qualification serve as a fixed point for Pauline chronology. By contrast, Acts and Orosius provide an unintentional and thus all the more noteworthy congruency for A.D. 49. An edict hostile to the Jews in this year also fits well with what we otherwise know about Claudius' religious policies during his later period, about the particular situation in Rome itself, and about the rest of the history of early Christianity.

---

256. My reconstruction is now largely confirmed and partly refined by H. Botermann, *Das Judenedikt des Kaisers Claudius* (1996) 44-140. It is to be hoped that her work will prove decisive on this question. Other literature on the edict since 1993 (see pp. 158-60, note 5 above) includes L. Alexander in G. F. Hawthorne et al., eds., *A Dictionary of Paul and His Letters* (1993) 120; J. A. Fitzmyer, *Romans* (1993) 30-32; O. Wittstock, *Sueton* (1993) 310f., 549, note 135; C. A. Evans in B. Chilton and C. A. Evans, *Studying the Historical Jesus* (1994) 457f.; B. Rapske, *Paul in Roman Custody* (1994) 330f.; E. A. Judge, *TynBul* 45 (1994) 361f.; J. Taylor, *Les deux actes des apôtres* V (1995) 312-14; R. Brändle and E. W. Stegemann, *NTS* 42 (1996) 1-11; J. Murphy-O'Connor, *Paul* (1996) 9-15; C. Wolff, *Der erste Brief des Paulus an die Korinther* (1996) 3; B. Wander, *Trennungsprozesse zwischen frühem Christentum und Judentum* ([3]1997) 224-26; T. Holtz in *Festschrift P. Stuhlmacher* (1997) 244-47.

§11

Paul and Gallio

11.1. The Achaian Proconsulate of Gallio

11.1.1. The Rise of Gallio

Gallio was born perhaps around 5 B.C.[1] as the eldest son of the rhetorician L. Annaeus Seneca the elder under the name L. Annaeus Novatus.[2] We unfortunately know very little about his *cursus honorum*. According to a remark made by his brother L. Annaeus Seneca the younger, he seems to have been quite ambitious, at least at the beginning (Seneca, *Dial.* xii.7: *"honores industria consecutus"*). The banishment of Seneca the Younger at the beginning of Claudius' reign (Dio Cassius, *Hist.* lxi.10) perhaps did not affect Gallio as strongly, since his patron L. Junius Gallio[3] protected him.[4] But Gallio's rise to the highest offices doubtless could not begin until after his brother Seneca returned from exile in the year A.D. 49 (see p. 105 above). Presupposing that Gallio occupied a consulate in the year A.D. 50/51, K. Wieseler thus already calculated the proconsulate in Achaia to the year A.D. 51/52,[5] and this date is

1. Cf. W. Rees, *Scrip* 4 (1949/51) 16.

2. Concerning Gallio, cf. further O. Rossbach, *PRE* I 1 (1894) 2236f.; L. Cantarelli, *Rendiconti della R. Accademia Nazionale dei Lincei* V/32 (1923) 157-75; K. Lake, *BC* V (1933) 460-64; L. Hennequin, *DBS* II (1934) 364-68; E. Groag, *Die römischen Reichsbeamten von Achaia* (1939) 32-35; W. Rees, *Scrip* 4 (1949/51) 11-20 (contains in part undocumented assertions relating to facts); A. Stein and L. Petersen, *Prosopographia Imperii Romani, Saec. I.II.III.* vol. IV (²1952-1966) 335f.; G. Scarpat, *Il pensiero religioso di Seneca* (1977) 118-24; W. Elliger, *Paulus in Griechenland* (1978) 231-37; B. Reicke, *EDNT* I (1990) 234; R. K. Jewett, *A Chronology of Paul's Life* (1979) 38-40; J. Murphy-O'Connor, *St. Paul's Corinth* (1983) 141-52; *JBL* 112 (1993) 315-17; K. Haacker, *ABD* II (1992) 901-3. Earlier bibliography can be found in J. Dauvillier, *Les Temps Apostoliques* (1970) 16.

3. Concerning him, cf. B. Gerth, *PRE* I 19 (1918) 1035-39.

4. Cf. W. Rees, *Scrip* 4 (1949/51) 14f.

5. *Chronologie des apostolischen Zeitalters* (1848) 119f. Pliny the Elder, *HN* xxxi.62, mentions this consulate without dating it. K. Wieseler's calculation was based on

indeed suggested by the Gallio-inscription to be discussed below. To be sure, the name of Gallio is not found in the *fasti consulares* under Claudius known to us,[6] and the year A.D. 51 is hardly a possibility, while in A.D. 50 there are eight or nine vacancies.[7] The assumption that Claudius appointed Gallio *extra sortem* (cf. Dio Cassius, *Hist.* lx.25.6),[8] with Gallio thus serving as proconsul for two years,[9] cannot be adequately supported by his designation as friend of the emperor (ὁ φίλος μου) in the inscription (*SIG*[3] II 801, line 6).[10] Achaia was not elevated again to a senatorial province until A.D. 44 (Dio Cassius, *Hist.* lx.24), and it is improbable that the emperor would have deviated this early from the normal appointment procedure by the senate for one year. The rise of Novatus might also have been aided by the fact that he was adopted by L. Junius Gallio either shortly before the latter's death (A.D. 49 or 50) or else in his last will and testament (Tacitus, *Ann.* vi.3.1), and thenceforth bore the name L. Junius Annaeus Gallio.

11.1.2. The Gallio-Inscription

The first four fragments of this document were published in 1905 by E. Bourguet;[11] their significance for Pauline chronology was then popularized by W. M. Ramsay for English-speaking scholars,[12] by A. Deissmann for German Protestants,[13] and by E. Dubowy for German Catholics.[14] Although A. Brassac[15] in 1913 and D. Plooij[16] in 1919 had already published the three additional fragments that could be fitted into the inscription, the discussion in

---

the practice applicable under Sulla, namely, that the proconsulate followed immediately upon the one-year consulate period. After 53 B.C., a period of five years was required during the Republic (Dio Cassius, *Hist.* xl.46.2). In the time of the emperors, too, there were no fixed rules regarding the proconsulate. Cf. G. Wesenberg, *PRE* I 23.1 (1957) 1232-34.

6. Cf. E. M. Smallwood, *Documents Illustrating the Principates of Gaius, Claudius, and Nero* (1967) 2-7.

7. Cf. P. A. Gallivan, *CQ* 88 (1978) 407-26.

8. So esp. L. Hennequin, *DBS* II (1934) 365-67.

9. So L. Cantarelli, *Rendiconti della R. Accademia Nazionale dei Lincei* V/32 (1923) 167f.

10. Cf. A. Deissmann, *Paulus* ([2]1925) 218 (Eng. trans., *Paul* [[2]1926]); E. Groag, *Die römischen Reichsbeamten von Achaia* (1939) 34; J. Dauvillier, *Les Temps apostoliques* (1970) 209.

11. *De Rebus Delphicis imperatoriae aetatis capita duo* (1905) 63.

12. *Exp* VII/7 (1909) 467-69.

13. *Paulus* (1911) 159-77.

14. *BZ* 10 (1912) 143-54.

15. *RB* 10 (1913) 36-53.

16. *De chronologie van het leven van Paulus* (1919) 27-31, with a photo as frontispiece.

general was influenced all the way up to E. Haenchen[17] by the publications of A. Deissmann[18] and H. Pomtov (*SIG*³ II 801D), which were actually based only on these first four fragments (of altogether nine). A. Plassart then undertook a new edition of all the fragments,[19] creating thus a secure point of departure for subsequent studies.[20]

The actual recipient of this rescript of Claudius is a matter of dispute.[21] A. Plassart thought he could recognize in line 17 (εἰς τῶν [. . .]εια σε ἐντέλλομαι ἵν[α]) a personal pronoun of the second person, and concluded that this was a writing from the emperor to Gallio's successor in office.[22] Against this, J. H. Oliver argued that ἐντέλλομαι is normally construed with the dative (σοι), and that one must thus organize the sequence of letters (ειασε εντελλομαι ιν) such that σε constitutes a verbal ending.[23] From the designation of Gallio as proconsul (line 6: Γαλλίων ὁ φ[ίλος] μου κα[ὶ ἀνθύ]πατος), Oliver concluded that he still occupied that office when the letter was sent. A further investigation of the question by C. J. Hemer[24] seems to favor Oliver's view, even if the latter, like Plassart, organized the lacunae in part incorrectly. Hemer does emphasize, however, that Plassart's interpretation also remains a possibility. J. Murphy-O'Connor follows Plassart's lead by drawing attention to a construction of ἐντέλλομαι with the accusative possible in the New Testament, and to the identical word sequence in Mk. 13:34.[25] But this loan

17. E. Haenchen, *Acts* (Eng. trans., 1971) 66f. So previously, among others, also K. Lake, *BC* V (1933) 460-62; L. Hennequin, *DBS* II (1934) 355-63; E. Gabba, *Iscrizione greche e latine per lo studio della Bibbia* (1958) 74-76; C. K. Barrett, *The New Testament Background: Selected Documents* (1961) 48f.; J. Finegan, *Handbook of Biblical Chronology* (1964) 316-18; G. Ogg, *The Chronology of the Life of Paul* (1968) 104-8; A. Suhl, *Paulus und seine Briefe* (1975) 324f. Additional earlier bibliography can be found in A. Deissmann, *Paulus* (²1925) 210, note 3 (Eng. trans., *Paul* [²1926]); L. Hennequin, *DBS* II (1934) 373; A. J. and M. B. Mattill, *A Classified Bibliography of Literature on the Acts of the Apostles* (1966) 227f.; A. Plassart, *RÉG* 80 (1967) 374f., note 4; J. Dauvillier, *Les Temps apostoliques* (1970) 16.

18. *Paulus* (²1925) 205-21; here A. Deissmann also discusses an inscription from Plataea — unfortunately now lost — which perhaps similarly presupposes the Achaian proconsulate of Gallio (*ibid.*, 223-25).

19. *Fouilles de Delphes III: Épigraphie 4.3* (1970) no. 286 (26-32, and plate VII).

20. Easily accessible renderings of the Greek text can be found in H. M. Schenke and K. M. Fischer, *Einleitung in die Schriften des Neuen Testaments* I (1978) 50f.; J. Murphy-O'Connor, *St. Paul's Corinth* (1983) 173-76.

21. The discussion of this question in R. Jewett, *A Chronology of Paul's Life* (1979) 128f., note 138, is unsatisfactory. The same applies to the discussion of the Gallio-inscription in D. Slingerland, *JBL* 110 (1991) 444-46, who essentially addresses only the older explications of G. Ogg, *The Chronology of the Life of Paul* (1968) 104-11.

22. *RÉG* 80 (1967) 375-77; *Fouilles de Delphes III: Épigraphie 4.3* (1970) 27, 30.

23. *Hesp* 40 (1971) 239f.

24. In *Festschrift F. F. Bruce* (1980) 6-8.

25. *St. Paul's Corinth* (1983) 175f.

from New Testament grammar encounters two difficulties: (1) Although verbs of command are indeed also construed with the accusative in the New Testament,[26] it is precisely for ἐντέλλομαι that we have no witness. Mk. 13:34 undeniably uses the dative (καὶ τῷ θυρωρῷ ἐνετείλατο ἵνα γρηγορῇ). (2) Something possible in New Testament Greek would after all be fairly astonishing as a solecism[27] in an official document. Murphy-O'Connor's objection that Oliver has provided no reconstruction attempt based on his presuppositions is, given the discussion of Hemer,[28] no longer valid.

Murphy-O'Connor similarly concludes from the contents of the imperial rescript that it was addressed to Gallio's successor.[29] An imperial order to the depopulated city of Delphi, even for the purpose of providing for the settling of new inhabitants, allegedly would not have made sense. This interpretation is possible, but not certain. The emphasis on the emperor's interest in the city and especially the veneration of the Pythian Apollo (lines 3-4) would fit just as well in a writing to the Delphians. The exhibition of a copy of the rescript in the temple of Apollo at Delphi also points in this direction. Of significance, however, is Murphy-O'Connor's reference[30] to the fact that Claudius, as a friend of Greek culture (Suetonius, *Claudius* 42), had a special preference for the province of Achaia.[31] From this perspective one can thus conclude that with this rescript the emperor was reacting immediately to a report from his representative. This, as the chronological evaluation of the inscription will show, also militates against the assumption that Gallio had already served as *proconsul extra sortem* in Achaia since A.D. 50.

For our own inquiry, it is important that neither option regarding the addressee decisively changes the chronological implications.[32] Gallio is mentioned as proconsul in the third person (line 6). The document is dated to the period after the twenty-sixth acclamation of Claudius as Imperator (lines 1-2), and to this one can add, according to an inscription from Cos in Caria (*BCH* 11 [1887] 306-8), the twelfth year of his tribunal power.[33]

26. Cf. Blass, Debrunner, Rehkopf, §409.1.

27. Cf. LSJ 575b.

28. In *Festschrift F. F. Bruce* (1980) 7f. Hemer considers the following to be a possibility: ανα[. . . φ]ημί [[τ]οῖς μέντ]οι ἄλλοις οὓς ὁ Γαλλίων πεισθ]εὶς τῶν [κατοίκων] εἴασε ἐντέλλομαι ἵν[α].

29. *St. Paul's Corinth* (1983) 144f.

30. *Ibid.*, 148f.

31. The close connection can also be seen in the fact that one calculated dates in Thessaly according to a Claudius-era. Cf. H. Kramolisch, *Chiron* 5 (1975) 337-47.

32. Cf. C. J. Hemer, *The Book of Acts in the Setting of Hellenistic History* (1989) 168f., 252f.

33. Cf. A. Plassart, *RÉG* 80 (1967) 377; H. M. Schenke and K. M. Fischer, *Einleitung in die Schriften des Neuen Testaments* I (1978) 52.

The twenty-fourth acclamation is dated to the year A.D. 51 (*CIL* III [1977]). Since the twenty-seventh acclamation can be dated by combining information from Frontinus (*De Aquaeductis* i.13) with a founder's inscription on the aqueduct Aqua Claudia (*CIL* VI 1256 = *ILS* 218) to 1 August A.D. 52,[34] this imperial rescript must have been written before this date. The *terminus post quem* is the beginning of the twelfth tribunal year in January A.D. 52; actually, this *terminus* can be shifted even further into this year. On the basis of Tacitus' reports of military operations in Bretagne and in Cilicia (*Ann.* xii.38-40, 55), scholars of ancient history almost unanimously assume that the twenty-sixth acclamation is to be dated in the spring of A.D. 52,[35] and given the customs of Roman military practice it can hardly be dated before April.[36]

According to an edict of Tiberius (Dio Cassius, *Hist.* lvii.14.5), the proconsular term of office in senatorial provinces probably began on July 1, since a departure was supposed to take place within the time of the new moon in June.[37] If Claudius arranged the departure of the proconsuls from Rome for 1 April (Dio Cassius, *Hist.* lx.11.6) and later for the middle of this month (Dio Cassius, *Hist.* lx.17.3), this hardly was intended to determine anew when the term of office should begin, but rather to guarantee a seamless transition without any interregnum.[38] If the imperial rescript was addressed to Gallio's successor, then Gallio's latest possible year in office is 1 July A.D. 51 to 30 June A.D. 52. The imperial rescript is referring to a recent report from Gallio concerning the problems of the depopulation of Delphi (lines 5-6). Assuming that his term of office began on 1 July A.D. 52, one must accommodate within a single month Gallio's own report and its dispatch to Rome as well as the emperor's response. As especially E. Haenchen has quite justifiably emphasized,[39] this time frame does not seem possible.[40] This means that even assuming the document was addressed to the Delphians,

---

34. Cf. J. Murphy-O'Connor, *St. Paul's Corinth* (1983) 142f.

35. Cf. A. Plassart, *RÉG* 80 (1967) 377f., and A. Deissmann, *Paulus* (²1925) 215f. (Eng. trans., *Paul* [²1926]); K. Lake, *BC* V (1933) 462f.; L. Hennequin, *DBD* II (1934) 359-62; G. Ogg, *The Chronology of the Life of Paul* (1968) 108-10; H. M. Schenke and K. M. Fischer, *Einleitung in die Schriften des Neuen Testaments* I (1978) 52f.; J. Murphy-O'Connor, *St. Paul's Corinth* (1983) 143f.

36. Cf. J. Murphy-O'Connor, *St. Paul's Corinth* (1983) 143f.

37. How B. Reicke, *EDNT* I (1990) 234, concludes that the accession to office took place in the autumn also does not become clear in B. Reicke, *Neutestamentliche Zeitgeschichte* (³1982) 234f.

38. Cf. T. Mommsen, *Römisches Staatsrecht* II (1888) 256; W. Larfeld, *NKZ* 34 (1923) 638; A. Deissmann, *Paulus* (²1925) 219f.

39. E. Haenchen, *Acts* (Eng. trans., 1971) 66, note 3.

40. Cf. also R. Jewett, *A Chronology of Paul's Life* (1979) 39f.; C. K. Barrett and C. J. Thornton, *Texte zur Umwelt des NT* (1991) 59f.

one arrives at A.D. 51/52 as Gallio's latest possible year in office. This date fits exceedingly well with his career as figured after the return of Seneca (§11.1.1).

11.1.3. Gallio's Illness

Several scholars assume that Gallio broke off his term of office in Achaia prematurely.[41] A remark made by his brother Seneca prompted this assumption: *"Illud mihi ore erat domini mei Gallionis, qui cum in Achaia febrem habere coepisset, protinus navem ascendit clamitans non corporis esse, sed loci morbum"* (Seneca, *Ep. Mor.* 104.1). This incident is to be distinguished from the later health crisis after Gallio's *suffectus*-consulate under Nero, which prompted him to take a trip to Egypt. Pliny the Elder reports concerning this crisis, conveying the impression of a personality inclined to hypochondria (Pliny the Elder, *HN* xxxi.33.62). E. Groag has objected that Gallio could ill afford a step such as the premature end to his proconsulate in Achaia without endangering his career under Claudius, and the reference is in any case only to leaving the locale, and not the province.[42] Indeed, Seneca's manner of expression is not completely clear. The political argument, however, does not seem very persuasive. After Claudius' death, Gallio in fact was not particularly flattering toward the emperor (Dio Cassius, *Hist.* lx.35.4), and we probably know one reason for this. The fact that Gallio became *consul suffectus* for the year A.D. 55 immediately after the accession of Nero (cf. Pliny the Elder, *HN* xxxi.62)[43] suggests that in the last years of Claudius he had fallen from favor. It thus remains possible that Gallio ended his term of office in Achaia prematurely, perhaps even before the end of shipping (§16.1) in October A.D. 51.[44]

41. So, e.g., L. Cantarelli, *Rendiconti della R. Accademia Nazionale dei Lincei* V/32 (1923) 173; L. Hennequin, *DBS* II (1934) 368; C. J. Hemer, in *Festschrift F. F. Bruce* (1980) 8; R. Jewett, *A Chronology of Paul's Life* 1979) 40 (as a possibility which he also incorrectly ascribes to A. Deissmann, *Paulus* [²1925] 219); J. Murphy-O'Connor, *St. Paul's Corinth* (1983) 147.

42. *Die römischen Reichsbeamten von Achaia* (1939) 34.

43. This dating now seems well secured by a combination of various dates. Cf. A. Stein and L. Petersen, *Prosopographia Imperii Romani, Saec. I.II.III,* vol. IV (²1952-66) 335; E. M. Smallwood, *Hist* 17 (1968) 384; W. Eck, *Hist* 24 (1975) 339, 342.

44. Cf. J. Murphy-O'Connor, *St. Paul's Corinth* (1983) 147f.

11.2. The Trial before Gallio in Corinth

11.2.1. Chronological Information

The legal-historical objections raised against the portrayal of Paul's indictment before Gallio in Corinth (Acts 18:12-17) are not valid.[45] The procedure can be understood as a *cognitio extra ordinem* at which it was left to the discretion of the governor whether to accept a new kind of accusation. Sometime between 1 July A.D. 51 and 30 June A.D. 52, the apostle must have stood face to face with Gallio before the Corinthian podium *(bema)* that was subsequently excavated.[46] If one assumes a premature departure, then the time frame is reduced to between 1 July and the end of October. Before the trial, Acts mentions that Paul was there for a year and six months (Acts 18:11), and afterward it yet speaks about ἡμέραι ἱκαναί (Acts 18:18). Several scholars thus assume that Paul left Corinth not long after the trial, and the year-and-a-half can be calculated forward from the accession of the proconsul as almost the complete duration of Paul's stay.[47] This is without a doubt the impression one has at first reading. "The scene" seems "set toward the end of Paul's Corinthian stay and at the beginning of the proconsulate of Gallio."[48] K. Haacker,[49] however, has justifiably drawn attention to two uncertain elements: Γαλλίωνος δὲ ἀνθυπάτου ὄντος must not necessarily mean "Gallio became proconsul," and the information concerning "days" in Acts 18:18 can certainly also refer to a longer period of time.[50]

How long, according to Luke's view, did the apostle's mission in Corinth last altogether? Judging from the analogy of his stay in Ephesus (§12.1.3), where two periods of time are mentioned for activity inside and outside the synagogue, the year and six months in Acts 18:11 presumably encompasses the two corresponding phases in Corinth. The vision recounted in Acts 18:9f. explains why Paul "settled" (Acts 18:11: ἐκάθισεν) in the city for such an unusually long time.[51] It is not quite clear whether one should

---

45. Cf. A. N. Sherwin-White, *Roman Society and Roman Law in the New Testament* (1963) 99f.; J. Molthagen, *Hist* 40 (1991) 57-63; K. Haacker, *ABD* II (1992) 902; H. Botermann, *ThBeitr* 24 (1993) 75-78. Concerning the *cognitio extra ordinem*, cf. I. Buti, *ANRW* II 14 (1982) 29-59.

46. Cf. E. Dinkler, *Das Bema zu Korinth* (1940); W. Elliger, *Paulus in Griechenland* (1978) 225-27; R. Riesner, *GBL* II (1988) 816f.

47. Cf. esp. B. Schwank, *BZ* 15 (1971) 265f. Further representatives of this view can be found in R. Jewett, *A Chronology of Paul's Life* (1979) 38.

48. R. Pesch, *Die Apostelgeschichte* II (1986) 150.

49. *BZ* 16 (1972) 252-55.

50. Cf. already K. Lake, *BC* V (1933) 464.

51. Cf. G. Schneider, *Die Apostelgeschichte* II (1982) 251.

include the "sufficient days" in this year and six months,[52] or should add them.[53] Given the Ephesus-analogy, we would expect the latter. The duration of the overall stay, however, probably did not encompass much more than a year and six months, since otherwise Luke probably (as in the case of Ephesus) would have mentioned the number of about two years. Taken by itself, the expression ἡμέραι ἱκαναί (Acts 18:18) can refer to a longer period of time (cf. 1 Kgs. 2:38f. LXX). In Acts, however, this expression once refers to an indeterminate period of time (Acts 9:23) and once to what is certainly an extremely short period of a few days (Acts 27:7).

Historical considerations suggest that the procedure against Paul did indeed take place at the beginning of Gallio's term of office, as suggested also by the first impression of the account in Acts. If the Corinthian Jews had already had experience with the new governor over a longer period of time, what was for them a negative resolution of the procedure could have been foreseen. Gallio and his brother Seneca had a close relationship (Seneca, *Nat. Quaest.* iv.a *praef.* 10f.; cf. *Ep. Mor.* 104.1), something also shown by the fact that the philosopher dedicated to his brother the dialogues *De ira* and *De vita beata* (Seneca, *Dial.* iii-v, vii).[54] One may therefore assume that Gallio shared Seneca's anti-Jewish attitude (see p. 105 above). The account in Acts concurs completely with this: although Gallio does indeed confirm the Jewish right as a *religio legitima* to regulate its own internal affairs (Acts 18:15), he demonstrates anything but special sympathy (Acts 18:16), and does not even concern himself with antisemitic assaults (Acts 18:17). Naturally, the events of the year A.D. 49 in Rome (§10) also influenced his handling of this case, events Gallio himself had witnessed in the imperial capital. This historical background remains credible even if Luke has undeniably subjected this scene to literary stylization.[55]

Let us as a precaution juxtapose first the two most extreme possibilities of chronological reconstruction: (1) Assuming one year and six months as the time of Paul's stay before an indictment quite close to the accession of Gallio, the earliest possible time being the beginning of May, to which one then adds at most only a few extra days in Corinth, according to the information in Acts the last possible date for Paul's own arrival in Corinth would be November/Decem-

---

52. So C. J. Hemer, *The Book of Acts in the Setting of Hellenistic History* (1989) 119, note 48.

53. So J. A. T. Robinson, *Wann entstand das Neue Testament?* (1986) 44.

54. Cf. R. Hanslik, *KP* II (1967) 686.

55. Because he sets redactional and historical angles of vision too severely against one another, G. Lüdemann, *Das frühe Christentum* (1987) 205 (Eng. trans., *Early Christianity* [1989]), must criticize as historicizing exegesis burdened with aporia the reference made by W. Elliger, *Paulus in Griechenland* (1978) 236f., to the antisemitic undertones in Gallio's behavior. Cf. by contrast the conclusion of a scholar of ancient history such as J. Wiseman, *ANRW* II 7.1 (1979) 504.

ber A.D. 49. (2) If one assumes a trial at the end of Gallio's proconsulship, with the larger part of Paul's stay lasting at least one year and six months in Corinth beginning only in the period after this, the latest possible departure date is then the end of A.D. 53. Between these two possibilities, of course, extremely varied combinational solutions are also possible. Because of Gallio's anti-Jewish attitude and the possibility of a premature end to his term of office, I am inclined to accept the assumption that the trial took place at an early date and that accordingly Paul arrived in Corinth fairly early. A trial in July (the probable month of accession to office) or August, and the apostle's departure perhaps in September before the end of shipping, would be conceivable. One would then date Paul's arrival in Corinth in February/March A.D. 50. But here, too, only correlation with other dates can provide more certainty (§18.5.2).

11.2.2. Acts 18:1-17

The significance of the Gallio-incident as a fixed point of Pauline chronology would be placed in an entirely different light if G. Lüdemann's literary-critical analysis of this section were correct.[56] In Acts 18:1-11 and Acts 18:12-17 he finds two different redacted traditions concerning Paul's founding visit in Corinth as well as an additional stay. In his literary argument, Lüdemann points to the position of the chronological information concluding Acts 18:1-11, but not Acts 18:1-17. But in the case of the stay in Ephesus, too, Luke provides chronological information in the account itself, and only later recounts the actual duration of the overall stay (see pp. 208f. above). The commencement in Acts 18:12, which Lüdemann characterizes as "abrupt,"[57] can very well represent Luke's own intended impression: the accession of this proconsul also meant the end of Paul's successful activity in the city.

Furthermore, Lüdemann considers it significant, favoring the assumption of two different stays in Corinth, "that in v. 8 the ruler of the synagogue is Crispus . . . where in v. 17 Sosthenes is given this title."[58] He does not discuss the possible assumption of F. J. de Waele,[60] namely, that given the considerable size of the Corinthian Jewish community[59] there were at least two synagogues. W. Wiefel's explanation,[61] namely, that Crispus lost his office after converting to the new messianic faith (Acts 18:8: Κρίσπος δὲ ὁ ἀρχισυνάγωγος ἐπίστευσεν τῷ κυρίῳ σὺν ὅλῳ τῷ οἴκῳ αὐτοῦ), Lüdemann rejects

---

56. G. Lüdemann, *Paul: Apostle to the Gentiles* (1984) 157-77; *idem, Early Christianity according to the Traditions in Acts* (Eng. trans., 1989) 195-204.
57. G. Lüdemann, *Paul. Apostle to the Gentiles* (1984) 159.
58. *Ibid.*
59. Cf. J. Wiseman, *ANRW* II 7.1 (1979) 503f.
60. *Corinthe et St. Paul* (1961) 96.
61. *Jud* 26 (1970) 75, note 77.

as an argument that "historicizes in a way that is inappropriate to the text."[62] He argues that "such a view would be possible only if Luke were an eyewitness or if he derived the basic material of the *entire* chapter from the diary of a companion of Paul."[63] In his own analysis of Acts 18:1-17, however, Lüdemann himself infers a whole series of redacted traditions which in his opinion contain historical information, and among which he expressly includes as "specific pieces of information and untendentious . . the report of the conversion of Crispus, the president of the synagogue"[64] and as one of the "elements of tradition" in the following section "the name of Sosthenes, the synagogue president."[65] In the original version of his work *(Habilitationsarbeit)*, Lüdemann rejected the suggestion that Crispus lost his synagogal office after his conversion because this would presuppose too strenuous an opposition between Christianity and Judaism for this early period.[66] Although the published version lacks this (more than) questionable argument, it does retain its consequences. In this case one really does have the impression that literary and historical criticism first create the problems they then want to solve.

11.2.3. Gallio and Pauline Chronology

G. Lüdemann's thesis, which through literary criticism tears apart the Corinthian account in Acts and dates this founding stay according to his questionable dating of the edict of Claudius (§10) prior to A.D. 41, is at first glance quite revolutionary. At the same time, however, the reconstruction contains a peculiarly conservative element which actually contradicts Lüdemann's own premises. The association of Paul's activity with an imperial edict, and his noncondemnation by a Roman governor, accords strikingly well with the salvation-historical and pro-Roman/apologetical inclinations of which Luke is accused and which otherwise make one suspicious that he has actually invented information commensurate with this inclination. D. Slingerland thus asks quite justifiably why Lüdemann actually maintains the historicity of the two items.[67] Apparently, a new Acts, too, can do without neither Luke nor Gallio. Hence it is not surprising that all more recent commentaries to the Corinthian letters continue to take the Gallio-incident as the point of departure for their chronological reconstructions.[68]

---

62. G. Lüdemann, *Paul: Apostle to the Gentiles* (1984) 159.
63. *Ibid.,* 185, note 53.
64. *Early Christianity according to the Traditions in Acts* (Eng. trans., 1989) 199.
65. *Ibid.*
66. Cf. R. Jewett, *A Chronology of Paul's Life* (1979) 82.
67. *JBL* 109 (1990) 687f.
68. Cf. the overview in R. Bierlinger, *EThL* 72 (1991) 125-28; and now C. Wolff, *Der erste Brief des Paulus an die Korinther* (1996) 3-5.

§12

Later Chronology

12.1. Paul in Ephesus

12.1.1. The Affliction in Asia

Right at the beginning of his second letter to the Corinthians, Paul informs the congregation: "We do not want you to be unaware, brothers and sisters, of the affliction we experienced in Asia; for we were so utterly, unbearably crushed that we despaired of life itself (ὥστε ἐξαπορηθῆναι ἡμᾶς καὶ τοῦ ζῆν). Indeed, we felt that we had received the sentence of death so that we would rely not on ourselves but on God who raises the dead. He who rescued us from so deadly a peril will continue to rescue us . . . " (2 Cor. 1:8-10). M. Carrez associates this severe affliction in the province of Asia[1] with the cryptic remark at the end of the first letter to the Corinthians:[2] "If with merely human hopes I fought with wild animals (ἐθηριομάχησα) at Ephesus, what would I have gained by it? If the dead are not raised, [then] 'Let us eat and drink, for tomorrow we die' " (1 Cor. 15:32). This apparently presupposes that the apostle was mortally threatened in the provincial capital of Asia.[3] If with many exegetes since Hippolytus (*Comm. in Dan.* 3.29) one understands literally this reference to battle with animals,[4] then Paul would also have been taken prisoner in Ephesus.[5] Although a condemnation *ad bestias* must not necessarily contradict the apostle's Roman citizenship (see Excursus I),[6] several considerations suggest that Paul's expression here is to be understood figuratively.[7] If with "wild animals"

---

1. Contra an understanding of this as a serious illness, cf. R. P. Martin, *2 Corinthians* (1986) 15f.; U. Heckel, *Kraft in Schwachheit* (1993) 262, note 279.
2. *La deuxième Épître de Saint Paul aux Corinthiens* (1986) 52f.
3. Cf. G. D. Fee, *The First Epistle to the Corinthians* (1987) 770f.
4. Representatives can be found in R. E. Osborne, *JBL* 85 (1966) 225f.
5. So, among modern authors, esp. J. F. Collange, *L'épître de Saint Paul aus Philippiens* (1973) 26.
6. Cf. E. A. Judge, *JAC* 15 (1972) 25f.
7. Cf. R. E. Osborne, *JBL* 85 (1966) 226-30; A. J. Malherbe, *JBL* 87 (1968) 71-80.

he is picking up on Hab. 2:17 (cf. 1QpHab 11:16–12:5) and referring to religious adversaries,[8] then one might construe a connection with the account in Acts, which mentions both Gentile (Acts 19:23-26) and Jewish opposition (cf. Acts 19:9, 33f.).

Even if one assumes the presence of figurative language in 1 Cor. 15:32, or even rejects any connection with 2 Cor. 1:8-10, the possibility of a Pauline imprisonment in Ephesus still remains worthy of consideration. The name Ἀσία (2 Cor. 1:8) could (as in Acts 20:16) stand for the provincial capital Ephesus. V. P. Furnish points to the close connections between 2 Cor. 1:8-10 and Philippians 1–2,[9] that is, a letter which many date to an Ephesian imprisonment. Especially after the studies of W. Michaelis[10] and G. S. Duncan,[11] studies which do admittedly differ in the details of their reconstruction, probably the majority of scholars today, including J. Knox,[12] G. Lüdemann,[13] and R. Jewett,[14] do reckon with this possibility.[15] A. Deissmann had already advocated the likelihood of an imprisonment in Ephesus,[16] one which with the anti-Marcionite prologue to the letter to the Colossians[17] also had the support of an older tradition. Paul's reference in Rom. 16:4 to Aquila and Priscilla's having "risked their necks" for him, and in the same context to Andronicus and Junia(s) as his (former) "fellow prisoners" (Rom. 16:7: συναιχμαλώτους), might be alluding to an incarceration in Ephesus (cf. 1 Cor. 16:19).[18] Although according to many scholars the political and geographical circumstances presupposed for Paul's imprisonment in the letter to Philemon support the assumption of an imprisonment in Ephesus,[19] Caesarea is certainly also a serious possibility.[20]

This is also the place to say something concerning the question of Paul's date of birth. In the letter to Philemon he calls himself an "old man (πρεσβύτης)" (Phlm. 9). When the apostle compares his own zeal in persecut-

8. Cf. R. E. Osborne, *loc. cit.,* 229f.

9. *II Corinthians* (1984) 123.

10. *Die Gefangenschaft des Paulus in Ephesus* (1925).

11. *St. Paul's Ephesian Ministry* (1929). The concluding form of his hypothesis is summarized in the chronological table in *NTS* 5 (1958/59) 43-45.

12. *Chapters in a Life of Paul,* rev. ed. (1987) 61.

13. *Paul: Apostle to the Gentiles* (1984) 263 (as a possibility).

14. *A Chronology of Paul's Life* (1979) 103.

15. Additional representatives can be found in G. F. Hawthorne, *Philippians* (1983) xxvi-xxxix; J. Gnilka, *Der Philipperbrief* (⁴1987) 19f.

16. In *Festschrift W. M. Ramsay* (1923) 121-27.

17. Text in E. Preuschen, *Analecta* II (²1910) 85f.

18. Cf. F. F. Bruce, *Paul* (1977) 298.

19. Cf. P. Stuhlmacher, *Der Brief an Philemon* (³1989) 20-23; J. Molthagen, *Hist* 40 (1991) 63-65.

20. Cf. C. J. Thornton, *Der Zeuge des Zeugen* (1991) 203-16.

ing the Christian church with that of members of his own age group (Gal. 1:14: καὶ προέκοπτον ἐν τῷ Ἰουδαϊσμῷ ὑπὲρ πολλοὺς συνηλικιώτας ἐν τῷ γένει μου), he points out that he was rather young then. The possibility thus arises that Luke's designation of Paul as νεανίας in Acts 7:58 preserves an accurate piece of information. The expression refers to a man "from about the 24th to the 40th year."[21] If the letter to Philemon was composed around A.D. 52/54 (§17.1.4), and most certainly if it was composed around A.D. 57-59 (§12.4), the apostle would thus have been at least fifty years old, and probably older. Hence one need not seek refuge in the conjecture πρεσβευτής,[22] but rather may with T. Zahn understand the word πρεσβύτης in this sense: Paul "would hardly have said this to his friend Philemon if he really were already an old man according to the number of years. This remark fits better coming from a man who has attained or just passed his mid-50s, and notices that the vigor of his earlier years has begun to decrease under the constant effects of an exciting and grinding professional life, cf. 2 Cor. 4:16."[23] The apostle's birth may thus be dated cautiously around the turn of the century, something that also fits well with our considerations of his father's acquisition of the *civitas Romana* (Excursus I/1).

The silence of Acts regarding an imprisonment in Ephesus should not be taken to militate against the assumption, especially given the same book's obvious gaps regarding the dangers Paul encountered (2 Cor. 11:23-25). Luke does portray — and does so quite extensively — the difficulties Paul encountered in the provincial capital (Acts 19:23-40). Here the portrayal of the apostle's Ephesian ministry is strikingly two-faced. On the one hand, precisely the report of disturbances clearly exhibits features of local color,[24] and perhaps

21. BAGD 534. Agrippa I is called νεανίας in Josephus, *Ant.* xviii.197, even though at that time he was at least forty years old. For Varro, someone was a young man until forty-five, and was old at sixty (according to E. Jacquier, *Les Actes des Apôtres* [²1926] 238). In antiquity, the determination of the stages of life was closely connected to various numerical speculations. Thus the forty-ninth year of life could be described as the threshold of old age (7 × 7 years), though also the fifty-ninth (assuming four stages in life of twenty years each). Cf. F. Boll, *NJKlA* 16 (1913) 89-145. It is uncertain whether Luke consciously distinguished between νεανίας and νεανίσκος, as T. Zahn, *Die Apostelgeschichte des Lucas* I (1919) 264f., supposes. It appears that νεανίας sounded a bit more refined. Cf. J. de Zwaan, *BC* II (1933) 35.

22. So, among others, A. Oepke, in K. H. Rengstorf, *Das Paulusbild in der neueren Forschung* (1969) 439.

23. *NKZ* 15 (1904) 31.

24. Cf. W. Elliger, *Ephesos — Geschichte einer antiken Weltstadt* (1985) 137-48. "Regarding no other station along the journeys of Paul does Acts report as extensively as regarding Ephesus, and Ephesus is, after Athens, the city whose local color Acts has captured best" (*ibid.,* 137). R. F. Stoops, *JBL* 108 (1989) 73-91, shows that the portrayal of the Demetrius-disturbances in Acts 19:23-41 represents not a piecing together of

this portrayal can be associated with events at the time. It is striking that with regard to the problematical marriage between Claudius and Agrippina in A.D. 49 as well as to her elevation to Augusta in A.D. 50 (see p. 96 above), in the year A.D. 50/51 in Ephesus two types of silver commemorative coins *(cistophori)* were struck.[25] The permission to coin silver, though also the unusual Latin legend, suggests that this city had a special relationship with the imperial household. The second type of coin bears next to a double portrait of the imperial couple *recto* a representation of Diana Ephesia on the reverse side. Bronze coins commemorating the divine marriage *(THEOGAMIA)* of the imperial couple support the assumption that a syncretistic cult of Diana and of the empress was propagated in Ephesus.[26] Such a connection between the cult of the emperor and that of Artemis makes the resonating political undertones (Acts 19:40) especially understandable.[27] Just how ticklish was competition with the Ephesian Artemis can be seen in an oracle in seventeen hexameter verses from the second century A.D. with which priests of Artemis threatened judgment over the city if the goddess's cult were neglected (cf. Acts 19:27).[28] The author of Acts apparently also knew that the legal citizens' assembly (Acts 19:39: ἔννομος ἐκκλησία) met in the theater (cf. Acts 19:29).[29] The assumption that the office of the ἀσιάρχαι mentioned in Acts 19:31 was temporarily suspended in the first century is incorrect. In Titus Claudius Hiero around A.D. 55 we even know one of the occupants of the office during the period of Paul's Ephesian stay.[30] Since the rights of Jews in

different sources, but rather a story consciously composed by Luke. The background includes those particular Jewish claims to tolerance and autonomy in the Greek cities of the eastern Mediterranean basin which the *auctor ad Theophilum* in a certain way also claims for Christians. Although this apologetic agenda does explain the choice and broad portrayal of precisely this incident in the metropolis of Asia Minor, it does not necessarily mean that it is a literary fiction. The details seem too precise for that to be the case (see discussion below). Concerning the local color of Acts 19, cf. now also T. R. Schnackenburg, *BZ* 35 (1991) 43-54; G. H. R. Horsley, *NT* 24 (1992) 121-58; P. Lampe, *BZ* 36 (1992) 59-76; R. A. Kearsley, *NewDoc* VI (1992) 203-6; W. Theissen, *Christen en Ephesus* (1995) 90-246; R. Strelan, *Paul, Artemis, and the Ephesian Jews* (1996).

25. C. H. V. Sutherland, *The Roman Imperial Coinage* I (^{2}1984) 130f.

26. Cf. *ibid.,* 120.

27. Cf. L. J. Kreitzer, *JSNT* 30 (1987) 59-70.

28. Reference to this finding according to the *Süddeutsche Zeitung* 37 (15 February 1988) 10. Professor Dieter Knibbe (University of Vienna) has related to me that the inscription is to be published in *JÖAI*. The income of the cult of Artemis was enormous. According to another inscription (*JÖAI* 59 [1989] 75f.), in the mid-second century the *boulē* fixed the fees for priestesses at yearly 5,000 (!) drachmae each.

29. Cf. A. N. Sherwin-White, *Roman Society and Roman Law in the New Testament* (1963) 87.

30. Cf. R. A. Kearsley, *AnSt* 38 (1988) 43-51. My thanks to Professor Benedikt Schwank, OSB (Beuron), for referring me to this article.

Asia Minor were regulated directly by the emperor (Josephus, *Ant.* xvi.165), the Asiarchs, as protectors of the imperial temples, were especially involved in cases of anti-Jewish disturbances (cf. Acts 19:33f.; cf. Josephus, *Ant.* xiv.227).[31]

On the other hand, Luke's account is remarkably incomplete and allusive. It gives the impression that Paul founded the church in Ephesus (Acts 19:8-10); however, the disciples of John (Acts 19:1-7)[32] as well as problematical Jewish Christians such as Apollos (Acts 18:24-26) and Paul's fellow workers Aquila and Priscilla ministered in the metropolis in Asia Minor before the apostle himself (Acts 18:26f.). Within what Luke does after all figure to have been a ministry lasting around three years (Acts 20:31; cf. Acts 19:8, 10) for the apostle, the *auctor ad Theophilum* provides, in addition to the story of the disciples of John, only the other two stories about the sons of Sceva (Acts 19:11-20)[33] and the Demetrius-disturbances (Acts 19:23-40). The latter account leaves unclear just why several Christians and even favorably disposed Asiarchs prevent Paul from justifying himself before the assembly of the people in the theater (Acts 19:30f.). M. Carrez has voiced the suspicion that in Ephesus Paul regained his freedom in an illegal manner, either through his friendship with these Asiarchs[34] or through a bribe paid by the Christian church.[35] This hypothesis might explain why Luke is silent concerning imprisonment in Ephesus, and why the apostle met the elders of Ephesus in Miletus rather than in Ephesus itself (Acts 20:17f.). The possibiliy of an illegal release was probably also made easier by the political circumstances of the time, circumstances we will briefly discuss.

12.1.2. A Chronological Fixed Point?

M. Carrez believes that the peculiar plural ἀνθύπατοι in Acts 19:38, considering that Luke otherwise mentions proconsuls by name,[36] points to the time after the murder of the proconsul Silanus.[37] This view is not new, having been

---

31. Cf. R. F. Stoops, *JBL* 108 (1989) 85. Immediately after the elevation of Octavius to Augustus, the cultic veneration of the emperor began in Ephesus in private quarters. Cf. P. Scherrer, *JÖAI* 60 (1990) 87-101.

32. Cf. in this regard esp. H. Lichtenberger, *ZThK* 84 (1987) 47-51.

33. Concerning the interesting possibility that Sceva might be an ἀρχιερεύς within the cult of the emperor, cf. J. A. Fitzmyer, in *Festschrift G. Schneider* (1991) 299-305.

34. The historicity of this feature would be more easily accepted if R. A. Kearsley, *ABD* I (1992) 495-97; in A1CS II (1994) 363-76, were correct in distinguishing the office of the Asiarch as a civil office from the religious office of the ἀρχιεροσύνη for Asia.

35. In *Festschrift J. Dupont* (1985) 772, 775.

36. Acts 13:7 (Sergius Paulus); 18:12 (Gallio).

37. *Loc. cit.,* 773-75.

formulated by H. M. Luckock[38] and then adopted by G. S. Duncan.[39] The conservative scholar W. M. Ramsay has criticized this hypothesis even though it did seem to offer a historical confirmation for information in Acts.[40] Immediately after the death of Claudius (13 October A.D. 54), Nero's mother, Agrippina, gave the order to have Silanus murdered (Tacitus, *Ann.* xiii.1; Dio Cassius, *Hist.* lxi.6.4f.); this took place at the latest in December A.D. 54 or January A.D. 55.[41] Ramsay was correct in pointing out that the two murderers, the *eques* Publius Celer and the freedman Helius, could not be these "proconsuls," since during the interregnum the administration resided in the hands of three deputies. It is possible, however, that the generalizing plural ἀνθύπατοι is referring to these deputies in the sense of "there are (officials like) proconsuls."[42] Murky circumstances of power during this interregnum could on the one hand have posed a serious threat to Paul's position, and yet on the other hand made possible the apostle's unofficial release. A date that assumes Paul left Ephesus at the beginning of the year A.D. 55 fits well into the remaining Pauline chronology (§16.1.4).

12.1.3. The Duration of the Stay

The information in Acts concerning the duration of Paul's missionary work in Ephesus does not give the impression of a completely schematic structuring. The assertion of a three-month initial proclamation in the synagogue (Acts 19:8) may have been rounded off because of the number's symbolic value (cf. Acts 17:2). Luke allows two years for Paul's instructional activity in the hall of Tyrannus (Acts 19:10). The *auctor ad Theophilum* then mentions an indefinite period of time subsequent to this (Acts 19:22: αὐτὸς ἐπέσχεν χρόνον εἰς τὴν Ἀσίαν). One can ask with D. Georgi "whether Luke's mention of a continuation of Paul's stay in Ephesus 'for some time longer' is not the last, faint recollection of this imprisonment at the end of the Ephesian stay — particularly since Luke does not justify or explain this reference, and since on the other hand it does, after all, stand within the context surrounding the Demetrius-incident."[43] When in his discourse before the elders in Miletus Paul describes his stay rhetorically as having lasted three years (Acts 20:31: μνημονεύοντες ὅτι τριετίαν νύκτα καὶ ἡμέραν οὐκ ἐπαυσάμην μετὰ δακρύων νουθετῶν ἕνα ἕκαστον), this does not

---

38. *Footprints of the Apostles as Traced by St. Luke* II (1897) 189 (non vidi).

39. *St. Paul's Ephesian Ministry* (1929) 102-7.

40. *Exp* VI/2 (1900) 334f.

41. Cf. M. Carrez, *Festschrift J. Dupont* (1985) 774f.

42. Cf. F. F. Bruce, *Paul* (1977) 295f.; *The Acts of the Apostles* (³1990) 421; C. J. Hemer, *The Book of Acts in the Setting of Hellenistic History* (1989) 123, note 63.

43. *Die Geschichte der Kollekte des Paulus für Jerusalem* (1965) 64 (Eng. trans., *Remembering the Poor* [1992].

contradict Luke's own assertion that the stay lasted a bit less than three years.[44] But the (relative) reliability of the Lukan information must prove itself by being reconcilable with the rest of Pauline chronology (§17.1.4).

12.2. The Journey to Jerusalem for Pentecost

K. Wieseler already tried to calculate the day of the week on which the fifteenth of Nisan of that particular Passover festival fell which Paul, according to Acts 20:6, spent in Philippi.[45] According to Wieseler, calculations lead to Tuesday, 28 March A.D. 58, and O. Gerhardt[46] is inclined to support this reconstruction. To the extent that modern scholars do see the possibility of carrying out such calculations,[47] however, they subscribe to the form argued by W. M. Ramsay[48] and D. Plooij.[49] Nowhere in Acts does one find such a plethora of detailed information about time periods than in the we-account concerning the seven-week journey from Philippi to the Pentecost festival in Jerusalem (Acts 20:6–21:15). One has the impression of great haste, and may from that conclude that Paul left Philippi immediately after the end of the Christian Passover celebration (Acts 20:6).[50] The "first day of the week" (ἐν τῇ μιᾷ τῶν σαββάτων) in Troas (Acts 20:7) can, given the analogy of Lk. 24:1, only have been a Sunday. Since Luke figures a day from sunrise to sunrise (Acts 4:3-5; 10:3-23; 20:7-11; 23:12-32),[51] the worship service portrayed here took place not on Saturday evening, but rather on Sunday evening, and the departure on Monday morning.[52] Since the apostle stayed in Troas for seven full days (Acts 20:6), he arrived here on Tuesday of the preceding week. If one figures back the five days' journey from Philippi (Acts 20:6), this yields a departure date of Friday, and then a Thursday as both the beginning and end of the Passover festival. Between A.D. 52 and 60, the fourteenth of Nisan fell on a Thursday probably only on 7 April A.D. 57.[53] Of course,

---

44. Cf. also R. Jewett, *A Chronology of Paul's Life* (1979) 55.

45. *Chronologie des apostolischen Zeitalters* (1848) 99-115.

46. *NKZ* 33 (1922) 89-114.

47. F. F. Bruce, *Paul* (1977) 340; C. J. Hemer, in *Festschrift F. F. Bruce* (1980) 9-12; *The Book of Acts in the Setting of Hellenistic History* (1989) 169f.; R. Jewett, *A Chronology of Paul's Life* (1979) 47-50.

48. *Exp* V/3 (1896) 336-45.

49. *De chronologie van het leven van Paulus* (1919) 83-85.

50. Cf. C. J. Hemer, in *Festschrift F. F. Bruce* (1980) 9-10.

51. Cf. J. Morgenstern, *CrozQ* 26 (1949) 232-40.

52. Cf. also I. H. Marshall, *Acts* (1980) 325f.

53. Concerning the new moons, cf. H. H. Goldstine, *New and Full Moons* (1973) 88f.

one cannot be completely certain that the departure from Philippi really did take place immediately on the day after the ending of the festival of Unleavened Bread,[54] and thus this calculation cannot stand on its own. But it does warrant our attention because of its possible close correlation with other dates.

12.3. The Egyptian Agitator

According to Acts 21:38, the military tribune who had Paul arrested at the temple plaza thought the apostle could be the "Egyptian who recently stirred up a revolt and led the four thousand assassins out into the wilderness." According to Josephus, this insurgency attempt (Josephus, *B.J.* ii.261-63/*Ant.* xx.167-72) took place after the death of Claudius (cf. Josephus, *Ant.* xx.158ff.). Because the leader, an Egyptian Jew, escaped at that time (Josephus, *Ant.* xx.171), it seemed to have been both hoped and feared that he could repeat this venture.[55] Because the insurrection was preceded by measures such as the territorial reorganization ordered by Nero (Josephus, *Ant.* xx.158f.), Felix's fight against the Zealot leader Eleazar, son of Dinaeus (Josephus, *Ant.* xx.160-62), as well as by the conspiracy to murder the high priest Jonathan (Josephus, *Ant.* xx.163f.), one would have to go back at least to the year A.D. 55.[56] Because of the sabbatical year A.D. 55/56, B. Z. Wacholder considers Nisan A.D. 56 as the most probable date for the emergence of the Egyptian,[57] a date coinciding well with our own dating of Paul's arrest at Pentecost A.D. 57.

12.4. Paul before Felix and Festus

12.4.1. The Accession of Felix

Although the beginning of this procuratorship is dated almost universally to A.D. 52,[58] D. R. Schwartz has presented what are to a large extent persuasive arguments against this placement.[59] Because Josephus mentions the accession

---

54. Cf. the objections in G. Ogg, *The Chronology of the Life of Paul* (1968) 140-45; E. Haenchen, *Die Apostelgeschichte* ([7]1977) 558.

55. Cf. M. Hengel, *Die Zeloten* ([2]1976) 237, note 4 (Eng. trans., *The Zealots* [1989]).

56. Cf. R. Jewett, *A Chronology of Paul's Life* (1979) 40.

57. *HUCA* 46 (1975) 126.

58. Cf. merely Schuerer I, 460; E. M. Smallwood, *The Jews under Roman Rule* ([2]1981) 269.

59. In *Studies in the Jewish Background of Christianity* (1992) 223-36.

of Felix between the dismissal of Cumanus and the expansion of the territory of Agrippa II, which occurred at the end of the twelfth year of Claudius (A.D. 53) (Josephus, *B.J.* ii.245-47/*Ant.* xx.136-38), scholars too self-evidently conclude that Cumanus' term of office extended to A.D. 52. Schwartz concludes from a comparison between Josephus, *B.J.* ii.223, and Josephus, *Ant.* xx.103f., that in the later account the Jewish historian was correcting, based on the source before him, the false impression given by the older portrayal, namely, that Cumanus was appointed only after the death of Herod of Chalcis, which occurred toward the end of A.D. 48 or in the first weeks of A.D. 49 (cf. Josephus, *Ant.* xx.104).[60] The beginning of A.D. 49 would thus be the *terminus ante quem* for the beginning of the procuratorship of Cumanus. Although no exact information can be gleaned from Josephus concerning this beginning, his portrayal of this term of office (cf. Josephus, *B.J.* ii.232-44/*Ant.* xx.118-33) gives the impression that it hardly lasted more than a year, and is thus to be dated A.D. 48/49.

The resulting early dating for the beginning of Felix's own term of office is also supported by information in Tacitus, information which previously has presented great difficulties for scholarship. Within the context of the year A.D. 52, the Roman historian reports an event that took place when Cumanus in Galilee and Felix in Samaria were simultaneously procurators (Tacitus, *Ann.* xii.54). Schwartz correctly points out that this is ordered not chronologically but thematically, in order to denounce Pallas through the misbehavior of his brother Felix.[61] Tacitus is alluding rather to the fact that the episode happened "when Felix had already ruled Judea for some time *(iam pridem Iudaeae impositus)*," sometime in the interval between *("interim")* the time of Caligula and A.D. 52 *(ibid.)*. D. R. Schwartz alters a hypothesis of his elder namesake E. Schwartz[62] to explain Tacitus' statements regarding the simultaneous activity of two procurators, statements which seem to contradict so completely the picture we get from Josephus. D. R. Schwartz assumes that Tacitus misunderstood a source that reported disturbances in the year A.D. 49 as well as the intervention of the Syrian legate Ummidius Quadratus, a source to which Josephus also had access. Tacitus incorrectly concluded from the source before him that at that time Judea devolved to Syria, and made Cumanus and Felix into procurators of the two regions entangled in the disturbances, Samaria and Galilee. Since the historian knew that after the death of Agrippa I (A.D. 44) Judea became a Roman province again,[63] he

---

60. *Ibid.*, 224-27.

61. In *Studies in the Jewish Background of Christianity* (1992) 231-36.

62. *NGWG* (1907) 286f.

63. Tacitus, *Hist.* v.9.3: *"Claudius, defunctis regibus aut modicum redactis, Iudaeam provinciam equitibus Romanis aut libertis permisit."*

viewed the situation for A.D. 49 described in his source as something new, and he noted as much in the corresponding chronological context of his work (Tacitus, *Ann.* xii.23.1). He then saved the details for later because of the reason mentioned. This explanation seems more plausible than other attempts at harmonizing[64] or explaining as errors[65] the accounts of Josephus and Tacitus. Within this understanding, the portrayal of the Roman historian also supports an accession of Felix in A.D. 49. Since he was a favorite of the empress Agrippina, an appointment in just this year is quite possible (§6.3.3).

The administrative transition from Felix to Porcius Festus mentioned in Acts 24:27 also presents problems. Different scholars offer different dates between A.D. 54 and A.D. 61 for this political change. The year A.D. 54, however, must actually already be eliminated because of the marriage at that time between Felix and Drusilla (see p. 104 above) (cf. Acts 24:24). Recently, however, a later dating within this period seems to be gaining support,[66] and, indeed, the more weighty evidence does support it.

12.4.2. The Fall of Pallas

Josephus reports that at Felix's dismissal, the latter was spared worse treatment as a result of the intervention of his brother Pallas (see p. 95 above) (Josephus, *Ant.* xx.182). This has prompted the conclusion that his dismissal occurred[67] before Pallas lost his office as head of the imperial finance administration in A.D. 55 (Tacitus, *Ann.* xiii.14). Nero's motives prompting this dismissal were to lessen the influence of the imperial widow Agrippina and to transfer to Seneca the restructuring of financial policy. However, for Pallas, the proverbially wealthy (Juvenal, *Sat.* i.109) bachelor, this loss of public office by no means meant the lost of influence. Anyone from whom the emperor himself wanted to draw an inheritance (Dio Cassius, *Hist.* lxii.14.3) could also pur-

---

64. According to F. F. Bruce, *JSS* 29 (1984) 42, at the dismissal of Cumanus, Felix was promoted from a subordinate post in Samaria to procurator. By contrast, M. Aberbach, *JQR* 40 (1949/50) 1-14, believes that Felix previously governed Galilee.

65. E. M. Smallwood, *The Jews under Roman Rule* (²1981) 256, note 1, believes that Tacitus confused Herod Agrippa I with Herod of Chalcis.

66. Cf. J. J. Gunther, *Paul: Messenger and Exile* (1972) 140f.; M. Stern, CRINT I/1 (1974) 74, note 2; R. K. Jewett, *A Chronology of Paul's Life* (1979) 43; J. A. T. Robinson, *Wann entstand das Neue Testament?* (1986) 54, note 52; F. F. Bruce, *The Book of Acts* (1988) 448f.; C. J. Hemer, *The Book of Acts in the Setting of Hellenistic History* (1989) 171; M. A. Hubaut, *Paul de Tarse* (1989) 47; additional representatives can be found in D. A. Carson, D. J. Moo, and L. Morris, *An Introduction to the New Testament* (1992) 230, note 56.

67. So, e.g., K. Lake, *BC* V (1933) 464-67, 470-73; M. Sordi, *StRo* 8 (1960) 401-5; H. Conzelmann, *Acts. Hermeneia* (Eng. trans., 1987) 194f.; E. Haenchen, *Die Apostelgeschichte* (⁷1977) 83f.; D. R. Schwartz, *Tarb* 52 (1982/83) 182-86; G. Schille, *Die Apostelgeschichte* (1983) 436; and esp. C. Saumagne, in *Festschrift M. Piganiol* (1966) 1373-86.

chase mild treatment for his brother. Indeed, one year after this loss of office, the indictment against Pallas was completely dropped, and potentially damaging evidence from the imperial financial administration was even burned at the order of the court (Tacitus, *Ann.* xiii.23). The dismissal must have taken place already before the birthday of Britannicus on 13 February A.D. 55 (cf. Tacitus, *Ann.* xiii.15.1). However, it seems utterly impossible to compress within four months the measures undertaken by Felix as reported by Josephus for the reign of Nero (after 13 October A.D. 54) (Josephus, *B.J.* ii.247-70/*Ant.* xx.160-81).[68] Hence, from this perspective the only *terminus ante quem* for the dismissal of Felix remains the poisoning of Pallas ordered by Nero in the year A.D. 62 (Tacitus, *Ann.* xiv.65), an event probably connected with the fall of the praetorian prefect Afranius Burrus (cf. Tacitus, *Ann.* xiv.51).[69]

12.4.3. The Information in Eusebius

The *Chronicon* of Eusebius, according to the Armenian version, dates the dismissal to the last year of Claudius (Eusebius, *Chron.* [ed. Schöne II 152]), and in the edition of Jerome to the second year of Nero (Eusebius, *Chron.* [ed. Helm 181f.]), that is, A.D. 54 or 56. E. Schürer denied the information in Eusebius any independent reliability, and viewed it merely as a misunderstanding of the Josephus-text, which shortly before the dismissal of Felix had mentioned the first year of Nero (Josephus, *Ant.* xx.158).[70] C. Erbes,[71] however, dedicated an exhaustive study to this question, one D. Plooij then picked up and in part continued.[72] Eusebius definitely understood the change in procurators not to have taken place until Nero, a fact proven not only by the rendering of the *Chronicon* in Syncellus (Eusebius, *Chron.* [ed. Schöne II 152]), but also by the corresponding assertion in his *Ecclesiastical History* (Eusebius, *HE* ii.22). Since in this chronological context Jerome is generally inclined to date things one year later, one can postulate that the original text of Eusebius mentioned the first year of Nero (A.D. 54/55).[73] This also makes comprehensible the fact that the information in the Armenian version could slip into the preceding, final year of

68. Cf. Schuerer I, 466, note 42. The argument of D. Georgi, *Die Geschichte der Kollekte des Paulus für Jerusalem* (1965) 95f. (Eng. trans., *Remembering the Poor* [1992]), is uncertain; Georgi finds that a later date for the change in procurators is suggested by the beginning of disturbances between Gentiles and Jews in Caesarea at the time of the change in procurators (Josephus, *B.J.* ii.270 [prior to this]; *Ant.* xx.182ff. [a bit after this]), disturbances which led to the outbreak of the Jewish War.

69. Cf. S. I. Oost, *AJPh* 79 (1958) 133-38.

70. *Geschichte des jüdischen Volkes* I ($^{3/4}$1901) 577f., note 38.

71. *TU* 19.1 (1899) 16-36.

72. *De chronologie van het leven van Paulus* (1919) 49-61.

73. Cf. C. Erbes, *TU* 19/1 (1899) 26f.

Claudius. This date was significant for Eusebius because at the beginning of the third century A.D., the Liberian Catalogue of Popes (*TU* 19/1, 5) already dated the arrival of Paul in A.D. 55.[74] The change of procurators is also noted under the tenth year of Agrippa II, though Eusebius incorrectly understands his reign to have begun in the year after the death of his father, Agrippa I, that is, in A.D. 45. If Eusebius derived this information from a source — and much suggests Justus of Tiberias[75] — then from the perspective of the correct starting year of A.D. 50 one would arrive at A.D. 59.

K. Lake objects that following this calculation requires one to date the accession of Festus as well, for whom both versions provide the date of A.D. 51, to A.D. 56, and thus under Nero instead of under Claudius.[76] But Lake, whom modern authors follow a bit too uncritically,[77] has overlooked the fact that Erbes[78] already offered a plausible answer to this. This time the source really is Josephus, whom Eusebius does expressly mention in connection with Felix. The church historian, like many modern scholars after him, (mis)understood Josephus, *Ant.* xx.137f. (§12.4.1), to read that Felix became procurator before the twelfth year of Claudius (A.D. 52/53). With G. B. Caird[79] and R. Jewett[80] one can take seriously the date of A.D. 59 derived from the pre-Eusebian tradition, since it is supported by other, independent information.

12.4.4. Numismatic Evidence

The last coins unquestionably dating from Felix's term of office can be dated to the first year of Nero (A.D. 54/55). A noticeably large number of coins were struck in Judea in the emperor's fifth year (A.D. 58/59),[81] a situation possibly signaling the arrival of a new procurator.[82] More recent numismatic publications[83] are increasingly inclined to accept this assumption.[84]

74. Cf. *ibid.*, 1-16.

75. Cf. *ibid.*, 34-36.

76. In *BC* V (1933) 472.

77. So, e.g., J. A. T. Robinson, *Wann enstand das Neue Testament?* (1986) 54, note 49.

78. *TU* 19.1 (1899) 30.

79. *IDB* I (1962) 604f.

80. *A Chronology of Paul's Life* (1979) 44.

81. Cf. G. F. Hill, *BMC Palestine* (1914), nos. 1-28; Y. Meshorer, *Jewish Coins of the Second Temple Period* (1967) 103.

82. So, e.g., H. J. Cadbury, *The Book of Acts in History* (1955) 9f.; M. Stern, CRINT I/1 (1974) 76, note 5.

83. Cf. F. Sternberg, *Antike Münzen* (1976) 49f.; A. Kindler, *Israel Numismatic Journal* 5 (1981) 20f.

84. My thanks to Dr. Arie Kindler of the Museum Haaretz in Jerusalem for cordial correspondence concerning this detail.

12.4.5. Additional Information in Acts

Other chronological references in Acts also support a change of office in the year A.D. 59.[85] If Paul was arrested in Jerusalem at Pentecost A.D. 57 (§12.2), then the two years of imprisonment that passed until the change in procurators (Acts 24:27) lead to A.D. 59. A consideration of Acts 24:10 (see above) already makes highly improbable any interpretation of διετία as referring to the duration of Felix's term of office. Moreover, Luke nowhere exhibits any interest in the duration of any particular procurator's term of office, but does indeed exhibit such interest with regard to the duration of Paul's imprisonment (Acts 28:30).[86] E. Haenchen also admits that at least Luke did refer this information to the apostle's imprisonment, even though the source from which he drew — so Haenchen — was referring to the procurator's term of office.[87] This source-critical conclusion loses its basis as a result of the chronological reconstruction of Felix's term of office presented here. Since the procurator exercised rule in Palestine at least since A.D. 52, and probably already since A.D. 49, one can likely understand literally what Acts 24:10 has Paul say: "knowing that for many years (ἐκ πολλῶν ἐτῶν) you have been a judge over this nation."[88]

12.5. Transport to Rome

12.5.1. Departure from Kaloi Limenes

Although "Fair Havens" (Καλοὶ Λιμένες) and the neighboring city Lasea (Λασαία) are well attested in ancient sources, they are at the same time so insignificant that their mention (Acts 27:8) is best explained as a result of eyewitness accounts.[89] The information concerning time in Acts 27:9 also sounds relatively precise: "Since much time had been lost and sailing was now dangerous, because even the Fast had already gone by . . . (διὰ τὸ καὶ

---

85. So, among others, E. M. Smallwood, *The Jews under Roman Rule* (²1981) 269; R. Jewett, *A Chronology of Paul's Life* (1979) 40-44; F. F. Bruce, *The Book of the Acts* (1989) 448f.; C. J. Hemer, *The Book of Acts* (1989) 171.

86. Cf. further G. Schneider, *Die Apostelgeschichte* I (1982) 353, note 25.

87. E. Haenchen, *Acts* (Eng. trans., 1971) 661; cf. *ibid.*, 68-71.

88. Because of, among other things, Luke's negative-ironic portrayal of Felix, the scholar of ancient history G. Rinaldi, *RBI* 39 (1991) 423-66, assumes that Luke's information is reliable.

89. Cf. C. J. Hemer, *The Book of Acts in the Setting of Hellenistic History* (1989) 136f., and now esp. C. J. Thornton, *Der Zeuge des Zeugen* (1991) 326-41, as well as *NewDoc* IV (1987) 115f.

τὴν νηστείαν ἤδη παρεληλυθέναι).'' The Festival of Booths, which Jewish tradition[90] viewed as the end of the period of safe sea travel, had apparently not yet passed, since it otherwise would have been mentioned. The conversation reported in what follows would thus have taken place in the five days between the two festivals Yom Kippur and Succoth. From the second καί, W. P. Workman concluded that besides the fasting on the Great Day of Atonement (10 Tishri), yet another date critical for sea travel, namely the equinox, had already passed.[91] His comparative texts from Caesar's *Gallic Wars* (Caesar, *Bell. Gall.* iv.36.2; v.23.5), however, refer to the situation specific to the campaigns in Britain.[92] Workman's further observation, however, is correct, namely, that on the basis of the following information,[93] the Atonement Festival should be dated as late as possible. Of the years in question (between A.D. 57 and 60), A.D. 59 was structured such that 10 Tishri fell on 5 October.[94] This seems noteworthy because of its agreement with the date for Felix's dismissal (§12.4).

12.5.2. The Stay in Rome

According to the most likely chronology suggested thus far, Paul would have arrived in Rome in the spring of A.D. 60.[95] If one follows the reflections of E. M. Smallwood[96] and D. R. Schwartz[97] concerning the term of office of the high priest Ishmael ben Phiabi, then according to a Talmudic reference to a function of ten years (*b. Yoma* 9a), he (after A.D. 49) occupied the office until A.D. 58/59. A change in the high-priestly office might help explain why

---

90. Billerbeck II, 771f.

91. *ET* 11 (1899/1900) 316-19.

92. Cf. C. J. Hemer, *The Book of Acts* (1989) 138, note 109.

93. A model calculation in R. Jewett, *A Chronology of Paul's Life* (1979) 51f.

94. Cf. R. A. Parker and W. H. Dubberstein, *Babylonian Chronology* (1956) 47.

95. R. Jewett, *A Chronology of Paul's Life* (1979) 44f., still follows D. Plooij, *De chronologie van het leven van Paul* (1919) 81-83, by assuming that the majority text (including sy[h**]) to Acts 28:16 (τῷ στρατοπεδάρχῳ) presupposes the responsibility of a single prefect. Since the last single occupant of this office, Afranius Burrus (cf. Tacitus, *Ann.* xiv.51), died in January A.D. 62 (cf. Tacitus, *Ann.* xiv.51f.; Dio Cassius, *Hist.* lxii.13), A.D. 61 would be the last possible year for Paul's arrival in Rome (so also already K. Wieseler, *Chronologie des apostolischen Zeitalters* [1848] 83f.). But quite apart from the secondary character of the majority text in this passage (B. M. Metzger, *A Textual Commentary* [²1975] 501), it remains uncertain just which military person is being referred to by the designation "Stratopedarch." Cf. C. J. Hemer, *The Book of Acts* (1989) 199f. Hence one should disregard this possibility of a *terminus ad quem*.

96. *The Jews under Roman Rule* (²1981) 262.

97. In *Studies in the Jewish Background of Christianity* (1992) 218-42. See pp. 133f. above.

charges were not immediately brought against the apostle (cf. Acts 28:17-31). Acts 23:2 (ὁ δὲ ἀρχιερεὺς Ἀνανίας) seems to support the majority opinion, according to which Ananias son of Nebedaeus occupied the office till approximately A.D. 59.[98] Admittedly, the title "high priest," attributed to him by both Luke (Acts 23:2) and Josephus (*Ant.* xx.162; *B.J.* ii.243) for the time after A.D. 49, is not an absolutely certain indication, since earlier office-holders were also so called (Excursus II/2).[99] Whether one dates the journey of Ishmael to Rome, his attendant imprisonment as hostage and subsequent deposal (Josephus, *Ant.* xx.194-96) to A.D. 58/59 or after 59, the circumstances emerging from this account do illuminate the situation at the time Paul himself was transported to and arrived in the imperial capital. Despite the intercession of the emperor's wife Poppea (Josephus, *Ant.* xx.195; cf. *Vita* 16), the political situation at the court was still precarious for Jews. The ambassadors under Ishmael were only able to effect a compromise.[100] As late as A.D. 64, Josephus had to work to procure the release of priests[101] who had been apprehended under Felix (A.D. 49-59) (Josephus, *Vita* 13-16). This event, too, fits our own solution better, namely, that of dating the end of Felix's procuratorship to A.D. 59 rather than around A.D. 55/56.

It is beyond the scope of this study to address Paul's legal situation in the two years following his arrival in Rome (Acts 28:30). More recent studies suggest that he was released after the *biennium* because the Sanhedrin neglected to continue the indictment within the prescribed time.[102] Neither can we discuss further whether this enhances once again the value of ancient church tradition which associates the apostle's death with the Neronian persecution of Christians after A.D. 64.[103] In any event, a chronology of Acts that finds Paul in Rome in A.D. 62 presents fewer riddles than does his

98. Cf. Schuerer, II, 231; R. Jewett, *A Chronology of Paul's Life* (Philadelphia: Fortress, 1979) 44 (bibliography); C. J. Hemer, *The Book of Acts in the Setting of Hellenistic History* (1989) 170f.

99. M. Goodman, *The Ruling Class of Judaea* (1987) 142, note 5: "In favour of Schwartz' detailed hypothesis, note that Ananus in *c.* A.D. 54 [according to our calculations: A.D. 59] was no longer obviously the High Priest in the eyes of an uninformed observer, since St. Paul had to be told about his status according to Acts 23:2."

100. Cf. T. Rajak, *Josephus* (1983) 39.

101. Cf. H. Lichtenberger, in *Festschrift H. Schreckenberg* (1993) 251-53.

102. Cf. C. J. Hemer, *The Book of Acts in the Setting of Hellenistic History* (1989) 383-404; J. Méleze-Modrezejewski, in *Festschrift J. Imbert* (1989) 403-11; H. W. Tajra, *The Trial of St. Paul* (1989) 172-96; S. Légasse, *Paul apôtre* (1991) 242-45.

103. Cf. in this regard, among others, L. P. Pherigo, *JBL* 70 (1951) 277-84; R. Jewett, *A Chronology of Paul's Life* (1979) 45f.; A. Moda, in *Festschrift J. Dupont* (1985) 289-315; J. A. T. Robinson, *Wann entstand das Neue Testament* (1986) 149-60; W. Rordorf, in *Festschrift E. E. Ellis* (1987) 319-27; H. W. Tajra, *The Martyrdom of Paul* (1994).

disappearance from the history of early Christianity after a stay in Jerusalem in the year A.D. 52 or at latest A.D. 55, as suggested by the reconstruction of G. Lüdemann.[104]

104. *Paul: Apostle to the Gentiles* (1984) 108f., 263.

II. Stages of Pauline Missionary Strategy

INTERIM CONSIDERATIONS
Geographic Sequences in Paul's Letters

Hitherto we have dealt with possible individual dates of Pauline chronology. In the following chapter we will attempt to arrive at a relatively coherent picture of the early Pauline mission to the extent our sources allow. Taking the apostle's own statements as our point of departure whenever possible, we will then immediately ask to what extent the information from Acts is commensurate with them, contradicts them, or perhaps historically explicates or complements them. Our consistent heuristic principle will be the question whether the Pauline statements allow us to infer a specific geographic sequence characterizing his missionary activities (§§13-15). If such a geographic movement is indeed discernible, we acquire thereby an important tool for corroborating Luke's portrayal. If we can reconstruct in its main features the geographic sequence of Paul's activity, this also will make it easier to arrive at a synthesis using individual chronological dates (§17).

A directly sequential evaluation of the information from Paul's letters and from Acts might prompt the objection that this constitutes a regression behind the distinction between primary and secondary sources for Pauline chronology (§1.4). A common treatment of the Pauline and Lukan material will be undertaken here primarily for one reason: as the survey of scholarship (§1) has already shown, and as will become even more clear in what follows, the outlines that do not make use of Acts are much too optimistic regarding what can be derived from the Pauline letters alone.[1] I believe that three sequences can be derived from the letters with virtual certainty.

---

1. J. J. Gunther, in B. C. Corley, *Colloquy on New Testament Studies* (1983) 328, remarks in the discussion of the outlines of R. K. Jewett and G. Lüdemann that "to the extent that Acts has explicit statements, they have to be given greater value sometimes than a statement in Paul's letters which is ambivalent and open to half a dozen interpretations — if you will dig the commentaries out. And if you claim this one interpretation, a chronological interpretation of a certain statement in Paul's letters, as the one by which you exclude an explicit contrary statement in Acts, you are not being very historical in your method."

The *first* sequence emerges from the apostle's autobiographical retrospective in the letter to the Galatians:

Conversion near
Damascus (implied by Gal. 1:17)
Arabia (Gal. 1:17)
Damascus (Gal. 1:17)
 after three years
Jerusalem (Gal. 1:18)
Syro-Cilicia (Gal. 1:21)
 after fourteen years
Jerusalem (Gal. 2:1)
Letter to the Galatians.

Unlike G. Lüdemann,[2] I do not believe that the "apologetic letter" assumed by H. D. Betz[3] represents a genre whose formal characteristics have been demonstrated sufficiently to apply them without further qualification to Gal. 1:6–2:14.[4] Hence it is by no means certain that the so-called Antiochene incident (Gal. 2:11ff.) represents a thematic retrospective and is to be dated before the Apostolic Council of Gal. 2:1ff. One can, however, translate the introductory sentences of Gal. 2:11ff. in the pluperfect, and thus on the basis of purely grammatical considerations date the Antiochene conflict before the Apostolic Council.[5] One's understanding of this matter will be determined by the overall reconstruction of the events surrounding the Apostolic Council. Thus O. Böcher, for example, believes that a historically correct understanding of Paul in this passage is possible only with the help of Luke, namely, by identifying Gal. 2:11ff. and Acts 15:1f. (not Acts 15:37-39).[6] The writing itself does not allow us to determine with any certainty just when the founding of the churches in "Galatia," presupposed by the letter, took place. It is equally unclear how much time passed between the meeting in Jerusalem of Gal. 2:1ff. and the composition of the letter.

---

2. *Paul: Apostle to the Gentiles* (1984) 46-59.
3. *NTS* 21 (1975) 353-79; *Galatians* (1979) 14-25.
4. Cf. W. A. Meeks, *JBL* 100 (1981) 304-7; E. A. Russell, *Irish Biblical Studies* 6 (1984) 156-60; R. Y. K. Fung, *The Epistle to the Galatians* (1987) 28-32; R. N. Longenecker, *Galatians* (1990) cix-cxiv; T. Söding, *BN* 56 (1991) 32, note 4; W. B. Russell, *BS* 150 (1993) 351-58. Further bibliography can be found in B. R. Gaventa, *NT* 28 (1986) 311, note 4.
5. Cf. G. Stählin, *Die Apostelgeschichte* ([6]1978) 206, 209f. A prepositioning is already considered by Augustine, *Ep.* 82.10, and then esp. by T. Zahn, *Die Apostelgeschichte* II (1921) 539f., and H. M. Féret, *Pierre et Paul à Antioche et à Jérusalem* (1955). Additional earlier advocates can be found in J. Dupont, *Études sur les Actes des Apôtres* (1967) 187; A. Wechsler, *Geschichtsbild und Apostelstreit* (1991) 155, note 125.
6. In *Festschrift J. Gnilka* (1989) 331.

The *second* sequence for a mission in Greece emerges from the first letter to the Thessalonians:

Philippi (1 Thess. 2:2)
Thessalonica (1 Thess. 2:2; cf. Phil. 4:15f.)
Athens (1 Thess. 3:1)
First letter to the Thessalonians

One cannot decide alone on the basis of information from the letter to the Thessalonians or from the apostle's other writings whether this journey took place before or after the Apostolic Council of Gal. 2:1ff. It is quite probable, if not entirely certain, that an additional station can be added to this journey:

Corinth (cf. 2 Cor. 11:7-9)

The *third* sequence is associated with a collection in the Pauline churches (§15.5.2) allowing us to present for the letters the sequence 1 Corinthians — 2 Corinthians — Romans; any more precise detailing based on hypotheses involving a division of the second letter to the Corinthians is questionable (§15.4.1):

Ephesus (1 Cor. 16:8)
First letter to the Corinthians
Troas (2 Cor. 2:12)
Macedonia (2 Cor. 2:13)
    Plan to visit Judea (2 Cor. 1:16; cf. 1 Cor. 16:3f.) and Corinth
    (2 Cor. 9:4) as well as a mission beyond Corinth (2 Cor. 10:16f.;
    cf. Rom. 15:20)
Second letter to the Corinthians

The relationship between the collection alluded to in Gal. 2:10 (see p. 16 above) and this collection activity is uncertain. 1 Cor. 16:1 by no means compels us to conclude simultaneity.[7] Gaius Δερβαῖος (Acts 20:4), one of Paul's companions on his final trip to Jerusalem, was in all probability not a representative of the Galatian churches.[8] A Galatian collection could already long previously have been concluded and delivered (see p. 297 below). In any event, in Rom. 15:26 the apostle speaks exclusively of collections in Achaia and Macedonia.

Since it was probably in Corinth that Paul wrote his letter to the Romans (§15.5.2), a letter which in any case does presuppose that the collection had been concluded (Rom. 15:25f.), one may assume that the apostle was able to

7. Cf. C. J. Thornton, *Der Zeuge des Zeugen* (1991) 230.
8. Cf. *ibid.,* 256f.

233

carry out his plan to visit this city. Hence the final sequence to emerge in the series which one can discern with certainty is:

> Corinth (cf. Rom. 16:23)
> Letter to the Romans
> > Anticipated journeys (Rom. 15:23-29) to
> Jerusalem, Rome, Spain

Again, the letters alone do not allow us to determine how much time separates the stay in Ephesus and the one, certain, previous visit to Corinth. If with respect to the relative Pauline chronology we do not wish to make do merely with ascertaining three unconnected sequences,[9] no other choice is available than to attempt a critical combination with dates from Acts and other evidence. A modest element of hope already resides in the fact that Luke offers more or less clear parallels to the sequences already ascertained.[10]

---

9. J. Knox, *Chapters in a Life of Paul*, rev. ed. (1987) 346f., admits that a connection independent of Acts is possible only by way of surmise. The direct connection between the first and second sequence established by J. Murphy-O'Connor, *RB* 89 (1982) 90f., in order to demonstrate a mission to Greece already before the Apostolic Council, is more suggestive than argumentative. See also p. 28, note 112 above.

10. A summarizing overview can be found in T. F. Campbell, *JBL* 74 (1955) 87, and in J. A. Fitzmyer, *According to Paul* (1993) 38-40.

§13
The Beginning of the Mission

13.1. Calling to the Gentile Mission

13.1.1. Christophany and Mission to the Gentiles

Paul described his call to be a missionary most clearly in Gal. 1:15-17: "But when God, who had set me apart before I was born and called me through his grace, was pleased to reveal his Son to me, so that I might proclaim him among the Gentiles (ἀποκαλύψαι τὸν υἱὸν αὐτοῦ ἐν ἐμοὶ ἵνα εὐαγγελίζωμαι αὐτὸν ἐν τοῖς ἔθνεσιν), I did not confer with any human being, nor did I go up to Jerusalem to those who were already apostles before me, but I went away at once into Arabia, and afterward I returned to Damascus." It is perfectly clear that when composing the letter to the Galatians the apostle was convinced that the self-revelation of the resurrected Jesus near Damascus already contained his commission to the Gentiles. Scholars of extremely varying directions have thus concluded further that Paul began his proclamation to Gentiles immediately after his conversion, with the geographic specification "Arabia" providing a clue to the first locus of his work.[1] Even though probably the majority of contemporary exegetes takes this position, M. Hengel quite correctly advises caution: "The duration and purpose of this Arabian sojourn remain uncertain. It may have been limited to a few months. Perhaps Paul did make his first missionary attempts in 'Arabia'; this is, however, by no means certain."[2]

The formulation in Gal. 1:16, strictly speaking, says first of all only that the Christophany near Damascus contained the mission to the Gentiles

1. Cf. H. Conzelmann, *Acts* (Eng. trans., 1987) 74; F. F. Bruce, *New Testament History* (London, 1969) 250-62; E. Haenchen, *Acts* (Eng. trans., 1971) 333-35; M. Grant, *Saint Paul* (1976) 15f.; G. Bornkamm, *Paulus* ([6]1987) 48f. (Eng. trans., *Paul, Paulus* [1971]). Further bibliography can be found in R. Y. K. Fung, *The Epistle to the Galatians* (1988) 68, notes 33-36. So also already Ambrosiaster (*CSEL* 81/III, 15).

2. *Zur urchristlichen Geschichtsschreibung* ([2]1984) 73. But see now M. Hengel and A. M. Schwemer, *Paul between Damascus and Antioch* (1997) 106-26.

as its goal (ἵνα . . .).[3] Paul does not say whether the resurrected Jesus commissioned him directly through a vision or through words, and it is therefore possible that the initiation of the mission to the Gentiles represents a realization that emerged for the apostle only sometime later from this Christophany.[4] It is not the intention of the section Gal. 1:15ff. to render a detailed account of Paul's missionary activity. Regrettably, we do not learn just what he did in "Syria and Cilicia" (Gal. 1:21) (§14.1). In this context, the geographic information clearly functions to establish that Paul stayed far away from Jerusalem at that time, and was thus independent of the authorities there. The same apologetic intention is served by pointing out that following his conversion he immediately went to Arabia (Gal. 1:17). Whatever he had in mind and actually did there, Paul was in any event not in Jerusalem at that time, and this fact receives the entire emphasis.[5]

By contrast, a matter of decisive significance for understanding the Pauline mission is clear: as demonstrated by the concurrence even in its wording, Gal. 1:15 (ὁ ἀφορίσας με ἐκ κοιλίας μητρός μου καὶ καλέσας) is formulated with unmistakable reference to Isa. 49:1 (ἐκ κοιλίας μητρός μου ἐκάλεσεν τὸ ὄνομά μου). Elsewhere, too, Paul understood his own conversion as a prophetic calling analogous to that of the Deutero-Isaianic Servant of God (as shown, e.g., by Rom. 15:20f. [Isa. 52:15] and 2 Cor. 6:2 [Isa. 49:8 LXX]). Although this view, presented particularly by L. Cerfaux,[6] has indeed been criticized,[7] a new study by K. O. Sandnes[8] has clearly confirmed its essential features.[9] It should be pointed out that the Pauline self-witness here concurs with the portrayal of Acts (Acts 13:47; cf. Isa. 49:6; Acts 26:16-18, cf. Isa. 42:6, 16).[10] In the Old Testament, the most unequivocal statements of hope concerning the Gentile world appear in the second part of the book of

---

3. Cf. in this regard esp. T. Zahn, *Der Brief des Paulus an die Galater* (1905) 63-68. J. Jeremias, *Der Schlüssel zur Theologie des Apostels Paulus* (1971) 26, 30, note 24, refers to the analogy of Acts 26:17f., which, according to Acts 22:17-21, is similarly to be understood intentionally.

4. So, among others, R. Liechtenhan, *Die urchristliche Mission* (1946) 78-80; A. Fridrichsen, *LUÅ* 3 (1947) 13.23; E. P. Blair, *BR* 10 (1965) 19-33; A. Oepke, *Der Brief des Paulus an die Galater* ([2]1957) 33; F. Mussner, *Der Galaterbrief* ([5]1987) 51f.

5. Cf. O. Linton, *StTh* 3 (1949) 84, and F. Mussner, *loc. cit.*, 92.

6. In *Recueil Lucien Cerfaux* II (1954) 439-54; *The Christian in the Theology of St. Paul* (1967) 75-107.

7. So by M. D. Hooker, *Jesus and the Servant* (1959) 116-23.

8. *"Paul — One of the Prophets?"* (1991) 48-71.

9. Cf. further esp. A. M. Denis, *EThL* 33 (1957) 245-318; T. Holtz, *ThLZ* 91 (1966) 321-30; O. Haas, *Paulus der Missionar* (1971) 10-15; W. P. Bowers, *Studies in Paul's Understanding of His Mission* (1976) 135-43 (137, note 1: further bibliography).

10. Cf. W. P. Bowers, *loc. cit.*, 142; K. O. Sandnes, *"Paul — One of the Prophets?"* (1991) 75-77.

Isaiah (Isa. 45:20-22; 51:4f.; 56:1-8), specifically in connection with the figure of the Servant of God (Isa. 42:1, 3f., 6; 49:1, 6, 22). Since Paul offers us no direct explanation in this regard, we must rely on additional considerations of how specifically this understanding of his own calling emerged for him from the Christophany.[11] We may refer here to a geographic factor as *one* possible element, emphasizing all the while the extremely hypothetical nature of many of these considerations.

13.1.2. The Light of the Messiah in the Land of Damascus

What Acts states explicitly (Acts 9:3; 22:6; 26:12), Paul confirms implicitly (Gal. 1:17: καὶ πάλιν ὑπέστρεψα εἰς Δαμασκόν): his conversion through an encounter with the resurrected Jesus occurred near Damascus.[12] The apostle (2 Cor. 4:6) confirms Luke's portrayal (Acts 9:3; 22:6; 26:13) in yet another important element as well: the Christophany was accompanied by a luminous phenomenon.[13] Was it of particular significance for Paul that the light of the Messiah was shown for him precisely in the vicinity of Damascus? 2 Corinthians 4:6 (ὁ θεὸς ὁ εἰπών: ἐκ σκότους φῶς λάμψει, ὃς ἔλαμψεν ἐν ταῖς καρδίαις ἡμῶν πρὸς φωτισμὸν τῆς γνώσεως τῆς δόξης τοῦ θεοῦ ἐν προσώπῳ Ἰησοῦ Χριστοῦ) recalls not only Gen. 1:3 LXX (καὶ εἶπεν ὁ θεὸς Γενηθήτω φῶς), but also Isa. 9:1 LXX (ὁ λαὸς ὁ πορευόμενος ἐν σκότει . . . φῶς λάμψει ἐφ' ὑμᾶς).[14] The light of creation is for Paul identical with the eschatological light that radiated about him at his conversion. The promise in Isa. 9:1 belongs to a particular geographic context that was not a matter of indifference to part of Jewish and Christian expectation: "In the former time he [God] brought into contempt the land of Zebulun and the land of Naphtali, but in the coming time he will make glorious the way of the sea, the land beyond the Jordan,

---

11. Concerning the significance of the Damascus-revelation for the Pauline view of the Gentile mission, cf. esp. S. Kim, *The Origin of Paul's Gospel* ([2]1984) 46-55, and C. Dietzfelbinger, *Die Berufung des Paulus als Ursprung seiner Theologie* (1985) 137-47. Note also the title of a Groningen dissertation of 1855: C. P. Hofstede de Groot, *Pauli Conversio, praecipuus theologiae Paulinae fons.*

12. Cf. H. Schlier, *Der Brief an die Galater* ([5]1971) 58f.; A. Oepke, *Der Brief des Paulus an die Galater* ([4]1979) 62, for a critical view of the eccentric understanding of E. Barnikol, *Die vorchristliche und frühchristliche Zeit des Paulus* (1929) 76-88; *Die Christwerdung des Paulus in Galiläa und die Apostelberufung vor Damaskus und im Tempel* (1935) 7-52, according to which, after his conversion in Galilee, Paul allegedly returned to Damascus, which belonged to Arabia (Gal. 1:17c as epexegesis of 1:17b). The Sanhedrin's legal authority, apparently presupposed for Damascus, represents a genuine problem (Acts 9:2). But cf. F. F. Bruce, *The Acts of the Apostles* ([3]1990) 233; K. Haacker, *ANRW* II 26.2 (1995) 878-91; and F. Millar, *The Roman Near East* (1993) 56f.

13. Cf. S. Kim, *The Origin of Paul's Gospel* ([2]1984) 5-13.

14. So as possibility also S. Kim, *loc. cit.,* 8f., note 9.

Galilee of the nations (דרך הים עבר הירדן גליל הגוים; LXX ὁδὸν θαλάσσης καὶ οἱ λοιποὶ οἱ τὴν παραλίαν κατοικοῦντες καὶ πέραν τοῦ Ἰορδάνου, Γαλιλαία τῶν ἐθνῶν, τὰ μέρη τῆς Ἰουδαίας). The people who walked in darkness have seen a great light; those who lived in a land of deep darkness —on them light has shined (נָגַהּ אוֹר; LXX φῶς λάμψει)" (Isa. 8:23–9:1 [Eng. 9:1-2]).

For Josephus, the territory of the tribe of Naphtali extended to Damascus (Josephus, *Ant.* v.86). The *Genesis Apocryphon* from Qumran exhibits a striking interest in the topography of the northern land of East Jordan (1Qap-Gen 21:28–22:10). Abraham's pursuit of the conquered kings (Gen. 14) extends "to Helbon which is north of Damascus" (1QapGen 22:10). It seems that Essenizing circles understood the patriarch's victory as a model for the eschatological victory won by the messiah.[15] The settlement of Essenic groups in the "land of Damascus" (CD 6:5, 19; 8:21; 19:34; 20:12: ארץ דמשק)[16] was obviously prompted by the anticipation that the messianic age would begin there.[17] It was hoped that the messianic star of Num. 24:17 would rise in the region of Damascus (CD 7:14-18). The region around Mount Hermon appears in the Enoch-tradition (*1 Enoch* 13:7ff.) and in the *Testament of Levi* (*T. Levi* 2:3ff.) as the locus of special revelatory reception.[18] Isolated rabbinic traditions such as *Lev. Rab.* 9 (111a) and *S. Dtn.* 41 (79b) also attest the eschatological significance of the land in the north.[19]

Several Christian groups also give special attention to the northern part of East Jordan as a *terra Messianica*.[20] Jerome records a Jewish-Christian interpretation of Isa. 8:23–9:1 (Jerome, *Comm. in Is.* 9:1 [*PL* 24, 125]), according to which in fulfillment of this prophecy Jesus first liberated Zebulun and Naphtali from the yoke of Jewish tradition (*"prima terra Zabulon et terra*

15. Cf. N. Wieder, *JJS* 30 (1969) 86-88.

16. Concerning the historicity of an exodus of Essenes to this region, cf. S. Iwry, *EI* 9 (1969) 80-88; F. M. Strickert, *RQ* 12 (1986) 334-37; H. Stegemann, in J. Trebolle Barrera and L. Vegas Montaner, *The Madrid Qumran Congress I* (1992) 146-48. It is thus not necessary to view the "land of Damascus" as a cover name for Qumran. This alone refutes the assumption of S. Sabugal, *Análisis exegético sobre la conversión de San Pablo* (1976) 163-224; in M. Delcor, *Qumrân* (1978) 403-13, that Paul's conversion took place in the region of the Essene monastery.

17. Cf. N. Wieder, *The Judean Scrolls and Karaism* (1962) 1-5. The Jews living in Damascus viewed Abraham as the former king of this city (Nicolaus of Damascus [Josephus, *Ant.* i.159]; cf. Pompeius Trogus [Justin, *Epit.* 36.2]). Since the tradition of an Ἀβράμου οἴκησις was attached to a *village* (κώμη) in this area (Josephus, *Ant.* i.160), one might ask whether the bearers of this tradition were not Essenic groups in the "land of Damascus."

18. Cf. G. W. E. Nickelsburg, *JBL* 100 (1981) 582-90.

19. Billerbeck I 160f.; IV/2, 789. Cf. R. Riesner, *TynBul* 38 (1987) 55.

20. Cf. J. Daniélou, *Primitive Christian Symbols* (1964) 102-23.

Nephtali . . . gravissimum traditionum Iudaicarum iugum excussit de cervicibus suis").[21] In atypical fashion, the messiah thus begins his salvific activity precisely where for Israel disaster and judgment began (Isa. 9:3; cf. 2 Kgs. 15:29). Justin gave an extremely peculiar interpretation to Isa. 8:4 ("he will carry away the wealth of Damascus and the spoil of Samaria"): at the moment of Jesus' birth, when the magi (Mt. 2:1ff.) began to follow the star, the power of the evil spirit in Damascus was broken (Justin, *Dial.* 78.9). Hence the eschatological light encounters the first Gentiles in the region of Damascus, from which for Justin the magi originally came (Justin, *Dial.* 78.2, 10). Mt. 4:13-16 understands Jesus' ministry in northern Galilee and in the adjoining land of East Jordan as the fulfillment of Isa. 8:23–9:1 (together with Num. 24:17), and thus as an anticipation of the illumination of the Gentiles.[22] The apocryphal Jewish-Christian *Testament of the Redeemer in Galilee,* difficult to date, portrays Paul, in fulfillment of Isa. 8:4, preaching to the Gentiles in the area around Damascus (*T. Gal.* 44 [PO 9, 215]), and thus one must ask seriously whether this does not reflect an Old Testament-salvific-historical way of thinking of the sort that also affected the apostle himself after his conversion. Jerome, too (*Comm. in Is.* 9:1 [*PL* 24, 125]), reports that at least some Jewish Christians viewed Isa. 8:23–9:1 as coming to complete fulfillment in Paul's activity.

In a fundamental reflection on the Old Testament justification of the mission to the Gentiles, Paul cites Isa. 11:10: "The root of Jesse shall come, the one who rises to rule the Gentiles; in him the Gentiles shall hope" (Rom. 15:12). Naturally, the apostle considered the "root of Jesse" in this passage of the book of Isaiah to be none other than the eschatological ruler from the house of David according to Isa. 9:5f. The passages Num. 24:17; Isa. 9:1; and Isa. 11:1 could for Jewish exegesis (cf. Mt. 4:16; Lk. 1:78f.) once again be especially evoked by the play with the related concepts "rising star" (ἀνατελεῖ ἄστρον, דרך כוכב)/"shining light" (φῶς λάμψει, נגה אור)/"sprouting branch" (ἄνθος ἀναβήσεται [ח]ונצר יפרה).[23] Hence it does not seem far-fetched that Paul came to understand the shining of the messianic light near Damascus as the beginning of the eschatological ingathering of the Gentiles. Such a possibility takes on special force if the Jewish Christians in and around Damascus with whom the apostle had his first positive contacts were of an Essenic character.[24]

21. Concerning the actual foundation of a Jewish-Christian-Hebrew targum, cf. recently R. A. Pritz, *Nazarene Jewish Christianity* (1988) 64f. The doubts of A. F. J. Klijn, *RSR* 60 (1972) 251f., note 46, are thus unnecessary.

22. Cf. R. Riesner, *TynBul* 38 (1987) 49-51.

23. Cf. R. H. Gundry, *Matthew* (1982) 60f.; R. Riesner, *TynBul* 38 (1987) 50f.

24. F. A. Schilling, *AThR* 16 (1934) 203-5, following H. Preisker, *ThBl* 8 (1929) 49-54, assumed that Paul wanted to expand the persecution to include Damascus precisely because the new messianic faith enjoyed particularly quick acceptance among the Essenic

O. Michel[25] has asked whether the theological reworking of the Damascus revelation in 2 Cor. 4:6 does not exhibit similarities to the language of the Essene-like *Testament of Levi*,[26] the bearers of which tradition G. W. E. Nickelsburg[27] seeks in the region of Mount Hermon.[28]

As representative of the circle of disciples, Peter made his own confession to the messiah in the same area around Caesarea Philippi (Mt. 16:13/Mk. 8:27), qualified by the expression σάρξ καὶ αἷμα οὐκ ἀπεκάλυψέν σοι ἀλλ' ὁ πατήρ μου (Mt. 16:17). Perhaps in Gal. 1:15f. (εὐδόκησεν ὁ θεὸς . . . ἀποκαλύψαι . . . οὐ προσανεθέμην σαρκὶ καὶ αἵματι) Paul is referring

---

Jews there. Cf. also R. E. Osborne, *CJTh* 10 (1964) 16-20. The discourse delivered by the חָסִיד (Acts 22:12: ἀνὴρ εὐλαβής) Ananias in Acts 22:14 concerning the messiah as "the Righteous One" recalls *1 Enoch* 38:2; 53:6. Cf. R. Riesner, *ANRW* II 26.2 (1995) 1862f. By contrast, the assumption of C. S. Mann, *ET* 99 (1988) 331-34, according to which Damascus was of particular strategic importance to the Jerusalem temple nobility because there one allegedly tested the orthodoxy of the pilgrims from the eastern Jewish settlements areas, is nothing but conjecture. Whereas Byzantine tradition locates Paul's conversion close to Damascus, a crusader tradition asserts that it took place at the village of Kaukab, 15 kilometers southwest of the city (J. Nasrallah, *Souvenirs de St. Paul* [1944] 13-22; O. F. A. Meinardus, *BA* 44 [1981] 58f.). Although the remains of a Byzantine church (B. Bagatti, *LA* 11 [1960/61] 295-300) might attest earlier veneration, the unsystematic excavations (Y. Samara, *an-Ni'ma* II/2 [1963] 65-69) make it difficult to draw any conclusions (J. Nasrallah, *MBib* 31 [1983] 35f.). This Kokhba ("Star [Village]"; cf. Num. 24:17) was apparently a settlement of Essenizing Jewish Christians. Cf. B. Pixner and R. Riesner, *GBL* II (1988) 801f. J. Daniélou, *Primitive Christian Symbols* [1964] 119, assumed that this (subsequently distorted) local tradition has something to do with Paul's having once stayed here after his conversion. This suspicion might at least help explain the Essenic conceptual and linguistic forms in Paul (cf. esp. J. Murphy-O'Connor, ed., *Paul and Qumran* [1968]; J. Daniélou, *Les manuscripts de la mer Morte et les origines du christianisme* [²1974] 91-96; H. W. Kuhn, in D. Dimant and U. Rappaport, *The Dead Sea Scrolls* [1992] 327-37), forms which are quite remarkable coming from a former Pharisee. However, one cannot completely exclude the possibility that a certain fascination with the Essene quarter on the southwestern hill in Jerusalem may already have captivated Paul during his time there (see p. 87 above). Cf. M. Hengel, *ThBeitr* 21 (1990) 185f.

25. In *Festschrift C. K. Barrett* (1978) 45.

26. In *T. Levi* 18:3f. we read about the messianic high priest: "And his star shall arise in heaven as of a king, lighting up the light of knowledge as the sun the day; and he shall be magnified in the world. He shall shine forth as the sun on the earth, and shall remove all darkness from under heaven." Later (*T. Levi* 18:9) the prediction is made: "And in his priesthood the Gentiles shall be multiplied in knowledge upon the earth, and enlightened through the grace of the Lord."

27. *JBL* 100 (1981) 588-90.

28. With respect to 1 Corinthians 7, A. Oepke, in K. H. Rengstorf, *Das Paulusbild in der neueren Forschung* (1969) 431, writes: "Paul most closely resembles certain mildly ascetic currents within Hellenistic Judaism such as those in evidence, besides in Philo, especially in the *Testaments of the Twelve Patriarchs*."

antithetically to the Petrine confession;[29] attention has also been drawn to possible parallels between the story of the transfiguration (Mt. 17:1-8 par.), which appears localized in the area around Mount Hermon,[30] and Gal. 1:15f.[31] These and similar observations are relevant to the question whether this sort of geographic thinking can possibly be presupposed for Paul. Occasionally, later rabbinic tradition also attests the expectation (one possibly previously suppressed because of anti-Christian tendencies) that the light of the messiah would bring a great many proselytes to Judaism (*Midr. Cant.* 1:3 [85b], Billerbeck I, 162). Thus there may well have been several previous Jewish and Jewish-Christian sources providing the impetus for Paul, too, to find in his own Christophany, one taking place precisely near Damascus, an element of eschatological hope for the Gentile world.

13.2. Geographic Framework of the Mission

13.2.1. Romans 15:19

If anywhere there is any indication that Paul based his mission activity on a specific geographic concept, then it is Rom. 15:19 in its context: ὥστε με ἀπὸ Ἰερουσαλὴμ καὶ κύκλῳ μέχρι τοῦ Ἰλλυρικοῦ πεπληρωκέναι τὸ εὐαγγέλιον τοῦ Χριστοῦ. In a dissertation unfortunately not yet published, W. P. Bowers presents a thorough exegesis of this text[32] which I can largely follow here.[33] A. S. Geyser has admittedly raised a fundamental objection to any specifically geographic understanding of Rom. 15:19b,[34] asserting that Paul was here claiming only in a general fashion as a *nota apostoli* that he was preaching to the boundaries of the earth. However, the command to undertake mission activity (Mt. 28:18-20) is a much too narrow and late basis from which to claim this sort of characteristic apostolic identification,[35] especially since at

---

29. Cf. J. Chapman, *RBén* 29 (1912) 133-47; B. C. Butler, *DR* 66 (1948) 370-72; J. B. Orchard, *Galatians* (1969) 1175; D. Wenham, *Paul* (1995) 200-205.

30. Cf. R. Riesner, *TynBul* 38 (1987) 57f.; *GBL* II (1988) 562f.

31. Cf. J. Bligh, *Galatians* (1970) 131-33; D. Wenham, *Paul* (1995) 357-63 (on 2 Cor. 4:6).

32. *Studies in Paul's Understanding of His Mission* (diss., Cambridge, 1976) 18-26. The treatment in U. Maiburg, *JAC* 26 (1983) 42, is unfruitful.

33. Cf. recently also M. Hengel, in *idem* and U. Heckel, eds., *Paulus und das antike Judentum* (1991) 219f.

34. *NTS* 67 (1959/60) 156-59. Similarly also U. Wilckens, *Der Brief an die Römer* III (1982) 119f.

35. Cf. in this regard the criticism of W. P. Bowers, *Studies in Paul's Understanding of His Mission* (1976) 206-9.

that time Illyricum was not exactly thought to lie at the ends of the earth. Our own treatment of the Pauline missionary routes will try to show in detail that there are no insuperable historical difficulties involved in understanding Rom. 15:19 as Paul's geographically summarizing retrospective of his previous activity. Three questions must be briefly clarified: (1) What does "from Jerusalem and far around [a circle]" mean? (2) Is "as far as Illyricum" to be understood inclusively or exclusively? (3) To what extent could Paul speak of having "fulfilled the gospel of Christ" at the time of the letter to the Romans within the geographic framework thus indicated?

(1) The expression ἀπὸ Ἰερουσαλὴμ καὶ κύκλῳ is often understood as meaning "from Jerusalem and its surroundings,"[36] and taken to refer either only to Judea or as including even Damascus and Arabia (Gal. 1:17). In this case, however, one should expect the definite article and formulations such as καὶ τῆς κύκλῳ χώρας or καὶ τοῦ κύκλῳ,[37] or the plural rendering καὶ τῶν κύκλῳ. Similarly, a formulation meaning "from . . . to" would lack a connecting element. Hence it is better to follow those older[38] and more recent[39] exegetes who understand the expression adverbially (Bauer-Aland, Wörterbuch 928 [BAGD 457a]) in the sense of a circular movement through which Paul went during his activity between Jerusalem and Illyricum. The witnesses adduced by Bowers from Xenophon (An. vii.1.14), Appian (Mithrid. 101), and especially Philo of Alexandria (Leg. ad Gaium 250) show that not only a complete circle, but also a half circle can be intended.[40] The expression "from Jerusalem," rather than referring generally to Paul's proclamatory activity in the holy city (Acts 9:29; 26:20), likely refers to the special significance this locale possesses for the beginnings of his Gentile mission (§13.4), which alone is the concern of the overall context of Romans 15. The special position Jerusalem possesses here for the apostle's work militates against the assumption of a mere Lukan construction; Paul repeatedly seeks contact with the Christian churches of the holy city.[41]

(2) It is noteworthy that as a geographic boundary for his work in the west, Paul does not mention the Adriatic, nor any city (e.g., Thessalonica or Corinth), but rather a designation referring to a Roman province, namely,

36. So, e.g., U. Wilckens, *Der Brief an die Römer* III (1982) 120.
37. Cf. C. E. B. Cranfield, *The Epistle to the Romans* II (²1981) 761.
38. Oecumenius (*PG* 118.621d); John Chrysostom, *In Ep. ad Rom. Hom.* 29 (*PG* 60.656); Theodoret, *Interpret. Ep. ad Rom. cop.* 15 (*PG* 82.213b); Gennadius (ed. K. Staab 416).
39. So, e.g., T. Zahn, *Der Brief des Paulus an die Römer* (1910) 599, note 33; M. J. Lagrange, *Saint Paul: Épître aux Romains* (²1922) 353; O. Michel, *Der Brief an die Römer* (⁵1978) 460; E. Käsemann, *Romans* (Eng. trans., 1980) 394; R. Pesch, *Römerbrief* (1983) 104f.
40. *Studies in Paul's Understanding of His Mission* (1976) 24f.
41. Cf. also P. Stuhlmacher, *ZThK* 86 (1989) 148-55.

Dalmatia, which after its separation from Pannonia (A.D. 6-9) was called *superior provincia Illyricum* (*LAW* 1374f.). Although one might possibly interpret this as that part of Macedonia which is considered ethnically Illyrian,[42] this seems less likely because in the immediate context Paul also mentions other provinces, namely, Spain (Rom. 15:24, 28) as well as Macedonia and Achaia (Rom. 15:26). The assumption that the reference is to the name of a province is supported here especially by the fact that the apostle uses the otherwise uncommon Latinized form Ἰλλυρικόν, whereas the Greek designations were Ἰλλυρία or Ἰλλυρίς.[43] W. Wiefel remarks concerning this passage that "Paul began thinking early, as it were, in terms of provinces."[44] The question is whether this "early" can be specified a bit more closely (§15.1). It is not necessary to assume actual entry into the province of Illyricum itself, since μέχρι can mean "to the boundary of."[45] But Illyricum being mentioned at all might mean that Paul also missioned in the western part of Macedonia (§15.3.2) abutting the southern boundary of Illyricum.

(3) The apostle's assertion that he "fulfilled the gospel of Christ from Jerusalem in a circle as far as Illyricum" similarly yields (with respect to Acts) geographic sense. From the perspective of the holy city, the apostle was active in a coherent area of neighboring provinces: Syria-Cilicia, Cyprus, Lycia-Pamphylia, Galatia, Asia, Macedonia, and Achaia. The fulfillment of the gospel also included the fact that the apostle had not merely preached in these areas, but had also founded viable churches in important centers from which Christianity could spread into the surrounding areas.[46] The vision of the mission in Rom. 15:19 is eschatologically conceived in a sense comparable to that in Mk. 13:10,[47] as our investigation into the Old Testament background will also demonstrate (§13.2.3). But this eschatological orientation should not mislead one into concluding falsely that perspectives on missionary strategy and church establishment were irrelevant for Paul. The work of W. P. Bowers can counter any absolutizing of this eschatological factor here.[48] The attention the apostle gave to churches such as those in Ephesus, Philippi, Thessalonica,

---

42. Cf. Appian, *Illyrica* i.7; Josephus, *B.J.* ii.369; Strabo vii.7.4. Concerning the boundaries of the provinces of Macedonia, Thrace, and upper Illyricum, as well as concerning the expansion of the Illyrian linguistic sphere in western Macedonia, cf. the maps in *ANRW* II 7.1 (1979) after pp. 216 and 304.

43. Cf. W. P. Bowers, *Studies in Paul's Understanding of His Mission* (1976) 21, note 3, and already A. Souter, *Exp* VIII/1 (1911) 341.

44. *Kairos* 17 (1975) 219.

45. Cf. U. Wilckens, *Der Brief an die Römer* III (1982) 119, note 583.

46. Cf. W. P. Bowers, *Studies in Paul's Understanding of His Mission* (1976) 18-80; *JETS* 30 (1987) 185-98.

47. Cf. C. K. Barrett, *The Epistle to the Romans* (²1962) 276f.

48. *Studies in Paul's Understanding of His Mission* (1976) 81-123.

or Corinth through longer sojourns, multiple visits, as well as through his dispatch of letters and fellow workers, would be inexplicable if this eschatological orientation were referring to a mere punctiliar proclamation of the gospel without any consideration for consolidation. Thus M. Dibelius writes quite correctly that Paul "himself was content to conduct his mission in a few towns, most of which were communication centres; from there the gospel was carried further afield by others"; Dibelius continues: "Although his belief that the end was approaching meant that time was a vital factor, he saw the possibility of fruitful and unmolested work as a charge from God, who bade him stay and work on."[49]

From Illyricum, the eastern shore of the Adriatic, the apostle directs his gaze across the sea to the imperial capital Rome, albeit merely as a way station rather than as an independent mission goal (Rom. 15:23f.); the goal lies rather in Spain (Rom. 15:24, 28) in the westernmost part of the known world at that time. Peculiarly, Paul does not seem, in contrast to his position concerning the east, to have envisioned any mission in the provinces between Rome and Spain (and thus especially Gaul), even though in all probability these, too, represented areas "where Christ had not already been named" (Rom. 15:20). W. P. Bowers did not sufficiently address the question of how Paul arrived at the geographic understanding of his activity evident in Rom. 15:19 and the context. He considers two possible explanations: (1) "One might speculate that the daily progress of light from east to west, which pictured for Paul the spreading gospel, might also have held special directional meaning for him, inasmuch as his mission was in any case already tending on that course."[50] (2) Bowers asks, following the lead of W. M. Ramsay,[51] whether Paul as a Roman citizen did not quite consciously prefer a mission in the *imperium Romanum*.[52] Although this may represent an additional motive,[53] the real explanation is probably found elsewhere. When one sees how Paul repeatedly tries to understand his apostolic activity in the light of the holy Scriptures, the question arises whether the apostle did not perhaps find his missionary route prefigured in the Old Testament. This view accepts rather than denies that Rom. 15:19ff. also has something to do with the agreements reported in Gal. 2:7ff. (§15.1).

49. Martin Dibelius, *Paul,* ed. W. G. Kümmel (Eng. trans., London, 1953) 68f.
50. *Studies in Paul's Understanding of His Mission* (1976) 75. In note 1, W. P. Bowers refers to Rom. 10:18 (cf. Ps. 19:4) and 2 Cor. 4:6, though neither mentions either sunlight or any specific direction.
51. In *Pauline and Other Studies* ([2]1906) 49-100; *The Cities of St. Paul* (1907) 48-78, 423-35; *St. Paul the Traveller and the Roman Citizen* ([14]1920) 125f., 135-40.
52. *Studies in Paul's Understanding of His Mission* (1976) 76f.
53. Cf. M. Hengel, in M. Hengel and U. Heckel, eds., *Paulus und das antike Judentum* (1991) 201f.

244

13.2.2. Romans 15:16-28 and Isaiah 66:18-21

Could Paul find any support in the Old Testament for the geographic breadth of his own mission? The eschatological commission of the Servant of God to the Gentiles extends, according to Isa. 49:6, a decisive text for Paul's theological understanding of the Damascus-event,[54] to the ends of the earth (ἕως ἐσχάτου τῆς γῆς). Only Isa. 66:19, however, provides a more specific geographic description within the context of eschatological hope for the Gentiles.[55] F. Delitzsch introduced his exegesis of the section Isa. 66:18ff. with the following words: "Prophecy now clearly describes the path Israel's history will take. It is the same which Paul, the apostolic prophet, presents in Romans 9–11 as the circuitous but praiseworthy path of divine mercy to its all-encompassing goal.[56] Although this statement does lack historical-critical precision, it can nonetheless direct our attention to the way Paul read this text as someone who was convinced that Scripture was referring to the eschatological fulfillment in which he had been living since the advent of Jesus (cf. 1 Cor. 9:10; 10:11). Considering the significance the book of Isaiah, and especially chapters 40–66, had for Paul,[57] it is difficult to believe that he did not also give special attention to its concluding chapter. J. Muilenburg summarizes the perspective at the end of the book of Isaiah as follows: "The journey is a triumphant procession to the holy mountain of Jerusalem.

54. Cf. O. Betz, in *Festschrift G. Stählin* (1970) 117f.

55. When I wrote the following section, I believed that the significance of this text for the apostle's activity had never before been addressed. Only in C. Spicq, *Helm* 15 (1964) 52, note 21, did I find reference to Isa. 66:19 as evidence that Spain represented the western border of the inhabited world for Paul, the former pupil of Gamaliel. Only after concluding this work did I become aware of R. D. Aus, *NT* 21 (1979) 232-62. I am heartened that we ascribe equally high value to the significance of Isaiah 66 for the Pauline mission, and that many details of our exegeses of Romans 15 are also parallel. This independently acquired concurrence may attest that the interpretation presented here does not merely represent the speculation of a single individual. To be sure, I do diverge occasionally from R. D. Aus; e.g., I do not believe that Paul understood Tarshish as Spain (*loc. cit.,* 242-46). Also, I hope to demonstrate in greater detail the significance of Isa. 66:19 for the geographic framework of the Pauline mission, which R. D. Aus, *loc. cit.,* 240f., similarly sees. O. Hofius, *ZTK* 83 (1986) 297-324, shows in the case of Romans 11 how an additional dimension of depth can reside behind the primary sense precisely by way of the apostle's scriptural exegesis.

56. *Jesaja* (³1879) 679.

57. T. Holtz, *TLZ* 91 (1966) 327, concludes that "it [the book of Isaiah], represented by twenty-one explicit citations, is the Old Testament book he most frequently uses. Of these twenty-one citations, thirteen come from chapters 40–66 alone." Cf. further E. E. Ellis, *Paul's Use of the Old Testament* (²1981) 150-85. Concerning the textual form of Isaiah used by Paul, cf. D. A. Koch, *Die Schrift als Zeuge des Evangeliums* (1986) 48-51, 59-70.

God has sent a sign in the world, and the nations stream to Zion to bring their cereal offerings to the Lord. In this description the vision is again summarizing the eschatology of all the poems of Second Isaiah (43:6; 49:22) as well as of Third Isaiah (60:1-22)."[58]

In one text-critically reconstructed form (see pp. 248, 252 below), Isa. 66:18-21 reads: "(18) But I am coming to gather all nations and tongues; they shall come and shall see my glory. (19) I will set signs among them. Some of those who have escaped I will send to the nations, to Tarshish, Put, and Lud, Meshech and Tubal and Javan, to the farthest islands that have not heard of my fame or seen my glory; and they shall declare my glory among the nations. (20) They shall bring all your kindred from all the nations as an offering to Yahweh, on horses, and in chariots, and in litters, and on mules, and on dromedaries, to my holy mountain Jerusalem, says Yahweh, just as the Israelites bring a grain offering in clean hands to the house of Yahweh. (21) From these I will take priests and Levites, says Yahweh."

Our hypothesis is that Paul read this text as being fulfilled in his own activity, and traces of this exegesis stand behind Rom. 15:16-24. The entire fifteenth chapter of the letter to the Romans is characterized by direct citations from and allusions to the Old Testament.[59] Right at the beginning, the apostle formulates programmatically: "For whatever was written in former days was written for our instruction, so that by steadfastness and by the encouragement of the scriptures we might have hope" (Rom. 15:4). In the first part of the chapter, Paul addresses in a fundamental and concluding fashion the problems that have arisen in the congregation through Jewish Christians who are especially conscientious regarding food and drink (Rom. 14), and in so doing the apostle establishes a double relation between Christ and the unity of the church of Jews and Gentiles: Jesus' own example obligates us to selfless sacrifice (Rom. 15:1-7). But his redemptive-historical identification as "the servant of circumcision on behalf of the truth of God in order that he might confirm the promises given to the patriarchs" (Rom. 15:8) demonstrates that without an origin rooted in the ancient Jewish people of God, neither is there any hope for the Gentiles (Rom. 15:8-13). Paul cites Isa. 11:10: "The root of Jesse shall come, the one who rises to rule the Gentiles; in him the Gentiles shall hope" (Rom. 15:12).

The reign of the Christ over the nations will begin when "by the word and deed" of Paul he "wins obedience from the Gentiles (εἰς ὑπακοὴν

---

58. *The Book of Isaiah (Chapters 40–66)* (1956) 772.
59. Concerning the direct citations as related to the Gentile mission, cf. esp. A. Bertrangs, *ETL* 30 (1954) 391-415, as well as O. Haas, *Paulus der Missionar* (1971) 36-41.

ἐθνῶν)" (Rom. 15:18). Just as Christ became "a servant for circumcision (διάκονος περιτομῆς)" (Rom. 15:8) in order to put into effect for the Gentiles the promises to the patriarchs (Rom. 15:9), so also does Paul now understand himself "because of the grace given me by God to be a minister of Christ Jesus to the Gentiles (λειτουργὸν Χριστοῦ Ἰησοῦ εἰς τὰ ἔθνη) in the priestly service of the gospel of God (ἱερουργοῦντα τὸ εὐαγγέλιον τοῦ θεοῦ), so that the offering of the Gentiles may be acceptable (ἵνα γένηται ἡ προσφορὰ τῶν ἐθνῶν εὐπρόσδεκτος)" (Rom. 15:15f.). Although "generally, he [Paul] avoids a sacral understanding of his ministry," so E. Käsemann, nonetheless "as already in 12:1f. cultic terms and motifs are here used in a transferred eschatological sense."[60] It is precisely because this notion of priestly service is so unusual in Paul that one should inquire after an Old Testament background. O. Michel's commentary on Rom. 15:16 suggests that "ἡ προσφορὰ τῶν ἐθνῶν (gen. appos.) recalls Isa. 66:20, where the diaspora Jews brought back to Jerusalem appear as an offering for the eternal one. To be sure, Isaiah uses the term מִנְחָה there, which means 'sacrificial gift, offering,' and in the LXX is rendered by δῶρον."[61] Do these differences disqualify Isaiah 66 as a background source? In the eleventh chapter, the apostle gave the Roman congregation a glimpse into the mystery revealed to him, namely, that the entry of the "full number of the Gentiles" constitutes the condition for the eschatological deliverance of Israel (Rom. 11:25-27). In Isa. 66:19, proclamation of God's glory among the "nations . . that have not heard of my fame" is the condition for the diaspora Jews being "brought as an offering . . . to the holy mountain Jerusalem" (Isa. 66:20). From this perspective, it would not be surprising for Paul to consider it his commission first to win the "full number of the Gentiles" (πλήρωμα τῶν ἐθνῶν)" (Rom. 11:25) — a number predetermined by God — to a certain extent as an offering, by "fulfilling the gospel of Christ (πεπληρωκέναι τὸ εὐαγγέλιον τοῦ Χριστοῦ)" (Rom. 15:19) through his geographically expansive proclamation. That was his task; he is silent here concerning the obligation of others to engage in a vigorous mission to the Jews (cf. Gal. 2:7-9). "That there is also a προσφορὰ τῶν Ἰουδαίων goes without saying," as C. E. B. Cranfield remarks concerning this passage.[62]

Could Paul see Isa. 66:18ff. coming to fulfillment in other ways as well as in his apostolic work? In order to answer this question, one must juxtapose the Hebrew and Greek texts of Isa. 66:19a:

---

60. *Romans* (Eng. trans., 1980) 393.

61. *Der Brief an die Römer* ([5]1978) 457f., note 13. Billerbeck III 315, and Nestle-Aland[26], 762, already note the possible allusion in Rom. 15:16 to Isa. 66:20.

62. *The Epistle to the Romans* II ([2]1981) 757.

וְשַׂמְתִּי	καὶ καταλείψω
בָהֶם אוֹת	ἐπ' αὐτῶν σημεῖα
וְשִׁלַּחְתִּי	καὶ ἐξαποστελῶ
מֵהֶם פְּלֵיטִים	ἐξ αὐτῶν σεσωσμένους
אֶל הַגּוֹיִם	εἰς τὰ ἔθνη
. . .	. . .
וְהִגִּידוּ . . .	καὶ ἀναγγελοῦσιν . . .

This is the only time, apart from the Servant prophecies, that the Old Testament speaks about proclamation to the Gentiles by human agents.[63] C. Westermann remarks concerning this half-verse: "This is the first unequivocal mention of mission in the sense we understand it: The sending of individuals to distant nations to proclaim the glory of God. This corresponds precisely to the apostolic mission at the beginning of the Christian church. One can only note with astonishment that here, on the periphery of the Old Testament, God's path from the small sphere of the chosen people into the wide world at large is already envisioned."[64] A prophecy of this sort must have attracted Paul's attention. The apostle could have associated the sign (MT singular) God performs with God's deed in the cross and resurrection of Jesus,[65] especially since that sign apparently occurs in Jerusalem, where God assembles the nations (Isa. 66:18). Yet such usage of σημεῖον is not attested in Paul. If one takes as a point of departure the better-attested reading (σημεῖα) of the LXX text, which is also supported by 1QIsa[a] (אותות),[66] then the reference is to "signs" in the plural which God "leaves behind" and which are followed by a sending (ἐξαποστέλλω). One might ask whether the notion of the "signs of the apostle (τὰ σημεῖα τοῦ ἀποστόλου)" (2 Cor. 12:12), a notion unique in Paul, perhaps also has some connection with this passage. In Rom. 15:19, Paul's mission to the Gentiles is similarly accompanied by "signs" (ἐν δυνάμει σημείων καὶ τεράτων).

The emissaries of Isa. 66:19 are sent to those "who have not yet heard my name (οἱ οὐκ ἀκηκόασίν μου τὸ ὄνομα [so LXX, which differs from MT])." Paul evangelizes "where the name Christ has not yet been named (οὐχ ὅπου ὠνομάσθη Χριστός)" (Rom. 15:20). Although in support Paul

63. Paul did, however, also associate Isa. 52:7 with the eschatological apostolic mission to the nations (Rom. 10:15). Cf. P. Stuhlmacher, in *The Gospel and the Gospels* (Eng. trans., 1991) 156-66.

64. *Das Buch Jesaja (Kap. 40–66)* ([3]1879-[5]1986) 337 (Eng. trans., *Isaiah 40–66* [1969]).

65. According to R. D. Aus, *NT* 21 (1979), 238f., Paul would have thought concretely of the fulfillment of Isa. 7:14 and 11:10-12 (Tg אות, interpreted messianically).

66. Cf. J. C. Trever, *Scrolls from Qumrân Cave I* (1972) 122f. The variant reading is not noted in *BHS*.

specifically cites Isa. 52:15 LXX, for a former scriptural scholar this passage was not very far removed from Isaiah 66. According to the largely unanimous opinion of modern commentaries, however, the emissaries of Isa. 66:19 represent Gentiles who have escaped judgment (cf. Isa. 66:18). Exegetes do also admit, however, that the text is somewhat difficult to understand insofar as the emissaries are sent to the nations even though they, the emissaries, are themselves described as belonging to those nations.[67] An earlier exegete such as F. Delitzsch even asked whether according to Zech. 14:14 these emissaries do not also include Jews that have come under judgment.[68] Although this may well be a harmonizing insertion, precisely as such it is not all that far from Paul's own thinking. For an interpreter schooled as he was in rabbinic exegesis, an understanding of מהם that included Jews as well hardly represented a major difficulty when everything else fit so well.

Paul viewed himself as an ἀπόστολος τῶν ἐθνῶν; Isa. 66:19 speaks about eschatological emissaries to the nations. Survivors (σεσῳσμένοι) are sent (Isa. 66:19); Paul, too, understood himself to be a survivor (Rom. 5:9; cf. 8:24). The conclusion to the section Isa. 66:18-21 announces: "From these I [God] will take priests and Levites (καὶ ἀπ' αὐτῶν λήμψομαι ἐμοὶ ἱερεῖς καὶ Λευίτας)" (Isa. 66:21). This sentence is an interesting parallel to Isa. 66:19 inasmuch as here, too, it is not immediately clear just who is meant by מהם/ἀπ' αὐτῶν. In the case of Isa. 66:21, modern interpreters do not even agree whether the eschatological priests and Levites are referring to Jews[69] or Gentiles[70] or both.[71] For the Pauline understanding of Isa. 66:19 about which we are speculating, it is revealing to note which path earlier Jewish exegesis took in order to avoid the conclusion that in Isa. 66:21 the eschatological priests and Levites are indeed referring to Gentiles.[72] So here, too, it is possible that Paul associated these statements with eschatological Jewish emissaries such as himself. In that case, we would also have a basis for the concept of his priestly service in connection with the proclamation of the gospel to the Gentiles (Rom. 15:16). It would then also be no accident that after providing information concerning his anticipated journey to Spain (Rom. 15:22-24), which was to bring the gospel to fulfillment in the west as well (cf. Rom. 15:19), Paul now comes to speak about the collection for Jerusalem

---

67. Cf. A. Dillmann and R. Kittel, *Jesaja* ([6]1898) 531; K. Marti, *Das Buch Jesaja* (1900) 413; F. Feldmann, *Das Buch Isaias* II (1926) 294; J. Fischer, *Das Buch Isaias* II (1939) 213.

68. *Jesaja* ([3]1879) 680.

69. So, e.g., B. Duhm, *Das Buch Jesaja* ([4]1922) 488f.

70. So, e.g., A. S. Herbert, *The Book of the Prophet Isaiah (Chapters 40–66)* (1975) 197.

71. So C. Westermann, *Jesaja II* ([5]1986) 338 (Eng. trans., *Isaiah 40–66* [1969]).

72. Cf. the authors in F. Delitzsch, *Jesaja* ([3]1879) 683f.

(Rom. 15:25-28). This monetary collection for the earthly Jerusalem could also be understood as a material concretion of the fact that the apostle was bringing the Gentiles into the eschatological Jerusalem as an offering of the end time (Isa. 66:20).[73] The delivery of gifts by Gentiles from the ends of the earth was a familiar theme in rabbinic eschatology.[74]

If a Pauline understanding of the prophecy in Isa. 66:18-21, as proposed here, seems possible, then it would also be of interest to consider the particular geographic information which the apostle could understand as a guide for a mission encompassing the Gentile world. The LXX text of Isa. 66:19 which, except for individual graphic variants, attests only a single deviation (noted below; ed. J. Ziegler, 368f.), provides important keys concerning the contemporary understanding of the individual regions:

(1)	תרשיש	Θαρσις
(2)	פול	καὶ Φουδ
(3)	ולוד	καὶ Λουδ
(4)	משכי	καὶ Μοσοχ
(5)	קשת	. . .
(6)	תבל	Θοβελ
(7)	ויון	καὶ εἰς τὴν Ἑλλάδα
(8)	האיים הרחקים	καὶ εἰς τὰς νήσους τὰς πόρρω

(1) Tarshish was long viewed with virtual unanimity as Tartessus in western Spain,[75] even though not a single writer from antiquity made this equation. At present, a whole series of identifications are advocated, extending from Rhodes to Carthage.[76] Josephus provides the only express geographic explanation[77] of the Greek name Θαρσίς from the New Testament period. He

---

73. Concerning the collection as an eschatological thanksgiving offering of the Gentiles and its obvious connection with the notion of the pilgrimage of the nations, cf. the various approaches of J. Munck, *Paul and the Salvation of Mankind* (Eng. trans., 1959) 301-5; D. Georgi, *Die Geschichte der Kollekte des Paulus für Jerusalem* (1965) 29f. (Eng. trans., *Remembering the Poor* [1992]); K. F. Nickle, *The Collection* (1966) 130, 138-42; W. Wiefel, *Kairos* 17 (1975) 226; W. P. Bowers, *Studies in Paul's Understanding of His Mission* (1976) 64-66; J. Eckert, *Festschrift F. Mussner* (1981) 65-80. Cf. also §15.5.2. Concerning the significance for the unity of the people of God composed of Jews and Gentiles, cf. K. Berger, *NTS* 23 (1977) 180-204.

74. Cf. R. D. Aus, *NT* 21 (1979) 246-57.

75. Cf. merely A. Schulten, *PRE* II 8 (1932) 2446f.

76. Cf. E. A. Speiser, *Genesis* (1964) 66; G. J. Wenham, *Genesis 1–15* (1987) 218; D. W. Baker, *ABD* VI (1992) 332f.

77. The rendering of the term "ships of Tarshish" אניות תרשיש (cf. J. Simons, *The Geographical and Topographical Texts of the Old Testament* [1959] 89) in the LXX does not help much, since this had already been the "customary designation for large merchant ships" since the eighth century B.C. (M. Rehm, *Das erste Buch der Könige* [1979]

not only identifies Tarshish of the Table of Nations in Gen. 10:4 with Tarsus in Cilicia (Josephus, *Ant.* i.127), but also understands the prophet Jonah (Jonah 1:3; 4:2) as having fled to this city (Josephus, *Ant.* ix.208). The rabbis seem to have understood Tarshish similarly.[78] In his *Onomasticon,* Eusebius mentioned Josephus' view, but then also mentioned the rendering of the corresponding passages from Ezekiel in the LXX with Carthage, and even noted the opinion of some who believed that Tarshish was referring to India (Eusebius, *Onom.* [ed. E. Klostermann 100.23ff.]). Jerome then translated this passage literally and without any additions (*loc. cit.,* 101.23ff.).

(2) Old Testament Put (to be emended according to the LXX instead of MT Pul) probably refers to a North African locale, most likely Libya, and perhaps even more specifically Cyrene.[79] The LXX usually renders Put with Libya (Jer. 26:9 [MT Jer. 46:9]; Ezek. 27:10; 30:5; 38:5; Nah. 3:9). According to Josephus, Phut (Gen. 10:6) colonized Libya (Josephus, *Ant.* i.132). In the book of Judith, however, Φουδ καὶ Λουδ are associated with Cilicia (Jdt. 2:23; cf. 2:24). Rassis, mentioned in the same context (Jdt. 2:23), might be referring to Tarsus.[80]

(3) The Ludim of Gen. 10:13 are to be distinguished from Lud in Gen. 10:22.[81] Because of the frequent juxtaposition with Egypt (Gen. 10:13f.; 1 Chr. 1:11) and other North African areas (Jer. 46:9; Ezek. 30:5), modern scholarship tends to identify the Ludim with North Africa, most likely with Libya,[82] though Ezek. 27:10 associates the Ludim with Persia. In Gen. 10:22, the ancestor Lud is apparently already referring to the Lydians of Asia Minor,[83] and this reference also recommends itself for Isa. 66:19.[84] In any case, Josephus identifies Lud (Gen. 10:22) with the ancestor of the Lydians (Josephus, *Ant.* i.144),[85] and Symmachus wrote Λύδους in Isa. 66:19 (ed. J. Ziegler 369).

---

118). The LXX renders (1) πᾶν πλοῖον θαλάσσης (Isa. 2:16); (2) Carthaginian merchants (Καρχηδόνιοι ἔμποροι [Ezek. 27:12]) or their ships (Isa. 23:1, 14; Ezek. 27:25), or (3) πλοῖα [ναῦς] Θαρσις (1 Kgs. 10:22; [22:49]; Ps. 47:8 [LXX]; 2 Chr. 9:21; 20:36). North Africa may possibly be the reference in *Tg. Jon. 1 Kgs.* 22:48; *Tg. Jon. Jer.* 10:9.

78. Cf. A. Neubauer, *La Géographie du Talmud* (1868) 424. Given the geographic context, which points to the eastern Mediterranean basin, the examples from *y. Meg.* 71b/*Gen. Rab.* 37 (22c)/*Tg. Jon. I Gen.* 10:4/*Tg. 1 Chr.* 1:7, which Billerbeck assembles in III 27, probably all refer to Tarsus. Cf. also Billerbeck II 691.

79. Cf. S. Balter, *EJ* XIII (1973) 1414f.; W. S. Lasor, *ISBE* III (1986) 1059; G. J. Wenham, *Genesis 1–15* (1987) 221; D. W. Baker, *ABD* V (1992) 560.

80. Cf. P. Giffin, *Judith* (1969) 405.

81. Cf. S. Herrmann, *BHH* II (1964) 1108; G. J. Wenham, *Genesis 1–15* (1987) 224.

82. Cf. W. S. Lasor, *ISBE* III (1986) 178; D. W. Baker, *ABD* IV (1992) 397.

83. Cf. G. J. Wenham, *Genesis 1–15* (1987) 228-30.

84. Cf. S. Herrmann, *BHH* II (1964) 1108; G. Fohrer, *Jesaja III* (²1986) 282.

85. The rabbis understand Lud (without any reference to the passages in Genesis) only as the Palestinian coastal city Lydda. Cf. Billerbeck V 281f.

(4) Today, Meshech is generally identified as the Μόσχοι of the Greek sources (see below), a people who inhabited central and eastern Anatolia.[86] Herodotus identified them with the Phrygians (Herodotus, i.14; cf. vii.78). According to Josephus, in his day the Meshechians (Μεσχῆνοι), founded by Meshech (Gen. 10:2), were called Cappadocians (Καππαδόκες [Josephus, *Ant.* i.125]). The rabbis occasionally identified Meshech with Mysia (*y. Meg.* 71b; *b. Yoma* 10a).[87]

(5) The קשׁת standing in the fifth position in the MT presents problems. It interrupts the juxtaposition of Meshech and Tubal attested in other sources, and is almost certainly an insertion from Jer. 46:9 (the Ludim as those who draw the bow), and thus is to be deleted commensurate with the LXX.[88]

(6) Cuneiform sources mention Tubal together with Meshech, and in Greek writers the tribes of the Μόσχοι and Τιβαρηνοί stand together (e.g., Herodotus iii.94; vii.78).[89] According to Josephus, the descendants of Tubal (Gen. 10:2) are now called Ἴβηρες, though he also calls the Spaniards (e.g., *Ap.* ii.40) and a people in the Caucasus (*Ant.* xiii.421; xviii.97) by this name. The rabbis, on the other hand, equate Tubal with Bithynia.[90]

(7) In Isa. 66:19, Javan refers perhaps first to the Greeks inhabiting the coast of Asia Minor,[91] as it does in the Persian documents from the time of Darius.[92] In the late strata of the Old Testament, apparently all Greeks are already so designated (Dan. 8:21; 10:20; 11:2), and the LXX, too, reads Ἑλλάς in this passage. For Josephus, Javan was the ancestor of all Greeks (Josephus, *Ant.* i.124), regardless of whether they lived in Aeolia, Cilicia, or Cyprus (Josephus, *Ant.* i.127). The rabbis apparently identify Javan with Macedonia (*b. Yoma* 10a).[93]

(8) With the "distant islands," the concluding gaze moves toward the west to the boundaries of the earth,[94] which is often designated by islands (cf. Sir. 47:17).

86. Cf. R. K. Harrison, *ISBE* III (1986) 328; G. J. Wenham, *Genesis 1–15* (1987) 217; D. W. Baker, *ABD* IV (1992) 711.

87. Cf. A. Neubauer, *La Géographie du Talmud* (1868) 423; Billerbeck II 741.

88. It is incomprehensible how one can arrive from the LXX at the conjecture משׁך ורשׁ (C. Westermann, *Das Buch Jesaja [Kap. 40–66]* [⁵1986] 336, note 2). This can only be referring to an emendation according to MT Ezek. 38:2; 39:1. Cf. B. Duhm, *Das Buch Jesaja* (⁴1922) 488.

89. Cf. G. J. Wenham, *Genesis 1–15* (1987) 217; D. W. Baker, *ABD* VI (1992) 670.

90. Cf. A. Neubauer, *La Géographie du Talmud* (1868) 422f.; Billerbeck II 741f.

91. Cf. G. J. Wenham, *Genesis 1–15* (1987) 217.

92. Cf. G. L. Borchert, *ISBE* II (1982) 971.

93. Cf. A. Neubauer, *La Géographie du Talmud* (1868) 422.

94. Cf. J. Fischer, *Das Buch Isaias II* (1939) 214.

What picture of the spread of the eschatological Gentile mission could emerge for Paul from Isa. 66:18-21? The movement obviously takes Jerusalem as its point of departure, to which God comes for the gathering of the nations (Isa. 66:18).[95] According to the more authentic LXX text, the path of the rescued emissaries involves seven stations (Isa. 66:19), which might indicate a self-enclosed quality intended by God. According to the most probable contemporary understanding, in the New Testament period one envisioned the following areas in Isa. 66:19: (1) Tarsus in Cilicia; (2) Libya (Cyrene) or Cilicia; (3) Lydia in Asia Minor; (4) Cappadocia or Mysia; (5) the Caucasus or Bithynia; (6) Greece or Macedonia; and (7) the western end of the world. No countries are mentioned east or south of Palestine. Later (especially rabbinic) identifications even make a geographically fairly coherent understanding possible: (1) Tarsus; (2) Cilicia (Jdt.); (3) Lydia; (4) Mysia; (5) Bithynia; (6) Macedonia; and (7) the farthest west. This movement, beginning from Jerusalem and proceeding in a northwesterly arc to the most extreme west, would correspond to the conception lying behind Rom. 15:19 (§14.2.1).[96] The assertion here is not that the Pauline missionary plans were from the very outset oriented toward Isa. 66:19, nor that this prophecy represents the only or even most important basis for the routes taken by the apostle. In what follows, however, we will investigate whether at decisive stations along his way Paul was not *also* influenced by this Old Testament missionary prediction.

13.2.3. Driving and Inhibiting Factors

The early Christian missionary offensive, carried forward during the first century by itinerant preachers and teachers, is a remarkable phenomenon. Not even the Jewish attraction of proselytes[97] constitutes any real model for

---

95. Cf. *ibid.*, 213f.

96. This movement also corresponds conspicuously to the distribution of the sons of Japheth (cf. Y. Aharoni and M. Avi-Yonah, *The Macmillan Bible Atlas* [²1977] 21), according to Genesis 10. Concerning the Table of Nations in rabbinic exegesis, cf. S. Krauss, *MGWJ* 39 (1895) 1-11, 49-63; concerning cartography during this period, cf. O. A. W. Dilke, *Mathematics and Measurement* (1987) 35-39. See now J. M. Scott, *Paul and the Nations* (1995), in which he addresses in great detail the history of Jewish tradition regarding Genesis 10. Scott views Rom. 15:19 against the background of the Table of Nations, and believes that at the Apostolic Council Paul was entrusted with the mission to the sons of Japheth. Scott similarly finds in Isa. 66:19 a significant text for the apostle, albeit one not exclusively focused on the sons of Japheth and thus mentioning the addressees of the Pauline mission only in part.

97. Cf. H. Gressmann, *ZMR* 39 (1924) 169-83; W. G. Braude, *Jewish Proselyting in the First Five Centuries* (1940); D. Georgi, *The Opponents of Paul in Second Corinthians* (Eng. trans., 1986) 83-151; H. Kasting, *Die Anfänge der urchristlichen Mission* (1969) 11-32; M. Simon, in *Festschrift A. Dupont-Sommer* (1971) 509-20; Schuerer III/1 (1986)

it, though this phenomenon did indeed provide one of the preparatory pre-suppositions for the early Christian mission.[98] And this aggressive evangelization of the early period was never matched through the course of the following four centuries.[99] A. von Harnack remarked concerning the third century: "The church missions much more through its very existence and through its sacred possessions and ordinances than through professional missionaries."[100] The second part of the statement would have to be formulated in an even more limiting fashion, since at that time there were hardly any missionaries in the sense we understand them today.[101] By contrast, as far as Paul was concerned: "Theologian and missionary . . . Paul is both: one can read hardly a line in his letters without recognizing him in both roles. As a missionary he had a message that was theology; as a theologian he had a theology that demanded communication."[102] The problem contemporary theology still often has with this realization is also illustrated by the fact that some current surveys of scholarship do not take the praxis of the Pauline mission as a theme.[103]

Our concern here is not with the details of the strategy and method of the Pauline mission,[104] but rather primarily with the geographic factor. Even

---

150-76; D. Piatelli, in G. Ghiberti, ed., *La missione nel mondo antico* (1990) 87-100. Additional bibliography can be found in W. P. Bowers, *Studies in Paul's Understanding of His Mission* (1976) 201-4; S. McKnight, *A Light among the Gentiles* (1991); L. H. Feldman, *Jew and Gentile in the Ancient World* (1993); and E. Will and C. Orrieux, *"Prosélytisme juif"?* (1992).

98. Cf. K. Axenfeld, in *Festschrift G. Warneck* (1904) 1-80; F. M. Derwacter, *Preparing the Way for Paul* (1930); E. Lerle, *Proselytenwerbung und Urchristentum* (1960); R. Pesch, *ThJb(E)* (1987) 348f. (bibliography); M. Goodman, in J. Lieu, J. North, and T. Rajak, eds., *The Jews among Pagans and Christians* (1992) 53-78; *Mission and Conversion* (1994).

99. Cf. K. Holl, in *idem, Gesammelte Aufsätze* III (1928) 117-29.

100. *Die Mission und Ausbreitung des Christentums* (⁴1924) 557 (Eng. trans., *The Mission and Expansion of Christianity in the First Three Centuries* [1908]).

101. Cf. E. Molland, in H. Frohnes and U. W. Knorr, eds., *Kirchengeschichte als Missionsgeschichte* I (1974) 51-67; N. Brox, in K. Kertelge, ed., *Mission im Neuen Testament* (1982) 215-32. In the second century, the picture was in part somewhat different. Cf. T. Zahn, in *Skizzen aus dem Leben der alten Kirche* (1905) 178f.

102. C. K. Barrett, *ZTK* 86 (1989) 32.

103. K. H. Schelkle, *Paulus: Leben — Briefe — Theologie* (1981); H. Hübner, *ANRW* II 25.4 (1987) 2649-2840.

104. Cf. in this regard, e.g., T. Zahn, in *Skizzen aus dem Leben der Alten Kirche* (1894) 117-54; H. Weinel, *Paulus als kirchlicher Organisator* (1899); E. Weber, *Die Beziehungen von Röm. 1–3 zur Missionspraxis des Paulus* (1905); W. M. Ramsay, in *Pauline and Other Studies in Early Christian History* (1906) 49-102; T. G. Soares, *BW* 34 (1909) 326-36; P. Wernle, *Paulus als Heidenmissionar* (²1909); A. Freytag, *ZM* 2 (1912) 114-25; J. Warneck, *Paulus im Lichte der heutigen Heidenmission* (1913);

if Paul found extensive directions for his missionary work in the prophet's words, they by no means fixed any concrete steps or routes. In an almost completely overlooked work, E. Stange has tried to collect together the various motives influencing the apostle's choice of missionary fields and places of sojourn.[105] The most important factors include: (1) taking the Jewish synagogue congregations as a point of departure (2 Cor. 11:24f.; Rom. 1:16; cf. Rom. 10:1) along with the circle of proselytes and "God-fearers" often found around them;[106] (2) favorable or unfavorable travel conditions (1 Cor. 16:5f.); (3) an orientation toward the Roman provinces and their centers (1 Cor. 16:1-

A. Oepke, *Die Missionspredigt des Apostels Paulus* (1920); A. von Harnack, *Die Mission und Ausbreitung des Christentums* (⁴1924) 60-86 (Eng. trans., *The Mission and Expansion of Christianity in the First Three Centuries* [1908]); A. Deissmann, *Paulus* (²1925) 170-95 (Eng. trans., *Paul* [²1926]); K. Pieper, *Paulus. Seine missionarische Persönlichkeit und Wirksamkeit* (1929) 142-263; M. Schlunk, *Paulus als Missionar* (1937); R. Liechtenhan, *Die urchristliche Mission* (1946) 67-91; A. Freytag, *Paulus baut die Weltkirche* (1951); H. Turlington, *RExp* 51 (1954) 168-86; R. Allen, *Missionary Methods: St. Paul's or Ours* (⁴1956); F. W. Maier, *Paulus als Kirchengründer und kirchlicher Organisator* (1961); F. Hahn, *Das Verständnis der Mission im Neuen Testament* (1963) 80-94; M. Dibelius, *Paul,* ed. W. G. Kümmel (Eng. trans., London, 1953) 67-84; R. G. Villoslada, *MisEx* 11 (1964) 215-27; J. A. Grassi, *A World to Win: The Missionary Methods of Paul the Apostle* (1965); P. Seidensticker, *Paulus, der verfolgte Apostle Jesu Christi* (1965); G. Schille, *Die urchristliche Kollegialmission* (1967); H. Kasting, *Die Anfänge der urchristlichen Mission* (1969) 105-8; H. Clavier, in *Festschrift G. Stählin* (1970) 171-87; O. Haas, *Paulus der Missionar* (1971); M. Hengel, *NTS* 18 (1971/72) 15-38; W. D. Davies, *The Gospel and the Land* (1974) 180-85; W. Wiefel, *Kairos* 17 (1975) 218-31; E. M. B. Green, *Evangelisation zur Zeit der ersten Christen* (1977); E. E. Ellis, in *Prophecy and Hermeneutics in Early Christianity* (1978) 3-22; W. H. Ollrog, *Paulus und seine Mitarbeiter* (1979); C. T. Bennett, *EMQ* 16 (1980) 133-38; W. P. Bowers, *NT* 22 (1980) 316-23; R. F. Hock, *The Social Context of Paul's Ministry* (1980) 26-49; R. B. Cook, *Missiology* 9 (1981) 485-98; E. G. Hinson, *The Evangelization of the Roman Empire* (1981) 33-39; D. Zeller, in K. Kertelge, ed., *Mission im Neuen Testament* (1982) 164-89; P. Stuhlmacher, *TBei* 12 (1983) 107-35; A. J. Hultgren, *Paul's Gospel and Mission* (1985) 125-50; W. P. Bowers, *JETS* 30 (1987) 185-98; W. Klaiber, in *Festschrift P. J. Borgen* (1987) 89-106; E. Plümacher, *Identitätsverlust und Identitätsgewinn* (1987) 31-34; M. L. Soards, *The Apostle Paul* (1987) 27-36; H. Doohan, *Paul's Vision of Church* (1989) 11-38; P. Iovino, in G. Ghiberti, *La missione nel mondo antico e nella Bibbia* (1990) 155-84; L. Legrand, *Unity and Plurality* (1990) 107-30; W. P. Bowers, *JSNT* 44 (1991) 89-111; J. Y. Pak, *Paul as Missionary* (1991); E. P. Sanders, *Paul* (1991) 19-25; J. Murphy-O'Connor, *Paul* (1995) 173-75, 234-37. Additional bibliography in W. P. Bowers, *Studies in Paul's Understanding of His Mission* (1976) 186-92.

105. *Paulinische Reisepläne* (1918). Not even the monograph of O. Haas, *Paulus der Missionar* (1971), mentions E. Stange. No doubt the book's date of publication has not recommended it.

106. Cf. H. Gülzow, in H. Frohnes and U. W. Knorr, eds., *Kirchengeschichte als Missionsgeschichte* I (1974) 194-210; J. Molthagen, *Hist* 41 (1991) 46-48.

19; Rom. 15:19);[107] (4) a positive reception of (1 Cor. 16:8f.) or opposition to (cf. 1 Thess. 2:18) the gospel; (5) work in areas previously not the object of missionary activity (2 Cor. 10:16; Rom. 15:20f., 23; cf. 1 Cor. 1:17; Rom. 1:14f.); (6) the building and nurturing of viable churches (1 Thess. 3:10; 2 Cor. 1:15; 2:10f.); and finally also (7) the Pauline conviction of not only being bound generally to God's will (Phil. 2:24; 1 Cor. 4:19; 16:7; Rom. 1:10; 15:32), but also of receiving concrete guidance through the Holy Spirit (Gal. 2:2; 2 Cor. 2:12f.). From the perspective of these presuppositions, let us now try to understand the geographic movements that become visible in Paul's letters and in a critical comparison between these letters and Acts.

13.3. Paul in Arabia

13.3.1. The Geographic Designation "Arabia"

From the two different temporal indications in Acts 9:19b (ἐγένετο δὲ μετὰ τῶν ἐν Δαμασκῷ μαθητῶν ἡμέρας τινάς) and Acts 9:23 (ὡς δὲ ἐπληροῦντο ἡμέραι ἱκαναί), scholars have concluded that Luke is alluding to an interruption in Paul's stay in Damascus.[108] But this is an unnecessary harmonization; the *auctor ad Theophilum* either knew nothing about any early trip the apostle took to "Arabia" (Gal. 1:17), or considered it unnecessary to mention what was in any event perhaps merely a brief interlude.[109] The two possibilities would again become especially comprehensible if Ἀραβία were referring to an area in the vicinity of Damascus. Contra the speculations of earlier scholars,[110] most

---

107. E. Stange, *Paulinische Reisepläne* (1918) 25-28, largely rejects this factor in the section entitled "Strategic Considerations." Perhaps the background for this rejection is the disinclination, quite comprehensible after the First World War, against any sort of military thinking or power politics, and especially against any exaggerated nationalism (cf. the "preliminary remark" [*Vorbemerkung*], *loc. cit.,* 7). Before this World War, headings such as "Paul: A Hero" (J. Warneck, *Paulus* [1913] III) or "The Statemanship of Paul" (W. M. Ramsay, *Pauline and Other Studies* [1906] 49) were not uncommon. The two authors just mentioned, however, justifiably emphasize the concentration on accessible routes and "key cities" (J. L. Kelso, *BS* 79 [1922] 481-86). The significance of this factor became completely clear in the sociological study of W. A. Meeks, *The First Urban Christians* (1983).

108. So, among others, W. M. Ramsay, *St. Paul the Traveller and the Roman Citizen* (1895) 380; P. M. Barnard, *Exp* V/9 (1899) 317-20.

109. Cf. contra W. M. Ramsay already, and justifiably, J. A. Cross, *Exp.* V/3 (1896) 78-80.

110. Lacking any text-critical basis, S. A. Fries, *ZNW* 2 (1901) 150f., conjectured the existence of a Galilean place called Ἄραβα, which Josephus (also Josephus, *Vita* 265), however, calls Γαβαρά (C. Möller and G. Schmitt, *Siedlungen Palästinas nach Flavius Josephus* [1976] 56f.). Regarding an identification of "Arabia" with the eastern Diaspora, see note 154.

contemporary scholars assume that by Ἀραβία Paul is referring in Gal. 1:17 to the Nabatean kingdom.[111] Use of the geographic name in ancient sources, however, is vague.[112] Doubtless, in the New Testament period the Nabatean kingdom was understood primarily as Ἀραβία,[113] though Pliny can just as well include parts of the Decapolis in Arabia (Pliny the Elder, *HN* v.16.74), and the *Epistle of Aristeas* (*Ep. Arist.* 119) and occasionally Josephus[114] simply refer to East Jordan by this name. Given this wide usage, it is also more understandable that Justin includes Damascus in Arabia (Justin, *Dial.* 78.10), and is followed by Tertullian (Tertullian, *Adv. Jud.* 9; *Adv. Marc.* 3.13).

Hence scholarly consideration of areas other than the Nabatean is not necessarily misguided. Following the lead of H. Graetz, J. Klausner[115] decided in favor of Auranitis, which as a result of its association with the Herodian kingdom (cf. Josephus, *B.J.* i.398; ii.95, 215) also had a Jewish settlement. In his own turn, T. Schlatter considered "the cities south of Damascus belonging to the Decapolis, between the Jordan and the steppe, or perhaps the areas north of Damascus with Palmyra, which everywhere included not insignificant Jewish communities."[116] Similarly, fifty years later H. Bietenhard conjectured that Paul was active in the Decapolis, and even that the apostle may have founded the church at Pella, though he also emphasized the completely hypothetical nature of such assumptions.[117]

111. So, e.g., H. Schlier, *Der Brief an die Galater* ([5]1971) 58; A. Oepke, *Der Brief des Paulus an die Galater* ([4]1979) 61f.; F. F. Bruce, *The Epistle of Paul to the Galatians* (1982) 95f.; F. Mussner, *Der Galaterbrief* ([5]1987) 91f.; R. Y. K. Fung, *The Epistle to the Galatians* (1988) 68; F. Millar, *The Roman Near East* (1993) 56f.; M. Hengel and A. M. Schwemer, *Paul between Damascus and Antioch* (1997) 110-13.

112. Cf. H. Bietenhard, *ANRW* II 8 (1977) 227-30.

113. So in Josephus from the Hasmonean period onward, though it is not always clear whether the reference is to the political entity or merely to the region primarily encompassed by that entity. Cf. A. Schalit, *Namenwörterbuch zu Flavius Josephus* (1968) 14, minus the passages mentioned in the following note.

114. Josephus, *B.J.* i.89 (Gilead and Moab); iii.47; v.160; *Ant.* viii.179; *Ap.* i.133; ii.25; cf. also *B.J.* i.161.

115. *Von Jesus zu Paulus* (1950) 313f. Similarly W. Feneberg, *Paulus der Weltenbürger* (1992) 89f.

116. *NKZ* 36 (1925) 507f., note 2. Recollection of the famous father extinguished in many later scholars the fact that the son Theodor was also a New Testament scholar. The article is incorrectly ascribed to Adolf Schlatter, e.g., in B. Rigaux, *Paulus und seine Briefe* (1964) 100, note 4 [corrected in *The Letters of St. Paul* (Eng. trans., 1968) 205, note 4, albeit with incorrect periodical citation]; G. Schneider, *Die Apostelgeschichte* I (1982) 131, note 48.

117. *ANRW* II 8 (1977) 255f.

13.3.2. Mission among the Nabateans?

Although it is by no means certain that by Arabia Paul was referring to the Nabatean region, a whole series of both earlier and more recent scholars[118] are certain that the apostle also preached in Petra, and the Pauline map of a respected biblical reference work depicts his route all the way to this city.[119] The only possible topographical reference to the time in Arabia is Gal. 4:25: τὸ δὲ Ἁγὰρ Σινᾶ ὄρος ἐστὶν ἐν τῇ Ἀραβίᾳ. Here, however, it is already difficult to decide whether during the New Testament period the Mount of Moses was sought on the Sinai Peninsula[120] or beyond the Gulf of Aqaba.[121] Above all, however, nothing in this context allows us to conclude with certainty that the apostle is here speaking from firsthand acquaintance with the locale, or to what extent he is merely passing on a popular tradition concerning the name. It is also unclear whether he became acquainted with such tradition during his time in "Arabia,"[122] or whether the geographic learning of the rabbinic pupil is manifesting itself here.

W. A. Meeks formulates yet another argument, asserting that we can be certain Paul missioned in Nabatea: "The Ethnarch of the Nabatean king Aretas IV tried to have Paul arrested in Damascus (2 Cor. 11:32). It is evident that Paul had stirred up this official hostility not by meditating in the desert nor by wandering from village to village, but by preaching in flourishing Hellenistic cities such as Petra, Gerasa, Philadelphia, and Bostra. . . ."[123] But if our reconstruction of the background to the flight from Damascus is accurate (§5.4.2), then this argument, too, is not compelling. For all these reasons, one

---

118. So, e.g., D. Stanley, *Sinai and Palestina,* 50 (after J. A. Montgomery, *Arabia and the Bible* [1934] 34); M. Lindner, *Petra und das Königreich der Nabatäer* (³1980) 74.

119. G. Stählin and E. Höhne, eds., *Der östliche Mittelmeerraum zur Zeit des Apostels Paulus.* Beilage zu BHH (²1968). Concerning highway conditions in New Testament Transjordan, cf. M. Du Buit, *DBS* X (1985) 1040-51; R. Rademacher and F. Schlaich, *TAVO* B 17.2 (1988); D. F. Graf, *MBib* 59 (1989) 54-56; D. F. Graf, B. Isaac, and I. Roll, *ABD* VI (1992) 782-87.

120. So G. I. Davies, *VT* 22 (1972) 152-63; *PEQ* 111 (1979) 87-101; P. Maiberger, *Topographische und historische Untersuchungen zum Sinaiproblem* (1984) 101-4.

121. So J. Koenig, *RHPR* 43 (1963) 2-31; H. Gese, in *Vom Sinai zum Zion* (1974) 49-62.

122. J. B. Lightfoot, *The Epistle of St. Paul to the Galatians* (¹⁰1890) 87-90, considered whether Paul did not acquire his own understanding of the law through meditation on the Damascus-event during a pilgrimage to Sinai, but he himself considers such reflections clearly to be "speculation."

123. *The First Urban Christians* (1983) 10. Similarly, e.g., F. F. Bruce, *Paul* (1977) 81f.; A. Oepke, *Der Brief des Paulus an die Galater* (⁴1979) 62; J. Murphy-O'Connor, *CBQ* 55 (1993) 732-37; M. Hengel and A. M. Schwemer, *Paul* (1997) 106-13.

should be cautious in making any bold assumptions regarding which routes the apostle took in "Arabia," since we are not certain concerning the exact location of this area as far as Paul is concerned.

If it is not even certain whether Paul entered the primary Nabatean territory in the first place, then it is completely uncertain that he missioned among the Nabateans. One consideration, however, might yet support this assumption. During the Hellenistic period, some Jews and even non-Jews (Apollonius Molon [Eusebius, *HE* ix.9.1-3]) viewed the Nabateans as well as other Arab tribes as Ishmaelites, and thus as (albeit it in Jewish eyes illegitimate) sons of Abraham.[124] In writings such as the book of *Jubilees* and the *Testaments of the Twelve Patriarchs,* one finds a relatively positive estimation of the Ishmaelites.[125] It is thus conceivable that in his missionary activity among the Nabateans Paul could have picked up on this assumed blood kinship, though the relationships between the Jews and the Arab tribes had taken a dramatic turn for the worse as a result of political events since the Hasmoneans and Herod the Great.[126] Roman attempts to ameliorate the tensions had no real success. The enormity of this mutual hatred was illustrated most shockingly by the horrors perpetrated by the already feared (Tacitus, *Hist.* v.1) Nabatean auxiliary troops on the Jewish population during the rebellion of A.D. 70 (Josephus, *B.J.* ii.68ff.; vii.550f.; *Ant.* xvii.290).[127] Above all, however, it is quite uncertain whether the connection Nabatean/Ishmaelites played a role in Judaism apart from Josephus (e.g., Josephus, *Ant.* i.239-41).[128]

Against a mission among the Nabateans, however, at least the following reasons can be adduced.[129] Whereas the transition from the pure mission among the Jews to that among the Samaritans was accompanied by an element not only of blood kinship but also of religious kinship, the latter factor was completely absent with regard to the Nabateans. What we know of their

---

124. Cf. I. Ephal, *JNES* 35 (1976) 231-35. Concerning the question of continuity with the Edomites, cf. J. R. Bartlett, *PEQ* 111 (1979) 53-66.

125. Cf. D. Mendels, *The Land of Israel as a Political Concept in Hasmonean Literature* (1987) 145-54.

126. Cf. A. Kasher, *Jews, Idumaeans, and Ancient Arabs* (1988) 126-91.

127. Cf. *ibid.,* 200-203.

128. Cf. F. Millar, *JJS* 44 (1993) 28-38. The only passage from intertestamental literature with a (positive) reference to this connection is perhaps *Jub.* 20:11-13, though even this remains uncertain given its contradiction with *Jub.* 15:30 and the difficult textual tradition.

129. We will hold in abeyance here the question to what extent a mission within the actual Nabatean territory would also encounter a certain linguistic barrier. Nabatean, a dialect of Aramaic, survived into the fourth century A.D. Inscriptions, documents, and coin legends from the New Testament period are almost wholly composed in Nabatean. Cf. F. Millar, *JJS* 38 (1987) 152-54.

religion[130] had to make them appear to be the most grievous idolators in Jewish eyes. It is also striking that in no other passage does Paul mention churches in "Arabia" or disclose any plans to visit such. Of course, one can try to explain this by suggesting that his initial missionary attempts there remained fruitless.[131] Indeed, we know absolutely nothing of any Christian communities in the region of Petra during the pre-Constantine period,[132] and as late as *ca.* A.D. 400, the population there put up stubborn resistance to Christianity (*Sozomen* vii.15), although there was in Bostra a "bishop of the Arabs" in the mid-third century (Eusebius, *HE* vi.20.2). Another of the apostle's statements possibly also suggests that the Gentile mission had not begun already in "Arabia," namely Rom. 15:19, which associates the beginnings of his missionary work with Jerusalem (§13.4).

It thus remains a possibility worthy of consideration that for some time after the encounter with the resurrected Jesus at Damascus Paul lived in "Arabia" somewhat reclusively.[133] W. W. Müller has only recently suggested again that both Gal. 1:17 and Isa. 10:9 LXX (addition of Ἀραβία next to Damascus) are referring to "the rocky wilderness area southeast of Damascus."[134] Another possibility would be a sojourn with a group of Jewish Christians in Kokhba (see pp. 239f., note 24 above), which at least Epiphanius in the fourth century A.D. expressly includes as part of Arabia (ἐν τῇ Ἀραβίᾳ ἐν τῇ Κωχάβῃ) (Epiphanius, *Pan.* 40.1). It is also possible that Paul did mission work under the Jews living in the Nabataean territory.[135] But with regard to these assumptions, too, A. von Harnack's exhortation to exercise caution applies: "What drove him to Arabia, and what he did there, simply is beyond the scope of our knowledge."[136]

130. Cf. J. Starcky, *DBS* VII (1966) 985-1016; M. Gawlikowski, *ANRW* II 18.4 (1990) 2659-2677.

131. So, e.g., S. Perowne, *The Journeys of St. Paul* (1973) 32-34; E. Haenchen, *Acts* (Eng. trans., 1971) 334; G. Bornkamm, *Paulus* (⁶1987) 48f. (Eng. trans., *Paul* [1971]).

132. Cf. A. von Harnack, *Die Mission und Ausbreitung des Christentums* (1924) 702 (Eng. trans., *The Mission and Expansion of Christianity in the First Three Centuries* [1908]).

133. So, e.g., H. Clavier, in *Festschrift G. Stählin* (1970) 176; D. Guthrie, *Galatians* (1974) 71, and recently esp. (albeit not always with persuasive reasons) N. Taylor, *Paul, Antioch and Jerusalem* (1992) 67-74. Additional advocates can be found in W. P. Bowers, *Studies in Paul's Understanding of His Mission* (1976) 33, note 1.

134. *Neues Bibel-Lexikon* I (1991) 144.

135. For the Jewish presence there cf. S. Noja, *BeO* 21 (1979) 203-316; M. Hengel and A. M. Schwemer, *Paul between Damascus and Antioch* (1997) 112f., 388f., note 585.

136. *Die Mission und Ausbreitung des Christentums* (1924) 699, note 5 (Eng. trans., *The Mission and Expansion of Christianity in the First Three Centuries* [1908]).

13.3.3. The Obstructed Route to the South and East

W. H. Ollrog remarks concerning Paul's brief account of his flight from Damascus under the ethnarch of Aretas in 2 Cor. 11:32f.: "This section, which belongs substantively to the peristasis-catalog, reads like an insertion, and seems out of place after the solemn conclusion in 11:31."[137] Ollrog thus attempts a psychological explanation: The writer did not notice that Paul interrupted the dictation to tell an anecdote! But then one must additionally assume that the apostle did not read through his letter again, or that he did not notice this error when reading it again. It was earlier popular to eliminate this remark as an interpolation,[138] and the view was even advocated that a Pauline fragment actually belonging between Gal. 1:17 and Gal. 1:18 was erroneously inserted into the second letter to the Corinthians.[139] However, one can very well also present reasons why the apostle inserted such an example precisely here.[140]

The context does indeed prove to be consciously structured.[141] Parallels in contemporary peristasis-catalogs have been adduced for the insertion of an isolated episode.[142] But no one has hitherto explained in this way why Paul selected precisely this event. Because he repeatedly had to defend his apostolic authority, Paul often spoke of the Christophany near Damascus (cf. Gal. 1:15-17), including to the Corinthians (cf. 1 Cor. 15:8ff.). By means of the emphatically prepositioned indication of place "in Damascus" (ἐν Δαμασκῷ), which shortly thereafter is repeated in a slightly varied form, the apostle could awaken the expectation among the readers of the letter that he would now again speak about this revelation. But then he relates, so to speak, a reverse Damascus-experience. At this city, he was not only, as it were, elevated to heaven, but under considerably less brilliant circumstances[143] he was also lowered down the city wall. J. Zmijewski[144] has justifiably drawn attention to this movement countering the upward visionary climb (2 Cor. 12:1-4).

Even if Acts 9:23-25 is literarily independent of 2 Cor. 11:32f.,[145] it was not without reason that A. Schlatter pointed out that Luke "relates the same occurrence . . . in a version closely resembling Paul's sentence, whereas

---

137. *Paulus und seine Mitarbeiter* (1979) 10.

138. Discussed, e.g., by E. B. Allo, *Seconde Épître aux Corinthiens* (1937) 300f.

139. Suggested, following J. R. Harris, by E. F. F. Bishop, *ET* 64 (1952/53) 188f.

140. A survey of more recent opinions can be found in R. P. Martin, *2 Corinthians* (1986) 384.

141. Cf. K. T. Kleinknecht, *Der leidende Gerechtfertigte* (²1988) 284-89.

142. A. Fridrichsen, *SO* 7 (1928) 29.

143. E. A. Judge, *JCE* 9 (1966) 45, pointed out that for Roman soldiers it was especially glorious to be the first to climb the city wall.

144. *Der Stil der paulinischen "Narrenrede"* (1978) 289.

145. Cf. C. Burchard, *Der dreizehnte Zeuge* (1970) 150-60.

Acts otherwise exhibits no verbatim concurrence with the language of Paul's letters."[146] Schlatter explained this by suggesting that "it shows that Paul often related this event because it was an especially vivid illustration of the way in which weakness and strength, danger and deliverance were paired in his work from the very outset."[147] Earlier exegetes, e.g., J. Calvin *("haec persequtio fuit quasi primum tyrocinium Pauli"),*[148] already advocated the view that this event made a strong impression on the apostle's memory. Its resonance with the Old Testament story of the spies (Josh. 2:15) might indicate that it was frequently passed on in an already relatively fixed form.[149] H. J. Klauck speaks in this context of a "witness for the existence of a personal Pauline tradition,"[150] and A. von Harnack even assumed that what Luke narrated in Acts 9:1-28 he owed directly to Paul himself.[151]

Yet another consideration can make it understandable why Paul often related this particular event. If through this Christophany near Damascus he had basically also received his calling to missionary work (Gal. 1:16), then his flight from this city concluded the first phase of his activity, regardless of whether such proclamation before Gentiles was merely announced or had already begun. With the persecution by the ethnarch of Aretas, Paul now had the Nabatean authorities against him. They, however, controlled the caravan routes that passed through the Sinai or the Arabian desert to the south, as well as the routes to the east,[152] thereby making difficult or even impossible any continued missionary thrust in these directions.[153] In this context, perhaps the apostle directed his attention to the fact that the description of the areas of the eschatological Gentile mission in Isa. 66:19 mentioned neither the east nor the south (§13.2.2).[154] In any event, the apostle left the Nabatean area of influence and turned first toward Jerusalem.

146. *Paulus, der Bote Jesu* (1934) 657.

147. *Ibid.*

148. *Commentarius in Epistolam Secundam ad Corinthios. CR* 78, 135.

149. Cf. A. Schlatter, *Paulus, der Bote Jesu* (1934) 657, note 1. This was adopted, e.g., by M. Carrez, *La deuxième épître de Saint Paul aux Corinthiens* (1986) 225; H. J. Klauck, *2. Korintherbrief* (1986) 91.

150. *2. Korintherbrief* (1986) 91.

151. *Die Apostelgeschichte* (1908) 139.

152. Cf. P. C. Hammond, *The Nabataeans* (1973) 65-69; G. W. Bowersock, *Roman Arabia* (1983) 173-81.

153. This is why the assumption of E. Pax, *BibLeb* 15 (1974) 203-6, that on his first missionary journeys Paul above all followed routes determined by Nabatean trading colonies, is not very probable. Is this hypothesis a product of the Jerusalem Franciscan exegete's love for Jordan?

154. The assertion of C. W. Briggs, *BW* 41 (1913) 255-59, that "Arabia" refers to the eastern (Babylonian) Diaspora falters not least because he adduces not a single witness for this linguistic usage.

13.4. Jerusalem as Point of Departure for the Gentile Mission

According to the concurring accounts of both Paul (Gal. 1:18) and Acts (Acts 9:26ff.), the apostle went from Damascus to Jerusalem. According to Luke's portrayal, Paul experienced a vision in the temple in which the exalted Jesus himself directed him to proclaim the gospel among the Gentiles (Acts 22:17-21). H. Conzelmann is certain that "the account here cannot be harmonized with Gal. 1:17–2:2."[155] To be sure, he also ascertains an inner-Lukan contradiction with Acts 9:29f., and thus assumes that a pre-Lukan tradition stands behind the vision account. C. Burchard doubts the self-contradiction, but does agree with the irreconcilability with Gal. 1:15ff., though he does add the strikingly cautious remark: "The provenance of the tradition is uncertain. It is not Pauline if we are correct in assuming that from the very outset Paul understood himself to be sent to the Gentiles."[156] The exegetical presupposition of Luke-criticism, however, is certainly questionable in this passage (see pp. 235f. above). If our understanding of Rom. 15:19 is correct, then Paul viewed Jerusalem exclusively as the point of departure for his mission to the Gentiles (§13.2.1). If one tries to explain how this view could arise, one is directed in one way or another to Paul's first sojourn in the holy city after his conversion. The question can remain open here whether Luke accurately knew about a visionary experience[157] — in any case, Gal. 2:1 (κατὰ ἀποκάλυψιν) does offer a structural analogy — or whether he illustrated in the form of a legend an insight Paul had in Jerusalem (mediated by Hellenists [cf. Acts 9:29]?).[158] In view of the Christ-vision in the temple (Acts 22:17-21), one can at least venture the cautious formulation: "Perhaps Luke is here picking up a tradition connected with Paul's own self-witness in Rom. 15:19 according to which the Pauline mission began in Jerusalem itself."[159]

155. *Acts* (Eng. trans., 1987) 187.
156. *Der dreizehnte Zeuge* (1970) 164. Opinions are peculiarly distributed regarding the question whether Acts 22:17-21 possesses any traditionary basis. R. Pesch, *Die Apostelgeschichte* II (1986) 231, reckons with a purely Lukan composition. For G. Lüdemann, *Early Christianity according to the Traditions in Acts* (Eng. trans., 1989) 239, "despite Lukan linguistic elements, the basic structure of this section, without v. 20, is tradition."
157. So, e.g., P. Seidensticker, *Paulus, der verfolgte Apostel Jesu Christi* (1965) 23; F. F. Bruce, *The Book of Acts* (1988) 418f.
158. Concerning this possibility, cf. esp. O. Betz, in *Festschrift G. Stählin* (1970) 113-23.
159. M. Hengel, *Zur urchristlichen Geschichtsschreibung* (^{2}1984) 76. Cf. also W. P. Bowers, *Studies in Paul's Understanding of His Mission* (1976) 20, 34.

§14

Pushing Forward to the Northwest

14.1. Syro-Cilicia

14.1.1. Considerations of Missionary Strategy?

Paul's conviction of being sent in a special way to the Gentiles, attained at last during his visit in Jerusalem, might also explain why he left the city again so quickly. The reason Luke mentions is the dispute with the Hellenistic Jews and the concern of the early Jerusalem church that he might be murdered (Acts 9:29). Although this may be true, it would be consistent with Luke's irenic tendencies not to mention that the apostle had failed to gain much support for his notion of missioning to the Gentiles.[1] Such reticence was understandable insofar as such an undertaking would have made the position of the Jerusalem Jewish Christians even more precarious two to three years after the expulsion of the Christian Hellenists. Luke seems to allude to this when after Paul is sent away (ἐξαπέστειλαν) to Tarsus (Acts 9:30) he writes: "the church throughout Judea, Galilee, and Samaria had peace . . ." (Acts 9:31). One is tempted to read between the lines in Acts: did Luke in fact know that at that time Paul was "encouraged" to leave Jerusalem? In any event, his departure did essentially ease the situation of his Jewish-Christian dialogue partners.

The apostle was now faced with the question of where, specifically, he should turn. Among the possibilities, the caravan routes to the east and south had become problematical for the apostle because of the Nabatean controls, and the prophetic oracle in Isa. 66:19 also excluded these two directions. By way of Alexandria, Paul could have gone to the southwest toward Libya (Lud) or Carthage (Tarshish?). If he was already following his principle of working wherever possible in areas that had not already been subject to missionary activity, that probably militated against this potential destination.[2] Although we

---

1. Cf. also M. Hengel, *Zur urchristlichen Geschichtsschreibung* ([2]1984) 74f.
2. So also W. P. Bowers, *Studies in Paul's Understanding of His Mission* (1976) 73f., note 1.

264

are largely dependent on conjecture, especially because of the almost complete annihilation of Egyptian Judaism (A.D. 115-17 and 132-35), it is nonetheless quite probable that even in the earliest period, and presumably directly from Jerusalem (cf. Acts 18:25 D), Jewish-Christian churches emerged among the sizable Jewish communities in Egypt.[3] The numerous Jews of Cyrenaica (Josephus, *Ant.* xiv.114)[4], whose varied connections with the holy city are occasionally reflected in the New Testament (Mk. 15:21 par.;[5] Acts 2:10; 6:9;[6] 11:19f.; cf. 13:1), might also have been addressed quite early by the mission of the Palestinian Jewish Christians. One can ask whether some of the Cyrenian Hellenists driven from Jerusalem (Acts 11:20) did not return to their home.[7] Hence the nearest route for Paul led to the north. The first geographic goal of the eschatological mission mentioned in Isa. 66:19 is Tarshish, which during the New Testament period was identified with Tarsus in Cilicia (see pp. 250f. above). However odd it may seem to us, we cannot preclude the possibility that Paul ascribed special significance to the fact that his own place of birth (Acts 22:3)[8] was mentioned in this prophetic oracle. In any event, the apostle under-

---

3. Cf. already T. Zahn, in *Skizzen aus der alten Kirche* (1894) 300, note 33, and esp. J. M. Fennelly, *The Origins of Alexandrian Christianity* (1967); C. H. Roberts, *Manuscript, Society and Belief in Early Christian Egypt* (1979) 26-48; J. J. Gunther, *EQ* 54 (1982) 219-23; B. A. Pearson, in B. A. Pearson and J. E. Goehring, eds., *The Roots of Egyptian Christianity* (1986) 132-59; A. F. J. Klijn, *ibid.*, 161-75; and P. F. Beatrice in *ANRW* II 2612 (1995) 1232-75. J. J. Gunther, *EQ* 54 (1982) 223-33; 55 (1983) 21-29, presents several interesting arguments supporting the thesis that Barnabas and John Mark, after their separation from Paul in connection with the Apostolic Council (Acts 15:36-39) and a shorter stop on Cyprus, worked in Egypt from approximately A.D. 50 to 57. A. Deissmann, *Paulus* ([2]1925) 176f., attributed the Pauline omission of Egypt to the Jewish disturbances that broke after A.D. 38 under Caligula (§6.2.3). This assumption, of course, is possible only if one presupposes a late conversion date (§4).

4. Josephus' assumption is supported by epigraphic material deriving almost exclusively from the period before A.D. 115. Cf. G. Lüderitz, *Corpus jüdischer Zeugnisse aus der Cyrenaika* (1983). Cf. further Schuerer III/1 (1986) 60-62. Concerning the rabbinic material, cf. Billerbeck II 612.

5. Simon being called a Κυρηναῖος can also be a reference to Cyrenian citizenship. Cf. G. Lüderitz, *loc. cit.,* 41f. An ossuary discovered in 1942 by E. L. Sukenik in the Kidron Valley (N. Avigad, *IEJ* 12 [1962] 1-12) probably bears the name of the Alexander mentioned here, son of Simon of Cyrene. Cf. J. P. Kane, *JSS* 23 (1978) 278f.; R. Riesner, *GBL* I (1987) 177f.; G. Kroll, *Auf den Spuren Jesu* ([11]1990) 356-58.

6. Cf. Billerbeck II 663.

7. So, e.g., W. S. Lasor, *ISBE* I (1979) 845.

8. The apostle's origin in Tarsus is also supported by G. Lüdemann, *Early Christianity according to the Traditions in Acts* (Eng. trans., 1989) 241. It is striking in the larger sense how seldom this bit of Lukan information has been doubted by skeptical scholarship. Has this also had something to do with a certain theological preference for the diaspora Jew Paul, to whom syncretic tendencies might sooner be attributed?

stood himself (like a new Jonah?) to be "set apart" already "in the womb" for his missionary task (Gal. 1:15; cf. Isa. 49:1).

14.1.2. Tarsus in Syria-Cilicia

Acts does indeed have Paul now proceed directly from Jerusalem by way of Caesarea and the sea route to Tarsus (Acts 9:30). E. Haenchen[9] views this route description as contrasting with Gal. 1:21: ἔπειτα ἦλθον εἰς τὰ κλίματα τῆς Συρίας καὶ τῆς Κιλικίας. Haenchen is apparently assuming that the mention of Syria requires the land route to Cilicia. Tarsus, however, like all of Cilicia Pedias before the creation of the separate province Cilicia by Vespasian in the year A.D. 72, belonged to the double province Syria-Cilicia, with the capital at Antioch. The linguistic usage both of Acts (Acts 15:23, 41) and Paul in Gal. 1:21 can be understood as the name of the double province if in Acts 15:41 and Gal. 1:21 one follows the reading represented especially by ℵ (omission of the second article before Cilicia).[10] Hence Acts and Paul's own self-witness do not have to exhibit merely approximate concurrence regarding the goal. As a missionary base, Tarsus offered the apostle several advantages. Here his Roman and perhaps also his Tarsan citizenship offered protection (Excursus 1). The most important city[11] in the province after the metropolis Antioch probably had a sizable Jewish community.[12] Its proximity to the sea and to the Cilician Gates (Cicero, *Att.* v.20.2) made Tarsus an ideal point of departure for missionary activity to the north and west.[13]

---

9. E. Haenchen, *Acts* (Eng. trans., 1971) 333.

10. Cf. E. M. B. Green, *ET* 71 (1959/60) 52f.; C. J. Hemer, *The Book of Acts in the Setting of Hellenistic History* (1989) 172, 179.

11. Cf. W. Ruge, *PRE* II 8 (1932) 2413-39; C. B. Welles, *MUSJ* 38 (1962) 43-75; J. Finegan, *The Archaeology of the New Testament* II (1981) 51-54; S. E. Johnson, *Paul the Apostle and His Cities* (1987) 25-34; C. J. Hemer, *ISBE* IV (1988) 734-36; W. W. Gasque, *ABD* VI (1992) 333f.

12. Two inscriptions from Jaffa mention Tarsan Jews (*CIJ* II 925, 931). Concerning Philostratus, *VA* iv.34, see p. 148 above; concerning the synagogue of the Cilicians (Acts 6:9) in Jerusalem, which the rabbis perhaps know as that of the Tarsans (Billerbeck II 663f.), see p. 153 above. Cf. further W. M. Ramsay, *Exp* VI/5 (1902) 19-33; W. Ruge, *PRE* II 8 (1932) 2420f.; Schuerer III/1 (1986) 33f.

13. During the New Testament period, Tarsus was directly connected with the sea by the Cydnus and a lagoon (Rhegma; Strabo xiv.5.10-12; Pliny the Elder, *HN* v.27). Cf. W. Ruge, *PRE* II 8 (1932) 2438; C. Schilling, *GBL* III (1989) 1530. Concerning the general traffic and highway conditions, cf. A. Steinmann, *Zum Werdegang des Paulus* (1928) 7-9; W. Ruge, *loc. cit.,* 2435f.

14.1.3. The Nature of the Mission

According to E. Haenchen, the author of Acts assumes "that Paul now remains quietly for a while in his hometown of Tarsus,"[14] though it remains unclear just how Haenchen supports this conviction. Luke is simply silent regarding Paul's activity; from his silence, however, one can as little conclude that the apostle was inactive as one can conclude from the fact that Peter is not mentioned after Acts 15 that the latter retired after the Apostolic Council. Rather, in Acts 15:41 Luke presupposes that Paul's activity in Syro-Cilicia resulted in the founding of Christian churches, for according to the Lukan portrayal only Paul had hitherto worked as a missionary in Cilicia. An explicit self-witness from the apostle concerning his missionary activity in this period is found in Gal. 1:23, where Paul passes on the conclusions of the Judean churches, conclusions at which they had arrived probably through news of the "Hellenists": "The one who formerly was persecuting us is now proclaiming the faith he once tried to destroy." Presumably, some of the persecutions and tribulations enumerated in 2 Cor. 11:24ff. derive from the period during which Paul missioned from his base in Tarsus. One might also ask whether at that time the apostle had not also pushed forward into Cappadocia,[15] which since A.D. 17 was a Roman province. Although during the early Roman period there were very few cities there, the area did have important trade routes (especially the κοινὴ ὁδός) to the north. Jews are known to have lived in Cappadocia since the Hasmonean period (1 Macc. 15:22-24; cf. Acts 2:9), and already during the first century B.C. their number seems to have been significant (Josephus, *Ant.* xiv.104). Josephus considered this area to be the Meshech of Isa. 66:19, and it could thus be understood as part of that eschatological geography (see p. 252 above).

The fact that a mission in Cappadocia is nowhere attested does not necessarily mean that none was known; there may be another explanation. In the Roman world, the Cappadocians had the reputation of being crude and stupid because Hellenistic culture had spread only very slowly among them. Perhaps a dual geographic division must also be assumed. In the more densely settled eastern part (Melitene), accessible through the Euphrates valley, Christianity was firmly entrenched in the second half of the second century (Tertullian, *Apol.* 5.6; Eusebius, *HE* v.2.2-6). By contrast, the western part accessible from Tarsus was quite thinly populated. Like the rest of eastern and northern Asia Minor, Cappadocia seems at least later to have belonged to the Petrine missionary territory (1 Pet. 1:1; see p. 292, note 66 below). Regarding any assumption that during this period Paul undertook a

14. E. Haenchen, *Acts* (Eng. trans., 1971) 333.
15. Cf. R. Teja, *ANRW* II 7.2 (1980) 1083-1124.

more extensive mission, the fact that he himself, in Gal. 1:21, mentions only Syro-Cilicia should serve as an admonition to exercise reserve. He would have been very well served by mentioning Cappadocia, since it lay even farther from Jerusalem and its authorities. By contrast, Paul did not have to mention Cyprus and Lycia-Pamphylia (Acts 13–14), since the Galatians no doubt were already themselves familiar with the route he took to get to them. If the apostle, like the writer of the book of Judith, understood as Cilicia the locale mentioned in second position in Isa. 66:19, namely, Put, that would be yet another factor making it more comprehensible that he concentrated his efforts so long in this area before a pneumatic experience (§14.3) called him to a different task.

Paul had not only received his "academic" training in the holy city, but had also undergone his elementary schooling in Jerusalem (Acts 22:3: ἀνατεθραμμένος δὲ ἐν τῇ πόλει ταύτῃ, παρὰ τοὺς πόδας Γαμαλιὴλ πεπαιδευμένος).[16] As a result one occasionally finds the apostle's thoughts expressed in Aramaic linguistic forms.[17] In the house of the teacher Gamaliel, Paul doubtless became familiar with the Septuagint,[18] and it is not surprising, therefore, that Luke portrays Paul in close contact with Greek-speaking Jews (Acts 9:29; cf. Acts 6:9 [see pp. 153f. above]) in Jerusalem.[19] Later in Tarsus, however, he doubtless deepened his knowledge of the Greek translation along with its recensions.[20] Even with regard to the period in Syria-Cilicia, the conclusion of M. Hengel is worthy of consideration: "It is certainly possible, and indeed even probable, that as a missionary the early Paul did not yet understand himself to be sent to the non-Jews with such unequivocally exclusive precedence as in the later period, before and certainly after the 'Apostolic Council.' In the initial years after his conversion, he might *also* — presumably largely without success — have made attempts to win his fellow Jews for the gospel, despite his basic message of salvation that was free of the law."[21]

16. Cf. W. C. van Unnik, in *Sparsa Collecta* I (1973) 259-320, 321-27; K. W. Niebuhr, *Heidenapostel aus Israel* (1992) 43-48. In passing we might mention that T. Zahn, *NKZ* 15 (1904) 32, already remarked (with respect to Acts 22:3) that Paul "was sent to Jerusalem while still a boy, and when he had reached the required age, was introduced to the house of the teacher Gamaliel." See also Excursus I/4 (pp. 154f.).

17. Cf. W. C. van Unnik, in *Sparsa Collecta* I (1973) 129-43, 144-59.

18. Cf. R. Riesner, *Jesus als Lehrer* (³1988) 61, 385.

19. Concerning Paul's training, cf. recently M. Hengel, in *idem,* and U. Heckel, eds., *Paulus und das antike Judentum* (1991) 212-65; P. Stuhlmacher, *Biblische Theologie des Neuen Testaments* I (²1997) 229f.

20. Cf. T. Zahn, in *Skizzen aus dem Leben der alten Kirche* (1894) 133.

21. *Zur urchristlichen Geschichtsschreibung* (²1984) 76; emphasis in the original.

14.2. Early Mission in Greece?

14.2.1. The Origin of Titus

Depending on which year one takes for his conversion (§4), Paul remained in Tarsus and its environs between three and ten years (§17.1.3-4). It is thus understandable that, when assuming a longer duration for this period, scholars who consider the framework of Acts to be completely secondary assume that Paul was involved in more extensive activities than merely a mission in Cilicia. J. Knox[22] found evidence confirming a European mission prior to the Apostolic Council in the fact that, apart from Gal. 2:1-3, it is only in the Corinthian correspondence that Paul mentions Titus, who is not mentioned in Acts (2 Cor. 2:13; 7:6, 13f.; 8:6, 16, 23; 12:18). Titus, according to Knox, was among the first converts in Europe. A tradition traceable at least to the beginning of the fourth century A.D. seems to name Antioch as Titus's hometown.[23] Even if this ultimately represents a conclusion from Gal. 2:1-3 (Titus accompanies Paul and Barnabas from Antioch to Jerusalem), it does in any case remain one possible consideration.[24] Paul could have taken Titus along consciously as a new fellow worker in the place of the Jerusalemite Silas on what is known as the third missionary journey.[25] This choice would have made equally clear both his continued association with and his increasing independence from Antioch. Titus apparently did not occupy the same position as Silas, for he is never mentioned in the prescripts to letters. This would make more comprehensible why Luke was able to pass over him in silence. An even more important reason might admittedly be that Acts, given its irenic character, intentionally passes over the tensions between the apostle and the church in Corinth.[26]

14.2.2. Philippians 4:15

G. Lüdemann is convinced: "Since Paul formulates primarily from his own perspective in Phil. 4:15 and not from the perspective of the Philippians, ἐν ἀρχῇ τοῦ εὐαγγελίου is best translated as 'in the beginning of my proclamation of the gospel,' for Paul views his mission in Greece, begun from Mace-

---

22. *Chapters in a Life of Paul* (1950) 59.
23. The text of an anonymous African from the period around A.D. 310 was edited anew by T. Zahn, *Festschrift A. Hauck* (1916) 52-63. T. Zahn gives a summary of his discussion of this writing in *Die Apostelgeschichte* II (1921) 399-405; a brief critique of his views can be found in H. J. Cadbury, *BC* V (1933) 492f.
24. Cf., e.g., F. F. Bruce, *The Pauline Circle* (1985) 58f.
25. Cf. W. H. Ollrog, *Paulus und seine Mitarbeiter* (1979) 34f.
26. Cf. C. K. Barrett, *Essays on Paul* (1982) 118f.

donia, as the initial period of his evangelistic activity."[27] According to this understanding, one would have to assume that after a relatively short period of time, Paul fundamentally changed his mind in this case as well, since later, in Rom. 15:19, he designates Jerusalem as the point of departure of his proclamation of the gospel (§13.2.1). Lüdemann mentions the passage from Romans only in a single footnote, and even there his concern is with the meaning of μέχρι τοῦ Ἰλλυρικοῦ.[28] F. C. Baur considered the entire fifteenth chapter of the letter to the Romans to be an interpolation of a Paulinist standing close to Luke,[29] probably also because he quite justifiably feared that a passage such as Rom. 15:19 might bring Acts and the Pauline letters too close to one another. If one does not wish to take refuge in this kind of violent maneuver, then one must explain how this Pauline statement can be reconciled with Lüdemann's understanding of Phil. 4:15. The traditional, almost unanimously advocated understanding,[30] namely, that here the letter is being formulated from the perspective of the Philippians, who after all are being addressed directly (οἴδατε δὲ καὶ ὑμεῖς Φιλιππήσιοι), spares us the embarrassment of having Paul contradict himself yet again. The choice of the unusual expression might also have been influenced by the fact that Philippi and Macedonia were important for the apostle as the beginning of the missionary work in Europe (see pp. 292f. below). But this possible geographic undertone does not stand in opposition to the traditional understanding of the passage. Despite all reservation regarding the value of the *argumentum e silentio,* one must also remember that in the letter to the Galatians the apostle is utterly silent regarding any mission to Europe before coming to Galatia, even though by mentioning such he could additionally and impressively have underscored his independence from Jerusalem.

Lüdemann writes further: "In view of Paul's relative understanding of ἀρχή, it is quite possible that Paul could have reckoned his provably prior activity in Arabia (uncertain), Damascus, Syria/Cilicia, and south Galatia (probable) to the initial period (i.e., the early phase) of his proclamation of the gospel. Since Christian congregations probably existed in these localities at a very early date, and since Paul does not want to preach where ὠνομάσθη Χριστός, ἵνα μὴ ἐπ' ἀλλότριον θεμέλιον οἰκοδομῶ (Rom. 15:20), it is understandable that Paul left Palestine/Syria soon after his conversion and came to Greece."[31] If one reflects on the geographic and chronological implications,

27. *Paul: Apostle to the Gentiles* (Eng. trans., 1984) 106.
28. *Ibid.,* 135, note 185.
29. *Paulus, der Apostel Jesu Christi* (1845) 398-416.
30. An overview of the variously advocated solutions can be found in G. F. Hawthorne, *Philippians* (1983) 204; P. T. O'Brien, *Philippians* (1991) 531f.
31. *Paul: Apostle to the Gentiles* (1984) 106.

then even the use of the word "relative" seems highly relative. That is, in Phil. 4:15, Paul would have subsumed geographically his activity in a large part of the eastern Mediterranean basin (Syria, Asia Minor) under the rubric of the mission in Greece. From a temporal perspective, at least six years separate the apostle's conversion and his transition to Europe in Lüdemann's chronological reconstruction as well,[32] and thus the term "soon" is also to be taken only quite "relatively." Finally, how do we know that Christian congregations already existed in Cilicia and south Galatia prior to Paul's own activity, such that he would not have counted them among his own missionary territories? The whole struggle for the (south) Galatian congregations becomes incomprehensible if the apostle did not view them at least as results of his own efforts as (co-)founder. Assuming Paul did mean what Lüdemann believes, why did he not then write at least ἐν ἀρχῇ τοῦ εὐαγγελίου μου? Neither the exegetical basis of Phil. 4:15 nor Lüdemann's historical assumption that the Claudian edict concerning the Jews is to be dated in A.D. 41 (§10) sufficiently grounds the assumption of a Pauline mission to Europe prior to the Apostolic Council.

14.3. Transition to Antioch

According to Acts, Barnabas took Paul from Tarsus to Antioch (Acts 11:25), which then became the center for a geographically expansive, aggressive Gentile mission (Acts 13:1ff.). The Pauline letters only indirectly confirm this portrayal. The way Paul speaks about Barnabas in the letter to the Galatians (Gal. 2:1, 9, 13) suggests the two participated in a common mission (see pp. 288f. below). Antioch emerges as the most important base for such a mission (Gal. 2:11): whatever was decided there, so the apostle's conviction, would also be implemented in the churches of Galatia (Gal. 2:12ff.). The notion that Paul once worked as a missionary in an equal, if not subordinate role ("junior partner"), seems impossible to Lüdemann in view of the apostle's own statements especially in Gal. 1–2.[33] Here, however, "Paul has to interpret in retrospect an event which to the highest degree seemed to witness in favor of his adversaries and unfavorably for him. . . . The Pauline inclination, obviously in Galatians 2 as well, is to demonstrate the autonomy and independence of his apostolate and his message."[34] The old list in Acts 13:1 is weighty evidence suggesting that for a

---

32. *Ibid.,* 262f.

33. In B. C. Corley, ed., *Colloquy on New Testament Studies* (1983) 292.

34. P. Stuhlmacher, *Das paulinische Evangelium* I (1968) 85. W. Stenger, *Festschrift F. Mussner* (1981) 123-140, speaks with respect to Gal. 1:11–2:14 about "idealized biography." Cf. further also J. Becker, *Paulus* (1989) 19-21 (Eng. trans., *Paul* [1993]).

time in Antioch, Paul belonged to the local church leadership together with others of equal status.[35] If one not only views theological statements in an isolated fashion, but also considers historical and sociological circumstances, then it is highly probable that before the incident of Gal. 2:11ff. Paul stood in a certain position of dependency with regard both to Jerusalem and to Antioch.[36]

The transition from what was perhaps fairly autonomous activity (in Tarsus) to missionary work in which Paul was not the only leader is remarkable, and demands an explanation. Perhaps we possess in Paul's letters an indication of why the apostle entered into this undertaking. T. Zahn assumed that the ecstatic experience alluded to in 2 Cor. 12:2ff. is connected with Paul's transition to the Antiochene mission,[37] and this view continues to find isolated advocates even today.[38] Unfortunately, nothing certain concerning the content of the heavenly revelation can be retrieved from Paul's own portrayal. Given the context, it apparently had something to do with his apostolic office.[39] The most likely support for a connection between the revelation and the transition to Antioch is our chronological reconstruction (§17.1.4), which on the other hand excludes the Damascus event[40] or the vision in the Jerusalem temple (§13.4).[41] In the period between A.D. 40 and 44, the continuation of the Gentile mission seems to have been a topic in other ways as well in early Christian prophecy (§7.1.4).

14.4. Mission on Cyprus

According to Acts, Barnabas and Paul, together with their companion John Mark, turned first to Cyprus (Acts 13:4-13). Although Paul's letters make absolutely no mention of such an undertaking, several historical factors speak

35. Cf. A. Zimmermann, *Die urchristlichen Lehrer* ([2]1988) 118-40.

36. Cf. B. Holmberg, *Paul and Power* (1978) 14-34. N. Taylor, *Paul, Antioch and Jerusalem* (1992), now also (over-)emphasizes this.

37. *Einleitung in das Neue Testament* II (1900) 635 (Eng. trans., *Introduction to the New Testament* II [1909]).

38. So P. Bachmann, *Der zweite Brief des Paulus an die Korinther* (1918) 391f.; E. B. Allo, *Saint Paul: Seconde Épître aux Corinthiens* (1937) 307 (additional, earlier representatives), 321f.; J. J. Gunther, *Paul: Messenger and Exile* (1972) 26-29. As a possibility also H. Windisch, *Der zweite Korintherbrief* (1924) 373; R. P. Martin, *2 Corinthians* (1986) 399.

39. Cf. P. Bachmann, *loc. cit.,* 392; J. J. Gunther, *loc. cit.,* 27.

40. So esp. C. H. Buck and G. R. Taylor, *Saint Paul* (1969) 222-26; opposed also A. F. Segal, *Paul the Convert* (1990) 36f.

41. So, among others, N. Hyldahl, *Die paulinische Chronologie* (1986) 118-20. Additional representatives can be found in R. Jewett, *A Chronology of Paul's Life* (1979) 54f., note 37, who correctly voices the criticism that 2 Cor. 12:2-4 is referring to something inexpressible, while the content of the vision of Acts 22:17 could be described publicly.

in favor of this destination. Barnabas came from Cyprus (Acts 4:26), and apparently felt a strong obligation toward the mission on his home island (cf. Acts 15:39). Perhaps Hellenists who were driven from Jerusalem and originally came from Cyprus (Acts 11:19f.) provided further connections with the island.[42] Since the time of the Hasmoneans (1 Macc. 15:23), a rapidly growing Jewish population group existed there,[43] so that Philo could say that Cyprus was counted among the islands "full of Jewish colonies (μεσταὶ τῶν Ἰουδαϊκῶν ἀποικιῶν)" (Philo, *Leg. ad Gaium* 282). It thus seems credible that Salamis had several synagogues (Acts 13:5), and judging from findings from the second/fourth centuries A.D., Jewish communities could be found also outside the larger cities.[44] At least some Jews belonged to the upper class (Josephus, *Ant.* xviii.131), and that might have facilitated the establishment of a larger group of "God-fearers." The account (Acts 13:6-12) of the encounter between the early Christian missionaries and the proconsul Sergius Paul(l)us and his court astrologer Elymas reflects the remarkable attraction Judaism genuinely was able to exert even on members of the highest circles (§9). The account in Acts does exhibit an acquaintance with the locale insofar as it knows that the harbor in Cyprus lying opposite Seleucia was Salamis, and that Paphos was situated at the other end of the island (Acts 13:4-6).

14.5. Pushing Forward to Galatia

14.5.1. Reasons for the Chosen Route

Thereafter, Luke recounts the passage to Perga in Pamphylia (Acts 13:13) and missionary activity in the Galatian provincial cities Pisidian Antioch (Acts 13:14-50),[45] Iconium (Acts 13:51–14:5), and Lystra (Acts 14:6-20). Since

42. Cf. R. Pesch, *Die Apostelgeschichte* II (1988) 23.

43. Cf. M. Stern, CRINT I/1 (1974) 154f.; Schuerer III/1 (1986) 68f.

44. Cf. S. Applebaum, CRINT I/2 (1976) 711f.; T. B. Mitford, *ANRW* II 7.2 (1980) 1380f. On Cyprus generally, see A. Nobbs in A1CS II (1994) 279-90; D. W. J. Gill, *TynBul* 46 (1995) 219-28.

45. This city was situated on the Phrygian boundary with Pisidia, and is thus sometimes correctly ascribed to the former (Strabo xii.6.4; Ptolemy v.5), and sometimes incorrectly to the latter (Pliny the Elder, *HN* v.24.94; Ptolemy v.4.9). Cf. W. Stengel, *PRE* I 1 (1894) 2446, as well as esp. B. M. Levick, *Roman Colonies in Southern Asia Minor* (1967) 18, and 33, note 2. The original reading of Acts 13:14 with "Pisidian Antioch" (Ἀντιόχειαν τὴν Πισιδίαν) refers probably to its proximity to the boundary (C. J. Hemer, *The Book of Acts in the Setting of Hellenistic History* [1989] 109, 228f.; concerning Πισίδια as an adjective, cf. *NewDoc* IV 90), whereas the later (D and Majority Text) variant (Ἀντιόχειαν τῆς Πισιδίας) apparently reflects circumstances after the fourth century A.D. (F. F. Bruce, *The Epistle of Paul to the Galatians* [1982] 6, note 17).

273

Acts contains no indication of Pauline activity in the territory of Galatia, and since other reasons also militate against this (§15.2.1), one may view Paul's letter to the churches in Galatia (Gal. 1:2: ταῖς ἐκκλησίαις τῆς Γαλατίας) as a witness for the existence of Pauline churches in the southern part of the province Galatia.

One can attempt to understand the route from Cyprus into this region on the basis of several presuppositions of Pauline missionary strategy which emerge more clearly later. It should be kept in mind, however, that during this phase of "collaborative mission" the apostle still had to consider the opinion of Barnabas. By way of the Cilician Gates either to the north or west, Galatia was the nearest Roman province bordering on Syria-Cilicia. Sizable Jewish communities could be found in the southern parts of Galatia for over two hundred years.[46] Admittedly, the next directions following upon Tarshish and Put (Cilicia) in Isa. 66:19 point toward Lydia (Lud) and Mysia (Meshech), and to the north (Tubal) into the region of the Black Sea coast (see pp. 251f. above). A larger Roman highway probably led inward from Perga to the Black Sea coast. The discovery of Augustan milestones (6 B.C.) attests the existence of an improved highway leading to Pisidian Antioch from the south.[47] Furthermore, two inscriptions found in modern Antalya confirm the construction of a Roman highway from Attalia to Perga and thence to the north in the direction of Antioch.[48] It is uncertain where exactly the boundary was situated between the double province Lycia-Pamphylia, founded anew by Claudius in A.D. 43, and Galatia.[49] At least in the late Flavian period under Domitian, an improved highway led from Pisidian Antioch to Cotyaeum (Kutahyah) and Dorylaeum (Eskişehir) in the north. From Cotyaeum the way was open to Mysia. From the great traffic crossroad Dorylaeum,[50] it was possible to travel either directly to the north to the Bithynian coast of the Black Sea, or in a northeasterly direction via Ancyra to the Pontus coastal area.[51] One may assume that the Flavian highways had precursors in early times. Although we do not know how well constructed these highways were,[52] it is clear that many different routes led from Perga into the interior of the country.

The missionaries' route from Perga to Antioch cannot be determined

46. Cf. Schuerer III/1 (1986) 32-34.
47. Cf. D. H. French, *ANRW* II 7.2 (1980) 707f.
48. Cf. S. Mitchell, *Chiron* 16 (1986) 23-25, and *NewDoc* IV (1987) 129.
49. Cf. A. S. Hall, *AnSt* 18 (1968) 59. Concerning this history, cf. R. Syme, in *Roman Papers* I (1979) 120-48.
50. Cf. J. Bérard, *RA* VI/5 (1935) 80f.
51. Cf. D. H. French, *ANRW* II 7.2 (1980) 707-12.
52. It seems that paving was not customary before the Flavian period. Cf. D. H. French, *Roman Roads and Milestones of Asia Minor* I (1981) 32A.

exactly. W. M. Ramsay suspected that a highway ran along the eastern side of the Valley of the Cestrus (Aksu), and believed that the earlier name of Adada, namely, Kara Bavlo, preserved a recollection of this Pauline route.[53] This derivation of the name, however, is philologically difficult,[54] and the route is geographically improbable from the perspective of the journey itself.[55] Regardless of whether the apostle took the route via the Roman colonies Cremna and Sagalassus (Aghlasun), or further to the west via Comama and Apollonia/Pisidia,[56] it is noteworthy that he did not continue on into nearby[57] Apamea. At this crossroad of the *Via Sebaste*[58] the highway forked toward Cotyaeum on the one hand, and Dorylaeum on the other, and the missionaries would have encountered here a strong Jewish community (Cicero, *Flacc.* 28-68).[59] Perhaps another circumstance can help explain the route they did in fact take.

14.5.2. Sergius Paullus and Galatia

If one identifies the Sergius Paullus of the New Testament with the member of the senatorial family mentioned in a Claudian Tiber-inscription (*CIL* VI 31545; §9.2.3), then it is possible that the missionaries' transition to south Galatia also had something to do with the connections between the Sergii and this region. This was the suggestion of E. Groag,[60] and other scholars have continued to concur with him.[61] S. Mitchell assumes it was "virtually certain that the proconsul himself advised Paul to continue his journey to Pisidian Antioch, where he could provide introductions to the upper class of the Roman

53. *The Church in the Roman Empire before A.D. 170* (1893) 19-22. So also E. A. Judge, *ISBE* III (1986) 767.

54. Cf. K. Lake, *BC* V (1933) 224.

55. Cf. J. Bérard, *RA* VI/5 (1935) 64f.; T. R. S. Broughton, *Festschrift K. Lake* (1937) 131-33.

56. Cf. the highway map in J. Bérard, *RA* VI/5 (1935) 62.

57. According to Strabo xii.6.5, the locale was separated from Sagalassos by a single day's journey.

58. Its Greek name, βασιλικὴ ὁδός, appears in *Acts Pet.* 3. Cf. T. Pekary, *Untersuchungen zu den römischen Reichsstraßen* (1968) 156f.

59. Cf. further Schuerer III/1 (1986) 28-30.

60. *PRE* II 4 (1923) 1718.

61. So, e.g., G. A. Harrer, *HTR* 33 (1940) 30-32; W. Hartke, *Vier urchristliche Parteien und ihre Vereinigung zur apostolischen Kirche* II (East Berlin, 1961) 415f. (with confusion concerning the area of the Roman provinces Syria-Cilicia, Cyprus, and Galatia); G. Kehnscherper, *TU* 87 (1964) 433-38; M. F. Baslez, *Saint Paul* (1991) 125f. Cf. now generally C. Breytenbach, *NTS* 39 (1993) 396-413; *Paulus und Barnabas in der Provinz Galatien* (1996) 31-49, 180-87; P. Trebilco, *Jewish Communities in Asia Minor* (1991) 21-23; G. W. Hansen in A1CS II (1994) 377-95; and J. Taylor in *ANRW* II 26/2 (1995) 1189-1231.

colony,"[62] and G. H. R. Horsley finds this assumption "attractive."[63] At least during the Flavian period, the Sergii Paulli owned land in the vicinity of Vetissus (Emirler) in rural central Anatolia (*MAMA* VII 319, 321, 330f., 485),[64] and S. Mitchell, given the analogy of other circumstances of property ownership in this area, assumes they acquired these properties already during the Julio-Claudian period.[65] Other evidence suggesting a special relationship between the family and the Roman colony of Pisidian Antioch founded in 25 B.C. under Augustus[66] includes an inscription[67] erected there in honor of L. Sergius L. f. Paullus filius, who was probably the proconsul's grandson (§9.2.3). According to Acts, this city was apparently the conscious destination after the departure from Paphos (Acts 13:13f.). By contrast, in the Lukan portrayal the significant city of Perga[68] served the missionaries only as a stopover point (Acts 13:13).[69] In any case, Antioch, which was economically important,[70] had a significant Jewish community probably composed mainly of merchants (Acts 13:14)[71] and with extensive influence over Gentiles (Acts 13:16, 26).[72]

62. *ANRW* II 7.2 (1980) 1074, note 134. Cf. now S. Mitchell, *Anatolia* II (1993) 5-8.

63. *NewDoc* IV (1987) 138.

64. Cf. W. M. Ramsay, *JRS* 16 (1926) 202f.; W. M. Calder, *Klio* 24 (1930/31) 59f.

65. *ANRW* II 7.2 (1980) 1073f.; *ABD* I (1992) 264. Cf. also H. Halfmann, *Die Senatoren aus dem östlichen Teil des Imperium Romanum* (1979) 30, 55f., 101f., 105.

66. Cf. B. M. Levick, *Roman Colonies in Southern Asia Minor* (1967) 33-38, 56-67, 130-44, *et passim.* W. D. Davies, *The Gospel and the Land* (1974) 181, draws a false conclusion when he writes: "It is not clear that Antioch in Pisidia, Lystra, Iconium, Derbe were 'significant' centres of Roman penetration." Every more reliable historical map of Asia Minor shows that Antioch represented an important highway crossroad. The least significant was Lystra. Cf. D. Magie, *Roman Rule in Asia Minor* I (1950) 463.

67. Cf. W. M. Ramsay, *The Bearing of Recent Discovery on the Trustworthiness of the New Testament* ([4]1920) 151. Cf. also M. T. Rapsaet-Charlier, *Prosopographie des femmes de l'ordre sénatorial* (1987) 561-62.

68. Cf. W. M. Ramsay, *The Church in the Roman Empire before A.D. 170* (1893) 16-24; W. Ruge, *PRE* 37 (1937) 694-704; D. Magie, *Roman Rule in Asia Minor* II (1950) 1334f., note 7.

69. The mention in Acts 14:25 of Attalia as the departure harbor is not a contradiction resulting from lack of familiarity with the locale. During the New Testament period, Perga was connected with the sea (Strabo xiv.42), probably by a connecting canal from the Cestrus River. Cf. D. Magie, *loc. cit.,* 1139, note 16; G. Bean, *Turkey's Southern Shore* (1968) 45. The assumption is also worth considering that the passage was made directly from Cyprus to Perga, whereas a coastal ship would put in at Attalia. Cf. C. J. Hemer, *The Book of Acts in the Setting of Hellenistic History* (1989) 109.

70. Cf. B. M. Levick, *Roman Colonies in Southern Asia Minor* (1967) 58, 94, 99f.

71. The additional reference of G. Kehnscherper, *TU* 87 (1964) 435, note 2, to Josephus, *B.J.* vii.43, is the result of having confused Syrian with Pisidian Antioch.

72. Cf. B. M. Levick, *loc. cit.,* 58, 99, 189.

14.5.3. Reasons for Return Routes

Whatever the case may have been regarding the influence of Sergius Paullus and the original northern missionary plan, the path of Barnabas and Paul did not, according to Acts, lead from Antioch/Pisidia either to the north (Bithynia), northeast (Cappadocia), or west (Lydia), as one might have expected from Isa. 66:19 (see pp. 251f. above), but rather toward the east to Iconium (Acts 13:51). Several explanations for this change of direction are possible, and all may have played a part. During this period, Paul still had to take Barnabas into consideration in making travel plans. It is uncertain whether already during the Claudian period an improved highway led to the north from Antioch (§14.5.1). Only a little north of Antioch began an area in which Phrygian was still spoken.[73] Although Greek was naturally also spoken in Hellenized cities such as Philomelium, Amorion, or Orkistos, the language barrier could have been perceived as a definite hindrance (see pp. 283f. below). According to an inscription found in 1987, the Sergii could have owned real estate in Iconium as well.[74] Perhaps the missionaries had decided to take the land route back to Antioch through the Cilician Gates. The continuation of the Augustan *Via Sebaste* probably led via Iconium and Lystra to the east,[75] both of which, like Antioch, were Roman colonies.[76] In the larger sense, the *Via Sebaste* seems to have functioned to connect such colonies with one another,[77] and it is thus possible that Paul's concentration on Roman colonies — a concentration clearly visible later — began already at this time (see p. 149 above). Lystra and Iconium were prospering economically.[78] Iconium at least had a Jewish community (Acts 14:1), and one can conclude the presence of Jews and "God-fearers" in Lystra (Acts 16:1-3; cf. 2 Tim. 1:5).

73. Cf. W. M. Calder, in *MAMA* VII (1956) xliv.

74. N. Ehrhardt, *ZPE* 81 (1990) 185-88 (187, note 16).

75. Cf. M. H. Ballance, *AnSt* 8 (1958) 223-34; in *MAMA* VIII (1962) xi; A. S. Hall, *AnSt* 18 (1968) 61.

76. Concerning Lystra, cf. B. M. Levick, *Roman Colonies in Southern Asia Minor* (1967) 51f., 153-56, 195-97, *et passim,* and concerning Iconium, cf. *ibid.,* 165, 183, *et passim.* New numismatic evidence (H. von Aulock, *Münzen und Städte Lykaoniens* [1976] nos. 297-99) make it clear that Iconium bore the title *colonia* not just honorifically, as has been the *communis opinio* since the studies of W. M. Ramsay, but was also founded by Augustus. Since Claudius, both a colony *(Colonia Iulia Augusta Iconium)* and a *polis* ΚΛΑΨΔΕΙΚΟΝΙΕΩΝ existed side by side in the city. This confirms the high degree of Hellenization suggested by Acts 14:1. Cf. S. Mitchell, *Hist* 28 (1979) 411-25.

77. Cf. D. H. French, *ANRW* II 7.2 (1980) 707f.

78. Cf. M. P. Charlesworth, *Trade-Routes and Commerce in the Roman Empire* (1924) 82f., and esp. B. M. Levick, *Roman Colonies* (1967) 99, who remarks in this context that "Antioch and Iconium, like Lystra, were visited by St. Paul, whose journeyings took him along well-established routes."

If the missionaries did intend to reach Syrian Antioch by the land route, then this admittedly raises questions concerning the repeated change of direction in Derbe, leading to a return along the same route (Acts 14:20-25). The explanation is inadequate[79] which points to the fact that the territory of the Roman province of Galatia ceased at Derbe (Acts 14:20),[80] where the client kingdom of Commagene began.[81] In any case, the next journey reported by Acts (Acts 15:41–16:1) took Paul along the direct route via the Taurus Passes through the non-Roman territory of Commagene. Perhaps the approaching winter[82] precluded returning by way of the snowed-in Taurus Passes.[83] Yet even without this external circumstance, it might have seemed advisable to Paul and Barnabas to visit once more and to consolidate the newly founded churches that found themselves under attack (cf. Acts 14:21-23).

This time, the return journey from Pisidia to Pamphylia (Acts 14:24) is accompanied by a report of a proclamation of the gospel in this territory as well, one in which a larger number of Jews had been living since the

79. Cf. W. M. Ramsay, *St. Paul the Traveller and the Roman Citizen* ([17]1930) 110-13.

80. The political status of Derbe during the New Testament period is disputed. Based on inscriptional evidence (M. H. Ballance, *AnSt* 7 [1957] 147-51), it can today be identified with Kerti Hüyük lying further to the East. Cf. further M. H. Ballance, *AnSt* 14 (1964) 139f.; B. van Elderen, *Festschrift F. F. Bruce* [1970] 156-61. G. Ogg, *NTS* 9 (1962/63) 367-70, has correctly pointed out that this new location increases the possibility that Derbe lay outside the *provincia Galatia*. From Strabo xii.6.3, one might, however, conclude that Derbe belonged to Galatia. Cf. F. F. Bruce, *The Epistle of Paul to the Galatians* (1982) 5, note 15. But at the latest since A.D. 41, Laranda (Karaman), situated about twenty kilometers south-southwest, no longer belonged to this province, as attested by coins struck there under Antiochus IV of Commagene (D. Magie, *Roman Rule in Asia Minor* II [1950] 1368, note 49). Experts in the historical geography of Asia Minor come to different conclusions in view of our limited knowledge and the fluctuating situation regarding precisely this boundary. G. Stählin and E. Höhne, *Der östliche Mittelmeerraum zur Zeit des Apostels Paulus. BHH Beilage* ([2]1968), and S. Mitchell, *ANRW* II 7.2 (1980), fig. 1 (after p. 1056), reckon Derbe to Galatia. R. K. Sherk, *loc. cit.*, fig. 1 (after p. 960) and I. Pill-Rademacher, *et al., TAVO* B V 8 (1988), do not.

81. Soon after the establishment of the province (25 B.C.), Augustus assigned Rugged Cilicia *(Cilicia Tracheia)* and eastern Lycaonia *(Lycaonia Antiochiana)* to the kingdom of his ally Archelaus of Cappadocia (Strabo xiv.5.6; cf. Dio Cassius, *Hist.* liv.9.2; Josephus, *Ant.* xvi.131). Antiochus IV of Commagene received this area temporarily under Caligula, and then permanently under Claudius after A.D. 41 (Dio Cassius, *Hist.* lix.8.2; Ptolemy, v.6.16; Tacitus, *Ann.* xii.55).

82. Cicero even asserted *"Nam Taurus propter nives ante mensem Iunium transiri non potest"* (Cicero, *Ad. Att.* v.21.14).

83. So W. M. Ramsay, *The Church in the Roman Empire before A.D. 170* (1893) 69f., followed by, among others, E. Stange, *Paulinische Reisepläne* (1918) 78, and G. Kehnscherper, *TU* 87 (1964) 435.

Hasmonean period (1 Macc. 15:23; Philo, *Leg. ad Gaium* 39; cf. Acts 2:9).[84] The apostles' preaching in Perga is mentioned explicitly (see p. 276 above) (Acts 14:25), and D also claims the same took place in Attalia (εὐαγγελι-ζόμενοι αὐτούς). In this version, the gospel would have been preached in the capital of the double province Lycia-Pamphylia as well. In any event, Attalia is mentioned as the harbor from which they departed in returning to Antioch (Acts 14:26), whose seaport Seleucia Luke had mentioned earlier (Acts 13:4).[85]

279

§15

The Way West

15.1. Effects of the Apostolic Council

After their shared missionary journey through south Galatia, Paul and Barnabas spent considerable time in Antioch (Acts 14:26-28: διέτριβον δὲ χρόνον οὐκ ὀλίγον), during which the demands of pharisaically influenced Palestinian Jewish Christians for the circumcision of Gentiles precipitated a crisis for their new ministry (Acts 15:1-5). At least one historically identifiable factor contributing to the reemergence of this problem with this particular severity, a problem that demanded fundamental theological clarification, was the strengthening of the Zealot movement toward the end of the A.D. 40s (§6.3). The Zealots' hatred was directed first of all toward those among their countrymen whom they suspected of collaborating with the Roman occupation army or of mingling with Gentiles.[1] "Following Old Testament models, they believed that in this world ruled by antidivine forces one could make room for God's holy will only by means of the sword, and men such as Jesus and Paul had to appear to them to be dangerous dreamers."[2] The transformation from a Gentile mission free from the law to a proselyte movement would have taken dangerous pressure off the Palestinian early church. It is certainly possible that propagandists for this course of accommodation also came as far as south Galatia, promising the churches there that in this way "they would not be persecuted for the cross of Christ" (Gal. 6:12).[3] Disturbances in Antioch

---

1. In a study of the coexistence of different nationalities in the *imperium Romanum,* D. B. Saddington, *ANRW* II 2 (1975) 132, concludes that "something approaching 'nationalism' can be found in one area at this period [A.D. first century], Judaea. . . . The factors which lay behind Jewish opposition to Rome formed a special case. The major one was a religious intolerance which found attitudes typified by *interpretatio Romana* anathema. A second was a strong feeling of exclusiveness. Thirdly, there was little room for political accommodation when the ultimate Jewish aim was theocracy. The Jewish situation must be regarded as atypical."

2. M. Hengel, *Die Zeloten* (²1967) 231 (Eng. trans., *The Zealots* [1989]).

3. Cf. R. K. Jewett, *NTS* 17 (1970/71) 198-212. In general, the theme of "per-

(see p. 196 above) and Rome (§10.7) in the years A.D. 48 and 49 suggest that the effects of Zealot agitation were felt even as far as the Diaspora.

We can concern ourselves here only with that which the Apostolic Council meant with respect to Pauline missionary strategy. U. Wilckens writes in this regard: "A redemptive-historical missionary conception lies behind Rom. 15:19; and one may ask whether this conception as such did not experience the hour of its birth in the negotiations of the Apostolic Council (cf. Gal. 2:9) — or at least the hour of its first official designation — thence acquiring also its pan-ecclesiastical/ecumenical validity. When Paul speaks of it here, he is not emphasizing specifically himself with *his* mission, but rather is subsuming it under the overriding context of a universal understanding of gospel and mission whose validity he also can assume is both familiar and recognized in Rome."[4] In any event, Paul separated from Barnabas after the Apostolic Council (Acts 15:35-39; cf. Gal. 2:11-13), and from now on he could freely follow his own notions about the geographic expansion of his mission. Thus also do his intentions become immediately clear, namely, to proceed, after a visit of consolidation to the churches in Syro-Cilicia (Acts 15:40) and south Galatia (Acts 16:1-6), to the province of Asia, about whose heartland, Lydia, Isa. 66:19 spoke in third position (see p. 251 above).

15.2. Altered Routes in Asia Minor

15.2.1. Through Phrygo-Galatia to Mysia

Paul's letters do not reveal the route along which he reached Europe. Since Acts mentions Derbe and Lystra as the stations (Acts 16:1) following Syro-Cilicia (Acts 15:41 [§14.1.2), the route through the Cilician Gates is presupposed. We then read: "As they [Paul and Silas] went from town to town, they delivered to them for observance the decisions that had been reached by the apostles and elders who were in Jerusalem" (Acts 16:4). It is not our task here to address the question how Luke could associate Paul with what is known as the "Apostolic Decree" (Acts 15:23-29);[5] we are concerned here

---

secution" has long been too neglected in the interpretation of the letter to the Galatians. Cf. E. Baasland, *StTh* 38 (1984) 135-50.

4. *Der Brief an die Römer* III (1982) 120 (emphasis by the author).

5. The difficulty would be eliminated if the second part of Acts 16:4, which in the D-text constitutes a doublet to Acts 15:41, were a gloss. So A. S. Geyser, in *Festschrift J. de Zwaan* (1953) 136-38, and as a possibility also F. F. Bruce, *The Book of Acts* (1988) 305. This solution, however, founders on the secondary character of the D-text. Nevertheless, some more recent authors also consider the decree to be historical, such as G. Stählin, *Die Apostelgeschichte* (⁶1978) 210f.; R. Pesch, *Die Apostelgeschichte* II (1986) 84-90;

only with the underlying geographic presuppositions. As far as the "cities" are concerned, apart from the previously mentioned locales of Derbe and Lystra, Luke can be thinking only of the cities evangelized on the first missionary journey, namely, Iconium and Pisidian Antioch (cf. Acts 15:36). The route we must presuppose thus leads to the northwest.

In what follows, this relatively detailed route-description is given (Acts 16:6-8): "They went through (διῆλθον δὲ τὴν Φρυγίαν καὶ Γαλατικὴν χώραν), having been forbidden by the Holy Spirit to speak the word in Asia (κωλυθέντες ὑπὸ τοῦ ἁγίου πνεύματος λαλῆσαι τὸν λόγον ἐν τῇ Ἀσίᾳ). When they had come opposite Mysia (ἐλθόντες δὲ κατὰ τὴν Μυσίαν), they attempted to go into Bithynia (ἐπείραζον εἰς τὴν Βιθυνίαν πορευθῆναι), but the Spirit of Jesus did not allow them; so, passing through Mysia, they went down to Troas (παρελθόντες δὲ τὴν Μυσίαν κατέβησαν εἰς Τρῳάδα)." According to the regnant understanding, Paul would have traveled from Lystra (via Iconium) to the north through eastern Phrygia into the territory of Galatia in central Anatolia.[6] Although Luke's account says nothing direct about any missionary activity, it is inferred from the fact that διέρχομαι is a *terminus technicus* for such activity.[7] But the parallel adduced as witness, namely Acts 8:4, says that the Hellenists driven from Jerusalem "went from place to place, proclaiming the gospel (διῆλθον εὐαγγελιζόμενοι)." Hence a double expression is used that as a matter of fact does not occur in Acts 16:6, raising doubts whether without further qualification one can indeed understand simple διέρχομαι as a reference to missionary activity.

This widespread understanding also encounters geographic difficulties. Even today, the region of eastern Phrygia presupposed for Paul, as well as the southern part of the territory of Galatia, both belong to the least-densely populated regions of Anatolia. Without actually becoming acquainted with the locale firsthand, scholars perhaps are inclined to give too little consideration to the fact that immediately north of Iconium a semi-desert begins. If along this route the apostle wanted to found churches, this could have happened only in the area around Pessinus or the provincial capital Ancyra situated to its east, that is, in the northern part of the territory of Galatia. It is difficult to imagine a mission in the steppe region of eastern Phrygia. In this completely rural area, the Phrygian and Celtic tribal languages still predominated until

---

O. Böcher, in *Festschrift J. Gnilka* (1989) 325-33. From earlier scholarship one might emphasize T. Zahn, *Die Apostelgeschichte* II (1921) 537-41; K. Bornhäuser, *NKZ* 34 (1923) 391-438; A. Wikenhauser, *Die Apostelgeschichte* (1938) 109-11; E. Lerle, *Proselytenwerbung und Urchristentum* (1960) 120-31.

6. So, e.g., R. Pesch, *Die Apostelgeschichte* II (1986) 101.

7. Cf. *ibid.*, 100.

the beginning of the Byzantine period.[8] Although the upper classes were Hellenized in the first century A.D., the broad masses of the population were not.[9] Still, anyone in the area around Ancyra who wants to reach Bithynia does not turn in an almost right angle westward to the vicinity of the Mysian boundary. Even assuming that Galatia is referring only to the area around Pessinus, the mention of Mysia still does not really make sense. Bithynia lay immediately to the north, whereas Phrygian territory separated the city from Mysia in the west.

According to G. Schneider, the expression Γαλατικὴ χώρα is referring to "the district inhabited by the Galatians, including the cities of Nakoleia, Dorylaeum, Pessinus, and Ancyra, though Paul must not necessarily have gone into the territory of the latter two cities (Haenchen)."[10] One anticipates finding in E. Haenchen's commentary on Acts some evidence that Nakoleia and Dorylaeum belonged to the territory of Galatia;[11] instead, Haenchen refers the reader further to M. Dibelius, who writes: "One must not necessarily understand by 'region of Galatia' the actual territory of Galatia itself with Ancyra and Pessinus," and he supports this with the justified question "how could Paul have gotten so far to the east on his way to Bithynia?"[12] Dibelius continues: "Along this route, however, lay Amorion, Orkistus, and Nakoleia — all of which could conceivably be part of the Γαλατικὴ χώρα insofar as there, too, Celtic was presumably spoken."[13] Dibelius is thus aware that Nakoleia did not belong to the territory of Galatia; in support of the linguistic-historical argument, he refers to K. Lake, who apparently also represents an unnamed source for Schneider's statement.

Lake writes that " 'Phrygia and Galatian country' means territory in which sometimes Phrygian and sometimes Gaelic was the language of the villagers. His route may have been through Laodicea [Combusta], Amorion, and Orkistos (surely a Gaelic place) to Nakoleia and perhaps Dorylaeum. Either Nakoleia or

8. Cf. R. Schmitt, *ANRW* II 29.2 (1983) 566-68, who remarks with regard to neo-Phrygian inscriptions of the first-fourth centuries A.D. (from the area between Eskişehir [Dorylaeum] — Eğridir — Konya [Iconium] — Tuz Gölü [Palus Tattaeus]): "As the most recent direct witnesss of a pre-Greco/pre-Roman language in Asia Minor," they are "a clear indication that those regions of the interior that were not so easily accessible became completely Hellenized only at a very late date" (*loc. cit.,* 566).

9. Cf. K. Bittel, *Proceedings of the Xth International Congress of Classical Archaeology* I/3 (1978) 169-74.

10. *Die Apostelgeschichte* II (1982) 205, note 12.

11. E. Haenchen, *Acts* (Eng. trans., 1971) 483, note 2.

12. In *Aufsätze zur Apostelgeschichte* (1951) 169, note 2. The eccentricity of such a route becomes esp. clear on the map provided by G. Stählin and E. Höhne, eds., *Der östliche Mittelmeerraum zur Zeit des Apostels Paulus. Beilage zu BHH* (²1968).

13. In *Aufsätze zur Apostelgeschichte* (1951) 169, note 2.

Dorylaeum might be said to be κατὰ τὴν Μυσίαν."[14] Although Lake's statement is not completely clear, he probably means that for him the mixed linguistic area extended approximately to Orkistos, whereas Nakoleia and Dorylaeum merely designate the possible endpoints of Paul's route. Indeed, the two cities (like the entire territory after Laodicea Combusta) were situated politically in *Asia proconsularis*,[15] and the missionaries would have disobeyed the instructions of the Spirit and would have "spoken the word in Asia" (Acts 16:6). Both Nakoleia and Dorylaeum belonged not to the Celtic, but rather to the Phrygian linguistic territory, something true even of the locales to the south which Lake mentions.[16] Neither were the cities he enumerates connected by any ancient highway.[17] Hence there is no historically persuasive support for the assertion that the "Galatian country" is referring to the area around Nakoleia and Dorylaeum.

Moreover, one would have to assume that Paul had deviated from his consistently evident strategy of missioning in the larger Hellenized cities (§13.2.3). As far as any Jewish presence in the territory of Galatia is concerned, the same applies today as in the days of W. M. Ramsay, namely, that "the evidence is very sparse."[18] The alleged mention of Ancyra in the pro-Jewish edict of Augustus (Josephus, *Ant.* xvi.162-65) actually involves only a conjecture by J. J. Scaliger; in all likelihood, however, the decree was issued in the Roma-temple of Pergamum.[19] More recent possible epigraphic evidence for Jews or Judaizing tendencies in the territory of Galatia seems to derive largely from the Byzantine period.[20] Only a single Jewish inscription, probably from the third century A.D. (Amastris), is known from the neighboring northern territory of Paphlagonia.[21] What else could have prompted Paul to mission in an area whose special characteristic (according to Lake) was its linguistic inaccessibility? M. Dibelius saw this problem clearly: "If, as is possible, difficulties of language made it possible for them to speak to only a part of the population, Paul had to try all the harder to reach a wider sphere of activity to the north in the towns of Bithynia."[22]

14. In *BC* V (1933) 236.

15. To be sure, the western route from Antioch to Ancyra, although leading over Asiatic territory, seems to have been under the supervision of the governor of Galatia (*MAMA* VII 193).

16. Cf. W. M. Calder, in *MAMA* VII (1956) ix-xvi; F. F. Bruce, *BJRL* 52 (1969/70) 257f.; *The Epistle of Paul to the Galatians* (1982) 11f.

17. Cf. C. J. Hemer, *The Book of Acts in the Setting of Hellenistic History* (1989) 285f.

18. Schuerer, III/1 (1986) 34.

19. Cf. *ibid.*, 34f.

20. Cf. *ibid.*, 35.

21. B. Lifshitz, *Donateurs et fondateurs dans les synagogues juives* (1967) no. 35 (36f.).

22. *Paul*, ed. W. G. Kümmel (Eng. trans., 1953) 76. Concerning the particular suitability of Greek as an early Christian missionary language, cf. C. Mohrmann, *ZMR* 38

Given the historical geography of Asia Minor, a more satisfactory interpretation of Acts 16:6-8 suggests itself. Luke alludes to the fact that Paul's journey had as its goal all the areas of the province Galatia evangelized on what is known as his first missionary journey (§14.5). Iconium and Antioch lay in that part of Phrygia assigned to Galatia. If following profuse evidence one understands Φρυγία as an adjective, which in agreement with grammatical parallels and substantive analogies is through the word καί combined into a substantive unity with Γαλατική,[23] then ἡ Φρυγία καὶ Γαλατικὴ χώρα is referring to precisely this region, namely, Phrygian-Galatia.[24] This is also suggested by the single article, placed only once at the beginning. This understanding of the double expression would be additionally supported if the aorist participle κωλυθέντες were to be understood in the sense of an action following upon this.[25] The following plausible route can then be reconstructed. Paul used the *Via Sebaste* from Lystra via Iconium to the west as far as Antioch near Pisidia. There, where the highway forks off to Apamea, leading through the Lycus Valley to the Asiatic provincial capital Ephesus, the apostle was prevented "by the Spirit" from missioning in the province of Asia (Acts 16:6). One possible question here is whether another factor might also have been at work, namely, that the Jewish-Christian mission had already, even before Paul, reached Ephesus, with its strong Jewish population[26] (Acts 18:24-26).[27]

The related passage Acts 18:23 seems to militate against understanding this geographic information as referring to the provincial region "Phrygian-Galatia." After his mission in Greece and a visit to Jerusalem (Acts 18:22), Paul set out from Syrian Antioch and "went from place to place through the Galatian territory and Phrygia (διερχόμενος καθεξῆς τὴν Γαλατικὴν χώραν καὶ Φρυγίαν), strengthening all the disciples" (Acts 18:23). The linguistic parallel is incomplete. The position of καί and the word καθεξῆς indicate that

---

(1954) 103-11. Perhaps it was also true (despite Rom. 1:14) for the apostle what K. Holl states generally concerning the problem of languages in the early church: "It never occurred to a Greek for the sake of Christianity to learn a foreign language so that he might translate the Bible for another people" (in H. Frohnes and U. W. Knorr, eds., *Kirchengeschichte als Missionsgeschichte* I [1974] 393). On the other hand, see note 113 below.

23. Cf. C. J. Hemer, *JTS* 27 (1976) 122-26; 28 (1977) 99-101; *BJRL* 60 (1977/78) 45f., and *New Doc* IV (1987) 174.

24. Cf. further C. J. Hemer, *Themelios* 2 (1977) 84f.; F. F. Bruce, *The Epistle of Paul to the Galatians* (1982) 11, note 42; T. S. Mitchell, *ABD* II (1992) 871.

25. Cf. G. M. Lee, *NT* 9 (1967) 41f.; 17 (1975) 199; *Bibl* 51 (1970) 235-37.

26. Concerning the Jews of Asia Minor, cf. Schuerer, III/1 (1986) 17-32; P. Trebilco, *Jewish Communities in Asia Minor* (1991). Rabbinic witnesses can be found in Billerbeck II, 611f. Concerning Ephesus, cf. esp. C. J. Hemer, *The Letters to the Seven Churches of Asia in Their Local Setting* (1986) 36-41.

27. Cf. also W. P. Bowers, *Studies in Paul's Understanding of His Mission* (1976) 45f.

the reference is to two separate geographic designations, and thus Φρυγία is to be understood here as a substantive. Here Luke might be referring in addition to (Lycaonic and Phrygian) Galatia[28] to the Phrygia that belongs to the province of Asia.[29] This would fit well with the fact that the crossing of the upper country in Acts 19:1 (διελθόντα τὰ ἀνωτερικὰ μέρη) is presumably referring to the high road leading to the Cestrus Valley.[30] The fact that according to the letter to the Colossians Paul was originally known neither in Colossae nor in Laodicea (Col. 2:1), and that Hierapolis also did not represent a church founded by Paul (cf. Col. 4:12f.),[31] can be explained by assuming that at least at that time the apostle did not travel through the Lycus and Meander Valleys.

15.2.2. The Addressees of the Letter to the Galatians

If this understanding of the geographic information in Acts 16:6-8 and Acts 18:23 is correct, then, according to Luke, Paul never set foot in the region of Galatia. The only remaining arguments supporting an address to churches in this region are those taken from the letter to the Galatians itself. W. G. Kümmel, to whose *Introduction* repeated references have been made in this context, mentions two such reasons: "(1) If Gal was addressed to churches founded on the so-called first missionary journey, Paul would scarcely have written (2:1), 'Then I came into the regions of Syria and Cilicia,' but, 'Then I came to Syria and Cilicia, and on to you.'"[32] Quite apart from the fact that the apostle did not necessarily have to inform his readers about something they really did already know, even presupposing the regional hypothesis the silence concerning the first missionary journey remains problematical. Mention of south Galatia could have underscored the apostle's intentions in Galatians 1–2 (§13.1.1; 14.3): he is independent and far removed from Jerusalem! If indeed there were churches in south Galatia founded by Paul, then one can hardly understand why Palestinian Jewish Christians concentrated their own activities — activities directed against Paul's gospel, which was free from the law — precisely in the remote interior of Anatolia. Why did they spare south Galatia, which was both accessible and settled by Jews, so that the apostle did not have to direct his writing to Christians in this area? Especially if one

28. So already in the fourth century the Pontic bishop Asterius of Amasea (*ABD* II [1992] 871).

29. Cf. C. J. Hemer, *The Book of Acts in the Setting of Hellenistic History* (1989) 120.

30. Cf. *ibid.* A different view is taken by J. A. Bérard, *RAr* VI/5 (1935) 86f.

31. This information seems credible to me even assuming pseudonymity. Concerning the question of a connection with the Pauline school, see p. 31, note 7, above.

32. *Introduction to the New Testament* (Eng. trans., 1975) 298.

suspects the Galatian churches around Pessinus, technical considerations affecting travel already virtually insured that the Judaizers would move through south Galatia; after all, at that time there were no direct flights between Tel Aviv and Ankara.

Hence the final, and indeed stronger, remaining argument is: "(2) Paul could not possibly have written to the Lycaonians or the Pisidians, 'O you Galatians' (Gal 3:1), since that usage is not attested anywhere."[33] But how could the apostle have addressed Lycaonians, Phrygians, Pisidians, Greek speakers, and Roman colonists together other than with reference to their common province?[34] F. F. Bruce has justifiably objected to the psychological argument according to which the emphasis of one ethnic designation would have alienated the members of other population groups: "If Paul's readers found anything objectionable in being called 'foolish Galatians,' the objection arose from the adjective 'foolish' rather than from the substantive 'Galatians.' "[35] Since the time of Tiberius, attempts had been made to create a certain independent provincial identity through a strong propagation of the cult of the emperor in the sanctuaries in Ancyra, Pessinus, and Antioch.[36] Other epigraphic material also points in a similar direction.[37] For the Claudio-Neronian period, the comprehensive name *provincia Galatica* (e.g., *ILS* 9499, ll. 6f. [Ephesus, A.D. 54-66]) or ἐπαρχεία Γαλατική (e.g., *CIG* I 3991 [Iconium, A.D. 54]) also seems to have become established in addition to the enumeration of individual areas belonging to the province. The provincial designation *Galatia*/Γαλατία is attested in ancient writers (Ptolemy v.14; Tacitus, *Hist.* ii.9; *Ann.* xiii.35), as well as in the New Testament (1 Pet. 1:1).[38] C. J. Hemer has shown on the basis of inscriptional material the considerable degree to which the use of Γαλάτης, Γαλάται fluctuated at that time.[39]

There are at least two possible witnesses for an expanded meaning of the name Γαλάτης.[40] We must thus view as too dogmatic the assertion that

33. *Ibid.*

34. Cf. by contrast already T. Zahn, *Der Brief des Paulus an die Galater* ([3]1922) 11f. In the foreword to the reprint, M. Hengel speaks about a "stale argument" (1990, vii).

35. *The Epistle of Paul to the Galatians* (1982) 16.

36. Cf. S. Mitchell, *Chiron* 16 (1986) 33.

37. Cf. C. J. Hemer, *The Book of Acts in the Setting of Hellenistic History* (1989) 290-99.

38. Here the name stands amid the provincial designations "Pontus, Galatia, Cappadocia, Asia, and Bithynia," whose sequence probably has something to do with the letter courier's route. The enumeration is one possible indication that the letter was composed before A.D. 72, when Vespasian united Cappadocia with Galatia. Cf. C. J. Hemer, *ET* 89 (1978) 239-43.

39. *The Book of Acts in the Setting of Hellenistic History* (1989) 299-305.

40. In an inscription (A.D. 57) from Apollonia in Phrygia Galatica, the founder gives thanks that Zeus "brought [him] back to his home, the land of the Galatians (Γαλατῶν γαίης ἤγαγες εἰς πατρίδα)" (*MAMA* IV 140). W. M. Ramsay, *A Historical Commentary*

south Galatian churches could not be addressed by Ὦ Γαλάται.[41] Theologians would do well to consider the cautious conclusion of a historian of ancient history such as H. Volkmann: "The ambiguous term Galatia makes it difficult to decide whether the addressees of the Pauline letter to the Galatians are to be found in the entire Roman province or only in Galatia proper."[42] The address "you foolish Galatians" (Gal. 3:1) contains at most a possible indication, and by no means a compelling argument against the South Galatian understanding. It seems of considerably more weight that we have certain knowledge about south Galatian churches founded by Paul, whereas the conclusion from Acts concerning a Pauline mission in the region of Galatia has not been proved. If one postulates that Paul was active in the region of Galatia and that Luke simply knew nothing of such activity,[43] then in addition to the problems attaching to any such *argumentum e silentio* there still remain the historico-geographic reservations mentioned above.[44]

One can adduce other, if not compelling then at least supporting arguments for the view that the letter to the Galatians was addressed to churches in the southern part of the Roman province. To mention but two[45]: (1) The impor-

---

on St Paul's Epistle to the Galatians (1900) 135, already made reference to this. In Tacitus, *Ann.* xv.6, *"simul Pontica et Galatarum Cappadocumque auxilia"* might be referring to auxiliary troops from the province of Galatia. F. Mussner, *Der Galaterbrief* (⁵1987) 8, note 38a, cites in this context a letter from H. Bengston: "For the rest, I fear that in general the material does not allow a clear decision concerning the question of whether in the other sources the province of Galatia or the Galatians themselves are meant."

41. James M. Scott, in his study *Paul and the Nations* (1995), opens a completely new avenue of investigation by asking how Paul understood Γαλάται from the perspective of his own Jewish-geographic presuppositions. Josephus, *Ant.* i.123, identifies the Galatians with the descendants of Japheth's son Gomer (Gen. 10:2f.), and ascribes to them the area of the Roman province of Galatia as their home (Josephus, *Ant.* i.126). This refutes the main argument of the North Galatian hypothesis according to which Γαλάται could be referring only to the Celtic inhabitants of the region of Galatia. Josephus also uses the expression Phrygian-Galatia in a manner comparable to Acts 16:6 (*ibid.,* 201-8).

42. *KP* II (1962) 670.

43. Considered a possibility by G. Schille, *EDNT* I (Eng. trans., 1990) 233.

44. D. Lührmann, *Der Brief an die Galater* (1978) 10, e.g., writes thus: After his separation from Antioch, Paul allegedly journeyed "through the middle of Asia Minor toward the west" in the year A.D. 49, "perhaps with the goal of getting to Rome, the imperial capital, as quickly as possible. Along the way, he was held up for a time in Galatia. . . . This Galatia, approximately in the area of the modern Turkish capital Ankara, was a rather inhospitable, mountainous region." A glance at the map, however, shows that anyone wanting to get from Antioch to Rome as quickly as possible does not climb into the mountains, but rather onto a ship. And anyone who does choose the overland route hardly undertakes an additional round-trip to the north.

45. Cf. further W. Michaelis, *Einleitung in das Neue Testament* (³1961) 183-87; D. Guthrie, *Galatians* (1974) 15-27; F. F. Bruce, *The Epistle of Paul to the Galatians* (1982) 3-18; R. Y.-K. Fung, *The Epistle to the Galatians* (1988) 1-3.

tant role Barnabas plays in the writing (Gal. 2:1, 9, 13), and the way in which Paul speaks about him, better fit the assumption that the Cypriot Levite participated in the founding of the churches.[46] There are even fewer indications for Barnabas's having been active in north Galatia than for Paul's having missioned there. (2) Even granting that one must be cautious with the assertion that Paul uses names exclusively of provinces,[47] his preference for them is nonetheless unmistakable (1 Thess. 1:7; 4:10; 1 Cor. 16:15, 19; 2 Cor. 1:8; 8:1; 9:2, 4, 9; 11:10; Rom. 15:26; 16:5).[48] It is especially important to demonstrate why within the narrow context of 1 Corinthians 16 we can be certain the apostle is speaking about the provinces Macedonia (1 Cor. 16:5), Achaia (1 Cor. 16:15), and Asia (1 Cor. 16:19: αἱ ἐκκλησίαι τῆς Ἀσίας), and yet by "Galatia" (1 Cor. 16:1: ταῖς ἐκκλησίαις τῆς Γαλατίας) is referring exclusively to the region. The assumption of locating the Galatian churches in the southern part of the province Galatia is supported by weighty historico-geographic considerations, and is also by no means the domain of conservative scholars, as the example of J. Knox shows.[49] T. S. Mitchell, perhaps the foremost living authority on ancient Galatia, has even concluded that "the most authoritative champion of the South Galatian Theory was the great explorer of Asia Minor, W. M. Ramsay, and although the North Galatian Theory finds many supporters, his work should long ago have put the matter beyond dispute."[50]

46. Cf. R. J. Bauckham, *JSNT* 2 (1979) 61-70; F. Watson, *Paul* (1986) 56f.

47. The counterexamples presented by W. G. Kümmel, *Introduction to the New Testament* (Eng. trans., 1975) 297, however, are hardly persuasive. (1) Concerning "Syria and Cilicia" (Gal. 1:21) not being taken as "the Seleucid territory in which Antioch lay" *(ibid.),* but rather as the name of the double province, cf. §13.1.2. (2) How is it certain that the apostle is always thinking of the region when using the term Judea? In 2 Cor. 1:16, Judea stands next to the provincial designation Macedonia. It is difficult to say how much the name Judea encompasses in 1 Thess. 2:14. Cf. T. Holtz, *Der erste Brief an die Thessalonicher* (²1990) 99f. Luke's use of Ἰουδαία is extremely variable, and includes its use as a provincial designation (Lk. 3:1; 23:6). Cf. M. Hengel, *ZDPV* 99 (1983) 151. (3) In Gal. 1:17 it is uncertain whether "Arabia" is referring to Nabatean territory (§13.3.1), and whether one should thus demand the "official name for the Nabataean realm" *(ibid.).* In any case, at that time (before A.D. 106) there existed as yet no *provincia Arabia.* The question is not whether Paul used regional names, but rather whether in the case of concurrence between regional and provincial names one should think sooner of the former than the latter.

48. Cf., in this regard, O. Haas, *Paulus der Missionar* (1971) 83-86; W. P. Bowers, *Studies in Paul's Understanding of His Mission* (1976) 70-72.

49. *Chapters in a Life of Paul,* rev. ed. (1987) 57-60. The most recent advocates of the Province Hypothesis include R. N. Longenecker, *Galatians* (1990) lxi-lxxi; H. W. Neudorfer, *JET* 5 (1991) 47-62; D. A. Carson, D. J. Moo, and L. Morris, *An Introduction to the New Testament* (1992) 290-93; D. Wenham in *The Book of Acts in Its Literary Setting* (1993) 226-43; and C. Breytenbach, *Paulus und Barnabas in Galatien* (1996). Earlier bibliography can be found in J. Rohde, *Der Brief des Paulus an die Galater* (1989) 6f.

50. *ABD* II (1992) 871.

What is known as the first missionary journey emerges as the *terminus post quem* for dating the letter to the Galatians, presupposing a south Galatian address. It is widely assumed that Gal. 4:13 ("you know that it was because of a physical infirmity that I τὸ πρότερον announced the gospel to you") presupposes an earlier visit.[51] Now, in Hellenistic Greek, πρῶτος as a rule means "the first of two times," whereas τὸ πρότερον usually only means "earlier," or "the only earlier time."[52] Even assuming the first meaning, τὸ πρότερον could also suggest the double visit to the south Galatian churches on the outward and return trips during the first missionary journey.[53]

One should consider only with the greatest caution the argument that the thematic proximity of the letters to the Galatians and to the Romans also allows us to conclude their temporally proximate composition.[54] Several more recent studies emphasize justifiably that Paul already must have arrived at the basic outline of his understanding of the law and salvation soon after the events at Damascus.[55] Scholars often assume that Paul's position regarding the question of the law is more highly developed in the letter to the Romans, and the letter to the Galatians is thus removed temporally a bit from the former.[56] More recently, G. Howard has even adduced the argument of a theological development from Galatians to Romans to support an extremely early dating of the letter to the Galatians (before the Apostolic Council).[57] The dating of the letter to the Galatians is closely related to the question of how in connection with Galatians 1–2 and Acts 9–15 one reconstructs the events surrounding the "Apostolic Council" (§17.1.3), something which is, however, utterly controversial.[58] Our own geographic-chronological reconstruction yields two conclusions: (1) The

51. So, e.g., W. G. Kümmel, *Introduction to the New Testament* (Eng. trans., 1975) 302.

52. This is emphasized by two commentators as different as H. D. Betz, *Galatians* (1979) 224, note 52, and F. F. Bruce, *The Epistle of Paul to the Galatians* (1982) 209.

53. Cf. C. J. Hemer, *Themelios* 2 (1977) 83, note 7.

54. So especially U. Borse, *Der Standort des Galaterbriefes* (1972) 120-39. A classic formulation of this argument can already be found in J. B. Lightfoot, *The Epistle of St. Paul to the Galatians* (1865) 44-50.

55. Cf. S. Kim, *The Origin of Paul's Gospel* (²1984) 269-329; C. Dietzfelbinger, *Die Berufung des Paulus als Ursprung seiner Theologie,* 90-137. See also p. 395, note 8 below.

56. Cf. most recently C. K. Barrett, *ZTK* 86 (1989) 22: "We may also see how his thinking develops. In the letter to the Galatians, the law appears as an intermezzo. . . . In the letter to the Romans, Paul says even more clearly that the law stepped in so that sin would become even more powerful, but now he has seen how the gospel upholds the law (Rom. 3:31)."

57. *Paul: Crisis in Galatia* (1979) (maintained in ²1990, ix).

58. Here, too, the history of scholarship is thoroughly instructive. Cf. A. Wechsler, *Geschichtsbild und Apostelstreit* (1991).

addressees of the letter to the Galatians are churches in the southern part of the province of Galatia, founded on the first missionary journey (before A.D. 49), which itself thus represents a *terminus post quem* for its composition. (2) Since Paul probably visited these churches only once (cf. Gal. 1:6; 4:13), the beginning of the second journey to Asia Minor (probably A.D. 52) constitutes the *terminus ante quem.* Chronological possibilities for composition then include the two datings either before the Apostolic Council from Antioch,[59] or at the end of the second missionary journey in Corinth.[60] Compared to the position often advocated that the letter was composed in Ephesus, both these views have the advantage of making comprehensible why, despite the severity of the Galatian crisis, Paul wrote only one letter, but did not announce a visit soon (see pp. 395f. above). Whatever conclusion one reaches here, it is worth noting that a scholar of ancient history of the stature of F. Millar calls the letter to the Galatians "almost certainly the earliest" of all the Pauline letters.[61]

15.2.3. Through Mysia to Troas

If Paul found the way into the province of Asia closed off, then this involved not only the heartland Lydia, but also Mysia, mentioned thereafter in fourth position in Isa. 66:19 (Meshech [see p. 252 above]). "On the heights of Mysia (ἐλθόντες κατὰ τὴν Μυσίαν)," perhaps at an important crossroad such as Dorylaeum (Eskişehir), or more likely Cotyaeum (Kutahyah),[62] the apostle thus tried to reach Bithynia (Tubal), mentioned in fifth position in the prophecy (Acts 16:7). However, the mission in this area, too, with its large Hellenistic cities such as Nicomedia[63] and its strong Jewish colonies (Philo, *Leg. ad Gaium* 281)[64] was prohibited "by the Spirit of Jesus" (Acts 16:7). Once again, one can ask[65] whether news of already existing Jewish-

---

59. Recently advocated most extensively by R. N. Longenecker, *Galatians* (1990) lxi-c, followed by I. H. Marshall, *The Acts of the Apostles* (1992) 93-95; and R. Bauckham in *The Book of Acts in Its Palestinian Setting* (1995) 415-80. The view advocating a composition of Galatians during the Apostolic Council (before the Apostolic Decree was passed!), as argued by F. J. Badcock, *The Pauline Epistles* (1937) 14-27, represents an anomaly.

60. Cf. esp. T. Zahn, *Introduction to the New Testament* (Eng. trans., 1909) 1.193-202; M. Albertz, *Die Botschaft des Neuen Testaments* I/2 (1952) 227; W. Michaelis, *Einleitung in das Neue Testament* (³1961) 190f. (as a possibility), and recently J. R. Armogathe, *Paul* (1980) 208; A. Wainwright, *JSNT* 8 (1980) 66-70; H. Binder, in R. F. Collins, ed., *The Thessalonian Correspondence* (1990) 90.

61. *JJS* 44 (1993) 38.

62. Cf. F. F. Bruce, *The Book of Acts* (1988) 306f.

63. Cf. B. F. Harris, *ANRW* II 7.2 (1980) 866-69.

64. Cf. Schuerer, III/1 (1986) 37f.

65. So also W. P. Bowers, *Studies in the Understanding of Paul's Mission* (1976) 72, note 1.

Christian churches played a role here.[66] W. Elliger rejects the assumption that the sparse geographic information in this passage (only regions, but no locales such as, e.g., in Acts 20:1ff.) is a result primarily of Luke's own lack of knowledge. Rather, Luke allegedly wanted to use this concentration on only a few designations to make clear the goal-oriented guidance of the Spirit into the new mission area of Europe (cf. Acts 16:9f.).[67] According to our own understanding, it is striking that Luke mentions precisely three thwarted destinations to which Paul was directed by Isa. 66:19: Asia (Lydia), Mysia (Meshech),[68] and Bithynia (Tubal). This might indicate that the *auctor ad Theophilum* did indeed possess more specific knowledge here regarding the apostle's original intentions.[69] The first we-account begins immediately following (Acts 16:11ff.).

W. P. Bowers has drawn attention to one difficulty with the Lukan account[70]: if Acts 16:8 (παρελθόντες δὲ τὴν Μυσίαν κατέβησαν εἰς Τρῳάδα) means that from a point of departure such as Dorylaeum[71] or, more likely, Cotyaeum[72] Paul traveled directly through the region of Mysia, then contra his otherwise habitual pattern he did not use a main highway.[73] A larger road would have run in a northwesterly direction to Apamea on the Propontis (Sea of Marmara), from which Paul then could have traveled further either along

66. Pilgrims from Pontus are mentioned already in connection with the first Pentecost in Jerusalem (Acts 2:9). Paul's later co-worker Aquila came from Pontus, which had been united into a double province with Bithynia (Acts 18:2). Although he was already a Christian when the apostle met him in Corinth (see pp. 190f. above), his conversion can naturally also have taken place in Rome. 1 Pet. 1:1 presupposes churches (founded during a Petrine mission before the Apostolic Council? [so C. P. Thiede, *Simon Peter* (1986) 155], but established at least before A.D. 72 [see note 38]) which were already quite strong at the beginning of the second century (Pliny the Younger, *Ep.* x.96).

67. *Paulus in Griechenland* (²1987) 24-28.

68. Although Acts 16:7f. does not mention Mysia as one of Paul's original goals, the statement that the missionaries did pass through this region (Acts 16:8: παρελθόντες) suggests one should probably associate the Spirit's prevention of the proclamation (Acts 16:7) commensurately with Mysia as well.

69. Concerning the possible itinerary, cf. also F. F. Bruce, *The Book of Acts* (1988) 357. Even J. Knox, *Chapters in a Life of Paul,* rev. ed. (1987) 50, expresses optimism here.

70. *Studies in Paul's Understanding of His Mission* (1976) 41-43; *JTS* 30 (1979) 507-11. Cf. also C. J. Hemer, *The Book of Acts in the Setting of Hellenistic History* (1989) 112f.

71. So J. Bérard, *RA* VI/5 (1935) 80-82.

72. Cf. T. R. S. Broughton, *Festschrift K. Lake* (1937) 135.

73. Although such a highway was conjectured by J. A. R. Munro and H. M. Anthony, *GJ* 9 (1897) 256-58 (with a map after p. 248), evidence supports only a highway through the Troada (W. P. Bowers, *JTS* 30 [1979] 509). But cf. also T. S. Broughton, *loc. cit.,* 136-38.

the coastal highway or by ship.[74] The fact that he apparently set out for Troas by the most direct route possible might be related to the fact that it was the most important seaport for passage to Macedonia.[75] Theoretically, the journey from Troas could also have led to a seaport such as Maroneia in the province (since A.D. 44) of Thrace. Although Theodoret was convinced of this in the first half of the fifth century (*In Ep. ad Rom.* 15 [PG 82.213B]), this doubtless represents merely a conclusion from the καὶ κύκλῳ of Rom. 15:19.[76]

Several conceivable factors might explain why Paul, against his usual custom of entering into neighboring provinces, excluded Thrace, which may be seen to constitute the connecting link between Asia Minor and Macedonia. His exclusion of this province probably did not owe primarily to the slight Jewish presence there,[77] nor to the fact that at that time the Thracians themselves were only slightly Hellenized,[78] but rather to the fact that after Bithynia (Tubal), the next (sixth) goal mentioned in Isa. 66:19 was Greece or Macedonia (see p. 252 above). In addition, the sea route to Neapolis was not much farther than to one of the Thracian seaports. In his own turn, Luke mentions that the choice of Macedonia as a missionary area resulted from pneumatic experiences and decisions (Acts 16:9f.).[79] The emphasis in Acts on the transition to Europe as a pronounced stage might well have reflected Paul's own feelings.[80] Although his reference to the "beginning of the gospel, when I left Macedonia" (Phil. 4:15: ἐν ἀρχῇ τοῦ εὐαγγελίου, ὅτε ἐξῆλθον ἀπὸ Μακεδονίας) is indeed formulated from the perspective of the Philippians (§14.2.1), a consideration of geographic significance for Paul himself may be resonating as well: Macedonia was the beginning of his mission in a part of Hellas, indeed of Europe, that had hitherto been utterly untouched by the gospel.

74. Cf. W. M. Ramsay, *St. Paul the Traveller and the Roman Citizen* (1893) 197; J. Bérard, *RA* VI/5 (1935) 82f.

75. Cf. W. P. Bowers, *JTS* 30 (1979) 510f. Concerning Troas, cf. further §15.4.2 below.

76. Cf. R. Pillinger, *AÖAW.PH* 120 (1983) 201.

77. Cf. Schuerer, III/1 (1986) 72.

78. Although the Roman province Thrace did include the Macedonian coastal strip east of the Nestus as well as the islands of Samothrace (cf. Acts 16:11) and Thassos (B. Gerov, *ANRW* II 7.1 [1979] 231f.), the interior mountain region was inhabited largely by autochthonal Thracians. A final, great popular uprising against the Romans occurred in A.D. 26 (Tacitus, *Ann.* iv.46-51). Cf. C. M. Danov, *ANRW* II 7.1 (1979) 142-45. The Thracian language was still quite widespread in the first century. Cf. R. Schmitt, *ANRW* II 29.2 (1983) 563-65.

79. W. P. Bowers, *JTS* 30 1979) 511, remarks in this regard: "Paul's experience of supernatural guidance did not generate his human intention but rather responded to the intention already formed."

80. Cf. W. Elliger, *Paulus in Griechenland* (²1987) 27f. The tripartite division of the world into Europe, Asia, and Libya had been valid in the entire ancient world since Herodotus iv.42. Cf. H. Treidler, *KP* II (1967) 448f.

15.3. Initial Activity in Europe

15.3.1. From Neapolis to Thessalonica

The first we-account of Acts begins with the two-day journey from Troas, past Samothrace, and on to Neapolis (Acts 16:11). The concentration on Roman colonies is demonstrated yet again by the fact that no activity is mentioned in connection with the seaport itself,[81] the report focusing rather on the immediate journey to Philippi.[82] This preference does not represent merely one of Luke's literary peculiarities, but rather quite apparently corresponded also to Paul's own intentions (see pp. 149, 277 above). A. N. Sherwin-White has suggested that the disturbances in Philippi (Acts 16:19-24; cf. 1 Thess. 2:2) were also enflamed by the news of Claudius' edict against the Jews of Rome.[83] For chronological and other reasons, however, one must rather suspect that Paul learned of this measure in Thessalonica (§18.4.2-4).

The description of the journey in Acts 17:1, beginning in Philippi ("they passed through Amphipolis and Apollonia and came to Thessalonica, where there was a synagogue of the Jews"), presupposes that the apostle completed this trip on the great imperial east-west highway, the *Via Egnatia*, in the shortest possible time (§16.2.4). The description of the route alone suggests that Paul did not engage in missionary activity in either of the two interim stations.[84] This is noteworthy insofar as Amphipolis was the main city of the first district of Macedonia and, in part because of its favorable location near the mouth of the river Strymon, constituted a clearly significant center.[85] Paul quite obviously had the provincial capital in mind as a goal with Thessalonica (§18.1).

81. Concerning Neapolis, cf. P. Collart, *Philippes* (1937) 102-32; W. Elliger, *loc. cit.*, 32-77; R. Riesner, *GBL* II (1988) 1037f. (bibliography); F. Papazoglou, *Les villes de Macédoine* (1988) 403f.

82. Cf. P. Collart, *Philippes ville de Macédoine* (1937); P. Lemerle, *Philippes et la Macédoine Orientale* (1945) 7-68; J. Finegan, *The Archaeology of the New Testament* II (1981) 101-6; F. Papazoglou, *Les villes de Macédoine* (1988) 405-13; R. Riesner, *GBL* III (1989) 1196-99; and now especially P. Pilhofer, *Philippi* (1995).

83. *Roman Society and Roman Law in the New Testament* (1963) 81.

84. Contra E. von Dobschütz, *Die Thessalonicher-Briefe* (⁷1909) 9, cf. R. Riesner, *BK* 44 (1989) 79-81.

85. This is shown by excavations (D. Lazaridis, Ἀμφίπολις καὶ Ἄργιλος [1972]; *AncMac* IV [1986] 353-64) which still have not been concluded. My thanks to the present archaeologist, Professor Kalliope Lazaridis (University of Thessalonica), for an on-site introduction. Concerning the history of the city, cf. O. Hirschfeld, *PRE* I 2 (1894) 1949-52; F. Papazoglou, *Les villes de Macédoine* (1988) 392-97. M. F. Unger, *BS* 119 (1962) 38, is completely incorrect in asserting that "at this period it [Amphipolis] possessed no great importance."

15.3.2. Failure of the Initial Plan for Rome?

According to his own witness, Paul had already long harbored a plan to go to Rome: "I want you to know, brothers, that I have often (πολλάκις) intended to come to you, but thus far have been prevented (καὶ ἐκωλύθην ἄχρι τοῦ δεῦρο)" (Rom. 1:13). Not only had the apostle already been prevented several times from coming (Rom. 15:22: ἐνεκοπτόμην τὰ πολλὰ τοῦ ἐλθεῖν πρὸς ὑμᾶς), but his wish to visit them was already several years old (Rom. 15:23: ἐπιποθίαν δὲ ἔχων τοῦ ἐλθεῖν πρὸς ὑμᾶς ἀπὸ πολλῶν ἐτῶν). Rome was apparently also already on the apostle's mind when he set foot on European soil for the first time. G. Bornkamm remarks in this regard: "We can assume with relative certainty that at the latest since Asia Minor and his trip through Macedonia to Thessalonica, Rome appeared to him as a distant goal. This is indicated by his own statements in the later letter to the Romans."[86] It could be that Paul wanted to push forward on the *Via Egnatia*[87] as far as the Illyrian coast of the Adriatic, perhaps to Dyrrhachium, the seaport and Roman colony with Italian privilege[88] (cf. Rom. 15:19).[89] From the Macedonian coast of the Adriatic, the apostle could then have reached Brundisium (Brindisi) in Italy after a short crossing passage, and then come to Rome on the *Via Appia*. Our own reconstruction of the events in Thessalonica and Beroea also suggests that Paul originally wanted to journey on farther to the west (§18.4).

The alteration of the route to the south, however, prompted by adverse circumstances, may not have been construed as an embarrassing solution for the apostle. Isa. 66:19 LXX has not only Macedonia, but all of Greece in view (Ἑλλάς). The altered route westward and the difficulties in Macedonia may thus have been considered divine indications that, commensurate with the prophetic preview, Paul now undertake a missionary push into the Greek heartland, the province of Achaia. Paul's route from Thessalonica via Athens and on to Corinth as portrayed by Acts (Acts 17:1, 15; 18:1) is confirmed by the self-witness of the letters (1 Thess. 2:2; 3:1; Phil. 4:15f.; 2 Cor. 11:7-9).[90] In Achaia, too, the apostle concentrated his activity in the provincial capital,

---

86. *Paulus* ([5]1983) 70 (Eng. trans., *Paul, Paulus* [1971]).

87. Regarding the course of the highway in its western portion, cf. F. O'Sullivan, *The Egnatian Way* (1972) 36-91; P. A. MacKay, *AncMac* II (1977) 201-10; N. G. L. Hammond, *JRS* 64 (1974) 185-94; *AncMac* IV (1986) 247-53; F. W. Walbank, *AncMac* IV (1986) 671-80.

88. Cf. F. Papazoglou, *ANRW* II 7.1 (1979) 358-60.

89. A. Suhl, *Paulus und seine Briefe* (1975) 92-110, 342 (similarly also F. Laub, *1. und 2. Thessalonicherbrief* [1985] 8f.), believes that Paul did in fact journey from Thessalonica to the Illyrian coast of the Adriatic, and only turned around there; but chronological difficulties militate against this assumption (§18.4.2).

90. Cf. T. F. Campbell, *JBL* 74 (1955) 82f.

Corinth,[91] with its old and significant Jewish community[92] (Acts 18:1-18).
When Paul broke off his stay in Corinth soon after the end of the proconsulate
of Gallio (§11), Claudius was still in power, and his Roman edict concerning
the Jews prompted the apostle to view for the moment the way west as closed
off. He found no support in Isa. 66:19 for journeying to the north, into the
provinces either of Illyricum or Moesia; moreover, it is doubtful that either
region had any Jewish communities. Ultimately there were other reasons as
well for returning to the east as long as the way west was not open.

15.4. Closing a Gap: Asia

15.4.1. Ephesus

Among the eschatological missionary areas prefigured in Isa. 66:19, in the
east it was above all the region of the province of Asia that was still outstanding. But it was not only the prophetic oracle that could suggest to Paul that
he now close this gap in his work. There was no connecting link between the
churches in south Galatia responsible to him (cf. 1 Cor. 16:1) and those in
Macedonia and Achaia.[93] If Paul could create such, then the danger would
diminish that the Galatian churches could be alienated from their cofounder.
Thus the apostle journeyed from Corinth's eastern harbor, Cenchreae (cf. Acts
18:18),[94] to Ephesus (Acts 18:19-21), the capital of the province of Asia, and
indeed the metropolis of Asia Minor in the larger sense. According to Acts,
Paul preached only before the Jews; neither is any Christian congregation
mentioned. One may speculate whether the enigmatic remark that Paul separated from Aquila and Priscilla in Ephesus (κἀκείνους κατέλιπεν), even
though at the same time he preached in the synagogue there (Acts 18:19), is
perhaps an indication that these fellow workers went to a Jewish-Christian

91. Cf. J. Wiseman, *ANRW* II 7.2 (1980) 438-548; J. Murphy-O'Connor, *St. Paul's Corinth* (1983); *ABD* I (1992) 1134-39; W. Elliger, *Paulus in Griechenland* (³1987) 200-251; V. P. Furnish, *BAR* 15/3 (1988) 14-27; R. Riesner, *GBL* II (1988) 815-19 (bibliography).

92. The letter of Agrippa I to Caligula mentions, in addition to Argos, Corinth as the only city among the Jewish groups in European territories (Philo, *Leg. Gai.* 281). Concerning the (relatively) plentiful Jewish inscriptions, cf. Schuerer, III/1 (1986) 65f. Of particular interest is *SEG* 29 (1979) 300: διδάσ[καλος] καὶ ἀρχ[ισυνάγωγ]ος τῆ[ς συναγω-γῆς?]. Cf. *NewDoc* IV (1987) 213f.

93. This consideration also comes to expression in a certain fashion in J. Knox, *Chapters in a Life of Paul*, rev. ed. (1987) 350.

94. Concerning Cenchreae, cf. J. Wiseman, *The Land of the Ancient Corinthians* (1978) 64-69; J. Murphy-O'Connor, *St. Paul's Corinth* (1983) 17-22; R. Riesner, *GBL* II (1988) 775 (bibliography).

church already existing there, or that they founded such a church there.⁹⁵ Luke has Paul depart shortly thereafter without explanation, though the apostle does admittedly express the hope that he will soon return (Acts 18:21). F. J. A. Hort remarked concerning this brief visit that "on his return to the East, though he had little time to spare, it would seem that he could not be satisfied without at least setting foot in Ephesus."⁹⁶

An equally brief and in some sense puzzling remark asserts that Paul traveled to Caesarea, and from there "went up to greet the church (ἀναβὰς καὶ ἀσπασάμενος τὴν ἐκκλησίαν), and then went down to Antioch" (Acts 18:22). "The church" can only be referring to the church of Jerusalem.⁹⁷ There is no real reason why Luke should have invented the apostle's Nazirite vows and the Palestine journey.⁹⁸ Even if we should move the usual dating of the letter to the Galatians to the period thereafter, no insuperable hindrance arises concerning the historicity of this journey, since in Galatians 1–2 the apostle is concerned with enumerating his journeys to Jerusalem only within the time frame from his conversion to the Apostolic Council (Gal. 2:1ff.) or to the Antiochene incident (Gal. 2:11ff.). This journey to the seat of the earliest church does make sense if Paul could hope to secure his own missionary work — now being carried out independently — through discussions with the leaders there.⁹⁹

It is also possible that the apostle's commitment to the Jerusalem collection (§15.5.2), whose preparations become evident at the latest after A.D. 54 in Corinth, and previously already in Galatia (1 Cor. 16:1f.), can be traced back to this visit to the holy city.¹⁰⁰ Anyone who considers such efforts to be beneath the apostle's theological dignity should at least consider the advantages of practical congregational work: with regard both to distance and to technical considerations of travel, south Galatia lay nearer to Jerusalem than to Macedonia and Achaia. Paul could not be indifferent to the kinds of influence coming into the northwest from the Jewish Christians of Palestine. Perhaps the apostle heard about such problems, or even experienced corresponding difficulties himself in

95. See now W. Thiessen, *Christen in Ephesus* (1995) 28-89.
96. Cited after W. M. Ramsay, in *Pauline and Other Studies* (²1906) 77.
97. Cf. G. Schneider, *Die Apostelgeschichte* II (1982) 256.
98. Cf. R. Pesch, *Die Apostelgeschichte* II (1986) 157. G. Lüdemann, in B. C. Corley, *Colloquy on New Testament Studies* (1983) 300, also concludes that "the absence of a direct reference to Jerusalem is a sure sign that we are dealing with a tradition, and not redaction, for Luke usually expresses special interest for trips to Jerusalem."
99. In 1 Cor. 9:6, Paul speaks more positively about Barnabas than one might expect following their disagreement (Acts 15:36-40; cf. Gal. 2:13?). Perhaps the apostle met with his former missionary companion during this trip to Judea and Syria and was able to smooth out differences. Contra J. Georgi, *Der Armen gedenken* (1994) 117.
100. Cf. C. J. Hemer, *The Book of Acts in the Setting of Hellenistic History* (1989) 257, and J. Sanchez Bosch, *NTS* 37 (1991) 346.

Ephesus, and Luke — following his own irenic inclinations — passed over these in silence.[101] But theologically, too, Paul did not necessarily have to be less prepared to come to an understanding at that time than during the period in which he wrote the letter to the Romans. Thus one can agree with R. Pesch that "in all probability, one may assume that after his great successes in Galatia, Macedonia, and Achaia, Paul wanted to establish connections between his own churches and the headquarters just mentioned [Jerusalem, Antioch], thus securing the unity of the emerging church."[102]

One can see how important to Paul was the connection with the south Galatian congregations from the fact that from Palestine he did not journey to his destination, Ephesus, by ship, but rather took upon himself the longer, more arduous overland route. In this way he could "strengthen all the disciples" (ἐπιστηρίζων πάντας τοὺς μαθητάς) as he traveled through "the Galatian territory and Phrygia" (see pp. 285f. above) (Acts 18:23). The apostle made the provincial capital of Asia[103] his center of activity for several years (§12.1.3), during which churches were also founded in the surrounding area (1 Cor. 16:19). From Ephesus, Paul maintained contact with Greece by means of letters, of which at least the so-called[104] first letter to the Corinthians has come down to us (cf. 1 Cor. 16:8: ἐπιμενῶ δὲ ἐν Ἐφέσῳ). This writing is probably to be dated toward the end of the Ephesian period (cf. 1 Cor. 15:32; 16:5-9) (§12.1), when, despite considerable resistance, the apostle was still hoping for significant missionary successes (1 Cor. 16:9). One possible congruency between this letter and the book of Acts is the sending of Timothy to Macedonia (Acts 19:22) or Corinth (1 Cor. 16:10f.; cf. 4:17).[105] 1 Cor. 7:26 (ἀνάγκη ἐνεστῶτα) might be referring to the effects of a previous famine (between A.D. 52 and 54) (see p. 130 above).

In my opinion, both the assumption of an interim visit to Macedonia and certain hypotheses concerning letter division[106] become superfluous if

101. Cf. also D. T. Rowlingson, *JBL* 69 (1950) 342f.

102. *Die Apostelgeschichte* II (1986) 157f.

103. Cf. D. Knibbe and W. Alzinger, *ANRW* II 7.2 (1980) 748-830; W. Elliger, *Ephesos* (1985); R. E. Oster, *ABD* II (1992) 542-49; and P. Treblico in A1CS II (1994) 291-363. Concerning Jews in Ephesus, cf. G. H. R. Horsley, *NewDoc* IV (1987) 231f.; *NT* 34 (1992) 121-27; D. Knibbe, H. Engelmann, and B. Iplikcioglu, *JÖAI* 59 (1989) 219f.; P. Trebilco, *Jewish Communities in Asia Minor* (1991) 310 (index). Concerning bibliography at large, cf. R. E. Oster, *A Bibliography of Ancient Ephesus* (1987).

104. According to 1 Cor. 5:9, it was at least the second letter.

105. Cf. D. Georgi, *Die Geschichte der Kollekte des Paulus für Jerusalem* (1965) 94 (Eng. trans., *Remembering the Poor* [1992]).

106. After surveying modern commentaries, R. Bieringer, *ETL* 72 (1991) 120, concludes that "the original unity of the second letter to the Corinthians should again be seriously considered." Concerning the basic problematic of the division hypotheses, cf. Excursus III/1 (pp. 404-6).

one follows the basic features of N. Hyldahl's reconstruction:[107] the "letter of tears" (2 Cor. 2:3f.; 7:8f.) is referring — as patristic exegesis (e.g., Theodoret, Ephraem, Ambrosiaster) consistently assumed[108] — to the first letter to the Corinthians, which was dispatched in place of a delayed visit. The second letter to the Corinthians (esp. 2 Cor. 10–13), too, functioned as a renewed *ersatz* for the apostle's own visit. But now, at the third attempt, Paul really will come (2 Cor. 13:1: τρίτον τοῦτο ἔρχομαι πρὸς ὑμᾶς). Neither does 2 Cor. 2:1 (μὴ πάλιν ἐν λύπῃ πρὸς ὑμᾶς ἐλθεῖν) necessarily refer to a previous interim visit. The context suggests that in 2 Cor. 1:23–2:2, Paul is picking up again the theme of the abandoned travel plans (2 Cor. 1:15f.). The apostle did not again come to Corinth (2 Cor. 1:23: οὐκέτι ἦλθον εἰς Κόρινθον) after the basic proclamation together with Silvanus and Timothy (2 Cor. 1:19). Hence πάλιν is not to be taken with ἐλθεῖν, but rather with ἐν λύπῃ: at his (first) return to Corinth, the apostle does not want to come in sadness. The strong epistolary contact with the Corinthians confirms the Lukan picture (Acts 18:1-18) of Corinth as having been an especially important center for Paul.

15.4.2. Troas

Paul did not write the second letter to the Corinthians from Ephesus. The apostle broke off his missionary work in Ephesus apparently because of "the affliction we experienced in Asia (2 Cor. 1:8: τῆς θλίψεως ἡμῶν τῆς γενο-μένης ἐν τῇ Ἀσίᾳ)." These afflictions probably included imprisonment in Ephesus, during which many consider the letter to Philemon to have been composed (§12.1.1). Since the letter to the Philippians seems to imply that Paul and Timothy had not visited the church again since its founding, this writing also might belong to the period of the Ephesian imprisonment.[109] Paul now shifted the center of his activity to (Alexander) Troas, where he experienced greater success (2 Cor. 2:12: ἐλθὼν δὲ εἰς τὴν Τρῳάδα εἰς τὸ εὐαγγέλιον τοῦ Χριστοῦ, καὶ θύρας μοι ἀνεῳγμένης ἐν κυρίῳ). With this stay in yet another Roman colony and at a significant traffic crossroad,[110] he had now expanded his work to include Mysia as well. The Pauline gospel was able to spread on the great coastal highway along the Propontis into Bithynia. At this time, Paul could genuinely have the impression that in the eastern part of the

107. *ZNW* 64 (1973) 289-306, and both revised and somewhat modified in *Die paulinische Chronologie* (1986) 88-106.

108. Cf. E. Golla, *Zwischenbesuch und Zwischenbrief* (1922) 10-19.

109. Cf. N. Hyldahl, *Die paulinische Chronologie* (1986) 18-21, with express agreement from R. Jewett, *JBL* 107 (1988) 549.

110. Cf. W. Ruge, *PRE* II 13 (1939) 526-83; J. M. Cook, *The Troad* (1973) 16-21; C. J. Hemer, *TynBul* 26 (1975) 79-112; M. Brändl, *GBL* III (1989) 1599-1601 (bibliography); E. M. Yamauchi, *ABD* VI (1992) 666f.

Mediterranean basin, within the parameters provided by the prophecy of Isa. 66:19, "the gospel of Christ had been fulfilled (πεπληρωκέναι)" (Rom. 15:19).

All that was missing now was the great push to the boundaries of the west. For this, too, the way was opened in connection with the end of the mission in Ephesus: Claudius died on 13 October A.D. 54, and his successor, Nero, seems soon thereafter to have lifted the restrictions for Jews coming to Rome (see p. 200 above). Although Luke is silent concerning this stay in Troas, he does associate this plan with the end of the Ephesian ministry: "Now after these things had been accomplished, Paul resolved in the Spirit to go through Macedonia and Achaia, and then to go on to Jerusalem. He said, 'After I have gone there, I must also see Rome'" (Acts 19:21). Indeed, Paul was already considering at least the possibility of an additional trip to Jerusalem[111] during the composition of the first Corinthian letter (1 Cor. 16:4: ἐὰν δὲ ἄξιον ᾖ τοῦ κἀμὲ πορεύεσθαι . . .), and by the second Corinthian letter this had become his firm intention (2 Cor. 1:16: ὑφ' ὑμῶν προπεμφθῆναι εἰς τὴν Ἰουδαίαν).

15.5. Via Greece and Jerusalem to Rome and Spain

15.5.1. Macedonia and Achaia

The same geographic sequence found in Acts can also be inferred from Paul's own letters. When Paul wrote the second Corinthian letter, he was already in Macedonia (2 Cor. 2:13; 7:5; 8:1; 9:1f.; cf. Acts 20:1) and was planning a visit to Corinth (2 Cor. 9:4; 12:14; 13:1f.; cf. Acts 20:2f.). His attention, however, was already directed considerably farther than he allowed the Corinthians to know. We want "to proclaim the gospel in lands beyond you (εἰς τὰ ὑπερέκεινα ὑμῶν εὐαγγελίσασθαι), without boasting of work already done in someone else's sphere of action" (2 Cor. 10:16). Resonance with Rom. 15:20 suggests that this passage is already definitively alluding to plans for Spain. When the apostle wrote the second Corinthian letter in Macedonia (2 Cor. 2:13; 7:5; cf. 8:1), a year had already passed (2 Cor. 8:10: ἀπὸ πέρυσι) since the beginning of the collection, mentioned already in the first Corinthian letter (1 Cor. 16:1-3). From this, G. Lüdemann has correctly concluded that one winter must have passed between the composition of 1 Corinthians 16 and 2 Corinthians 8.[112] The second Corinthian letter was quite obviously the

---

111. A detailed attempt at reconstructing this final collection journey can be found in C. J. Thornton, *Der Zeuge des Zeugen* (1991) 229-67.

112 G. Lüdemann, *Paul: Apostle to the Gentiles* (Eng. trans., 1984) 97-99.

ersatz for the apostle's visit announced in 1 Cor. 16:5-7 and then postponed (2 Cor. 1:15-17).

One might ask whether on his final trip to Macedonia Paul also pushed into the eastern part of this province, as various scholars assume.[113] Mention of the province Illyricum (see p. 243 above) as the limit of his activity in the western part of the Mediterranean basin would then be more easily understandable. Scholars have also sought in various ways to associate with this period the suggestion in the letter to Titus that Paul planned to spend the winter in the Roman colony[114] Nicopolis, founded by Augustus to commemorate the victory at Actium in 31 B.C. and at that time the most important city on the entire Dalmatian coast[115] (Titus 3:12).[116] But such conjectures involve far too many unknowns. Paul would then also have reached the region of Epirus in the northern half of the province of Achaia, which under Nero was apparently elevated to the status of an independent province.[117] The apostle could then have said with even greater justification that his task had been fulfilled in all of Greece (Isa. 66:19).

15.5.2. The Collection for Jerusalem

In his letter to the Romans, Paul announced that before his stay in the imperial capital and his continued journey to Spain, he wanted to visit Jerusalem in

---

113. So, e.g., P. Vielhauer, *Geschichte der urchristlichen Literatur* (1975) 80; C. E. B. Cranfield, *The Epistle to the Romans* II (²1981) 761f. (p. 762: "The period of time indicated by the last few words of v. 1 and the two participial clauses of v. 2 of Acts 20 may well have been long enough to allow such a journey"); F. F. Bruce, *The Book of the Acts* (²1988) 381, who even assumes Paul wanted to spend a few weeks learning Latin in the southern part of Latin-speaking South Illyricum so that he might be better equipped for the Spanish mission (*Paul* [1977] 315f.; *BJRL* 61 [1978/79] 354). Even M. Dibelius, *Die Pastoralbriefe* (1955) 115 (Eng. trans., *The Pastoral Epistles* [1972]), wrote that "it seems credible that Paul was once in Nicopolis and Epirus."

114. Cf. F. Schober, *PRE* II 17.1 (1937) 511-39.

115. Cf. N. G. L. Hammond, *Epirus* (1967) index.

116. G. S. Duncan, *St. Paul's Ephesian Ministry* (1929) 217-21, dates this news to the period before Acts 28. W. Metzger, *Die letzte Reise des Apostels Paulus* (1976) 42f., though thinking of the time after this, writes further: "In contrast to the second missionary journey [§18.4.2-3] . . . he must have travelled west on the third journey. This is also his reference when in Rom. 15:19 he writes to Rome that he fully proclaimed the gospel 'to Illyricum,' i.e., either as far as or across the Illyrian border with Macedonia. Only if at that time he had already founded a church in Nicopolis, after having journeyed through Macedonia, turned south, and reached the Adriatic Sea, is it comprehensible that he now, on his last great journey, could dispatch Titus there (Titus 3:12)." Such a route is depicted on the map of G. Stählin and E. Höhne, *Der östliche Mittelmeerraum zur Zeit des Paulus. BHH Beilage* (²1968).

117. Cf. E. Meyer, *KP* II (1967) 286f.

order to deliver a collection from his churches in Macedonia and Achaia (Rom. 15:25-28). Although Luke mentions this collection only once, and as an aside (Acts 24:17), perhaps Paul's companions on this trip (Acts 20:4) are also to be viewed as those commissioned to deal with the collection in the individual regions (cf. 1 Cor. 16:3; 2 Cor. 8:18-20).[118] This project similarly establishes a close connection between 1 Corinthians (1 Cor. 16:1-4), 2 Corinthians (2 Cor. 8–9), and Romans (Rom. 15:25-28) (pp. 233f.). Paul apparently wanted to travel to the holy city directly from Corinth (perhaps on a pilgrim ship to the Passover festival), but then decided to journey to Macedonia instead because of a Jewish conspiracy against his life (Acts 20:3). In a fairly detailed itinerary (§12.2), Acts then recounts the journey from the seaport of Philippi (Neapolis) to Troas (Acts 20:6 [here the second we-account begins]), and then farther to Assos (Acts 20:13), Mitylene (Acts 20:14), past Chios via Samos to Miletus (Acts 20:15), finally via Cos and Rhodes to Patara (Acts 21:1),[119] and ultimately south past Cyprus to Tyre (Acts 21:3) and via Ptolemais (Acts 21:7) to Caesarea (Acts 21:8).[120]

For A. Suhl,[121] S. Dockx,[122] and N. Hyldahl,[123] a Sabbatical Year which they date in A.D. 54/55 plays an important role in dating the apostle's final trip to Jerusalem to A.D. 55. The collection would have reached the holy city when the effects of the failure to sow became noticeable. The Sabbatical Year, however, must be dated one year later (A.D. 55/56).[124] Paul had been organizing the collection at least since A.D. 54 (§12.1). Even if it was directly related to the Sabbatical Year, it is by no means certain that the apostle was successful with his own timetable. The Corinthian correspondence attests delays affecting his travel plans to Achaia and thus also his arrival in Jerusalem (§15.4.1-2). One cannot thus exclude the possibility that a journey planned already for A.D. 56 was not undertaken until A.D. 57. The Sabbatical Year in and of itself does not constitute a certain dating criterion capable of refuting other, more unequivocal evidence.

118. Cf. K. F. Nickle, *The Collection* (1966) 68-70; F. F. Bruce, *The Book of the Acts* (1988) 382f.

119. The presumed variant of the extremely late P[41] (eighth century A.D.), which moreover belongs only to the textual category III (K. Aland and B. Aland, *The Text of the New Testament* [Eng. trans.; rev. ed., 1989] 98), does not demonstrate that the addition of Myra in the D-text is original. In any event, the circumstances of the journey militate against this. Cf. F. F. Bruce, *The Book of Acts* (1988) 398, note 4.

120. Cf. C. J. Hemer, *The Book of Acts in the Setting of Hellenistic History* (1989) 188f.

121. *Paulus und seine Briefe* (1975) 327-33.

122. *Chronologies néotestamentaires* ([2]1984) 137-50.

123. *Die paulinische Chronologie* (1986) 120.

124. Cf. B. Z. Wacholder, *HUCA* 46 (1975) 216.

The letter to the Romans belongs in the period immediately prior to the apostle's departure for Jerusalem (cf. Rom. 15:25: νυνὶ . . πορεύομαι εἰς Ἰερουσαλήμ). It was obviously composed in Corinth,[125] since Romans 16 constitutes an integral part of the writing (see p. 191 above), and "Erastus, the city treasurer (ὁ οἰκονόμος τῆς πόλεως)" may be identified with an inscriptionally attested aedile[126] from Corinth.[127] In Corinth, sufficient news could have reached the apostle from the imperial capital (§16.3.3), as the letter presupposes especially in its final, parenetic section (Rom. 13–15).[128] The taxation problems addressed in Rom. 13:1-7 can be associated with specific difficulties in Rome.[129] The tax burden had presumably been increased yet again by Claudian legislation at the end of his reign in the years A.D. 53/54 (cf. Tacitus, *Ann.* xii.60; Suetonius, *Claudius* 12),[130] so that in A.D. 58 massive grievances and an extensive reform by Nero resulted (Tacitus, *Ann.* xiii.50f.; cf. Suetonius, *Nero* 10). The apostle's admonitions become more comprehensible the closer to the events of this year one dates the composition of the letter.[131] The strategic religious significance possessed by the imperial capital in the view of antiquity can be seen in the irresistible power with which founders of sects were drawn to Rome.[132] If Paul directed his attention to the farthest west, then he had to keep Rome free at his rear if he did not want to sever the connection with his own churches in the eastern Mediterranean basin.

125. So most recently, among others, H. Schlier, *Der Römerbrief* (1977) 2; O. Michel, *Der Brief an die Römer* (⁵1978) 25f.; R. Pesch, *Römerbrief* (1983) 5; P. Stuhlmacher, *ZNW* 77 (1986) 189; J. D. G. Dunn, *Romans 1-8* (1988) xliv; J. A. Fitzmyer, *Romans* (1993) 85-88.

126. J. H. Kent, *Corinth* VIII/3 (1966) 232 (99f.). Another, extremely fragmentary inscription that mentions a Vitellius Frontinus Erastus (*SEG* 29 [1979] 301), comes only from the second century A.D. Cf. A. C. Clarke, *TynBul* 42 (1991) 146-51.

127. Cf. G. Theissen, in *Studien zur Soziologie des Urchristentums* (²1983) 236-45; W. A. Meeks, *The First Urban Christians* (1983) 58f.; V. P. Furnish, *BAR* 15/3 (1985) 20; D. W. J. Gill, *TynBul* 40 (1989) 293-302; *Secular and Christian Leadership in Corinth* (1993) 46-56. The tombstone of another Christian *aedile* comes from the third century A.D. (*Corinth* VIII/3 [1966] 558).

128. Cf. P. Stuhlmacher, *ZNW* 77 (1986) 187-98.

129. Cf. J. Friedrich, W. Pöhlmann, and P. Stuhlmacher, *ZTK* 73 (1976) 156-59.

130. Cf. A. Strobel, *BHH* III (1966) 2225.

131. M. F. Baslez, *Saint Paul* (1991) 378f., note 125, dates the letter before the autumn of A.D. 54, since Narcissus (Rom. 16:11) is referring to the famous freedman of Claudius (Suetonius, *Claudius* 28), who committed suicide at that time! This name, however, was quite common in Rome as the name of freedmen. Cf. P. Lampe, *Die stadt-römischen Christen* (²1989) 136.

132. Cf. T. Zahn, in *Skizzen aus dem Leben der alten Kirche* (1905) 190f.

15.5.3. The Plan for Spain

Why did Paul not have any plans to evangelize at least in Gaul? This would have been consistent with his strategy in the eastern half of the empire of founding churches in a chain of contiguous or at least neighboring provinces. F. F. Bruce attempts to explain this as follows: "If Spain beckoned to him as his next mission-field, that was probably because the other lands bordering on the Mediterranean (including the North African coast west of Cyrenaica) were already being evangelized. Narbonese Gaul (the present-day Provence), part of which had been colonized by Ionian Greeks centuries before and still maintained close links with the Aegean world, came to be regarded as falling within the sphere of the churches of Asia."[133] Although Bruce is correct in assuming this for Italy (cf. Acts 28:13-15) and North Africa (see p. 265 above), his assertion is questionable in the case of Gaul. References to the bishop's office of Irenaeus of Asia Minor in Lyon, and to the martyrs of A.D. 177 in the same city (Eusebius, *HE* v.1) as witnesses to the non-Pauline character of the mission in Gaul, are balanced by a reference in the Pastoral Epistles, whereby one need only accept their origin within the Pauline school and a knowledge of some historical traditions regarding places and persons, but not necessarily their authenticity (see p. 31 above). When 2 Tim. 4:10 asserts that the Pauline pupil Crescens went εἰς Γαλατίαν, the author of the second letter to Timothy would already have understood by this not Galatia in Asia Minor, but rather Gaul, which in Greek is similarly called Γαλατία,[134] and would have done so even before part of the later manuscript tradition (ℵ and others: εἰς Γαλλίαν) as well as before later church tradition did so (e.g., Eusebius, *HE* iii.4.8; Epiphanius, *Pan.* 51.11).[135] Precisely the fact that southern Gaul had already been Hellenized, and that compared to Spain[136] it was far more likely to have a significant number of Jews,[137] would have made this region attractive to Paul.

133. *Paul* (1977) 315.

134. Cf. C. Spicq, *Saint Paul. Les Épîtres Pastorales* II (⁴1969) 811-13.

135. Cf. further F. X. Pölzl, *Die Mitarbeiter des Weltapostels Paulus* (1911) 349-56.

136. W. P. Bowers, *JTS* 26 (1975) 395-402, fundamentally calls into question the presence of Jews in Spain before A.D. 70. And, indeed, only two Jewish inscriptions before the fourth century have hitherto been found. Cf. H. Solin, *ANRW* II 29.2 (1983) 749-51. To be sure, the witness of Seneca, who was born in Cordoba, is weighty: *"Cum interim usque eo sceleratissimae gentis consuetudo convaluit, ut per omnes iam terras recepta sit"* (in Augustine, *Civ. Dei* vi.11 [ed. M. Stern I 431]).

137. Cf. Schuerer, III/1 (1986) 84f. Admittedly, views concerning the strength of Jewish settlements in Gaul vary greatly. Cf. H. Solin, *ANRW* II 29.2 (1983) 753-55, and *New Doc* I (1981) 120.

If Isa. 66:19 was directing the apostle's plans from the eastern Mediterranean basin directly to the western boundary of the known world at that time (see p. 252 above), then his omission of Gaul becomes more comprehensible. In contemporary geographic descriptions, Spain constitutes "the boundaries of the world" (Lucian, *Pharsalia* iii.454). For Juvenal, the known world extended "from Gades to the Ganges" (*Sat.* x.1f.), for Strabo from the "Don to Gades" (Strabo ii.5.9). For Silius Italicus, too, this city in western Spain lay "at the end of the world" (*Punica* xvii.637).[138] This broad outreach to the most extreme west can best be explained if, for Paul, Spain concluded his own commission in the west. The letter to the Romans contains nothing to indicate that Spain was just a tactical missionary goal from which to move into other areas.[139] Apparently at that time, too, Paul anticipated the parousia in the very near future: νῦν γὰρ ἐγγύτερον ἡμῶν ἡ σωτηρία ἢ ὅτε ἐπιστεύσαμεν. ἡ νὺξ προέκοψεν, ἡ δὲ ἡμέρα ἤγγικεν (Rom. 13:11f.).

15.6. The Fulfilled Mission in the East

In addition to the mission-strategic motives customarily addressed by scholarship, we have also tried to understand Paul's geographic movements, as these emerge from his letters and from Acts, against the background of a prophecy such as Isa. 66:19 concerning the eschatological mission. Although much in our considerations must remain hypothetical, let us once more point out those features that are more easily comprehensible given these presuppositions: (1) For the contemporary geographic understanding, the Isaianic prophecy presented a route neither to the east nor to the south. We have no reliable information to the effect that the apostle undertook missionary activity in these directions, or even planned such. This is all the more astonishing because for Paul as an educated Jew, the civilized world was by no means restricted to the Mediterranean basin, but extended rather at least to the Euphrates and the Rhine.[140] (2) This prophecy expressly mentions as the first station Tarsus, and

---

138. Concerning the possibility that Acts 1:8 (ἕως ἐσχάτου τῆς γῆς) is referring to Spain, cf. E. E. Ellis, in *Festschrift G. Schneider* (1991) 277-87.

139. Contra W. P. Bowers, *Studies in Paul's Understanding of His Mission* (1976) 62f.: "That the journey to Spain would involve bypassing other western lands need prove problematic only if the mission to Spain is viewed, as to Paul's mind, somehow climactic, if one assumes that for Paul Spain was to be not a starting point but the stopping point." Here W. P. Bowers is basically contradicting two points he himself emphasizes: (1) Paul normally moves from province to province (*loc. cit.,* 18-48, 70-73); (2) from the perspective of the Old Testament, Spain as the "end of the earth" possesses an eschatological symbolic value (*loc. cit.,* 56-62).

140. Philo, *Leg. ad Gaium* 10, mentions these two rivers as boundaries of the area in which in his opinion most human beings dwelled, and which alone actually deserves

then (in an understanding applicable at that time) Cilicia. This can help explain the apostle's remarkably long sojourn in his own city of birth and its environs. (3) Immediately after the commencement of his independent mission, Paul tried to reach precisely those areas subsequently mentioned in the prophecy, namely, Asia (Lydia), Mysia (Meshech), and Bithynia (Tubal). (4) The apostle's path then led not to the nearest province, Thrace, but rather, in agreement with Isa. 66:19 (Javan), to Macedonia and Achaia, that is, to Greece proper. (5) From here Paul turned neither to the north into neighboring Moesia and Illyricum, nor to the west and Italy. Rather, he tried to close the gap in western Asia Minor by staying in the heart of the province of Asia. (6) After "fulfilling" his missionary work in the east (Rom. 15:19), Paul did not plan any activity in Italy or Gaul, but rather turned his attention immediately to the most extreme boundaries of the west (Isa. 66:19), to Spain. (7) In the prophecy, the eschatological missionary movement begins in the holy city and leads back there. The apostle not only viewed Jerusalem as the point of departure of his mission to the Gentiles, but also understood himself to be directed toward the holy city in the future. These considerations, too, show that the traditional distinction between a "second" and "third missionary journey" is not really commensurate with the circumstances. For Paul, the mission in the east Aegean sphere constituted a nexus.[141]

the name "world" (τῶν πλείστων καὶ ἀναγκαιοτάτων μερῶν τῆς οἰκουμένης, ἃ δὴ καὶ κυρίως ἄν τις οἰκουμένην εἴποι).
141. Cf. also D. T. Rowlingson, *JBL* 69 (1950) 341-44.

§16

The Apostle's Rate of Travel

The first and second Christian centuries represent a period of great mobility, and one of the most mobile groups was the early Christians.[1] Since the reign of Augustus, journeys over long distances had become possible as never before and for long afterward. The *Pax Romana* had eliminated most boundaries between countries, and it insured relative security from robbers at least on the main traffic routes.[2] An expanded network of roads[3] connected the most distant

1. Cf. T. Zahn, in *Skizzen aus dem Leben der alten Kirche* (1894) 156-95, 302-9; W. M. Ramsay, *Exp* VI/8 (1903) 401-22; *DB* (Extra Volume) (1904) 375-402; E. Delaye, *Études* 131 (1912) 443-61; A. Steinmann, *Die Welt des Paulus im Zeichen des Verkehrs* (1915) 20-54; E. Stange, *Paulinische Reisepläne* (1918) 31-34; L. Friedlaender, *Darstellungen aus der Sittengeschichte Roms* ([10]1922) 1.318-98; R. H. Pope, *On Roman Roads with Saint Paul* (1939); H. Metzger, *St. Paul's Journeys in the Greek Orient* (Eng. trans., 1955); M. Rostovtzeff, *The Economic History of the Roman Empire* II ([2]1957) 609f., note 24; G. A. Barrois, *IDB* IV (1962) 681-83; S. V. McCasland, *ibid.,* 690-93; E. M. Small-wood, *Philonis Alexandrini Legatio ad Gaium* ([2]1970) 167, 283-85; A. Suhl, *Paulus und seine Briefe* (1975) 360 (Index); L. Casson, *Reisen in der antiken Welt* ([2]1978); É. Cothenet, in *Cahiers Évangiles* (1978) 27f.; J. R. Armogathe, *Paul* (1980) 79-92; G. Lüdemann, *Paulus, der Heidenapostel* I (1980) 142f., note 180 [not in Eng. trans.]; R. Jewett, *A Chronology of Paul's Life* (1979) 55-57; A. J. Malherbe, *Social Aspects of Early Christianity* ([2]1983) 62-65, 94-96; W. A. Meeks, *The First Urban Christians* (1983) 16-23; M. Hengel, *SHAW.PH (1983/84)* (1984) 44-46; A. Hamman, *Die ersten Christen* (1985) 31-46; C. Wells, *The Roman Empire* (1984) 262-66; J. Stambaugh and D. Balch, *The Social World of the First Christians* (1986) 35-41; E. Ferguson, *Background of Early Christianity* (1987) 64-67; S. Mittmann, *GBL* II (1988) 515-19; *GBL* III (1989) 1284-86; M. Adinolfi, *La prima lettera ai Tessalonicesi* (1990) 135-43; F. Meijer and O. van Nijf, *Trade, Transport, and Society in the Ancient World* (1991); F. F. Bruce, *ABD* VI (1992) 648-53; S. R. Llewelyn, *NewDoc* VII (1994) 58-92; B. M. Rapske in A1CS II (1994) 1-48. Earlier bibliography can be found in A. Steinmann, *loc. cit.,* 21, note 1.

2. The New Testament (Lk. 10:30; 2 Cor. 11:26) already shows that one really can speak only of relative security. Cf. further L. Friedlaender, *Darstellungen aus der Sitten-geschichte Roms* I ([10]1922) 352-59; H. C. Schneider, *Altstrassenforschung* (1982) 116-20; B. Isaac, *HCSP* 88 (1984) 171-203.

3. Cf. V. W. von Hagen, *The Roads That Led to Rome* (1967); T. Pekary, *Unter-suchungen zu den römischen Reichsstraßen* (1968); R. Chevallier, *Roman Roads* (Eng.

parts of the empire with the capital, where at the "Golden Milestone" all paths took their symbolic point of departure. Since Pompey, the reign of the pirates in the eastern Mediterranean had been broken, and regular shipping took care especially of the grain imports from Egypt and Syria to Rome.[4] Of course, not even under the Romans did travel become completely free of danger, as shown precisely by Paul's own experiences (2 Cor. 11:25-27). It was especially seasonal factors and the ancient means of travel as such that imposed limits on mobility, limits which need to be considered in presenting any chronology for the apostle.

16.1. Wintering

During the New Testament period, as today, the eastern Mediterranean became increasingly stormy from the end of September on.[5] According to Vegetius (fourth century A.D.), shipping in general closed down from November 11 to March 10: *"maria clauduntur"* (Vegetius, *De rei milit.* iv.39). Pliny the Elder, too, reports that shipping did not reopen until spring: *"ver aperit navigantibus maria"* (Pliny the Elder, *HN* ii.47). Shortly before the end of the *mare clausum,* the festival *navigium Isidis* was celebrated (Apuleius, *Met.* xi.7ff.); according to the oldest known calendars it fell on March 5 (*CIL* I/1, 260, 280, 311). Beyond this, the periods from March 10 to May 27, and from September 14 to November 11, were considered dangerous for sea travel (Vegetius, *De rei milit.* iv.39, cf. Pliny the Elder, *HN* ii.47). The rabbis thus advised taking sea journeys only between Pentecost and the Feast of Booths, that is, from May to the end of October (*Gen. Rab.* 6 [12a]; *y. Šabb.* 5b). But it was not just winter storms that made sea travel uncertain. Before the invention of the compass, overcast skies and longer nights made navigation difficult, increasing the chances of running onto rocks or shallows.[6] There were, of course, exceptions, especially in the case of military campaigns or urgent matters of state, but as a rule people adhered to these cautionary

---

trans., 1976) 186f.; G. Radke, *PRESup* 13 (1973) 1417-86; H. E. Herzig, *ANRW* II 1 (1974) 593-648; H. Bender, *Römischer Reiseverkehr* (1978); J. Siat, *MBib* 5 (1978) 16-22; D. French in A1CS II (1994) 49-58.

    4. Cf. M. P. Charlesworth, *Trade-Routes and Commerce of the Roman Empire* (1924); J. Rougé, *Recherches sur l'organisation du commerce maritime en Méditerranée sous l'empire Romain* (1966); L. Casson, *Ships and Seamanship in the Ancient World* (1971) 141-48, 270-99, 365-70; O. Höckmann, *Antike Seefahrt* (1985) 52-93.

    5. On a trip during the final week of September 1986, stormy weather kept us from leaving the Cyclades island of Milos.

    6. Cf. L. Casson, *Ships and Seamanship in the Ancient World* (1971) 270-72.

measures.[7] Precisely this is demonstrated by the account in Acts concerning the transport of the imprisoned apostle to Rome (Acts 27:12; 28:11: παραχ-ειμάζειν).[8] Philostratus then later renounced all sea journeys during the winter (Philostratus, *VA* 4.13), preferring instead a departure in the spring (*VA* 5.5).

Vegetius asserted further that land journeys were also halted during the period between mid-November and mid-March (*De rei milit.* iv.39), and witnesses from a somewhat later period confirm this.[9] Snowed-in mountain ranges such as the Taurus (see p. 278 above) as well as swollen rivers (cf. 2 Cor. 11:26: κίνδυνοι ποταμῶν) often rendered roads completely impassable during the winter and early spring. In the case of Asia Minor, it can by no means be presupposed that all imperial highways were traversable during the entire year as a result of meter-thick macadamization and stone paving (see p. 274, note 52 above). Both his letters (1 Cor. 16:6; cf. Titus 3:12) and Acts (cf. Acts 20:2f.) equally allow the conclusion that, as a rule, Paul spent the winter months in secure quarters.

16.2. Land Journeys

16.2.1. Riding and Walking

Paul doubtless traversed long stretches of his missionary journeys *per pedes apostolorum.* He may have had in mind the express example of Jesus when in 2 Cor. 11:26 he emphasizes the ὁδοιπορίαι among his afflictions, referring in all probability not only to journeys in general, but to foot journeys in particular (cf. Jn. 4:6).[10] For the journey from Troas to Assos, Acts seems explicitly to presuppose such (Acts 20:13), though it is not certain whether πεζεύειν must be understood in the etymological sense. In this instance, the contrast is between a land journey and a sea journey, and does not necessarily imply a foot journey as distinct from riding on an animal or in a carriage.[11] One can by no means exclude the possibility that Paul occasionally used a riding animal or a carriage.[12] The following considerations should be noted

7. A. Steinmann, *Die Welt des Paulus im Zeichen des Verkehrs* (1915) 43f., fails to recognize the character of such exceptions. Contra E. de Saint-Denis, *RÉL* 25 (1947) 196-214, who reckons only with restricted shipping during the winter months, cf. J. Rougé, *RÉA* 54 (1952) 316-25, and W. M. Ramsay, *DBSup* (1904) 376f.

8. Cf. J. Rougé, *loc. cit.,* 317.

9. Cf. W. M. Ramsay, *DBSup* (1904) 377.

10. Cf. E. F. F. Bishop, *BS* 117 (1960) 14-18.

11. Cf. F. F. Bruce, *The Book of Acts* (1988) 386, note 33. See also p. 313 below.

12. Scholars as different as G. Lüdemann, *Paulus, der Heidenapostel* I (1980) 143, note 180, and F. F. Bruce, *loc. cit.,* 386, note 33 assume this.

in this regard: (1) One should not object to the likely use of means of travel which cost money. This applies especially to passage by ship,[13] which the apostle seems to have preferred if serious circumstances did not advise against such (cf. Acts 20:3). (2) The travel preparations indicated by the verb ἐπισκευάζεσθαι (Acts 21:15) can also have included the procurement of a riding animal.[14] The D-text of the following verse (Acts 21:16) apparently presupposes a two-day journey from Caesarea to Jerusalem, which for a distance of approximately 100 km. would not have been possible by foot.[15] (3) Mention of stations along the *Via Egnatia* in Acts 17:1 might indicate a trip by vehicle or riding animal (§16.2.4). During the New Testament period, it was not possible for a private citizen to take advantage of the swiftness[16] of the official postal service *(cursus publicus)*.[17] Even for a provincial governor such as Pliny the Younger, the issuing of a *diploma* to his wife for using this service was exceptional.[18] An organized network of private travel, however, was also available.[19] The account of the journey of a certain Theophanes, who between A.D. 317 and 323 traveled the route between Antioch on the Orontes and Pelusium (Port Said) in eighteen days (*PRyl* IV [ed. A. Hunt 106f.]), allows us to assume an average speed of travel for vehicles to have been 25-30 miles per day, that is, about 38-45 km.,[20] although individual instances of a day's journey of over 40 miles or 60 km. were also possible.[21]

---

13. Cf. C. J. Thornton, *Der Zeuge des Zeugen* (1991) 307f.

14. Cf. W. M. Ramsay, *St. Paul the Traveller* ([14]1920) 302.

15. Cf. A. Steinmann, *Die Welt des Paulus im Zeichen des Verkehrs* (1915) 49.

16. Cf. W. M. Ramsay, *JRS* 15 (1925) 60-74; F. F. Bruce, *ABD* VI (1992) 649f.

17. Cf. in this regard H. Bender, *Römischer Reiseverkehr* (1978) 6-16; H. C. Schneider, *Altstrassenforschung* (1982) 90-101; S. R. Llewelyn, *NewDoc* VII (1994) 1-25. Local provision of the necessary means for the rapid post was a continual source of dispute. These problems have recently been illustrated quite well by an inscription, published by S. Mitchell, *JRS* 66 (1976) 106-31, from the region of Sagalassus (Aghlasun) in Pisidia, dating from the beginning of the reign of Tiberius and providing help in removing the *crux interpretum* κανών (here: delimited area) in 2 Cor. 10:13, 15, 16 (E. A. Judge, *NewDoc* I [1981] 36-45).

18. Cf. J. P. V. D. Balsdon, *The Early Roman Empire* 1-3 (1980) 107.

19. Cf. A. Steinmann, *Die Welt des Paulus* (1915) 46-48; L. Friedlaender, *Darstellungen aus der Sittengeschichte Roms* I ([10]1922) 332f.; L. Casson, *Reisen in der antiken Welt* ([2]1978) 206-27 (Eng. trans., *Travel in the Ancient World* [1974]).

20. So already W. M. Ramsay, *DBSup* (1904) 386.

21. Cf. L. Casson, *Reisen in der antiken Welt* ([2]1978) 220-23. Additional examples, prompting extremely varied interpretations, can be found in G. Radke, *PRESup* 13 (1973) 1474-77. Naturally, rates of travel depended above all on road conditions. Weather permitting, carriages traveled on leveled, unpaved side roads. The most significant roads apparently also had a pounded layer of loam on top of the paving, which (in dry weather) made smooth travel possible. Cf. T. Pekary, *Untersuchungen zu den römischen Reichsstraßen* (1968) 31f.

Hence Cicero needed one day to travel the 55 km. between Ephesus and Tralles, a route Paul might also have traversed more than once (Cicero, *Att.* v.14.1).

In presenting a Pauline chronology, however, methodological caution prompts us first to reckon the minimal duration of journeys according to the rate of travel by foot. Archaeology of Roman roads shows that the average distance between the *mansiones* was 30-36 km. A passage in Vegetius allegedly suggests that this distance corresponded approximately to the normal marching performance *(iter iustum)* of a legionnaire.[22] The military author, however, is referring to the (exceptional) training performance of recruits (Vegetius, *De rei milit.* i.9). Archaeological experiments show that in the case of marches of several weeks, even well-trained persons have an upper limit of 30 km. for a day's march.[23] After three days of forced marching *(magnum iter),* Roman soldiers had a day of rest.[24] Although both Josephus (*Vita* 269f.) and the rabbis (*m. Taʿan.* 1.3; *b. Pesaḥ.* 93b) concur that the average performance for one day for Palestine was about 40 km., one must remember that the goal of almost all journeys there could be reached in three to four days. Neither should one's determination of the average performance by foot be miscalculated on the basis of astonishing records of the sort ancient authors love to emphasize.[25] Two examples[26] can illustrate normal performances: (1) Strabo refers to the distance from Sagalassus (Aghlasun) to Apamea (just over 30 km.) as a journey of one day (Strabo xii.6.5). (2) Official determinations of time periods assume a day's journey of 20 miles (*ca.* 30 km.) (Gaius, *Dig.* ii.11.1; *ILS* 7212, lines 29f.). It is thus probably realistic to follow earlier scholars and modern experts in reckoning, in the case of longer journeys over fairly normal terrain, a day's journey by foot as covering from 15-20 miles, or 20-30 km.[27]

22. Cf. R. Chevallier, *Les voies Romaines* (1972) 213f.

23. Cf. M. Junkelmann, *Die Legionen des Augustus* (1986) 233f.: Regardless of whether only light traveling gear was taken along *(ambulatio)* or full marching gear, the average output per day, or 540 km. in 21 marching days, was 25.7 km.

24. Cf. R. Chevallier, *loc. cit.,* 224.

25. This is the source of the one-sided nature of the material presented by L. Friedlaender, *Darstellungen aus der Sittengeschichte Roms* I ([10]1922) 333-36, on which G. Lüdemann, *Paulus, der Heidenapostel* I (1980) 142f., note 180, depends too heavily in assuming a daily average of 37.5 km. Caesar calls this distance (25 miles) an exceptional accomplishment at the battle against the Aedui (Caesar, *Bell. Gall.* vii.40f.). Concerning other record performances, including Acts 10:3, 7-9, cf. M. Hengel, *ZDPV* 99 (1983) 172f.

26. Cf. further Strabo xi.2.17; xii.2.9.

27. Cf. W. M. Ramsay, *DBSup* (1904) 386; C. Lécrivain, *DAGR* V (1912) 817-20; L. C. Purser, in H. J. Lawlor, *Eusebiana* (1912) 235f. S. V. McCasland, *IDB* IV (1962) 693; L. Casson, *Reisen in der antiken Welt* ([2]1978) 220; A. Hamman, *Die ersten Christen* (1985) 35; B. J. Beitzel, *ABD* VI (1992) 646f.

16.2.2. The Route from Jerusalem to Corinth

R. Jewett has calculated a duration of at least 91, and more likely 201 weeks for this itinerary as undertaken by Paul according to the account in Acts of what is known as the second missionary journey.[28] The assumption of a travel time between almost two and four years generates far-reaching consequences for the chronology of Acts. Because Jewett dates the apostle's arrival in Corinth in the winter of 49/50, the widespread dating of the Apostolic Council to 48 or 49 is problematical for him. He thus believes, on the basis of the temporal strictures this generates, that the assembly must be dated to the period after the mission in Greece (A.D. 51), and identified with the visit to Jerusalem alluded to in Acts 18:22.[29] Jewett, however, has unnecessarily boxed himself into a corner.[30] His calculation is problematical particularly for two reasons: (1) Because there was no Pauline mission in the region of Galatia (§15.2), the calculation can subtract at least six and at most twelve months for any activity there. (2) Of course, this also necessitates reducing the land route by at least 500 of what Jewett[31] calculates as over 2,700 kilometers. According to his determination of an average rate of 30 km. daily, this means subtracting seventeen days' minimum time and (according to Jewett) around five weeks' normal time. (3) Whereas the stay in Thessalonica, which includes the founding of the church, could indeed have lasted three to four months (§18.5.1), the stays in other places, such as Antioch (seven weeks to four months), Troas (two weeks to two months), or Philippi (three months to one year), seem too high.[32] But even following Jewett's extremely generous calculations, this yields a time frame between 57 weeks' minimum time and 132 weeks' normal time, that is, a median of 95 weeks, or less than two years.[33] Jewett's calculations are, however, of relative value insofar as they do demonstrate the probability that Paul spent one winter along the route from Jerusalem to Corinth, especially considering that journeys through the wintry Taurus mountains were undertaken only in exceptional instances.[34]

28. *A Chronology of Paul's Life* (1979) 58-62. Concerning several extremely subjective factors in R. Jewett's calculations, cf. the critical remarks of A. Suhl, *TLZ* 109 (1984) 817f.

29. Cf. R. Jewett, *A Chronology of Paul's Life* (1979) 91f.

30. Cf. also the criticism of C. J. Hemer, *The Book of Acts in the Setting of Hellenistic History* (1989) 256f., note 24; 267f.

31. R. K. Jewett, *A Chronology of Paul's Life* (1979) 61.

32. *Ibid.,* 59f.

33. It is interesting in the context to note that the journey of the imprisoned bishop Ignatius from Antioch to Rome can be calculated at around 100 days, which harmonizes well with the duration one can infer from his letters (approximately July 6 to October 7). Cf. W. M. Ramsay, *DBSup* (1904) 386.

34. Cf. W. M. Ramsay, *DBSup* (1904) 377. See also p. 278 above.

16.2.3. From Corinth via Jerusalem to Ephesus

According to our determination, Paul left Corinth in the autumn of A.D. 51 before the end of shipping (§12.2), and traveled by ship, with a brief interruption in Ephesus, to Caesarea (Acts 18:21), all of which took from ten to fourteen days (see p. 315 below). A visit to Jerusalem (Acts 18:22) was followed by an apparently longer stay in Antioch (Acts 18:23a: καὶ ποιήσας χρόνον τινά) and a strengthening of churches in Phrygia-Galatia (Acts 18:23b), before Paul reached Ephesus (Acts 19:1). The approximately eighteen-hundred-kilometer land route from Jerusalem to the provincial capital of Asia could have been made in sixty to ninety days on foot. The presupposed visits and wintry conditions in the Taurus range as well as in the Anatolian highlands make it impossible for the apostle to have reached his goal in the same year. He doubtless spent the winter somewhere en route (perhaps in Antioch), and reached Ephesus shortly before early summer in the year A.D. 52.

16.2.4. The Via Egnatia from Philippi to Thessalonica

The account of Paul's stay in Philippi is followed by this route description: "They passed through (διοδεύσαντες) Amphipolis and Apollonia, and came to Thessalonica" (Acts 17:1). This clearly presupposes the route along the great imperial east-west highway, the *Via Egnatia,* one of the most important transportation arteries in the entire empire.[35] Amphipolis as the capital of the first district of Macedonia,[36] and Apollonia (referring to the *mansio* of this name, and not to the city situated farther to the southwest in the mountains, Ἀπολωνία ἡ Μυγδονική),[37] are apparently mentioned as interim stations on a three-day journey.[38] This betrays genuine familiarity with the locale insofar as the distances of twice approximately fifty and once sixty kilometers really could be traversed in three days if one used a carriage.[39] While on the first two stages one also had to deal with a slight incline, the third was almost exclusively downhill.

35. Cf. F. O'Sullivan, *The Egnatian Way* (1972); J. P. Adams, *AncMac* IV (1986) 17-42; W. Elliger, *Paulus in Griechenland* (²1987) 45-47.

36. Cf. C. M. Danoff, *KP* I (1964) 449; F. Papazoglou, *Les villes de Macédoine* (1988) 218-22.

37. Cf. C. I. Makaronas, *AncMac* II (1977) 189-94.

38. Cf. R. Jewett, *A Chronology of Paul's Life* (1979) 32; C. J. Hemer, *The Book of Acts in the Setting of Hellenistic History* (1989) 115.

39. Contra G. Schneider, *Die Apostelgeschichte* II (1982) 223. According to Livius xlv.33, the Roman field general Aemilius Paullus, from his camp near Amphipolis, reached Pella, *ca.* 50 km. from Thessalonica, in a forced march of five days.

16.2.5. Highway Stations near Rome

According to Acts 28:15, Christians from Rome came as far as the Forum of Appius and Three Taverns to meet the apostle (ἦλθαν εἰς ἀπάντησιν ἡμῖν ἄχρι Ἀππίου Φόρου καὶ Τριῶν Ταβερνῶν). These two locales are correctly presupposed as stopover points along the *Via Appia*.[40] Although knowledge of the larger Forum Appius might conceivably have been acquired from hearsay, such an explanation cannot be considered for the otherwise insignificant Three Taverns, which is still awaiting rediscovery.[41] If one does not assume that Luke was familiar with Cicero's letters, which mention the *mansio* several times (Cicero, *Att.* i.13.1; 2.10; ii.12.2; 13.1), the best explanation is that the we-account really does derive from eyewitness recollections. Local circumstances also explain why some Roman Christians came even as far as the Forum of Appius to meet the prisoner transport. It was here that the canal ended coming from Terracina and led through the Pomptine Marshes parallel to the *Via Appia,* a canal which according to the witness of Horace enabled travelers to advance more quickly (Horace, *Sat.* i.5.1-19; cf. Strabo v.3.6). Perhaps the prisoner transport also used the canal,[42] as presupposed by the *Acts of Peter* (ed. R. A. Lipsius II/1, 306), and in any event, the Forum of Appius provided a sure meeting place.[43]

16.3. Sea Journeys

Since sailing depends on changing weather conditions, it is only with great caution that one can assert for the Roman period an average speed of 180-270 km. per day under favorable conditions.[44] Ancient sources, however, do contain information for important sea routes in the Mediterranean which mention travel times under optimal conditions (especially in the case of northerly trade winds in the summer), information based in part on the experiences of generations:[45]

---

40. Cf. C. J. Hemer, *The Book of Acts in the Setting of Hellenistic History* (1989) 156.

41. Cf. K. Miller, *PRE* II 4.2 (1932) 1875; B. Mariani, in *S. Paolo* (1963) 87-140; A. Esch, *AW* 19 (1988) 15-20; R. Riesner and C. P. Thiede, *GBL* III (1989) 1595.

42. Cf. H. Balmer, *Die Romfahrt des Apostels Paulus* (1905) 484f.; E. Jacquier, *Les Actes des Apôtres* (1926) 753.

43. Cf. B. Schwank, *EA* 36 (1960) 189f.; A. Esch, *AW* 19 (1988) 25.

44. Cf. H. Bender, *Römischer Reiseverkehr* (1978) 28f.

45. Cf. T. Zahn, in *Skizzen aus dem Leben der alten Kirche* (1905) 303, note 6; L. Friedlaender, *Darstellungen aus der Sittengeschichte Roms* I ([10]1922) 336-42; M. P. Charlesworth, *Trade-Routes and Commerce of the Roman Empire* (1924) 84f.; E. de Saint-Denis, *RA* VI/18 (1941) 121-38; R. van Compernolle, *BIHBR* 30 (1957) 5-30; L. Casson, *TAPA* 82 (1951) 136-48; *idem, Ships and Seamanship in the Ancient World* (1971) 281-96; *Reisen in der Antiken Welt* ([2]1978) 173-77; J. Rougé, *Recherches sur l'organisation du commerce maritime en Méditerranée sous l'empire Romaine* (1966) 101-4.

Alexandria-Ephesus	(Achilles Tatius v.15.1; 17.1)	5
Ashkelon-Thessalonica	(MarcD, *Vit. Porph.* 6)	12
Byzantium-Gaza	(MarcD, *Vit. Porph.* 27)	10
Byzantium-Rhodes	(*ibid.,* 55)	5
Dyrrhachium-Brundisium	(Livius xlv.41)	1-2
Crete-Egypt	(Strabo x.475)	3-4
Messina-Alexandria	(Pliny the Elder, *HN* xix.3f.)	7
Ostia-Gibraltar	(*ibid.*)	7
Ostia-Massilia	(*ibid.*)	3
Puteoli-Carthage	(cf. Pliny the Elder, *HN* xv.74)	2
Puteoli-Corinth	(Philostratus, *VA* 7.10)	5
Rhodes-Alexandria	(Diodorus Siculus iii.33)	4
Troas-Alexandria	(Lucian, *Pharsalia* ix.1004f.)	7

For the most frequently undertaken trip, namely, Rome-Alexandria, one had to reckon with a travel time of ten to thirteen days,[46] though occasionally a record of nine days was attained (Pliny the Elder, *HN* xix.3). Grain ships on this route, ships Paul also used (Acts 27:5f.),[47] even followed a kind of schedule.[48] Under unfavorable wind conditions, the journeys lasted two to three times as long, or one had to cancel the trip entirely until more favorable weather.[49] Under inclement conditions, a trip from Alexandria to Rome could take forty-five days, and from Ephesus to the imperial capital two entire months.[50] We will examine more closely here only three of the routes with an eye to their implications for Pauline chronology and for the accuracy of details in Acts.

16.3.1. From Troas to Neapolis

We have seen that Troas was the most important crossroad for traffic from northern Asia Minor to Greece (see p. 299 above). The we-account of Acts provides one day for the passage to Samothrace, and a second for the continued journey to Neapolis (Acts 16:11). The island was a familiar landmark for sailors.[51] Titus Livius also assumes a single day for passage to this island lying exactly in the middle of the route (Livius xliv.45). By contrast, under

46. Cf. L. Casson, *TAPA* 82 (1951) 146.

47. Concerning reconstruction of the normal routes, cf. L. Casson, *TAPA* 81 (1950) 43-56. The criticism of B. S. J. Isserlin, *TAPA* 86 (1955) 319f., was addressed persuasively by L. Casson, *TAPA* 87 (1956) 239f. Cf. also R. R. Llewelyn, *NewDoc* VII (1994) 112-29.

48. Cf. L. Casson, *Ships and Seamanship in the Ancient World* (1971) 297-99.

49. Cf. *ibid.,* 289-91.

50. Cf. A. Hamman, *Die ersten Christen* (1985) 33f.

51. Cf. C. J. Hemer, *The Book of Acts* (1989) 113.

different wind conditions in the spring (Passover period), the passage
Neapolis-Troas could last five days (Acts 20:6).

16.3.2. From Greece to Palestine

Paul's plan to travel from Greece to Palestine at the end of what is known as
the third missionary journey after the Passover festival (Acts 20:6), and to
arrive by Pentecost (Acts 20:16), was realistic, since this was a season dominated almost exclusively by northerly winds. According to our chronological
determinations, Paul left Philippi on 15 April A.D. 57 (§12.2), and Pentecost
fell in this year on May 29.[53] Since under favorable wind conditions the
journey lasted twelve to fourteen days (see p. 315 above), there was also
enough time for several interim stops (Acts 20:6, 17; 21:2, 4). We lack any
direct material from contemporary sources with which to compare the information from the we-passages concerning the number of days involved in the
sea journey from Philippi to Caesarea (Acts 20:5, 15; 21:1). Regarding the
accuracy of other details of the account, however, one can draw attention to
a series of observations:[54] (1) In Troas (Acts 20:6), the apostle — who was
in great haste — could anticipate a favorable transportation opportunity.
(2) Because of the special coastal circumstances, the land route (on riding
animal or carriage) from Troas to Assos (Acts 20:13f.) was shorter, so that
Paul could extend his stay in Troas a bit if he chose this route. (3) The change
of ships in Patara (Acts 21:1f.) reflects the importance of this transfer harbor
for the Roman grain fleet.

16.3.3. Connections between Corinth and Rome

Under favorable wind conditions, a letter could travel by ship from Corinth
to Rome in about one week (see p. 315 above). The journey on the land route
with passage across the Adriatic took about fifteen days: Corinth-Aulon nine
days,[55] passage across the Adriatic one day (Livius xlv.41), and Brundisium-
Rome five days (Plutarch, *Cat. Ma.* 35). The shipping route between Aulon
and Brundisium seems to have been used with relative regularity even during
the winter.[56] Since the transport of passengers and goods across the isthmus

---

52. Cf. L. Casson, *Ships and Seamanship in the Ancient World* (1971) 272f.

53. Cf. H. H. Goldstine, *New and Full Moons* (1973) 88f.

54. Cf. esp. C. J. Hemer, *The Book of Acts in the Setting of Hellenistic History*
(1989) 124f.

55. For the route between the harbor opposite Corcyra to Delphi, Aemilius Paulus
needed five days (Livius xlv.41). For Corinth-Delphi and Buthrotum-Aulon, one must
probably reckon another two days each.

56. Cf. W. M. Ramsay, *JRS* 15 (1925) 71.

enabled sailors to avoid a trip around the stormy capes in the south of the Peleponnes, Corinth, with its western harbor of Lechaeum, maintained excel- lent connections with the imperial capital.[57] Hence Paul did not have to write the letter to the Romans to a congregation completely unknown to him; rather, "the friends he mentions in Romans 16 could have informed him easily (and regularly) concerning circumstances in Rome."[58]

57. Cf. J. Rougé, *Recherches sur l'organisation du commerce maritime* (1966) 131f. Concerning the central position of Rome also in the shipping traffic of the Roman Empire, cf. L. Casson, *Die Seefahrer der Antike* (1979) 353-78.
58. P. Stuhlmacher, *ZNW* 77 (1986) 188.

§17

Attempt at a Chronological Synthesis

17.1. Acts and the Letters of Paul

Previously, we attempted to establish individual chronological dates for Paul's life (§§3-12). Then we were concerned with determining whether the letters, critically compared with Acts, might yield an understanding of the geographic movements of the apostle's activity (§§13-15). We will now attempt a relatively plausible chronological summary with the aid of three further series of dates. We have yet at our disposal direct information concerning time spans (1) in Paul's letters and (2) in Acts, and we also have (3) minimum time spans inferable from the geographic movements (§16.2). In the process, we will move from stages of Pauline activity for which we have access to a tighter weave of dates, back to those for which conjectures necessarily play a greater role.

17.1.1. From Philippi via Jerusalem to Rome (A.D. 57-62)

A whole series of dates stands at our disposal regarding this period: (1) The transition of the Judean governorship from Felix to Festus (Acts 24:27) and thus the transport of Paul to Rome can be dated in A.D. 59 (§12.4). (2) This seems even more likely if in this year the date of the Atonement Festival, a date critical for sea travel (Acts 27:9), came extremely late (§12.5.1). (3) The credibility of this information strengthens our trust in Luke's exact information concerning a sea journey from Philippi to Jerusalem (Acts 20:6–21:8), which leads to A.D. 57 (§12.2). (4) If Paul came to the holy city during the Pentecost festival of this particular year, then it would have been quite possible for him to be viewed as the Egyptian agitator (Acts 21:38) who presumably appeared at the Passover Festival in A.D. 56 (§12.3). (5) Above all, between the apostle's arrival in Jerusalem (A.D. 57) and his departure for Rome (A.D. 59), we have precisely those two years (Acts 24:27) which Luke provides for the imprisonment in Caesarea (§12.4.5). (6) This encourages us to take seriously also the assertion of "two whole years (ἐνέμεινεν δὲ διετίαν ὅλην)" for his Roman

318

imprisonment (Acts 28:30) (§12.5.2). The portrayal of Acts thus extends approximately to the spring of A.D. 62. (7) A dating of the letter to the Romans at the beginning of A.D. 57 fits the oppressive tax situation he addresses (Rom. 13:1-7), which in A.D. 58 led to a wave of grievances and to the reforms of Nero (see p. 303 above).

17.1.2. From Thessalonica to Ephesus (A.D. 49-52)

For this period, we have access especially to four dates: (1) If Paul abandoned his first Rome-plan in Thessalonica because of Claudius' Roman edict concerning the Jews, issued in A.D. 49 (§10; cf. Acts 18:2), then he must have received news of this at latest in the spring of A.D. 50 (§18.5.2). (2) The year-and-a-half Paul stayed in Corinth (Acts 18:11) leads, even with generous calculations, to the conclusion that the apostle left this city at the latest at the end of A.D. 51 (§11.2.1). (3) This dating converges with the most probable reconstruction of the Gallio-incident. The Corinthian Jews presented the charges against Paul (Acts 18:12-17) before the governor immediately after Gallio's accession to office on 1 July A.D. 51. Not too long after this, the apostle traveled by ship to Jerusalem (§11), reaching it before November of the same year. (4) Given the travel circumstances (Acts 18:22–19:1), the beginning of the Ephesian ministry can be dated at the earliest in the early summer of A.D. 52 (§16.2.3).

17.1.3. From Conversion to the Apostolic Council (A.D. 31/32-48)

The problem here is that no single date can stand on its own. Only a multi-faceted correlation of variously reliable data can lead to a relatively satisfactory result: (1) Of the two dates regarding the apostle's conversion deriving from early church tradition, A.D. 31/32 proves somewhat superior to A.D. 36/37 (§4). (2) Although the time spans provided by Galatians 1–2 do offer a further possible corrective, their significance for Pauline chronology tends generally to be overestimated, since two open questions generate considerable room for play: (a) One cannot decide unequivocally whether the three (Gal. 1:18) or fourteen years (Gal. 2:1) for the first and second visits to Jerusalem are meant consecutively, or whether both refer back to the conversion (Gal. 1:15f.); grammatically, both are possible.[1] (b) Commensurate with the custom of ancient time reckoning, any fraction of the first and last years can be included

---

1. Cf. C. J. Hemer, *The Book of Acts in the Setting of Hellenistic History* (1989) 262f., who precisely formulates the problem: "While it is certain that ἔπειτα denotes sequence in time, the point at issue in Gal. 1:18–2:1 is whether we have here *consecutive* rather than *concurrent* sequence of time."

as a full year in the calculation.[2] The following juxtaposition of possibilities for the visits to Jerusalem can show how little legitimacy apodictic determinations[3] can claim:

Conversion	31/32	36/37
simultaneous (13/14 years)	43/45 (A)	48/50 (C)
consecutive (15/17 years)	45/48 (B)	50/53 (D)

If, with the majority of contemporary scholars, one identifies Galatians 2 and Acts 15, then within the overall framework of our chronology (especially given the Gallio-date), A.D. 50/53 (D) must be eliminated as a date for the Apostolic Council. A.D. 48/50 (C), while possible, is rather tight. Thus from this perspective as well, the later conversion date proves to be problematical. Whereas option A is eliminated, given this identification and the assumption of an early conversion date, reckoning consecutively fully seventeen years brings us in the case of B to A.D. 48. The minority opinion, advocated first apparently by J. Calvin,[4] namely, that Galatians 2 is to be identified with Acts 11:28-30, is at least chronologically possible only with option A. The historical background suggested for the Antiochene collection the end of the period between A.D. 41/42 and 44/45 (§8). Adherents of this identification also date, from the perspective of the Gallio-incident, the Apostolic Council to A.D. 48 or 49.[5] (3) The time necessary for the trip from Jerusalem to Macedonia and Greece (Acts 15:36–18:1) leads, with respect to its beginning, to A.D. 48, not 49 (§16.2.2).

17.1.4. From Ephesus to Greece (A.D. 52-57)

Although genuinely fixed dates are lacking here, too, this period can be fitted into the preceding and following periods already inferred: (1) Given Paul's arrival in Ephesus in the first half of the year A.D. 52, his stay of a bit less than three years (Acts 20:31) (§12.1.3) suggests a departure at the beginning of A.D. 55. (2) Because of the uncertainty of the political situation in the provincial capital of Asia (§12.1), the transition from A.D. 54 to 55 was a dangerous period for Paul as well. This fits the assumption of increasing

---

2. Cf. R. Y. K. Fung, *The Epistle to the Galatians* (1988) 73.

3. It is not justified when, e.g., R. Jewett, *A Chronology of Paul's Life* (1979) 52-54, insists on understanding this as exactly seventeen years to the month, or when A. Suhl, *Paulus und seine Briefe* (1975) 46f., as well as R. Pesch, *Simon-Petrus* (1980) 78f., allows only a simultaneous manner of reckoning. Concerning G. Lüdemann, see pp. 20-22 above.

4. *Commentarius in Epistolam ad Galatas,* Corpus Reformatorum 78.182.

5. Cf., e.g., F. F. Bruce, *Paul* (1977) 475 (A.D. 49); R. Y. K. Fung, *The Epistle to the Galatians* (1988) 27 (A.D. 48); C. J. Hemer, *The Book of Acts* (1989) 269 (A.D. 49).

difficulties at the end of his stay in Ephesus. (3) If 2 Corinthians is to be dated in A.D. 55/56 (§12.1; 15.4), then the ecstatic experience "fourteen years ago" (2 Cor. 12:2) took place *ca.* A.D. 42/44. If one associates this with Paul's transition to Antioch (§14.3) and adds the "entire year (ἐνιαυτὸν ὅλον)" of his joint activity with Barnabas in this church (Acts 11:25f.), one acquires at least an approximate date for the Antiochene collection of A.D. 44/45 (Paul's own participation being problematical). (4) The apostle's travel movements in the period following his stay in Ephesus (Acts 20:1-3) make it probable that he spent two further winters in Macedonia (A.D. 55/56) and Achaia (A.D. 56/57) (§15.5.1-2). This yields a connection with the apostle's departure from Philippi for Jerusalem, which is to be dated in April A.D. 57 (§12.2).

17.1.5. Synthesis

The table on the next page organizes the view of Pauline chronology emerging from all these considerations.

17.2. Chronology and Autopsy

The chronology we have produced can also make a modest contribution to two crucial introductory questions in the dual Lukan work: (1) Do the we-passages in Acts represent authentic recollections of one of Paul's companions, or merely a stylistic device? (2) Can the author of these we-passages be identical with the author of the dual work, or do precisely the chronological errors in the overall conception show how far the author of Acts was from the time of Paul?

17.2.1. General Evaluation

First, we must acknowledge that the overall framework of the sequence of events portrayed by Acts is chronologically possible and coherent (albeit, of course, not necessarily for individual episodes[6]). Real difficulties emerge only in connection with two dates (Excursus II, section IV.7-8): (1) The census of Quirinius (Lk. 2:1f.) lay outside the conscious experience of the *auctor ad Theophilum* in every suggested dating of Luke-Acts. (2) If with the overwhelming majority of scholars one dates the uprising of Theudas after A.D. 44 (Josephus, *Ant.* xx.97f.), then Luke did in fact commit an avoidable error

---

6. Here the comparison between the "dramatic episodic style" in Acts and in Hellenistic literature is helpful. Cf. E. Plümacher, *Lukas als hellenistischer Schriftsteller* (1972) 80-136.

Contemporary History		Early Christianity/Paul	
26	Pilate as Prefect	26/27	Public Appearance of John
27	Sabbatical Year (27/28)	27/28	Public Appearance of Jesus
28		28/29	Death of John the Baptist
29			
30		30	Crucifixion of Jesus
31	Fall of Sejanus	31/32	Martyrdom of Stephen
32			Conversion of Paul
33		33/34	Paul in Jerusalem
34		34-42	Paul in Syria-Cilicia
35			
36	Recall of Pilate		
37	Death of Tiberius	ca. 37	Designation "Christian" in
38			Antioch (Hellenist Mission)
39			
40	Death of Aretas IV		
41	Death of Caligula	41/42	Death of James of Zebedee
	Disturbances in Antioch		Peter leaves Jerusalem
42	41/42 Hunger in Rome		
43		42/44	Paul in Antioch
44	Death of Agrippa I		
	Dearth in Judea (44-49)	44/45	Antiochene Collection
45	Fadus as Procurator in Judea	45-47	Paul and Barnabas in
46	Tiberius Alexander as Procurator		Cyprus and south Galatia
47			
48	Jewish Disturbances in Antioch	48	in Antioch (Gal.??)
	Cumanus as Procurator		Council in Jerusalem
49	Felix as Procurator	49	Paul in Macedonia
	Roman Edict concerning the Jews	49/50	Paul in Thessalonica
50		50	in Corinth (Gal. ?? 1 Thess.)
51	Gallio in Achaia (51/52)	51	Paul before Gallio
	Hunger in Rome	51/52	Paul in Syria
52		52/55	Paul in Ephesus
53			
54	Death of Claudius	54/55	(1 Cor., Phil.?, Phlm.??)
55	Sabbatical Year (55/6)	55	Paul in Troas
		55/56	in Macedonia (2 Cor.)
56	Egyptian Agitator	56/57	Paul in Corinth (Rom.)
57		57	in Jerusalem
58	Roman taxation unrest	57-59	Caesarea imprisonment
			(Phlm.??)
59	Festus as Procurator in Judea	59	Paul to Rome
60		60-62	Paul in Rome

in Acts 5:36. For no ancient (or even modern) historian, however, can a single error constitute the determining factor regarding the overall value of his or her work. None of the other directly or indirectly determinable information concerning time departs necessarily from the chronological sequence, and, taken together, it does indeed yield a coherent nexus.

17.2.2. Evaluating Details

The specific chronological pieces of information are distributed quite disparately within the dual Lukan work. In what follows we provide a juxtaposition structured according to this Gospel,[7] the first part of Acts (Acts 1–15),[8] the we-passages,[9] and the remaining passages from the second part,[10] among which one can almost always assume the spatial and/or temporal proximity of the author of the we-passages. Furthermore, we will distinguish once again dates associated with events and/or persons from general history from other chronological information such as hours, days, festivals, or years.

	Gospel	**Acts, Part 1**	**We-passages**	**Rest of Acts, Part 2**
World history	2	3 (2)	—	4
Other dates	20	11 (3)	50	13

A crude statistical evaluation of these findings shows the material distributed about as follows: Gospel, ½; first part of Acts, ¼; second part, ¼. This means that only ¼ of the entire dual Lukan work (the we-passages and the remaining, second part of Acts) contains 67 of the *ca.* 103 pieces of chronological information, that is, approximately 66 percent. This relationship shifts even more strongly if one considers that some of this information (about five instances) is found in the first part of Acts (in parentheses) in close association with the collection from Antioch,[11] that is, with that particular city which a whole

---

7. Lk. 1:5, 8, 24, 26, (36), 56; 2:1f. (census), 42; 3:1f. (Tiberius), 23; 4:2 (Mk. 1:13), 40-42 (Mk. 1:32-34); 9:28 (diff. Mk. 9:2), 37; 10:21; 13:31; 22:1 (Mk. 14:1), 7 (Mk. 14:12), 66; 23:44 (Mk. 15:33), 56 (cf. Mk. 15:42); 24:1 (Mk. 16:1), 13, 33. When parallels in Mark are lacking, the information appears especially in pieces such as the prehistory or the Passion account, for which a basis in tradition in probable. Cf. also §3.2.

8. Acts 1:40; 2:1; 3:1; 4:5; 5:7, 36f. (Theudas and Judas); 9:9; 11:26, 28 (hunger under Claudius); 12:3f., 6, (18), 21ff. (death of Agrippa I); 13:44; 14:30.

9. Acts 16:11f., 25; 20:6 (ter), 11, 15 (bis), 16, 31; 21:1, 4, 7, 17f.; 27:3, 5, 9, 19 (bis), 27, (33), 33, (39); 28:7, 11, 12, 13 (bis), 14, 17, 30.

10. Acts 17:2; 18:2 (Claudius' edict), 11, 12 (Gallio); 19:6, 10; 20:2f.; 21:27, 30, 38 (Egyptian agitator); 23:11, 12, 23, 31, 32; 24:1, 11, 27 (Felix/Festus); 25:1, 6, 23.

11. Acts 11:26, 28 (famine); 12:3f., 6, (18), 21ff. (Agrippa I).

series of scholars continue to view as the hometown of the author of Acts.[12] Finally, one should point out that the we-passages, constituting less than 10 percent of the entirety of the dual Lukan work, contain the highest absolute number of pieces of chronological information, namely, fifty, or about half the total. Now, one could try to explain these statistical findings by pointing out that the purpose of the detailed information in the we-passages is precisely to lend to those passages, artificially, the flair of authenticity. However, caution is advised not least by the fact that the we-passages do indeed also contain unspecific information regarding time.[13]

It is especially striking, however, that by far the highest concentration of specific or detailed pieces of information regarding time, namely, festival dates and/or individual, unconventional time spans regarding days, are found in the we-passages: (1) for the passage from Troas to Philippi in Acts 16:11f. (§16.3.1); (2) with regard to the journey from Philippi to Jerusalem in Acts 20:6–21:8 (§12.2); and (3) with regard to the journey from Caesarea to Rome in Acts 27–28 (§12.5). Since this information can in part be related to dates from secular history, and since from the perspective of the last two we-passages a coherent chronology can be produced, caution is advised in assuming that the details represent merely literary convention. Contra the assertion that the Lukan account of the journey to Rome is following a widespread ancient fictive narrative genre,[14] a series of literary[15] as well as historical[16]

---

12. Cf. R. Riesner, *Jesus als Lehrer* (³1988) 25 (bibliography), and recently esp. J. A. Fitzmyer, *The Gospel according to Luke* I (1981) 41-47.

13. Cf. Acts 16:11, 18; 21:10; 27:7, 9, 14.

14. So, with a great deal of confidence, V. K. Robbins, "The We-Passages in Acts and Ancient Sea-Voyages," *BR* 20 (1975) 5-18; *"By Land and by Sea:* The We-Passages and Ancient Sea-Voyages," in C. H. Talbert, ed., *Perspectives on Luke-Acts* (Edinburgh, 1978) 215-42.

15. Cf. esp. C. K. Barrett, *Festschrift A. T. Hanson* (1987) 51-64.

16. Recently, H. Warnecke, *Die tatsächliche Romfahrt des Apostels Paulus* (1987), especially emphasizes the good geographic and nautical information found in Luke. This work, which prompted an unusual amount of attention in the press (e.g., in *Die Zeit* 52 [23 Dec. 1988] 33f.: "Paul was never on Malta. Biblical maps and popular translations of Acts must now be revised"), is interesting because of its considerable knowledge of ancient sea travel and of the nautical conditions in the eastern Mediterranean. The main point of the author's thesis, namely, that Μελίτη in Acts 28:1 is to be identified with the northwest Greek island Cephalonia, however, is unpersuasive, since it offers no witness to Cephalonia ever having been called Μελίτη. Other arguments, too, are questionable. For example, one can certainly assert that a different delimitation of the Adriatic (Acts 27:27) is possible than the one H. Warnecke, *loc. cit.,* 69-74, declares to be the only possible one. Cf. J. Rougé, *Recherches sur l'organisation du commerce maritime en Méditerranée sous l'empire Romaine* (1966) 42f. J. Wehnert, *ZTK* 87 (1990) 67-99; 88 (1991) 169-80, while offering justified criticism, nonetheless absolutizes too excessively in his own turn the interpretation of Acts in the tradition of M. Dibelius and H. Conzelmann. The weakness of the Cephalonia-thesis becomes

arguments can be adduced. The analysis of the individual pieces of chronological information in Acts thus supports the conclusions of those who consider the we-passages to be, in one way or another, eyewitness recollections.[17]

To this we can add that a disproportionately high number, namely, around 25 percent (with an overall share of about 15 percent), of detailed pieces of chronological information in Acts is similarly found in passages in which the author, according to the claim of the we-passages, stood in temporal and/or spatial proximity to the events portrayed: (1) The author apparently was in Philippi (cf. Acts 16:12-16) when news of the Claudian edict reached Greece (cf. Acts 18:2). In Philippi, he could also have learned that Paul left Corinth — after a stay of around one-and-a-half years — shortly after the trial before Gallio (Acts 18:11ff.). (2) The fact that the "we" stands both at the beginning (Acts 21:15-18) and end (Acts 27:1) of the account of Paul's final stay in Jerusalem apparently presupposes the presence of the author of the we-passages during this entire period. He can thus also have known (a) that the visit with James occurred on the day immediately after Paul's arrival (Acts 21:17f.), (b) that the incident in the temple took place at the end of the Nazirite period (Acts 21:26f.), (c) that Paul was taken before the High Council on the day after his arrest (Acts 22:30), (d) that a day later his life was threatened by a conspiracy of Sicarii (Acts 23:12), which is why he was escorted away "in the third hour of the night" (Acts 23:23) from Jerusalem to Caesarea, where five days later the high priest Ananias appeared (Acts 24:1), and, finally,

---

even more apparent in H. Warnecke and T. Schirrmacher, *War Paulus wirklich auf Malta?* (1992). Cf. P. Guillaumier, *The Sunday Times (Malta)* (1 November 1992) 30f.; (8 November 1992) 42f., who also offers the best modern defense for Malta (in M. Galea and J. Ciarlo, eds., *St. Paul in Malta* [1992] 53-114). G. Kettenbach, *Das Logbuch des Lukas* (1986), calls into question Luke's reliability based on nautical considerations, though his portrayal is also subject to serious questioning. For example, the wind so important for his fictive-symbolic interpretation (*loc. cit.,* 56-80), εὐρακύλων (Acts 27:14), can easily be identified with the help of ancient sources (C. J. Hemer, *JTS* 26 [1975] 100-111). One modern navy historian concludes: "The laconic account in Acts is probably the most dramatic and detailed witness of an ancient sea journey that we possess" (O. Höckmann, *Antike Seefahrt* [1985] 88f.). Concerning Paul's sea journey to Rome, cf. esp. C. J. Hemer, *TynBul* 36 (1985) 87-109; *idem, The Book of Acts in the Setting of Hellenistic History* (1989) 133-52. Earlier studies deserving consideration include F. Brannigan, *ThGl* 25 (1933) 170-86; J. Dauvillier, *BLÉ* 61 (1960) 11-25; J. Rougé, *VigChr* 14 (1960) 193-203; I. Maistrello, in B. Mariani, *S. Paolo da Cesarea a Roma* (1963) 163-92; L. Casson, *Die Seefahrer der Antike* (1979) 375-77.

17. A survey of the more recent discussion of the we-passages can be found in V. Fusco, *BeO* 25 (1983) 73-86; S. E. Porter, in D. W. J. Gill and C. Gempf, *The Book of Acts in Its Graeco-Roman Setting* (1994) 545-74; and S. M. Praeder, *NT* 29 (1987) 193-218, who closes with the more skeptical remark: "Comparative literary solutions assume that other ancient texts will illuminate the text of Acts. So far this has not been the case for the textual features of first person narration in Acts" (*loc. cit.,* 218). A more optimistic view of an orientation of Luke to ancient models is taken by E. Plümacher, *ZNW* 68 (1977) 2-22.

(e) that Paul then spent two years in prison (Acts 24:27), until the new governor, Festus, three days after his arrival, took up the investigation anew (Acts 25:1). A comparison of these relatively numerous, more exact remarks with the almost exclusively vague temporal details (μετὰ ταῦτα, ἐν ταῖς ἡμέραις ταύταις, etc.) in the Gospel or in the first part of Acts, strengthens the suspicion that the author of the we-passages and of the dual work are the same person.[18] This assumption is also commensurate with the observation that outside the we-passages, the best geographic information concerns the environs of places where their author found himself: Philippi (§16.2.4),[19] Jerusalem, and Caesarea.[20] Finally, A. von Harnack's conclusion can be mentioned: "All the temporal designations occurring in the we-passages — and some of these are unusual, including such not otherwise found in the New Testament — recur scattered in the other parts of the book."[21]

The analysis of such chronological and topographical details prompts us to recall the criterion T. Mommsen formulated for Luke: "The numerous small features — features not really necessary for the actual course of action, and yet which fit so well there — are internal witnesses for his reliability."[22] And the conclusion concerning Acts reached by a historian of the rank of E. Meyer — a historian not at all uncritical of Christianity itself — is still worthy of discussion: "For the history of Christianity, however, we have . . . the completely inestimable advantage — one hardly otherwise available in the case of great spiritual movements — of having access to a portrayal of the beginning stages of its development directly from the pen of one of its coparticipants. That alone ensures for the author an eminent place among the significant historians of world history."[23]

---

18. The literary form of the itinerary by no means militates against the possibility that an author is offering his own recollections. Cf. J. Reumann, in *Festschrift J. A. Fitzmyer* (1989) 335-57.

19. P. Pilhofer, *Philippi* I (1995) 248-54, even concludes that Luke was an inhabitant of this town, and at least a Macedonian.

20. Cf. M. Hengel, *ZDPV* 99 (1983) 152-75.

21. *SPAW.PH* (1907) 392. Also in *Die Apostelgeschichte* (1908).

22. *ZNW* 2 (1901) 87.

23. *Ursprung und Anfänge des Christentums* I ([4/5]1924) 2f. See now also H. Botermann, *Das Judenedikt des Kaisers Claudius* (1996).

Excursus II: Acts and World History

Within the context of his introductory chapter, "A Critical Survey of Research into the Chronology of Paul," G. Lüdemann presents the "Contradictions between Luke's Chronological Information and Data from World History."[1] Using military diction, Lüdemann precisely circumscribes his tactical and strategic goal: "In the following we shall launch a full-scale attack on the conventional chronology by means of fundamental criticism of the propriety of accepting any absolute datum of world history from Luke (without confirmation from Paul). We shall demonstrate that Luke's chronological references to world history are often incorrect and thereby deny the methodological right of developing a chronology of Paul on the basis of the reference to Gallio."[2] Although a thorough discussion is not possible, we will nonetheless evaluate the significance of and draw methodological conclusions from the eight examples Lüdemann mentions. That is, closer examination reveals that these represent extremely different situations requiring more differentiated treatment.

(1) Information in Favor of Luke

1. Earlier scholars accused Luke of having confused in Lk. 3:1 the tetrarch Lysanias of Abilene with the king of Ituraea by the same name who had already been executed in 34 B.C. by Antony at Cleopatra's behest (Josephus, *Ant.* xiv.330; xv.92).[3] As Lüdemann admits, however, "this suspicion has been dampened, though in my opinion not completely muffled, by the discovery that there was evidently another, later Lysanias (who died between 28 and 37

1. *Paul: Apostle to the Gentiles* (Eng. trans., 1984) 8-11.
2. *Ibid.,* 8-9.
3. Cf. R. Riesner, *GBL* II (1988) 904 (bibliography).

C.E.)."[4] Although the evidence accessible to us speaks in favor of Acts, Lüdemann nonetheless adduces Lk. 3:1 as a negative example. Apparently, Luke's own statements will in every case be used against him, regardless of what he writes.

2. According to Lüdemann, in Lk. 3:19f. Luke appropriately corrects Mk. 6:17 by eliminating the name Philip for the former husband of Herodias.[5] So at least here the *auctor ad Theophilum* might be viewed as an informed and careful historian. But Lüdemann objects that "Josephus gives a completely different reason for the imprisonment of John by Herod the tetrarch. Only with great difficulty can this reason be harmonized with that provided by Mark and Luke. For Josephus the reason is not John's moral condemnation of Herod but rather Herod's fear that political rioting might be incited by John's proclamation. *Ant.* xviii.118 reads: . . ."[6] The alternative presented here represents an utter anachronism for New Testament Palestine. The behavior of Herod Antipas cannot be compared with the fling of some politician in a permissive western society. John the Baptist accused the tetrarch of violating Mosaic law (cf. Lev. 18:16). Given the simultaneous presence of a theocratically motivated insurgency movement, this constituted a highly political accusation. As a rule, historians thus consider the different modes of portrayal to be compatible.[7]

(2) Information Lacking Comparative Material

3. Concerning Lk. 13:1, Lüdemann concludes that "the slaughter of the Galileans by Pilate has no parallel in Josephus."[8] Luke, according to Lüdemann, confused the incident with Pilate's blood bath among the Samaritans at Mount Gerizim (Josephus, *Ant.* xviii.85ff.) around A.D. 35. But Lüdemann supports this suspicion neither by providing a reason nor by referring to another study.[9] A study by J. Blinzler,[10] which with considerable specialized understanding of the period also addresses this alleged confusion on Luke's part, is dismissed as "uncritical" without any further discussion of its details.[11]

4. *Paul: Apostle to the Gentiles* (Eng. trans., 1984) 9.
5. *Ibid.* Concerning another possible explanation, see pp. 42f., note 46 above.
6. *Paul: Apostle to the Gentiles* (Eng. trans., 1984) 9f.
7. Cf. merely Schuerer I, 346, and cf. §3.2.2.
8. *Paul: Apostle to the Gentiles* (Eng. trans., 1984) 10.
9. The reference to Schuerer I, 385ff. (*loc. cit.*, 34, note 31), does not get us any further, since the identification Lüdemann advocates is as a matter of fact not carried out there.
10. *NovT* 2 (1958) 24-49.
11. G. Lüdemann, *Paul: Apostle to the Gentiles* (Eng. trans., 1984) 31, note 31.

(3) Information Whose Details May Be Imprecise,
But Which Are Not in General Incorrect

4. Acts 4:6 refers only to Annas (A.D. 6-15) as the high priest (χαὶ Ἅννας ὁ ἀρχιερεύς), even though immediately thereafter the real officeholder at that time (A.D. 18-37) is mentioned, namely, Caiaphas. By contrast, one can understand the grammatical construction in Lk. 3:2 (ἐπὶ ἀρχιερέως Ἅννα χαὶ Καϊάφα) such that both are conceived as high priests together at the time of John the Baptist's public appearance.[12] This would be inaccurate insofar as according to the Jewish view there could be only one legitimate high priest, and according to Roman directive also only one officeholder. A slightly different picture emerges if Luke — as in Lk. 3:2 (§3.2.1), so in Acts 4:6 — was following a Jewish-Christian source. Then Acts 4:6 can represent a Jewish linguistic custom with which the source of Acts picked up on "the judgment of public Palestinian opinion,"[13] which accorded the title only to the person whose claim to the office of high priest had religio-legal legitimacy.[14] One would then understand Lk. 3:2 either analogously as singular, or with plural meaning as an imprecise manner of expression on which one ought not base conclusions that are too far-reaching. Josephus, too, occasionally speaks of two former officeholders, Ananus (A.D. 62) and Jesus, son of Gamaliel (A.D. 63-64),[15] as high priests (ἀρχιερεῖς) in the plural (Josephus, *Vita* 193); and in general, the Jewish historian exhibits remarkable terminological flexibility regarding this matter.[16] Yet no one on this basis is likely to accuse him of being poorly informed concerning the religious and civil-legal background of the high-priestly office of the period before A.D. 70.

5. The sequence of more extensive local famines that probably took place during the reign of Claudius (A.D. 51-54) (§8.2) makes it seem not entirely illegitimate for Luke (Acts 11:28), in a fashion similar to Suetonius

---

12. Cf. I. H. Marshall, *The Gospel of Luke* (1978) 134.

13. H. Schürmann, *Das Lukasevangelium* (²1981) 151.

14. Documentation can be found in J. Jeremias, *Jerusalem zur Zeit Jesu* (³1962) 178 (Eng. trans., *Jerusalem in the Time of Jesus* [1969]). In addition to Annas and his son-in-law Caiaphas, Acts 4:6 mentions two others, John and Alexander, from the high-priestly family (ἐκ γένους ἀρχιερατικοῦ). The former is perhaps identical with a grandson of Annas, whose name was found in an Aramaic ossuary-inscription in the vicinity of Jerusalem (D. Barag and D. Flusser, *IEJ* 36 [1986] 39-44). If with D *it* one reads Jonathan instead, the reference might be to a son of Annas who was high priest in A.D. 36/37, and was probably a temple captain during the time of Acts 4:6. This would give us a *terminus ante quem.* Cf. J. Jeremias, *loc. cit.,* 222.

15. Cf. Schuerer II, 232.

16. Cf. *ibid.,* 233-36.

(*Claudius* 18.2), to speak about famine or dearth throughout the empire under this emperor.[17]

6. Regardless of whether one considers it an inaccurate generalization for Luke (like Suetonius?) to speak of the expulsion of "all" Jews from Rome under Claudius (Acts 18:2), the author of Acts does in any case, contra Lüdemann,[18] provide the correct chronology for this event (§12).

(4) Information about Which a Majority of Scholars Consider Luke to Have Made a Mistake

7. The problems attaching to an empire-wide census (ἀπογραφή) conducted apparently — according to Luke — under the Syrian governor Quirinius also in the territory of Herod the Great, are sufficiently familiar.[19] Nonetheless, it is questionable whether all the scholars who exercise reserve in assuming a Lukan error are addressed sufficiently by the assertion that "the attempts of Zahn and others to identify a census by Quirinius which differs from that mentioned by Josephus and to connect this one with Lk. 2:1ff. are apologetic."[20] Weighty historical and literary-critical concerns can also be raised against Josephus' chronological details regarding a census around A.D. 6 (Josephus, *Ant.* xvii.355; xviii.1-5).[21] The most recent monograph on this topic supports the objective accuracy of Luke's own information.[22] Other scholars grant him at least general credibility, all the while accepting a measure of terminological ambiguity, such as the assumption of a governor-

---

17. Contra G. Lüdemann, *Paul: Apostle to the Gentiles* (Eng. trans., 1984) 11.

18. *Ibid.,* 11.

19. Surveys of the discussion can be found in F. X. Steinmetzer, *RAC* II (1954) 969-72; G. Ogg, *ET* 79 (1967/68) 231-36; Schuerer I, 399-427; M. Stern, CRINT I/1 (1974) 372-74; P. Benoit, *DBS* VII (1981) 707-13; W. Brindle, *JETS* 27 (1984) 43-52; S. R. Llewelyn, *NewDoc* VI (1992) 119-32. The most recent study of the Roman census system by L. Neesen, *Untersuchungen zu den direkten Abgaben der römischen Kaiserzeit* (1980) 30-44, emphatically contests Luke's reliability; similarly also R. Syme, in *Roman Papers* III (1984) 869-84 (1973). Additional bibliography can be found in T. P. Wiseman, *NTS* 33 (1987) 479f.

20. G. Lüdemann, *Paul: Apostle to the Gentiles* (Eng. trans., 1984) 9.

21. Cf. T. Zahn, *NKZ* 4 (1893) 633-54; *FGNKAL* III 129-35, 751-55; *Das Evangelium des Lucas* (3/41920) 750-54; *Introduction to the New Testament* (Eng. trans., 1909) 3.95-100, 130f.; F. Spitta, *ZNW* 7 (1906) 290-303; W. Weber, *ZNW* 10 (1909) 307-19; and esp. W. Lodder, *Die Schätzung des Quirinius bei Flavius Josephus* (1930), as well as P. Benoit, *DBS* VII (1981) 704-7.

22. G. Firpo, *Il problema cronologico della nascita di Gesù* (1983) 119-260. Cf. also D. J. Hayles, *Buried History* 9 (1973) 113-32; 10 (1974) 16-31; P. W. Barnett, *ET* 85 (1973/74) 377-80; K. F. Doig, *New Testament Chronology* (1991) 99-108.

ship of Quirinius over Syria at that time (Lk. 2:2: ἡγεμονεύοντος τῆς Συρίας Κυρηνίου).[23] Hence one could also classify this particular problem in the preceding category.

8. The greatest chronological-historical difficulty in Luke is his mention of a rebel leader by the name of Theudas before the revolt of Judas the Galilean at the time of a census (ἐν ταῖς ἡμέραις τῆς ἀπογραφῆς) in a speech (Acts 5:36f.) which Gamaliel the Elder allegedly delivered before the death of Herod Agrippa I (cf. Acts 12:1ff.) in the year A.D. 44. Josephus mentions the revolt of one Theudas under the procurator Cuspius Fadus, who did not take office until after Agrippa I (Josephus, *Ant.* xx.97-99). Lüdemann[24] himself notes that more recently, as well,[25] scholars have considered the possibility that Josephus made a chronological error here.[26] Scholars are still considering cautiously the possibility that Luke and Josephus may be referring to two different persons.[27] The arguments Lüdemann raises against this latter possibility are not as strong as they appear at first glance. Given the materials now available, his assertion that "the name Theudas is extremely rare"[28] will have to be attenuated.[29] Within a time span covering forty years, Josephus also mentions four rebel leaders by the name of Simon, and within ten years three who were called Judas.[30] Finally, it is not inconceivable that Josephus himself could have left out a more significant insurgency movement under Herod the Great. The Jewish historian reports in part only quite summarily about the various disturbances in Judea after Herod's death (Josephus, *Ant.* xvii.269f.). Some have even thought specifically about the insurgency movement of

23. G. M. Lee, *CQR* 167 (1966) 431-36; A. Strobel, *Ursprung und Geschichte des frühchristlichen Osterkalenders* (1977) 82-84; P. Benoit, *DBS* VII (1981) 713-16; R. Laurentin, *Les Évangiles de l'Enfance du Christ* (²1983) 388f. (Eng. trans., *The Infancy Narratives of Christ* [1986]); W. Hinz, *ZDMG* 139 (1989) 301-3.

24. *Paul: Apostle to the Gentiles* (Eng. trans., 1984) 34f., note 34.

25. F. Dexinger, *Kairos* 17 (1975) 261, note 61. So also G. Stählin, *Die Apostelgeschichte* (⁶1978) 93.

26. A thorough attempt at grounding this argument can be found in T. Zahn, *Die Apostelgeschichte des Lucas* I (1919) 215f.

27. C. S. C. Williams, *The Acts of the Apostles* (²1964) 19f.; R. J. Cassidy, *Jesus, Politics, and Society* (1978) 17; I. H. Marshall, *The Acts of the Apostles* (1980) 122f.; R. N. Longenecker, *The Acts of the Apostles* (1981) 322f.; P. W. Barnett, *NTS* 27 (1981) 694, note 2; D. J. Williams, *Acts* (1985) 99.

28. G. Lüdemann, *Paul: Apostle to the Gentiles* (Eng. trans., 1984) 10f.

29. Cf. Schuerer I, 456, note 6; G. H. R. Horsley, *NewDoc* IV (1987) 183-85 ("the name, by no means common, but certainly better attested than the entries in MM and BAGD suggest" [*loc. cit.*, 183]). Present evidence does not allow us to decide whether Theudas could serve as an abbreviated form of Theodoros and/or Theodotos, nor which Semitic name it represented.

30. Cf. R. J. Knowling, *The Acts of the Apostles* (1912) 158.

Matthias, son of Margalothus, at the end of Herod's reign (Josephus, *Ant.* xvii.149-67).[31] Lüdemann[32] might admittedly be correct when contra F. F. Bruce[33] he considers Origen's remark concerning the revolt of one Theudas before the birth of Jesus (Origen, *Cels.* i.57) to be a mere conclusion from Acts 5:36f. In this connection, one might check once more the thesis of T. Zahn that Origen had access to additional information about the Jews under Tiberius, which he might have gotten from Philo of Alexandria.[34] Nonetheless, the concurrence of names between Luke and Josephus is so striking[35] that even conservative exegetes assume here that either Luke himself or the tradition preceding him made an error.[36] The possible Hebraism γίνεσθαι εἰς (היה ל) in Acts 5:36 might betray the use of a source.[37]

(5) General Evaluation

After this detailed examination of the examples adduced by Lüdemann for the historical unreliability of Luke, some fundamental methodological reflection is necessary. Even if in all these eight cases Luke really had reported falsely, that would prove first of all only that he, like every other ancient and modern historian, is susceptible to error.[38] Whether he was (according to ancient standards) an unreliable or on the whole credible historical writer can only be ascertained by the control test: how much does Luke report accurately?[39] Even

31. Cf. E. Jacquier, *Les Actes des Apôtres* ([2]1926) 178.
32. *Paul: Apostle to the Gentiles* (Eng. trans., 1984) 34f., note 34.
33. *The Acts of the Apostles* ([2]1952) 147.
34. *FGNKAL* VI (1900) 304f., note 3.
35. Cf. M. Hengel, *Die Zeloten* ([2]1976) 235 (Eng. trans., *The Zealots* [1989]).
36. A. Wikenhauser, *Die Apostelgeschichte* ([4]1961) 76; J. Munck, *The Acts of the Apostles* (1967) 46; G. A. Krodel, *Acts* (1986) 129f.
37. Cf. F. F. Bruce, *The Acts of the Apostles* ([2]1952) 147f.
38. Concerning the (extremely varied) standards of ancient historical writing, cf. E. Gabba, *JRS* 71 (1981) 50-62; M. Hengel, *Zur urchristlichen Geschichtsschreibung* ([2]1984) 11-35; D. Flach, *Einführung in die römische Geschichtsschreibung* (1985); L. Alexander, *NT* 28 (1986) 48-74; C. Nicolet, *L'inventaire du monde* (1988) 69-96; C. J. Hemer, *The Book of Acts in the Setting of Hellenistic History* (1989) 63-100; G. E. Sterling, *Historiography and Self-definition* (1992); A. Baum, *Lukas als Historiker der letzten Jesusreise* (1993) 39-102.
39. The most comprehensive treatment of this question is still A. Wikenhauser, *Die Apostelgeschichte und ihr Geschichtswert* (1921). In crucial sections, this work has now been continued and superseded by the unfortunately posthumous study of C. J. Hemer, *The Book of Acts in the Setting of Hellenistic History* (1989) 101-220. Cf. also the overview in F. F. Bruce, *ANRW* II 25.3 (1984) 2575-82; the presentation of the history of scholarship in W. W. Gasque, *A History of the Criticism of the Acts of the Apostles* (1975); and the series The Book of Acts in Its First Century Setting, ed. B. W. Winter (1993-).

this cursory treatment of difficulties has probably already made it clear that Luke looks considerably better than Lüdemann would have us believe. Considering the more extensive treatment of chronological questions presented here, one can suggest that apart from two genuinely problematical assertions (Quirinius-census, Theudas-revolt), Luke offers in at least six instances direct (fifteenth year of Tiberius) or indirect (famine under Claudius, death of Agrippa I, Roman edict concerning the Jews, governorship of Gallio, Egyptian agitator, transition from Felix to Festus) chronological information that can be understood meaningfully against the background of the contemporary history of the time.

Beyond this, a distinction must once more be made in the material offered by Luke. Where was he following sources whose reliability he could perhaps in part not check? And where was he claiming to report information based on his own experience or on direct research? One should remember that Luke probably found the two problematical items concerning the empire census and the Theudas-revolt in other sources. To be sure, especially the latter case involves information that possibly could have been checked in other ways even if with the majority of scholars one assumes that Acts is to be dated around A.D. 80.

III. Early Pauline Theology: The Apostle and the Church in Thessalonica

§18

Apology for a Hasty Departure

18.1. Thessalonica at the Time of Paul

18.1.1. History and Significance

When the apostle, probably in the neighborhood of the later Lete Gate,[1] entered Thessalonica,[2] he was entering the "metropolis of Macedonia," as

---

1. Topographical features as well as especially the discovery of a Roman milestone make it certain that the *Via Egnatia* came to Thessalonica not from the east, but rather exactly like the more modern road from Kavalla (Neapolis), from the north. Cf. C. I. Makaronas, *Festschrift D. M. Robinson* (1951) 391-98. Today, the milestone (C. Romiopolou, *BCH* 98 [1974] 813-16) is on exhibit in the new archaeological museum of Thessalonica (Inv. No. 1837); concerning the place along the road to Langadas where it was found, cf. B. Schwank, *EA* 39 (1961) 410f. Hence the modern "Hodos Egnatias," crossing the city in an east-west direction, bears its name illegitimately. Byzantine sources call this road ἡ λεωφόρος. Cf. M. Vickers, *JHS* 92 (1972) 162. The northwest gate, which the Byzantines called Λιτέα, whose basis apparently went back to the (late?) Roman period (W. Elliger, *Paulus in Griechenland* [1978] 100f.), was torn down at the beginning of the twentieth century by the Turkish city administration for road widening.

2. Cf. C. Diehl, *Salonique* (1920); J. Nehama, *Histoire des Israelites de Salonique* I/II (1935) 8-44; E. Oberhummer, *PRE* II 6 (1937) 143-48; H. Leclerq, *DACL* XV/1 (1950) 624-713; B. Rigaux, *Saint Paul: Les épîtres aux Thessaloniciens* (1956) 11-20; P. Rossano, *RBI* 6 (1958) 242-47; M. F. Unger, *BS* 119 (1962) 38-44 (unreliable); P. E. Davies, *BA* 26 (1963) 103-5; B. Schwank, *EA* 39 (1963) 409-13; A. Suhl and B. Reicke, *BHH* III (1966) 1968f.; R. M. Evans, *Eschatology and Ethics: A Study of Thessalonica and Paul's Letters to the Thessalonians* (1968) 1-83; F. O'Sullivan, *The Egnatian Way* (1972) 91-96; A. E. Vacalopoulos, *A History of Thessalonica* (1972) 3-18; M. Vickers, *JHS* 92 (1972) 156-70; W. Elliger, *Paulus in Griechenland* (1978) 68-113; J. Finegan, *The Archaeology of the New Testament* II (1981) 107-16; O. F. A. Meinardus, *Die Reisen des Apostels Paulus* (1981) 90-98; F. F. Bruce, *1 & 2 Thessalonians* (1982) xix-xxviii; N. Hugédé, *Saint Paul et la Grèce* (1982) 67-84; W. A. Meeks, *The First Urban Christians* (1983) 45-47; H. L. Hendrix, *Thessalonians Honor Romans* (1984); T. L. Donaldson, in R. K. Harrison, ed., *Major Cities of the Biblical World* (1985) 258-65; T. Holtz, *Der erste Brief an die Thessalonicher* (²1990) 9-23; R. Jewett, *The Thessalonian Correspondence* (1986) 118-32; S. E.

the geographer Strabo called it (Strabo vii, Fr. 21: ἡ μητρόπολις τῆς νῦν Μακεδονίας). The importance and economic power of Thessalonica, however, were connected then as today with the extremely favorable transportation location of the city on the Thermaic Gulf, which extends a considerable distance inland (Pliny the Elder, *HN* iv.10.17), a location the founders of the Hellenistic city had already used to their advantage.[3] This is the intersection of the shortest routes from the Bosporus to the Adriatic, and from the Balkans through the Axios (Vardar) Valley into the Danube region. West of the city, a fertile coastal plain opens up (Appian, *BC* iv.105; *Athen* xv.682B). The remains of an Ionian temple found in the western part of the old city come from the period of the first Macedonian dynasty in the sixth century B.C. Contemporary scholarship assumes almost unanimously that these first traces of a city settlement represent Therma mentioned by Herodotus (Herodotus vii.128), which also gave the gulf its name.[4] Strabo quite obviously assumes this identification (Strabo viii, Fr. 24). The name Therma probably derives not from the hot springs, but from the "heat" (θέρμη) of an ecstatic Dionysus-cult with roots in the religion of the original Thracian-Phrygian inhabitants.[5] In 316 or 315 B.C., the Macedonian king Cassander combined Therma with twenty-six other settlements into a new political unity (συνοικισμός), naming it after his wife, a half-sister of Alexander the Great, Θεσσαλονίκη (Strabo viii, Fr. 21, 24).[6]

Because of its favorably situated harbor (Herodotus vii.121; Livius xliv.10), Thessalonica soon became more important than the old Macedonian capital Pella, whose distance from the sea became increasingly greater as a result of heavy silting. In 168 B.C., after the fall of the independent Macedonian

---

Johnson, *Paul the Apostle and His Cities* (1987) 76-80; E. Krentz, *BiTod* 24 (1988) 328-37; F. Papazoglou, *Les villes de Macédoine à l'époque romaine* (1988) 189-212; D. H. Madvig, *ISBE* IV (1988) 836-38; R. Riesner, *GBL* III (1989) 1545-48; M. Adinolfi, *La prima lettera ai Tessalonicesi nel mondo greco-romano* (1990) 24-28; H. L. Hendrix, *ABD* VI (1992) 523-27. On Macedonia cf. D. W. J. Gill in A1CS II (1994) 397-417.

3. A. E. Vacalopoulos, *A History of Thessalonica* (1972) 3: "Thessaloniki is the only sea-board city of contemporary Greece that has never, from its foundation (316 B.C.) till today, lost its commercial importance."

4. Cf. M. Vickers, *Festschrift C. Edson* (1981) 327-33. A different view is taken by E. Oberhummer, *PRE* II/6 (1937) 145 (identification of Therma with hot springs twelve kilometers southeast of Thessalonica), and now more recently F. Papazoglou, *Les villes de Macédoine* (1988) 189-98, who is inclined to identify it with a locale which sources call Emathia.

5. Cf. G. Bakalakis, *Antike Kunst* Beiheft 1 (1963) 30-34; A. E. Vacalopoulos, *A History of Thessalonica* (1972) 5f.

6. Admittedly, Strabo falsely understood the founding of the city to have involved the destruction of this settlement and the violent centralization of the inhabitants. Cf. A. E. Vacalopoulos, *loc. cit.,* 6f.

kingdom at the battle of Pydna, the Roman general Aemilius Paullus made Thessalonica the capital of the second of four districts *(regiones)* of Macedonia (Livius xliv.32, 45; xlv.29.9; 30.4). In 146 B.C., after the suppression of the rebellion of the tanner Andriscus, a rebellion driven by strong social motives (Diodorus Siculus xxxii.9.15), Thessalonica was then elevated to the governor's residence of the newly founded senatorial province of the same name, which also encompassed Epirus and parts of Illyricum.[7] This central political function as well as the improvement of the *Via Egnatia,*[8] which connected the western and eastern halves of the empire, gave Thessalonica an even greater significance than it had previously possessed.[9] Because the city sided with the future victors Anthony and Octavia in the Roman civil war (Appian, *BC* iv.118; Plutarch, *Brut.* 46), it then received further privileges under the principate of Augustus. Thessalonica became a *civitas libera* (Pliny the Elder, *HN* iv.36). As a result, the inhabitants could govern themselves, strike their own coins, and had no Roman garrison inside the city walls. A special element of independence also came to expression in the fact that Thessalonica apparently never belonged to the κοινὸν τῶν Μακεδόνων.[10] After the reorganization of the Balkan region by Augustus, the city was relieved of its precarious position at the boundary of the empire and was able to enjoy the advantages of the *Pax Romana.* But when the imperial tax burden became oppressive, and the provinces of Achaia and Macedonia filed grievances with Tiberius, in A.D. 15 he abruptly withdrew from them the proconsular government and put them under his direct rule (Tacitus, *Ann.* i.76). Claudius then annulled this measure and reorganized Macedonia from A.D. 44 onward as a senatorial province. Thessalonica once again became the seat of the governor, who apparently did, however, also occasionally reside in Dyrrhachium on the Adriatic.[11]

7. Cf. F. Papazoglou, *ANRW* II 7.1 (1979) 302-69.

8. Polybius xxxiv.12.9 already attests a road from Apollonia/Illyricum to Byzantium, and in 56 B.C. Cicero mentions a military highway (Cicero, *De prov. cons.* 4). The name *Via Egnatia* is attested with certainty only for the section from Dyrrhachium or Apollonia to Thessalonica (Strabo vii.329 [Fr. 10, 13]). Cf. T. Pekary, *Untersuchungen zu den römischen Reichsstraßen* (1968) 10, 23, 129-31; F. O'Sullivan, *The Egnatian Way* (1972); G. Radke, *PRESup* 13 (1973) 1666f.; F. W. Walbank, *AncMac* IV (1986) 673-80, and the map in F. Papazoglou, *ANRW* II 7.1 (1979), after p. 304. The milestone found in Thessalonica attests the proconsul of Macedonia Cn. Egnatius C. f. as the builder of this particular section of the road (between 146 and 120 B.C.). Cf. G. H. R. Horsley, *NewDoc* I (1981) 81.

9. Cf. Livius xlv.30.4 *(urbs celeberrima);* Strabo vii.323; Antistius, *Anthol. Plant.* ix.428; *CIG* I 1969 (μητρόπολις, πρώτη Μακεδόνων).

10. Cf. F. Papazoglou, *Les villes de Macédoine* (1988) 206-8.

11. Cf. T. Pekary, *Untersuchungen zu den römischen Reichsstraßen* (1968) 130.

18.1.2. Archaeology

Despite the difficulties facing research involving a continuously inhabited city, the pioneer work of H. von Schoenebeck[12] as well as further investigations by M. Vickers[13] and J. M. Spieser[14] have made it possible to answer the main questions surrounding the expansion of Hellenistic Thessalonica (cf. the city map in illustration 3 [p. 418]). As it turns out, the course of the modern, late-Byzantine wall of the old city, except in the northeast,[15] is not identical with that of the ancient city. The most reliable source for determining earlier expansion is offered by the Hellenistic street-grid, still preserved in the map of the Turkish city before the conflagration of 1917 and the almost equally violent rebuilding program after the Second World War.[16] According to this grid, considerable parts of the contemporary northern part of the old city lay outside the city walls of the New Testament period. The two main modern thoroughfares, "Hodos Demetriou" and "Egnatia," correspond perhaps to the two main Roman east-west roads *(decumani)*. The original north-south axis *(cardo)* might be approximately identical with the contemporary Venizelos Street.

Finding the location of the Hellenistic agora presents problems. The partially excavated Roman forum with its cryptoporticus comes from the period of Antoninus Pius and Severus Alexander toward the end of the second century A.D.[17] Although there is almost no archaeological evidence for it, most scholars still assume there was a precursor to this tract in the Hellenistic period.[18] The strongest evidence is an inscription found in the vicinity (Hodos Olympou) (*IG* X/2.1 5), attesting an agora for 60 B.C. Another possible location would be the area near the "Platia Diikitiriou," where today the government presidium of Macedonia stands. In any event, this area at least included a kind of "holy

---

12. *Internationaler Kongreß für Archäologie* (1940) 478-82 (also in Θεσ-σαλονίκην Φιλίππου Βασιλίσσαν [1985] 346-50).

13. *Istanbul Arkeoloji Müzeleri Yiligi* 15/16 (1969) 313-18; in E. Birley, ed., *Roman Frontier Studies 1969* (1970) 249-55; *AncMac* I (1970) 239-51; *JGS* 92 (1972) 156-61.

14. *BCH* 98 (1974) 507-19.

15. Cf. G. Gounaris, *The Walls of Thessalonica* (1982) 29, and pl. 28-29. Special thanks to Professor Georgios Gounaris for his personal introduction to the problems of the archaeology of the ancient city during my stay in Thessalonica in October and November 1988.

16. Cf. B. Dimitriadis, Τοπογραφία τῆς Θεσσαλονίκης κατὰ τὴν ἐποχὴν τῆς Τουρκοκρατίας (1983), plan 54.

17. Cf. P. Petsas, *AAA* 1 (1968) 156-61; M. Vickers, *AncMac* I (1970) 50f.; C. Bakirtzis, *BSt* 14 (1972) 305f.; *AncMac* II (1977) 257-69.

18. Cf. M. Vickers, *JHS* 92 (1972) 163f.; W. Elliger, *Paulus in Griechenland* (1978) 103f.

precinct" (see p. 338 above, and pp. 379f. below). M. Vickers, commensurate with the recommendation of Aristotle, also assumes that a commercial agora was located in the harbor area (Aristotle, *Pol.* vii.11.2), probably in the vicinity of the modern harbor.[19] Because three gymnasial inscriptions were found near the church of St. Demetrius,[20] and because *insulae* are lacking in this area, Vickers believes the gymnasium was located immediately south of this church, and the stadium even farther south in the area leading to the forum.[21] Thessalonica was the site of the Olympic and Pythian festival games (*CIG* I 1068).[22] The acropolis, on which the exiled Cicero found refuge along with the other city inhabitants in the year 58 B.C. from an attack of barbarians (Cicero, *De prov. cons.* 2.4; *In pis.* 17.40), was located in the northeast on a spur of the Choriatis in the vicinity of the former Turkish citadel.

The Hellenistic street-grid also suggests that during the New Testament period the sea probably extended up to 400 meters further inland. The New Testament coastline may be indicated approximately by the streets "Hodos Hermou" and "Pavlou Mela."[23] Because Thessalonica had one of the best natural harbors in the Aegean, during the Roman period ships anchored at roadsteads along the entire seaward side of the city. Not until Constantine the Great (Zosimus, *Hist.* ii.22) at the beginning of the fourth century A.D. was an artificial basin constructed in the vicinity of today's harbor.[24] Given the circumference of the wall and the course of the coastline, the size of the Hellenistic-Roman city can be calculated at about 1.3 square kilometers; and given the usual assumptions of historical demography for ancient cities,[25] the population can be calculated at about sixty-five thousand inhabitants, though given the presence of settlements outside the walls, the overall number should probably be considerably higher, possibly even as high as one hundred thousand.[26] Hence Thessalonica was not only the most populous city of Macedonia (Strabo vii.7.4; cf. Lucian, *Asin.* 46), but because of this total population doubtless was counted among the preeminent larger cities in the Roman empire.

19. *JHS* 92 (1972) 163f.

20. The oldest, from 96/95 B.C., refers to the administration of the gymnasium (*IG* X/2.1 4); the other two, from the Roman period, mention ephebes (*IG* X/2.1 876).

21. *JHS* 92 (1972) 165. So also H. L. Hendrix, *ABD* VI (1992) 523.

22. Cf. A. E. Vacalopoulos, *A History of Thessalonica* (1972) 14.

23. My thanks to Dr. Aristoteles Mentzios of the Department of Archaeology and History of Art at the University of Thessalonica for this information. At a colloquy on 18 December 1988, he reported concerning his hitherto unpublished investigations.

24. Cf. M. Vickers, *JHS* 92 (1972) 169.

25. Various authors arrive at an average of forty to fifty persons on one thousand square meters. Cf. M. Broshi, *RB* 82 (1975) 5-7.

26. T. Zahn, *Introduction to the New Testament* (Eng. trans., 1909) 1.212, note 4, reckoned with eighty thousand. Concerning even higher estimates, cf. R. M. Evans, *Eschatology and Ethics* (1968) 233, note 353.

18.2. The Founding of the Christian Community

The account of Acts regarding the beginnings of the Christian community in Thessalonica (Acts 17:1-15) allows a more detailed comparison with Paul's own statements about his history with the Thessalonians.[27] This comparison can contribute somewhat to answering the question of the literary peculiarity and historical credibility of the *auctor ad Theophilum*. The most recent treatments of this section almost all assume the presence of partially[28] or largely[29] accurate information which Luke himself then used. One exception is the work of W. Stegemann, who, on the basis of linguistic indices, considers the Thessalonica-narrative to be a complete Lukan creation reflecting historically the experiences of Christians during the time of Domitian.[30]

The shape of Lukan language, of course, is not a problem for those who consider the *auctor ad Theophilum* to be a companion of Paul who also composed the we-passages (see pp. 412 below). Luke could then render in his own language and with his own agenda events about which he heard either

27. Concerning the relationship between the report of Acts and 1 Thessalonians, cf. especially J. B. Lightfoot, in *Biblical Essays* (1893) 253-69; C. Clemen, *NKZ* 7 (1896) 139-64; G. Milligan, *St. Paul's Epistles to the Thessalonians* (1908) xxvi-xl; E. von Dobschütz, *Die Thessalonicher-Briefe* (1909) 11-17; G. Wohlenberg, *Der erste und zweite Thessalonicherbrief* ([2]1909) 1-8; J. E. Frame, *The Epistles of St. Paul to the Thessalonians* (1912) 1-7; F. Durrleman, *Salonique et Saint Paul* (1919) 25-64; W. Neil, *The Epistle* [sic] *of Paul to the Thessalonians* (1950) ix-xiii; B. Rigaux, *Les épîtres aux Thessaloniciens* (1956) 20-32; L. M. Dewailly and B. Rigaux, *Les épîtres de Saint Paul aux Thessaloniciens* (1969) 9-11; E. Best, *The First and Second Epistles to the Thessalonians* ([2]1977) 4-7; W. Marxsen, *Der erste Brief an die Thessalonicher* (1979) 13-20; F. F. Bruce, *1 and 2 Thessalonians* (1982) xxii-xxvi; I. H. Marshall, *1 and 2 Thessalonians* (1983) 4-6; E. F. Palmer, *1 and 2 Thessalonians* (1983) xvi-xx; R. Pesch, *Die Entdeckung des ältesten Paulus-Briefes* (1984) 11-18; R. Trevijano Echeverria, *Salm 32* (1985) 265-68; J. L. Galanis, Ἡ πρώτη Ἐπιστολὴ τοῦ Ἀποστόλου Παύλου πρὸς Θεσσαλονίκεις (1985) 40-49; *DeltBiblMel* 14 (1985) 61-72; F. Laub, *1. und 2. Thessalonicherbrief* (1985) 6-8; T. Holtz, *Der erste Brief an die Thessalonicher* ([2]1990) 15-18; O. Knoch, *1. und 2. Thessalonicherbrief* (1987) 11-15; A. J. Malherbe, *Paul and the Thessalonians* (1987) 12-17; L. Morris, *The Epistles of Paul to the Thessalonians* ([2]1991) 1-6; C. U. Manus, in R. F. Collins, ed., *The Thessalonians Correspondence* (1990) 27-38; F. Bassin, *Les épîtres de Paul aux Thessaloniciens* (1991) 15-20; D. J. Williams, *1 and 2 Thessalonians* (1992) 2-6.

28. Cf. J. Roloff, *Die Apostelgeschichte* (1981) 249-53; G. Schille, *Die Apostelgeschichte* (1983) 350-53; G. Lüdemann, *Early Christianity according to the Traditions in Acts* (Eng. trans., 1989) 184-88; J. Molthagen, *Hist* 40 (1991) 53-57; H. Botermann, *TBei* 24 (1993) 79-81.

29. Cf. R. Pesch, *Die Apostelgeschichte* II (1986) 120-27 (Timothy as a source); H. W. Tajra, *The Trial of St. Paul* (1989) 30-44; F. F. Bruce, *The Acts of the Apostles* ([3]1990) 369-75; F. M. Gillman, in R. F. Collins, ed., *The Thessalonian Correspondence* (1990) 39-49; H. Binder, *ibid.,* 87.

30. *Zwischen Synagoge und Obrigkeit* (1991) 226-37.

already in Philippi (cf. Acts 16:11ff.) or later on the journey to Jerusalem (cf. Acts 20:5ff.). One should also distinguish quite clearly between stylization and invention. Without a doubt, the Lukan account of Paul's founding visit in Thessalonica is stylized, and reflects a tripartite structure: (1) proclamation of the gospel (Acts 17:1-4); (2) rejection by the majority of Jews (Acts 17:5-7); (3) partial discharge of the Christians (Acts 17:8f.). Connection with the synagogue, explication of Scripture, refusal of the Jews, the winning of aristocratic God-fearers or Gentiles, as well as the reaction of the civil authorities — all these are Lukan motifs. None of these taken in and for itself can be said to be either historical or unhistorical. Only detailed analysis can decide. If, on the basis of Paul's letters and the reconstruction of the overall historic context, one is convinced that the apostle did in fact mission among Jews,[31] then certainly he also did this in synagogues, where he naturally did not expound the Stoics and Epicureans or talk about the weather, but rather interpreted the holy Scriptures. If one must not assume on the basis of 1 Thessalonians that at the founding of this church Paul preached a purely apocalyptic message largely void of any christology or soteriology (§21), then one will hardly be offended that Luke summarizes Paul's kerygma with the assertion "that it was necessary for the Messiah to suffer and to rise from the dead, and saying, 'This is the Messiah, Jesus whom I am proclaiming to you'" (Acts 17:3).

The postulation of a Domitian background to the Lukan narrrative of the events in Thessalonica also encounters difficulties. Just recently, scholars have vehemently disputed whether this particular emperor took any noteworthy measures against Christians.[32] W. Stegemann refers to the episode reported by Eusebius under the authority of Hegesippus, according to which the grandsons of Judas the brother of Jesus were brought before Domitian on suspicion of messianic conspiracy (Eusebius, *HE* iii.20). Now, as W. Stegemann admits, this account (over eighty years later), too, is vehemently disputed. Yet while he treats Luke, who according to his dating is writing only about forty years later, with extreme skepticism, Stegemann presents no supporting argument here, and is satisfied with citing one positive conclusion from secondary literature.[33] It is also peculiar that, on the one hand, Stegemann concludes that any "relationship between Acts 17 and the letter of Claudius to Alexandria, a letter known to us purely by chance [but what difference does that make?],

31. Cf. especially H. Botermann, *TBei* 24 (1993) 62-84; and M. Reiser, *BZ* 39 (1995) 76-91.

32. Cf. K. L. Gentry, *Before Jerusalem Fell* (1989) 259-332; M. Hengel, *Die Johanneische Frage* (1993) 312 (Eng. trans., *The Johannine Question* [1990]); J. C. Wilson, *NTS* 39 (1993) 589-97. R. B. Moberly, *Bibl* 74 (1993) 393, concludes: "There is almost no hard evidence that Christians were persecuted by Rome under Domitian."

33. *Zwischen Synagoge und Obrigkeit* (1991) 235, note 184.

is purely speculative,"[34] and on the other he uses precisely this writing to illuminate events fifty years later under Domitian(!).[35] But naturally, it is legitimate first to check whether a document from Claudius from the year A.D. 41 can throw light on events alleged to have happened during his reign around A.D. 50. Only if the Lukan placement proves to be impossible for historical reasons should one seek out other times and places.

18.2.1. The Missionaries' Route

Paul and Luke both agree that the apostle came to Thessalonica from Philippi, which he had to leave because of persecution (Acts 16:16-40; cf. 1 Thess. 2:2). His companions were Silvanus and Timothy, a fact emerging from their mention as co-signees of the letter (1 Thess. 1:1).[36] Luke expressly mentions Silas (Acts 17:4, 10), and Timothy's presence can be presupposed from the context (cf. Acts 16:1-3; 17:14f.; 18:5).

18.2.2. Connection with the Synagogue?

We do not know when the first Jews came to Thessalonica. It is possible that some of them settled there already during the decades following the founding of the rapidly blossoming Hellenistic harbor city.[37] According to Josephus, who cites the work of Hecataeus here, Jewish mercenaries took part in the campaigns of Alexander the Great (Josephus, *Ap.* i.200-204). During the Hasmonean period, there was brisk exchange between Judea and Greece (1 Macc. 12:2, 7; 15:22f.; 2 Macc. 5:9; Josephus, *Ant.* xii.225; xiv.149-55). For Athens, Jews are attested since the second century B.C. (*IG* II² 12609). The enumeration of regions inhabited by Jews in Herod Agrippa's letter to Caligula also mentions Macedonia (Philo, *Leg. ad Gaium* 281). Inscriptional evidence in Thessalonica itself is admittedly quite sparse.[38] Two sarcophagi with the menorah are almost certainly of Jewish origin, but difficult to date

---

34. *Ibid.,* 229, note 149.

35. *Ibid.,* 235.

36. Cf. T. Holtz, *Der erste Brief an die Thessalonicher* (²1990) 13f.

37. Cf. A. E. Vacalopoulos, *A History of Thessalonica* (1972) 9; A. Nar, Οἱ συναγῶγες τῆς Θεσσαλονίκης (1985) 16-19. J. Nehama, *Histoire des Israelites de Salonique* I/II (1935) 8-10, even believed that isolated seafaring Jews settled in Thessalonica as early as the preexilic period.

38. Cf. Schuerer III/1 (1986) 66f. *CIJ* I 66*, 67* (569f.) must be viewed as of Gentile origin. The information offered by R. Jewett, *The Thessalonian Correspondence* (1986) 199, is at least misleading: "Since the only evidence concerning Jewish population in Thessalonica is the account in Acts 17, and since no evidence of Greek synagogues or Jewish inscriptions has been found. . . ."

(*CIJ* I² 693b-c).[39] By contrast, an epitaph for "Abrameus and his wife Theodote" from the late Roman period (fourth century A.D.?) could also be of Christian origin (*CIJ* I² 693 = *IG* X/2.1 633).[40] Neither can we decide the origin of a tombstone — which has since disappeared — which a Παρασκευή erected for her daughter Φοίβη (cf. Rom. 16:1) in the year A.D. 155 (*IG* X/2.1 449).[41] Finally, an inscription that was similarly lost and thus can no longer be dated with any certainty (fourth century A.D.?), may also be of Jewish origin (*IG* X/2.1 632.1: ΕΒΣΑΛΙΤΟΥ = Εἰσραλίτου?). Most interesting is an inscription from the late second or early third century, only recently published (*ZPE* 102 [1994] 297-306), which speaks about ταῖς συναγωγαῖς, that is, either Jewish communities or religious buildings.[42]

We know nothing certain about where the synagogue stood during the New Testament period (Acts 17:1). Local Christian traditions locating the synagogue in the crypt of the Demetrius church or near a spring in the southeastern suburb Hagios Pavlos are late and fanciful.[43] Recent findings regarding the course of the coastline have rendered untenable the assumption that this place of prayer stood at the site of the oldest Sephardic synagogue Etz Chaim in the vicinity of the "Platia Eleftherias."[44] And it was always considered improbable that there was any continuity in local tradition between the Roman-Byzantine period and the arrival of the Jews expelled by the Spanish inquisition in the sixteenth century.

---

39. It is indeed noteworthy that one sarcophagus bears the inscription — one previously attested only as Christian — Κύριος μεθ᾽ ἡμῶν. Cf. B. Lifshitz and J. Schiby, *RB* 75 (1968) 377f. Both sarcophagi were found in what is primarily an early Christian necropolis in the eastern part of the city (T. Pazaras, *Mak* 21 [1981] 373-89), which does, however, already attest several Hellenistic graves (M. Vickers, *JHS* 92 [1972] 168f.). Dr. Euterpe Marki (Byzantine Museum, Thessalonica) is preparing a larger study of this particular cemetery (*The Early Christian Necropolis in Thessaloniki),* where Christian symbols have been found since the end of the second century A.D. Cf. already E. Marki, in Χριστιανική Θεσσαλονίκη (1990) 171-93. A Christian inscription (with palm branch), now unfortunately lost, probably dated already from this time and mentioned an Ἀπολλώνιος Ἀπολλωνίου πρεσβύτερος (*IG* X/2.1 431). A grave stela (*IG* X/2.1 1017), from the third century A.D or later, is also to be considered Christian based on the symbolic word ἰχθύς. The next early Christian inscriptions date after the fourth century A.D. and frequently mention the office of the ἀναγνώστης (e.g., *IG* X/2.1 789). Cf. C. Edson, *Inscriptiones Graecae Thessalonicae et viciniae* (1972) 310f. For the Christian inscriptions, however, this edition is difficult to apply. Cf. L. Robert, *RPh* 98 (1974) 188f.

40. C. J. Hemer, *The Book of Acts in the Setting of Hellenistic History* (1989) 115, incorrectly adduces this inscription as a witness to the existence of a synagogue in the second century A.D.

41. Cf. L. Duchesne and M. Bayet, *Mémoire sur une mission au Mont Athos* (1876) 65.

42. I. Levinskaya, *The Book of Acts in Its Diaspora Setting* (1996) 155f.

43. Cf. O. F. A. Meinardus, *Die Reisen des Apostels Paulus* (1981) 96f.

44. So B. Schiby, in Μακεδονικὸν Ἡμερολόγιον (1966) 55-58.

A bilingual Samaritan inscription (*CIJ* I² 693a = *IG* X/2.1 789) with the priestly benediction (Num. 6:22-27) was found at the southwest edge of the Roman forum in the vicinity of the Byzantine church "Panhagia Chalceon."[45] Hence the New Testament synagogue is often assumed to have stood here,[46] though the archaeological evidence is often misunderstood.[47] But in view of the tense relations between Jews and Samaritans, it is difficult to explain how a Jewish synagogue could have become a Samaritan one.[48] If the founder of the inscription Sirikios (*CIJ* I² 693a, line 16) was identical with the sophist Siricius from Neapolis (Shechem), who taught in Athens in the fourth century A.D.,[49] then the inscription would come from the same century. Although the script type does allow a dating as late as the sixth century A.D.,[50] the rather awkward letters make any more precise determination difficult.[51] The evidence probably indicates a synagogue,[52] something suggested especially by the choice of the priestly benediction, though building parts indicating a synagogue were not found. The founder's inscription of the "Panhagia Chalceon" of 1028 might indicate that this church was supposed to supplant a non-Christian cultic site.[53] The synagogue-inscription represents an additional, important witness for the expansion of the Samaritan

45. First published by S. Pelekidis, in Πεπραγμένα τοῦ θ' διεθνοῦς Βυζαντινολόγου συνεδρίου I (1955) 408 and pl. 84. Cf. B. Lifshitz and J. Schiby, *RB* 75 (1968) 368-78; J. Robert and L. Robert, *RÉG* 82 (1969) 476-78; J. M. Spieser, *Travaux et Mémoires* 5 (1973) 149f.; E. Tov, *RB* 81 (1974) 394-99; B. Lifshitz, *CIJ* I (²1975) 70-75; G. H. R. Horsley, *NewDoc* I (1981) 108-10. This inscription could subsequently no longer be located in the Archaeological Museum of Thessalonica.

46. So O. F. A. Meinardus, *Die Reisen des Apostels Paulus* (1981) 95; N. Hugédé, *Saint Paul et la Grèce* (1982) 79.

47. Thus E. Tov, *RB* 81 (1974) 394, mistakenly speaks about an inscription "found in a synagogue in Thessalonica," and K. P. Donfried, in *Harper's Bible Dictionary* (1985) 1065, about "a Samaritan synagogue (attested to on a recently found marble inscription)." The inscription, however, was already published in 1955 by S. Pelekidis in the acts of the Eighth Congress of Byzantinists of 1953 in Thessalonica (see note 45). R. Jewett, *The Thessalonian Correspondence* (1986) 120, even writes that "the fact that a Samaritan synagogue has been excavated[!] in Thessalonica, dating apparently from the third century B.C.E.[!] . . ." The misunderstandings probably derive in part from the title of the article by B. Lifshitz and J. Schiby, *RB* 75 (1968) 368-78: "Une synagogue samaritaine à Thessalonique." Apart from the superscription, however, the authors do not touch on the question of a synagogue edifice.

48. Admittedly, archaeological and epigraphic findings on Delos raise the question whether Jewish and Samaritan communities existed in immediate proximity to one another, or whether the Jewish prayer site replaced a Samaritan one. Cf. Schuerer III/1 (1986) 70f.

49. So the late discoverer of the inscription Professor Stratos Pelekidis (University of Thessalonica). Cf. B. Lifshitz and J. Schiby, *RB* 75 (1968) 369.

50. Cf. J. D. Purvis, *BASOR* 221 (1976) 121-23.

51. Cf. R. Pummer, in A. D. Crown, *The Samaritans* (1989) 149f.

52. With considerable reservation F. Millar, in Schuerer III/1 (1986) 67.

53. Cf. J. Schiby, *Zion* 42 (1977) 106.

Diaspora.[54] In the designation of a tower as Πύργος τῆς Σαμαρείας, local tradition preserved up to the beginning of the twentieth century[55] the recollection of the presence of a Samaritan community in Thessalonica.[56]

The oldest evidence for the location of the Jewish quarter, in a sermon of the archbishop Leon Mathematikos of Thessalonica from the year A.D. 842 (*ST* 232 [1964] II 281f.), suggests that during the Byzantine period it was the area between the Roman forum and the probable site of the temple of Dionysus (§19.2.1) in the area of the Byzantine basilica "Panhagia Achiropiitos," also known as "Hagia Paraskevi."[57] If there is any continuity with the Jewish settlement in the Hellenistic-Roman period, the New Testament synagogue would be located there. Perhaps another local tradition can reinforce this assumption. Late Byzantine sources (*Acta Dionysiou* [ed. N. Oikonomides 95]) mention a church of St. Paul in the vicinity of the Roman forum, and the archaeologist E. Marki assumes this has some connection with the site of the synagogue.[58] Based on information in Simeon of Thessalonica (*EEThS* 21 [1976] 134), the old church of St. Paul is more specifically to be sought in the vicinity of the Achiropiite church *ca.* 150 meters west of the forum.[59] Perhaps the early Christian fresco found in a room bordering on the cryptoporticus of the Roman forum in the south, displaying two orants on either side of a cross,[60] has something to do with a tradition of Paul's activity in the vicinity of this agora (cf. Acts 17:5). As we have seen (see p. 340 above), it is unfortunately not quite certain whether the Hellenistic agora was located in the area of the Roman forum. By no means, however, does the lack hitherto of any evidence from outside the New Testament constitute a reason for doubting the existence of a synagogue during the period of Paul's arrival in Thessalonica.[61]

54. Cf. B. Lifshitz and J. Ṣchiby, *RB* 75 (1968) 376f.; and in general A. D. Crown, in *The Samaritans* (1989) 195-217.

55. Cf. O. Tafrali, *Topographie de Thessalonique* (1913) 112; J. Schiby, *Zion* 42 (1977) 106f.

56. Cf. B. Lifshitz and J. Schiby, *RB* 75 (1968) 368.

57. Cf. G. Bakalakis, *AncMac* III (1983) 31-43.

58. Communication by letter (December 5, 1988). Concerning earlier attempts at finding this location, cf. N. Oikonomides, *Acte de Dionysiou* (1968) 94.

59. Cf. R. Janin, *Les églises et les monastères des grands centres byzantins* (1975) 405. Today there is only a single church of St. Paul in Thessalonica, built in 1950, whose predecessor comes from the nineteenth century. Cf. E. Dassmann, *Paulus in früh-christlicher Frömmigkeit und Kunst* (1982) 8.

60. Cf. D. Pallas, *Les monuments paléochrétiens du Grèce* (1977) 65-68; A. Xyn-gopoulos, Βυζαντινά 9 (1977) 411-16.

61. Contra the assertion of an anachronistic use of συναγωγή for the period before A.D. 70 in the dual Lukan work by H. C. Kee, *NTS* 36 (1990) 1-24; cf. R. E. Oster, *NTS* 39 (1993) 178-208; R. Riesner in R. Bauckham, *The Book of Acts in Its Palestinian Setting* (1995) 180-201.

Even if the account of the apostle's synagogue-visit exhibits Lukan stylization (Acts 17:2: κατὰ δὲ τὸ εἰωθὸς τῷ Παύλῳ εἰσῆλθεν πρὸς αὐτοὺς [εἰς τὴν συναγωγήν]), at least two elements confirm the connection between the Pauline mission in Thessalonica and worship services in the synagogue community: (1) Jason,[62] in whose house the newly founded church apparently met (Acts 17:5f.), bore a typical Jewish name ('Ιάσων instead of 'Ιησοῦς),[63] and if he is identical with the Jason in Rom. 16:21,[64] he was indeed a Jew. This equivalency is also supported by the fact that he is mentioned next to Sosipater, who can be identified as Sopater of Beroea (Acts 20:4).[65] The Thessalonian Aristarchus (Acts 20:4; cf. Col. 4:10f.; Phlm. 24) was certainly of Jewish lineage.[66] He, like the Thessalonian Secundus mentioned along with him (Acts 20:4), might have belonged to the city's first Christians (see pp. 350f. below). (2) The fact that the persecution was co-initiated by Jewish circles (§18.3.1) would suggest that missionary activity was carried out among them.

18.2.3. Jewish and Gentile Christians

Whereas only a few Jews joined the church, Luke speaks of a larger number of "God-fearers," including several of the leading women (Acts 17:4: καὶ τινες ἐξ αὐτῶν ἐπείσθησαν καὶ προσεκληρώθησαν τῷ Παύλῳ καὶ τῷ Σιλᾷ, τῶν τε σεβομένων Ἑλλήνων πλῆθος πολύ, γυναικῶν τε τῶν πρώτων οὐκ ὀλίγαι). An inscription from Thessalonica (first century A.D. or later), now unfortunately lost, might indeed demonstrate that Gentiles expressed considerable interest in the Jewish faith; it read: Θεῷ Ὑψίστῳ κατ' ἐπιταγὴν ΙΟΥΕΣ (*CIJ* I 693d = *IG* X/2.1 72). The Jewish background is suggested by the final word, which apparently represents an attempt at circumscribing the tetragrammaton.[67] Several inscriptions have been found in Macedonia (Beroea, Edessa,

---

62. In the case of his name, even W. Stegemann, *Zwischen Synagoge und Obrigkeit* (1991) 228, note 141, is tempted to assume a pre-Lukan tradition.

63. Cf. M. Hengel, *ZTK* 72 (1975) 175; Blass, Debrunner, Rehkopf, §53.3d. Perhaps Aristion of Pella, in his dialogue 'Ιάσωνος καὶ Παπίσκου ἀντιλογία περὶ Χριστοῦ (Origen, *Cels.* iv.52), already imagined the Jewish-Christian disputant as Jason from Thessalonica. Cf. T. Zahn, *Die Apostelgeschichte* II (¹/²1921) 589f., note 27.

64. Concerning this possibility, cf. U. Wilckens, *Der Brief an die Römer* III (1982) 146. Ancient church tradition subscribes wholly to this identification. Cf. F. X. Pölzl, *Die Mitarbeiter des Weltapostels Paulus* (1911) 230.

65. Cf. F. M. Gillman, in R. F. Collins, ed., *The Thessalonian Correspondence* (1990) 40.

66. Cf. E. von Dobschütz, *Die Thessalonicher-Briefe. ND* (1974) 11; W. H. Ollrog, *Paulus und seine Mitarbeiter* (1979) 40f., 46f.

67. Cf. Schuerer III/1 (1986) 67. C. Edson, *Inscriptiones Thessalonicae et viciniae* (1972) 36, expresses doubt in this interpretation.

Kozane, Pydna) dealing with the worship of "Zeus Hypsistos,"[68] and one may come from Thessalonica (*IG* X/2.1 62*). At present, there is justifiably considerable doubt whether these represent witnesses for a syncretistic cult influenced by Judaism.[69] In any event, this inclination toward henotheism did contain an anticipatory element both for the Jewish attraction of proselytes and for the early Christian mission.[70] Acts 16:17 may be alluding to the confluence of Jewish and pagan influences when in this passage a pagan medium in Philippi calls Paul and Silas δοῦλοι τοῦ θεοῦ τοῦ ὑψίστου.[71]

The first letter to the Thessalonians could be taken to suggest that the apostle is writing exclusively to Gentile Christians. Paul speaks of the Thessalonians' having turned from idols to the one true God (1 Thess. 1:9: πῶς ἐπεστρέψατε πρὸς τὸν θεὸν ἀπὸ τῶν εἰδώλων δουλεύειν θεῷ ζῶντι καὶ ἀληθινῷ; cf. 1 Thess. 2:14; 4:15). However, the letters to the Corinthians (1 Cor. 12:2; cf. 1 Cor. 6:11) and to the Galatians (Gal. 4:8) present similar problems for us, even though the presence of a Jewish-Christian minority is even more certain in the case of these churches than in that of Thessalonica. But neither does the first letter to the Thessalonians compel us to assume that its addressees were exclusively persons who did not have any more extensive contact with Judaism. As a rule, the "God-fearers" had a pagan past, and their status was characterized precisely by the fact that they had not undergone any clear conversion to Judaism.[72] If one is not prepared to assume that Paul largely misread the intellectual capacity of his readers, then the linguistic form of this letter, too, indicates that many of his readers formerly had some contact with the synagogue. Its language is "influenced essentially by Jewish Greek, and in large part would be fully comprehensible only to someone . . . who knew that Greek."[73] Luke portrays the situation correctly insofar as he, too, asserts that the Jewish Christians constituted a minority (τίνες ἐξ αὐτῶν ἐπείσθησαν) over against the Gentile Christians (τῶν τε σεβομένων Ἑλλήνων πλῆθος πολύ) (Acts 17:4). Although Luke could indeed give the impression that the new converts came only from the synagogal sphere of influence, his account of the apostle's further activity in the community is so brief that the proclamation could possibly have influenced Thessalonians outside this particular milieu as well.

68. Cf. Schuerer III/1, 68.

69. Cf. M. Hengel, *Judaism and Hellenism* (Eng. trans., 1974) 1.297-99; G. H. R. Horsley, *NewDoc* I (1981) 25-29; I. Levinskaya, *Diaspora Setting* (1996) 83-103.

70. Cf. A. D. Nock, C. Roberts, and T. C. Skeat, *HTR* 29 (1936) 39-88.

71. Cf. W. Elliger, *Paulus in Griechenland* (1978) 67-69; G. H. R. Horsley, *NewDoc* I (1981) 28; C. J. Hemer, *The Book of Acts in the Setting of Hellenistic History* (1989) 231, correctly draws attention to the clear evidence of local color in this epithet.

72. Cf. A. J. Hultgren, *Paul's Gospel and Mission* (1985) 140-42.

73. T. Holtz, *Der erste Brief an die Thessalonicher* (²1990) 10.

18.2.4. The Social Composition

It is commensurate with Luke's literary agenda to emphasize the conversion of persons of some status, in this case of "not a few of the leading women (γυναικῶν τε τῶν πρώτων οὐκ ὀλίγαι)" (Acts 17:4). This can evoke a one-sided picture of the sociological composition of the church in Thessalonica. Neither, however, does Luke expressly assert that those of high rank constituted the majority. Mention of the ἀγοραῖοι ἄνδρες in Acts 17:5 might reflect knowledge that the church of Thessalonica had contacts with this segment of society as well (see pp. 376f. below).

The treatment of the theme of manual trades in 1 Thessalonians allows the cautious assumption that the majority of church members to whom the apostle is writing belong to the working (either middle or lower) class (§19.3). The letter does not, however, exclude the possibility that the church also had some more aristocratic and wealthy members. Judging from the analogy of 1 Corinthians (1 Cor. 16:15f.: οἴδατε τὴν οἰκίαν Στεφανᾶ . . . ἵνα καὶ ὑμεῖς ὑποτάσσησθε τοῖς τοιούτοις καὶ παντὶ τῷ συνεργοῦντι καὶ κοπιῶντι),[74] the κοπιῶντες ἐν ὑμῖν καὶ προϊστάμενοι ὑμῶν mentioned in 1 Thess. 5:12 enjoyed a higher social status.[75] R. Jewett remarks with respect to the admonition to submit to the κοπιῶντες and προϊστάμενοι: "In all likelihood the leaders in question were patrons and patronesses of the house churches in Thessalonica as well as the socially prominent members of the congregation, assuming that the social profile of other Pauline churches is relevant."[76]

This is also suggested by individual personal remarks Luke makes, remarks usually viewed as accurate. With Jason, who accommodated the church (apparently in a larger house; Acts 17:5f.) and was able to post a bail (Acts 17:9),[77] we are acquainted with at least one of the obviously more well-to-do Christians in Thessalonica.[78] Secundus also came from this city, and is mentioned in connection with the last trip to Jerusalem as one of the church representatives and Paul's companions (Acts 20:4) who are to deliver the collection with him (see p. 302 above). Secundus is one of the inscription-

---

74. Cf. D. Wenham, *Themelios* 13 (1988) 55f.

75. Concerning the social status of the leading Christians in Corinth (e.g., Stephanas), cf. G. Theissen, in *Studien zur Soziologie des Urchristentums* (²1983) 231-71.

76. *The Thessalonian Correspondence* (1986) 103.

77. G. Lüdemann, *Early Christianity according to the Traditions in Acts* (Eng. trans., 1989) 186f., also considers the name and bail to be elements of tradition.

78. Cf. W. A. Meeks, *The First Urban Christians* (1983) 62f.; A. J. Malherbe, *Paul and the Thessalonians* (1987) 15; F. M. Gillman, in R. F. Collins, ed., *The Thessalonian Correspondence* (1990) 41.

ally most frequently attested names in Thessalonica, and in over 80 percent of cases is the *cognomen* of Roman citizens.[79] This fact reinforces the suspicion[80] that the New Testament Secundus was also a *civis Romanus*.[81] Although we do not know the date of the conversion of Secundus, his participation in a task requiring such responsibility suggests that he was among the "first converts" (cf. 1 Cor. 16:15; Rom. 16:4) of the mission in Thessalonica.

Although the emphasis on leading female congregation members is commensurate with Luke's preferences as visible elsewhere as well (Lk. 8:2f.; Acts 13:7-12; 17:34, *et passim*),[82] here it may also have as its background the significant position of women within Macedonian society[83] (see p. 356 below). We do in fact know of considerable missionary successes among matrons during the early period of Christianity.[84] Here, too, the connection between the Christian mission and the synagogue is evident. Grave inscriptions suggest that women constituted 50 percent of the proselytes and 80 percent of the "God-fearers" among only 40 percent of the sepulchral inscriptions relating to women.[85] P. W. van der Horst, to whom we owe the systematic evaluation of the epigraphic material regarding this complex, expressly comments regarding the considerable extent to which this inscriptional evidence confirms Luke's portrayal (also in Acts 17:4-6).[86]

79. Simple name: *IG* X/2.1 58, 243, 262, 312, 630B-C. As *cognomen* for men: *IG* X/2.1 37, 58, 68, 69, 114, 126, 193, 239, 244, 247, 290, 323, 616, *734; for women: *IG* X/2.1 545, 630, *726, *734; Σεκουνδ-: *IG* X/2.1 *986.

80. Cf. E. A. Judge, *Rank and Status in the World of the Caesars and St. Paul* (1982) 36, note 20.

81. T. Zahn, *Introduction to the New Testament* (Eng. trans., 1909) 1.213, note 6, even assumed that "the occurrence of the name Γάϊος Ἰούλιος Σεκοῦνδος in Thessalonica (Duchesne and Bayet, *Mission au Mont Athos*, p. 50, No. 78 [*IG* X/2.1 290]) gives the ground for the conjecture that the Secundus of Acts xx.4 may be identified with the Macedonian Gaius, who in Acts xix.29 is similarly associated with Aristarchus, and that in distinction from (Gaius) Secundus of Thessalonica the other Gaius is designated as from Derbe (Cod. A ὁ Δερβαῖος)." C. Edson, *Inscriptiones Thessalonicae et viciniae* (1972) 117, however, dates the inscription no earlier than the second or third century A.D. Ancient church tradition peculiarly contains no information about Secundus. Cf. F. X. Pölzl, *Die Mitarbeiter des Weltapostels Paulus* (1911) 333.

82. Cf. W. A. Meeks, *The First Urban Christians* (1983) 61f.

83. Cf. F. F. Bruce, *1 and 2 Thessalonians* (1982) xxv.

84. Cf. A. von Harnack, *Die Mission und Ausbreitung des Christentums* (⁴1924) 589-611 (Eng. trans., *The Mission and Expansion of Christianity* [1908]).

85. Cf. P. W. van der Horst, *Ancient Jewish Epitaphs* (1991) 102-13.

86. *BZ* 36 (1992) 171.

18.3. Persecution of the Community

18.3.1. The Instigators of the Persecution

Paul confirms that difficulties arose even as he was founding the church (1 Thess. 1:6: δεξάμενοι τὸν λόγον ἐν θλίψει πολλῇ), persecutions associated with a hostile populace (1 Thess. 2:14: ἐπάθετε καὶ ὑμεῖς ὑπὸ τῶν ἰδίων συμφυλετῶν). Acts draws an animated picture of the outbreak of the persecution against the young Christian church. The Jews of Thessalonica are jealous (Acts 17:5: ζηλώσαντες δὲ οἱ Ἰουδαῖοι) of the missionary successes (cf. Acts 17:4) and incite street ruffians into a public riot which then leads to proceedings before the city government (Acts 17:6). This envy over the winning away of actual or potential adherents of high social status is certainly understandable as the persecutory motive of a group[87] which, like the Jews of Thessalonica, was dependent on the intercession of influential patrons (§19.3.2). Despite this, some exegetes consider Luke's portrayal difficult to reconcile with Paul's own statements[88] in 1 Thess. 2:14: "For you, brothers and sisters, became imitators of the churches of God in Christ Jesus that are in Judea, for you suffered the same things from your own compatriots (ὑπὸ τῶν ἰδίων συμφυλετῶν) as they did from the Jews." It is disputed whether the term συμφυλετής can be said to exclude or include Jews.[89] In New Testament Greek, this word had apparently already lost its reference to ethnicity.[90] But even if it refers here to the Gentile compatriots of the Thessalonians, the Jews are not excluded as co-instigators.[91]

Such exclusion would make it incomprehensible for Paul to mention them in this context in the first place. The apostle becomes so agitated about their resistance that he adduces not only the Deuteronomistic topos of Israel as the murderer of the prophets,[92] but probably also the Jesus-tradition in its criticism of the Pharisees (cf. Mt. 23:31-36).[93] He even approximates the

---

87. Cf. also J. Roloff, *Die Apostelgeschichte* (1981) 250.

88. So especially E. Haenchen, *Acts* (Eng. trans., 1971) 510f.; R. Jewett, *The Thessalonian Correspondence* (1986) 117f.

89. From her overall view of the Pauline mission, H. Botermann, *TBei* 24 (1993) 83, note 55, even finds in the συμφυλεταί of the Thessalonian Christians exclusively Jews.

90. Cf. B. Rigaux, *Les épîtres aux Thessaloniciens* (1956) 443.

91. Cf. E. Dobschütz, *Die Thessalonicherbriefe* (⁷1909) 109f.

92. Cf. especially I. Broer, *BN* 20 (1983) 59-91.

93. Cf. especially J. B. Orchard, *Bibl* 19 (1938) 19-42; D. Wenham, in R. T. France and D. Wenham, eds., *Gospel Perspectives* II (1981) 361f., and also C. A. Wanamaker, *The Epistles to the Thessalonians* (1990) 116 (bibliography).

linguistic devices of ancient Gentile Jewish polemic[94] when he writes: "[The Jews] who killed both the Lord Jesus and the prophets, and drove us out; they displease God and oppose everyone" (1 Thess. 2:15). It is not only the Jews about whom Paul's language here seems to generalize. One could also (mis)understand him to be saying that all the fellow citizens were hostile toward the Thessalonian Christians. Even if one could translate in a limiting fashion (the Judean Jewish Christians suffered the same thing "from the Jews who killed the Lord Jesus"),[95] the language remains harsh. This comes easily from the lips of a person who has himself suffered such miserable experiences in the not-too-distant past. Paul is probably also thinking of the events in Thessalonica when he accuses the Jews: "they hinder us from speaking to the Gentiles" (1 Thess. 2:16). Particularly, however, the only aorist in a long series of verbs (1 Thess. 2:15) is apparently speaking about a specific occasion:[96] "and they drove us out (ἐκδιωξάντων)." The account in Acts is able to illuminate the apostle's experience here and to make his shockingly harsh manner of expression at least historically comprehensible.[97]

B. A. Pearson argued in favor of a later interpolation[98] of 1 Thess. 2:13-16 also by pointing out that we know nothing of any Jewish persecution of Christians between the reign of Agrippa I (§7.2) and the outbreak of the Jewish War (A.D. 66-70).[99] But we have already discussed the possibility that Jewish unrest in the year A.D. 48 in Antioch had an anti-Christian edge (see p. 196 above), and it is even chronologically possible for Paul to have experienced this trouble himself. Neither can one exclude the possibility that, given the surge of Zealot sentiment in Judea after the reestablishment of the Roman province (§6.3), attacks against Jewish Christians occurred here as well as in Syria. This newly awakened Zealotism was related to two events that might

---

94. Possible parallels can be found in B. Rigaux, *Les épîtres aux Thessaloniciens* (1956) 448; M. Adinolfi, *La prima lettera ai Tessalonicesi* (1990) 96-103. But cf. the cautious judgment of I. Broer, *BN* 20 (1983) 79-82. It is interesting that this problem passage had no real influence on anti-Judaism in the ancient church. Cf. R. Kampling, in *Festschrift H. Schreckenberg* (1993) 183-213.

95. So F. Gilliard, *NTS* 35 (1989) 481-502; J. A. Weatherly, *JSNT* 42 (1991) 84-88.

96. Cf. I. H. Marshall, *1 and 2 Thessalonians* (1983) 79.

97. Concerning the assumption of an interpolation of the section, cf. W. G. Kümmel, *Festschrift O. Cullmann* (1962) 218-21; R. F. Collins, *Studies in the First Letter to the Thessalonians* (1984) 103-5 (bibliography), 131f.; K. P. Donfried, *Interpretation* 38 (1984) 242-53; T. Holtz, *Der erste Brief an die Thessalonicher* (²1990) 27, 110-12; R. Jewett, *The Thessalonian Correspondence* (1986) 36-41; B. C. Johanson, *To All the Brethren* (1987) 81-100; I. Broer, in R. F. Collins, ed., *The Thessalonian Correspondence* (1990) 137-59; J. A. Weatherly, *JSNT* 42 (1991) 79-98, and generally Excursus III (pp. 404-11).

98. Cf. T. Holtz, *loc. cit.,* 107.

99. *HTR* 64 (1971) 86.

throw some light on Paul's difficult assertion: "but the wrath has overtaken them (ἔφθασεν δὲ ἐπ᾽ αὐτοὺς ἡ ὀργὴ) — εἰς τέλος"[100] (1 Thess. 2:16).

E. Bammel[101] suggests that the actualization of the commencing judgment of wrath can be found in Claudius' Roman edict concerning the Jews, about which Paul must have heard immediately before composing the letter (§18.4.2). R. Jewett[102] considers the possibility that the reference is to the Passover disturbances of the year A.D. 49, during which, Josephus alleges, twenty to thirty thousand Jews were killed in Jerusalem (Josephus, *B.J.* ii.224-27/*Ant.* xx.112). One does not, however, have to decide in favor of a single event, but rather can formulate with F. F. Bruce: "At the time when 1 Thessalonians was written, the coincidence of troubles for the Jews in so many parts of the world might have been thought to presage the end-time judgement."[103] If Paul's remarks in 1 Thess. 2:13-16 had a specific, concrete background, then one must be cautious in drawing any overly fundamental conclusions from them concerning Paul's theological judgment of Judaism at that time.[104] Perhaps one can understand the ζηλώσαντες δὲ οἱ Ἰουδαῖοι in Acts 17:5 as a relatively specific expression associated with the escalation of Zealot fervor in the years A.D. 48/49.

18.3.2. Popular Assembly and Politarchs

Since the agitation against the new messianic group was instigated within Jewish circles, while at the same time affecting a group composed largely of Gentile Christians, it could not have been merely a matter of synagogal jurisdiction. Neither do we know whether the Thessalonian Jews even had been granted this limited degree of self-jurisdiction.[105] In contrast to the

100. Translations of εἰς τέλος diverge widely: "in full, completely" (F. F. Bruce, *1 and 2 Thessalonians* [1982] 48 [bibliography]; T. Holtz, *Der erste Brief an die Thessalonicher* [²1990] 108 [note 513 contains bibliography]); "finally, at last" (U. Luz, *Das Geschichtsverständnis des Paulus* [1968] 91, note 109; I. Broer, *BN* 20 [1983] 85); "to the end" (C. A. Wanamaker, *The Epistles to the Thessalonians* [1990] 117f.).

101. *ZTK* 56 (1959) 295, 306. E. Bammel mentions P. Schmidt, *Der erste Thessalonicherbrief* (1885) 87-90, as his precursor. Further advocates included W. Brückner, *Die chronologische Reihenfolge* (1890) 198; C. Clemen, *NKZ* 7 (1896) 154; and J. Moffatt, *An Introduction to the Literature of the New Testament* (²1912) 73. E. Bammel is followed by A. Strobel, *BHH* III (1966) 2224, and W. Wiefel, *Kairos* 17 (1975) 225.

102. *NTS* 17 (1970/71) 205, note 5. R. Jewett does not mention that J. A. Bengel, *Gnomon Novi Testamenti* (³1885) 799, already advocated the same view.

103. *1 and 2 Thessalonians* (1982) 49.

104. Neither T. Holtz, in R. F. Collins, *The Thessalonian Correspondence* (1990) 284-94, nor J. A. Weatherly, *JSNT* 42 (1991) 79-98, see any fundamental break between 1 Thess. 2:13-16 and Rom. 9–11.

105. W. Elliger, *Paulus in Griechenland* (1978) 92, suspects that the Jews joined together in a religious association similar to that formed by a group from Asia Minor for

comparatively vague descriptions of attacks against Paul in Pisidian Antioch (Acts 13:50) and Iconium (Acts 14:4-6), the account of the events in Thessalonica is characterized by more specific details and local color. The original purpose of the mob scene[106] was to bring Paul and his companions before the popular assembly (Acts 17:5: προαγάγειν εἰς τὸν δῆμον),[107] to which Thessalonica, as a *civitas libera* (see p. 339 above) had access.[108] A. N. Sherwin-White remarks in this regard that "though Acts makes no reference to this, the energetic action of the Jews against Paul and Silas might have been inspired by the knowledge that the hands of the city authorities, unlike those of Ephesus, were not directly under Roman control."[109]

When the missionaries were not found at the assembly site of the house church, the mob dragged their patron, Jason, before the politarchs functioning as city magistrates (Acts 17:6). The expression πολιτάρχαι was unattested in any other literary source of antiquity except this passage in Acts, and accordingly gave rise to doubts. This title, although not unique to Macedonia, is nonetheless a thoroughly typical one, deriving already from the pre-Roman period;[110] it has in the meantime been attested in at least sixty-four inscriptions,[111] of which no fewer than thirty come from Thessalonica and its environs, and twenty-two more from Macedonia.[112] An inscription of white marble affixed to the former southwest

---

the worship of Dionysus (*IG* X/2.1 309). Concerning θίασος of the *Asiani,* cf. C. Edson, *HTR* 41 (1948) 154-58.

106. E. A. Judge, *The Social Pattern of the Christian Groups in the First Century* (1960) 26, sees here a typical element in the life of a larger Hellenistic city: "For the purpose of expressing its opinion, the citizenry had this means of unofficial, though organized demonstrations, which are virtually characteristic of Hellenistic city life. Even though they were illegal, they often attained their goal without much ado." Concerning the *acclamatio,* cf. further T. Klauser, *RAC* I (1950) 216-33.

107. This is a juristic *terminus technicus* (cf. H. Conzelmann, *Acts* [Eng. trans., 1987] 135), and is to be taken in that sense here as well. Cf. E. A. Judge, *RThR* 30 (1971) 2. A different view is taken by W. Elliger, *Paulus in Griechenland* (1978) 94f., who understands δῆμος (as in Acts 12:22; 19:30, 33) simply as "crowd of people."

108. Concerning the city government during the New Testament period, cf. R. M. Evans, *Eschatology and Ethics* (1968) 8-15.

109. *Roman Society and Roman Law in the New Testament* (1963) 96.

110. This view, advocated by B. Helly, *AncMac* II (1977) 531-44, has now been definitively proven by an inscription from Amphipolis dating from the period between 179 and 171 B.C. Cf. C. Koukouli-Chrysanthaki, in *Festschrift C. Edson* (1981) 229-41.

111. Cf. L. Robert, *RPh* 98 (1974) 207-12; F. Papazoglou, *Hist* 35 (1986) 438-48; G. H. R. Horsley, *ABD* VI (1992) 384-89 (386-88: list); in A1CS II (1994) 419-32. E. Haenchen, *Acts* (Eng. trans., 1971) 508, note 1, and even G. Schneider, *Die Apostelgeschichte* I (1982) 225, note 33, mention E. W. Burton, *AJT* 2 (1898) 598-632, as the most recent treatise on this institution.

112. πολιτάρχης: *IG* X/2.1 *30, 37, 137, 163; πολιταρχέω: *IG* X/2.1 27, 28, 31, 32, 50, 86, 109, 126-*129, *133, 199, 214, *226, 962; πολιταρχικός: *IG* X/2.1 162, 197,

gate (Vardar Gate) of the Byzantine city wall (*IG* X/2.1 126)[113] mentions six politarchs and, as J. B. Lightfoot already pointed out,[114] is also interesting from the perspective of the local color of the Acts account insofar as it contains the name Secundus (cf. Acts 20:4) (see pp. 350f. above), and draws attention to the prominent position of several women in Thessalonica (cf. Acts 17:4).

18.3.3. The Accusations against the Christians

Luke formulates the charges brought against Jason before the politarchs as follows: "These people who have been turning the empire upside down (οἱ τὴν οἰκουμένην ἀναστατώσαντες οὗτοι)[115] have come here also, and Jason has entertained them as guests. They are all acting contrary to the decrees of the emperor (οὗτοι πάντες ἀπέναντι τῶν δογμάτων Καίσαρος πράσσουσιν), saying that there is another king named Jesus (βασιλέα ἕτερον λέγοντες εἶναι Ἰησοῦν)" (Acts 17:7).[116] It is immediately noteworthy that Luke reports a political charge against the Christians that was not easily refuted. Emperor Claudius mistrusted any empire-wide religious movements that could cause upheavals. As we have seen, his letter regarding the Alexandrian disturbances in the year A.D. 41 shows this quite clearly (§6.2.3). Although earlier commentators drew attention to the charge of the *crimen maiestatis*,[117] this was already forbidden as a breach of public peace, and not just by special ordinances of the emperor,[118] of which Luke seems to be thinking here. A. N. Sherwin-White, against his usual position, thus considered Luke's account here to be somewhat confused.[119]

E. A. Judge, a scholar of ancient history, has contributed significantly to a clarification of this situation.[120] Judge associates the charge with the imperial edicts against astrologers and diviners issued by Augustus (Dio Cassius, *Hist.*

228, *252; πολιταρχ-: *IG* X/2.1 226; πτολιαρχός: *IG* X/2.1 848, as well as *IG* X/2.1 181, 201; *CIG* II 1967; *Mak* 9 (1969) 143f.

113. The gate was torn down in 1878, and the inscription is now in the British Museum. Cf. P. E. Davies, *BA* 26 (1963) 103. A facsimile can be found in *GBL* III (1989) 1546.

114. In *Biblical Essays* (posthumous) (1893) 246, 256.

115. The verb ἀναστατόω is an equivalent of *tumultuare/i,* used by Suetonius (*Claudius* 25.4 [§10.2.2]).

116. In the eastern part of the empire, the emperor was called βασιλεύς (Jn. 19:15; 1 Pet. 2:13, 17). Cf. further the documentation in G. Schneider, *Die Apostelgeschichte* II, 225, note 38!

117. So, e.g., E. Jacquier, *Les Acts des Apôtres* (1926) 515; E. Haenchen, *Acts* (Eng. trans., 1971) 510.

118. Cf. C. W. Chilton, *JRS* 45 (1955) 73-81; R. A. Baumann, *Impietas in Principem* (1974).

119. *Roman Society and Roman Law* (1963) 96.

120. *RThR* 30 (1971) 1-7. Similarly also K. P. Donfried, *NTS* 31 (1985) 342-44.

lvi.25.5f.) and Tiberius (Dio Cassius, *Hist.* lvii.15.8 [δόγμα!]).[121] Predictions concerning the health and life of the emperor were particularly threatened with severe punishment not only in Rome itself, but also in the provinces (cf. Tacitus, *Ann.* ii.27-32; Paulus, *Sententiae* v.21). Municipal administrators and other local authorities were apparently bound by oath to insure these edicts were upheld. Paul's messianic proclamation (Acts 17:3) could have been exploited as such an insinuation. The first letter to the Thessalonians reinforces this interpretation (see pp. 379-81 below). Not only did Paul speak generally about Christ's parousia, his proclamation also encompassed apocalyptic expositions about "the times and the seasons" (1 Thess. 5:1). He could associate contemporary events with apocalyptic expectation (§18.3.1). Occasionally he could even make it clear that the Christians' view of the future was in a certain sense at odds with the political program of the Roman state *(pax et securitas):* "When they say, 'There is peace and security (εἰρήνη καὶ ἀσφάλεια),' then sudden destruction will come upon them ..." (1 Thess. 5:3). The behavior of some church members, prompted by a misunderstanding of Pauline preaching, could also raise the suspicion that revolutionary expectations for the future were being disseminated (§19.2).

Although Judge assumed that the change in choice of jurisdictional authority had something to do with the alteration of the accusation, he found himself unable to explain this change.[122] Perhaps the Claudian edict can help here.[123] As we suspect based on considerations elsewhere (§18.4.2), news of this edict reached Thessalonica at precisely that time (perhaps only one or two days after Paul's departure). Could it be that after this edict became known, the agitated Gentile Thessalonians now preferred to avoid any connection with the Jewish community, and now formulated their accusation against the background of the new imperial decree? In connection with this edict, we expressed our suspicion that the emperor had also become suspicious of both Jews and Jewish Christians because of their apocalyptic expectations (§10.7.1). The agitation of the politarchs and of other citizens (Acts 17:8: ἐτάραξαν) was understandable insofar as both this accusation and the mob scene could potentially cost the city its legal privileges as well as its good relationships with Roman patrons (§19.3.2). The memory was still fresh of how they lost the administrative seat under Tiberius, not receiving it back until five years earlier (A.D. 44) through the personal favor of Claudius himself (see p. 339 above).

With regard to the charges identified by Luke against Paul's mission and the resulting church in Thessalonica, two important historical objections obtain:

---

121. Cf. F. H. Cramer, *Astrology in Roman Law and Politics* (1954) 248-81; R. MacMullen, *Enemies of the Roman Order* (1966) 128-62.

122. *RThR* 30 (1971) 2.

123. W. Neil, *The Acts of the Apostles* (1973) 188, also already suspected some connection.

(1) In the accusation of an empire-wide movement of insurrection, is Luke not anachronistically bringing to expression the experiences of his own time, more specifically of the persecution under Domitian (see p. 343 above)?[124] Even in the particular situation of Thessalonica, however, this accusation does not seem absurd. In the eyes of Gentiles, the new messianic faith could still hardly be distinguished from its Jewish origins. Accusations against Jews could easily turn into allegations against the Christians. In A.D. 41, Jewish disturbances in the second-largest city of the empire, Alexandria, prompted Claudius to intervene (§6.2.3). Around A.D. 48, there were apparently also disturbances surrounding the Jewish question in the third-largest city as well, namely, Antioch (see p. 196 above). And now one also heard that the imperial capital itself was affected, and that the emperor had reacted by issuing an edict of expulsion (§10). Later history has provided us with significantly less serious occasions that have led to the charge of a worldwide Jewish conspiracy.

(2) Another criticism asks how, in the face of such serious accusations, the matter could have been resolved so indulgently. In the final analysis, however, benevolent analysis would reveal that the charges were in fact false. Even a complete acquittal by the politarchs would have been possible. The fact that they apparently imposed a ban and security might prompt speculation whether this was not perhaps a diplomatic measure designed, first, to assuage the agitated city populace and, second, to keep a potential source of unrest at a distance. The fact that the politarchs, despite the volatile nature of the accusations, did not immediately refer the procedure to the proconsul, who similarly resided in Thessalonica, reminds us that no municipal government proud of its own independence will lightly surrender its authority. Indeed, one wonders if the Christians — Secundus comes to mind (see pp. 350f. above) — might have had some influential patrons protecting them.

18.4. The Apostle's Flight

18.4.1. The Unclear Circumstances of His Flight

When the mob in front of Jason's house demanded that he surrender the missionaries, they found — according to Luke — that the latter were not

124. So also H. Botermann, *TBei* 24 (1993) 80f., who otherwise rates the historical value of Acts fairly high. By contrast, another scholar of ancient history is more cautious. J. Molthagen, *Hist* 40 (1991) 56, although he considers the charge unsuitable for the situation in Thessalonica, writes: "But this does not yet allow the conclusion that the formulation is simply to be ascribed to Luke's literary phantasy. The charge of creating a disturbance among Jews everywhere in the world seems rather to be a Jewish accusation against the Pauline missionary activity."

there (Acts 17:5f.). We do not learn where Paul and his companions had hidden themselves. It remains similarly unclear why the apostle in fact did not appear before the politarchs if he was, after all, still staying in the city. Finally, neither do we know why "that very night (εὐθέως) the believers sent Paul and Silas off to Beroea" (Acts 17:10). If the hope was that the missionaries' departure would calm the situation for the new Christian community, then at least according to Luke this was indeed fulfilled: the politarchs accepted the bail from Jason (Acts 17:9: λαβόντες τὸ ἱκανόν[125]). Perhaps this was tied to the promise not to take Paul in again, thus preventing his return.[126] This sort of ban would explain why Paul's attempts to return were futile (1 Thess. 2:17f.).

Luke's account is unclear in many details, and we do not know whether he simply lacked information or rather wanted to keep silent the circumstances of the apostle's precipitate departure. What does in any case become clear is that Paul's departure was unplanned and sudden, so that he was hardly able to take his leave of the whole community. The letter also confirms that he left Thessalonica in flight. The apostle's defense in 1 Thess. 2:1-8 presupposes that not everyone understood his unexpected departure (§18.7). The fact that Paul's return was "blocked by Satan" (1 Thess. 2:18) apparently means that, for some reason, things had become too risky for him in Thessalonica. Since there was no common legal jurisdiction between cities, every change of locale brought Paul into secure surroundings.[127]

18.4.2. The Futile Attempt to Push Farther West

We have seen that probably during his first stay in Europe, Paul was already thinking about a journey to the imperial capital Rome (§15.3.2). T. Zahn[128] considered whether the local tradition for the apostolic memorial Στοὺς Ἀποστόλους (cf. 1 Thess. 2:7) near the old Macedonian capital and Augustan colony[129] Pella contains a kernel of history. According to this tradition, Paul would indeed have pushed forward a bit (a journey of one to two days) to the west on the *Via Egnatia* toward the Adriatic, but then have turned south for some reason (Acts 17:10). If news of Claudius' Roman edict concerning the Jews (§10) reached the apostle at this time, something chronologically quite

---

125. This expression renders Latin *satis accipere,* which also otherwise designates the Greek praxis taken over by the Romans (*OGIS* 484.50; 629.100f.). Cf. A. N. Sherwin-White, *Roman Society and Roman Law in the New Testament* (1963) 95f.

126. So W. Neil, *The Acts of the Apostles* (1973) 188. Cf. also H. W. Tajra, *The Trial of St. Paul* (1989) 43f.

127. Cf. A. N. Sherwin-White, *Roman Society and Roman Law* (1963) 97.

128. *Introduction to the New Testament* (Eng. trans., 1909) 214.

129. Cf. F. Papazoglou, *ANRW* II 7.1 (1979) 358.

possible (§18.5), then this change of direction is understandable.[130] A. Suhl believes that Paul did in fact reach the Adriatic at that time (cf. Rom. 15:19), and then missioned in *Illyris Graeca* and Epirus.[131] Quite apart from the contradiction with Acts, the period of two to three months which Suhl himself provides in his outline seems a bit too tight.[132]

18.4.3. The Stay in Beroea

It is striking that because of the news of the Claudian edict, Paul escaped to Beroea (Acts 17:10).[133] That is, this city is not located on the great highway to the south (cf. Cicero, *In Pisonem* 36: *"oppidum devium"*), which ran close to the coastline, but rather a bit off to the southwest at the foot of Mt. Bermius.[134] Acts 17:14 correctly assumes a considerable distance from the city to the sea.[135] Paul withdrew to Beroea apparently in the hope of returning to Thessalonica after things had settled down. One is probably correct in associating with Beroea one of at least two (see p. 363 below) attempts at returning mentioned in 1 Thessalonians (1 Thess 2:18: διότι ἠθελήσαμεν ἐλθεῖν πρὸς ὑμᾶς, ἐγὼ μὲν Παῦλος καὶ ἅπαξ καὶ δίς, καὶ ἐνέκοψεν ἡμᾶς ὁ σατανᾶς).

Despite its location away from the coastal highway, Beroea was not an insignificant city[136] with a Roman trading colony[137] and a Jewish community[138] with a synagogue (Acts 17:10). The fact that the Jews of Beroea meet Paul amicably (Acts 17:11f.) represents a departure from Luke's usual mode

---

130. Cf. E. Bammel, *ZTK* 56 (1959) 304, note 4; F. F. Bruce, *1 and 2 Thessalonians* (1982) xxvif.

131. *Paulus und seine Briefe* (1975) 92-110, 342. A. Suhl is followed by W. Marxsen, *Der erste Brief an die Thessalonicher* (1979) 15f.

132. Cf. T. Holtz, *Der erste Brief an die Thessalonicher* (1986) 20f.

133. This was already noted by, among others, C. Clemen, *Paulus* (1904) I, 266; II, 159; E. Stange, *Paulinische Reisepläne* (1918) 32.

134. Cf. F. Papazoglou, *ANRW* II 7.1 (1979), map after p. 304.

135. The map of G. Stählin and E. Höhne, *Der östliche Mittelmeerraum zur Zeit des Apostels Paulus. Beilage zu BHH III* (²1968), incorrectly has the Thermaic Gulf extend to Beroea. The location of Aloros, however, does insure that the coastal line extended much farther to the east. Cf. F. Papazoglou, *ibid.*

136. It had a large population (D. H. Madvig, *ISBE* I [1979] 462), and according to the witness of an inscription (J. M. R. Cormack, *AncMac* II [1977] 139-50) had access to a gymnasium at least since the second century B.C., and in the New Testament period — like Thessalonica — to a city government led by politarchs (G. H. R. Horsley, *NewDoc* II [1982] 35). Cf. further F. Papazoglou, *Les villes de Macédoine* (1988) 141-48.

137. Cf. F. Papazoglou, *ANRW* II 7.1 (1979) 356.

138. Two Jewish funerary inscriptions are known from the late Roman period (*CIJ* I² 694a-b). Consecratory inscriptions to Zeus Hypsistos (but see pp. 348f. above) were also found. Cf. Schuerer III/1 (1986) 68.

of portrayal, and thus suggests the presence of redacted material.[139] When, however, agitators dispatched by the synagogal community in Thessalonica similarly protest against Paul in Beroea (Acts 17:13), apparently the native Christians there, too, encourage him to move on (Acts 17:14). The text (εὐθέως δὲ τότε τὸν Παῦλον ἐξαπέστειλαν οἱ ἀδελφοὶ πορεύεσθαι ἕως ἐπὶ τὴν θάλασσαν) implies a sea journey to Athens (Acts 17:15),[140] beginning perhaps from Pydna or Dion, which was not only a well-known pilgrimage site associated with Dionysos (§19.2.1), but in addition to Cassandreia also one of the first two Roman colonies[141] in Macedonia; Dion even possessed the *ius Italicum* (Diogenes Laertius 15.8).

18.4.4. The Sending of Timothy

Since all the apostle's attempts to visit the church again himself had foundered, he decided to send[142] his co-worker Timothy (1 Thess. 3:1f.).[143] One of Timothy's tasks was to strengthen spiritually the young, as yet unsecured, Christian congregation (1 Thess. 3:2: εἰς τὸ στηρίξαι ὑμᾶς καὶ παρακαλέσαι ὑπὲρ τῆς πίστεως ὑμῶν), Paul demonstrating here remarkable psychological insight into the new converts' distress (§19.1). The dispatch of Timothy, however, also quite obviously served to allay any misunderstandings or accusations arising from the apostle's unanticipated departure (§18.7). Most scholars consider the information in the letter to be irreconcilable with the movements of Paul's co-workers as presupposed in Acts.[144] According to Luke, it seems that Paul was alone in Athens the entire time (cf. Acts 17:16; 18:1), since he had left Silas and Timothy behind in Beroea (Acts 17:14), and the two are not mentioned again until they arrive in Corinth from Macedonia (Acts 18:5). 1 Thess. 3:1f. (διὸ μηκέτι στέγοντες εὐδοκήσαμεν καταλειφθῆναι ἐν Ἀθήναις μόνοι, καὶ ἐπέμψαμεν Τιμόθεον . . .) is understood almost universally to mean that Paul

139. Cf. T. Holtz, *Der erste Brief an die Thessalonicher* ([2]1990) 17.

140. Contra T. Zahn, *Introduction to the New Testament* (Eng. trans., 1909) 1.214, cf. C. J. Hemer, *The Book of Acts in the Setting of Hellenistic History* (1989) 116.

141. Cf. F. Papazoglou, *ANRW* II 7.1 (1979) 357-59.

142. Concerning the dispatch of messengers in the surrounding Greco-Roman world, cf. M. M. Mitchell, *JBL* 111 (1992) 641-62.

143. E. von Dobschütz, *Die Thessalonicherbriefe* (1909) 15f., assumed that it was through one of the church members from Beroea (Acts 17:15) that Paul instructed Timothy to return from there once more to Thessalonica. But then it is not quite clear why Paul "decided to remain behind alone in Athens" (1 Thess. 3:1).

144. So, e.g., E. Best, *The First and Second Epistles to the Thessalonians* ([2]1977) 131f.; W. Marxsen, *Der erste Brief an die Thessalonicher* (1979) 13f.; G. Lüdemann, *Paul: Apostle to the Gentiles* (Eng. trans., 1984) 14; J. Knox, *Chapters in a Life of Paul*, rev. ed. (1987) 72, note 15. Even an exegete as conservative as F. F. Bruce, *1 and 2 Thessalonians* (1982) 61, speaks of the "incompleteness of his [Luke's] information."

sent Timothy to Thessalonica from Athens, and thus contrary to the appearance in Acts was not alone the entire time in Athens. This tension has resulted in a number of extremely complicated attempts at harmonization.[145]

But as K. P. Donfried has shown, the conventional understanding of this passage from 1 Thessalonians is by no means compelling, and indeed is not even the most obvious.[146] The word ἐπέμψαμεν in 1 Thess. 3:2 is to be understood as a redactional plural, requiring the plural μόνοι and able to refer thus to Paul alone. The apostle could have dispatched Timothy even before his stay in Athens.[147] The rhetorical situation of the letter also suggests that Paul wants to emphasize here that he was *completely alone* in Athens. The congregation in Thessalonica is so important to the apostle that for its sake he is even willing to do without the companionship of his much-valued co-worker Timothy. One can naturally only surmise the tasks with which Silas was engaged in his absence from Paul. Although A. Wainwright believes he delivered the letter to the Galatians, written at that time,[148] he more likely performed some service in the newly founded churches of Philippi and Beroea. Paul sent Timothy to Thessalonica either already from Beroea, or at the latest as he departed by ship.[149] Since the apostle was apparently also prevented from visiting Thessalonica even after Timothy's arrival in Corinth, he sent a letter as a substitute for his own presence in the church.[150]

18.5. Chronological Evaluation

18.5.1. The Duration of the Stay

According to Acts, Paul preached in the synagogue on three sabbaths (Acts 17:2); because no other information regarding time is then given, one might

---

145. An especially thorough discussion can be found in T. Zahn, *Introduction to the New Testament* (Eng. trans., 1909) 1.205f. Surveys of the various attempts can be found in A. Stegmann, *Silvanus* (1917) 17f.; E. von Dobschütz, *Die Thessalonicherbriefe* (1909) 14f.; B. Rigaux, *Les épîtres aux Thessaloniciens* (1956) 30f.

146. In *Festschrift O. Knoch* (1991) 189-96.

147. Cf. B. Rigaux, *Les épîtres aux Thessaloniciens* (1956) 467.

148. *JSNT* 8 (1980) 66-70.

149. B. Rigaux, *Saint Paul: Les épîtres aux Thessaloniciens* (1956) 467, remarks regarding 1 Thess. 3:1: "This fear of remaining alone in Athens accords extremely well with what Acts tells us: Paul has to slip away from Beroea precipitately. Through the believers who have accompanied him as far as Athens, Paul sends to Silas and Timothy instructions to come and rejoin him ὡς τάχιστα, as soon as possible, Acts 17:15."

150. It was a notion otherwise widespread in antiquity as well, namely, that a letter can represent its sender. Cf. K. Thraede, *Grundzüge griechisch-römischer Brieftopik* (1970) 146-50.

have the impression that he left Thessalonica immediately thereafter. Scholars often assume an irreconcilable contradiction here between Luke and Paul,[151] since the letter clearly assumes that Paul spent a considerably longer period of time there. Several of the arguments in favor of the latter assumption are anything but compelling. Even if Paul was in Thessalonica for only a single month, he could still refer to the example of his own work "night and day" (1 Thess. 2:9). Neither is any real information about the duration of his stay provided by the fact that certain members were in charge within the congregation (1 Thess. 5:12) and that during his absence some (more than two?) church members had died (1 Thess. 4:13). A more promising reference is that to Phil. 4:16: "For even when I was in Thessalonica, you [already] sent me help for my needs καὶ ἅπαξ καὶ δίς." The Greek expression is probably best rendered by "more than once,"[152] though because of the doubled καί one can also translate "both [when I was] in Thessalonica and more than once [in other places]."[153] In that case, the Philippians (probably at their own initiative) sent help to the apostle in Thessalonica only once, something that, given the five to six days' journey by foot, could be accommodated even in the case of a stay of one month.[154] Even more recent commentators thus occasionally maintain the assertion that his stay was that short.[155]

The letter, however, witnesses to a congregation in which the great majority of members were Gentile Christians, suggesting a stay encompassing more than just one three- to four-week proclamation in the synagogue. Neither does Luke's portrayal necessarily exclude the possibility that Paul remained a bit longer in the city. The reference to the "three sabbaths" probably also intends, with its symbolical numerical value, to designate the divinely willed conclusion of the Jewish mission in Thessalonica. A. J. Malherbe justifiably draws attention to the fact that one can also understand Luke's stereotypical account such that after the break with the synagogue, Paul's subsequent activity resulted in a church's forming in Jason's house just as it did in Titus Justus' house in Corinth (Acts 18:6f.).[156] The agitators did in any event know that this house served as headquarters for the missionaries (Acts 17:5), and they did in fact find "several believers" there in addition to the owner, Jason

---

151. So, e.g., E. Best, *The First and Second Epistles to the Thessalonians* ([2]1977) 5; R. Jewett, *The Thessalonian Correspondence* (1986) 117.

152. Cf. T. Holtz, *Der erste Brief an die Thessalonicher* ([2]1990) 116f.

153. L. Morris, *NT* 1 (1956) 208. So already J. E. Frame, *The Epistles of St. Paul to the Thessalonians* (1912) 120f.

154. Cf. C. Clemen, *NKZ* 7 (1896) 146; *Paulus* II (1904) 158; J. E. Frame, *The Epistles of St. Paul to the Thessalonians* (1912) 7.

155. So L. Morris, *1 and 2 Thessalonians* (1956) 16f.; I. H. Marshall, *1 and 2 Thessalonians* (1983) 5.

156. *Paul and the Thessalonians* (1987) 13f.

(Acts 17:6). Although it is likely, then, that Paul was present for more than a month, one should probably not reckon with much more than that. The apostle had to break off his stay prematurely (§18.3.1), leaving behind a congregation that still lacked important instruction (1 Thess. 3:10: εἰς τὸ . . . καταρτίσαι τὰ ὑστερήματα τῆς πίστεως ὑμῶν). The overall chronological framework also precludes anything much over two to fourth months.

18.5.2. Dating the Stay and the Letter

The period of the apostle's stay in Thessalonica can be approximately determined. If he received news of the Claudian edict soon after leaving the city (§18.4.2), an edict issued in the eighth year of the emperor (§10), we are led to February A.D. 50 as a *terminus ante quem*. This concurs with the fact that according to our interpretation of the Gallio-date, Paul reached Corinth (§11.2) in February/March A.D. 50, that is, just as (coastal) shipping was being re-opened (cf. Acts 17:15 [§18.4.3]). Paul had spent the winter following the "Apostolic Council, " that is, A.D. 48/49, in Syria or Asia Minor (§16.2.2), and the distances covered by the routes suggest that he did not make the passage to Macedonia until the second half of A.D. 49. Even with extremely generous reckoning, hardly more than eight months remain for the period from Neapolis to Athens, of which again at least two to three months must be reckoned for founding the churches in Philippi and Beroea, as well as a month for traveling. So from this perspective, too, we arrive at a figure of at most four, and probably fewer months for Paul's stay in Thessalonica.

Several *subscriptiones* (e.g., A K L)[157] mention Athens as the place where 1 Thessalonians was composed.[158] One fact militating against this attribution is that according to 1 Thess. 3:1 (εὐδοκήσαμεν καταλειφθῆναι ἐν Ἀθήναις μόνοι), Paul was not accompanied in Athens by Silvanus[159] and probably also not by Timothy (§18.4.4). By contrast, according to 2 Cor. 1:19, Paul, Silvanus, and Timothy together founded the church in Corinth, and all three also appear as co-signees in the prescript to 1 Thessalonians (1 Thess. 1:1). Hence the majority of exegetes today justifiably assume the letter was composed in Corinth (see note 161). Moreover, "one can point out that contrary to Paul's custom elsewhere, the end of the letter contains no greetings from others. This can only mean that no church existed at the place where

---

157. Cf. in this regard E. von Dobschütz, *Die Thessalonicherbriefe* (1909) 17f., note 4.

158. Cf. Excursus III/3 (pp. 407-9) concerning the hypotheses of H. M. Schenke and K. M. Fischer, as well as R. Pesch, who divide 1 Thessalonians into two writings: one from Athens and one from Corinth.

159. Cf. B. Rigaux, *Saint Paul: Les épîtres aux Thessaloniciens* (1956) 467; T. Holtz, *Der erste Brief an die Thessalonicher* (²1990) 124.

the letter was composed which could enter into a connection with the recipient congregation, and that no other co-workers of Paul except Silvanus and Timothy were present who had any connection with them. This militates decisively for a date soon after the founding of the church [in Corinth]."[160] This conclusion, too, concurs with the regnant consensus within contemporary scholarship.[161] The various possibilities for place of composition, however, would not involve any essential changes in dating.

The view competing with this dating, following W. Lütgert,[162] W. Hadorn,[163] and W. Michaelis,[164] and advocated today especially by W. Schmithals,[165] asserts that the letter was not written until during what is known as the third missionary journey. Most of the reasons adduced are so weak[166] that only three will be addressed here briefly:[167] (1) The difficulty raised by the fact that 1 Thess. 3:1f., contra Acts 17:4; 18:5, presupposes that Timothy was present in Athens, is nonexistent (§18.4.4), and thus one need not challenge the identity of the sojourns. (2) The assertion is made that during his brief stay in Athens, Paul could not have made several futile plans for returning to Thessalonica. But 1 Thess. 2:17f. does not say that the apostle entertained these thoughts in Athens. As we have seen (p. 360 above), he could already have considered returning while he was in Pella and Beroea. (3) The assumption of an "interim visit" in Corinth required by a late dating is a superfluous hypothesis (§15.4.1).

Elements in the writing itself suggest that only a brief period separated the founding visit and the letter. The apostle was orphaned only "for a short time (πρὸς καιρὸν ὥρας)" by the separation from his congregation (1 Thess. 2:17). The numerous allusions to his founding visit (esp. 1 Thess. 1:5; 2:1, 5, 9, 10) bear the mark of "fresh recollections."[168] Through Timothy's return,

---

160. T. Holtz, *loc. cit.,* 11.

161. So also, among others, B. Schwank, *BZ* 15 (1971) 265f.; W. G. Kümmel, *Introduction to the New Testament* (Eng. trans., 1975) 259f.; N. Flanagan, *Friend Paul* (1986) 41; T. Holtz, *Der erste Brief an die Thessalonicher* ([2]1990) 11f., 19; R. Jewett, *The Thessalonian Correspondence* (1986) 30f.; W. Trilling, *ANRW* II 25.4 (1987) 3384.

162. *Die Vollkommenen in Philippi und die Enthusiasten in Thessalonich* (1919) 55-59.

163. *Die Abfassung der Thessalonicherbriefe in der Zeit der dritten Missionsreise des Paulus* (1919/20); *ZNW* 19 (1919/20) 67-72.

164. *Die Gefangenschaft des Paulus in Ephesus und das Itinerar des Timotheus* (1925) 41-67.

165. In *Festschrift R. Bultmann* (1964) 295-315; *Paulus und die Gnostiker* (1965) 133f.

166. Cf. W. G. Kümmel, *Introduction to the New Testament* (1975), 257-59.

167. A condensed critique can also be found in B. Rigaux, *Saint Paul: Les épîtres aux Thessaloniciens* (1956) 45-50.

168. W. G. Kümmel, *Introduction to the New Testament* (1975), 259.

Paul had only just learned that the church even still existed, and how it was faring (1 Thess. 3:2-6). This letter was the immediate answer to his news. The circumstances of the apostle's departure made necessary a speedy acknowledgment by letter (§18.7), and the problems addressed in the writing are in part typical for new converts (§19.1). These observations also militate decisively against 2 Thessalonians's having been composed prior to this.[169] By contrast, it would be possible that Timothy brought along a letter from the Thessalonians, as C. E. Faw has concluded with reference to the περί-passages (1 Thess. 4:9, 13; 5:1, 12),[170] though one can also explain this formula as reflecting a Christian pedagogical situation.[171] According to our chronology, the apostle's departure from Thessalonica and his letter to the church there were separated by little more than six months.

18.6. Acts and 1 Thessalonians

R. Jewett objects in strong language to the credulity still demonstrated toward the account of Acts regarding the founding of the church in Thessalonica, credulity maintained despite the work of critical commentators (esp. E. Haenchen, H. Conzelmann, and G. Schneider).[172] To be sure, the voices of the modern exegetes he cites are extremely varied. On balance, even Jewett himself seems to consider more information in Acts to be wholly or at least approximately correct than completely false. It will be helpful to summarize those specific pieces of Lukan information that can be verified. That which can be verified either directly or through elements within 1 Thessalonians include: (1) the route starting from Philippi; (2) persecution there; (3) Silas

---

169. C. A. Wanamaker, *The Epistles to the Thessalonians* (1990) 37-45, with reference to precursors such as J. Weiss, *Das Urchristentum* (1917) 217-19; T. W. Manson, *BJRL* 35 (1952/53) 428-47; C. H. Buck and G. R. Taylor, *Saint Paul* (1969) 140-45, and R. W. Thurston, *ET* 85 (1973/74) 52-56 (additional advocates since Hugo Grotius [1641] can be found in W. G. Kümmel, *Introduction to the New Testament,* 263), now advocates the reversal of the traditional sequence. He does this with a great deal of circumspection, but must, following G. Lyons (see p. 369 below), largely extract the *exordium* (1 Thess. 1:2-10) and *narratio* (1 Thess. 2:1–3:10) from any contemporary background as provided in so illuminating a fashion by the account in Acts, and views the whole a bit too excessively as a Pauline *exercitium* in rhetoric. By contrast, cf. especially R. Jewett, *The Thessalonian Correspondence* (1986) 19-30.

170. *JBL* 71 (1952) 217-25. J. R. Harris, *Exp* V/8 (1898) 161-80, first drew attention to this possibility.

171. Cf. E. Baasland, *ST* 42 (1988) 69-87.

172. *The Thessalonian Correspondence* (1986) 114-21. In the meantime, this has come to be considered an indisputable result even in popular publications (so, e.g., I. Havener, *BiTod* 24 [1988] 324).

and Timothy as cofounders of the church in Thessalonica; (4) connection with the synagogue there; (5) a congregation composed largely of Gentile Christians, to whom Paul proclaims (6) the messiahship, (7) suffering, and (8) resurrection of Jesus; all of which led (9) to politically motivated accusations against the Christians, and (10) to persecution by the inhabitants of Thessalonica, in which (11) Jews also played a role; (12) a premature breaking off of Paul's activity; (13) the continued journey to Athens; (14) Paul's sojourn there alone; and (15) perhaps the issuing of the Claudian edict at that time.

Six additional pieces of information appear only in Acts, of which four are doubtless accurate: (16) the stations along the *Via Egnatia* leading to Thessalonica; (17) the inscriptionally attested government of Thessalonica by politarchs; (18) the correctly conceived legal situation of a free city; and (19) the special role occupied by Jason in the newly founded church, which hardly a single exegete doubts.[173] The more specific description of the accusation as (20) an empire-wide insurgency movement, and as (21) a transgression against imperial decrees, is at least historically possible.

Finally, we also have pieces of information for which we cannot immediately establish any congruency between the letter and Acts: (22) Luke possibly portrayed an abbreviated version of the Pauline sojourn. (23) The letter neither confirms nor strictly denies that the city mob played a role in the persecution of the church. This feature might, however, yet contain a recollection of the social tensions in which the Christian congregation, because of its composition as presupposed in the letter, also participated. (24) The reference to the existence of higher-standing church members is not false, as our knowledge of several concrete persons shows. As a characterization of the social composition of the church, however, Luke's description is in a certain sense tendentious. (25) The *auctor ad Theophilum* either was not able or did not want to provide any information concerning the exact circumstances of the apostle's flight.

Hence, of the altogether twenty-five individual pieces of information in the Lukan account of the founding, eighteen to nineteen are either directly or indirectly confirmed by 1 Thessalonians. Of the independent pieces of information in Luke, four can be checked, and two seem possible. Although the imposition of extremely strict standards might enable us to view four of the Lukan details as doubtful or one-sided, none of them is impossible. On the whole, these are quite admirable findings for an ancient historian.[174]

---

173. Neither does R. Jewett, *The Thessalonian Correspondence* (1986) 116f., see any reason to do so.

174. The concurrences between Acts and the letter cannot be explained by asserting that Luke was familiar with 1 Thessalonians, as suggested recently by M. D. Goulder, *PerspRelSt* 13 (1986) 107-9. The resonance between 1 Thess. 4:8 and Lk. 10:16, and

18.7. The Necessity of Written Justification

18.7.1. Rebuke of Paul

As we will see, the apostle takes a pastorally sensitive approach in his letter to the problems of his new converts, who through this step had variously isolated themselves from their families, friends, and their entire social surroundings (§19.1). Even though this particular concern, as well as the queries of the Thessalonians themselves concerning open ethical and eschatological questions, represents the primary motivation for the apostle's writing, an additional reason is similarly unmistakable. A scholar as early as C. Clemen already drew attention to a potential hazard in Paul's relationship with the Thessalonians: "Finally, however, one need only view Paul from the perspective of the pagan rhetoricians in order to find in him deceptive and even ambitious and greedy intentions for the sake of which he would flatter people."[175] After M. Dibelius,[176] it was then especially A. J. Malherbe[177] who worked out parallels between 1 Thess. 2:1-12 and the picture of the ideal moral philosopher such as appears especially in Dio Chrysostomus. One probably must, however, reckon with the probability that Paul came by some of the *topoi* not directly through any contact with schools of rhetoricians or philosophers, but rather as a former rabbinic pupil. Hence, with regard to the image of the apostle as a "nurse" (1 Thess. 2:7: ἐγενήθημεν ἤπιοι ἐν μέσῳ ὑμῶν. ὡς ἐὰν τροφὸς θάλπῃ τὰ ἑαυτῆς τέκνα),[178] an image especially important to Malherbe, one can refer to Qumran. The great Psalm Scroll (11QPsᵃ

---

between 1 Thess. 5:1-3 and Lk. 21:34-36, can be understood as literary dependence only by someone who entertains a completely unhistorical picture of the emergence and transmission of the Gospel-traditions. C. M. Tuckett, in R. F. Collins, ed., *The Thessalonian Correspondence* (1990) 160-82, largely disputes any knowledge of Jesus-traditions in 1 Thessalonians. M. A. Thompson, *Clothed with Christ* (1991) 28-38, develops useful criteria for allusions to such traditions. A comprehensive treatment of the question "Paul and the Jesus-traditions" remains a desideratum. Cf. R. Riesner, *Festschrift P. Stuhlmacher* (1997) 347-65.

175. *NKZ* 7 (1896) 152.
176. *An die Thessalonicher* I, II (²1937) 10f.
177. *NovT* 12 (1970) 203-17; 25 (1983) 242-45; *Paul* (1987) 52-60.
178. The cynic background assumed by A. J. Malherbe would be considerably less persuasive if with the best manuscripts (P⁶⁵ ℵ* B* D*) one were to read νήπιοι (cf. B. M. Metzger, *A Textual Commentary on the Greek New Testament* [²1975] 629f.). More recent commentaries, however, uniformly follow the minority reading (ℵᶜ A C² D²). Cf. T. Holtz, *Der erste Brief an die Thessalonicher* (²1990) 82, note 337 (bibliography). K. P. Donfried, *NTS* 31 (1985) 338, 340, considers the possibility that the apostle is referring here antithetically to religions which, like the Dionysus-cult and the mysteries of Samothrace, attested various notions of "nurses."

21:14f.) contains the word עלה (nurse) parallel with מלמד (teacher).[179] All the same, the comparative features demonstrated by Malherbe do remain impressive.

18.7.2. Reality and Rhetoric

One cannot follow Malherbe when he challenges the notion that Paul had any real reason to defend himself against accusations of behaving like a third-class philosopher.[180] Attributing merely parenetic concern[181] to the overall section 1 Thess. 1–3 does not do justice to all the statements made there.[182] It would be astonishing if the apostle of Christ (1 Thess. 2:7) had compared himself to a philosopher merely for reasons of admonition. This text becomes immediately comprehensible as coming from the hand (or dictation) of Paul if he is thinking of very real or at least of potential accusations of deception, impure motives, and trickery (1 Thess. 2:3: πλάνη, ἀκαθαρσία, δόλος), of flattery or concealed greed (1 Thess. 2:5: λόγος κολακείας, πρόφασις πλεονεξίας).

We can leave open the question whether the apostle had heard of such accusations from the church itself,[183] or, as 1 Thess. 3:5f. might also suggest, had put himself in the situation of the Thessalonians before their pagan and Jewish[184] critics. Especially the apostle's precipitate departure, as portrayed

179. Cf. R. Riesner, *Jesus als Lehrer* (³1988) 172. Cf. also 1QH 7:20-22.

180. It is even less persuasive to explain the justifying retrospective in 1 Thess. 1–2, as does E. von Dobschütz, *Die Thessalonicherbriefe* (1909) 106f., as a result of the melancholy mood into which the apostle sank as a result of being separated from his church. Beyond this, one must grant to E. von Dobschütz that Timothy's return eliminated any occasion for this mood: "The sober observer may ask: Why does Paul even still speak of it? But anyone familiar with the human heart knows that after such times of care it must first give vent to its emotions" (*loc. cit.,* 107). This psychologizing interpretation does not do justice to the careful disposition of this section, nor to the genuine dangers threatening an unsecured Christian minority under the pressure of a pagan metropolis.

181. So also G. Lyons, *Pauline Autobiography* (1985) 177-221; D. E. Aune, *The New Testament in Its Literary Environment* (1987) 206.

182. Cf. especially I. H. Marshall, *1 and 2 Thessalonians* (1983) 60-75; T. Holtz, *Der erste Brief an die Thessalonicher* (²1990) 66-95; R. Jewett, *The Thessalonian Correspondence* (1986) 91-109.

183. So, e.g., C. Clemen, *NKZ* 7 (1896) 152f.; K. P. Donfried, *NTS* 31 (1985) 351. The construct of a group of adversarial gnostics in the church is utterly off the mark (W. Schmithals, in *Paul and the Gnostics* [Eng. trans., 1972] 124-218). Cf. by contrast E. Best, *The First and Second Epistles to the Thessalonians* (²1977) 16-22; I. H. Marshall, *1 and 2 Thessalonians* (1983) 17-19; R. Jewett, *The Thessalonian Correspondence* (1986) 147-49.

184. Jewish adversaries (as well) are suspected of being behind the apology of 1 Thess. 1–2 by, e.g., E. Best, *loc. cit.,* 16f.; I. H. Marshall, *loc. cit.,* 17; T. Holtz, *Der erste Brief an die Thessalonicher* (²1990) 94.

clearly in Acts, could elicit slander (cf. Dio Chrysostomus, *Or.* 32.11). Hence the following picture probably approximates the actual events: "Paul is presupposing that the Thessalonians are being subjected to the massive influence of their pagan fellow citizens, citizens intent upon extracting them from this fellowship that has suspended or at least called into question all previous social ties and prescribed for them a completely new, rigorous lifestyle. One excellent way to accomplish this is to level the apostle into that host of itinerant preachers who, along with their message, have long become transparent for what they really are. Because Paul sees that this represents a serious threat, one to which the church has indeed not yet succumbed, but which encounters them as a repressive force along their path, he composes this 'apology.' For the message stands or falls with its messenger."[185]

185. T. Holtz, *Der erste Brief an die Thessalonicher* ([2]1990) 94.

§19

Christians under the Pressure
of a Pagan Metropolis

19.1. Problems of Alienation among Converts

19.1.1. The Situation of the Thessalonians

In two essays that have received little attention, the Franciscan exegete E. Pax has shown how the language and content of the first letter to the Thessalonians betray that, above all, it is addressing typical problems of converts.[1] Pax already drew attention to comparative material from the Jewish solicitation of proselytes (esp. the novel *Joseph and Aseneth [JSHRZ* II/4]) and from the philosophical schools. This initiative was carried forward by A. J. Malherbe[2] who, despite substantial differences, does justifiably emphasize that both in pagan philosophical writings and in Paul, the emotional problems of converts are already being portrayed with astonishing psychological insight. For many of the new converts, this change to the new messianic faith involved a break with familial bonds and friendships, as well as, in a city characterized by pagan state cults (§19.2), social isolation. Insofar as the converts came from the sphere of the "God-fearers," this was perhaps already their second, even more difficult experience of alienation.

Another typical problem of recent converts is the cooling of their initial enthusiasm; having initially seemed transported into a completely new world, they soon discover the concerns of daily life catching up with them. Newly founded churches lacking any real tradition, in an environment of rejection, can be kept intact only through particularly intensive personal engagement. Although Paul knew this as well, adverse external circumstances hindered him from maintaining precisely this contact, so decisive in the beginning stages. It is therefore not a mere manner of speech when the apostle speaks of several

---

1. *SBFLA* 21 (1971) 220-61; *BibLeb* 13 (1972) 24-37.
2. *Paul and the Thessalonians* (1987) 35-52; *NTS* 36 (1990) 375-91.

failed attempts to visit (1 Thess. 2:17f.). Without the personal encouragement of its founding figure, encouragement which experience shows to be of crucial importance for many converts in dealing with these changes, a church as young as that in Thessalonica could easily completely collapse (cf. 1 Thess. 3:5).

The entire problematic with which Paul, only a few months after founding the church, found himself confronted while composing the first letter to the Thessalonians, can be summarized in his reference to "being orphaned (1 Thess. 2:17: ἀπορφανίζεσθαι)," "which Paul tactfully applies to himself while in reality it describes the situation of the addressees themselves, who probably complained to Timothy about it."[3] Although this word is a New Testament hapax legomenon, it (or its equivalent) does appear often in Jewish proselyte literature.[4] E. Pax described quite well the mood in which the apostle wrote the first letter to the Thessalonians: "Paul considers it vital to help the Thessalonians through their difficulties. It is only through *personal engagement* that the converts' crisis can be overcome, and this is why the letter is written. For the letter is, as such, a presence, a living reality. Its content is of value only if it bears the personality of the writer, who tries to secure his contact with the addressees by attempting to revivify the recent event of conversion for them, thus turning recollection itself into genuine presence. Here his personal participation is so decisive that, by comparison, other tasks become secondary. Even though Paul is planning an extensive missionary journey, he finds time to attend to what is basically a small church."[5]

19.1.2. The Apostle's Pastoral Response

This problem of an unsecured church without its founder does indeed consistently characterize the letter Paul sent to Thessalonica as a substitute for his own presence. The length of the grateful retrospective is already striking (1 Thess. 1:2–3:13). A reminder of the commonly experienced time of fulfillment at the beginning (1 Thess. 1:5-10) encourages the Thessalonians to hold fast to their faith both now and in the future. The apostle knew that the small church could survive in its pagan environment only if it constituted itself as a family-like fellowship with close personal ties. This is why this section of the letter is dominated by the language of family ("brethren": 1 Thess. 1:4; 2:1, 9, 14, 17; 3:7; 4:10, 13; 5:1, 4, 12, 14, 15;[6] Paul as mother and father of

---

3. E. Pax, *BibLeb* 13 (1972) 32f.

4. Cf. E. Pax *SBFLA* 21 (1971) 244.

5. *BibLeb* 13 (1972) 35f. Emphasis in the original.Cf. now also J. Chapa, *NTS* 40 (1994) 150-60.

6. Compared with these fourteen occurrences of the address "brothers" ("brothers and sisters," "beloved," so NRSV), only ten occur in the letter to the Romans, which is over four times as long.

the church: 1 Thess. 2:7, 12) and friendship (1 Thess. 4:9: φιλαδελφία). Paul consciously avoids asserting the authority of his office (1 Thess. 2:7; cf. 1 Thess. 1:1 [the absence of ἀπόστολος in the prescript]), and tries to strike a tone of warm cordiality (1 Thess. 2:8, 17, 19f.; 3:1, 5, 8f.).

Paul tries to address his new converts' disappointment at the difficulties they continue to encounter by pointing out that even as he founded the church, he did not conceal these things from them (1 Thess. 3:4; cf. 1 Thess. 1:6). The θλίψεις doubtless refer not only to genuine persecutory measures as such, but also to every internal and external tribulation encountered by the young believers. This word occurs in non-Christian literature as well in connection with the problems of converts.[7] The apostle's self-defense (§18.7) also constituted help for the new converts insofar as any doubts in the integrity of the church founder could easily have precipitated the end of their own faith. By authenticating himself, the apostle strengthened the congregation both internally and externally. The apostle's explicit admonitions also demonstrate the kinds of threats emerging for the young church both from their own, as yet unsecured existence and from the pressures of their pagan environment.

19.2. Threats from Pagan Cults

19.2.1. The Dionysus-Cult in Thessalonica

Apart from the treatment of questions of social life (1 Thess. 4:10b-12), U. Schnelle finds that all the other admonitions in the letter represent merely customary parenesis.[8] Given the multireligious situation in Thessalonica, this is at least questionable. The Dionysus-cult[9] is attested epigraphically in Thessalonica without interruption for the period from the second pre-Christian to the second post-Christian century (*IG* X/2.1 28, 59, 258). It is almost certain that a Dionysus-temple stood in the area of the later Byzantine basilica "Hagia Achiropiitos," since one of the three altars found there (*IG* X/2.1 260, 503, 506) was positioned *in situ*,[10] and even in the late Byzantine period this general location was still familiar (see pp. 374f. below). The Serapeion of Thessalonica (see pp. 373f. below) contains evidence of an amalgamation of the cults of Osiris

7. Cf. E. Pax, *BibLeb* 13 (1972) 33f.; A. J. Malherbe, *Paul* (1987) 37f., 46-48.
8. *NTS* 32 (1986) 209.
9. Among the more recent studies of this cult, one might mention M. Daraki, *Dionysos* (1985); S. Goldhill, *JHS* 107 (1987) 58-76. Concerning the spread of mystery religions during the New Testament period, cf. A. J. M. Wedderburn, *Baptism and Resurrection* (1985) 90-163; H. J. Klauck, *Die religiöse Umwelt des Urchristentums* I (1995) 77-128.
10. Cf. C. Edson, *HTR* 41 (1948) 118-40.

and Dionysus.[11] Although at least in the Republican period the veneration of the god of wine and fertility was also a state religion (*IG* X/2.1 28), his cult was cultivated above all in private religious associations.[12] It is possible, however, that these θίασοι had some connection with the state cult.[13] The significance of the worship of Dionysus in all of Macedonia is demonstrated by the excavations in Dion[14] beneath the Olympus mountain range, which on a relatively clear day can be seen from Thessalonica across the Thermaic Gulf. The Dionysus-cult not only exerted an attraction through its promise of a joyous beyond, but also was able to offer something in the here and now.[15]

19.2.2. 1 Thessalonians 4:1-9; 5:4-8

A scholar as early as J. B. Lightfoot already suspected that in 1 Thess. 2:3 (ἀκαθαρσία), Paul was distancing himself from the orgiastic practices typical of the Cabirus-cult (§19.3.2) and the mysteries of Samothrace.[16] Two other admonitions might also have some connection with the mysteries, and especially with the Dionysus-cult.

Apart from the traditional catalog of vices in Gal. 5:19, this sort of warning against fornication does not otherwise appear in Paul except in the Corinthian correspondence (1 Cor. 5:1; 6:13, 18; 2 Cor. 12:21) and 1 Thess. 4:3-8. This does not, to be sure, allow us to assume without further qualification that the background is one of cultic prostitution,[17] since such practices are attested in Corinth for the Greek period, but not for the Roman one.[18] A polemical connection with the Dionysus-cult would be possible if in 1 Thess. 4:4 σκεῦος were understood as *membrum virile,* and the sense of the expression εἰδέναι ἕκαστον ὑμῶν τὸ ἑαυτοῦ σκεῦος κτᾶσθαι were circumscribed as "controlling one's sexual urge."[19] In an allusion to corresponding rites,

11. Cf. H. L. Hendrix, *ABD* VI (1993) 524.

12. Cf. W. Elliger, *Paulus in Griechenland* (1978) 97f.

13. Cf. C. Edson, *HTR* 42 (1948) 139-41.

14. Cf. D. Pandermalis, *Dion* (1987) 7f. One giant Dionysus-mosaic in a Roman villa has not yet been published. A Dionysus-statue from the last quarter of the second century B.C. was found not too long ago (*Frankfurter Allgemeine Zeitung* 226 [September 29, 1988] 31).

15. Concerning its general spread, cf. V. J. Hutchinson, *JRA* 4 (1991) 222-30. One should note, however, that during the time of the emperors, many Dionysian *thiasoi* "had become popularly accepted traditional associations" (M. Hengel, *Der Sohn Gottes* [²1977] 48, note 56; Eng. trans., *The Son of God* [1976]).

16. In *Biblical Essays* (posthumous) (1893) 257f.

17. Contra K. P. Donfried, *NTS* 31 (1985) 341f.

18. Cf. R. Riesner, *GBL* II (1988) 818.

19. J. Whitton, *NTS* 28 (1982) 142f., with reference to 1 S. 21:6. He is followed by G. P. Carras, in R. F. Collins, ed., *The Thessalonian Correspondence* (1990) 310. K. P.

the area of the former Dionysus-temple was still known as Φάλλος during the Byzantine period.[20] The qualifying remark "not in lustful passion, like the Gentiles (μὴ ἐν πάθει ἐπιθυμίας καθάπερ καὶ τὰ ἔθνη) who do not know God" (1 Thess. 4:5) would be directed not against pagan fornication in general, but rather against pagan cults in particular.[21] This admonitory distancing would also be present if one were to choose the meaning "body" for σκεῦος, translating then "keeping ["controlling," so NRSV] your own body in holiness and honor." N. Baumert, in a thorough terminological study and exegesis of 1 Thess. 4:3-8, has suggested that σκεῦος (in substantive, not terminological correspondence to Gen. 2:18) can be understood in a manner similar to the rabbinic expression כלי as "support, help," with the section then speaking about the correct behavior of Christian men in courting brides. Baumert's interpretation has the advantage of offering an extremely coherent understanding of the entire context.[22]

One might also ask whether the warning against sleep and the nocturnal inebriation "of the others" (1 Thess. 5:4-8) intends a delimitation from Bacchanalian excesses, though neither can one exclude the possibility that the apostle is referring merely to the kinds of sexual and alcoholic offerings typical — then as today — of any large seaport. In any case, Paul's ethical instructions to the Thessalonians are characterized largely by Jewish traditions, with the goal of giving the church an unmistakable identity of its own to insure it would not be confused with other religious *collegia*.[23]

19.3. Social Unrest and Political Pressure

19.3.1. The Social Situation

After the civil war and the acquisition of many privileges (§18.1.1), Thessalonica, like Corinth and in contrast to the rest of Greece, experienced an

---

Donfried, *NTS* 31 (1985) 342, refers for this meaning of σκεῦος to Antistius Vetus (*Anthol. Plan.* iv.243) and Aelianus (*Hist. Animal.* xvii.1.1).

20. Cf. G. Bakalakis, in Θεσσαλονίκην Φιλίππου Βασιλίσσαν (1985) 978-92.

21. H. Ulonska, *TZ* 43 (1987) 213f., suspects that in either Asia Minor or Athens, Paul himself witnessed the *Aphrodisia* festival. Cf. also R. Hodgson, *BiTod* 24 (1988) 347f.

22. In R. F. Collins, ed., *The Thessalonian Correspondence* (1990) 318-39. Baumert's interpretation is not affected by the criticism of M. McGehee, *CBQ* 51 (1989) 82-89, of the conventional reference to rabbinic parallels.

23. Cf. P. Perkins, in *Festschrift J. A. Fitzmyer* (1989) 325-34; G. P. Carras, in R. F. Collins, *The Thessalonian Correspondence* (1990) 306-15; and U. Heckel, in *Festschrift M. Hengel* (1993) 282-91.

increasing economic upswing as a seaport and industrial city.[24] The city was subject to an influx of immigrants from Italy, Asia Minor, Moesia, and the rest of Greece, as well as to considerable building activity.[25] The distribution of this newly emerging wealth, however, was extremely inequitable. Although the middle class of manual workers and small merchants, especially numerous in the larger cities, did indeed have, in a few instances, the possibility of rising into the upper classes, more often than not the extravagent burden of taxation threatened to drag it down into the lower classes. Because of a relatively high unemployment rate, the urban proletariat represented a special social problem.[26] As in other large cities, so also in Thessalonica, a considerable part of this population probably lived on the public distribution of grain *(frumentatio)*,[27] either from the city or from rich private individuals.[28] Lack of insurance rendered the status of the unemployed or of seasonal workers in a certain sense even worse than that of domestic slaves, toward whom owners had legal obligations. The city's prosperity attracted those in search of work, simultaneously increasing the social tensions already exisiting. This social fermentation probably had something to do with the fact that in 88 B.C., many Macedonians joined the attempted rebellion of Mithridates VI Eupator from Pontus,[29] whose program included the liberation of slaves and the remission of debts (Appian, *Mith.* 46f.). The problematical position of many of the city's inhabitants led to two different reactions. Many simply let themselves go, making Juvenal's famous saying *"panem et circenses"* into their life's motto, a situation also resulting in a crisis in individual ethics: unstable marriages and the exposure of children were the order of the day.[30] Others tried to escape the downward social and moral spiral by joining private religious associations.

We find a reflection of the social problems in Thessalonica in Luke's portrayal of a staged mob scene. The τῶν ἀγοραίων ἄνδρες τίνες πονηροί (Acts 17:5) were apparently unemployed persons loitering around the agora who for a bit of money could easily be goaded into causing a public demonstration. Paul speaks in 2 Cor. 8:2-4 of the great poverty (ἡ κατὰ βάθος

24. Cf. M. Rostovtzeff, *History of the Roman Empire* ([2]1957) 91-93; R. M. Evans, *Eschatology and Ethics* (1968) 18-21, 29-33.
25. Cf. R. M. Evans, *loc. cit.,* 21, 47; W. Elliger, *Paulus in Griechenland* (1978) 88f.
26. Cf. R. M. Evans, *loc. cit.,* 55f.
27. A *frumentarius* by the name of Aurelius Statius Theodorus is attested in Thessalonica from the third century A.D. (*IG* X/2.1 207).
28. Cf. R. M. Evans, *Eschatology and Ethics* (1968) 42-46. Concerning this practice in general, cf. A. R. Hand, *Charities and Social Aid in Greece and Rome* (1968) 62-95; R. MacMullen, *Roman Social Relations* (1974) 57-87.
29. Cf. R. M. Evans, *Eschatology and Ethics* (1968) 42.
30. Cf. *ibid.,* 58-61.

πτωχεία αὐτῶν) of the Macedonian churches. The first letter to the Thessalonians shows that these social tensions extended into the Christian congregation as well. The exhortation to engage in the work of one's own hands (1 Thess. 4:11) presupposes that a considerable portion of the church members were workers or artisans. Paul probably won many of them to the new faith during his own work (1 Thess. 2:9) in a shop at the marketplace.[31] Hence scholars usually assume justifiably that the majority of the congregation in Thessalonica belonged to the working classes.[32]

Two difficulties Paul addresses, however, also show that at least some members of the congregation must have been better positioned in the ranks of patrons, as Acts presupposes (§18.2.4). After praising love for fellow Christians among the Thessalonians, the apostle writes: "But we urge you, beloved, to do so more and more, to aspire to live quietly, to mind your own affairs, and to work with your hands (φιλοτιμεῖσθαι ἡσυχάζειν καὶ πράσσειν τὰ ἴδια καὶ ἐργάζεσθαι ταῖς [ἰδίαις] χερσὶν ὑμῶν), as we directed you, so that you may behave properly toward outsiders and be dependent on no one (καὶ μηδενὸς χρείαν ἔχητε)" (1 Thess. 4:10-12). Here, like Dio Chrysostomus (*Or.* 3.124f.),[33] Paul is speaking against the mentality widespread among the proletariat[34] of living from either public or private support. If the new Christian congregation was governed by love for fellow Christians (1 Thess. 4:9: φιλαδελφία), it was only too natural for some of the poorer members to expect support from those few who were better off. This alone explains Paul's admonition,[35] though certain eschatological attitudes might possibly also have played a role.[36] Over against the regnant paternalistic

---

31. Cf. R. F. Hock, *The Social Context of Paul's Ministry* (1980) 26-49; A. J. Malherbe, *Paul and the Thessalonians* (1987) 17-20. According to W. Magass, *Kairos* 26 (1984) 156, 1 Thess. 2:10 (ὑμεῖς μάρτυρες) is alluding to the situation of the public marketplace.

32. So, among others, R. M. Evans, *Eschatology and Ethics* (1968) 87-95; E. Best, *The First and Second Epistles to the Thessalonians* (²1977) 176; W. A. Meeks, *The First Urban Christians* (1983) 64; R. Jewett, *The Thessalonian Correspondence* (1986) 120-22; A. J. Malherbe, *loc. cit.,* 15.

33. Cf. R. F. Hock, *The Social Context of Paul's Ministry* (1980) 42-46.

34. Cf. S. Mott, in G. F. Hawthorne, ed., *Current Issues in Biblical and Patristic Interpretation* (1975) 60-72.

35. So already J. E. Frame, *The Epistles of St. Paul to the Thessalonians* (1912) 162; and B. N. Kaye, *NT* 17 (1975) 47-57; G. Schöllgen, *NTS* 34 (1988) 76; R. Russel, *NTS* 34 (1988) 105-19. Concerning the important role of Christian εὐεργέται (cf. Rom. 13:3f.; 1 Pet. 2:14f.), cf. recently B. W. Winter, *JSNT* 34 (1988) 87-103; TynBul 40 (1989) 105f., 303-15; see also *Seek the Welfare of the City* (1994) 41-60.

36. So especially R. M. Evans, *Eschatology and Ethics* (1968) 172-76 (eschatological enthusiasm); R. Jewett, *The Thessalonian Correspondence* (1986) 173-75 (politically colored millenarianism). A survey of other views can be found in T. Holtz, *Der erste Brief an die Thessalonicher* (²1990) 176-79.

welfare-state mentality, Paul tried through the example of his own manual trade to encourage the congregation to adopt an ethos of working in cooperation and partnership.[37]

If the new fellowship was indeed characterized by great intimacy, did one then also need, within the Christian congregation (or at all?), any socially or religiously motivated subordination? Hence in 1 Thess. 5:12f., Paul did have to exhort his members to respect patrons (see p. 350 above); the ἄτακτοι (1 Thess. 5:14) might be referring to those who resisted all authority. The meaning of this Greek word, as ascertained by C. Spicq in his characteristic minute and well-documented manner, involves resistance to the divine or natural order.[38] Those in 1 Thess. 4:9-12 who resist work can, based on contextual considerations, be identified with these "renitents."[39] Apparently there was in Thessalonica a circle of poorer believers representing the position that although the more wealthy members were not supposed to say anything, they were indeed supposed to pay. This egalitarian tendency, too, can be explained adequately as a result of this fellowship being based on love for one's fellow members. Moreover, possession of spectacular charismatic gifts (cf. 1 Thess. 5:19-22) could lead to feelings of superiority that did not even stop before the authority of Paul himself.[40] In 1 Thess. 4:9 (ὑμεῖς θεοδίδακτοί ἐστε), Paul encourages the mutual social responsibility of the believers with a possible reference to Jesus' commandment of love (εἰς τὸ ἀγαπᾶν ἀλλήλους).[41]

37. Cf. E. A. Judge, *JRH* 11 (1980/81) 214; R. Russell, *NTS* 34 (1988) 113, 118f., note 75.

38. *ST* 10 (1956) 1-13; *Notes de Lexicographie Néo-Testamentaires* I (1978) 159.

39. Cf. F. Laub, *Eschatologische Verkündigung und Lebensgestaltung nach Paulus* (1973) 145f.; D. A. Black, *JETS* 25 (1982) 307-21.

40. Cf. R. Jewett, *The Thessalonian Correspondence* (1986) 100-105.

41. A certain terminological parallelism with Philo obtains with the expression θεοδίδακτος, apparently newly coined by Paul. Cf. C. J. Roetzel, in A. Vanhoye, ed., *L'Apôtre Paul* (1986) 324-31. But one can also refer to the eschatological promise in Isa. 54:13, which is appropriated in Jn. 6:45. 1 Thess. 4:9b agrees verbatim with Jn. 13:34, and one can by no means exclude the possibility that Paul is in contact here with pre-Johannine tradition. Cf. C. Spicq, in *Festschrift A. Robert* (1957) 510f.; F. F. Bruce, *1 and 2 Thessalonians* (1982) 90, as well as already T. I. Tambyah, *ET* 44 (1933) 527f. The use of ζάω also suggests some proximity between 1 Thessalonians and John. Cf. J. G. van der Watt, in R. F. Collins, ed., *The Thessalonian Correspondence* (1990) 356-69. An allusion to Lev. 19:18 (cf. Mk. 12:31) is a possibility in 1 Thess. 4:9 (D. Lührmann, in *Festschrift A. J. Malherbe* [1990] 337-49). Despite all the interesting passages adduced as witnesses, the view of J. S. Kloppenborg, *NTS* 39 (1993) 278-89, is off the mark, according to which Paul wanted to use the word θεοδίδακτος to enlist the Dioscuri, who were worshiped in Thessalonica, as models for φιλαδελφία.

19.3.2 The Public Cult

Apart from the Dionysus-cult, the worship of Zeus, Hercules, Asclepius and Pythian Apollo, Aphrodite, Demeter, and Pallas Athene, as well as other deities is attested in Thessalonica.[42] The phenomenon most typical of Thessalonica, however, was the cult of the mystery god Cabirus.[43] In contrast to other Greek cities, he was worshipped in Thessalonica as *one* (i.e., a single) God,[44] though there was perhaps also a blending with the Dionysus-cult.[45] It was expected that Cabirus, who was murdered by his two brothers and interred with royal insignia, would return and help the city of Thessalonica and especially the poor. Inscriptions (*IG* X/2.1 199B) and coins suggest that the Cabirus-cult was absorbed by the official city cult since the Augustan period.[46] This development created a religious vacuum: "By the time of the first century in Thessalonica, the city-cult had meaning only for those most directly interested in the welfare of the city. Thus the transformation is complete. The Cabiri rose to be identified with the city god of Thessalonica, but in so doing lost their religious value and contact with the lower classes."[47] This vacuum was filled by the mystery cults from the east, and for Christianity, too, this precarious religious situation provided mission possibilities. This may be one more reason that members of the lower classes turned to the new faith in greater numbers.

Connections between the Thessalonian upper classes and Rome were especially intensive. Ever since the Augustan period, there was a *conventus civium Romanorum* (*IG* X/2.1 32, 33).[48] This close relationship is attested not least by the organization of the public cult.[49] The leading personalities of the city apparently made an immediate demonstration of their gratitude for the privileges granted to Thessalonica after the victory of Anthony and Octavia

---

42. Cf. A. E. Vacalopoulos, *A History of Thessalonica* (1972) 14.

43. Cf. C. Edson, *HTR* 41 (1948) 188-202; B. Hemberg, *Die Kabiren* (1950); P. Rossano, *RBI* 6 (1958) 246f.; R. M. Evans, *Eschatology and Ethics* (1968) 68-71; R. E. Witt, *AncMac* II (1977) 67-80; K. P. Donfried, *NTS* 31 (1985) 338-41; R. Jewett, *The Thessalonian Correspondence* (1986) 127-32; M. H. Blanchaud, *AncMac* IV (1986) 81-86.

44. The presentation of R. M. Evans and W. Elliger, *Paulus in Griechenland* (1978) 98f., is to be corrected at this point.

45. Cf. H. L. Hendrix, *ABD* VI (1992) 524.

46. Cf. C. Edson, *HTR* 41 (1948) 189-92. Concerning the Romanization of north Macedonian cults generally, cf. S. Düll, *AncMac* III (1983) 77-87.

47. R. M. Evans, *Eschatology and Ethics* (1968) 71.

48. Cf. F. Papazoglou, *Les villes de Macédoine* (1988) 208f.

49. Cf. C. Edson, *HCSP* 51 (1940) 127-36; R. M. Evans, *Eschatology and Ethics* (1968) 65-68; W. Elliger, *Paulus in Griechenland* (1978) 96f.; H. L. Hendrix, *Thessalonians Honor Romans* (1984) 98-139; *ABD* VI (1992) 324f.; K. P. Donfried, *NTS* 51 (1985) 342-46; R. Jewett, *The Thessalonian Correspondence* (1986) 123-26.

at Actium (§18.1.1) by establishing a temple for Caesar and the two εὐεργέται
(*IG* X/2.1 31).[50] This temple probably stood in the northern part of the
Hellenistic sacral precinct in the area of the modern "Hodos Stratigiou
Doumbiotou."[51] Perhaps the archaic temple (see p. 338 above) was also
incorporated into the cult of the emperor during the Augustan period.[52] A cult
of the Roma was established still during the first century B.C.,[53] and since 27
B.C. coins attest the designation of Julius Caesar as θεός (Gaebler II, no. 43).[54]
This development especially made it possible to identify personal piety and
loyalty to the state. H. L. Hendrix summarizes this state of affairs as follows:
"[While] 'the gods' of the city were due honors as the source of Thessalonica's
continued well-being, important foreign agents of its immediate interests were
acknowledged in concert with its divine sustainers . . . Honors *for* the gods
and Roman benefactors expressed a hierarchy of benefaction extending from
the divine sphere into human affairs."[55]

    Against this background, the accusation of having disseminated
prophecies concerning the end of the present ruler and the advent of a new
one (§18.3.2) was naturally especially dangerous. R. Jewett summarizes as
follows the political situation for the Christian community from the perspective of the governing classes of the city: "An unwelcome and certainly
unintended result, from the perspective of the Thessalonian politarchs, was

---

50. Cf. H. L. Hendrix, *loc. cit.,* 42. Lost inscriptions include one found in 1874
in the western part of the city (Kalimari Gate) between the foundation remnants of a
building (serving the cult of the emperor?) (L. Duchesne and M. Bayet, *Mémoire sur une
mission au Mont Athos* [1876] 11f.). Concerning the cult of the 'Ρωμαῖοι εὐεργέται in
Macedonia generally, cf. F. Papazoglou, *ANRW* II 7.1 (1979) 307f.

51. A statue of Augustus, now on exhibit in the Archaeological Museum, was
found there in 1939, and the headless statue of another emperor in 1957. Cf. M. Vickers,
AncMac I (1970) 247f.; *JHS* 92 (1972) 164. W. Elliger, *Paulus in Griechenland* (1978)
96f., assumed a location at the Latomus monastery in the northeastern part of the present
old city; this is not a possibility, however, because in all probability this area lay outside
the Hellenistic city walls. Since the statue of Augustus comes from the time of Caligula
or Claudius, Paul very likely saw it.

52. Cf. H. L. Hendrix, *ABD* VI (1992) 524.

53. Just where R. Jewett, *The Thessalonian Correspondence* (1986) 126, discovered the "impressive archaeological remains of the large temple of Roma," remains a
secret known only to him.

54. Cf. W. Elliger, *Paulus in Griechenland* (1978) 97; H. L. Hendrix, *Thessalonians Honor Romans* (1984) 170-73, 293-95; K. P. Donfried, *NTS* 31 (1985) 346.

55. *Thessalonians Honor Romans* (1984) 336. One other witness to the close bonds
between the city and Rome is the relatively large number of Thessalonians inscriptionally
attested as Roman soldiers. A collection from 1977 encompassing about 250 Macedonian
members of the military (T. C. Sarikakis, *AncMac* II [1977] 431-62) mentions among the
most frequent places of origin Scupi with fifty-seven, Philippi (!) with fifty-two, and
Thessalonica with thirty-six representatives.

that if a figure like the heroic Cabirus were perceived to have returned on behalf of the laborers of the city in a form not under the control of the civic cult, it would pose a threat of revolutionary dimensions. The παρουσία of any religious figure structurally similar to Cabirus would therefore naturally be perceived as subversive to Roman rule."[56] Catchwords for subversive insinuations could easily be extracted from Paul's preaching. Both in Thessalonica and elsewhere, terms such as βασιλεία (1 Thess. 2:12), παρουσία (1 Thess. 2:19; 3:13; 4:15; 5:23), ἀπάντησις (1 Thess. 4:17), and κύριος (1 Thess. 1:6; 3:12; 4:6, 15-17; 5:27) had political connotations.[57]

In connection with the problems of refusal to work and the rejection of authority (see pp. 376-78 above), we already encountered possible signs of millenarianism, prompted by high apocalyptic tensions, of the sort especially R. Jewett[58] and C. A. Wanamaker[59] conceive as the background of the problems in the church of Thessalonica. Such a suggestion runs the risk of any all-encompassing model of having to exclude certain parts of reality.[60] Nonetheless, this political suspicion may not have been completely unjustified with regard to at least some members of the church in Thessalonica. One of Paul's admonitions might be understood as warning against political aspirations: Παρακαλοῦμεν . . . φιλοτιμεῖσθαι ἡσυχάζειν καὶ πράσσειν τὰ ἴδια (1 Thess. 4:11)! E. von Dobschütz (with reference to the exegesis of H. Zwingli) found here "a political element as a contrast [to the quiet life, namely]: concerning oneself with public matters, seeking to control the affairs either of the state or of the city at the marketplace according to a program of Christian eschatology."[61] If this is referring to activities of eschatologically excited members of the congregation from the lower classes, then the counterargument is useless according to which politics in antiquity was considered to be the business of philosophers, aristocrats, and the wealthy.[62] In a city like Thessalonica, the recollection of the socio-revolutionary attempt at rebellion by Andriscus (§18.1.1) was probably just as fresh as that of the socio-reformist

56. *The Thessalonian Correspondence* (1986) 132.

57. Cf. E. Best, *The First and Second Epistles to the Thessalonians* ([2]1977) 199; K. P. Donfried, *NTS* 31 (1985) 344; R. H. Gundry, *NTS* 33 (1987) 161-69; E. Krentz, *BiTod* 26 (1988) 338; P. Perkins, in *Festschrift J. A. Fitzmyer* (1989) 328; J. S. Kloppenborg, *NTS* 39 (1993) 275-77.

58. *The Thessalonian Correspondence* (1986) 159-78.

59. *Neotest* 21 (1987) 1-10.

60. Concerning criticism of an early form of the thesis presented by R. Jewett, cf. I. H. Marshall, *1 and 2 Thessalonians* (1983) 19f. G. Schöllgen, *NTS* 34 (1988) 71-82, correctly draws attention to the extremely limited data basis for any socio-historical explanatory model.

61. *Die Thessalonicher-Briefe* (1909) 180.

62. So E. Best, *The First and Second Epistles to the Thessalonians* ([2]1977) 174f.

program of Mithridates VI (see p. 376 above).[63] Besides this, Thessalonica as *civitas libera* offered certain possibilities for democratically exerting one's influence.

The political interpretation of 1 Thess. 4:11, frequently presented before the First World War,[64] has fallen a bit from fashion. R. F. Hock, however, has added to the witnesses for a political background already mentioned (Plato, *R.* iv.496D, cf. *R.* iv.433A; Dio Cassius, *Hist.* lx.27)[65] additional ones (e.g., Dio Chrysostomus, *Or.* 34.52; 47.2; Plutarch, *Praec. Ger. Reip.* 798E-F).[66] The fact that Luke has loiterers at the marketplace (τῶν ἀγοραίων ἄνδρες τινὲς πονηροί)[67] participate in a mob scene against the Christian community (Acts 17:5) might yet be a reflection of a situation in which congregation members from the lower classes expressed themselves among their acquaintances and colleagues at the Agora in a way that could be understood as subversive.

63. Cf. also W. W. Tarn and A. T. Griffith, *Hellenistic Civilization* (³1952) 121; M. Rostovtzeff, *The Social and Economic History of the Roman Empire* II (²1957) 939f.; R. M. Evans, *Eschatology and Ethics* (1968) 40-42.

64. Representatives can be found in J. E. Frame, *The Epistles of St. Paul to the Thessalonians* (1912) 161.

65. Contra the attractive suggestion of G. Schimanowski, in *Festschrift M. Hengel* (1993) 305-11, that one should view ἡσυχάζειν (cf. Philo, *Spec. Leg.* ii.56ff.; *Vit. Mos.* ii.209ff.; Lk. 23:56) as an allusion to the sabbath rest, one can point out that (1) such an admonition is unmotivated in this context, and would represent (2) a unique occurrence in Paul otherwise as well; (3) moreover, the situation in Thessalonica was in fact so politically tense for Christians that the closest parallel would probably be 2 Thess. 3:6-13, regardless of how one actually dates the passage.

66. *The Social Context of Paul's Ministry* (1980) 46f., 90f., notes 191-92. Cf. also A. J. Malherbe, *Paul and the Thessalonians* (1987) 95-107.

67. Cf. A. J. Malherbe, *Paul and the Thessalonians* (1987) 17: "Significant for our purpose is that *agoraios* in such contexts retains its association with the marketplace (*agora*) and the small tradespeople and manual laborers who gathered there, whom it describes pejoratively [e.g., Plutarch, *Aem.* 38.3; Dio Chrysostomus, *Or.* 1.33]. Against this background, Luke's usage is remarkable."

§20

A Concrete Eschatological Question

20.1. Yearnings for the Beyond in Thessalonica

The apostle begins his exposition of the question concerning deceased Christians with the sentence: "But we do not want you to be uninformed, brethren, about those who have died, so that you may not grieve as others do who have no hope" (1 Thess. 4:13). A whole series of ancient grave stelae from the area around Thessalonica movingly attest human grief.[1] Neither can one emphasize strongly enough the fact that according to the witness of grave inscriptions in the Roman empire, not even half of all people reached the age of twenty-five; hardly 5 percent reached fifty.[2]

In Thessalonica, the older cult of the dead was associated with the divine figure of Hermes (cf. Acts 14:12).[3] The yearning for life after death created numerous adherents for the Isis- and Serapis-cult in Macedonia even though this Egyptian religion ran counter to the Greek inclination toward rationality. This cult is also attested precisely in places Paul visited, such as Philippi, Amphipolis, Apollonia, and Beroea.[4] Already in the third pre-Christian century, there was in the western part of Thessalonica a Serapis temple in which numerous inscriptions have been found, including a long Isis-aretalogy (*IG* X/2.1 254).[5] These two Egyptian gods could without difficulty be identified with the Greek deities

---

1. So, e.g., the portrayal of a young girl from Nea Kallikratia/Chalcidice (fifth century B.C.) or a grave relief from Liti crafted by an artist from Beroea (first century A.D.). Cf. M. Andronicos, *Museum Thessaloniki* (1988) 64, 74.

2. Cf. A. R. Burn, *PaP* 4 (1943) 1-31.

3. Cf. S. Düll, *AncMac* I (1970) 320f.

4. Cf. R. E. Witt, *AncMac* I (1970) 324-33. To be sure, R. E. Witt, *loc. cit.*, 332f., goes too far when he relates the allusion to the ἄνθρωπος τῆς ἀνομίας in 2 Thess. 2:3 to Caligula, interpreting thus: "I might consider Paul in this Anomos passage to be hitting out possibly at a Thessalonian cult in which Emperor worship was combined with the cult of Isis and Serapis" (*loc. cit.*, 332).

5. Cf. C. Edson, *HTR* 41 (1948) 180-87; W. Elliger, *Paulus in Griechenland* (1978) 81-86; G. H. R. Horsley, *NewDoc* I (1981) 30-32; K. P. Donfried, *NTS* 31 (1985) 337.

Demeter and Dionysus. Evidence found in the Serapeion, which was renovated during the early Christian era, shows how "the gods had become guarantors of a comforting notion of the beyond, and how thus the Homeric conception of the gods as a reflection of experienced reality had been abandoned once and for all."[6] Probably several of the Pauline converts came from those associated with this cult, and for them the question of the Christian understanding of the fate of the deceased of necessity became an especially burning issue.[7] From the Serapeion we have a late-Hellenistic inscription (*IG* X/2.1 107.1) in which a son consecrates his parents to Osiris (Ὀσείριδι). Since the apostle anticipated the resurrection of the body, these pagan yearnings for the beyond were without hope (1 Thess. 4:13f.).[8]

20.2. The Thessalonians' Problem

20.2.1. Insufficient Instruction?

Although in answering two of the Thessalonians' questions (περί) Paul expressly emphasizes that they really need no instruction (1 Thess. 4:9-12: love for one's fellows; 1 Thess. 5:1-11: times and seasons), the apostle introduces the middle theme with the words οὐ θέλομεν δὲ ὑμᾶς ἀγνοεῖν (1 Thess. 4:13). G. Lüdemann quite correctly remarks concerning this sentence that "Paul often used this introductory formula to introduce something new or to present his congregations with previously unknown information."[9] Lüdemann also persuasively criticizes[10] the view of W. Schmithals[11] and W. Harnisch[12] according to which Paul is allegedly polemicizing in 1 Thess. 4:13-17 against gnostics who have shaken the Thessalonians' hope in resurrection. A similarly unconvincing view holds that the Thessalonians were concerned that the deceased Christians would not be able to participate in the interim messianic kingdom.[13] Quite aside from the problem of whether one can indeed presuppose this notion for Paul and his congregations, it still hardly explains the profound lack of hope on the part of the Thessalonians, which makes them like the pagans (ἵνα μὴ λυπῆσθε καθὼς καὶ οἱ λοιποὶ οἱ μὴ ἔχοντες ἐλπίδα [1 Thess. 4:13]). However, considerable problems are also generated by the

6. W. Elliger, *loc. cit.,* 83.
7. P. Rossano, *RBI* 6 (1958) 245f., already suspected this.
8. Cf. B. Schwank, *EA* 39 (1963) 411f.
9. *Paul: Apostle to the Gentiles* (Eng. trans., 1984) 214.
10. *Ibid.,* 206-9.
11. In *Paulus und die Gnostiker* (1965) 118f.
12. *Eschatologische Existenz* (1973) 16-51.
13. So G. Friedrich, *Der erste Brief an die Thessalonicher* ([14]1976) 201f.

answer offered by W. Marxsen[14] and Lüdemann,[15] according to which Paul basically had not yet spoken at that time about the resurrection of Christians (§20.3.2).

An explanation commensurate both with the letter and with Acts (§18.4-7), however, consists in the reference to Paul's founding visit, which was both brief and prematurely broken off.[16] It is not necessary even to assume that the apostle had said nothing about the future resurrection of the dead. H. Giesen points out "that ἀγνοεῖν is not only — indeed not even primarily — to be understood in the cognitive sense, but rather in the sense of total comprehension of the given subject matter. It is not Paul's intention merely to inform the Thessalonians, thereby increasing their knowledge; rather, they are to be shown how to apply the doctrine of the resurrection of Jesus also to the fate of those who have already died."[17] It suffices to assume that Paul mentioned the resurrection of Christians as merely one of several topics without making it the fully addressed theme of his instruction. If the Thessalonians were particularly impressed by the portrayal of the rapture of the living at the parousia, then they could easily fall prey to the misunderstanding that the dead would not participate in this parousia at all, since rapture from death was not possible.[18] One might also imagine that Paul was misunderstood as having implied that an immediately imminent parousia[19] would exclude the death of any Christians until then.[20] If, like other Pauline congregations, the Thessalonians also met in different houses, or if Paul's instruction often took place in personal conversations, then it would be possible that only part of the members of the congregation had heard anything on this particular topic.[21] The apostle's imploring admonition to read the letter to *"all* the brethren" (1 Thess. 5:27) may be alluding to the fact that a full assembly of the congregation was not simply a given. In addition to lacking sufficient

14. *Der Erste Brief an die Thessalonicher* (1979) 65.

15. *Paul: Apostle to the Gentiles* (Eng. trans., 1984)

16. So, among others, B. N. Kaye, *NT* 17 (1975) 48, note 6; I. H. Marshall, *1 and 2 Thessalonians* (1983) 120-22; C. J. Hemer, *The Book of Acts in the Setting of Hellenistic History* (1989) 186.

17. *SNTU* 10 (1985) 126.

18. So H. Giesen, *SNTU* 10 (1985) 135f., with reference to J. Plevnik, *CBQ* 46 (1984) 274-83 (and previously already in *Festschrift D. M. Stanley* [1975] 199-277).

19. H. Giesen, *loc. cit.,* 135: "The proclamation of the expectation of the parousia (cf. 1:10) could so have impressed the Thessalonians that from the possibility that the Lord could come at any moment (5:2) they concluded that the parousia of the Lord was indeed temporally imminent."

20. Cf. L. Morris, *1 and 2 Thessalonians* (1956) 83.

21. L. M. Dewailly and B. Rigaux, *Les épîtres de Saint Paul aux Thessaloniciens* (³1969) 49, note e, also assume that only a portion of the congregation was affected by this question.

instruction, some specific experience of the congregation may also have aggravated the question concerning the fate of deceased Christians.

20.2.2. Executed Christians?

K. P. Donfried,[22] keying on the legal background of the persecution of the church as assumed in the present work as well (§18.3), presented once again the earlier thesis[23] that instances of martyrdom had made the Thessalonians' question especially virulent. Here one can refer to the analogy Paul establishes between the persecution of the Judean congregations and the problems in Thessalonica (1 Thess. 2:14-16: τὰ αὐτὰ ἐπάθετε). Since at least the grammatical possibility exists for connecting — as did church fathers such as John Chrysostom and Ephraem — διὰ τοῦ Ἰησοῦ with τοὺς κοιμηθέντας (1 Thess. 4:14),[24] one could find here, too, an allusion to Christians who died as martyrs.[25]

One difficulty with the assumption of martyrdoms is naturally the silence of Acts, which in this passage, however, one could explain relatively easily as a result of the author's own agenda, particularly since Luke never reports anything from Pauline churches during the apostle's absence. But even the potential allusions in Paul himself are not unequivocal enough to allow any reasonably secure assumption. If the reconstruction of the juristic background is correct, then one must admit that even a bloody persecution cannot be excluded. The oath of loyalty to the imperial house taken by the inhabitants

22. *NTS* 31 (1985) 349-51. Independent of K. P. Donfried, the same view is now also taken by J. S. Pobee, *Persecution and Martyrdom in the Theology of Paul* (1985) 113f.

23. K. P. Donfried, *loc. cit.,* 349, found only in F. F. Bruce, *The Acts of the Apostles* (1951) (= ²1952) 327f. But cf. already K. Lake, *The Earlier Epistles of St. Paul* (1911) (= ²1919) 88; J. Weiss, *Das Urchristentum* (1917) 222; P. Nepper-Christensen, *ST* 19 (1965) 137f. G. Friedrich, *Der erste Brief an die Thessalonicher* (¹⁴1976) 242; H. Schlier, *Der Apostel und seine Gemeinde* (²1973) 77 (as a rejected possibility). Even earlier representatives can be found in J. E. Frame, *The Epistles of St. Paul to the Thessalonians* (1912) 169f., and G. Wohlenberg, *Der erste und zweite Thessalonicherbrief* (²1909) 101. Although K. P. Donfried, *loc. cit.,* 355, note 83, is mistaken in asserting that F. F. Bruce, *1 and 2 Thessalonians* (1982), does not refer to the possibility of martyrdom, Bruce, *loc. cit.,* 98, did for all practical purposes abandon the thesis.

24. Cf. E. von Dobschütz, *Die Thessalonicherbriefe* (1909) 190f.; B. Rigaux, *Saint Paul: Les épîtres aux Thessaloniciens* (1956) 536; K. Staab, *Die Thessalonicherbriefe* (⁴1965) 34f. The majority of exegetes today, however, support the connection with the following verb ἄξει. Cf. T. Holtz, *Der erste Brief an die Thessalonicher* (²1990) 193 (bibliography).

25. J. Jeremias, *Unknown Sayings of Jesus* (Eng. trans., 1957) 64-67, considered whether the saying of the earthly Jesus — interpreted in 1 Thess. 4:15 and as background in 1 Thess. 4:16f. — (cf. Mt. 24:30f. par. Mk. 13:26f.) was not focusing especially on the fate of martyrs. See also note 55.

of Paphlagonia since the third century B.C. included violent measures against obvious enemies of the state.[26] In any event, assuming that the background to the situation in Thessalonica was indeed this serious would explain even better why Paul was unable to return to the city. Similarly, the accusations of some Thessalonians of having to endure — in contrast to Paul — a difficult situation of persecution (1 Thess. 2:1f., 14-16; 3:4), accusations implicitly addressed in the letter, would then be more understandable.

20.3. 1 Thessalonians 4:13-18 and 1 Corinthians 15:51f.

In the nineteenth century, it was especially O. Pfleiderer[27] and E. Teichmann[28] who applied the idea of development to Pauline eschatology,[29] assuming an evolution away from materialistic Jewish apocalyptic expectations and toward more sublime Hellenistic notions in three phases: (1) In 1 Thess. 4:13-17, Paul taught a resurrection as revivification at the parousia. (2) 1 Cor. 15:50-57 represented a transitional stage in which the apostle expected a transformation of the earthly body into a heavenly one at the parousia. (3) Finally, 2 Cor. 5:1-10 and Phil. 1:21-24 retain the idea of resurrection at most in name only, the real notion being the reception of a spiritual body at the moment of death. Although this construction never lacked adherents, it did recede quite strongly into the background for a while.[30] Recently, however, this thesis has experienced a remarkable resurrection, one that does, admittedly, seem more like a revivification than a transformation.[31] It is not the task of the present study

---

26. Text in V. Ehrenberg and A. H. M. Jones, *Documents Illustrating the Reigns of Augustus and Tiberius* (1949) 315.

27. *Paulinism: A Contribution to the History of Primitive Christian Theology,* 2 vols. (Eng. trans., 1891).

28. *Die paulinischen Vorstellungen von Auferstehung und Gericht und ihre Beziehungen zur jüdischen Apokalyptik* (1896).

29. Concerning this stage in the history of scholarship, one can still consult A. Schweitzer, *Paul and His Interpreters: A Critical History* (Eng. trans., 1912) 22-99.

30. Especially since J. Jeremias, *NTS* 2 (1955/56) 151-59, following A. Schlatter, *Paulus der Bote Jesu* (1934) 441f., showed that 1 Cor. 15:50 is to be translated: "Neither the living (σάρξ καὶ αἷμα) nor the dead (ἡ φθορά) can inherit the kingdom of God." The idea of bodily resurrection is thus not alien to the passage (so O. Pfleiderer, E. Teichmann, *et al.*), but rather is decisively supported by it.

31. Cf. in different variations, e.g., W. Wiefel, *TZ* 30 (1974) 65-81; C. L. Mearns, *NTS* 27 (1981) 137-57; *JSNT* 22 (1984) 19-35; H. H. Schade, *Apokalyptische Christologie bei Paulus* (²1984); G. M. M. Pelser, *Neotest* 20 (1986) 37-46 (peculiarly without any reference to G. Lüdemann); U. Schnelle, *NTS* 32 (1986) 210-14; *Wandlungen im paulinischen Denken* (1989) 37-48. A survey of scholarship can be found in H. Hübner, *ANRW* II 25.4 (1987) 2779-94.

to address with the appropriate thoroughness the question of possible developments in Pauline eschatology.[32] Let us recall, however, that since many scholars date the letter to the Philippians to the Ephesian imprisonment,[33] and thus into immediate temporal proximity with the first and second letters to the Corinthians, the element of temporal duration cannot have played any great role for the last part of the evolution as construed. Here we can limit ourselves to G. Lüdemann's interpretation[34] of 1 Thess. 4:13-17 in comparison with 1 Cor. 15:50f., since from this he draws a relatively specific argument for his own chronology: between these two texts, he sees differences requiring (1) a temporal separation of at least ten years, and thus (2) an early dating of the first letter to the Thessalonians.

20.3.1. The Number of Dead

The "viable chronological criterion for determining the date of texts and traditions from the early period of Christianity," as formulated by G. Lüdemann, is: "A text which presupposes that Christians do not have to die before the arrival of the eschaton probably arose during the period that followed directly on the death and resurrection of Jesus, that is, not long after 27/30 c.e. On the other hand, a text that limits the number of those who will not die or assumes that all will die should be considered as belonging chronologically to the end of the first generation (47-57) or to a later generation. Though chronologically exact datings cannot be expected when this criterion is employed, approximate datings can be."[35] The cautious qualification expressed at the conclusion is all too justified. Whoever assumes that the conviction was that *all* Christians would experience the parousia would have to discount the authenticity of that particular Jesus-saying anticipating the possi-

---

32. Cf. esp. B. F. Meyer, *TS* 47 (1986) 363-87. This article shows in an exemplary fashion how a complicated question can be clarified rather than inappropriately simplified by a concise portrayal concentrating on essentials. Cf. also further J. Baumgarten, *Paulus und die Apokalyptik* (1975) 236-38; B. Lindars, *BJRL* 67 (1985) 766-82; J. Plevnik, *Toronto Journal of Theology* 6 (1991) 86-99; B. Witherington, *Jesus, Paul, and the End of the World* (1992). The situationally determined nature of Paul's various eschatological expositions is correctly emphasized by J. Delobel, in R. F. Collins, ed., *The Thessalonian Correspondence* (1990) 340-47, and A. Lindemann, *NTS* 37 (1991) 373-99. Over the course of time, the apostle is concerned with systematic understanding and the development of technically more precise terminology. Cf. J. Gillmann, *CBQ* 47 (1985) 263-81.

33. Representatives can be found in G. F. Hawthorne, *Philippians* (1983) xxxviiif.; J. Gnilka, *Der Philipperbrief* (⁴1987) 19-24.

34. *PerspRelSt* 7 (1980) 195-201; in B. C. Corley, *Colloquy on New Testament Studies* (1983) 305-7; *Paul: Apostle to the Gentiles* (Eng. trans., 1984) 201-61.

35. *Paul: Apostle to the Gentiles* (Eng. trans., 1984) 204.

bility of martyrdom for his followers.[36] Moreover, such a belief could probably not be maintained even once for a full year. And indeed, not a single passage from the Gospels adduced by Lüdemann[37] in this context says anything of the sort (Mt. 10:23; Mk. 9:1; 13:10; Jn. 21:23). However, the other part of the criterion is also precarious, since we know neither the average age of Jesus' followers nor their life expectancy. Depending on those figures, the majority of eyewitnesses could already have died by about A.D. 40, or they could still be living around A.D. 60. The only really unequivocal limit was the complete dying off of the eyewitness generation (cf. Jn. 21:23) around *ca.* A.D. 100.

Concerning 1 Thess. 4:15 (ἡμεῖς οἱ ζῶντες οἱ περιλειπόμενοι εἰς τὴν παρουσίαν τοῦ κυρίου οὐ μὴ φθάσωμεν τοὺς κοιμηθέντας), Lüdemann remarks: "[Paul] radicalizes and actualizes the statement [of his Jewish source] that a remnant will be caught up into the air to the Lord by impressing on it the imminent expectation he nurtured at the time of 1 Thessalonians: 'We who are alive, who are left.' The statement now reads as if no further deaths are 'planned.' "[38] One page later, he asserts even more specifically "that Paul . . . does *not* think that there will be further deaths."[39] At this point, the extremely personal tone of the letter should be considered (§19.1.2). Paul is not lecturing in any fundamental fashion, but rather is giving personal, timely encouragement: "if the Lord returns tomorrow, then *we* who are alive will. . . ."[40] The apostle makes no direct statement here whether additional Thessalonians can yet die before the parousia. One can ask, however, whether the second participle so noticeable after ἡμεῖς οἱ ζῶντες, namely, οἱ περιλειπόμενοι, does not have a more specifically qualifying meaning: "We, the living, insofar as we remain behind until the parousia of the Lord, will have no advantage over those who have died."[41] In this case, the statement would imply that other Thessalonians could die as well, and the possibility is even kept open that the living, "those left behind," will then constitute only a remnant.[42]

From several passages in 1 Corinthians, Lüdemann concludes that at the time of its composition, in contrast to the situation in Thessalonica,

---

36. Cf. by contrast R. Riesner, *Jesus als Lehrer* ([3]1988) 453-75.
37. *Paul: Apostle to the Gentiles* (Eng. trans., 1984) 202-4.
38. *Ibid.,* 233.
39. *Ibid.,* 234. Emphasis in the original.
40. Also H. Giesen, *SNTU* 10 (1985) 139, assumes a "literary we."
41. *Ibid.,* 137.
42. W. Schmithals, in *Paul and the Gnostics* (Eng. trans., 1972) 181-91, concluded from this very passage that the first letter to the Thessalonians belonged to a later period, namely, that of what is known as the third missionary journey, and *after* the first letter to the Corinthians. Contra this dating, which is problematical for other reasons, cf. §18.5.2.

instances of death had already ceased to be the exception[43]: (1) "In 1 Cor. 15:51-52 precisely the inverse appears to be the case. This is evident from Paul's formulation in v. 51b: πάντες οὐ κοιμηθησόμεθα, πάντες δὲ ἀλλαγη-σόμεθα ('We shall not all sleep, but we shall all be changed')."[44] But do we know whether the apostle meant 40, 60, or 80 percent by "not all"? (2) "1 Cor. 11:30 mentions that many (ἱκανοί) have fallen asleep."[45] To this A. J. M. Wedderburn correctly objects that in Pauline usage (Rom. 15:23; 1 Cor. 15:9; 2 Cor. 2:6, 16; 3:5), this word means "quite enough": "Paul is stressing the seriousness of the physical consequences of the Corinthians' sin: 'quite enough' of their number have died as a consequence and that again need be no more than two."[46] (3) "The formula in 1 Cor. 6:14, ὁ (. . .) θεὸς καὶ τὸν κύριον ἤγειρεν καὶ ἡμᾶς ἐξεγερεῖ, for which 1 Corinthians 15 provides a commentary . . . assumes that death has become the normal case."[47] But if one wants to press this formula, then one can also conclude that Paul and *all* the Corinthians will die before the parousia, for how else could the apostle assert without qualification that "the Lord will raise *us*"? This would utterly contradict Lüdemann's own assumption that at the time 1 Corinthians was composed, too, Paul was yet firmly convinced that he himself would experience the parousia.[48] (4) "The statement that τινες of the five hundred brethren, to whom the Lord appeared (1 Cor. 15:6), have died also assumes an advanced situation."[49] But Paul does not write "of whom most have died, though some are still living," but rather ἐξ ὧν οἱ πλεόνες μένουσιν ἕως ἄρτι, τινὲς δὲ ἐκοιμήθησαν. This sentence would in all probability also be valid fourteen years after the resurrection (Lüdemann's date of 1 Thessalonians). (5) "Paul speaks in a self-evident manner of οἱ κοιμηθέντες ἐν Χριστῷ (1 Cor. 15:18)."[50] Why should the apostle not speak this way about deceased *Christians,* regardless of whether it was two, twenty, or two hundred? The deceased Thessalonians, too, were νεκροὶ ἐν Χριστῷ for him (1 Thess. 4:16) without Lüdemann concluding from this that the reference must be to more than two.[51]

43. *Paul: Apostle to the Gentiles* (Eng. trans., 1984) 240f.
44. *Ibid.,* 240.
45. *Ibid.,* 241.
46. *ET* 92 (1981) 106.
47. G. Lüdemann, *Paul: Apostle to the Gentiles* (Eng. trans., 1984) 241.
48. *Ibid.,* 241f.
49. *Ibid.,* 241.
50. *Ibid.*
51. Cf. *ibid.,* 205f. Yet another weakness in G. Lüdemann's argument was brought up in the discussion: "*Lüdemann:* . . . But I would restate my point that Paul — whatever the differences of the communities were — had to deal with the fact of death. And, secondly, his early preaching in Thessalonica and Corinth implied the survival of most Christians. If you could agree to that then we have taken one step together. I think

20.3.2. The Nature of the Resurrection

G. Lüdemann sees a clear distinction between the two letters in Paul's understanding of the resurrection of the dead: "We saw above that the description of the resurrection in 1 Thess. 4:13-18 can be called realistic and that the concept of a transformation should not be associated with this passage. The resurrection was mentioned in the context of the assertion that the living do not have any advantage over the dead, and its function was to place the dead on equal footing with the living so that they might be withdrawn together. An analogous depiction of the resurrection was found in the *Syriac Apocalypse of Baruch,* where the living recognize the raised dead. In 1 Corinthians, by contrast, the resurrection is depicted within a *dualistic* framework, where the present *sōma psychikon* is distinguished from the *sōma pneumatikon,* the product of the transformation. Both conceptions of the resurrection, the realistic conception and the supernatural conception that involves the notion of a transformation, were known to Paul from Judaism. They are even found alongside one another in the *Syriac Apocalypse of Baruch* (50–51). Surely Paul did *not* use the notion of the resurrection that involved the transformation to explicate the Christ-event at the time of the composition of 1 Thessalonians because the resurrection of Christians could not yet have been a separate, developed theme in his theology."[52]

To this one can respond: (1) Lüdemann himself relativizes the religio-historical argument. *2 Bar.* 50:1–51:3 (*JSHRZ* V/2 155f.) detaches resurrection and transformation briefly from one another only for obviously apologetic reasons. A more appropriate reference for the apostle than this apocalypse would be a passage such as Dan. 12:2f. (cf. Phil. 2:15), where the resurrected are transformed into an angel-like existence (cf. Dan. 8:10). The general expectation of resurrection was already a constituent part of the faith of Paul the Pharisee.[53] (2) The brevity of the text prevents us from determining whether such recognition, which Lüdemann correctly presupposes, requires mere revivification. One can ask, however, which was the most likely model Paul would have been using. It seems a bit artificial, however, when Lüdemann

---

everybody has to agree to that. *Koester:* Very briefly, I don't find this persuasive because as you move closer to the parousia, that is, the later it is in time, the fewer people you would expect to die. So you could just turn it around and come to the opposite result. *Hurd:* If the parousia is tomorrow, then most of us who are here will be there for the parousia. *Koester:* Ten years before the parousia you would expect that quite a few will die, but one day before the parousia you would expect that everybody would still be alive. *Hurd:* Well, eschatology is not an exact science, is it! It breaks out unexpectedly . . ." (in B. C. Corley, ed., *Colloquy on New Testament Studies* [1983] 333).

52. *Paul: Apostle to the Gentiles* (Eng. trans., 1984) 242.
53. Cf. E. Best, *The First and Second Epistles to the Thessalonians* (²1977) 181.

insists on distinguishing between 1 Thessalonians, whose reference to the resurrection of Jesus he alleges is concerned exclusively with the "that" of the argumentation, and 1 Corinthians, which is allegedly concerned with drawing conclusions concerning the "how" of the process. All the resurrection stories preserved for us presuppose a transformation of Jesus (Mk. 16:12; Lk. 24:31, 36-53; Jn. 20:19-23). If Paul was familiar with such traditions (cf. 1 Cor. 15:3-5; Rom. 4:25; 8:34), then it is difficult to understand why he had not always viewed the resurrection of Jesus as being prototypical for the resurrection of Christians.[54] (3) Finally, as for the assertion that the resurrection of Christians did not yet represent an independent theme for Paul at the time of the letter to the Thessalonians, one can point out that the apostle gives his answer with the help of a *tradition* available to him.[55]

One might also recall that even in Lüdemann's chronology, at least ten years separate the crucifixion of Jesus in A.D. 27 and the founding of the church in Thessalonica (after A.D. 36). Certainly, more than two Christians died in this period, so that it is difficult to see how Paul could escape reflection on the fate of the deceased Christians. For the founding visit in Corinth some five years later (A.D. 41), Lüdemann does at least assume that "teaching about the resurrection (of Christians) was a subordinate part of the founding proclamation in Corinth."[56] Paul's complete or partial silence concerning this topic in Thessalonica, fourteen or twenty years after the cross and resurrection, remains astonishing, and is probably best explained on the basis of the external factors discussed above. Yet one should remember that even in the less situationally dependent and essentially more thorough letter to the Romans, the resurrection of the dead does not represent an independent instructional theme,

54. Cf. B. F. Meyer, *TS* 47 (1986) 376f.

55. G. Lüdemann, *Paul: Apostle to the Gentiles* (Eng. trans., 1984) 221-31, assumes that the λόγος κυρίου in 1 Thess. 4:15-17 represents an early Christian prophetic saying in the form of a small Jewish apocalypse. By contrast, I, as well as R. H. Gundry, *NTS* 33 (1987) 164-66, now as before, consider a connection with a saying of the earthly Jesus to be more likely. R. H. Gundry does overlook the fact, however, that regarding his own suggestion, Jn. 11:25f. has already been subjected to a thorough argumentative attempt by P. Nepper-Christensen, *ST* 19 (1965) 136-54. Concerning the possible presence of an agraphon, cf. R. N. Longenecker, *NTS* 31 (1985) 90f. Concerning the possibility of connections with the synoptic apocalypse, cf. L. Hartman, *Prophecy Interpreted* (1966) 181-90; D. Wenham, *The Rediscovery of Jesus' Eschatological Discourse* (1984) 89f., 304-6. D. Gewalt, *Ling-Bibl* 51 (1982) 105-13, refers to Mk. 9:1. F. F. Bruce, *1 and 2 Thessalonians* (1982) 104, suspects that the Thessalonians' misunderstandings concerning the relationship between parousia and resurrection might be related to a false understanding of a saying such as Mk. 9:1. O. Hofius, in P. Stuhlmacher, *The Gospel and the Gospels* (Eng. trans., 1983) 357-60, thinks it is neither an early Christian prophetic saying nor a saying of Jesus.

56. *Paul: Apostle to the Gentiles* (Eng. trans., 1984) 243.

but rather follows from the resurrection of Jesus. It is thanks to the Corinthian errors that we possess at least 1 Corinthians 15.

20.4. Retrospective Chronological Conclusions?

The reasons mentioned by Lüdemann do not require that a decade separate 1 Thessalonians and 1 Corinthians. Neither can they support an early dating of the founding of the church in Thessalonica at the end of the first decade after the crucifixion and resurrection of Jesus. The only chronological information that Paul's discussion of the resurrection of Christians in 1 Thess. 4:13-18 yields is that the apostle probably stayed only a fairly short time in Thessalonica itself, a situation either hindering any more extensive treatment of the theme or at least making it possible for misunderstanding to arise. This retrospective conclusion from the letter thus represents yet another confirmation of the impression evoked by Acts: the founding visit in Thessalonica was relatively brief, and was broken off prematurely.

§21
Absent Doctrine of Justification?

The view represented especially by W. Wrede,[1] namely, that Paul developed his conviction concerning justification apart from the law only later, and as a combative doctrine against Judaism and nomistic Jewish Christianity, has recently once again attracted staunch advocates.[2] After G. Strecker[3] and H. H. Schade,[4] it is now especially U. Schnelle who claims that "at the time of the composition of 1 Thessalonians, Paul obviously did not yet have access to the conceptions of his later doctrine of law and grace; it was only the conflict in Galatia that first led to the development of a terminologically mature doctrine of justification characterized by a negative conception of the law and a positive conception of grace."[5]

21.1. Pauline Nomology and Chronology

21.1.1. Chronology of the Galatian Conflict

This problem also involves a close connection between theology and chronology. Schnelle's assertion is possible only if the letter to the Galatians was composed on what is known as the third missionary journey. Even if this understanding corresponds to the conviction of the majority of scholars today, it still faces considerable difficulties. According to Gal. 4:20, the apostle himself would like to be present in the churches (ἤθελον δὲ παρεῖναι πρὸς

---

1. *Paulus* (1904) 72-79.
2. Concerning the similarly inclined attempts of H. Räisänen, *Paul and the Law* (1983), and E. P. Sanders, *Paul and Palestinian Judaism* (1977), cf. H. Hübner, *NTS* 26 (1979/80) 445-73; *ANRW* II 25.4 (1987) 2723-26; S. Kim, *The Origin of Paul's Gospel* ([2]1984) 345-58; and M. A. Seifrid, *Justification by Faith* (1992).
3. In *Festschrift E. Käsemann* (1976) 479-508.
4. *Apokalyptische Christologie bei Paulus* ([2]1984) 49f., 112f.
5. *NTS* 32 (1986) 218. The complete argumentation can be found in U. Schnelle, *Gerechtigkeit und Christusgegenwart* ([2]1986) 33-103.

ὑμᾶς ἄρτι, καὶ ἀλλάξαι τὴν φωνήν μου, ὅτι ἀποροῦμαι ἐν ὑμῖν). It is abundantly clear that a visit by Paul himself would be urgently necessary to overcome this serious crisis. Nowhere, however, does Paul announce any firm intentions to make such a visit, nor does he mention that he is even planning something of this sort. From this, J. Knox concluded that a higher authority was preventing Paul from doing so, and that the letter therefore may have been written during imprisonment in Caesarea.[6] But given the analogy of other letters from prison, one can hardly believe that precisely here the apostle would have concealed such information (cf. Gal. 5:11; 6:17). The conventional view dating the letter to the Galatians during the Ephesian ministry, however, cannot persuasively explain why Paul did not undertake the visit. Presupposing the regional hypothesis, the north Galatian churches were not more difficult to reach from Ephesus (excepting good sailing conditions) than Corinth, for which an interim visit is assumed because of the problems there.

U. Borse[7] has tried to demonstrate in a careful study[8] that the letter to the Galatians was written in Macedonia. He assumes the following sequence: (1) 2 Cor. 1–9, during the middle of Paul's stay in Macedonia in late autumn A.D. 57; (2) then the letter to the Galatians; (3) 2 Cor. 10–13, a few weeks after 2 Cor. 1–9 and shortly before the apostle's departure for Corinth; (4) the letter to the Romans toward the end of the three-month winter stay in this city. The letters to the Galatians and the Romans were thus separated by not much more than three months.[9] Then, however, another question posed by J. Knox becomes compelling: "We may wonder how Paul in Romans can be so complacent about his work 'from Jerusalem and as far round as Illyricum' and can feel that he no longer has 'any room for work in these regions' (Rom. 15:19, 23) so soon after the grave disturbances in Galatia. . . ."[10] For chronological reasons it is virtually impossible that within the reconstruction of Borse Paul was already writing the

6. *IDB* II (1962) 343.

7. *Der Standort des Galaterbriefes* (1972).

8. U. Borse, has not, however, been able to convince everyone. For example, H. Hübner, *NTS* 26 (1979/80) 458, note 56, insists that Galatians was written before 1 Corinthians, since *"the concept* σῶμα Χριστοῦ *is not found in Galatians,* even though it is tailor-made for the argumentation in Galatians 3!" In general, H. Hübner, *Das Gesetz bei Paulus* (³1982), as well as J. W. Drane, *Paul: Libertine or Legalist* (1975), both assume that considerable development took place between the letters to the Galatians and Romans. J. W. Drane also advocates an early dating of Galatians before the Apostolic Council (*Paulus* [1978] 35-48).

9. But considering the circumstantial nature of ancient writing (writing material, dictation) (O. Roller, *Das Formular der paulinischen Briefe* [1933] 4-18, 250-304), and assuming Paul himself had already started having copies made (H. von Soden, *Griechisches Neues Testament* [1913] vii; L. Hartman, in *Festschrift K. Stendahl* [1986] 139), then this quick succession already seems problematical not least for simple technical reasons.

10. *Chapters in a Life of Paul,* rev. ed. (1987) 73.

letter to the Romans with the knowledge that his letter to the Galatians had immediately brought about a resolution of the situation. Because of the *mare clausum* in the winter months, messengers were largely confined to the land routes. From Macedonia to the region of Ancyra, they had to travel over one thousand kilometers, and for the return to Corinth over five hundred kilometers more. Even assuming they used a carriage and made fairly quick progress (§16.2.1), the routes (with no stops) would require between sixty and seventy days. A more realistic assumption would be three months, though still in the hope that the emissaries were not caught in the snow. Neither can Borse's dating explain why Timothy, Paul's co-worker who was so important for Galatia, is not mentioned in the prescript, whereas he does appear as co-signee of the second letter to the Corinthians (2 Cor. 1:1). Finally, in connection with his planned journey from Jerusalem to Rome, Paul could have chosen the land route and thus been able to announce (or threaten) a visit to the Galatians.

Both difficulties — the lack of any possibility for a visit and the silence regarding Timothy — can be explained by the two hypotheses that date the letter earlier by assuming a south Galatian address: (1) Assuming an early dating before the Apostolic Council, Timothy was not yet converted, and Paul was on his way from Antioch to Jerusalem. (2) According to a dating at the very beginning of the Corinthian ministry (a view advocated especially by T. Zahn[11]), Timothy had not yet returned from Thessalonica, and the apostle was hindered in any immediate return plans to the east by the uncertainty of the condition of that congregation as well as by the promising beginning of the missionary work in the provincial capital of Achaia. Both these chronological decisions would also involve far-reaching consequences for the question of the age of the Pauline doctrine of justification. According to both hypotheses, the letter to the Galatians would be Paul's oldest writing, and 1 Thessalonians would have to be interpreted with this in mind. It is not possible here to address further the complex question of the exact chronological dating of the letter to the Galatians. The arguments presented against the regional hypothesis (§15.2.1-2) do in any case show that even if one identifies Gal. 2 with Acts 15, the question of dating Galatians before the stay in Ephesus is not as certain as one recent research survey seems to imply.[12]

11. *Einleitung in das Neue Testament* I ([3]1924) 138-44 (Eng. trans., *Introduction to the New Testament* III [1909]). Concerning C. Clemen, cf. §1.4.2. For additional representatives, see p. 291, note 60 above.

12. A. Suhl, *ANRW* II 25.4 (1987) 3077: "To be sure, it is generally acknowledged that the letter must have been written during what is known as the third missionary journey. . . ." A. F. J. Klijn, *An Introduction to the New Testament* ([2]1980) 95: "There are no really conclusive arguments . . . to support any particular date for this letter. The evidence may be slightly in favour of an early date. . . ." See also H. D. Betz, *Galatians* (1979) 9-12; R. A. Martin, *Early Paul* (1993) 238-40.

21.1.2. The Damascus-Event and the Doctrine of Justification

The assumption that a development of the doctrine of justification began only in connection with the Galatian conflict also reflects an inadequate understanding of the Damascus-event. It is neither possible nor necessary to repeat here the arguments presented especially by S. Kim,[13] P. Stuhlmacher,[14] and C. Dietzfelbinger[15] supporting the emergence of the Pauline understanding of law and justification in the Christophany at Damascus. With regard to the more recent attempts at a late dating of the Pauline doctrine of the law, the conclusion of Dietzfelbinger can be cited as a summary: "The Damascus-experience, namely, that it was the law that brought the Kyrios onto the cross, and that the law thus, although believed to be a factor of salvation, nonetheless had functioned as a factor of quite the opposite, and that both its task and its history must thus be completely rethought — this experience does not receive the attention it deserves. If, however, one does note what is indeed to be noted here, one finds that the Damascus-experience is chronologically the place forcing Paul to rethink the Torah. *From the very outset,* then, the problem of the law had to dominate his theology, and he had to respond in theological reflection to this new view of the Torah and to transform it into the language of preaching."[16] Historically it is indeed hardly conceivable that Paul, given his Pharisaic background and his Damascus-experience, could have treated the law as "adiaphoron," to use a formulation by G. Strecker.[17] Hence, one does not have to deny that Paul came to a more precise understanding of his view in the Galatian conflict; the self-witness of the letter to the Galatians itself also shows, however, that it did not represent a new creation, but rather the consequence and development of the Christophany at Damascus.[18]

21.2. The Communication Situation

21.2.1. The Situation of the Church

According to U. Schnelle, not only "the theological conception of the doctrine of justification," but also that of "the theology of the cross, of the church as

---

13. *The Origin of Paul's Gospel* (^{2}1984) 269-311.

14. In *The Gospel and the Gospels* (Eng. trans., 1991) 152-69.

15. *Die Berufung des Paulus als Ursprung seiner Theologie* (1985) 90-125.

16. *Ibid.,* 115. Emphasis in the original.

17. In *Festschrift E. Käsemann* (1976) 480.

18. P. Stuhlmacher, in *The Gospel and the Gospels* (Eng. trans., 1991) 156, note 20: "In Galatians 1 and 2, as much as in 2 Corinthians 4 and Philippians 3, Paul discusses the experience of his call as he looks back upon an event that occurred decades earlier."

the body of Christ, and of baptism as being buried with Christ — all these are apparently unknown to 1 Thessalonians."[19] Here one must once again recall the situation and character of 1 Thessalonians. The letter was written only a few months after the founding of the church. Teachers had not yet come into the church from the outside, thus requiring Paul to address the problem of the law in any way. Even against W. Schmithals, U. Schnelle correctly concludes that "the so-called 'apology' in 2:1-12 does not allow any conclusions concerning disputes Paul may have had with (gnostic) adversaries; rather, Paul has a good relationship with the congregation (3:5; cf. further 2 Cor. 8:1ff.)."[20] In his hasty response, the apostle concentrated on what was immediately necessary: he defended himself against the (possible) charge of having departed too quickly, encouraged the besieged new converts, responded to their concrete ethical and eschatological problems, and added several of his own helpful admonitions for the urban church of Thessalonica. There was as little occasion here as in the letter to Philemon to develop his doctrines of justification, of the cross, and of baptism, all of which were yet fresh in the memory of the letter's recipients. 1 Thessalonians consistently presupposes that the congregation has received relatively precise instruction and is familiar with various pieces of tradition (1 Thess. 1:6, 9f.; 3:3f.; 4:1f., 6, 9, 12; 5:2).[21]

21.2.2. The Thessalonians' Previous Knowledge

In no other Pauline letter does one find expressions such as αὐτοὶ γὰρ οἴδατε (1 Thess. 2:1; 3:3; 5:2), καθὼς οἴδατε (1 Thess. 1:5; 2:2, 5; 3:4), καθάπερ οἴδατε (1 Thess. 2:11), or οἴδατε γάρ (1 Thess. 4:2) as frequently as in 1 Thessalonians. In contrast to three additional formulations of this sort in other writings (Gal. 4:13; Phil. 4:14; 1 Cor. 12:2), these always refer back to the apostle's initial proclamation.[22] This peculiarity of 1 Thessalonians can be explained well on the basis of the historical and chronological situation surrounding its origin. The Thessalonians' recollection of Paul's fundamental guidance was still fresh. In contrast to other situations, the apostle's doctrine was not a point of dispute between him and the congregation but rather could constitute the commonly accepted foundation of their communication.

19. *NTS* 32 (1986) 207.
20. *Ibid.,* 219, note 6.
21. Cf. especially T. Holtz, in *Festschrift E. Schweizer* (1983) 55-78; *Der erste Brief an die Thessalonicher* (²1990) 11f., as well as I. Havener, *SBL Seminar Papers* (1981) 105-28, and the earlier study by G. Müller, in *Festschrift G. Warneck* (1904) 81-102.
22. Cf. J. Plevnik, in R. F. Collins, *The Thessalonian Correspondence* (1990) 53f.

21.3. Presupposed Doctrinal Points

21.3.1. Christology and Ecclesiology

Among the items of which Paul could presuppose an understanding among his readers in 1 Thessalonians were basic christological facts; even a scholar such as E. Richard admits this, who otherwise assumes considerable development took place in Pauline theology.[23] Jesus is not only the Χριστός for the apostle, but also the κύριος and the υἱός (τοῦ θεοῦ). "In 1 Thessalonians, Paul is already using, indeed is offering up almost the entire breadth of christological designations that occur in his letters as a whole."[24] Paul brings God and Jesus together in a way that must have seemed almost di-theistic to his Jewish contemporaries (1 Thess. 1:1; 3:11; cf. 5:28). In 1 Thessalonians, Jesus is already understood exclusively as a mediator of salvation (1 Thess. 1:10; 5:9). The substance of the formula so typical for Paul, namely, ἐν Χριστῷ, is also found (1 Thess. 1:1; 2:14; 4:16). Here "the designation of the church in Thessalonica as 'ecclesia . . . in God the Father and the Lord Jesus Christ' (1:1) presupposes reflected ecclesiology."[25]

21.3.2. The Gospel of the Cross and Resurrection of Jesus

Paul is apparently using the term εὐαγγέλιον as an abbreviation for the content of his proclamation in Thessalonica (1 Thess. 1:5; 2:2, 4, 8, 9; 3:2). The assumption that the apostle understood the gospel already to have the same content here that emerges so clearly in his other letters, is at least as legitimate as the assumption that he understood something completely different by it here than later. In any case, in 1 Thessalonians the gospel already represents for Paul something invariable, something one entrusts to others to be passed on further (1 Thess. 2:4: καθὼς δεδοκιμάσμεθα ὑπὸ τοῦ θεοῦ πιστευθῆναι τὸ εὐαγγέλιον οὕτως λαλοῦμεν). Since Paul expressly refers his own description of its content in 1 Cor. 15:3ff. to appropriated tradition (probably already from Jerusalem [cf. 1 Cor. 15:11]) (παρέδωκα γὰρ ὑμῖν ἐν πρώτοις, ὃ καὶ παρέλαβον), this content (ὅτι Χριστὸς ἀπέθανεν ὑπὲρ τῶν ἁμαρτιῶν ἡμῶν κατὰ τὰς γραφάς . . .) may also already be presupposed for the instructions given the Thessalonians.

Indeed, an expression recalling this confession also appears in 1 Thess. 5:9f. ('Ιησοῦ Χριστοῦ τοῦ ἀποθανόντος ὑπὲρ ἡμῶν). Reference has often

---

23. In J. M. Bassler, ed., *Pauline Theology* I (1991) 44, 50. Cf. also M. Casey, in *Festschrift C. K. Barrett* (1982) 124f.

24. O. Merk, in *Festschrift F. Hahn* (1991) 104.

25. J. Eckert, in J. Hainz, ed., *Theologie im Werden* (1992) 294f.

been made[26] to the formulaic character (cf. Rom. 5:6, 8; 14:15; 2 Cor. 5:15), which assumes more extensive familiarity on the part of the Thessalonians, perhaps even of the Eucharist tradition.[27] According to U. Wilckens, "the atonement meaning is consistently to be presupposed wherever abbreviated reference is made to Jesus' death ὑπὲρ ἡμῶν — corresponding to περὶ αὐτῶν in Lev. 4:20."[28] Another reflex of congregational instruction on this theme can be found in the similarly traditional-sounding expression in 1 Thess. 4:14 (πιστεύομεν ὅτι Ἰησοῦς ἀπέθανεν καὶ ἀνέστη).[29]

Against this background, one may then also read 1 Thess. 1:10 (ἀναμένειν τὸν υἱὸν αὐτοῦ ἐκ τῶν οὐρανῶν ὃν ἤγειρεν ἐκ τῶν νεκρῶν, Ἰησοῦν τὸν ῥυόμενον ἡμᾶς ἐκ τῆς ὀργῆς τῆς ἐρχομένης), concluding that "here Paul proclaims Christ as the Savior from the coming wrath of God in a way no different from that in Rom. 7:24f.; 8:31-39; and 11:26."[30] The eschatological main theme is probably already being anticipated when the formulation of 1 Thess. 1:9f., which contains elements of tradition,[31] speaks not of faith in Christ, but rather of hope in his return.[32] Such anticipatory glances are customary in the *exordium* of a letter.

Finally, the use of "our [i.e., my] message of the gospel" (1 Thess. 1:5: τὸ εὐαγγέλιον ἡμῶν), compared with 2 Cor. 4:3 as well as Rom. 2:16

26. E.g., by W. Neil, *The Epistle* [sic] *of Paul to the Thessalonians* (1950) 118; B. Rigaux and L. M. Dewailly, *Les épîtres de Saint Paul aux Thessaloniciens* (³1969) 53; E. Best, *The First and Second Epistles to the Thessalonians* (²1977) 217f.; F. F. Bruce, *1 and 2 Thessalonians* (1982) 113f.; I. H. Marshall, *1 and 2 Thessalonians* (1983) 140. L. Morris, *1 and 2 Thessalonians* (1956) 96, already correctly remarked: "Indeed, it is difficult to think that he [Paul] could have alluded to Christ's death in this fashion unless it was already a familiar, non-controversial topic to the Thessalonians."

27. Cf. T. Holtz, *Der erste Brief an die Thessalonicher* (²1990) 231. The reference to the imitation of Jesus' suffering by the Thessalonians (1 Thess. 1:6) similarly suggests a certain familiarity with Passion traditions. One can also note the proximity of this passage (δεξάμενοι τὸν λόγον ἐν θλίψει πολλῇ μετὰ χαρᾶς) to Mt. 13:20f. par. Mk. 4:16f. (τὸν λόγον μετὰ χαρᾶς λαμβάν[ουσιν] . . . γενομένης δὲ θλίψεως) and Lk. 8:13 (μετὰ χαρᾶς δέχονται τὸν λόγον). B. Rigaux, *Saint Paul: Les épîtres aux Thessaloniciens* (1956) 382, considers it possible that at least the expression δέχεσθαι τὸν λόγον might have some connection with Jesus-sayings.

28. *Der Brief an die Römer* I (1978) 240.

29. Cf. B. Rigaux, *Saint Paul: Les épîtres aux Thessaloniciens* (1956) 534: Apart from Old Testament citations (Rom. 15:12, cf. Isa. 11:10; 1 Cor. 10:7, cf. Ex. 32:6) and this passage, Paul uses the verb ἀνίστημι instead of ἐγείρειν only in 1 Thess. 4:16, and there also under the influence of this passage.

30. P. Stuhlmacher, in *Das Evangelium und die Evangelien* (1983) 164, note 20 (Eng. trans., *The Gospel and the Gospels* [1991]).

31. Cf. the survey of the discussion in T. Holtz, *Der erste Brief an die Thessalonicher* (²1990) 54-62; C. A. Wanamaker, *The Epistles to the Thessalonians* (1990) 84-89.

32. Cf. J. Munck, *NTS* 9 (1962/63) 110.

and Rom. 16:25, can very well be related to the particular understanding of the Pauline gospel culminating in justification without works.[33]

21.3.3. Election and the Bestowal of the Spirit

From a forensic perspective rather than primarily from that of being ἐν Χριστῷ, one can see that for the Thessalonians, election (ἐκλογή) is certain (1 Thess. 1:4; cf. 1 Thess. 2:12; 4:7; 5:24). Their being is essentially determined as being in responsibility "before (ἔμπροσθεν) God our Father" (1 Thess. 1:4; 3:9, 13) or "before our Lord Jesus Christ" (1 Thess. 2:19).[34] Even if the terminology of justification is absent, there is still substantive agreement with the doctrine of grace found in the other Pauline letters: "Election by God harmonizes with Paul's teaching on justification by faith; no one can be a Christian through his own achievement but only because a gracious God enables him through the death and resurrection of Christ. In this sense election is one aspect of the grace of God."[35]

Paul associates the Thessalonians' election with the gospel and with their being loved by God (1 Thess. 1:4f.). 1 Thess. 5:9 shows how already during the period when the church was founded in Thessalonica, the gospel of God's love was actualized in Jesus' salvific death: "For God has destined (ἔθετο, i.e., chosen[36]) us not for [the judgment of] wrath but for obtaining salvation (εἰς περιποίησιν σωτηρίας)." The Thessalonians appropriate salvation, however, διὰ 'Ιησοῦ Χριστοῦ. And this does not occur merely because Jesus Christ is the ruler of the end time; rather, this appropriation is grounded with the formulaic expression "because he died for us" (1 Thess. 5:10a), alluding to Jesus' representative atoning death (see pp. 399f.).

The Thessalonians were assured of their election by the gift of the Holy Spirit (1 Thess. 1:4f.), just as, according to the letter to the Galatians, the Spirit is the pledge of deliverance without works of the law (Gal. 3:2-5). This connection between the bestowal of the Spirit and the close relationship of believers with God as their Father does not first appear only in Rom. 8:14-16, but rather also already in the introduction to 1 Thessalonians: the existence of the Thessalonians comes to fulfillment "before God our Father, for we know, brethren, beloved by God, that he has chosen you, because our message of the gospel came to you not in word only, but also in power and in the Holy Spirit" (1 Thess. 1:3-5). Even in the preservation of the believers

---

33. Cf. E. Best, *The First and Second Epistles to the Thessalonians* (²1977) 175f.

34. Cf. H. Hübner, *NTS* 26 (1979/80) 455-58.

35. E. Best, *The First and Second Epistles to the Thessalonians* (²1977) 72.

36. Cf. I. H. Marshall, in R. F. Collins, *The Thessalonian Correspondence* (1990) 266f.

until the return of Jesus, God remains active: "The one who calls you (ὁ καλῶν ὑμᾶς) is faithful, and he will do this" (1 Thess. 5:24).

To demand more extensive exposition of the doctrine of justification than 1 Thessalonians actually offers would be asking too much of a situationally prompted letter.[37] One must also constantly recall that according to our chronology, Paul wrote 1 Thessalonians at a point when the disputes leading to the Apostolic Council were already behind him[38] and when, according to his own statements, he was proclaiming a gospel in Corinth concentrating on the cross (1 Cor. 1:17ff.; 2:1f.).

21.4. Antiochene and/or Pauline Theology?

Various scholars have recently pointed out that 1 Thessalonians, both in regard to its greater themes and to its individual expressions, recalls theological notions of the sort assumed for the Jewish-Hellenistic church in Antioch[39] and which become tangible not least in Luke himself.[40] Examples include the significance of pneumatic phenomena accompanying the initial proclamation (1 Thess. 1:5; cf. Acts 14:3, 10; 15:12; 19:11) and the use of the term ἐπι-στρέφειν (1 Thess. 1:9; cf. Acts 14:15; 26:18, 20; 28:27, et passim). The question arises whether this represents a traditional early form of Pauline theology from which he increasingly distanced himself after his independence from Antioch. It is true that Paul's other letters are by no means free of connections with tradition which the apostle is not merely dragging along behind him, but which precisely in letters such as Galatians (Gal. 4:4f.) and Romans (Rom. 1:3f.; 3:25) functions constitutively.[41] For traditions used there, too, Antioch can occasionally be considered as the place of origin or at least of transmission. One can attempt to connect the striking increase of tradition in 1 Thessalonians again with the particular situation surrounding its composition. Hence, according to F. Laub, the reason for the particular appearance

37. To be sure, situationally specific writing on the one hand, and authority on the other, are not mutually exclusive for Paul. Cf. Excursus III/1 (pp. 404f.).

38. This is now also emphasized esp. by J. Sanchez Bosch, *NTS* 32 (1991) 336-47.

39. So, e.g., S. Schulz, *TZ* 41 (1985) 236; J. Becker, in *Die Anfänge des Christentums* (1987) 112; *Paulus* (1989) 110-13; and especially A. Dauer, *Paulus und die Christliche Gemeinde im syrischen Antiochia* (1996).

40. A list of parallels can be found in K. P. Donfried, in R. F. Collins, ed., *The Thessalonian Correspondence* (1990) 21f.

41. R. B. Hays, *The Faith of Jesus Christ: An Investigation of the Narrative Substructure of Galatians 3:1–4:11* (1983), in an original initiative, emphasizes the significance of a christologically determined "narrative substructure" as the foundation of Paul's individual statements.

of the notion of the parousia is "not to be found in any occasional flaring up
of imminent expectation in Paul . . . but rather in the proximity of this letter
to the apostle's oral missionary proclamation in Thessalonica."[42] The more
profuse allusion to tradition in this writing may thus result from the fact that
memory of the congregational catechism was still fresh, and Paul's communication with the congregation could be enhanced either by referring to
commonly shared basic convictions or by implicitly presupposing them.

So one is at least not compelled to view the first letter to the Thessalonians as a document originating before the specifically Pauline theology
was developed in times of crisis.[43] Both the situation surrounding its origin
and references in the writing itself suggest that Paul is presupposing considerably more than he actually discusses more broadly in the way of individual
thematic material. "If this view is correct, then Paul's theology as evident in
1 Thessalonians, compared with that of his later letters, cannot simply be
characterized as a theology in the early stages of development; rather, it is
situationally determined, and only those specific themes move to the foreground which the apostle's pastoral concerns consider necessary. The question
remains open whether his initial proclamation in Thessalonica addressed additional themes as well."[44] Perhaps our own experiential horizon makes it
particularly difficult for us to imagine that there are times in which not
everything is controversial, times in which a broad consensus concerning
matters of faith really can exist.[45]

---

42. *Eschatologische Verkündigung und Lebensgestaltung nach Paulus* (1973) 33f.
43. Cf. also I. H. Marshall, in *Festschrift C. K. Barrett* (1982) 173-83; N. T.
Wright, in J. M. Bassler, *Pauline Theology* I (1991) 183-211.
44. J. Eckert, in J. Hainz, *Theologie im Werden* (1992) 297.
45. Cf. R. Riesner, *JETS* 10 (1996) 118-22.

Excursus III: The Unity of 1 Thessalonians

(1) Basic Considerations

The conclusion of W. G. Kümmel still applies, namely, that "in antiquity there are no parallels" for someone other than the original author "piecing together" several letters by that author.[1] The most recent studies by W. G. Doty,[2] S. K. Stowers,[3] and L. J. White,[4] all of which compare ancient and early Christian letters, are indeed silent concerning hypotheses of letter division.[5] Neither abbreviations and omissions in letter outlines, nor portions added as addenda, represent an analogy to the situation postulated here.[6] Although a one-time occurrence is naturally not impossible, this hypothesis involves other serious problems as well, quite apart from the not entirely persuasive motivation ascribed to the compiler.[7]

Given the tenacity of the New Testament text, such letter compositions are conceivable at all only in connection with the establishment of an authoritative collection of Pauline letters or in the period preceding this.[8] If with Y. K. Kim's[9] subtle paleographic arguments one could agree that P[46] is to be

1. *Introduction to the New Testament* (Eng. trans., 1975) 262.
2. *Letters in Primitive Christianity* (1973).
3. *Letter Writing in Greco-Roman Antiquity* (1986).
4. *ANRW* II 25.2 (1984) 1730-56; in D. E. Aune, *Greco-Roman Literature and the New Testament* (1988) 85-105.
5. A different view is taken by D. E. Aune, *The New Testament in Its Literary Environment* (1987) 208-10, who does not, however, adduce any parallels from outside the New Testament (cf. *loc. cit.*, 158-82). The same applies to H. Probst, *Paulus und der Brief* (1991).
6. Cf. L. J. White, *Light from Ancient Letters* (1986) 217f.
7. Cf. W. Michaelis, *TZ* 14 (1958) 321-26.
8. Cf. K. Aland, in *Studien zur Überlieferung des Neuen Testaments und seines Textes* (1967) 35-57.
9. *Bibl* 69 (1988) 248-57.

dated in the late first century A.D., then the collection of Pauline letters would also already belong in this period. The implementation of the division hypotheses, however, also involves other hardly conceivable auxiliary historical constructions. Paul's letters were addressed to places extremely distant from one another, such as Thessalonica, Philippi, and Corinth on the one hand, and Galatia (wherever one locates it) and Colossae (Philemon) as well as Rome on the other. Either the letters had previously not been exchanged between the various churches, and/or the compiler, after finishing his work, was able to destroy all the originals. Otherwise one can hardly explain why in the manuscript tradition we possess not a single piece of evidence of the earlier text form.

The two requisite auxiliary assumptions, however, are historically untenable. Even assuming pseudonymity, Col. 4:16 still attests that Paul's letters were exchanged between churches.[10] We encounter the beginnings of this custom in 1 Thessalonians. With the strongly formulated exhortation (1 Thess. 5:27; cf. *2 Bar.* 86:1f.), "I solemnly command you by the Lord that this letter be read to all the brethren (ἐνορκίζω ὑμᾶς τὸν κύριον ἀναγνωσθῆναι τὴν ἐπιστολὴν πᾶσιν τοῖς ἀδελφοῖς)," Paul inaugurates a reading of his own writings in the congregational worship service that is analogous to the Old Testament synagogue lectionary.[11] Several of the rhetorical stylistic devices employed similarly suggest a "life setting" in the worship service as well as a function transcending the unique occasion prompting the letter in the first place.[12] The churches could thus acknowledge this letter (like other similarly structured writings) as a challenge to read his letters repeatedly.[13] In view of the active contact between the young Christian communities (contact also presupposed by this letter; cf. 1 Thess. 1:7-9; 4:10), one may conclude further that letters (or copies of such) were soon exchanged. It would remain all the more puzzling that we encounter not the slightest trace in patristic literature of any discussion of the violence to which considerable parts of authoritative

10. Cf. R. F. Collins, in *Studies on the First Letter to the Thessalonians* (1984) 368-70, and further M. Hengel, *SHAW.PH 1983/84* (1984) 33-47. The active exchange of letters also raises questions concerning the assumption that both the self-recension and external recension of collections of Pauline letters involved considerable alterations or insertions, as assumed in an otherwise quite exciting study by D. Trobisch, *Paul's Letter Collection: Tracing the Origins* (Eng. trans., 1994). Regarding 1 Thessalonians, he remarks: "Although the earliest Pauline texts are redacted for inclusion within it, they are edited through the eyes of the late Paul" (*loc. cit.,* 137). For criticism of this view, cf. R. Riesner, *JET* 6 (1992) 164-68. Concerning the preparation of copies, see p. 395, note 9 above.

11. Cf. R. F. Collins, in *Studies on the First Letter to the Thessalonians* (1984) 365-67; I. Taatz, *Frühjüdische Briefe* (1991) 73f.

12. Cf. B. C. Johanson, *To All the Brethren* (1987) 175-87.

13. Cf. L. Hartman, in *Festschrift K. Stendahl* (1986) 137-39.

apostolic letters allegedly would have fallen victim. In the case of Thessalonica, we even have an interesting early indication which, should it be accurate, would not exactly favor any hypothetical assumptions of letters having been divided. According to Tertullian, Philippi and perhaps Thessalonica (some manuscripts lack it [CChr 216]) were among those cities in which the letters addressed to them were still being read from the original manuscript (Tertullian, *De praescr. haer.* 36).

(2) Earlier Division Hypotheses

Although basic considerations already prompt skepticism, the history of scholarship itself does not exactly enhance trust in the feasibility of letter division within 1 Thessalonians. Both the earlier survey of the discussion by C. Clemen[14] and the contemporary survey by R. F. Collins[15] demonstrate the considerable measure of subjectivity in these in part mutually exclusive hypotheses. The assumption of an interpolation of 1 Thess. 2:13-16 seems to have found the greatest resonance (§18.3.1). This is not the place to repeat the concerns raised especially by W. G. Kümmel,[16] A. Suhl,[17] I. H. Marshall,[18] R. F. Collins,[19] T. Holtz,[20] and R. Jewett[21] regarding the more recent attempts of E. Fuchs,[22] K. G. Eckart,[23] W. Schmithals,[24] E. Refshauge,[25] C. Demke,[26] H. M. Schenke and K. M. Fischer,[27] and W. Munro.[28] Apart from any possible criticism of details, one must point out that, again and again, two presuppositions lead to such hypotheses, namely, (1) that Paul employed a consistent

---

14. *Die Einheitlichkeit der paulinischen Briefe an der Hand der bisher mit bezug auf sie aufgestellten Interpolations- und Compilationshypothesen* (1894) 13-18.

15. In *Studies on the First Letter to the Thessalonians* (1984) 96-124.

16. In *Festschrift O. Cullmann* (1962) 213-25; *Introduction to the New Testament* (Eng. trans., 1975) 260-62.

17. *Paulus und seine Briefe* (1975) 96-102.

18. *1 and 2 Thessalonians* (1982) 11-16.

19. In *Studies on the First Letter to the Thessalonians* (1984) 124-35.

20. *Der erste Brief an die Thessalonicher* (²1990) 25-29.

21. *The Thessalonian Correspondence* (1986) 33-46.

22. *ThV* 7 (1959/60) 44-60.

23. *ZTK* 58 (1961) 30-44.

24. In *Festschrift R. Bultmann* (1964) 295-315; in *Paulus und die Gnostiker* (1965) 89-157, 225-45 (Eng. trans., *Paul and the Gnostics* [1972]). Modified again (!) in *Die Briefe des Paulus in ihrer ursprünglichen Form* (1984) 111-24.

25. *DTT* 34 (1971) 1-19.

26. In *Festschrift E. Fuchs* (1973) 103-24.

27. *Einleitung in die Schriften des Neuen Testaments* I (1978) 64-76.

28. *Authority in Peter and Paul* (1983) 82-93.

formula for his letters, and (2) that the apostle's language and thinking were consistent to the highest degree. The first presupposition is an unprovable assertion and the second is already called into question by the observation that especially in the passages suspected of being insertions, Paul uses Jewish and early Christian traditions.[29] Because R. Pesch endeavors to place his own division hypothesis into a real historical situation, and because he seems also to find greater acceptance,[30] we will examine his attempt a bit more closely here.

(3) The Hypothesis of Rudolf Pesch

R. Pesch[31] largely adopts the letter division in the form presented by H. M. Schenke and K. M. Fischer (note 27), augmenting it with a series of supporting arguments. He distinguishes a concerned letter of reference for Timothy from Athens, and a joyous letter of response after the co-worker's return. Pesch distributes the entire extant material between these two letters, and concludes that the compiler lost no material and got by with almost no redactional insertions:

The Letter from Athens		The Letter from Corinth	
		1:1	Prescript
2:13-16	Thanksgiving	1:2-10	Thanksgiving and
2:1-12	Retrospective		retrospective
2:17–3:5	Sending of Timothy	3:6-10	Timothy's return
		4:9-12	Love of one's fellows
		4:13-18	The deceased
		5:1-11	Times and seasons
4:1-8	Admonitions	5:12-22	Admonitions
3:11-13	Conclusion	5:23-27	Conclusion
		5:28	Concluding blessing

Neither Pesch's literary-critical/form-critical nor his historical arguments, however, make this hypothesis of the letter's division compelling. The repetition of εὐχαριστοῦμεν in 1 Thess. 1:2 and 2:13 does not allow one to assume without qualification the presence of two different thanksgivings.[32] Closer form analysis reveals a carefully constructed thanksgiving in

29. Cf. esp. T. Holtz, in *Festschrift E. Schweizer* (1983) 55-78.
30. Cf. F. Laub, *1. und 2. Thessalonicherbrief* (1985) 10f.; R. Bohlen, *TTZ* 96 (1987) 313-17; H. Ulonska, *TZ* 43 (1987) 210f.
31. *Die Entdeckung des ältesten Paulus-Briefes* (1986).
32. *Ibid.*, 42-44.

three parts (1 Thess. 1:2–2:12; 2:13–3:8; 3:9-13) culminating in an eschatological climax.[33] Its repetitions have good parallels in the exordia of Jewish-Hellenistic (e.g., 2 Macc. 1:11-17) and other Hellenistic letters.[34] The striking length of the retrospective thanksgiving can be explained effortlessly on the basis of Paul's particular situation in relationship to the Thessalonians (§18.7; 19.1). Pesch finds in 1 Thess. 4:1-8 and 1 Thess. 5:12-22 two different series of admonitions of which the second, in contrast to the first, allegedly is based on information brought by Timothy.[35] But 1 Thess. 4:1 (καθὼς καὶ περιπατεῖτε) also presupposes timely knowledge on Paul's part.[36] 1 Thess. 3:11-13 is not a doublet to the conclusion 1 Thess. 5:23-27,[37] but rather a typical doxology at the end of a thanksgiving.[38] At the same time, 1 Thess. 3:9-13 represents an indispensable transition between the letter's final two ring compositions (see p. 410 below).

In 1 Thess. 2:17–3:5, Pesch identifies a formulary for the dispatch of messengers, the forms εὐδοκήσαμεν (1 Thess. 3:1) and ἐπέμψαμεν (1 Thess. 3:2) representing epistolary aorists and thus to be understood as present.[39] Paul is thus allegedly talking about his intention to dispatch Timothy. Pesch claims to elevate the possibility of such language use to the status of probability by asserting that the description of the quality and commission of the messenger in 1 Thess. 3:2-5 suggests a present situation of dispatch. J. Murphy-O'Connor, however, correctly points out that in two other cases as well, the apostle mentions the circumstances of a mission that has already taken place: in 1 Cor. 4:17 (cf. 1 Cor. 16:11) regarding the sending of Timothy, and in 2 Cor. 2:1-13 and 2 Cor. 7:5-14 regarding the sending of Titus to Corinth.[40]

Finally, Pesch also traces various mood changes back to different historical situations.[41] Whereas 1 Thess. 2:17–3:5 reflects the worrisome time in Athens, 1 Thess. 3:6-10 mirrors the apostle's joy after Timothy's arrival in Corinth. Given the communication situation (§18.7; 19.1), however, the apostle understandably has to reveal both emotions to the Thessalonians

---

33. Cf. P. Schubert, *Form and Function of the Pauline Thanksgiving* (1939) 18; P. T. O'Brien, *Introductory Thanksgivings in the Letters of Paul* (1977) 141; R. F. Collins, in *Studies on the First Letter to the Thessalonians* (1984) 134f.; R. Jewett, *The Thessalonian Correspondence* (1986) 42f.; B. C. Johanson, *To All the Brethren* (1987) 67-72.

34. Cf. F. O. Francis, *ZNW* 61 (1970) 111-17; B. C. Johanson, *loc. cit.,* 69f.

35. R. Pesch, *Die Entdeckung des ältesten Paulus-Briefes* (1986) 52-55.

36. Cf. J. Murphy-O'Connor, *RB* 92 (1985) 456f.

37. R. Pesch, *Die Entdeckung des ältesten Paulus-Briefes* (1986) 50-52.

38. Cf. P. Schubert, *Form and Function of the Pauline Thanksgivings* (1939) 18f.; R. F. Collins, in *Studies on the First Letter to the Thessalonians* (1984) 135.

39. *Die Entdeckung des ältesten Paulus-Briefes* (1986) 46-50.

40. *RB* 92 (1985) 457.

41. *Die Entdeckung des ältesten Paulus-Briefes* (1986) 46-50.

in the same letter: his concern for their welfare after his sudden departure, and his joy at how well they have developed despite his absence. Pesch views the twofold mention of Paul's εἴσοδος among the Thessalonians as a further instance of doubling.[42] When, according to 1 Thess. 1:8f., there is already talk in Macedonia and Achaia, indeed "in every place (ἐν παντὶ τόπῳ)," about the apostle's arrival in the congregation, this allegedly — Pesch argues — betrays a later time than 1 Thess. 2:1f., where Paul is recalling his arrival from Philippi. Yet one should not make too much of this sort of hyperbolic manner of expression.[43] Following the assumption that Timothy was actually never in Athens (§18.4.4), there is absolutely no historical occasion for extracting from 1 Thessalonians a letter of reference for Paul's co-worker.

(4) Arguments for the Letter's Unity

Today, scholars are apparently again increasingly considering the possibility of more extensive participation of secretaries and/or co-authors in the Pauline letters.[44] H. Binder has presented an original attempt at explaining differently the phenomena in 1 Thessalonians generally thought to favor the divided-letter hypothesis.[45] He views the two letters to the Thessalonians as the common product of Paul and Silvanus, with only the latter responsible for the apocalyptic tone of the two writings. Binder's suggestion does, however, encounter fundamental and concrete difficulties. His assumption of an originally utterly unapocalyptic Paul stands contrary to what is here the almost unanimous consensus of scholarship. Similarly, for practical reasons it seems questionable that a letter ever would have been completed for which "specific analysis shows that Paul initiated his dictation fifteen times and that Silvanus made insertions fourteen times. Sometimes the one interrupts the other, as it were, in mid-sentence, such as when Silvanus, taking as his point of departure the catchword 'Jews' (2:14), which Paul has just uttered, inserts a polemic against the Jews. . . ."[46] Although in the two letters to the Thessalonians the name Paul stands in first position (1 Thess. 1:1; 2 Thess. 1:1), according to Binder only two-fifths of the first letter, and — worse yet — only a quarter of the second encompass genuine Pauline material — and that during a period when

---

42. *Ibid.*, 40-46.

43. Cf. T. Holtz, *Der erste Brief an die Thessalonicher* (²1990) 12.

44. Cf. M. Prior, *Paul the Letter-Writer* (1989) 37-49; E. R. Richards, *The Secretary in the Letters of Paul* (1991); and J. Murphy-O'Connor, *Paul the Letter-Writer* (1995) 1-41.

45. In R. F. Collins, *The Thessalonian Correspondence* (1990) 87-93.

the apostle, according to Binder's own dating, is also writing (alone!) the letter to the Galatians.[47] It is indeed worth considering, however, that Paul probably did discuss his letter with his co-signees, and that through Silvanus (cf. Acts 15:22, 27) the apostle had access to Jerusalem traditions,[48] including traditions concerning Jesus.[49] Traces of this may well have been left behind in the first letter to the Thessalonians.

B. C. Johanson[50] has recently presented an interesting attempt at demonstrating the unity of this letter. Anyone not intimidated by linguistic jargon will be richly rewarded by this study. Johanson presents impressive arguments demonstrating a carefully executed, threefold ring composition (1 Thess. 1:2–2:16; 2:17–3:13; 4:1–5:24) that is destroyed by all the division hypotheses (including the assumption of an interpolation of 1 Thess. 2:13-16). The assumption that the compiler created this artful composition does not explain the communicative-technical fact that the letter's strategy of persuasion is related to *Paul's* historical situation. If one does follow Johanson's analysis,

46. *Ibid.,* 91.

47. In R. F. Collins, ed., *The Thessalonian Correspondence* (1990) 92, 90. With his predilection for eccentric theses, M. D. Goulder, *JSNT* 48 (1992) 87-106, has suggested that Silas was the source of the errors Paul is combating in 1 Thessalonians. But this really does founder on the fact of the latter's identity as co-signee, and on the way in which Paul speaks about the alleged heretical leader in 2 Cor. 1:19.

48. In light of 1 Pet. 5:13, the resonance between 1 Pet. 1:1–2:3 and 1 Thess. 4:3-8 is interesting (P. Perkins, in *Festschrift J. A. Fitzmyer* [1989] 332). In 1 Thessalonians, both repentance and parenesis (M. Newton, *The Concept of Purity at Qumran and in the Letters of Paul* [1985] 102-4), though also the βασιλεία τοῦ θεοῦ (A. M. Schwemer, in M. Hengel and A. M. Schwemer, *Königsherrschaft Gottes und himmlischer Kult* [1991] 118) are conceived in cultic categories recalling Qumran. Concerning other Qumran-parallels in the letter, cf. H. W. Kuhn, in J. Trebolle Barrera and L. Vegas Montaner, *The Madrid Qumran Congress* I (1992) 339-53; K. P. Donfried, in *Festschrift K. Kertelge* (1996) 404-7. The original Jerusalem church apparently included a stronger contingent of Essene converts. Cf. R. Riesner, in B. Mayer, *Christen und Christliches in Qumran?* (1992) 139-55.

49. Concerning this topic in general, see pp. 367f., note 174; p. 378, note 41; and p. 392, note 55 above; concerning possible relationships between Paul and specifically Jerusalem Jesus-traditions, cf. R. Riesner, *TBei* 24 (1993) 243. 1 Thess. 1:6 recalls Lk. 8:13 (B. Rigaux, *Les épîtres aux Thessaloniciens* [1956] 381f., while 1 Thess. 5:1-3 recalls Lk. 21:34f. (J. Plevnik, *Bibl* 60 [1979] 82-84; D. Wenham, in R. T. France and D. Wenham, eds., *Gospel Perspectives* II [1981] 353-56; T. Holtz, in H. Wansbrough, ed., *Jesus and the Oral Gospel Tradition* [1991] 387f.). Contra the eccentric view of L. Aejmelaeus, *Wachen vor dem Ende* (1985) 131-37, namely, that Lk. 21:34-36 is also drawing from 1 Thess. 5:1-11, see the remarks concerning M. D. Goulder, p. 367f., note 174 above.

50. *To All the Brethren: A Text-Linguistic and Rhetorical Approach to 1 Thessalonians* (1987). For reasons of rhetorical structure, F. W. Hughes, in R. F. Collins, *The Thessalonian Correspondence* (1990) 102, similarly objects to an interpolation.

then one cannot deny that the apostle did possess a certain rhetorical mastery.[51] Precisely also in view of this original attempt at accessing the text, the conclusion of W. Trilling applies to the more recent attempts at division: "As long as no more conclusive arguments are presented, the conclusion *in possessione* is probably that 1 Thessalonians is to be viewed as a unified piece of writing."[52]

51. H. Koester, in *Festschrift G. H. Williams* (1979) 33, already concluded: "This carefully composed writing is actually an experiment in the composition of literature which signals the momentous entry of Christianity into the literary world of antiquity."Cf. also S. Walton, *TynBul* 46 (1995) 229-50.

52. *ANRW* II 25.4 (1987) 3384. W. Trilling, however, does not yet address R. Pesch. The most recent scholarly commentary by C. A. Wanamaker, *The Epistles to the Thessalonians* (1990) 28-37, argues vehemently against all hypotheses of division and interpolation.

SUMMARY
Chronology and Theology

The comparison of direct and indirect chronological information from Acts with dates from secular history produced a meaningful chronological sequence of events for Luke's portrayal. Above all, a close chronological connection can be maintained between an expulsion of Jews from Rome under Claudius (Acts 18:2) in the year A.D. 49 and Paul's trial before the proconsul Gallio in Corinth (Acts 18:12-17) between summer A.D. 51 and 52. The close weave of dates in connection with the we-account of the apostle's final journey to Jerusalem and his transport to Rome (Acts 20–28) proved to be strikingly reliable. The most satisfactory explanation here still seemed to be that this rendering of events is based on eyewitness accounts and that the author of the we-passages is identical with the author of Acts. The investigation thus supports in part the ancient church tradition (since Irenaeus, *Haer.* iii.1.1) concerning Luke, Paul's companion, as the author of the double work named after him.[1] The perspective of our line of questioning also confirms the conclusion of A. von Harnack: "A recognition of the book's credibility is thus enhanced by an exact study of its author's chronography, that is, where he speaks and where he is silent."[2]

By contrast, Paul's letters themselves were unable to provide even a marginally secure date for the apostle's life. This applies even to the Aretas-incident (2 Cor. 11:32f.). Chronological outlines of the sort J. Knox, G. Lüdemann, or N. Hyldahl claim to provide on the basis of the letters alone, have hitherto yielded neither concurring nor persuasive results. With the

---

1. Comprehensive argumentation has now been presented in this regard by C. J. Thornton, *Der Zeuge des Zeugen. Lukas als Historiker der Paulusreisen* (1991), who also offers effective criticism of the thesis that the we-accounts are actually literary fiction, as advocated again, e.g., by J. Wehnert, *Die Wir-Passagen der Apostelgeschichte. Ein lukanisches Stilmittel aus jüdischer Tradition* (1989). Cf. also the criticism of V. Fusco, *RBI* 39 (1991) 231-39. For Acts as an ancient historical monograph see D. W. Palmer in B. W. Winter and A. D. Clarke, *The Book of Acts in Its Ancient Literary Setting* (1993) 1-30; for the indebtedness of Luke to biblical history writing, B. S. Rosner, *ibid.*, 65-82.

2. *SPAW.PH* (1907) 391.

coercion inherent in any strict system, chronological information has been demanded of Pauline statements which they are unable to provide. By contrast, and despite the problems regarding details, considerable agreement with regard to the overall picture was attained between the framework of Acts and Paul's explicit or inferable information concerning the chronological or geographic parameters of his mission. A critical combination of Acts with the Pauline letters remains possible not just for individual Lukan traditions, but also for information regarding the larger framework. Hence, one should return to the relative consensus concerning the middle period of the Pauline ministry as was the case in scholarship for approximately seventy years after the discovery of the Gallio-inscription, until about 1980. The new chronological reconstructions by J. Becker,[3] L. Alexander,[4] E. Lohse,[5] and M. Hengel and A. M. Schwemer[6] represent hopeful signs; despite clear difference in specific arguments, these reconstructions exhibit striking parallels with the results of the present study. But even a study over a century earlier, such as that of C. F. Nösgen, already advocated the basic dates suggested here: A.D. 30, crucifixion of Jesus; 31/32, conversion of Paul; 48, Apostolic Council; 57, arrest in Jerusalem; 60-62, imprisonment in Rome.[7]

Luke's knowledge was not evenly distributed. He supplies excellent information in connection with the we-accounts, while in other areas he evidences gaps in his knowledge. Our admittedly limited investigation, however, yielded hardly any indications that the *auctor ad Theophilum* was making things up when he had no access to other information. As an ancient historian, Luke placed his material in the service of a specific literary agenda, a process during which as far as I can see he worked primarily with the devices of choice, organization, and effective stylistic structuring. The element of tension sometimes perceptible in Acts between the reworked material on the one hand, and Luke's redactional tendencies on the other, attests in its own way the author's ties to already extant information. The historiographic problem seems not to be that Luke simply invented whatever he needed, but rather that he often passed over in silence things he thought were either unpleasant or secondary. Hence he mitigated in particular internal church conflicts and often refrained from portraying problems with the pagan state. But by lending to his account of the origins of Christianity an appropriate chronological sequence, Luke did in his own way emphasize the importance of a connection between theology and chronology.

3. *Paulus. Der Apostel der Völker* (1989; ²1993) 17-33 (p. 32: table).

4. In G. F. Hawthorne et al., eds., *Dictionary of Paul and His Letters* (1993) 115-23.

5. *Paulus* (1996) 53-57.

6. *Paul between Damascus and Antioch* (1997) xi-xiv (Chronological Table).

7. *Commentar über die Apostelgeschichte* (1882) 63-70 (Zur Chronologie des apostolischen Zeitalters).

413

What is true of the Lukan work in the larger sense can also be shown to apply on a smaller scale to an important stage of the Pauline mission. The account Luke composed concerning the founding of the church in Thessalonica, even considering its literary tendencies and abbreviations, does agree to a noteworthy degree with the historical, social, and religious circumstances evident in 1 Thessalonians and illustrated by contemporary material. Paul founded the church in the winter of A.D. 49/50, and then had to leave it suddenly after approximately three months. His proclamation was misunderstood as being politically subversive. The resulting conflict with the city's government forced Paul to flee, and left him in an uncertain legal situation. After several attempts at returning failed, the apostle dispatched his co-worker Timothy even before arriving in Athens, and through him first reestablished contact with his church. As a reponse to the news from Thessalonica, and hardly six months after founding the church, Paul wrote the first letter to the Thessalonians from Corinth in the spring of A.D. 50. Here our reconstruction is close to that of R. Jewett.[8]

The first letter to the Thessalonians is truly a situationally determined piece of writing whose peculiarities can be explained on the basis of the historical circumstances. The apostle was writing to a congregation that as yet had not been influenced by other Christian teachers — false or otherwise. Hence it was not necessary to repeat basic features of the founding proclamation. In his hasty response, Paul oriented himself toward the congregation's external and internal situation. In a strikingly long, grateful retrospective on the founding visit (1 Thess. 1:2–3:13), the apostle combined his extremely personal encouragement of endangered new converts with a defense against actual and potential accusations regarding his own behavior, especially in connection with the sudden termination of his mission. 1 Thessalonians shows us in an especially personal fashion Paul as the founder and pastor of a church.

Similarly, the letter's admonitions do not follow abstract considerations or customary parenetic exposition, but rather take seriously the congregation's actual needs. The apostle framed his response to the Thessalonians' ethical and eschatological questions concerning such things as love of one's fellows and public behavior (1 Thess. 4:9-12), the unexpected deaths of Christians (1 Thess. 4:13-18), and "times and seasons" (1 Thess. 5:1-3) with warnings against external and internal threats such as pagan permissiveness (1 Thess. 4:1-8; 5:4-11) and problems of charismatic authority (1 Thess. 5:12-22). These expositions are similarly to be viewed against a concrete background, and were occasioned both by Timothy's own report and by the actual experiences of an urban missionary. The letter's uniqueness is misunderstood by expectations that it provided fundamental expositions about justification, the cross

---

8. *The Thessalonian Correspondence* (1986) especially 49-60.

and resurrection, or other basic statements of faith. The first letter to the Thessalonians is a reminder that in the Pauline understanding, both ethics and the practical establishment of church and congregation belong indispensably together with christology, soteriology, and anthropology.

Insofar as dogmatic themes resonate more strongly in the letter, this does not occur in a way that is essentially any different from statements of later letters. Especially the formulae of faith appearing frequently in this writing presuppose that the Thessalonians were already familiar with information the apostle only needed to recall by means of keywords. Nowhere does it become evident that the gospel proclaimed to this church was any different from that preached earlier in Galatia or immediately thereafter in Corinth. Far-reaching divergences in the eschatological views of 1 Thessalonians and 1 Corinthians seem to be the result of overly astute constructions. Although chronology was indeed one important factor in the *development* of Pauline theology, it cannot bear the burden of demonstrating radical, fundamental *transformation*.

APPENDIX
Illustrations

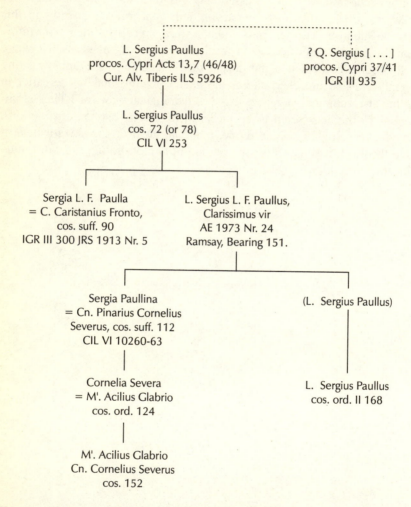

Illustration 1. Family Tree of the Sergii

This genealogy is inspired by J. Devreker, *Festschrift G. Sanders* (1991) 109-19 and H. Botermann, "Die Sergii Paulli und das Christentum." Mrs. Botermann (ancient historian at the University of Göttingen) was so kind as to show me her forthcoming article. Q. Sergius as brother and L. Sergius Paullus as son of the first L. Sergius Paullus remain somewhat hypothetical (see pp. 139-41 above).

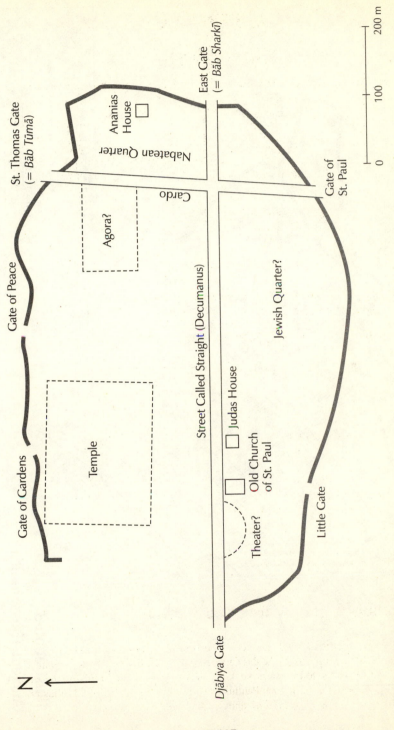

Illustration 2. Damascus
(present city walls, basic Hellenistic-Roman map and Christian memorial sites)

417

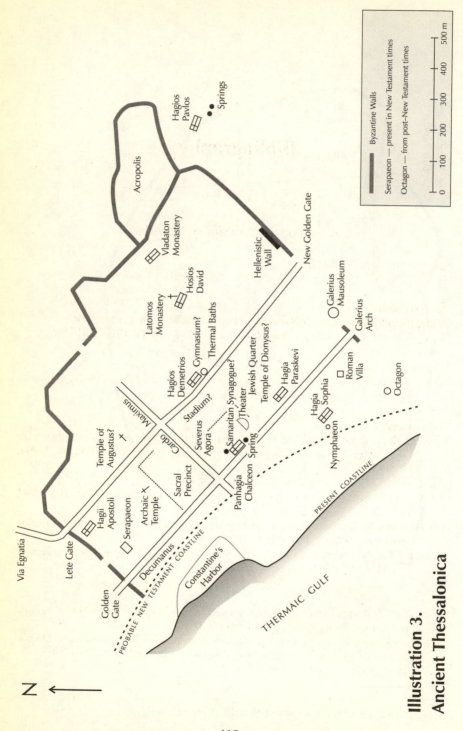

Illustration 3.
Ancient Thessalonica

Legend:
Byzantine Walls
Serapaeon — present in New Testament times
Octagon — from post–New Testament times

0 100 200 300 400 500 m

N ←

Labels on map:
Springs
Hagios Pavlos
Acropolis
Vladaton Monastery
Latomos Monastery
Hosios David
Hellenistic Wall
New Golden Gate
Gymnasium?
Thermal Baths
Hagios Demetrios
Galerius Mausoleum
Galerius Arch
Maximus
Stadium?
Samaritan Synagogue?
Jewish Quarter
Temple of Dionysus?
Theater
Hagia Paraskevi
Severus Agora
Roman Villa
Cardo
Hagia Sophia
Chalceon Spring
Nymphaeon
Octagon
Temple of Augustus?
Sacral Precinct
Panhagia
Archaic Temple
Hagii Apostoli
Serapaeon
Via Egnatia
Lete Gate
Decumanus
Golden Gate
PROBABLE NEW TESTAMENT COASTLINE
PRESENT COASTLINE
Constantine's Harbor
THERMAIC GULF

418

Bibliography

1. Sources and Auxiliary Material

Acta Martyrorum Paganorum:
Musurillo, H. *The Acts of the Pagan Martyrs. Acta Alexandrinorum* (London, 1954).

Old Testament:
Elliger, K., and Rudolph, W. *Biblia Hebraica Stuttgartensia* (Stuttgart, 1987).
Ziegler, J. *Isaias. Septuaginta — Vetus Testamentum Graecum* 14 (Göttingen, ²1967).

Ambrosiaster:
Ambrosiastri qui dicitur Commentarius in Epistulas Paulinas I: In Epistulam ad Romanos.
CSEL 81/1 (Vienna, 1966).

New Testament Apocrypha:
Hennecke, E., and Schneemelcher, W., eds. *Neutestamentliche Apokryphen in deutscher Übersetzung* II: *Apostolisches, Apokalypsen und Verwandtes* (Tübingen, ³1964, ⁵1989) [NTApo II].
James, M. R. *The Apocryphal New Testament* (Oxford, 1953).
Lipsius, R. A., and Bonnet, M. *Acta apostolorum apocrypha* (Leipzig; I: 1891; II/1: 1898; II/2: 1903).
Schneemelcher, W. *Neutestamentliche Apokryphen in deutscher Übersetzung* I; *Evangelien* (Tübingen, ⁵1987) (NTApo I).
Schneemelcher, W. and Wilson, R. M., eds. *New Testament Apocrypha* I-II (Eng. trans.; rev. ed. 1990, 1992) (*NTApoc*).

Apostolic Legends:
Schermann, T. *Propheten- und Apostellegenden nebst Jüngerkatalogen des Dorotheus und verwandter Texte. TU* N.S. 3.1 (Leipzig, 1907).
———. *Prophetarum Vitae Fabulosae. Indices Apostolorum Discipulorumque Domini Dorotheo — Epiphanio — Hippolyto Aliisque Vindicata* (Leipzig, 1907).
Zahn, T. *Acta Johannis* (Leipzig, 1880).

Appian:
White, H. *Appian: Historia Romana* I-IV. *LCL* (London, 1912/13).

Arabic Geographers:
Sauvaire, H. *Description de Damas. JA* 7 (1896) I, 369-459.

Epistle of Aristeas:
Meisner, N. *Aristeasbrief. JSHRZ* II/1 (Gütersloh, 1973) 35-87.
Shutt, R. J. H. "Letter of Aristeas." In J. H. Charlesworth, ed. *The Old Testament Pseude-pigrapha* II (Garden City, 1985) 7-34.

Ascension of Isaiah:
Charles, R. H. *The Ascension of Isaiah, translated from the Ethiopic Version, which, together with the new Greek Fragment, the Latin Versions and the Latin Transla-tion of the Slavonic, is here published in full* (London, 1900).
Detlef, C., and Müller, G. *The Ascension of Isaiah* (NTApoc II 603-20).
Hammershaimb, E. *Das Martyrium Jesajas. JSHRZ* II/1 (²1977) 16-34.
Knibb, M. A. "Martyrdom and Ascension of Isaiah." In J. H. Charlesworth, ed. *The Old Testament Pseudepigrapha* II (Garden City, 1985) 143-76.

Syriac Apocalypse of Baruch:
Klijn, A. F. J. *Die syrische Baruch-Apokalypse. JSHRZ* V/2 (Gütersloh, 1976) 103-91.
————. "2 (Syriac Apocalypse of) Baruch." In J. H. Charlesworth, ed. *The Old Testament Pseudepigrapha* I (Garden City, 1983) 615-52.

Dio Cassius:
Boissevain, U. P., Smilda, H., and Nawijn, W. *Cassii Dionis Cocceiani Historiarum Ro-manorum Quae Supersunt* I-V (Berlin, 1898-1931).
Cary, E. *Dio's Roman History* I-IX (London, 1914-1927).
Veh, O., and Wirth, G. *Cassius Dio: Römische Geschichte* Iff. (Zurich, 1985-).

Chronographers (Byzantine):
Dindorf, W. *Georgios Syncellus und Nicephorus Constantinopoleos. CSHB* 11/12 (Leipzig, 1829).
Mommsen, T. *Über den Chronographen vom J. 354. ASGW* 1 (Leipzig, 1850).

Claudius Caesar:
Lösche, S. *Epistula Claudiana. Der neuentdeckte Brief des Kaisers Claudius vom Jahre 41 n. Chr. und das Urchristentum. Eine exegetisch-historische Untersuchung* (Rot-tenburg, 1930).

Clement of Alexandria:
Stählin, O. *Clemens Alexandrinus II: Stromata I-VI. GCS* 52 (15) (Berlin, ³1960).
Stählin, O., and Früchtel, L. *Clemens Alexandrinus III: Stromata VII-VIII. GCS* 17 (Leipzig, 1909).

Dio Chrysostomus:
Budé, G. de. *Dio Chrysostomus: Orationes* (Leipzig, 1906).

Diodorus Siculus:
Oldfather, C. H. *(et al.). Diodorus Siculus* I-XI. *LCL* (London, 1936-1957).

Acts of Dionysus:
Oikonomides, N. *Actes de Dionysiou* (Texts) *Archives de l'Athos* IV/1 (Paris, 1968).

Doctrine of Addai:
Howard, G. *The Teaching of Addai.* SBL TT 16 *ECLS* 4 (Missoula, 1981).

Epiphanius of Salamis:
Holl, K. *Epiphanius I-III: Panarion Haer. GCS* 25, 31, 37 (Leipzig, 1915-1933).

Eusebius:
Heikel, I. A. *Eusebius VI: Demonstratio Evangelica. GCS* 23 (Leipzig, 1913).
Helm, R. *Die Chronik des Hieronymus. GCS* 47 (Berlin, 1956).
Klostermann, E. *Das Onomastikon der biblischen Ortsnamen. Eusebius Werke* III/1. *GCS* 11.1 (Leipzig, 1904).
Kraft, H. *Eusebius von Caesarea: Kirchengeschichte* (Darmstadt, 1967).
Mras, K. *Eusebius VIII/1-2: Praeparatio Evangelica. GCS* 43/1-2 (Berlin, 1954/56).
Schöne, A. *Eusebii Chronicorum Libri Duo* I-II (Dublin/Zurich, 1967) (= 1875).
Schwartz, E. *Kirchengeschichte. Kleine Ausgabe* (Leipzig, [4]1932).

1 Enoch (Ethiopic):
Charles, R. H. *The Book of Enoch . . .* (Oxford, [2]1912).

Herodotus:
Feix, G. *Herodot (Griechisch-Deutsch)* (Munich, 1963).

Jerome:
Migne, J. P. *Hieronymus: Liber de viris illustribus. PL* 23.631-766.

Hippolytus of Thebes:
Diekamp, F. *Hippolytus von Theben. Texte und Untersuchungen* (Münster, 1898)

Inscriptions:
Avigad, N. "A Depository of Inscribed Ossuaries in the Kidron Valley." *IEJ* 12 (1962) 1-12.
———. *Beth She'arim III* [Modern Hebrew] (Jerusalem, 1971).
Ballance, M. H. "The Site of Derbe: A New Inscription." *AnSt* 7 (1957) 147-51.
Barag, D., and Flusser, D. "The Ossuary of Yehohanah Granddaughter of the High Priest Theophilus." *IEJ* 36 (1986) 39-44.
Bonfioli, M., and Panciera, S. "Della Cristianità del *Collegivm qvod est in domo Sergiae Pavllinae.*" *RPARA* 44 (1971/72) 185-201.
———. " 'In domo Sergiae Paullinae.' Nota aggiuntiva." *RPARA* 45 (1972/73) 133-38.
Bourguet, E. *De Rebus Delphicis imperatoriae aetatis capita duo* (Paris, 1905).
Calder, W. M. *Monumenta Asiae Minoris Antiqua. Publications of the American Society for Archeological Research in Asia Minor* I-VIII (London, 1928-1962).
Clarke, A. D. "Another Corinthian Erastus Inscription." *TynBul* 42/1 (1991) 146-51.
Cormack, J. M. R. "The Gymnasiarchal Law of Beroea." *AncMac* II (1977) 139-49.
Corpus Inscriptionum Latinarum (Leipzig/Berlin, [2]1893-).
Corpus Inscriptionum Semiticarum. Pars Secundo: Inscriptiones Aramaicae continens (Paris, 1889-).

Cousin, G., and Deschamps, G. "Emplacements des ruines à la ville de Kus en Carie." *BCH* 11 (1887) 306-8.

Dessau, H. *Inscriptiones Latinae Selectae* I-III (Berlin, 1892-1916).

Duchesne, L., and Bayet, M. *Mémoire sur une mission au Mont Athos* (Paris, 1876).

Edson, C. E. *Inscriptiones Graecae* X/2: *Inscriptiones Graecae Epiri, Macedoniae, Thraciae, Scythiae*. Fasc. 1: *Inscriptiones Thessalonicae et viciniae* (Berlin, 1972).

Ehrhardt, N. "Eine neue Grabinschrift aus Iconium." *ZPE* 81 (1990) 185-88.

Frey, J. B. *Corpus Inscriptionum Judaicarum* I (ed. B. Lifshitz): *Europa* (Rome, 1936; New York, ²1975); II: *Asia et Africa* (Rome, 1952).

Frova, A. *"L'Iscrizione di Ponzio Pilato a Cesarea." RIL.L* 95 (1961) 419-34.

Gabba, E. *Iscrizioni greche e latine per lo studio della Bibbia. SOB* 3 (Rome, 1958).

Gibson, E. P. "The 'Christians for Christians' Inscriptions of Phrygia." *HTS* 32 (Missoula, 1978).

Hachlili, R. "The Goliath Family in Jericho: Funerary Inscriptions from a First Century A.D. Jewish Monumental Tomb." *BASOR* 235 (1979) 31-66.

Harding, G. L. *An Index and Concordance of Pre-Islamic Arabian Names and Inscriptions. NMES* 8 (Toronto, 1971).

Hogarth, D. G. *Devia Cypria* (London, 1889).

Ilan, T. "New Ossuary Inscriptions from Jerusalem." *Scripta Classica Israelica* 11 (Jerusalem, 1991/92) 149-59.

Isaac, B. "A Donation for Herod's Temple in Jerusalem." *IEJ* 33 (1983) 86-92.

Kent, J. H. *Corinth: Results of Excavations Conducted by the American School of Classical Studies at Athens,* VIII/3: *Inscriptions 1926-1950* (Princeton, 1966).

Knibbe, D., Engelmann, H., and Iplikcioglu, B. "Neue Inschriften aus Ephesos XI." *JÖAI* 59 (1989) 164-238.

Koukouli-Chrysanthaki, C. "Politarchs in a New Inscription from Amphipolis." *Ancient Macedonian Studies in Honor of Charles F. Edson* (Thessalonica, 1981) 229-41.

Levick, B. M. "Unpublished Inscriptions from Pisidian Antioch." *AnSt* 17 (1967) 101-21.

Lifshitz, B., *Donateurs et fondateurs dans les synagogues juives* (Paris, 1967).

Lifshitz, B., and Schiby, J. "Une synagogue Samaritaine à Thessalonique." *RB* 75 (1968) 368-78.

Lüderitz, G. *Corpus jüdischer Zeugnisse aus der Cyrenaika* (addendum by J. M. Reynolds). *BTAVO* B 53 (Wiesbaden, 1983).

Mitchell, S. "Requisitioned Transport in the Roman Empire, a New Inscription from Pisidia." *JRS* 66 (1976) 106-31.

Mitford, T. B. "Notes on Some Published Inscriptions from Roman Cyprus." *ABSA* 42 (1947) 201-30.

Plassart, A. *École Française d'Athènes: Fouilles de Delphes, III/3: Épigraphie (Inscriptions de la terrasse du temple et de la région nord du sanctuaire)* (Paris, 1970).

Reynolds, J. M., and Tannenbaum, R. *Jews and God-fearers at Aphrodisias: Greek Inscriptions with Commentary. Cambridge Philological Association Suppl* 12 (Cambridge, 1987).

Romiopoulou, C. "Un nouveau milliaire de la Via Egnatia." *BCH* 98 (1974) 813-16.

Roussel, J. *Supplementum Epigraphicum Graecum* (Leiden, 1923-).

Spieser, J. M. "Les inscriptions de Thessalonique." *Travaux et Mémoires* 5 (1973) 145-80.

Waddington, W. H. *Inscriptions grecques et latines receuillies en Grèce et an Asie Mineur* V (Paris, 1870).

West, A. B. *Corinth: Results of the Excavations Conducted by the American School of Classical Studies at Athens, VIII/2: Inscriptions 1896-1926* (Cambridge, Mass., 1931).

Irenaeus:
Harvey, W. W. *Irenaeus: Adversus Haereses I-II* (Cambridge, 1857).

Isidore of Seville:
Chaparro, Gomez C. *Isidorus Hispalensis, De ortu et obitu patrum. Introducción, edición crítica y traducción* (Paris, 1985).

Apocryphon of James:
Kirchner, D. *Brief des Jakobus. NTApo* I[5] (Tübingen, 1987) 234-44.
Williams, F. E. "The Apocryphon of James." In J. M. Robinson, ed. *The Nag Hammadi Library in English* (San Francisco, [2]1988) 29-37.

Josephus:
Feldman, L. H. "A Selective Critical Bibliography of Josephus." In L. H. Feldman and G. Hata. *Josephus, The Bible and History* (Leiden, 1989) 330-448.
Michel, O., and Bauernfeind, O. *De bello Judaico I-II* (Darmstadt, 1959 and 1963).
Schalit, A. *Namenwörterbuch zu Flavius Josephus: A Complete Concordance to Flavius Josephus.* Edited by K. H. Rengstorf. Supp. 1 (Leiden, 1968).
Thackeray, H. S.-J., Marcus, R., and Feldman, L. H. *Josephus Flavius I-IX* (London, 1926-1965).

Julius Africanus:
Migne, J. P. *PG* 10 (Paris, 1880) 63-94.
Routh, M. J. *Reliquiae Sacrae: Sive, Auctorum fere jam Perditorum Secundi Tertiique Saeculi post Christum Natum quae Supersunt* II (Oxford, [2]1846).

Justin Martyr:
Goodspeed, E. J. *Die ältesten Apologeten* (Göttingen, 1914).

Juvenal:
Friedländer, L. *D. Junii Juvenalis Saturarum Libri V* (with explanatory notes) I-II (Leipzig, 1895; repr. Hildesheim, 1967).

Maps:
Aharoni, Y., and Avi-Yonah, M. *The Macmillan Bible Atlas* (New York/London, [2]1971).
Calder, W. M., and Bean, G. E. *A Classical Map of Asia Minor. AnSt* 7 (1957) Supp. (London, 1957).
Kettenhofer, E., and Pohlmann, H. *Östlicher Mittelmeerraum und Mesopotamien in spätrömischer Zeit (337-527 n. Chr.). TAVO* B VI 4 (Wiesbaden, 1984).
Matthiae, K., and Thiel, W. *Biblische Zeittafeln. Geschichtliche Abrisse chronologische Übersichten, Überblickstafeln und Landkarten zur alt- und neutestamentlichen Zeit* (Neukirchen-Vluyn, 1985).
Olshausen, E., Wagner, J., and Stahl, W. *Kleinasien und Schwarzmeergebiet — Das Zeitalter Mithridates' I d. Gr. (121-63 v. Chr.). TAVO* B V 6 (Wiesbaden, 1981).
Pill-Rademacher, I., Podes, S., Rademacher, R., Wagner, J., and Pohlmann, H. *Vorderer Orient — Römer und Parther (14-138 n. Chr.). TAVO* B V 8 (Wiesbaden, 1988).
Rademacher, R., and Schlaich, F. *Die römischen Provinzen Palaestina und Arabien (70-305 n. Chr.). TAVO* B V 17.2 (Wiesbaden, 1988).
Stählin, G., and Höhne, E. *Der östliche Mittelmeerraum zur Zeit des Apostels Paulus. Beilage zu BHH* (Göttingen, [2]1968).

Wagner, J., and Stahl, W. *Östlicher Mittelmeerraum und Mesopotamien — Die Neuordnung des Orients von Pompeius bis Augustus (67 v. Chr.-14 n. Chr.). TAVO* B V 7 (Wiesbaden, 1983).

Church Fathers:

Altaner, B., and Stuiber, A. *Patrologie. Leben, Schriften und Lehre der Kirchenväter* (Freiburg,[8]1980).
Berardino, A. *Patrology* IV (Westminster, MD, 1986).
Quasten, A. *Patrology* I-III (Westminster, MD, 1950-66).
Zahn, T. "Ein Kompendium der biblischen Prophetie aus der afrikanischen Kirche um 305-325." *Geschichtliche Studien für Albert Hauck* (Leipzig, 1916) 52-63.

Lexika:

Bauer, W., Andt, W. F., Gingrich, F. W., and Danker, F. *A Greek-English Lexicon of the New Testament and Other Early Christian Literature* ([2]1979).
———. *Wörterbuch zum Neuen Testament* (Berlin, [5]1963).
———. *Wörterbuch zum Neuen Testament.* Edited by K. Aland and B. Aland (Berlin/New York, [6]1988).
Liddell, H. G., Scott, R., and Jones, H. S. *A Greek-English Lexicon.* New ed. (Oxford, 1968).
Petersen, L. *Prosopographia Imperii Romani. Saec. I.II.III,* Pars IV, Fasc. 3 (Berlin, 1966).
Rohden, P. von, and Dessau, H. *Prosopographia Imperii Romani. Saec. I.II.III.,* Pars III (Berlin, 1898).
Spicq, C. *Theological Lexicon of the New Testament* I-III (Eng. trans., Peabody, Mass., 1994).
Stein, A., and Petersen, L. *Prosopographia Imperii Romani. Saec. I.II.III,* vol. IV (Berlin, [2]1952-1966).

Livius:

Weissenborg, W., and Müller, M. *Livius* I-IV (repr., Leipzig, 1959).

Lucianus of Samosata:

Harmon, A. M. *Lucianus of Samosata* I-VII, *LCL* (London, 1913-).

Maccabees:

Kappler, W. *Maccabaeorum liber 1. SSLG* IX/1 (Göttingen, 1936).
Kappler, W., and Hanhart, R. *Maccabaeorum libri 2-3. SSLG* IX/2 (Göttingen, 1965).

Malalas:

Jeffreys, E., Jeffreys, M., and Scott, R. *The Chronicle of John Malalas: A Translation. Byzantina Australiensia* 4 (Melbourne, 1986).
Schenk von Stauffenberg, A. *Die Römische Kaisergeschichte bei Malalas. Griechischer Text der Bücher IX-XII und Untersuchungen* (Stuttgart, 1931).

Martyrologies:

Delehaye, H. *Commentarius Perpetuus in Martyrologium Hieronymianum.* In *ActaSS.Nov* II/1 (Brussels, 1931).
———. *Martyrologium Romanum.* In *Propylaeum ad ActaSS.Dec* (Brussels, 1940).
Dubois, J. *Le Martyrologe d'Usuard. Texte et Commentaire. SHG* 40 (Brussels, 1965).
Lietzmann, H. *Die drei ältesten Martyrologien. KlT* 2 (Bonn, 1903).

Coinage:

Aulock, H. von *Münzen und Städte Lykaoniens. Istanbuler Mitteilungen.* Beiheft 16 (1976).

Burnett, A. "The Coinage of King Agrippa I of Judaea and a New Coin of King Herod of Chalcis." In H. Huvelin, M. Christol, and G. Gautier, *Mélanges de numismatique offerts à Pierre Bastien* (Wetteren, 1987) 25-38.

Gaebler, H. *Die antiken Münzen von Makedonia und Paionia. Die antiken Münzen Nordgriechenlands* III/1-2 (Berlin, 1906 and 1935).

Grueber, H. A. *Coins of the Roman Republic in the British Museum* I (London, 1910).

Hill, G. F. *Catalogue of the Greek Coins of Palestine in the British Museum* (London, 1914).

Meshorer, Y. *Jewish Coins of the Second Temple Period* (Modern Hebrew) (Tel Aviv, 1966).

————. *Nabataean Coins. Qedem* 3 (Jerusalem, 1975).

————. *Ancient Jewish Coinage* II (Jerusalem, 1982).

————. *City-Coins of Eretz-Israel and the Decapolis in the Roman Period* (Jerusalem, 1985).

Mionnet, T. E. *Descriptions de médailles antiques, Grecques et Romaines, avec leur degré de rareté et leur estimation* V (Paris, 1811).

Saulcy, F. de. *Numismatique de la Terre Sainte* (Paris, 1874).

Spijkerman, A. *The Coins of the Decapolis and Provincia Arabia.* Edited and with historical and geographical introductions by M. Piccirillo. *SBFCMa* 25 (Jerusalem, 1978).

Sternberg, F. *Antike Münzen. Auktion Zürich* (25-26 November 1976).

Wroth, W. *Catalogue of the Greek Coins of Galatia, Cappadocia, and Syria in the British Museum* (London, 1899).

Nag Hammadi:

Robinson, J. M., ed. *The Nag Hammadi Library in English* (San Francisco, [2]1988).

New Testament:

Aland, K. *Vollständige Konkordanz zum griechischen Neuen Testament* II: *Spezialübersichten* (Berlin/New York, 1978).

Aland, K., and Aland, B. *The Text of the New Testament* (Eng. trans., rev. ed., Grand Rapids, 1989).

Aland, K., Black, M., *et al. Novum Testamentum Graece* (Stuttgart, [26]1979).

Blass, F., Debrunner, A. *Grammatik des neutestamentlichen Griechisch.* Edited by F. Rehkopf (Göttingen, [15]1979).

Blass, F., Debrunner, A., and Funk, R. W. *A Greek Grammar of the New Testament and Other Early Christian Literature* (Chicago, 1961).

Dickerson, G. F., ed. *Paul the Apostle and Pauline Literature: A Bibliography Selected from the ATLA Religion Database* (Chicago, [3]1982).

Mattill, A. J., and Mattill, M. B. *A Classified Bibliography of Literature on the Acts of the Apostles. NTTS* 7 (Leiden, 1966).

Metzger, B. M. *Index to Periodical Literature on the Apostle Paul. NTTS* 1 (Leiden, [2]1970).

————. *A Textual Commentary on the Greek New Testament* (London/New York, [2]1975).

Origen:

Koetschau, P. *Origenes II-III: Gegen Celsus. GCS* (Leipzig, 1899).

Orosius:

Lippold, A., and Andresen, C. *Die antike Weltgeschichte in christlicher Sicht* I-II (Zurich/Munich, 1985 and 1986).

425

Zangemeister, C. *Pauli Orosii, Historiarum adversum paganos libri VII rec. et commentario critico instruxit. CSEL* V (Vienna, 1882).

Papias:
Kürzinger, J. "Papias von Hierapolis und die Evangelien des Neuen Testaments." Eichstätter Materialien 4 (Regensburg, 1983) 89-138 (new edition and translation of the fragments).

Papyri:
Bell, H. I. *Jews and Christians in Egypt. The Jewish Troubles in Alexandria and the Athanasian Controversy: Illustrated by Texts from Greek Papyri in the British Museum* (Oxford, 1924).
Boak, A. E. R. "Papyri from Tebtunis 1,1." *Michigan Papyri* I (Ann Arbor, 1933).
Husselman, E. M. "Papyri from Tebtunis 2." *Michigan Papyri* V (Ann Arbor, 1944).
Hunt, A., *et al. Catalogue of the Greek Papyri in the John Rylands Library at Manchester* (Manchester, 1891-).
Tcherikover, V. A., and Fuks, A. *Corpus Papyrorum Judaicarum* I-III (Cambridge, Mass., 1957-1964).

Acts of Paul:
Gebhardt, O. von. *Passio S. Theclae Virginis. Die lateinischen Übersetzungen der Acta Pauli et Theclae. TU* N.S. 7.2 (Leipzig, 1902).
Schneemelcher, W., and Kasser, R. *The Acts of Paul* (NTApoc II, 213-70).

Gospel of Peter:
Mara, M. G. *Évangile de Pierre. Introduction, texte critique, traduction, commentaire et index. SC* 201 (Paris, 1973).
Maurer, C., and Schneemelcher, W. "The Gospel of Peter" (NTApoc I, 216-27).

Philo:
Cohn, L., and Wendland, P. *Philo von Alexandrien: Opera quae supersunt* I-VII (Berlin, 1896-1930).
Colson, F. H. *Philo X: The Embassy to Gaius. LCB* 379 (London, 1971).
Smallwood, E. M. *Philonis Alexandrini Legatio ad Gaium* (Leiden, [2]1970).

Pliny the Elder:
Detlefsen, D. *C. Plinii Secundi Naturalis Historia* I/II (Berlin, 1866/67).
Rackham, H., *et al. Pliny the Elder* I-X (London, 1938-1962).

Plutarch:
Babbit, F. C. *Plutarch's Moralia* IV-V. *LCL* (London, 1962).

Polybius:
Paton, W. R. *Polybios* I-VI. *LCL* (London, 1922-1927).

Old Testament Pseudepigrapha:
Charlesworth, J. H., ed. *The Old Testament Pseudepigrapha* I, II (New York, 1983, 1985).
Dupont-Sommer, A., and Philonenko, M. *La Bible. Écrits intertestamentaires* (Paris, 1987).
Riessler, P. *Altjüdisches Schrifttum außerhalb der Bibel* (Heidelberg, 1928; repr., [4]1982).

Pseudo-Clementines:

Irmscher, J., and Strecker, G. "The Pseudo-Clementines" (NTApoc II, 483-541).

Rehm, B., and Irmscher, I. *Pseudoclementinen* I: *Homilien. GCS* 42 (Berlin, 1953).

Rehm, B., and Paschke, F. *Pseudoclementinen* II: *Recognitionen in Rufins Übersetzung. GCS* 51 (Berlin, 1965).

Ptolemaeus (Gnostic):

Quispel, G. *Ptolemée: Lettre à Flora. SC* 26 (Paris, 1966).

Qumran:

Charlesworth, J. H. *Graphic Concordance to the Dead Sea Scrolls* (Tübingen/Louisville, 1991).

García Martínez, F. *The Dead Sea Scrolls Translated: The Qumran Texts in English* (Grand Rapids, [2]1996).

Jonge, M. de, and Woude, A. S. van der. "11Qmelchizedeq and the New Testament." *NTS* 12 (1965/66) 301-26.

Kuhn, K. G. *Konkordanz zu den Qumrantexten* (Göttingen, 1960).

Lohse, E., *Die Texte aus Qumran* (Hebrew-German) (Munich, [4]1986).

Milik, J. T. "Milkî-sedeq et Milkî-rešaʿ dans les anciens écrits juifs et chrétiens." *JJS* 23 (1972) 95-144.

Puech, É. "Notes sur le manuscript de 11QMelkîsédeq." *RQ* 12 (1987) 483-514.

Trever, J. C. *Scrolls from Qumrân Cave 1: The Great Isaiah Scroll. The Order of the Community. The Pesher to Habakkuk* (Jerusalem, 1972).

Rabbinic Literature:

Beer, G., Holtzmann, O., Krauss, S., *et al. Die Mischna. Text, Übersetzung und ausführliche Erklärung* (Gießen/Berlin, 1912-).

Danby, H. *The Mishnah, Translated from the Hebrew with Introduction and Brief Explanatory Notes* (Oxford, 1933).

Epstein, I. *Babylonian Talmud* I-XXXVI (New York, 1935-48).

Ginsburger, M. *Targum Jeruschalmi I: Targum Pseudojonathan* (Berlin, 1903).

Goldschmidt, L. *Der babylonische Talmud.* Berlin I-XII (Berlin, 1929-1936).

Strack, H. L., and Billerbeck, P. *Kommentar zum Neuen Testament aus Talmud und Midrasch* I: *Das Evangelium nach Mattäus* (Munich, [5]1969) (= 1926); II: *Das Evangelium nach Markus, Lukas und Johannes und die Apostelgeschichte* (Munich, [5]1969) (= 1924); III: *Die Briefe des Neuen Testaments und die Offenbarung Johannis* (Munich, [5]1969) (= 1926); V/VI: *Rabbinischer Index. Verzeichnis der Schriftgelehrten. Geographisches Register.* Edited by J. Jeremias (Munich, [4]1974).

Seneca:

Rouse, W. H. D. *Apocolocyntosis* (London, 1969).

Strabo:

Jones, H. L. *The Geography of Strabo* I-VIII (London, 1917-).

Suetonius:

Ailloud, H. *Suétone: Vies des Douzes Césars* II (Tibère-Caligula-Claude-Néron) (Paris, 1957).

Heinemann, M. *Cäsarenleben (übertragen und erläutert)* (Stuttgart, 1986).

Howard, A. A., and Jackson, C. N. *Index verborum C. Suetonii Tranquilli stilique eius proprietatum nonnularum* (Cambridge, Mass., 1922).
Mottershead, J. *Suetonius: Claudius* (Bristol, 1986).
Rolfe, J. C. *Suetonius* I-II (London, 1951).
Wittstock, O. *Sueton. Kaiserbiographien.* SQAW 39 (Berlin, 1993).

Sulpicius Severus:
Halm, C. *Sulpicius Severus: Chronica. CSEL* 1 (Vienna, 1866).

Syncellus:
Dindorf, W. *Syncellus Chronographia, Corpus scriptorum historiae Byzantiniae* (Bonn, 1829).

Syriac Texts:
Cureton, W., *Ancient Syriac Documents relative to the earliest establishment of Christianity in Edessa and the neighbouring countries, from the year after our Lord's ascension to the beginning of the fourth century* (Edinburgh/London, 1864).

Tacitus:
Borst, J., and Hross, H. *Historien. Lateinisch-Deutsch* (Munich, 1959).
Moore, C. H., and Jackson, J. *Histories — Annals* I (London, 1959).
Koestermann, E. *Annalen* I-IV (Heidelberg, 1963-1968).
Nipperdey, K., and Andresen, G. *Annalen* (Berlin, 1904).

Testaments of the Twelve Patriarchs:
Becker, J. *Die Testamente der zwölf Patriarchen. JSHRZ* III/1 (Gütersloh, ²1980).
Kee, H. C. "Testaments of the Twelve Patriarchs." In J. H. Charlesworth. *The Old Testament Pseudepigrapha* I (Garden City, 1983) 775-828.

Anthologies:
Barrett, C. K., ed. *The New Testament Background: Selected Documents* (New York, 1961, ²1987).
Barrett, C. K., and Thornton, C. J. *Texte zur Umwelt des Neuen Testaments. UTB* 1591 (Tübingen, 1991).
Ehrenberg, V., and Jones, A. H. M. *Documents Illustrating the Reigns of Augustus and Tiberius* (Oxford, 1949).
Horsley, G. H. R. *New Documents Illustrating Early Christianity. A Review of the Greek Inscriptions and Papyri, Macquarie University* I (1981), II (1982), III (1983), IV (1987), V (1989), VI (1992), VII (1996), VIII (1997).
Meijer, F., and Nijf, O. van. *Trade, Transport, and Society in the Ancient World: A Sourcebook* (London/New York, 1992).
Preuschen, E. *Analecta. Kurze Texte zur Geschichte der Alten Kirche und des Kanons* II (Leipzig, ²1910).
Reinach, T. *Textes dúteurs Grecs et Romains relatifs au Judaïsme. Réunis, traduits et annotés* (Paris, 1895; repr. Hildesheim, 1963).
Smallwood, E. M. *Documents Illustrating the Principates of Gaius, Glaudius and Nero* (Cambridge, 1967).
Stern, M. *Greek and Latin Authors on Jews and Judaism* I: *From Herodotus to Plutarch;* II: *From Tacitus to Simplicius* (Jerusalem, 1976 and 1980).
White, L. J. *Light from Ancient Letters* (Philadelphia, 1986).

Whittaker, M., *Jews and Christians: Graeco-Roman Views. Cambridge Commentaries in Writings of the Jewish and Christian World 200 BC to AD 200* (Cambridge, 1984).

Velleius Paterculus:
Stegmann, C. *Velleius Paterculus* (Leipzig, [2]1933).

2. Commentaries

Adinolfi, M. *La prima lettera ai Tessalonicesi nel mondo greco-romano. BPAA* 31 (Rome, 1990).

Allo, E. B. *Saint Paul: Seconde épître aux Corinthiens. ÉBib* (Paris, 1937).

Arrington, F. L. *The Acts of the Apostles: An Introduction and Commentary* (Peabody, Mass., 1988).

Bachmann, P. *Der zweite Brief des Paulus an die Korinther. KNT* 8 (Leipzig, [3]1918).

Barrett, C. K. *The Gospel According to St. John* (London, [2]1978).

———. *A Commentary on the Epistle of the Romans. BNTC* 6 (London, 1957).

———. *The Acts of the Apostles I: Preliminary Introduction and Commentary on Acts I-XIV. ICC* (Edinburgh, 1994).

Bassin, F. *Les épîtres de Paul aux Thessaloniciens. Commentaire Évangélique de la Bible* 13 (Vaux, 1991).

Bengel, J. A. *Gnomon Novi Testamenti. Editio Tertia.* Edited by E. Bengel (Tübingen, 1855). Eng. trans., *Gnomon of the New Testament* (Philadelphia, 1860).

Best, E. *The First and Second Epistles to the Thessalonians. BNTC* 10 (London, [2]1977).

Betz, H. D. *Galatians: A Commentary on Paul's Letter to the Churches in Galatia. Hermeneia* (Philadelphia, 1979).

Bligh, J. *Galatians: A Discussion of St. Paul's Epistle. Householder Commentaries* 1 (London, 1970).

Bock, D. L. *Luke II: 9:51–24:53.* Baker Exegetical Commentary on the New Testament 3B (Grand Rapids, 1996).

Boismard, M.-É., and Lamouille, A. *Les actes des deux apôtres I: Introduction — Textes. EB* n.s. 12 (Paris, 1990).

———. *Les actes des deux apôtres II: Le sens des récits. EB* n.s. 13 (Paris, 1990).

———. *Les actes des deux apôtres III: Analyses littéraires. EB* n.s. 14 (Paris, 1990).

Bruce, F. F. *The Acts of the Apostles* (London, [2]1952; Grand Rapids/Leicester, [3]1990).

———. *1 and 2 Corinthians. NCeB* (London, 1971).

———. *1 and 2 Thessalonians. WBC* 45 (Waco, 1982).

———. *The Book of Acts. NIC* (London, 1988).

Burton, E. W. *The Epistles to the Galatians. ICC* (Edinburgh, 1921).

Calmet, A. *Commentaire littéral . . . L'Évangile de S. Matthieu* (Paris, 1725).

Calvin, J. *Commentarius in Epistolam Secundam ad Corinthios. Commentarius in Epistolam ad Galatas.* In G. Baum, E. Cunitz, and E. Reuss, eds. *Ioannis Calvini Opera Quae Supersunt Omnia.* Vol. L, *CR* 78 (Braunschweig, 1893).

Carrez, M., *La deuxième épître de Saint Paul aux Corinthiens. CNT* 8 (Geneva, 1986).

Collange, J. F. *L'épître de Saint Paul aux Philippiens. CNT* Xa (Neuchâtel, 1973). Eng. trans. *The Epistle of Saint Paul to the Philippians* (London, 1979).

Conzelmann, H. *Acts of the Apostles. Hermeneia* (Eng. trans., 1987).

Cranfield, C. E. B. *A Critical and Exegetical Commentary on the Epistle to the Romans* I *(Introduction and Commentary on Romans I–VIII);* II *(Commentary on Romans IX–XVI and Essays). ICC* (Edinburgh, 1975, 1979).

Delitzsch, F. *Biblical Commentary on the Prophecies of Isaiah* (Eng. trans., Grand Rapids, 1960).

Dewailly, L. M., and Rigaux, B. *Les Épîtres de Saint Paul aux Thessaloniciens. SB(J)* (Paris, ³1969).

Dibelius, M. *An die Thessalonicher I, II. An die Philipper. HNT* 13 (Tübingen, ²1937).

———. *The Pastoral Epistles* (Eng. trans., Philadelphia, 1972).

Dillmann, A. *Der Prophet Jesaja. KEH* V. Edited by R. Kittel (Leipzig, ⁶1898).

Dobschütz, E. von. *Die Thessalonicher-Briefe.* Edited by F. Hahn (Göttingen, ⁷1909; repr. 1974).

Duhm, B. *Das Buch Jesaja. HK* III/1 (Göttingen, ⁴1922).

Duncan, G. S. *The Epistle of Paul to the Galatians. MNTC* (London, 1934).

Dunn, J. D. G. *Romans 1-8.* WBC 38A (Dallas, 1988).

Dupont, J. *Les actes des apôtres. SB(J)* (Paris, 1954).

Fee, G. D. *The First Epistle to the Corinthians. NIC* (Grand Rapids, 1987).

Feldmann, F. *Das Buch Isaias II (Kap. 40–66). EHAT* XIV/2 (Münster, 1926).

Fischer, J. *Das Buch Isaias. HSAT* VII/1,2 (Bonn, 1939).

Fitzmyer, J. A.. *The Gospel According to Luke I–IX. AB* 28 (New York, 1981).

———. *Romans.* AnB 33 (New York, 1993).

Fohrer, G. *Das Buch Jesaja III: Kapital 40–66. ZBK* XIX/3 (Zurich, ²1986).

Frame, J. E. *A Critical and Exegetical Commentary on the Epistles of St. Paul to the Thessalonians. ICC* (Edinburgh, 1912).

Friedrich, G. *Der erste Brief an die Thessalonicher. Der zweite Brief an die Thessalonicher. NTD* 8 (Göttingen, ¹⁴1976) 203-76.

Fung, R. Y.-K. *The Epistle to the Galatians. NIC* (Grand Rapids, 1988).

Furnish, V. P. *II Corinthians. AB* 32/A (New York, 1984).

Galanis, J. L. Ἡ Πρώτη Ἐπιστολὴ τοῦ Ἀπ. Παύλου πρὸς Θεσσαλονίκεις. Ἑρμηνεία Καινῆς Διαθήκης 11a (Thessalonica, 1985).

Gnilka, J. *Der Philipperbrief. HTKNT* X/3 (Freiburg, ⁴1987).

Gundry, R. H. *Matthew* (Grand Rapids, 1982, ²1994).

———. *Mark: A Commentary on His Apology for the Cross* (Grand Rapids, 1993).

Guthrie, D. Galatians. *NCeB* (London, 1974).

Haenchen, E. *Der Weg Jesu. Eine Erklärung des Markus-Evangeliums und der kanonischen Parallelen* (Berlin, ²1968).

———. *Acts* (Eng. trans., Philadelphia, 1971).

Hawthorne, G. F. *Philippians. WBC* 43 (Waco, 1983).

Herbert, A. S. *The Book of the Prophet Isaiah (Chapters 40–66). CBC* (Cambridge, 1975).

Holtz, T. *Der erste Brief an die Thessalonicher. EKKNT* XIII (Zurich/Neukirchen-Vluyn, 1986, ²1990).

Jacquier, E. *Les Actes des Apôtres. ÉBib* (Paris, ²1926).

Juel, D. H. *I Thessalonians. Augsburg Commentary* (Minneapolis, 1985) 211-54.

Käsemann, E. *Commentary on Romans* (Eng. trans., Grand Rapids, 1980).

Kistemaker, S. J. *Exposition of the Acts of the Apostles. New Testament Commentary* (Grand Rapids, 1990).

Klauck, H. J. *2. Korintherbrief. NEB* 8 (Würzburg, 1986).

Klostermann, E. *Das Lukasevangelium. HNT* 5 (Tübingen, ²1929).

Knoch, O. *1. und 2. Thessalonicherbrief. EKKNT* 12 (Stuttgart, 1987).

Knowling, R. J. *The Acts of the Apostles. The Expositor's Greek Testament* II (London, 1912) 3-554.

Krodel, G. A. *Acts. Augsburg Commentary on the New Testament* (Minneapolis, 1986).

Lagrange, M. J. *Saint Paul. Épître aux Romains. ÉBib* (Paris, ²1922).

Lake, K. *The Earlier Epistles of Paul* (London, 1911; [2]1919).

Lang, F. *Die Briefe an die Korinther. NTD* 7 (Göttingen, 1986).

Laub, F. *1. und 2. Thessalonicherbrief. NEB* 13 (Würzburg, 1985).

Lenski, R. C. H. *The Interpretation of I and II Corinthians* (Minneapolis, 1937).

Lietzmann, H. *An die Korinther I/II. HNT* 9 (Tübingen, [4]1931).

Lightfoot, J. B. *The Epistle of St. Paul to the Galatians* (London, 1865; [10]1890; repr. Grand Rapids, 1969).

Longenecker, R. N. *The Acts of the Apostles.* In F. E. Gaebelein, *The Expositor's Bible Commentary* IX (Grand Rapids, 1981) 207-573.

————. *Galatians. WBC* 41 (Dallas, 1990).

Lührmann, D. *Galatians. Continental Commentaries* (Minneapolis, 1992).

————. *Das Markusevangelium. HNT* 3 (Tübingen, 1987).

Luther, M. *In epistolam S. Pauli ad Galatas Commentarius (1531). WA* 40 I-II.

Marshall, I. H. *The Gospel of Luke. NIGTC* (Grand Rapids, 1978).

————. *The Acts of the Apostles. TNTC* (Leicester, 1980).

————. *1 and 2 Thessalonians. NCeB* (London, 1983).

Marti, K. *Das Buch Jesaja. KHC* X (Tübingen, 1900).

Martin, R. P. *2 Corinthians. WBC* 40 (Waco, 1986).

Marxsen, W. *Der erste Brief an die Thessalonicher. ZBKNT* 11.1 (Zurich, 1979).

Merklein, H. *Der erste Brief an die Korinther (Kapitel 1–4). ÖTK* 7/1 (Gütersloh/Würzburg, 1992).

Michel, O. *Der Brief an die Römer. KEK* IV (Göttingen, [5]1977).

Milligan, G. *St. Paul's Epistles to the Thessalonians* (London, 1908).

Moffatt, J., *The First and Second Epistles to the Thessalonians.* In W. R. Nicoll, ed. *The Expositor's Greek Testament* IV (1910) 1-54.

Moore, A. L. *1 and 2 Thessalonians. NCeB* (London, 1969).

Morris, L. *The Epistles of Paul to the Thessalonians* (London, [2]1991).

Muilenburg, J. *The Book of Isaiah (Chapters 40–66). IB* V (New York/Nashville, 1956) 381-775.

Munck, J. *The Acts of the Apostles. AB* 31 (London, 1967).

Mussner, F. *Die Apostelgeschichte. NEB* 5 (Würzburg, 1984).

————. *Der Galaterbrief. HTKNT* IX (Freiburg, [5]1987).

Neil, W. *The Epistle* [sic] *of Paul to the Thessalonians. MNTC* 12 (London, 1950).

————. *The Acts of the Apostles. NCeB* (London, 1973).

Nösgen, C. F. *Commentar über die Apostelgeschichte des Lukas* (Leipzig, 1882).

O'Brien, P. T. *The Epistle to the Philippians. NIGTC* (Grand Rapids, 1991).

Oepke, A. *Der Brief des Paulus an die Galater.* Edited by J. Rohde. *THKNT* 9 (East Berlin, [4]1979).

Orchard, B. *Galatians.* In R. C. Fuller, *et al. A New Catholic Commentary on Holy Scripture* (London, 1969) 1173-80.

Palmer, E. F. *1 and 2 Thessalonians. A Good News Commentary* (San Francisco, 1983).

Pesch, R. *Das Markusevangelium I: Einleitung und Kommentar zu Kap. 1,1–8,26. HTKNT* II/1 (Freiburg, [4]1984).

————. *Das Markusevangelium II: Kommentar zu Kap. 8,27–16,20. HTKNT* II/2 (Freiburg, [3]1984).

————. *Römerbrief. NEB* 6 (Würzburg, 1983).

————. *Die Apostelgeschichte (Apg 1–12). EKKNT* V/1; *(Apg 13–28). EKKNT* V/2 (Zurich/Neukirchen-Vluyn, 1986).

Plumptre, E. H. *The Acts of the Apostles.* In C. J. Ellicott, ed. *Commentary on the Whole Bible* 7/8 (no date; repr. Grand Rapids, 1959).

Preuschen, E. *Die Apostelgeschichte. HNT* IV/1 (Tübingen, 1912).

Quinn, J. D. *The Letter to Titus.* Edited by P. Boelter. *AB* 35 (New York, 1990).

Ramsay, W. M. *A Historical Commentary on St. Paul's Epistle to the Galatians* (London, [2]1900).

Rehm, M. *Das erste Buch der Könige. Ein Kommentar* (Würzburg, 1979).

Rigaux, B. *Saint Paul: Les Épîtres aux Thessaloniciens. ÉBib* (Paris, 1956).

Rohde, J. *Der Brief des Paulus an die Galater. THKNT* 9 (East Berlin, 1989).

Roloff, J. *Die Apostelgeschichte. NTD* 5 (Göttingen, 1981).

Rolston, H. *The First and Second Letters of Paul to the Thessalonians. LBC* 23 (Atlanta, 1963) 7-52.

Sanday, W., and Headlam, A. C. *A Critical and Exegetical Commentary on the Letter to the Romans. ICC* (Edinburgh, [5]1902).

Schille, G. *Die Apostelgeschichte des Lukas. THKNT* 5 (East Berlin, 1983).

Schlatter, A. *Der Evangelist Johannes. Wie er spricht, denkt und glaubt* (Stuttgart, 1930; repr. [3]1960).

———. *Paulus, der Bote Jesu. Eine Deutung seiner Briefe an die Korinther* (Stuttgart, 1934).

Schlier, H. *Der Brief and die Galater. KEK* 7 (Göttingen, [5]1971).

———. *Der Apostel und seine Gemeinde. Auslegung des Ersten Briefes an die Thessalonicher* (Freiburg, [2]1973).

———. *Der Römerbrief. THKNT* VI (Freiburg, 1977).

Schmidt, P. *Der erste Thessalonicherbrief neu erklärt. Nebst einem Excurs über den zweiten gleichnamigen Brief* (Berlin, 1885).

Schmithals, W. *Die Apostelgeschichte des Lukas. ZBKNT* 3/2 (Zurich, 1982).

Schnackenburg, R. *The Gospel According to St. John* I (Eng. trans., New York, 1990).

Schneider, G. *Die Apostelgeschichte* I *(Kap. 1,1–8,40);* II *(Kap. 9,1–28,31). HTKNT* V/2 (Freiburg, 1980 and 1982).

Schrage, W. *Der erste Brief an die Korinther (1 Kor. 1,1–6,11). EKKNT* VII/1 (Zurich/ Neukirchen-Vluyn, 1991).

Schweizer, E. *The Letter to the Colossians* (Eng. trans., Minneapolis, 1982).

Speiser, E. A. *Genesis. AB* 1 (Garden City, 1964).

Spicq, C. *Saint Paul: Les Épîtres Pastorales II. ÉBib* (Paris, [4]1969).

Staab, K. *Die Thessalonicherbriefe.* In *RNT* 7 (Regensburg, [4]1964) 5-63.

Stählin, G. *Die Apostelgeschichte. NTD* 5 (Göttingen, [6]1978).

Steinmann, A. *Die Apostelgeschichte. HSNT* 4 (Bonn, [4]1934).

Strobel, A. *Der erste Brief an die Korinther. ZBKNT* VI/1 (Zurich, 1989).

Stuhlmacher, P. *Der Brief an Philemon. EKKNT* 18 (Zurich/Neukirchen-Vluyn, [2]1981).

———. *Paul's Letter to the Romans* (Eng. trans., Louisville, 1994).

Tarazi, P. N. *1 Thessalonians: A Commentary. Orthodox Biblical Study* (Chesterwood/New York, 1982).

Taylor, J. *Les actes des deux apôtres V: Commentaire historique (Act. 9,1–18,22).* EB n.s. 23 (Paris, 1994).

Thomas, R. L. *1 Thessalonians.* In F. E. Gaebelein, ed. *The Expositor's Bible Commentary* 11 (Grand Rapids, 1978) 227-98.

Wanamaker, C. A. *The Epistles to the Thessalonians: A Commentary on the Greek Text. NIGNTC* (Grand Rapids/Exeter, 1990).

Ward, R. A. *Commentary on 1 and 2 Thessalonians* (Waco, 1973).

Weiser, A. *Die Apostelgeschichte (Kapitel 1–12). ÖTK* 5/1 (Gütersloh, 1981).

Wendt, H. H. *Kritisch-exegetisches Handbuch über die Apostelgeschichte* (Göttingen, 1888).

Wenham, G. J. *Genesis 1–15. WBC* 1 (Waco, 1987).

Westermann, C. *Das Buch Jesaja (Kap. 40/-66). ATD* 19 (Göttingen, [5]1986).

————. *Isaiah 40–66* (Eng. trans., Philadelphia, 1969).

Whiteley, D. E. H. *Thessalonians (in the Revised Standard Edition). NCBNT* 7 (Oxford, 1969).

Wieseler, K. *Commentar über den Brief Pauli an die Galater (mit besonderer Rücksicht auf die Lehre und Geschichte des Apostels)* (Göttingen, 1859).

Wikenhauser, A. *Die Apostelgeschichte. RNT* 5 (Regensburg, 1938; [4]1961).

Wilckens, U. *Der Brief an die Römer. EKKNT* VI (Zurich/Neukirchen-Vluyn), I *(Röm. 1–5)* (1978); III *(Röm. 12–16)* (1982).

Williams, C. S. C. *The Acts of the Apostles. BNTC* (London, [2]1964).

Williams, D. J. *1 and 2 Thessalonians. New International Biblical Commentary* 12 (Peabody, Mass., 1992).

Wohlenberg, G. *Der erste und zweite Thessalonicherbrief. KNT* 12 (Leipzig, [2]1909).

Wolff, C. *Der erste Brief des Paulus an die Korinther.* ThHK 6 (Berlin, 1996).

Zahn, T. *Das Evangelium des Johannes. KNT* 4 (Leipzig, [5/6]1921).

————. *Der Brief des Paulus an die Römer. KNT* VI (Leipzig, [2]1910).

————. *Das Evangelium des Lucas. KNT* 3 (Leipzig, [3/4]1920).

————. *Die Apostelgeschichte des Lucas* I *(Kap. 1–12);* II *(Kap. 13–28). KNT* V/1-2 (Leipzig, [3/4]1927).

————. *Der Brief des Paulus an die Galater. KNT* 9 (Leipzig, 1905).

————. *Der Brief des Paulus an die Galater.* Edited by F. Hauck. *KNT* 9 (Erlangen, [3]1922; repr. Gießen, 1990).

3. Monographs

Abbott, E. A. "John ii.20. Τεσσεράκοντα καὶ ἓξ ἔτεσιν οἰκοδομήθη ὁ ναὸς οὗτος." *CIR* 8 (1895) 89-93.

Abel, F. M. *Géographie de la Palestine II: Géographie politique. Les villes* (Paris, 1938).

Abel, K. "Seneca. Leben und Leistung." *ANRW* II 32.2 (Berlin/New York, 1985) 653-730.

Aberbach, M. "The Conflicting Accounts of Josephus and Tacitus Concerning Cumanus' and Felix' Terms of Office." *JQR* 40 (1949/50) 1-14.

Aberle, J. "Chronologie des Apostels Paulus von seiner Bekehrung bis zur Abfassung des Galaterbriefes." *BZ* 1 (1903) 256-79, 373-77.

————. "Chronologie des Apostels Paulus vom Apostelkonzile bis zum Märtyrertode des Apostels in Rom." *BZ* 3 (1905) 371-400.

Achtemeier, P. J. "An Elusive Unity: Paul, Acts, and the Early Church." *CBQ* 48 (1986) 1-26.

Adams, J. P. "Topeiros Thraciae, the Via Egnatia and the Boundaries of Macedonia." *AncMac* IV (Thessalonica, 1986) 17-42.

Adinolfi, M. "Giscala e San Paolo." *Ant* 41 (1966) 366-73.

————. "Etica 'commerciale' e motivi parenetici in 1 Tess. 4,1-8." *BeO* 19 (1977) 9-20.

Aejmelaeus, L. *Wachen vor dem Ende. Die traditionsgeschichtlichen Wurzeln von 1. Thess 5:1-11 und Luk 21:34-36. Schriften der Finnischen Exegetischen Gesellschaft* 44 (Helsinki, 1985).

Aland, K. "Glosse, Interpolation, Redaktion und Komposition in der Sicht der neutestamentlichen Textkritik." *Studien zur Überlieferung des Neuen Testaments und seines Textes. ANTT* 2 (Berlin) 35-57.

Albertz, M. *Die Botschaft des Neuen Testaments I/2: Die Entstehung des apostolischen Schriftenkanons* (Zurich, 1952).

Aletti, J. N. "La disposition rhétorique dans les épîtres pauliniens: proposition de méthode." *NTS* 38 (1992) 385-401.

Alexander, L. "Luke's Preface in the Context of Greek Preface-Writing." *NT* 28 (1986) 48-74.

———. "Chronology." In G. F. Hawthorne et al., eds. *Dictionary of Paul and His Letters* (Downers Grove and Leicester, 1993) 115-23.

Allen, R. *Missionary Methods: St. Paul's or Ours?* (London, ⁴1956).

Allo, E. B. "La portée de la collecte pour Jérusalem dans les plans de saint Paul." *RB* 45 (1936) 529-37.

Andresen, C. *Einleitung zu: Paulus Orosius: Die antike Weltgeschichte in christlicher Sicht I (Buch I-IV)* (Zurich/Munich, 1985) 5-57.

Andronicos, M. *Museum Thessaloniki. Ein neuer Führer durch seine Bestände* (Athens, 1988).

Applebaum, S. "The Legal Status of the Jewish Communities in the Diaspora." *CRINT* I/1 (Assen, 1974) 420-63.

———. "The Social and Economic Status of the Jews in the Diaspora." *CRINT* I/2 (Assen, 1976) 701-27.

Armogathe, J. R. *Paul ou l'impossible unité* (n.p. [Paris], 1980).

Armstrong, W. P., and Finegan, J. "Chronology of the New Testament." *ISBE* I (Grand Rapids, 1979) 686-93.

Askwith, E. H. " 'I' and 'We' in the Thessalonian Epistles." *Exp* 8th ser. 1 (1911) 149-59.

Atkinson, J. E. "Seneca's 'Consolatio ad Polybium'." *ANRW* II 32/2 (Berlin/New York, 1985) 860-84.

Aune, D. E. *Prophecy in Early Christianity and the Mediterranean World* (Grand Rapids, 1983).

———. *The New Testament in Its Literary Environment. Library of Early Christianity* 8 (Philadelphia, 1987).

Aus, R. D. "Paul's Travel Plans to Spain and the 'Full Number of the Gentiles' of Rom. XI 25." *NT* 21 (1979) 232-62.

Axenfeld, K. "Die jüdische Propaganda als Vorläuferin und Wegbereiterin der urchristlichen Mission." *Missionswissenschaftliche Studien. Festschrift zum 70. Geburtstag von Gustav Warneck* (Berlin, 1904) 1-80.

Baasland, E. "Persecution: A Neglected Feature in the Letter to the Galatians." *ST* 38 (1984) 135-50.

———. "Die περί-Formel und die Argumentation(ssituation) des Paulus." *ST* 42 (1988) 69-88.

Bacchiocchi, S. "Rome and Christianity until A.D. 62." *AUSS* 21 (1983) 3-25.

Bacon, B. W. "A Criticism of the New Chronology of Paul." *Exp* V/10 (1899) 351-430.

———. "Acts versus Galatians: The Crux of Apostolic History." *AJT* 11 (1907) 454-74.

Badcock, F. J. *The Pauline Epistles (and the Epistle to the Hebrews) in Their Historical Setting* (London, 1937).

Bagatti, B. "Ricerche su alcuni antichi siti Giudeo-Cristiani." *LA* 11 (1960/61) 288-314.

———. *Antichi villaggi cristiani di Galilea. SBFCMi* 13 (Jerusalem, 1971).

———. "Nuove testimonianze sul luogo della lapidazione de S. Stefano." *Ant* 49 (1974) 527-32.

———. *Recherches sur le site du Temple de Jérusalem (Iᵉʳ-VIIᵉ siècle). SBFCMi* 22 (Jerusalem, 1979).

Bailey, J. W. "Paul's Second Missionary Journey." *BW* 33 (1909) 414-23.

Bakalakis, G. "Therme-Thessaloniki." Antike Kunst Beiheft 1 (1963) 30-34.

———. "Ἱερὸ Διόνυσος καὶ φαλλικὰ δρώμενα στὴ Θεσσαλονίκη." AncMac III (Thessalonica, 1983) 31-43.

Baker, D. W. "Lud." ABD IV (New York, 1992) 397.

———. "Meshech." Ibid., 711.

———. "Put." ABD V (New York, 1992) 560.

———. "Tarshish (Place)." ABD VI (New York, 1992) 331-33.

———. "Tubal." Ibid., 670.

Bakirtzis, C. "D'une porte inconnue des remparts occidentaux de Thessalonique." BalS 14 (1972) 303-7.

———. "Περὶ τοῦ συγκροτήματος τῆς ἀγορᾶς τῆς Θεσσαλονίκης." AncMac II (Thessalonica, 1977) 257-604.

Baldwin, B. Suetonius (Amsterdam, 1983).

Ballance, M. H. "Derbe and Faustinopolis." AnSt 14 (1964) 139-45.

Balmer, H. Die Romfahrt des Apostels Paulus (Bern, 1905).

Balsdon, J. P. V. D. Romans and Aliens (London, 1979).

———. The Early Roman Empire and the Rise of Christianity 1-3: The Historical Background (Walton Hall, [2]1980).

Balter, S. "Put." EJ 13 (New York, 1973) 1414f.

Balz, H. "Παῦλος." EDNT III (1993) 59-62.

Bammel, E. "Philos tou Kaisaros." TLZ 77 (1952) 205-10.

———. "Judenverfolgung und Naherwartung. Zur Eschatologie des Ersten Thessalonicherbriefs." ZTK 56 (1959) 294-315.

———. "Jewish Activity against Christians in Palestine according to Acts." In R. Bauckham. The Book of Acts in Its Palestinian Setting. A1CS IV (Grand Rapids and Carlisle, 1995) 357-64.

Barbaglio, G. Paolo di Tarso e le origini Cristiane. Commenti e studi Biblici (Assisi, 1985).

Barclay, J. M. G. "Thessalonica and Corinth: Social Contrasts in Pauline Christianity." JSNT 47 (1992) 49-74.

Bardon, H. Les empereurs et les lettres latines d'Auguste à Hadrien (Paris, 1940).

Bardy, G. "Cérinthe." RB 30 (1921) 344-73.

———. "Le souvenir de Josèphe chez les Pères." RHE 43 (1948) 179-91.

Barnard, P. M. "Note on Acts IX.19ff." Exp V/9 (1899) 317-20.

Barnes, A. S. Christianity at Rome in the Apostolic Age: An Attempt at Reconstruction of History (London, 1938).

Barnes, T. D. "Legislation against the Christians." JRS 58 (1968) 32-50.

———. "The Date of Herod's Death." JTS 19 (1968) 204-9.

Barnett, P. W. "Ἀπογραφή and ἀπογράφεσθαι in Luke 2:1-5." ET 85 (1973/74) 377-80.

———. "'Under Tiberius All Was Quiet'." NTS 21 (1975) 564-71.

———. "The Jewish Sign Prophets — A.D. 40-70 — Their Intentions and Origins." NTS 27 (1981) 679-97.

Barnikol, E. Die vorchristliche und frühchristliche Zeit des Paulus. Nach seinen geschichtlichen und geographischen Selbstzeugnissen im Galaterbrief. FEUNTK 1 (Kiel, 1929).

———. Die drei Jerusalemreisen des Paulus. Die echte Konkordanz der Paulusbriefe mit der Wir-Quelle der Apostelgeschichte. FEUNTK 2 (Kiel, 1929).

———. Personen-Probleme der Apostelgeschichte. Johannes Markus, Silas und Titus. Untersuchungen zur Struktur der Apostelgeschichte und zur Verfasserschaft der Wir-Quelle. FEUNTK 3 (Kiel, 1931).

———. Römer 15. Letzte Reiseziele des Paulus: Jerusalem, Rom und Antiochien. Eine

Voruntersuchung zur Entstehung des sogenannten Römerbriefes. FEUNTK 4 (Kiel, 1931).

―――. "War Damaskus um 37 n. Chr. arabisch? 2. Kor 11,32-33 und Gal 1,17." *ThJb(H)* 1 (1933) 93-95.

―――. *Die Christwerdung des Paulus in Galiläa und die Apostelberufung vor Damaskus und im Tempel. FEUNTK* 9 (Kiel, 1935).

―――. "Kam Paulus vor Pfingsten zu Petrus? Die Entstehung der Hellenisten-Gemeinde in Jerusalem *nach* 40 n. Chr. um 42 n. Chr. und ihre Zerstreuung nach dem Martyrium des Stephanus *vor* 45 n. Chr. um 44 n. Chr." *ThJb(H)* n.s. 1 (1956) 16-20.

Barrett, A. "Chronological Errors in Dio's Account of the Claudian Invasion." *Britannica* 11 (1980) 31-35.

―――. *Caligula: The Corruption of Power* (London, 1989).

Barrett, C. K. "Titus." *Essays on Paul* (London, 1989) 118-31.

―――. "Paul Shipwrecked." In B. P. Thompson, ed. *Scripture and Meaning: Essays Presented to Anthony Tyrrell Hanson* (Hull, 1987) 51-64.

―――. "Paulus als Missionar und Theologe." *ZTK* 86 (1989) 18-32.

Barrois, A. "Damas." *DBS* II (Paris, 1934) 275-87.

Barrois, G. A. "Trade and Commerce." *IDB* IV (New York/Nashville, 1962) 677-83.

Bartlett, J. R. "From Edomites to Nabataeans: A Study in Continuity." *PEQ* 111 (1979) 53-66.

Bartlett, V. "Some Points in Pauline Chronology." *Exp* V/10 (1899) 263-80.

Baslez, M. F. *Saint Paul* (Paris, 1991).

Bauckham, R. "Barnabas in Galatians." *JSNT* 2 (1979) 61-70.

―――. "James and the Jerusalem Church." In R. Bauckham. *The Book of Acts in Its Palestinian Setting.* A1CS IV (Grand Rapids and Carlisle, 1995) 415-80.

Bauer, K. *Antiochia in der ältesten Kirchengeschichte* (Tübingen, 1919).

Baugh, S. M. *Paul and Ephesus: The Apostle among his Contemporaries* (diss., University of California, 1990).

Baum, A. D. *Lukas als Historiker der letzten Jesusreise* (Wuppertal/Zurich, 1993).

Bauman, R. A. *Impietas in Principem* (Munich, 1974).

Baumert, N. "Brautwerbung — das einheitliche Thema von 1 Thess 4,3-8." In R. F. Collins, ed. *The Thessalonian Correspondence.* BETL 87 (Leuven, 1990) 316-39.

Baumgarten, J. *Paulus und die Apokalyptik. Die Auslegung apokalyptischer Überlieferungen in den echten Paulusbriefen.* WMANT 44 (Neukirchen-Vluyn, 1975).

Baur, F. C. *Paul, The Apostle of Jesus Christ: His Life and Work, His Epistles and His Doctrine* (Eng. trans., London, 1876).

Bean, G. *Turkey's Southern Shore. An Archaeological Guide* (New York, 1968).

Beare, F. W. "Note on Paul's First Visit to Jerusalem." *FBL* 63 (1944) 407-10.

Beatrice, P. F. "Apollos of Alexandria and the Origins of Jewish-Christian Baptist Encratism." In W. Hasse. *ANRW* II 26/2 (Berlin and New York, 1995) 1232-75.

Bebber, J. van. *Zur Chronologie des Lebens Jesu* (Münster, 1898).

Becker, J. "Paulus und seine Gemeinden." *Die Anfänge des Christentums* (Stuttgart, 1987) 102-59.

―――. *Paul: Apostle to the Gentiles* (Eng. trans., Louisville, 1993).

Beckwith, R. T. "The Significance of the Calendar for Interpreting Essene Chronology and Eschatology." *RQ* 10 (1980/81) 167-202.

―――. "Daniel 9 and the Date of Messiah's Coming in Essene, Hellenistic, Pharisaic, Zealot, and Early Christian Computation." *RQ* 10 (1980/81) 521-42.

―――. "Cautionary Notes on the Use of Calendars and Astronomy to Determine the

Chronology of the Passion." In J. Vardaman and E. M. Yamauchi. *Chronos, Kairos, Christos. Nativity and Chronological Studies Presented to Jack Finegan* (Winona Lake, 1989) 183-205.

Beitzel, B. "Travel and Communication (Old Testament World)." *ABD* VI (New York, 1992) 644-48.

Beker, J. C. *Paul the Apostle: The Triumph of God in Life and Thought* (Philadelphia, 1980).

————. "Paul's Theology: Consistent or Inconsistent?" *NTS* 34 (1988) 364-77.

Bell, H. I. "Evidence of Christianity in Egypt during the Roman Period." *HTR* 37 (1944) 185-208.

Belser, J. E. "Pauli Reisen nach Korinth." *TQ* 76 (1894) 15-47.

————. "Zur Chronologie des Paulus." *TQ* 80 (1898) 353-79.

————. *Einleitung in das Neue Testament* (Freiburg, ²1905).

Bender, H. *Römischer Reiseverkehr. Cursus publicus und Privatreisen. Kleine Schriften zur Kenntnis der römischen Besetzungsgeschichte Südwestdeutschlands* 20 (Aalen, 1978).

Bengel, J. A. *Ordo temporum* (Stuttgart, ²1770).

Bengston, H. *Römische Geschichte. Republik und Kaiserzeit bis 284 n. Chr.* (Munich, ²1973).

Benko, S. "The Edict of Claudius of A.D. 49 and the Instigator Chrestus." *TZ* 25 (1969) 407-18.

————. "Pagan Criticism of Christianity during the First Two Centuries." *ANRW* II 23.2 (Berlin/New York, 1980) 1055-1118.

————. *Pagan Rome and the Early Christians* (Bloomington, 1986).

Bennett, C. T. "Paul the Pragmatist: Another Look at His Missionary Methods." *EMQ* 16 (1980) 133-38.

Benoit, P. "La deuxième visite de Saint Paul à Jérusalem." *Bibl* 40 (1959) 778-92.

————. "Quirinus (Recensement de)." *DBS* VII (Paris, 1981) 693-720.

Benzinger, I. "Antiocheia 1 (am Orontes)." *PRE* 1 (Stuttgart, 1894) 2442-45.

Bérard, J. "Recherches sur les itinéraires de Saint Paul en Asie Mineure." *RArch* VI/5 (1935) 57-90.

Berger, K. "Almosen für Israel: Zum Historischen Kontext der Paulinischen Kollekte." *NTS* 23 (1977) 180-203.

Bering-Staschewski, R. *Römische Zeitgeschichte bei Cassius Dio* (Bochum, 1981).

Bernard, J. H. "Traditionen über den Tod des Zebedäussohnes Johannes." In K. H. Rengstorf, ed. *Johannes und sein Evangelium. WdF* 82 (Darmstadt, 1973) 273-90.

Bernegger, P. M. "Affirmation of Herod's Death in 4 B.C." *JTS* 34 (1983) 526-31.

Bertrangs, A. "La vocation des gentils chez saint Paul. Exégèse et heuristique Pauliniennes des citations Vétéro-Testamentaires." *ETL* 30 (1954) 391-415.

Best, E. Review of R. Jewett, *Dating Paul's Life* (London, 1979). *SJT* 33 (1980) 487f.

Betz, H. D. "The Literary Composition and Function of Paul's Letter to the Galatians." *NTS* 21 (1975) 353-79.

————. "Galatians: Epistle to the." *ABD* II (New York, 1992) 872-75.

————. "Paul." *ABD* V (New York, 1992) 186-201.

Betz, O. "Die Vision des Paulus im Tempel von Jerusalem — Apg 22,17-21 als Beitrag zur Deutung des Damaskuserlebnisses." In O. Böcher and K. Haacker. *Verborum Veritas. Festschrift Gustav Stählin* (Wuppertal, 1970) 113-23.

————. "Probleme des Prozesses Jesu." *ANRW* II 25.1 (Berlin/New York, 1982) 565-647.

————. "Jesus in Nazareth. Bemerkungen zu Markus 6,1-6." *Jesus, der Messias Israels. Aufsätze zur biblischen Theologie. WUNT* 42 (Tübingen, 1987) 301-17.

437

————. "Kontakte zwischen Essenern und Christen." In B. Mayer, ed. *Christen und Christliches in Qumran? ESt* 32 (Regensburg, 1992) 157-75.

Betz, O., and Riesner, R. *Jesus, Qumran, and the Vatican: Clarifications* (London and New York, 1994).

Bickerman, E. J. "The Name of the Christians." *HTR* 42 (1949) 109-24 (repr. in *Studies in Jewish and Christian History. AGJU* 9 [Leiden 1986] 139-51).

————. *Chronologie* (Leipzig, ²1963).

————. *Chronology of the Ancient World, Aspects of Greek and Roman Life*. Edited by H. H. Scullard (London, 1968).

Bieringer, R. "Der 2. Korintherbrief in den neuesten Kommentaren." *ETL* 72 (1991) 107-30.

Bietenhard, H. "Die Dekapolis von Pompeius bis Traian. Ein Kapitel aus der neutestamentlichen Zeitgeschichte." *ZDPV* 79 (1963) 24-58.

————. "Die syrische Dekapolis von Pompeius bis Traian." *ANRW* II 8 (Berlin/New York, 1978) 220-61.

Bilde, P. "Josefus' berething om Jesus." *DTT* 44 (1981) 99-135.

Billerbeck, P. "Exkurs: Die Angaben der vier Evangelisten über den Todestag Jesu unter Berücksichtigung ihres Verhältnisses zur Halakha." In Billerbeck II (Munich, 1924) 812-53.

Binder, H. "Paulus und die Thessalonicherbriefe." In R. F. Collins, ed. *The Thessalonian Correspondence. BETL* 87 (Leuven, 1990) 87-93.

Birdsall, J. N. "The Continuing Enigma of Josephus' Testimony about Jesus." *BJRL* 67 (1985) 609-22.

Bishop, E. F. F. "Does Aretas Belong in 2 Corinthians or Galatians?" *ET* 64 (1952/53) 188f.

————. " 'Constantly on the Road'." *BS* 117 (1960) 14-18.

Bittel, K. "Die Galater, archäologisch gesehen." *Proceedings of the Xth International Congress of Classical Archaeology I/3, Ankara-Izmir 23-30/IX/1973* (1978) 169-74.

Black, D. A. "The Weak in Thessalonica: A Study in Pauline Lexicography." *JETS* 25 (1982) 307-21.

Black, M. "Paul and Roman Law in Acts." *ResQ* 24 (1981) 209-18.

Blair, E. P. "Paul's Call to the Gentile Mission." *BR* 10 (1965) 19-43.

Blake, E. C., and Edmonds, A. G. *Biblical Sites in Turkey* (Istanbul, 1987).

Blanchaud, M. H. "Les cultes orientaux en Macédoine Grecque dans l'antiquité." *AncMac* IV (Thessalonica, 1986) 83-86.

Blank, J. *Paulus und Jesus. Eine theologische Grundlegung. SANT* 18 (Munich, 1968).

Blass, F. "ΧΡΙΣΤΙΑΝΟΣ-ΧΡΕΣΤΙΑΝΟΣ," *Hermes* 30 (1895) 465-70.

Bleicken, J. "Provocatio." *PRE* I 23.2 (Stuttgart, 1959) 244-63.

————. *Die Verfassung der römischen Republik. Grundlagen und Entwicklung. UTB* 460 (Paderborn, 1975).

————. *Verfassungs und Sozialgeschichte des Römischen Kaiserreiches II. UTB* 839 (Paderborn, ²1981).

Blevins, J. L. "Acts 13–19: The Tale of Three Cities." *RExp* 87 (1990) 439-50.

Bligh, P. H. "The Pauline Chronology of John Knox." *ET* 83 (1972) 216.

Blinzler, J. "Die Niedermetzelung von Galiläern durch Pilatus." *NT* 2 (1957) 24-49.

————. "Rechtsgeschichtliches zur Hinrichtung des Zebedäiden Jakobus (Apg XII,2)." *NT* 5 (1962) 191-213.

————. *Der Prozeß Jesu* (Regensburg, ⁴1969).

————. "Zum Geschichtsrahmen des Johannesevangeliums." *Aus der Welt und Umwelt des Neuen Testaments. Gesammelte Aufsätze 1. SBB* (Stuttgart, 1969) 94-107.

Blosser, D. "The Sabbath Year Cycle in Josephus." *HUCA* 52 (1981) 129-39.

Bludau, A. "Die Juden Roms im ersten christlichen Jahrhundert." *Kath* 83 (1903) 113-34, 193-229.

————. "Die Militärverhältnisse in Caesarea im apostolischen Zeitalter." *ThPM* 17 (1907) 136-43.

Bockmuehl, M. Review of R. Jewett, *The Thessalonian Correspondence* (Philadelphia, 1986). *Themelios* 14 (1989) 71f.

Böcher, O. "Das sogennante Aposteldekret." In H. Frankemölle and K. Kertelge. *Vom Urchristentum zu Jesus. Festschrift Joachim Gnilka* (Freiburg, 1989) 325-36.

Boer, W. den. "Claudius." *RAC* III (Stuttgart, 1957) 179-81.

Boers, H. "The Form Critical Study of Paul's Letters. I Thessalonians as a Case Study." *NTS* 22 (1976) 140-58.

Böttger, P. C. "Paulus und Petrus in Antiochien. Zum Verständnis von Galater 2.11-21." *NTS* 37 (1991) 77-100.

Bohlen, R. "Die neue Diskussion um die Einheitlichkeit des 1. Thessalonicherbriefes. Eine Kurzinformation für die Verkündigung." *TTZ* 96 (1987) 313-17.

Boll, F. "Die Lebensalter. Ein Beitrag zur antiken Ethologie und zur Geschichte der Zahlen." *NJKA* 16 (1913) 89-145.

Borchert, G. L. "Javan." *ISBE* II (Grand Rapids, 1982) 971.

Borg, M. "A New Context for Romans 13." *NTS* 19 (1972/73) 205-18.

Bornhäuser, K. "Paulus und das Aposteldekret." *NKZ* 34 (1924) 391-438.

————. *Studien zur Apostelgeschichte* (Gütersloh, 1934).

Bornkamm, G. "Paulus, Apostel." *RGG*[3] V (Tübingen, 1961) 166-90.

————. *Paulus* (Stuttgart, [5]1983).

————. *Paul, Paulus* (Eng. trans., New York, 1971).

————. *Jesus of Nazareth* (Eng. trans., Minneapolis, 1995 [copyright 1960]).

Borse, U. *Der Standort des Galaterbriefs. BBB* 41 (Cologne/Bonn, 1972).

————. "Paulus und Jerusalem." In P. G. Müller and W. Stenger. *Kontinuität und Einheit. Festschrift Franz Mußner* (Freiburg, 1981) 43-64.

Botermann, H. "Paulus und das Urchristentum in der antiken Welt." *TRu* 56 (1991) 296-305.

————. "Der Heidenapostel und sein Historiker. Zur historischen Kritik der Apostelgeschichte." *TBei* 24 (1993) 62-84.

————. *Das Judenedikt des Kaisers Claudius. Römischer Staat und* Christiani *im 1. Jahrhundert*. Hermes E 71 (Stuttgart, 1996).

Boulvert, G. *Esclaves et affranchis impériaux dans l'Haut-Empire Romain (Rôle politique et administratif). Biblioteca di Labeo* 4 (Naples, 1970).

Bowen, C. R. "Paul's Collection and the Book of Acts." *JBL* 42 (1923) 49-58.

Bowers, W. P. *Studies in Paul's Understanding of His Mission* (diss., Cambridge, 1976).

————. "Jewish Communities in Spain in the Time of Paul the Apostle." *JTS* 26 (1975) 395-402.

————. "Paul's Route through Mysia. A Note on Acts XVI.8." *JTS* 30 (1979) 507-11.

————. "Paul and Religious Propaganda in the First Century." *NT* 22 (1980) 316-23.

———— "Fulfilling the Gospel: The Scope of the Pauline Mission." *JETS* 30 (1987) 185-98.

————. "Church and Mission in Paul." *JSNT* 44 (1991) 89-111.

Bowersock, G. W. *Roman Arabia* (Cambridge, Mass./London, 1983).

Bradford, E. *Paul the Traveller* (New York, 1974).

Brändl, M. "Troas." *GBL* III (Wuppertal/Gießen, 1989) 1604-6.

Brändle, R., and Stegemann, E. W. "Die Entstehung der ersten 'christlichen' Gemeinde Roms im Kontext der jüdischen Gemeinden." *NTS* 40 (1996) 1-11.

Brannigan, F. "Nautisches über die Romfahrt des heiligen Paulus." *TGl* 25 (1933) 170-86.

Brassac, A. "Une Inscription de Delphes et la chronologie de saint Paul." *RB* 10 (1913) 37-53, 207-17.

Braude, W. G. *Jewish Proselytizing in the First Five Centuries of the Common Era: The Age of the Tannaim and Amoraim* (Providence, 1940).

Braun, F. M. *Jean le Théologien et son évangile dans l'église ancienne. ÉBib* (Paris, 1959).

Braun, H. *Jesus — der Mann aus Nazareth und seine Zeit* (Stuttgart, 1984) (expansion of previous editions).

———. *Jesus of Nazareth. The Man and His Time* (Eng. trans., Philadelphia, 1979). (Not a translation of preceding, but rather of previous edition.)

Braund, D. C. *Rome and the Friendly King: The Character of Client Kingship* (London, 1984).

———. "Felix." *ABD* II (New York, 1992) 783.

Breytenbach, C. "Zeus und der lebendige Gott: Anmerkungen zu Apostelgeschichte 14,11-17." *NTS* 39 (1993) 396-413.

———. *Paulus und Barnabas in der Provinz Galatien. Studien zu Apostelgeschichte 13f.; 16,6; 18,23 und den Adressaten des Galaterbriefes.* AGAJU 38 (Leiden, 1966).

Briggs, C. W. "The Apostle Paul in Arabia." *BW* 41 (1913) 255-59.

Brindle, W. "The Census and Quirinius: Luke 2:2." *JETS* 27 (1984) 43-52.

Bringmann, K. "Sallusts Umgang mit der historischen Wahrheit in seiner Darstellung der Catilinarischen Verschwörung." *RMP* 114 (1971) 98-113.

———. "Zur Tiberiusbiographie Suetons." *RMP* 116 (1972) 268-85.

———. "Senecas 'Apocolocyntosis': Ein Forschungsbericht 1959-1982." *ANRW* II 32.2 (Berlin/New York, 1985) 885-914.

Bristol, L. O. "Paul's Thessalonian Correspondence." *ET* 55 (1943/44) 223.

Broer, I. " 'Antisemitismus' und Judenpolemik im Neuen Testament. Ein Beitrag zum besseren Verständnis von 1 Thess 2,14-16." *BN* 20 (1983) 59-91.

———. " 'Der ganze Zorn ist schon über sie gekommen': Bemerkungen zur Interpolationshypothese und zur Interpretation von 1 Thes 2,14-16." In R. F. Collins, ed. *The Thessalonian Correspondence.* BETL 87 (Leuven, 1990) 137-59.

Bronson, D. B. "Paul, Galatians, and Jerusalem." *JAAR* 35 (1967) 119-28.

Broshi, M. "La population de l'ancienne Jérusalem." *RB* 82 (1975) 5-12.

Broughton, T. R. S. "The Roman Army." *BC* V (London, 1933), 427-45.

———. "Three Notes on Saint Paul's Journeys in Asia Minor." *Quantalacumque. Festschrift Kirsopp Lake* (London, 1937) 131-38.

Brown, R. E., and Meier, J. P. *Antioch and Rome: New Testament Cradles of Catholic Christianity* (London, 1983).

Brox, N. "Zur christlichen Mission in der Spätantike." In K. Kertelge, ed. *Mission im Neuen Testament. QD* 93 (Freiburg, 1982) 190-237.

Bruce, F. F. "Christianity under Claudius." *BJRL* 44 (1961/62) 309-26.

———. "Paul and Jerusalem." *TynBul* 19 (1968) 3-25.

———. "Galatian Problems 2: North or South Galatians." *BJRL* 52 (1969/70) 243-66.

———. *Jesus and Christian Origins Outside the New Testament* (London, 1974).

———. "Is the Paul of Acts the Real Paul?" *BJRL* 58 (1976) 282-305.

———. *New Testament History* (London, 1971).

———. *Paul: Apostle of the Free Spirit* (Exeter, 1977).

———. "St. Paul in Macedonia." *BJRL* 61 (1978/79) 337-54.

440

————. *Men and Movements in the Primitive Church: Studies in Early Non-Pauline Christianity* (Exeter, 1979).

————. "Tacitus on Jewish History." *JSS* 29 (1984) 33-44.

————. "The Acts of the Apostles: Historical Record or Theological Reconstruction?" *ANRW* II 25.3 (Berlin/New York, 1984) 2569-2603.

————. *The Pauline Circle* (Grand Rapids/Exeter, 1985).

————. "Chronological Questions in the Acts of the Apostles." *BJRL* 68 (1986) 273-95.

————. "Travel and Communication: The New Testament World." *ABD* VI (New York, 1992) 648-53.

Brückner, W. *Die chronologische Reihenfolge, in welcher die Briefe des Neuen Testaments verfasst sind . . .* (Haarlem, 1890).

Bruggen, J. van. *"Na veertien Jaren." De datering van het in Galaten 2 genoemde overleg te Jeruzalem* (Kampen, 1973).

————. "The Year of the Death of Herod the Great." In T. Baarda, A. F. J. Klijn, and W. C. van Unnik. *Miscellanea Neotestamentica . . . II. NTSup* 48 (Leiden, 1978) 1-17.

Buchheim, K. *Der historische Christus. Geschichtswissenschaftliche Überlegungen zum Neuen Testament* (Munich, 1974).

Buck, C. H. "The Date of Galatians." *JBL* 70 (1951) 113-22.

Buck, C. H., and Taylor, G. R. *Saint Paul: A Study in the Development of His Thought* (New York, 1969).

Buit, M. du. "Routes aux temps biblique." *DBS* X (Paris, 1985) 1011-52.

Burchard, C. *Der dreizehnte Zeuge. Traditions- und kompositionsgeschichtliche Untersuchungen zu Lukas' Darstellung der Frühzeit des Paulus. FRLANT* 103 (Göttingen, 1970).

Burn, A. P. "Hic breve vivitur." *PaP* 4 (1943) 1-31.

Burton, E. W. "The Politarchs." *AJTh* 2 (1898) 598-632.

Buti, I. "La cognitio extra ordinem': da Augusto a Diocletiano." *ANRW* II 14 (Berlin/New York, 1982) 29-59.

Butin, J. D., and Schwartz, J. "Post Philonis Legationem." *RHPR* 65 (1985) 127-29.

Butler, B. C. "St. Paul's Knowledge and Use of St. Matthew." *DR* 66 (1948) 367-83.

Cadbury, H. J. "Roman Law and the Trial of Paul." *BC* V (1933) 297-338.

————. "Lucius of Cyrene." *Ibid.,* 489-95.

————. *The Book of Acts in History* (London, 1955).

Cadoux, C. J. "The Chronological Divisions of Acts." *JTS* 19 (1918) 333-40.

————. "A Tentative Synthetic Chronology of the Apostolic Age." *JBL* 56 (1937) 177-91.

Caird, G. B. "Chronology of the New Testament." *IDB* I (Nashville, 1961) 599-607.

————. *The Apostolic Age* (London, 1975).

————. Review of R. Jewett, *Dating Paul's Life* (London, 1979). *JTS* 31 (1980) 170-72.

Calder, W. M. "A Galatian Estate of the Sergii Paulli." *Klio* 24 (1930/31) 59-62.

Cambier, J. "Paul (Vie et doctrine de Saint)." *DBS* VII (Paris, 1966) 279-387.

Campbell, T. H. "Paul's 'Missionary Journeys' as Reflected in His Letters." *JBL* 74 (1955) 80-86.

Cantarelli, L. "Gallione proconsule di Acaia e San Paolo." *Rendiconti della R. Accademia Nazionale dei Lincei (Classe di scienze morali, storiche e filologiche)* V/32 (Rome, 1923) 157-75.

Cantineau, J. *Le Nabatéen II* (Paris, 1932).

Carcopino, J. *Daily Life in Ancient Rome.* Edited by H. T. Rowell (Eng. trans., New Haven, 1960).

Carney, T. F. "The Changing Picture of Claudius." *ACl* 3 (1960) 99-104.

————. "The Emperor Claudius and the Grain Trade." *Pro Munere Grates. Studies Presented to H. L. Gonin* (Pretoria, 1971) 39-57.

Carras, G. P. "Jewish Ethics and Gentile Converts: Remarks on 1 Thess. 4:3-8." In R. F. Collins. *The Thessalonian Correspondence. BETL* 87 (Leuven, 1990) 316-39.

Carrez, M. "Note sur les évènements d'Éphèse et l'appel de Paul à sa citoyenneté Romaine." *A cause de l'Évangile. Études sur les Synoptiques et les Actes offertes au P. Jacques Dupont, O.S.B. . . . LD* 123 (Paris, 1985) 769-77.

Carson, D. A., Moo, D. J., and Morris, L. *An Introduction to the New Testament* (Grand Rapids, 1992).

Casey, M. "Chronology and the Development of Pauline Christology." In M. D. Hooker and S. G. Wilson. *Paul and Paulinism. Essays in Honour of C. K. Barrett* (London, 1982) 124-34.

Cassidy, R. J. *Jesus, Politics, and Society: A Study of Luke's Gospel* (Maryknoll, 1978).

Casson, L. "The Isis and Her Voyage." *TAPA* 81 (1950) 43-56.

————. "Speed under Sail of Ancient Ships." *TAPA* 82 (1951) 136-48.

————. "The Isis and Her Voyage: A Reply." *TAPA* 87 (1956) 239f.

————. *Ships and Seamanship in the Ancient World* (Princeton, 1971).

————. *Travel in the Ancient World* (London, 1974).

Causse, A. "Le pèlerinage à Jérusalem et la première Pentecôte." *RHPR* 20 (1940) 120-41.

Cecchelli, C. "Il nome e la 'setta' dei Cristiani." *RivAC* 31 (1955) 55-73.

Cerfaux, L. "Saint Paul et le 'serviteur de Dieu' d'Isaïe." *Receuil Lucien Cerfaux II* (Gembloux, 1954) 239-54.

————. *The Christian in the Theology of St. Paul* (London, 1967).

Chantraine, H. "Zur Entstehung der Freilassung mit Bürgerrechtserwerb in Rom." *ANRW* I 2 (Heidelberg/New York, 1972) 59-67.

Chapa, J. "Consolatory Pattern? 1 Thess. 4:13, 18; 5:11." In R. F. Collins, *The Thessalonian Correspondence. BETL* 87 (Leuven, 1990) 220-28.

————. "Is First Thessalonians a Letter of Consolation?" *NTS* 40 (1994) 150-60.

Chapman, D. J. "St. Paul and the Revelation to St. Peter, Matt. XVI,17." *RBén* 29 (1912) 133-47.

Charlesworth, M. P. *Trade-Routes and Commerce of the Roman Empire* (Cambridge, 1924).

————. "Gaius and Claudius." *CAH* X (London, 1934) 653-701.

Chavel, B. "The Releasing of a Prisoner on the Eve of Passover in Ancient Jerusalem." *JBL* 60 (1941) 273-78.

Chevallier, R. *Roman Roads* (Eng. trans., Berkeley, 1976).

Chilton, C. W. "The Roman Law of Treason under the Early Empire." *JRS* 45 (1955) 73-81.

Cichorius, C. "Chronologisches zum Leben Jesu." *ZNW* 22 (1923) 16-20.

Clark, G. "The Social Status of Paul." *ET* 96 (1985) 110f.

Clarke, A. D. "Another Corinthian Erastus Inscription." *TynBul* 42 (1991) 146-51.

————. *Secular and Christian Leadership in Corinth: A Socio-Historical and Exegetical Study of 1 Corinthians 1–6.* AGAJU 18 (Leiden, 1993).

Classen, C. J. "Paulus und die antike Rhetorik." *ZNW* 82 (1991) 1-33.

Clavier, H. "Méthode et inspiration dans la mission de Paul." In O. Böcher and K. Haacker. *Verborum Veritas. Festschrift Gustav Stählin* (Wuppertal, 1970) 171-87.

Clemen, C. *Die Chronologie der paulinischen Briefe aufs Neue untersucht* (Halle, 1893).

————. *Die Einheitlichkeit der paulinischen Briefe an der Hand der bisher mit Bezug auf sie aufgestellten Interpolations- und Compilationshypothesen* (Göttingen, 1894).

————. "Paulus und die Gemeinde zu Thessalonike." *NKZ* 7 (1896) 139-64.

————. *Paulus. Sein Leben und Wirken* I: *Untersuchung;* II: *Darstellung* (Gießen, 1904).

Cohen, R. "New Light on the Date of the Petra-Gaza Road." *BA* 45 (1982) 240-47.

Cohen, S. J. D. "Respect for Judaism by Gentiles according to Josephus." *HTR* 80 (1987) 409-30.

Cole, R. A. "The Life and Ministry of Paul." In F. E. Gaebelein, ed. *The Expositor's Bible Commentary I: Introductory Articles* (Grand Rapids, 1979) 555-74.

Collart, P. *Philippes ville de Macédoine depuis ses origines jusqu'à la fin de l'époque romaine. École Française d'Athènes Travaux et Mémoires* 5 (Paris, 1937).

Collins, N. L. Review of D. R. Schwartz, *Agrippa I* (Tübingen, 1990). *NT* 34 (1992) 90-101.

Collins, R. F. "Recent Scholarship on the First Letter to the Thessalonians." *Studies on the First Letter to the Thessalonians. BETL* 64 (Löwen, 1984) 3-75.

————. "Apropos the Integrity of 1 Thess." *Ibid.,* 96-135.

————. " '. . . that this letter be read to all the brethren'." *Ibid.,* 365-70.

Colpe, C. "Aretas." *KP* I (Stuttgart, 1964) 529f.

Compernolle, R. van. "La vitesse des voiliers grecs à l'époque classique (V^e et IVe siècles)." *BIHBR* 30 (1957) 5-30.

Coninck, L. de. "Les sources documentaires de Suétone, 'Les XII Césars': 1900-1990." *ANRW* II 33.5 (Berlin/New York, 1991) 3675-3700.

Contenau, G. "L'Institut Français d'Archéologie et d'Art Musulmans de Damas." *Syr* 5 (1924) 203-11.

Conzelmann, H. *History of Primitive Christianity* (Eng. trans., Nashville/New York, 1973).

Cook, J. *The Troad* (Oxford, 1973).

Cook, R. B. "Paul, the Organizer." *Missiology* 9 (1981) 485-98.

Corsini, E. *Introduzione alle "Storie" di Orosio. Filologia Classica e Glottologia* II (Turin, 1968).

Corssen, P. "Die Urgestalt der Paulusakten." *ZNW* 4 (1903) 22-47.

Corwin, V. "St. Ignatius and Christianity in Antioch." *YPR* 1 (New Haven, 1960).

Cothenet, É. "Un grand voyageur." *Cahiers Évangiles* 26 (1978) 26-29.

————. "Premier voyage missionnaire." *Ibid.,* 30-48.

————. "Second voyage missionnaire." *Ibid.,* 49-62.

————. "Troisième voyage missionnaire." *Ibid.,* 63-69.

————. "Dernières années de Paul." *Ibid.,* 70-80.

Craig, W. L. "The Bodily Resurrection of Jesus." In R. T. France and D. Wenham. *Gospel Perspectives: Studies of History and Tradition in the Four Gospels* I (Sheffield, 1980) 47-74.

Cramer, F. H. *Astrology in Roman Law and Politics* (Philadelphia, 1954).

Cross, J. A. "Note on Acts IX.19-25." *Exp* V/3 (1896) 78-80.

Crown, A. D. "The Samaritan Diaspora." *The Samaritans* (Tübingen, 1989) 195-217.

Cumont, F. "Un rescript impérial sur la violation de sépulture." *RH* 163 (1930) 241-66.

Dahl, N. A. "Paul and Possessions." *Studies in Paul: Theology for the Early Christian Mission* (Minneapolis, 1977) 22-39.

Dalman, G. *Arbeit und Sitte in Palästina I: Jahreslauf und Tageslauf. 1. Hälfte: Herbst und Winter. BFCT* II/14 (Gütersloh, 1928; repr. Hildesheim, 1964).

Daniélou, J. *The Theology of Jewish Christianity: A History of Early Christian Doctrine before the Council of Nicaea* I. Edited by J. A. Baker (London/Philadelphia, 1964).

————. *Primitive Christian Symbols* (London, 1964).

————. *Les manuscrits de la mer Morte et les origines du christianisme* (Paris, ^{2}1974).

Danker, F. W. "Freedman — Synagogue of." *ISBE* II (Grand Rapids, 1982) 360f.

Danker, F. W., and Jewett, R. "Jesus as the Apocalyptic Benefactor in Second Thessalonians." In R. F. Collins. *The Thessalonian Correspondence. BETL* 87 (Leuven, 1990) 486-98.

Danoff [Danov], C. M. "Apollonia 3." *KP* I (Stuttgart, 1964) 449.

————. "Die Thraker auf dem Ostbalkan von der hellenistischen Zeit bis zur Gründung Konstantinopels." *ANRW* II 7.1 (Berlin/New York, 1979) 21-185.

Daraki, M. *Dionysos* (Paris, 1985).

Dassmann, E. *Paulus in frühchristlicher Frömmigkeit und Kunst. Rheinisch-Westfälische Akademie der Wissenschaften. Vorträge G* 256 (Opladen, 1982).

————. *Kirchengeschichte I: Ausbreitung, Leben und Lehre der Kirche in den ersten drei Jahrhunderten. Kohlhammer Studienbücher Theologie* 10 (Stuttgart, 1991).

Dauer, A. *Paulus und die christliche Gemeinde im syrischen Antiochia. Kritisch Bestandsaufnahme der modernen Forschung mit einigen weiterführenden Überlegungen. BBB* 106 (Weinheim, 1996).

Dautzenberg, G. "Der Wandel der Reich-Gottes-Verkündigung in der urchristlichen Mission." In G. Dautzenberg, H. Merklein, and K. Müller. *Zur Geschichte des Urchristentums. QD* 87 (1979) 11-32.

Dauvillier, J. "A propos de la venue de saint Paul à Rome. Notes sur son procès et son voyage maritime." *BLÉ* 61 (1960) 3-26.

————. *Les Temps Apostoliques — 1er siècle.* Histoire du Droit et des Institutions de l'Église en Occident II. Edited by G. Le Bras (Paris, 1970).

Davies, G. I. "The Significance of Deuteronomy I.2 for the Location of Mount Horeb." *PEQ* 111 (1979) 87-101.

Davies, P. E. "The Macedonian Scene of Paul's Journeys." *BA* 26 (1963) 91-106.

Davies, S. L. "John the Baptist and Essene Kashrut." *NTS* 29 (1983) 569-71.

Davies, W. D. "The Apostolic Age and the Life of Paul." In M. Black and H. H. Rowley, *Peake's Commentary on the Bible* (London, 1962) 870-81.

————. *The Gospel and the Land. Early Christianity and Jewish Territorial Doctrine* (Berkeley/Los Angeles, 1974).

Deissmann, A. *Bibelstudien. Beiträge zumeist aus den Papyri und Inschriften zur Geschichte der Sprache, des Schrifttums und der Religion des hellenistischen Judentums und des Urchristentums* (Marburg, 1895). Eng. trans., *Bible Studies* (Edinburgh, ²1909).

————. *Paul: A Study in Social and Religious History* (Eng. trans., London, ²1926).

————. "Zur ephesinischen Gefangenschaft des Apostels Paulus." In W. H. Buckler and W. M. Calder. *Anatolian Studies Presented to Sir William Mitchell Ramsay* (Manchester, 1923) 121-27.

Delaye, E. "Routes et courriers au temps de Saint Paul." *Études* 131 (1912) 443-61.

Delebecque, É. "Sur un problème de temps chez Saint Paul." *Bibl* 70 (1989) 389-95.

Delehaye, H. "Hagiographie et Archéologie Romaine." *AnBoll* 45 (1927) 297-322.

Delobel, J. "The Fate of the Dead according to 1 Thessalonians 4 and 1 Corinthians 15." In R. F. Collins. *The Thessalonian Correspondence. BETL* 87 (Leuven, 1990) 340-47.

Demke, C. "Theologie und Literarkritik im 1. Thessalonicherbrief. Ein Diskussionsbeitrag." In G. Ebeling, E. Jüngel, and G. Schunack. *Festschrift Ernst Fuchs* (Tübingen, 1973) 103-24.

Denis, A. M. "L'apôtre Paul, prophète 'messianique' des Gentils." *ETL* 23 (1957) 245-318.

Derwacter, F. M. *Preparing the Way for Paul: The Proselyte Movement in Later Judaism* (New York, 1930).

Dessau, H. "Der Name des Apostels Paulus." *Hermes* 45 (1910) 347-68.

————. *Geschichte der römischen Kaiserzeit* II/1 (Berlin, 1926).

Devreker, J. "Les Sergii Paulli: problèmes généalogiques d'une famille supposée chrétienne." In M. van Uytfanghe and R. Demeulenaere, *Aevum inter utrumque. Mélanges offerts à Gabriel Sanders* . . . (Instrumenta Patristica 23) (Steenbrugge, 1991) 109-19.

————. Review of B. Kreiler, *Die Statthalter Kleinasiens unter den Flaviern* (diss., Augsburg, 1975). *Epigraphica* 38 (1976) 179-88.

Dewailly, L. M. *La jeune église de Thessalonique. LD* 37 (Paris, 1957).

————. "Une communauté naissante: Thessalonique." *VS* 105 (1961) 254-69.

Dexinger, F. "Ein 'Messianisches Szenarium' als Gemeingut des Judentums." *Kairos* 17 (1975) 249-78.

Dibelius, M. "Rom und die Christen im ersten Jahrhundert." *SHAW* 32 (Heidelberg, 1942) 6-59.

————. "Die Apostelgeschichte im Rahmen der antiken Literaturgeschichte." *Aufsätze zur Apostelgeschichte.* Edited by H. Greeven (East Berlin, 1951) 163-74.

————. *Paul.* Edited by W. G. Kümmel (Eng. trans., London/New York/Toronto, 1953).

Dieckmann, H. *Antiochien ein Mittelpunkt urchristlicher Missionstätigkeit* (Aachen, 1920).

Diesner, H. J. *Isidor von Sevilla und seine Zeit. ATh* I/52 (Stuttgart, 1973).

Dietzfelbinger, C. *Die Berufung des Paulus als Ursprung seiner Theologie. WMANT* 58 (Neukirchen-Vluyn, 1985).

Dihle, A. *Greek and Latin Literature of the Roman Empire* (Eng. trans., London/New York, 1994).

Dilke, O. A. W. *Mathematics and Measurement* (London, 1987).

Dimitriadis, V. Τοπογραφία τῆς Θεσσαλονίκης κατὰ τὴν ἐποχὴν τῆς Τουρκοκρατίας *1430-1912* (Thessalonica, 1983).

Dinkler, E. "Das Bema zu Korinth. Archäologische, lexikographische, rechtsgeschichtliche und ikonographische Bemerkungen zu Apg 18,12-17." *Signum Crucis* (Tübingen, 1967) 188-33.

Dockery, D. S. "Acts 6–12: The Christian Mission beyond Jerusalem." *RExp* 87 (1990) 423-37.

Dockx, S. "Le 14 Nisan de l'an 30." In *Chronologie néotestamentaires et Vie de l'Église primitive. Recherches exégétiques* (Löwen, [2]1984) 21-29.

————. "Chronologie de la vie de saint Paul depuis sa conversion jusqu'à son séjour à Rome." *Ibid.,* 45-87.

————. "Barnabé et Saul." *Ibid.,* 89-95.

————. "Chronologie Paulinienne de l'année de la grande collecte." *Ibid.,* 137-49.

————. "Chronologie de la vie de saint Pierre." *Ibid.,* 161-78.

————. "Date de la mort d'Étienne le Protomartyr." *Ibid.,* 223-30.

————. "Deux nouvelles chronologies de la vie de saint Paul." *Ibid.,* 393-97.

————. "The First Missionary Voyage of Paul: Historical Reality or Literary Creation of Luke?" In J. Vardaman and E. M. Yamauchi. *Chronos, Kairos, Christos: Nativity and Chronological Studies Presented to Jack Finegan* (Winona Lake, 1989) 209-21.

Doer, B. " 'Civis Romanus sum.' Der Apostel Paulus als römischer Bürger." *Helikon* 8 (1968) 3-76.

Doig, K. F. *New Testament Chronology* (San Francisco, 1991).

Domaszewski, A. von. *Geschichte der römischen Kaiser* II (Leipzig, [2/3]1921).

Dominguez Del Val, U. "La utilización de los Padres por San Isidoro." *Isidoriana. Festschrift Manuel C. Díaz y Díaz* (Leon, 1961) 211-21.

Donaldson, T. L. "Thessalonica." In R. K. Harrison. *Major Cities of the Biblical World* (Nashville, 1985) 258-65.

Donfried, K. P. "Justification and Last Judgement in Paul." *ZNW* 67 (1976) 90-110.

———. "Paul and Judaism: I Thessalonians 2:13-16 as a Test Case." *Interpretation* 38 (1984) 242-53.

———. "The Cults of Thessalonica and the Thessalonian Correspondence." *NTS* 31 (1985) 336-56.

———."Thessalonica." *Harper's Bible Dictionary.* Edited by P. J. Achtemeier *et al.* (San Francisco, 1985) 1065f.

———. "The Theology of 1 Thessalonians as a Reflection of Its Purpose." In M. P. Horgan and P. J. Kobelski. *To Touch the Text: Biblical and Related Studies in Honor of Joseph A. Fitzmyer S.J.* (New York, 1989) 243-324.

———. "1 Thessalonians, Acts and the Early Paul." In R. F. Collins. *The Thessalonian Correspondence. BETL* 87 (Leuven, 1990) 3-26.

———. "War Timotheus in Athen? Exegetische Überlegungen zu 1 Thess 3,1-3." In J. J. Degenhardt. *Die Freude an Gott — unsere Kraft. Festschrift Otto Bernhard Knoch* (Stuttgart, 1991) 189-94.

———. "Chronology: New Testament." *ABD* I (New York, 1992) 1011-22.

———. "The Assembly of the Thessalonians: Reflections on the Ecclesiology of the Earliest Christian Letter." In R. Kampling and T. Söding. *Ekklesiologie des Neuen Testaments. Für Karl Kertelge* (Freiburg, 1996) 390-408.

Doohan, H. *Paul's Vision of Church. GNS* 32 (Wilmington, 1989).

Dorey, T. A. "Claudius und seine Ratgeber." *Altert* 12 (1966) 144-55.

Doty, W. G. *Letters in Primitive Christianity* (Philadelphia, 1973).

Downey, G. "The Size of the Population in Antioch." *TAPA* 89 (1958) 84-91.

———. *A History of Antioch in Syria from Seleucus to the Arab Conquest* (Princeton, 1961).

——— *Ancient Antioch* (Princeton, 1963).

Doyle, A. D. "Pilate's Career and the Date of the Crucifixion." *JTS* 42 (1941) 190-93.

Drane, J. W. *Paul: Libertine or Legalist* (London, 1975).

———. "Theological Diversity in the Letters of St. Paul." *TynBul* 27 (1976) 3-26.

———. *Paulus. Das Leben und die Briefe des Apostels* (Gießen, 1978). Eng. trans., *Paul: An Illustrated Documentary on the Life and Writings of a Key Figure in the Beginnings of Christianity* (New York, 1976).

———. "Why Did Paul Write Romans?" In D. A. Hagner and M. J. Harris. *Pauline Studies. Essays Presented to Professor F. F. Bruce* (Exeter, 1980) 208-27.

———. Review of R. Jewett, *Dating Paul's Life* (London, 1979). *JSNT* 9 (1980) 70-75.

Dschulnigg, P. "Die Rede des Stephanus im Rahmen der Berichtes über sein Martyrium (Apg 6,8–8,3). *Jud* 44 (1988) 195-213.

Dubowy, E. "Paulus und Gallio." *BZ* 10 (1912) 143-54.

Düll, S. "De Macedonum Sacris. Gedanken zu einer Neubearbeitung der Götterkulte in Makedonien." *AncMac* I (Thessalonica, 1970) 316-29.

———. "Die Romanisierung Nordmakedoniens im Spiegel der Götterkulte." *AncMac* III (Thessalonica, 1983) 77-87.

Duncan, G. S. *St Paul's Ephesian Ministry* (London, 1929).

———. "Paul's Ministry in Asia — The Last Phase." *NTS* 3 (1956/57) 211-18.

———. "Chronological Table to Illustrate Paul's Ministry in Asia." *NTS* 5 (1958/59) 43-45.

———. "Chronology." *The Interpreter's One-Volume Commentary on the Bible.* Edited by C. M. Laymon (New York/Nashville, 1961) 1271-82.

Dunn, J. D. G. "The Relationship between Paul and Jerusalem according to Galatians 1 and 2." *NTS* 28 (1982) 461-78.

Dupont, J. "Les problèmes du livre des Actes d'après les travaux récents." ALBO II 17 (Löwen, 1950).

———. "La famine sous Claude (Actes 11:28)." *Études sur les Actes des Apôtres. LD* 45 (Paris, 1967) 163-65.

———. "Les trois premiers voyages de Saint Paul à Jérusalem." *Ibid.,* 167-71.

———. "Pierre et Paul dans les Actes." *Ibid.,* 173-84.

———. "Pierre et Paul à Antioche et à Jérusalem." *Ibid.,* 185-215.

———. "La mission de Paul 'à Jérusalem' (Actes 12,25)." *Ibid.,* 217-41.

Dupraz, L. *De l'association de Tibère au principat à la naissance du Christ. Trois études. SF* n.s. 43 (Freiburg [Switzerland], 1966).

Durrleman, F. *Salonique et Saint Paul* (Paris, 1919).

Dussaud, R. "Numismatique des rois de Nabatène." *JA* 3 (1904) 189-238.

Eck, W. "Ergänzungen zu den Fasti Consulares des 1. und 2. Jh. n. Chr." *Hist* 24 (1975) 324-44.

Eckart, K. G. "Der zweite echte Brief des Apostels Paulus an die Thessalonicher." *ZTK* 58 (1961) 30-44.

Eckert, J. "Die Kollekte des Paulus für Jerusalem." In P. G. Müller and W. Stenger. *Kontinuität und Einheit. Festschrift Franz Mussner* (Freiburg, 1981) 65-80.

———. "Zur Erstverkündigung des Paulus." In J. Hainz. *Theologie im Werden. Studien zu den theologischen Konzeptionen im Neuen Testament* (Paderborn, 1992) 279-99.

Edmundson, G. *The Church in Rome in the First Century: An Examination of Various Controverted Questions Relating to Its History, Chronology, Literature and Traditions* (London, 1913).

Edson, C. "State Cults of Thessalonica (Macedonica II)." *HSCP* 51 (1940) 127-36.

———. "Cults of Thessalonica (Macedonica III)." *HTR* 41 (1948) 153-204.

Edwards, O. *Chronologie des Lebens Jesu und das Zeitgeheimnis der drei Jahre. Neue Gesichtspunkte zur Datierung seiner Geburt* (Stuttgart, 1978).

———. "Herodian Chronology." *PEQ* 114 (1982) 29-42.

Eger, O. *Rechtsgeschichtliches zum Neuen Testament* (Basel, 1919).

Eisler, R. ΙΗΣΟΥΣ ΒΑΣΙΛΕΥΣ ΟΥ ΒΑΣΙΛΕΥΣΑΣ. *Die messianische Unabhängigkeitsbewegung vom Auftreten Joh. d. Täufers bis zum Untergang Jakobus d. Gerechten nach der neuerschlossenen Eroberung von Jerusalem des Flavius Josephus und den christlichen Quellen dargestellt* I (Heidelberg, 1929).

Eisman, M. M. "Dio and Josephus: Parallel Analyses." *Lat* 36 (1977) 657-73.

Elderen, B. van. "Some Archaeological Observations on Paul's First Missionary Journey." In W. W. Gasque and R. P. Martin. *Apostolic History and the Gospel: Biblical and Historical Essays Presented to F. F. Bruce* (Exeter, 1970) 151-61.

Elliger, W. *Paulus in Griechenland. Philippi, Thessaloniki, Athen, Korinth. SBS* 92/93 (Stuttgart, 1978; repr. 1987).

———. *Ephesos — Geschichte einer antiken Weltstadt. Urban Taschenbücher* 375 (Stuttgart, 1985).

Ellis, E. E. *Paul's Use of the Old Testament* (Grand Rapids, 1957).

———. "Paul and His Co-Workers." *Prophecy and Hermeneutic in Early Christianity: New Testament Essays. WUNT* I/18 (Tübingen, 1978) 3-22.

———. "The Role of the Christian Prophet in Acts." *Ibid.,* 129-44.

———. "Midrash *Pesher* in Pauline Hermeneutics." *Ibid.,* 173-81.

———. "Exegetical Patterns in I Corinthians and Romans." *Ibid.,* 213-20.

———. "Die Datierung des Neuen Testaments." *TZ* 42 (1986) 409-30.

———. "Biblical Interpretation in the New Testament Church." *CRINT* II/1 (Assen, 1988) 691-725.

————. " 'Das Ende der Erde' (Apg 1,8)." In C. Bussmann and W. Radl. *Der Treue Gottes trauen. Beiträge zum Werk des Lukas für Gerhard Schneider* (Freiburg, 1991) 277-87.

Enslin, M. S. "Paul and Gamaliel." *JR* 7 (1927) 360-75.

Eph'al, I. " 'Ishmael' and 'Arab(s)': A Transformation of Ethnological Terms." *JNES* 35 (1976) 225-35.

Erbes, C. "Die Todestage der Apostel Paulus und Petrus und ihre römischen Denkmäler. Kritische Untersuchungen." *TU* 19/1 (Leipzig, 1899) 1-138.

————. "Die geschichtlichen Verhältnisse der Apostelgräber in Rom." *ZKG* 43 (1925) 38-92.

Esch, A. "Die Via Appia in der Landschaft." *AW* 19 (1988) 15-29.

Evans, C. A. "Jesus in Non-Christian Sources." In B. Chilton and C. A. Evans. *Studying the Historical Jesus: Evaluations of the State of Current Research.* NTTS 19 (Leiden, 1994).

Evans, R. M. *Eschatology and Ethics: A Study of Thessalonica and Paul's Letters to the Thessalonians* (diss., Basel, 1968).

Ewald, P. "Aretas." *RE*^{3} I (Leipzig, 1896) 795-97.

Fadinger, V. "L. S. Plautus." *KP* V (Munich, 1975) 137.

Farmer, W. R. Review of G. Lüdemann, *Paulus, der Heidenapostel I* (Göttingen, 1980). *JBL* 101 (1982) 296f.

Fascher, E. "Paulus." *PRESup* VIII (Stuttgart, 1958) 431-66.

Faw, C. E. "On the Writing of First Thessalonians." *JBL* 71 (1952) 217-25.

Feldman, L. H. *Josephus and Modern Scholarship* (Berlin/New York, 1984).

————. "The Omnipresence of the God-fearers." *BARev* 12/5 (1985) 58-63.

————. *Jew and Gentile in the Ancient World: Attitudes and Interactions from Alexander to Justinian* (Princeton, 1993).

Felten, J. *Neutestamentliche Zeitgeschichte. Judentum und Heidentum zur Zeit Christi und der Apostel* I (Regensburg, $^{2/3}$1925).

Feneberg, W. *Paulus der Weltenbürger. Eine Biographie* (Munich, 1992).

Fennelly, J. M. *The Origins of Alexandrian Christianity* (diss., Manchester, 1967).

Ferenczy, E. "Rechtshistorische Bemerkungen zur Ausdehnung des römischen Bürgerrechts und zum *ius Italicum* unter dem Prinzipat." *ANRW* II 14 (Berlin/New York, 1982) 1017-58.

Féret, H. M. *Pierre et Paul à Antioche et à Jérusalem* (Paris, 1955).

Ferguson, E. *Backgrounds of Early Christianity* (Grand Rapids, 1987).

Ferrari D'Occhieppo, K. *Der Stern der Weisen. Geschichte oder Legende?* (Vienna, ^{2}1977).

Feuillet, A. "Saint Paul et l'Église de Rome." *Petrus et Paulus Martyres. Commemorazione del XIX centenario del martirio degli apostoli Pietro e Paolo* (Milan, 1969) 85-113.

————. "Romains (Épître aux)." *DBS* X (Paris, 1985) 739-863.

Filmer, W. E. "The Chronology of the Reign of Herod the Great." *JTS* 17 (1966) 283-98.

Finegan, J. *Handbook of Biblical Chronology: Principles of Time Reckoning in the Ancient World and Problems of Chronology in the Bible* (Princeton, 1964).

————. *The Archaeology of the New Testament II: The Mediterranean World of the Early Christian Apostles* (Boulder/London, 1981).

Finn, T. M. "The God-Fearers Reconsidered." *CBQ* 47 (1985) 75-84.

Firpo, G. *Il Problema Cronologico della Nascita di Gesù. BCR* 42 (Brescia, 1983).

Fischer, K. M. *Das Urchristentum. Kirchengeschichte in Einzeldarstellungen* I/1 (East Berlin, 1985).

Fischer, T. Review of Y. Meshorer, *Nabataean Coins* (Jerusalem, 1975). *OLZ* 74 (1979) 239-44.

Fishbane, M. "Javan." *EJ* 9 (New York, 1973) 1301f.

Fitzmyer, J. A. "Qumran and the Interpolated Paragraph 2 Cor 6:14–7:1." *CBQ* 23 (1961) 271-80 = *Essays on the Semitic Background of the New Testament* (London, 1971) 205-17.

————. " 'A certain sceva, a Jew, a chief priest' (Acts 19:14)." In C. Bussmann and W. Radl. *Der Treue Gottes trauen. Beiträge zum Werk des Lukas für Gerhard Schneider* (Freiburg, 1991) 299-305.

————. "The Pauline Letters and the Lucan Account of Paul's Missionary Journeys." *According to Paul: Studies in the Theology of the Apostle* (New York and Mahwah, NJ, 1993) 36-46, 130-32.

Flach, D. "Zum Quellenwert der Kaiserbiographien Suetons." *Gym* 79 (1972) 273-89.

————. *Tacitus in der Tradition der antiken Geschichtsschreibung. Hyp* 39 (Göttingen, 1973).

————. *Einführung in die römische Geschichtsschreibung (Die Altertumswissenschaft)* (Darmstadt, 1985).

Flanagan, N. *Friend Paul: His Letters, Theology and Humanity. Background Books* 6 (Wilmington, 1986).

Flusser, D. "The Apocryphal Book of *Ascensio Isaiae* and the Dead Sea Sect." *IEJ* 3 (1953) 34-47 (repr. in *Judaism and the Origins of Christianity* [Jerusalem, 1988] 3-20).

————. ". . . To Bury Caiaphas, Not to Praise Him." *Jerusalem Perspective* 4 (1991) 23-28.

Foster, J. "Was Sergius Paulus Converted? Acts xiii.12." *ET* 60 (1948/49) 354f.

Fotheringham, D. R. "Acts xi.20." *ET* 45 (1933/34) 430.

Fotheringham, J. K. "The Evidence of Astronomy and Technical Chronology for the Date of the Crucifixion." *JTS* 35 (1934) 146-62.

Fowl, S. "A Metaphor in Distress: A Reading of ΝΗΠΙΟΙ in 1 Thessalonians 2.7." *NTS* 36 (1990) 469-73.

France, R. T. "Chronological Aspects of 'Gospels Harmony'." *VEv* 16 (1986) 33-59.

Francis, F. O. "The Form and Function of the Opening and Closing Paragraphs of James and I John." *ZNW* 61 (1970) 110-26.

Fredriksen, P. *From Jesus to Christ: The Origins of the New Testament Images of Jesus* (New Haven/London, 1988).

————. "Judaism, The Circumcision of Gentiles, and Apocalyptic Hope: Another Look at Galatians 1 and 2." *JTS* 42 (1991) 532-64.

French, D. "Acts and the Roman Roads of Asia Minor." In D. W. J. Gill and C. Gempf. *The Book of Acts in Its Graeco-Roman Setting.* A1CS II (Grand Rapids and Carlisle, 1994) 49-58.

French, D. H. "The Roman Road-system of Asia Minor." *ANRW* II 7.2 (Berlin/New York, 1980) 698-729.

————. *Roman Roads and Milestones of Asia Minor I: The Pilgrim's Road. British Institute of Archaeology at Ankara Monograph* 3 (Ankara, 1981).

Frend, W. H. C. *Martyrdom and Persecution in the Early Church: A Study of a Conflict from the Maccabees to Donatus* (Oxford, 1965).

Freudenberger, R. *Das Verhalten der römischen Behörden gegen die Christen im 2. Jh. MBPF* 52 (Munich, 1967).

Frey, J. B. "Les Communautés Juives à Rome aux premiers temps de l'Église." *RSR* 20 (1930) 269-97; 21 (1931) 129-68.

Freyne, S. *The World of the New Testament. New Testament Message* 2 (Dublin, 1988).

Freytag, A. "Die Missionsmethode des Weltapostels Paulus auf seinen Reisen." *ZM* 2 (1912) 114-25.

———. *Paulus baut die Weltkirche. Ein Missionsbuch* (Mödling, 1951).

Friedlaender, L. *Darstellungen aus der Sittengeschichte Roms in der Zeit von Augustus bis zum Ausgang der Antonine* I. Edited by G. Wissowa (Leipzig, [10]1922).

Friedrich, J., Pöhlmann, W., and Stuhlmacher, P. "Zur historischen Situation und Intention von Röm 13,1-7." *ZTK* 73 (1976) 131-66.

Fries, S. A. "Was meint Paulus mit Ἀραβία in Gal 1,17?" *ZNW* 2 (1901) 150f.

Fritz, K. von. "Tacitus, Agricola, Domitian and the Problems of the Principate." *CP* 52 (1957) 73-97.

Fuchs, E. "Hermeneutik?" *ThV* 7 (1959/60) 44-60.

Fuchs, H. "Tacitus über die Christen." *VC* 4 (1950) 65-93.

———. "Der Bericht über die Christen in den Annalen des Tacitus." In V. Pöschl. *Tacitus. WdF* 97 (Darmstadt, 1969) 558-604.

Fuhrmann, M. "Suetonius 2." *KP* V (Munich, 1975) 411-13.

Fuks, G. "Where Have All the Freedmen Gone? On an Anomaly in the Jewish Grave-Inscriptions from Rome." *JJS* 36 (1985) 25-32.

Funaioli, G. "C. Suetonius Tranquillus." *PRE* II/7 (Stuttgart, 1931) 593-641.

Funk, R. W. "The Enigma of the Famine Visit." *JBL* 75 (1956) 130-36.

Furnish, V. P. "Development in Paul's Thought." *JAAR* 38 (1970) 289-303.

———. "Corinth in Paul's Time — What Can Archaeology Tell Us?" *BARev* 15/3 (1988) 14-27.

Fusco, V. "Le sezioni-noi degli Atti nella discussione recente." *BeO* 25 (1983) 73-86.

———. "Ancora sulle sezioni-noi degli Atti." *RBI* 39 (1991) 231-39.

Gabba, E. "True History and False History in Classical Antiquity." *JRS* 71 (1981) 49-62.

Gaechter, P. "Jerusalem und Antiochia." *Petrus und seine Zeit. Neutestamentliche Studien* (Innsbruck, 1958) 155-212.

Gager, J. G. "Jews, Gentiles and Synagogues in the Book of Acts." *HTR* 79 (1986) 91-99.

Gaheis, A. "Claudius 256 (Ti. Claudius Nero Germanicus) VI: Schriftstellerische Tätigkeit." *PRE* I/6 (Stuttgart, 1899) 2836-39.

Gaiffier, B. de. "Le Breviarum Apostolorum (*BHL* 652). Tradition manuscrite et oeuvres apparantées." *AnBoll* 81 (1963) 89-116.

Galanis, J. L. "Ὁ ἀπόστολος Παῦλος καὶ ἡ Θεσσαλονίκη." *DeltBiblMel* 14 (1985) 61-72.

Galland-Hallyn, P. "Bibliographie suétonienne (Les 'Vies des XII Césars') 1950-1988. Vers une réhabilitation." *ANRW* II 33.5 (Berlin/New York, 1991) 3576-3622.

Gallivan, P. A. "The *fasti* for the Reign of Claudius." *CQ* 88 (1978) 407-26.

Gamble, H. A. *The Textual History of the Letter to the Romans: A Study in Textual and Literary Criticism* (Grand Rapids, 1977).

Gapp, K. S. *Famine in the Roman World from the Founding of Rome to the Time of Trajan* (diss., Princeton, 1934).

———. "The Universal Famine under Claudius." *HTR* 28 (1935) 258-65.

Garcia Del Moral, A. " 'Nosotros los vivos': ¿Convicción personal de Pablo o reinterpretación de un salmo? (I Tes 4,13–5,11)." *Communio* 20 (1987) 3-56.

Garnsey, P. "The Lex Iulia and Appeal under the Empire." *JRS* 56 (1966) 167-89.

———. *Social Status and Legal Privilege in the Roman Empire* (Oxford, 1970).

———. "Famine in Rome." In *idem* and C. R. Whittaker. *Trade and Famine in Classical Antiquity*. Cambridge Philological Society supplementary vol. 8 (Cambridge, 1983) 56-65.

———. *Famine and Food Supply in the Graeco-Roman World: Responses to Risk and Crises* (Cambridge, 1988).

Garnsey, P., and Saller, R. *The Roman Empire: Economy, Society and Culture* (London, 1987).

Garzetti, A. *From Tiberius to the Antonines: A History of the Roman Empire A.D. 14-192* (London, 1974).

Gascou, J. *Suétone historien. BEFAR* 255 (Rome, 1984).

Gasque, W. W. *A History of the Criticism of the Acts of the Apostles. BGBE* 17 (Tübingen, 1975).

————. "The Historical Value of Acts." *TynBul* (1989) 136-57.

————. "Tarsus." *ABD* VI (New York, 1992) 333f.

Gauger, J. D. *Beiträge zur jüdischen Apologetik. Untersuchungen zur Authentizität von Urkunden bei Flavius Josephus und im 1. Makkabäerbuch. BBB* 49 (Cologne/ Bonn, 1977).

Gaventa, B. R. "Galatians 1 and 2: Autobiography as Paradigm." *NT* 27 (1986) 309-26.

Gawlikowski, M. *Le Temple palmyrénien* (Warsaw, 1973).

————. "Les dieux des Nabatéens." *ANRW* II 18.4 (Berlin/New York, 1990) 2659-77.

Geiger, L. *Quid de Judaeorum moribus atque institutis scriptoribus Romanis persuasum fuerit. Commentatio historica* (Berlin, 1872).

Gempf, C. H. "The God-Fearers." In C. J. Hemer. *The Book of Acts in the Setting of Hellenistic History. WUNT* I/49 (Tübingen, 1989) 444-47.

Gentry, K. L. *Before Jerusalem Fell: Dating the Book of Revelation* (Tyler, 1989).

Georgi, D. *The Opponents of Paul in Second Corinthians: A Study of Religious Propaganda in Late Antiquity* (Eng. trans., Philadelphia, 1986).

————. *Remembering the Poor: The History of Paul's Collection for Jerusalem* (Nashville, 1992).

————. "Zu neuen Tendenzen gegenwärtiger Paulusforschung." *EvErz* 37 (1985) 462-79.

————. *Der Armen zu gedenken. Die Geschichte der Kollekte des Paulus für Jerusalem* (Neukirchen/Vluyn, 1994).

Gerhardt, O. "In welchem Jahre wurde der Apostel Paulus in Jerusalem gefangengesetzt?" *NKZ* 33 (1922) 89-114.

Gerov, B. "Die Grenzen der römischen Provinz Thracia bis zur Gründung des Aurelianischen Dakien." *ANRW* II 7.1 (Berlin/New York, 1979) 212-40.

Gerth, B. "Iunius Gallio." *PRE* 19 (Stuttgart, 1918) 1035-39.

Gese, H. "Τὸ δὲ Ἁγὰρ Σινᾶ ὄρος ἐστὶν ἐν τῇ Ἀραβίᾳ (Gal 4,25)." *Vom Sinai zum Zion. Alttestamentliche Beiträge zur biblischen Theologie. BEvT* 64 (Munich, 1974) 49-62.

Gewalt, D. "1 Thess 4,15-17; 1 Kor 15,51 und Mk 9,1 — Zur Abgrenzung eines 'Herrenwortes'." *Linguistica Biblica* 51 (1982) 105-13.

Geyser, A. S. "Paul, the Apostolic Decree and the Liberals in Corinth." *Studia Paulina in honorem Johannis de Zwaan Septuagenarii* (Haarlem, 1953) 124-38.

————. "Un essaie d'explication de Rm. XV.19," *NTS* 6 (1959/60) 156-59.

Giesen, H., "Naherwartung des Paulus in 1 Thess 4,13-18?" *SNTU* 10 (1985) 123-49.

Giet, S. "Le Second Voyage de Saint Paul à Jérusalem." *RevScRel* 25 (1951) 265-69.

————. "Les trois premiers voyages de Saint Paul à Jérusalem." *RSR* 41 (1953) 321-47.

————. "Nouvelles remarques sur les voyages de Saint Paul à Jérusalem." *RevScRel* 31 (1957) 329-42.

————. "Traditions chronologiques légendaires ou historiques," *Studia Evangelica I. TU* 73 (East Berlin, 1957) 607-20.

Gilbert, G. H. "The New Chronology of Paul's Life." *BS* 55 (1898) 244-58.

Gilchrist, J. M. "Paul and the Corinthians — The Sequence of Letters and Visits." *JSNT* 34 (1988) 47-69.

451

Gill, D. W. J. "Erastus the Aedile." *TynBul* 40 (1989) 293-302.

―――. "Corinth: A Roman Colony in Achaea." *BZ* 37 (1993) 259-64.

―――. "Macedonia." In D. W. Gill and C. Gempf. *The Book of Acts in Its Graeco-Roman Setting*. A1CS II (Grand Rapids and Carlisle, 1994), 397-418.

―――. "Achaia." *Ibid.*, 433-54.

―――. "Acts and Roman Policy in Judaea." In R. Bauckham. *The Book of Acts in Its Palestinian Setting*. A1CS IV (Grand Rapids and Carlisle, 1995) 15-26.

―――. "Paul's Travels through Cyprus (Acts 13:4-12)." *TynBul* 46 (1995) 219-28.

Gilliard, F. "The Problem of the Antisemitic Comma between 1 Thessalonians 2.14 and 15." *NTS* 35 (1989) 481-502.

Gillman, J. "Signals of Transformation in 1 Thessalonians 4:13-18." *CBQ* 47 (1985) 263-81.

―――. Review of R. Jewett, *The Thessalonian Correspondence* (Philadelphia, 1986). *CBQ* 50 (1988) 325.

―――. "Paul's Εἴσοδος: The Proclaimed and the Proclaimer (1 Thes 2,8)." In R. F. Collins. *The Thessalonian Correspondence*. BETL 87 (Leuven, 1990) 62-70.

Glueck, N. *Deities and Dolphins: The Story of the Nabateans* (London, 1966).

Gnilka, J. Review of G. Lüdemann, *Paulus, der Heidenapostel I* (Göttingen, 1980). *BZ* 25 (1981) 148-50.

―――. *Paulus von Tarsus. Zeuge und Apostel*. HThK Supplementband 6 (Freiburg, 1996).

Goetz, H. W. *Die Geschichtstheologie des Orosius* (Darmstadt, 1980).

Goguel, M. "Sur la chronologie Paulinienne." *RHR* 65 (1912) 285-339.

―――. *Jesus and the Origins of Christianity* (Eng. trans., New York, 1960).

Goldhill, S. D. "The Great Dionysia and Civic Ideology." *JHS* 107 (1987) 58-76.

Goldstine, H. H. *New and Full Moons 1001 B.C. to A.D. 1651* (Philadelphia, 1973).

Golla, E. *Zwischenbesuch und Zwischenbrief. Eine Untersuchung der Frage, ob der Apostel Paulus zwischen dem ersten und zweiten Korintherbrief eine Reise nach Korinth unternommen und einen uns verlorenen Brief an die Korinther geschrieben habe*. BibS(F) 20/4 (Freiburg, 1922).

Goodman, M. *The Ruling Class of Judaea: The Origins of the Jewish Revolt against Rome A.D. 66-70* (Cambridge, 1987).

―――. "Jewish Proselytizing in the First Century." In J. Lieu, J. North, and T. Rajak. *The Jews among Pagans and Christians in the Roman Empire* (London, 1992) 53-78.

Goodman, M. *Mission and Conversion: Proselytizing in the Religious History of the Roman Empire* (Oxford, 1994).

Goppelt, L. *Christentum und Judentum im ersten und zweiten Jahrhundert. Ein Aufriß der Urgeschichte der Kirche*. BFCT II/55 (Gütersloh, 1954).

―――. *Jesus, Paul and Judaism: An Introduction to New Testament Theology* (Eng. trans., London, 1964) (= translation of the first half of *Christentum und Judentum im ersten und zweiten Jahrhundert*).

―――. *Apostolic and Post-Apostolic Times* (Eng. trans., London, 1970).

Goudoever, J. van. *Biblical Calendars* (Leiden, ²1961).

Gough, M. *The Early Christians* (London, 1960).

Goulder, M. D. "Did Luke Know Any of the Pauline Letters?" *PerspRelSt* 13 (1986) 97-112.

―――. "Silas in Thessalonica." *JSNT* 48 (1992) 87-106.

Gounaris, G. "Παρατηρήσεις τινές ἐπὶ τῆς χρονολογίας τῶν τειχῶν τῆς Θεσσαλονίκης." *Mak* 11 (1971) 311-22.

―――. *The Walls of Thessaloniki. I.M.X.A. Guides* 8 (Thessalonica, 1982).

452

Graetz, H. *History of the Jews* (Eng. trans., Philadelphia, 1891-98).

Graf, D. F., Isaac, B., and Roll, I. "Roman Roads." *ABD* V (New York, 1992) 782-87.

Graf, D. F. "Les routes romaines d'Arabie Pétrée." *MBib* 59 (1989) 54-56.

———. "Aretas." *ABD* I (New York, 1992) 373-76.

———. "Nabataeans." *ABD* IV (New York, 1992) 970-73.

Grant, M. *The Jews in the Roman World* (New York, 1973).

———. *Saint Paul* (New York, 1976).

Grayston, K. Review of G. Lüdemann, *Paul: Apostle to the Gentiles* (Eng. trans., Philadelphia, 1984). *JTS* 37 (1986) 180-82.

Green, E. M. B. "Syria and Cilicia — A Note." *ET* 71 (1959/60) 52f.

———. *Evangelism in the Early Church* (Grand Rapids, 1970).

Green, J. B. "Festus (Porcius)." *ABD* II (New York, 1992) 794f.

Grégoire, H. Review of H. I. Bell, *Jews and Christians in Egypt* (London, 1924). *Byz* 1 (1924) 638-47.

Gressmann, H. "Jüdische Mission in der Werdezeit des Christentums." *ZMR* 39 (1924) 169-83.

Griffe, É. *Les persécutions contre les chrétiens aux Ier et IIe siècles* (Paris, 1967).

Griffin, M. T. *Nero: The End of a Dynasty* (London, 1984).

Groag, E. "Claudius 256 (Ti. Claudius Nero Germanicus) I-V." *PRE* I/6 (Stuttgart, 1899) 2778-2836.

———. "Sergius 34ff (Sergii Paulli)." *PRE* II/4 (Stuttgart, 1923) 1714-18.

———. *Die römischen Reichsbeamten von Achaia bis auf Diokletian. Schriften der Balkankommission (Antiquarische Abteilung)* 9 (Vienna/Leipzig, 1939).

Grosheide, F. W. "De chronologie van het leven van Paulus." *GThT* 19 (1918/19) 349-61.

Grundmann, W. *Die frühe Christenheit und ihre Schriften. Umwelt, Entstehung und Eigenart der neutestamentlichen Bücher* (Stuttgart, 1983).

Guarducci, M. "La data del martirio di san Pietro." *ParPass* 23 (1968) 81-117.

———. *The Tomb of St. Peter: The New Discoveries in the Sacred Grottoes of the Vatican* (Eng. trans., New York, 1960).

Gülzow, H. *Christentum und Sklaverei in den ersten drei Jahrhunderten* (Bonn, 1969).

———. "Soziale Gegebenheiten der altkirchlichen Mission." In H. Frohnes and U. W. Knorr. *Kirchengeschichte als Missionsgeschichte I: Die Alte Kirche* (Munich, 1974) 189-226.

Gugel, H. *Studien zur biographischen Technik Suetons. WStBH* 7 (Vienna, 1977).

Guillaumier, P. "New Perspective on the Historicity of St. Paul's Shipwreck on Melite." In M. Galea and J. Ciarlo. *St. Paul in Malta: A Compendium of Pauline Studies* (Malta, 1992) 53-114.

———. "The Melite-Cephalonia Deception." *The Sunday Times (Malta)* (1 November 1992) 30f.

———. "The Rise of Maltese Christianity and the Pauline Tradition." *The Sunday Times (Malta)* (8 November 1992) 42f.

Gundry, R. H. "The Hellenization of Dominical Tradition and the Christianization of Jewish Tradition in the Eschatology of 1-2 Thessalonians." *NTS* 33 (1987) 161-78.

Gunther, J. J. *Paul: Messenger and Exile: A Study in the Chronology of His Life and Letters* (Valley Forge, 1972).

———. "The Association of Mark and Barnabas with Egyptian Christianity." *EQ* 54 (1982) 219-33; 55 (1983) 21-29.

Guterman, S. L. *Religious Toleration and Persecution in Ancient Rome* (London, 1951).

Gutschmid, A. von. "Verzeichnis der nabatäischen Könige." In J. Euting. *Nabatäische Inschriften aus Arabian* (Berlin, 1885) 84-89.

Guyot, G. H. "The Chronology of St. Paul." *CBQ* 6 (1944) 28-36.

Haacker, K. "Die Gallio-Episode und die paulinische Chronologie." *BZ* 16 (1972) 252-55.

──────. "Die Berufung des Verfolgers und die Rechtfertigung des Gottlosen. Erwägungen zum Zusammenhang zwischen Biographie und Theologie des Apostels Paulus." *TBei* 6 (1977) 1-19.

──────. "Dibelius und Cornelius. Ein Beitrag formgeschichtlicher Überlieferungskritik." *BZ* 24 (1980) 234-51.

──────. "Erst unter Quirinius? Ein Übersetzungsvorschlag zu Lk 2,2." *BN* 38/39 (1987) 39-43.

──────. "Urchristliche Mission und kulturelle Identität. Beobachtungen zur Strategie und Homiletik des Apostels Paulus." *TBei* 19 (1988) 61-72.

──────. "Gallio." *ABD* II (New York, 1992) 901-3.

──────. "Zum Werdegang des Apostels Paulus. Biographische Daten und ihre theologische Relevanz." In W. Haase. *ANRW* II 26/2 (Berlin and New York, 1995) 815-938, 1924-33.

Haas, O. *Paulus der Missionar. Ziel, Grundsätze und Methoden der Missionstätigkeit des Apostels Paulus nach seinen eigenen Aussagen. Münsterschwarzacher Studien* 11 (Münsterschwarzach, 1971).

Hachlili, R., and Killebrew, A. "The Saga of the Goliath Family — As Revealed in Their Newly Discovered 2000 Year-Old Tomb." *BARev* 9/1 (1983) 44-53.

Hachlili, R., and Smith, P. "The Genealogy of the Goliath Family." *BASOR* 235 (1979) 67-70.

Haddad, G. *Aspects of Social Life in Antioch in the Hellenistic-Roman Period* (diss., Chicago, 1949).

Hadorn, W. *Die Abfassung der Thessalonicherbriefe in der Zeit der dritten Missionsreise des Paulus. BFCT* 24/3-4 (Gütersloh, 1919/20).

──────. "Die Abfassung der Thessalonicherbriefe auf der dritten Missionsreise und der Kanon des Marcion." *ZNW* 19 (1919/20) 67-72.

Haenchen, E. "The Book of Acts as Source Material for the History of Early Christianity." In L. E. Keck and J. L. Martyn. *Studies in Luke-Acts: Essays Presented in Honor of Paul Schubert* (New York/Nashville, 1966) 258-78.

Hagen, V. W. von. *The Roads That Led to Rome* (London, 1967).

Hahn, F. *Mission in the New Testament* (Eng. trans., Naperville, Ill., 1965).

Halfmann, H. *Die Senatoren aus dem östlichen Teil des Imperium Romanum bis zum Ende des 2. Jahrhunderts n. Chr. Hyp.* 58 (Göttingen, 1979).

Hall, D. R. "St. Paul and Famine Relief: A Study in Galatians 2,10." *ET* 82 (1971/72) 309-11.

Hall, R. G. *Revealed Histories: Techniques for Ancient Jewish and Christian Historiography. JSPSup* 6 (Sheffield, 1991).

Hamman, A. "Chrétiens et Christianisme vus et jugés par Suétone, Tacite et Pline le Jeune." *Forma Futuri. Studi in onore del Cardinale Michele Pellegrino* (Turin, 1975) 91-109.

──────. *Die ersten Christen* (Stuttgart, 1985).

Hammond, N. G. L. *Epirus: The Geography, the Ancient Remains, the History and the Topography of Epirus and Adjacent Areas* (Oxford, 1967).

──────. "The Western Part of the Via Egnatia." *JRS* 64 (1974) 185-94.

──────. "The Via Egnatia in Western Macedonia." *AncMac* IV (Thessalonica, 1986) 247-55.

Hammond, P. C., *The Nabataeans — Their History, Culture and Archaeology," SIMA* 37 (Gothenburg, 1973).

————. "Die Ausgrabung des Löwen-Greifen-Tempels in Petra (1973-1983)." In M. Lindner. *Petra. Neue Ausgrabungen und Entdeckungen* (Munich, 1986) 16-30.

Hand, A. R. *Charities and Social Aid in Greece and Rome* (Ithaca, 1968).

Hansen, G. W. "Galatia." In D. W. J. Gill and C. Gempf. *The Book of Acts in Its Graeco-Roman Setting*. A1CS II (Grand Rapids and Carlisle, 1994) 377-96.

Hanslik, R. "Claudius 39 (Ti. C. Nero Germanicus)." *KP* I (Munich, 1964) 1215-18.

————. "Gallio." *KP* II (Munich, 1967) 686.

Harding, G. L. *The Antiquities of Jordan* (London, ²1967).

Harding, M. "On the Historicity of Acts: Comparing Acts 9.23-5 with 2 Corinthians 11.32-3." *NTS* 39 (1993) 518-38.

Hardy, E. G. *Studies in Roman History* (London, 1906).

Hare, D. R. A. "Introduction" to J. Knox. *Chapters in a Life of Paul*. Rev. ed. (Macon, 1986) ix-xxii.

Harnack, A. von. *Geschichte der altchristlichen Litteratur bis Eusebius*. I: *Die Überlieferung und der Bestand;* II: *Die Chronologie* (Leipzig, 1893-).

————. *New Testament Studies I: Luke the Physician, the Author of the Third Gospel and the Acts of the Apostles* (Eng. trans., London, 1907).

————. "Die Zeitangaben in der Apostelgeschichte." *SPAW.PH 1907* I (Berlin, 1907) 375-99.

————. *New Testament Studies III. The Acts of the Apostles* (Eng. trans., London, 1909).

————. "Chronologische Berechnung des 'Tags von Damaskus.' " *SPAW.PH 1912* (Berlin, 1912) 673-82.

————. *Der kirchengeschichtliche Ertrag der exegetischen Arbeiten des Origenes (2. Teil)*. *TU* 42/4 (Leipzig, 1919).

————. *Die Mission und Ausbreitung des Christentums in den ersten drei Jahrhunderten* (Leipzig, ⁴1924). Eng. trans., *The Mission and Expansion of Christianity in the First Three Centuries* (London, 1908).

Harnisch, W. *Eschatologische Existenz. Ein exegetischer Beitrag zum Sachanliegen von 1 Thessalonicher 4,13–5,11*. FRLANT 110 (Göttingen, 1973).

Harrer, G. A. "Saul Who Also Is Called Paul." *HTR* 33 (1940) 19-33.

Harris, B. F. "Bithynia: Roman Sovereignty and the Survival of Hellenism." *ANRW* II 7.2 (Berlin/New York, 1980) 857-901.

Harris, J. R. "A Study in Letter Writing." *Exp* V/8 (1898) 161-80.

Harris, M. J. "References to Jesus in Early Classical Authors." In D. Wenham. *Gospel Perspectives V: The Jesus Tradition outside the Gospels* (Sheffield, 1985) 343-68.

Harrison, R. K. "Meshech." *ISBE* III (Grand Rapids, 1986) 328.

Hartke, W. *Vier Urchristliche Parteien und ihre Vereinigung zur apostolischen Kirche I/II*. SSA 24 (East Berlin, 1961).

Hartman, L. *Prophecy Interpreted: The Formation of Some Jewish Apocalyptic Texts and the Eschatological Discourse Mark 13 Par*. CBNT 1 (Lund, 1966).

————. "The Functions of Some So-Called Apocalyptic Timetables." *NTS* 22 (1976) 1-14.

————. " 'On Reading Others' Letter'." In G. W. E. Nickelsburg and G. W. MacRae. *Christians among Jews and Gentiles. Festschrift Krister Stendahl* (Philadelphia, 1986) 137-46.

Hausrath, A. *The Time of the Apostles* (Eng. trans., London, 1895).

Havener, I. "The Pre-Pauline Creedal Formulae of 1 Thessalonians." *SBL Seminary Papers* (Chico, 1981) 105-28.

————. "First and Second Thessalonians: An Introduction." *BiTod* 26 (1988) 324-27.

Hayles, D. J. "The Roman Census and Jesus' Birth. Was Luke Correct? I: The Roman

Census System." *Buried History* 9 (1973) 113-32; "II: Quirinius' Career and a Census in Herod's Day." *Buried History* 10 (1974) 16-31.

Hays, R. B. *The Faith of Jesus Christ. SBLDS* 56 (Chico, 1983).

Head, P. "Acts and the Problem of Its Text." In B. W. Winter and A. D. Clarke. *The Book of Acts in Its Ancient Literary Setting.* A1CS I (Grand Rapids and Carlisle, 1993) 415-44.

Heckel, U. *Kraft in Schwachheit. Untersuchungen to 2. Kor 10–13.* WUNT 11/56 (Tübingen, 1993).

———. "Das Bild der Heiden und die Identität der Christen bei Paulus." In R. Feldmeier and U. Heckel. *Die Heiden. Juden, Christen und das Problem des Fremden. WUNT* I/70 (Tübingen, 1993) 269-96.

Hedley, P. L. "Pilate's Arrival in Judaea." *JTS* 35 (1934) 56-58.

Helck, H. W. "Alexandreia." *KP* I (Munich, 1964) 244f.

Helly, B. "Politarques, poliarques et politophylaques." *AncMac* II (Thessalonica, 1977) 531-44.

Hemberg, B. *Die Kabiren* (Uppsala, 1950).

Hemer, C. J. "Alexandria Troas." *TynBul* 26 (1975) 79-112.

———. "Euraquilo and Melita." *JTS* 26 (1975) 100-111.

———. "The Adjective 'Phrygia'." *JTS* 27 (1976) 122-26.

———. "Phrygia: A Further Note." *JTS* 28 (1977) 99-101.

———. "Acts and Galatians Reconsidered." *Themelios* 2 (1977) 81-88.

———. "Luke the Historian." *BJRL* 60 (1977/78) 28-51.

———. "Observations on Pauline Chronology." In D. A. Hagner and M. J. Harris. *Pauline Studies: Essays Presented to Professor F. F. Bruce* (Exeter/Grand Rapids, 1980) 3-18.

———. "First Person Narrative in Acts 27–28." *TynBul* (1985) 79-110.

———. "The Name of Paul." *Ibid.,* 179-83.

———. *The Letters to the Seven Churches of Asia in Their Local Setting. JSNTSup* 11 (Sheffield, 1986).

———. "Tarsus." *ISBE* IV (Grand Rapids, 1988) 734-36.

———. *The Book of Acts in the Setting of Hellenistic History. WUNT* I/49. Edited by C. H. Gempf (Tübingen, 1989).

Hendrix, H. L. *Thessalonians Honor Romans* (diss., Harvard, 1984).

———. Review of R. Jewett. *The Thessalonian Correspondence* (Philadelphia, 1986). *JBL* 107 (1988) 763-66.

———. "Philippi," *ABD* V (New York, 1992) 313-17.

———. "Thessalonica." *ABD* VI (New York, 1992) 523-27.

Hengel, M. "Maria Magdalena und die Frauen als Zeugen." In O. Betz *et al. Abraham unser Vater. Festschrift Otto Michel.* AGSU 5 (Leiden, 1963) 243-56.

———. "Die Ursprünge der christlichen Mission." *NTS* 18 (1971/72) 15-38. Eng. trans., "The Origins of the Christian Mission." In *Between Jesus and Paul* (London/Philadelphia, 1983) 48-64.

———. "Christologie und neutestamentliche Chronologie. Zu einer Aporie in der Geschichte des Urchristentums." In H. Baltensweiler and B. Reicke. *Neues Testament und Geschichte. Festschrift Oscar Cullmann* (Zurich/Tübingen, 1972) 43-67. Eng. trans., "Christology and New Testament Chronology." In *Between Jesus and Paul* (London/Philadelphia, 1983) 30-47.

———. *Property and Riches in the Early Church: Aspects of a Social History of Early Christianity* (Eng. trans., Philadelphia, 1974).

————. *Judaism and Hellenism: Studies in Their Encounter in Palestine during the Early Hellenistic Period* (Eng. trans., Philadelphia, 1974).

————. "Zwischen Jesus und Paulus. Die 'Hellenisten,' die 'Sieben' und Stephanus (Apg 6,1-15; 7,54–8,3)." *ZTK* 72 (1975) 151-206. Eng. trans., "Between Jesus and Paul." In *Between Jesus and Paul* (London/Philadelphia, 1983) 1-29.

————. *Die Zeloten. Untersuchungen zur jüdischen Freiheitsbewegung in der Zeit von Herodes I. bis 70 N.Chr. AGSU* 1 (Leiden, [2]1976). Eng. trans., *The Zealots* (Edinburgh, 1989).

————. *Der Sohn Gottes. Die Entstehung der Christologie und die jüdisch-hellenistische Religionsgeschichte* (Tübingen, [2]1977). Eng. trans., *The Son of God: The Origin of Christology and the History of Jewish-Hellenistic Religion* (Philadelphia, 1976).

————. *Crucifixion in the Ancient World and the Folly of the Message of the Cross* (London, 1977).

————. *Zur urchristlichen Geschichtsschreibung* (Stuttgart, 1979; [2]1984). Eng. trans., *Acts and the History of Earliest Christianity* (London, 1979).

————. "Erwägungen zum Sprachgebrauch von Χριστός bei Paulus und in der 'vorpaulinischen' Überlieferung." In M. D. Hooker and S. G. Wilson. *Paul and Paulinism. Essays in Honour of C. K. Barrett* (1982) 135-59. Eng. trans., " 'Christos' in Paul." In *Between Jesus and Paul* (London/Philadelphia, 1983) 65-77.

————. "Der Historiker Lukas und die Geographie Palästinas in der Apostelgeschichte." *ZDPV* 99 (1983) 147-83. Eng. trans., "Luke as Geographer and Historian." In *Between Jesus and Paul* (London/Philadelphia, 1983) 97-128.

————. *Between Jesus and Paul: Studies in the Earliest History of Christianity* (London, 1983).

————. "Entstehungszeit und Situation des Markusevangeliums." In H. Cancik. *Markus — Philologie. Historische, literargeschichtliche und stilistische Untersuchungen zum zweiten Evangelium. WUNT* I/33 (Tübingen, 1984) 1-45. Eng. trans., "The Gospel of Mark: Time of Origin and Situation." In *Studies in the Gospel of Mark* (Philadelphia, 1985) 1-30.

————. *Die Evangelienüberschriften. SHAW.PH 1984/3* (Heidelberg, 1984). Eng. trans., "The Titles of the Gospels and the Gospel of Mark." In *Studies in the Gospel of Mark* (Philadelphia, 1985) 64-84.

————. "Jakobus der Herrenbruder — der erste 'Papst'?" In E. Grässer and O. Merk. *Glaube und Eschatologie. Festschrift Werner Georg Kümmel* (Tübingen, 1985) 71-104.

————. "Vorwort" zu T. Zahn, *Der Brief des Paulus and die Galater* (Wuppertal/Zürich, 1990) (repr. of *KNT* IX [Leipzig/Erlangen, [3]1922]) V-VII.

————. "Der vorchristliche Paulus." *TBei* 21 (1990) 174-95. Eng. trans., *The pre-Christian Paul*. In collaboration with Roland Deines (London/Philadelphia, 1991).

————. *Die johanneische Frage. Ein Lösungsversuch. WUNT* I/67 (Tübingen, 1993). Eng. trans., *The Johannine Question* (London/Philadelphia, 1990).

————. "The Geography of Palestine in Acts." In R. Bauckham. *The Book of Acts in Its Palestinian Setting.* A1CS IV (Grand Rapids and Carlisle, 1995) 27-78.

Hengel, M., and Schwemer, A. M. *Paul between Damascus and Antioch: The Unknown Years* (London, 1997).

Hennequin, L. "Delphes (Inscription de)." *DBS* II (Paris, 1934) 355-73.

Hennig, D. *L. Aelius Seianus. Untersuchungen zur Regierung des Tiberius. Vestigia* 21 (Munich, 1975).

————. "Zu neuveröffentlichten Bruchstücken der 'Acta Alexandrinorum'." *Chiron* 5 (1975) 317-35.

Herrmann, L. *Chrestos. Témoignages païens et juifs sur le christianisme du premier siècle.* *Collection Latomus* 109 (Brussels, 1970).

Herrmann, S. "Lud, Luditer." *BHH* II (Göttingen, 1964) 1108.

Herzig, H. E. "Probleme des römischen Straßenwesens. Untersuchungen zu Geschichte und Recht." *ANRW* II/1 (Berlin/New York, 1974) 592-648.

Hicks, E. L. "On Some Political Terms Employed in the New Testament." *ClR* 1 (1887) 4-8, 42-46.

Hild, J. A. "Les Juifs à Rome devant l'opinion et dans la littérature II: Depuis l'avènement d'Auguste jusqu'aux Antonins." *RÉJ* 11 (1885) 18-59.

Hilgenfeld, A. *Historisch-kritische Einleitung in das Neue Testament* (Leipzig, 1875).

————. "Paulus von Damascus bis zum Briefe an die Galater." *ZWTh* 31 (1888) 1-29.

Hill, C. E. "Paul's Understanding of Christ's Kingdom in I Corinthians 15:20-28." *NT* 30 (1988) 297-320.

Hillgarth, J. N. "The Position of Isidorian Studies: A Critical Review of the Literature since 1935." *Isidoriana. Festschrift Manuel C. Diáz y Diáz* (Leon, 1961) 11-74.

Hinson, E. G. *The Evangelization of the Roman Empire: Identity and Adaptability* (Macon, 1981).

Hinz, W. "Chronologie des Lebens Jesu." *ZDMG* 139 (1989) 301-9.

Hirschfeld, O. "Amphipolis." *PRE* I/2 (Stuttgart, 1894) 1949-52.

Hock, R. F. "Paul's Tentmaking and the Problem of His Social Class." *JBL* 97 (1978) 555-64.

————. *The Social Context of Paul's Ministry: Tentmaking and Apostleship* (Philadelphia, 1980).

Hodgson, R. "Gospel and Ethics in First Thessalonians." *BiTod* 26 (1988) 344-49.

Höckmann, O. *Antike Seefahrt. Beck's Archäologische Bibliothek* (Munich, 1985).

Hoehner, H. W. *Chronology of the Apostolic Age* (diss., Dallas Theological Seminary, 1965).

————. *Herod Antipas: A Contemporary of Jesus Christ* (Grand Rapids, ²1980).

————. *Chronological Aspects of the Life of Christ* (Grand Rapids, ⁵1981).

————. "The Date of the Death of Herod the Great." In J. Vardaman and E. M. Yamauchi. *Chronos, Kairos, Christos: Nativity and Chronological Studies Presented to Jack Finegan* (Winona Lake, 1989) 101-11.

————. "Chronology." *Dictionary of Jesus and the Gospels.* Edited by J. B. Green, S. McKnight, and I. H. Marshall (Downers Grove/Leicester, 1992) 118-22.

————. "Pontius Pilate." *Ibid.,* 615-17.

Hölscher, G. *Die Hohepriesterliste bei Josephus und die evangelische Chronologie.* *SHAW.PH 1939/40,* 3. Abhandlung (Heidelberg, 1940).

Hoennicke, G. "Die Chronologie des Lebens des Apostels Paulus." *NKZ* 13 (1902) 569-620.

————. *Die Chronologie des Lebens des Apostels Paulus* (Leipzig, 1903).

Hoerber, R. O. "Galatians 2:1-10 and the Acts of the Apostles." *CTM* 31 (1960) 482-91 (repr. in *Studies in the New Testament* [1991] 12-21).

————. "The Decree of Claudius in Acts 18:2." *CTM* 31 (1960) 690-94 (repr. *ibid.,* 22-26).

Hofius, O. "Unknown Sayings of Jesus." In P. Stuhlmacher. *The Gospel and the Gospels* (Eng. trans., Grand Rapids, 1991) 336-60.

————. "Gal 1,18: ἱστορῆσαι Κηφᾶν." *ZNW* 75 (1984) 73-85 (repr. in *Paulusstudien.* WUNT I/51 [Tübingen, ²1994]) 255-67).

————. "Das Evangelium und Israel. Erwägungen zum Römer 9–11." *ZTK* 83 (1986) 297-324 (repr. in *Paulusstudien,* 175-202).

Hofstede de Groot, C. P. *Pauli Conversio, Praecipuus Theologiae Paulinae Fons* (Groningen, n.d. [1855]).

Holl, K. "Kultursprache und Volkssprache in der altchristlichen Mission." In *Gesammelte Aufsätze zur Kirchengeschichte* II (Tübingen, 1928) 238-48 (repr. in H. Frohnes and U. W. Knorr, *Kirchengeschichte als Missionsgeschichte I: Die alte Kirche* [Munich, 1974] 389-96).

———. "Die Missionsmethode der alten und die der mittelalterlichen Kirche." *Gesammelte Aufsätze* III (Tübingen, 1928) 117-29 (repr. *ibid.,* 3-17).

Holmberg, B. *Paul and Power: The Structure of Authority in the Primitive Church as Reflected in the Pauline Epistles. CBNT* 11 (Lund, 1978).

Holtz, T. "Zum Selbstverständnis des Apostels Paulus." *TLZ* 91 (1966) 321-30.

———. "Traditionen im 1. Thessalonicherbrief." In U. Luz and H. Weder. *Die Mitte des Neuen Testaments. Festschrift Eduard Schweizer* (Göttingen, 1983) 55-78.

———. "The Judgment on the Jews and the Salvation of All Israel. 1 Thes 2,15-16 and Rom 11,25-26." In R. F. Collins. *The Thessalonian Correspondence. BETL* 87 (Leuven, 1990) 284-94.

———. "Paul and the Oral Gospel Tradition." In H. Wansbrough. *Jesus and the Oral Gospel Tradition. JSNTSup* 64 (Sheffield, 1991) 380-93.

———. "Die historischen und theologischen Bedingungen des Römerbriefes." In J. Ådna and O. Hofius. *Evangelium — Schriftauslegung — Kirche. Festschrift für Peter Stuhlmacher* (Göttingen, 1997) 238-54.

Holtzmann, O. *Neutestamentliche Zeitgeschichte* (Berlin, 1895).

———. "Die Jerusalemreisen des Paulus und die Kollekte." *ZNW* 6 (1905) 102-4.

Holzmeister, U. "Neuere Arbeiten über das Datum der Kreuzigung Christi." *Bibl* 13 (1932) 93-103.

———. "Wann War Pilatus Prokurator von Judaea?" *Bibl* 13 (1932) 228-32.

———. *Chronologia Vitae Christi — quam e fontibus digessit et ex ordine proposuit. SPIB* (Rome, 1933).

Homanner, W. *Die Dauer der öffentlichen Wirksamkeit Jesu. Eine patristisch-exegetische Studie. BibS(F)* XIII/3 (Freiburg, 1908).

Hommel, H. "Tacitus und die Christen. Ann XV 44,2-5." *ThV* 3 (1951) 1-30 (repr. in *Sebasmata. Studien zur antiken Religionsgeschichte und zum frühen Christentum* II [Tübingen, 1984] 174-99).

Hooker, M. D. *Jesus and the Servant: The Influence of the Servant Concept of Deutero-Isaiah in the New Testament* (London, 1959).

Horbury, W. "Herod's Temple and 'Herod's Days'." In W. Horbury. *Templum Amicitiae: Essays on the Second Temple Presented to Ernst Bammel. JSNTSup* 48 (Sheffield, 1991) 103-49.

Horsley, G. H. R. "The use of a double name." *NewDoc* I (Macquarie University, 1981) 89-96.

———. "Name Change as an Indication of Religious Conversion in Antiquity." *Numen* 34 (1987) 1-17.

———. "The Inscriptions of Ephesos and the New Testament." *NT* 34 (1992) 105-68.

———. "Names (Double)." *ABD* IV (New York, 1992) 1011-17.

———. "Politarchs." *ABD* V (New York, 1992) 384-89.

Horst, P. W. van der. "The Samaritan Diaspora in Antiquity." *Essays on the Jewish World of Early Christianity. NTOA* 14 (Freiburg [Switzerland]/Göttingen, 1990) 136-47.

———. "The Jews of Ancient Crete." *Ibid.,* 148-65.

———. "Jews and Christians in Aphrodisias in the Light of Their Relations in Other Cities of Asia Minor." *Ibid.,* 166-81.

———. "Das Neue Testament und die jüdischen Grabinschriften aus hellenistisch-römischer Zeit." *BZ* 36 (1992) 161-78.

———. *Ancient Jewish Epitaphs: An Introductory Survey of a Millennium of Jewish Funerary Epigraphy (300 B.C.E.-700 C.E.). Contributions to Biblical Exegesis and Theology* 2 (Kampen, 1991).

———. Review of G. E. Sterling, *Historiography and Self-Definition* (Leiden, 1992). *VC* 47 (1993) 203-6.

Howard, G. "The Beginnings of Christianity in Rome: A Note on Suetonius, Life of Claudius XXV.4." *RestQ* 24 (1981) 175-77.

———. *Paul: Crisis in Galatia: A Study in Early Christian Theology. SNTS.MS* 35 (Cambridge, 1979; ²1990).

Howell, E. B. "St. Paul and the Greek World." *GaR* 11 (1964) 7-29.

Hubaut, M. A. *Paul de Tarse. Bibliothèque d'Histoire du Christianisme* 18 (Paris, 1989).

Huber, W. *Passa und Ostern. Untersuchungen zur Osterfeier der alten Kirche. BZNW* 35 (Berlin, 1969).

Hudson, E. C. "The Principal Family at Pisidian Antioch." *JNEW* 15 (1956) 103-7.

Hübner, H. "Pauli theologiae proprium." *NTS* 26 (1979/80) 445-73.

———. *Das Gesetz bei Paulus. Ein Beitrag zum Werden der paulinischen Theologie. FRLANT* 119 (Göttingen, ³1982). Eng. trans., *Law in Paul's Thought* (Edinburgh, 1984).

———. Review of G. Lüdemann, *Paulus, der Heidenapostel I* (Göttingen, 1980). *TLZ* 107 (1982) 741-44.

———. "Paulusforschung seit 1945. Ein kritischer Literaturbericht." *ANRW* II 25.4 (Berlin/New York, 1987) 2649-2840.

Hugédé, N. *Saint Paul et La Grèce* (Paris, 1982).

Hughes, F. W. "The Rhetoric of 1 Thessalonians." In R. F. Collins. *The Thessalonian Correspondence. BETL* 87 (Leuven, 1990) 94-116.

Hughes, J. J. "Paulus, Sergius." *ISBE* III (Grand Rapids, 1986) 729f.

Huidekoper, F. *Judaism at Rome* (New York, 1880).

Hultgren, A. J. "Paul's Pre-Christian Persecutions of the Church: Their Purpose, Locale, and Nature." *JBL* 95 (1976) 97-111.

———. *Paul's Gospel and Mission: The Outlook from His Letter to the Romans* (Philadelphia, 1985).

Humphrey, J. W. *A Historical Commentary on Cassius Dio's Roman History (Book 59: Caius Caligula)* (diss., Vancouver, 1976).

Humphreys, C. J., and Waddington, W. G. "Dating the Crucifixion." *Nature* 306 (1983) 743-46.

———. "The Date of the Crucifixion." *JASA* 37 (1985) 2-10.

———. "Astronomy and the Date of the Crucifixion." In J. Vardaman and E. M. Yamauchi. *Chronos, Kairos, Christos: Nativity and Chronological Studies Presented to Jack Finegan* (Winona Lake, 1989) 165-81.

Hurd, J. C. *The Origin of 1 Corinthians* (London, 1965).

———. "Pauline Chronology and Pauline Theology." In W. R. Farmer, C. F. D. Moule, and R. R. Niebuhr. *Christian History and Interpretation: Studies Presented to John Knox* (Cambridge, 1967) 225-48.

———. "The Sequence of Paul's Letters." *CJT* 14 (1968) 189-200.

———. "Chronology (Pauline)." *IDBSup* (New York/Nashville, 1976) 166f.

———. "Seminar on Pauline Chronology: Introduction." In B. C. Corley. *Colloquy on New Testament Studies* (Macon, 1983) 265-70.

————. Review of G. Lüdemann, *Paul: Apostle to the Gentiles* (Eng. trans., Philadelphia, 1984). *Interp* 40 (1986) 323f.

Hurtado, L. W. "The Jerusalem Collection and the Book of Galatians." *JSNT* 5 (1979) 46-62.

Husband, R. W. "The Year of the Crucifixion." *TAPA* 46 (1915) 15-27.

Hutchinson, V. J. "The Cult of Dionysos/Bacchus in the Graeco-Roman World: New Light from Archaeological Studies." *Journal of Roman Archaeology* 4 (1991) 222-30.

Huzar, E. "Claudius — The Erudite Emperor." *ANRW* II 32.1 (Berlin/New York, 1984) 611-50.

Hyldahl, N. "Die Frage nach der literarischen Einheit des Zweiten Korintherbriefes." *ZNW* 64 (1973) 289-306.

————. "Paul og Arabien." In N. Hyldahl and E. Nielsen. *Hilsen til Noack* (Kopenhagen, 1975) 102-7.

————. *Die paulinische Chronologie.* ATDan XIX (Leiden, 1986).

Iovino, P. "Paolo: esperienza e teoria della missione." In G. Ghiberti. *La missione nel mondo antico e nella Bibbia. Ricerche Storico Bibliche* 1/1990 (Bologna, 1990) 155-84.

Isaac, B. "Bandits in Judaea and Arabia." *HSCP* 88 (1984) 171-203.

Isserlin, B. S. J. "The Isis and Her Voyage: Some Additional Remarks." *TAPA* 86 (1955) 319-21.

Iwry, S. "Was There a Migration to Damascus? The Problem of שבי ישראל" (Modern Hebrew). *EI* 9 (1969) 80-88.

Jacques, F. "Le nombre de sénateurs aux IIe et IIIe siècles." In *Epigraphia e ordine senatorio* I (*Tituli* 4) (Rome, 1982) 137ff.

Jalabert, L. "Damas." *DACL* IV (Paris, 1920) 119-45.

Janin, R. "Damas." *DHGE* XIV (Paris, 1960) 42-47.

————. *Les églises et les monastères des grands centres byzantins (Bithynie, Hellespont, Latros, Galésios, Trébizonde, Athènes, Thessalonique)* (Paris, 1975).

Janne, H. "Un passage controversé de la lettre de Claude aux Alexandriens." *RA* 35 (1932) 268-81.

————. "Impulsore Chresto." *AIPh* 2 *(Mélanges Bidez)* (Brussels, 1934) 531-53.

————. "La lettre de Claude aux Alexandriens." *AIPh* 4/1 *(Mélanges F. Cumont)* (Brussels, 1936) 273-95.

Janssen, L. F. " 'Superstitio' and the Persecution of the Christians." *VC* 33 (1979) 131-59.

Jaubert, A. *Les premiers chrétiens. Le temps qui court* 39 (Paris, 1967).

Jegher-Bucher, V. "Formgeschichtliche Betrachtung zu Galater 2,11-16. Antwort an James D. Hester." *TZ* 46 (1990) 305-21.

Jeremias, J. "Golgotha." ΑΓΓΕΛΟΣ 1 (Leipzig, 1926).

————. *Jerusalem zur Zeit Jesu B. Hoch und Niedrig, 1. Die Gesellschaftliche Oberschicht* (Gütersloh, 1929). Eng. trans., *Jerusalem in the Time of Jesus* (Philadelphia, 1969).

————. *The Eucharistic Words of Jesus* (Eng. trans., London, 1966).

————. *Jerusalem in the Time of Jesus* (Eng. trans., Philadelphia, 1969).

————. *Unknown Sayings of Jesus* (Eng. trans., New York, 1957).

————. "Zur Geschichtlichkeit des Verhörs Jesu." *Abba. Studien zur neutestamentlichen Theologie und Zeitgeschichte* (Göttingen, 1966) 139-44.

————. "Sabbatjahr und neutestamentliche Chronologie." *Ibid.,* 233-38.

————. " 'Flesh and Blood Cannot Inherit the Kingdom of God' (I Cor.XV.50)." *Ibid.,* 298-307 (previously in *NTS* 2 [1955/56] 151-59).

————. *Der Schlüssel zur Theologie des Apostels Paulus.* CH 115 (Stuttgart, 1971).

————. *New Testament Theology* (Eng. trans., New York, 1971).

Jervell, J. "The History of Early Christianity in the Acts of the Apostles." *The Unknown Paul: Essays on Luke-Acts and Early Christian History* (Minneapolis, 1984) 13-25.

———. "Paulus in der Apostelgeschichte und die Geschichte des Urchristentums." *NTS* 32 (1986) 378-92.

Jewett, R. "The Agitators and the Galatians Congregation." *NTS* 17 (1970/71) 198-212.

———. *Paul's Anthropological Terms. AGSU* 10 (Leiden, 1971).

———. *A Chronology of Paul's Life* (Philadelphia, 1979).

———. *Paulus-Chronologie. Ein Versuch* (Munich, 1982).

———. "Chronology and Methodology: Reflections on the Debate over Chapters in a Life of Paul." In B. C. Corley. *Colloquy on New Testament Studies. A Time for Reappraisal and Fresh Approaches* (Macon, 1983) 271-87.

———. *The Thessalonian Correspondence: Pauline Rhetoric and Millenarian Piety* (Philadelphia, 1986).

———. Review of N. Hyldahl, *Die paulinische Chronologie* (Leiden, 1986). *JBL* 107 (1988) 547f.

Johanson, B. C. *To All the Brethren: A Text-Linguistic and Rhetorical Approach to I Thessalonians. CBNT* 16 (Uppsala, 1987).

Johnson, D. " 'And They Went Eight Stades toward Herodeion.' " In J. Vardaman and E. M. Yamauchi. *Chronos, Kairos, Christos: Nativity and Chronological Studies Presented to Jack Finegan* (Winona Lake, 1989) 93-99.

Johnson, L. T. *The Writings of the New Testament: An Interpretation* (London, 1986).

Johnson, S. E. "The Apostle Paul and the Riot in Ephesus." *LexTQ* 14 (1979) 79-88.

———. *Paul the Apostle and His Cities. GNS* 21 (Wilmington, 1987).

Jones, A. H. M. *The Herods of Judaea* (Oxford, 1938).

———. "I Appeal unto Caesar." *Studies in Roman Government and Law* (Oxford, 1960) 53-65.

———. "Imperial and Senatorial Jurisdiction in the Early Principate." *Ibid.,* 69-98.

———. "Procurators and Prefects in the Early Principate." *Ibid.,* 117-25.

Jones, B. W. "Claudius (Emperor)." *ABD* I (New York, 1992) 1054f.

Jones, H. S. "Claudius and the Jewish Question at Alexandria." *JRS* 16 (1926) 17-35.

Jones, M. "A New Chronology of the Life of Paul." *Exp* 8th ser. 17 (1919) 363-83, 424-46; 18 (1919) 99-120.

Jones, P. R. "1 Corinthians 15:8: Paul the Last Apostle." *TynBul* 36 (1985) 3-34.

Judge, E. A. *The Social Pattern of the Christian Groups in the First Century* (London, 1960).

———. "The Decrees of Caesar at Thessalonica." *RThR* 30 (1971) 1-7.

———. "Claudius." *IBD* I (Leicester, 1980) 298.

———. "Thessalonica." *IBD* III (Leicester, 1980) 1557f.

———. "The Social Identity of the First Christians: A Question of Method in Religious History." *JRH* 11 (1980/81) 201-17.

———. "St. Paul and Classical Society." *JAC* 15 (1972) 19-36.

———. *Rank and Status in the World of the Caesars and St. Paul. University of Canterbury Publications* 29 (Canterbury, 1982).

———. "The Regional *Kanon* for Requisitioned Transport." *NewDoc* I (Macquarie University, 1981) 36-45.

———. "Greek Names of Latin Origin." *NewDoc* II (Macquarie University, 1982) 106-8.

———. "Perga." *ISBE* III (Grand Rapids, 1986) 767f.

Judge, E. A. "Judaism and the Rise of Christianity: A Roman Perspective." *TynBul* 45 (1994) 335-68.

Judge, E. A., and Pickering, S. R. "Papyrus Documentation of Church and Community in Egypt to the Mid-Fourth Century." *JAC* 20 (1977) 47-71.

Judge, E. A., and Thomas, G. S. R. "The Origin of the Church at Rome: A New Solution." *RThR* 25 (1966) 81-94.

Junkelmann, M. *Die Legionen des Augustus. Der römische Soldat im archäologischen Experiment. Kulturgeschichte der Antiken Welt* 33 (Mainz, 1986).

Juster, J. *Les Juifs dans l'empire Romain. Leur condition juridique, économique et sociale* II (Paris, 1914).

Kahrstedt, U. *Syrische Territorien in hellenistischer Zeit. AGWG.PH* n.s. 19.2 (Berlin, 1926).

Kampling, R. "Eine auslegungsgeschichtliche Skizze zu 1 Thess 2,14-16." In D. A. Koch and H. Lichtenberger. *Begegnungen zwischen Christentum und Judentum in Antike und Mittelalter. Festschrift Heinz Schreckenberg. Schriften des Institutum Judaicum Delitzschianum* 1 (Göttingen, 1993) 183-213.

Kane, J. P. "The Ossuary Inscriptions of Jerusalem." *JSS* 23 (1978) 268-82.

Karawidopoulos, J. "Ἀποστόλου Παύλου Α', Β' πρός Θεσσαλονικεῖς ἐπιστολές: Οἱ ἀπαρχές τῆς Χριστιανικῆς γραμματείας." In Χριστιανική Θεσσαλονίκη ἀπό τοῦ Ἀποστόλου Παύλου μέχρι καί τῆς Κωνσταντινείου ἐποχῆς (Thessalonica, 1990) 45-57.

Kasher, A. *The Jews in Hellenistic and Roman Egypt: The Struggle for Equal Rights. TSAJ* 7 (Tübingen, 1985).

————. *Jews, Idumaeans, and Ancient Arabs: Relations of the Jews of Eretz-Israel with the Nations of the Frontier and the Desert during the Hellenistic and Roman Era (332 B.C.E.–70 C.E.). TSAJ* 18 (Tübingen, 1988).

Kasting, H. *Die Anfänge der urchristlichen Mission. Eine historische Untersuchung. BEvT* 55 (Munich, 1969).

Kaye, B. N. "Eschatology and Ethics in 1 and 2 Thessalonians." *NT* 17 (1975) 47-57.

————. "Acts' Portrait of Silas." *NT* 21 (1979) 13-26.

Kearsley, R. A. "A Leading Family of Cibyra and Some Asiarchs of the First Century." *AnSt* 38 (1988) 43-51.

————. "Asiarchs." *ABD* I (New York, 1992) 495-97.

————. "Ephesus: Neokoros of Artemis." *NewDoc* VI (Macquarie University, 1992) 203-6.

————. "The Asiarchs." In D. W. J. Gill and C. Gempf. *The Book of Acts in Its Graeco-Roman Setting.* A1CS IV (Grand Rapids and Carlisle, 1994) 363-76.

Kee, H. C. "The Transformation of the Synagogue after 70 C.E.: Its Import for Early Christianity." *NTS* 36 (1990) 1-24.

Kehnscherper, G. "Der Apostel Paulus als römischer Bürger." *Studia Evangelica* II (*TU* 87) (East Berlin, 1964) 411-40.

Keim, K. T. *Jesu von Nazara III: Das apostolische Todesostern* (Zurich, 1872).

————. *Rom und das Christenthum. Eine Darstellung des Kampfes zwischen dem alten und dem neuen Glauben im römischen Reiche während der beiden ersten Jahrhunderte unserer Zeitrechnung* (Berlin, 1881).

Kellermann, U. "Ἡρῴδης." *EDNT* II (Grand Rapids, 1991) 122-23.

Kelso, J. L. "Paul's Roman Citizenship as Reflected in His Missionary Experiences and His Letters." *BS* 79 (1922) 173-83.

————. "Key Cities in Paul's Missionary Program." *BS* 79 (1922) 481-86.

Keresztes, P. "The Imperial Roman Government and the Christian Church I: From Nero to the Severi." *ANRW* II 23.1 (Berlin/New York, 1979) 247-315.

———. "The Nativity, the Star, the Crucifixion, and Roman History." *Imperial Rome and the Christians I: From Herod the Great to about 200 A.D.* (Lanham, 1989) 1-43.

———. "Paul, the Acts, and Imperial Rome." *Ibid.,* 45-66.

Kettenbach, G. *Das Logbuch des Lukas. EHS.T* 23/276 (Frankfurt/Bern/New York, 1986).

Kieffer, R. "L'eschatologie en 1 Thessaloniciens dans une perspective rhétorique." In R. F. Collins. *The Thessalonian Correspondence. BETL* 87 (Leuven, 1990) 206-19.

Kim, S. *The Origin of Paul's Gospel. WUNT* II/4 (Tübingen, [2]1984).

Kim, Y. K. "Palaeographical Dating of P[46] to the Later First Century." *Bibl* 69 (1988) 248-57.

Kindler, A., "A Re-Assessment of the Dates of Some Coins of the Roman Procurators of Judaea." *Israel Numismatic Journal* 5 (1981) 19-21.

Kinman, B. "Pilate's Assize and the Timing of Jesus' Trial." *TynBul* 42 (1991) 282-95.

Kirsch, J. P. "Le feste degli apostoli S. Pietro e S. Paolo nel Martirologio Geronimiano." *RivAC* 2 (1925) 54-83.

———. "Die beiden Apostelfeste Petri Stuhlfeier und Pauli Bekehrung im Januar." *JLW* 5 (1925) 48-67.

Klaiber, W. "Theorie und Praxis Paulinischer Gemeindearbeit." In P. W. Bøckman and R. E. Kristiansen. *Context: Essays in Honour of Peder Johan Borgen. Relieff* 24 (Trondheim, 1987) 89-106.

Klauck, H. J. *Die religiöse Umwelt des Urchristentums I: Stadt- und Hausreligion, Mysterienkulte, Volksglaube.* Studienbücher Theologie 9/1 (Stuttgart, 1995).

Klauser, T. "Akklamation." *RAC* I (Stuttgart, 1950) 216-33.

Klausner, J. *Jesus of Nazareth: His Life, Times, and Teaching* (Eng. trans., New York, 1943).

———. *From Jesus to Paul* (Eng. trans., New York, 1943).

Klein, P. "Zum Verständnis von Gal 2,1. Zugleich ein Beitrag zur Chronologie des Urchristentums." *ZNW* 70 (1979) 250f.

Kleinknecht, K. T. *Der leidende Gerechtfertigte. Die alttestamentlich-jüdische Tradition vom "leidenden Gerechten" und ihre Rezeption bei Paulus. WUNT* 13 (Tübingen, [2]1988).

Klijn, A. F. J. "Jerome's Quotations from a Nazorean Interpretation of Isaiah." *RSR* 60 (1972) 241-55.

———. *An Introduction to the New Testament* (Leiden, [2]1980).

———. "Jewish Christianity in Egypt." In B. A. Pearson and J. E. Goehring. *The Roots of Egyptian Christianity: Studies in Antiquity and Christianity* (Philadelphia, 1986) 161-75.

Kloner, A. "The 'Third Wall' in Jerusalem and the 'Cave of the Kings' (Josephus *War* V 147)." *Levant* 18 (1986) 121-29.

Kloppenborg, J. S. "Φιλαδελφία, θεοδίδακτος and the Dioscuri: Rhetorical Engagement in 1 Thessalonians 4.9-12." *NTS* 39 (1993) 265-89.

Knauf, E. A. "Zum *Ethnarchen* des *Aretas* 2 Kor II,32." *ZNW* 74 (1983) 145-47.

———. "Die Herkunft der Nabatäer." In M. Lindner, *Petra. Neue Ausgrabungen und Entdeckungen* (Munich, 1986) 74-86.

Knibbe, D., and Alzinger, W. "Ephesos vom Beginn der römischen Herrschaft in Kleinasien bis zum Ende der Principatszeit." *ANRW* II 7.1 (Berlin/New York, 1980) 748-830.

Knopf, R., Lietzmann, H., and Weinel, H. *Einführung in das Neue Testament* (Berlin, [5]1949).

Knox, J. " 'Fourteen Years Later': A Note on the Pauline Chronology." *JR* 16 (1936) 342-49.

———. "The Pauline Chronology." *JBL* 58 (1939) 15-29.

————. *Marcion and the New Testament* (Chicago, 1942; [2]1980).

————. *Chapters in a Life of Paul* (New York/Nashville, 1950).

————. "Galatians (Letter to the)." *IDB* II (New York/Nashville, 1962) 338-43.

————. "Chapters in a Life of Paul — A Response to Robert Jewett and Gerd Luedemann." In B. C. Corley. *Colloquy on New Testament Studies: A Time for Reappraisal and Fresh Approaches* (Macon, 1983) 339-64.

————. *Chapters in a Life of Paul.* Rev. ed. Edited by D. R. A. Hare (Macon, 1987).

Knox, W. L. *St. Paul and the Church of Jerusalem* (Cambridge, 1925).

————. *The Acts of the Apostles* (Cambridge, 1948).

————. *The Sources of the Synoptic Gospels I: St. Mark* (Cambridge, 1953).

Koch, D. A. *Die Schrift als Zeuge des Evangeliums. Untersuchungen zur Verwendung und zum Verständnis der Schrift bei Paulus. BHT* 69 (Tübingen, 1969).

Koenig, J. "La localisation du Sinaï et les traditions des scribes." *RHPR* 43 (1963) 2-31.

Kö[oe]ster, H. "I Thessalonians — Experiment in Christian Writing." In F. F. Church and T. George. *Continuity and Discontinuity in Church History: Essays Presented to George Huntston Williams. SHCT* 19 (Leiden, 1979) 33-44.

————. *Introduction to the New Testament* (New York, 1995-).

————. "Apostel und Gemeinde in den Briefen an die Thessalonicher." In D. Lührmann and G. Strecker. *Kirche. Festschrift Günther Bornkamm* (Tübingen, 1980) 287-98.

————. "From Paul's Eschatology to the Apocalyptic Schemata of 2 Thessalonians." In R. F. Collins. *The Thessalonian Correspondence. BETL* 87 (Leuven, 1990) 441-58.

————. *Ancient Christian Gospels: Their History and Development* (London/Philadelphia, 1990).

Koester, C. "The Origin and Significance of the Flight to Pella Tradition." *CBQ* 51 (1989) 90-106.

Koestermann, E. "Ein folgenschwerer Irrtum des Tacitus (Ann. 15,44,2ff)?" *Hist* 16 (1967) 456-69.

Kokkinos, N. "Which Salome Did Aristobulos Marry?" *PEQ* 118 (1986) 33-50.

————. "Crucifixion in A.D. 36: The Keystone for Dating the Birth of Jesus." In J. Vardaman and E. M. Yamauchi. *Chronos, Kairos, Christos: Nativity and Chronological Studies Presented to Jack Finegan* (Winona Lake, 1989) 133-63.

Kollwitz, J. "Antiochia am Orontes." *RAC* I (Stuttgart, 1950) 461-69.

Kornemann, E. *Römische Geschichte II: Die Kaiserzeit* (ed. H. Bengtson; Stuttgart, [7]1977 [[4]1959]).

Kraabel, A. T. "The Disappearance of the 'God-fearers'." *Numen* 28 (1981) 113-26.

————. "The Roman Diaspora: Six Questionable Assumptions." *JJS* 33 (1982) 445-62.

Kraeling, C. H. "The Jewish Community at Antioch." *JBL* 51 (1932) 130-60.

Kraft, B. "Euthalios." *LTK* III (Freiburg, 1959) 1206f.

Kraft, H. *Die Entstehung des Christentums* (Darmstadt, 1981).

Kramolisch, H. "Zur Ära des Kaisers Claudius in Thessalien." *Chiron* 5 (1975) 337-47.

Kraus, J. "Hippolyt von Theben." *LTK* V (Freiburg, 1960) 380.

Krauss, S. "Die biblische Völkertafel in Talmud, Midrasch und Targum." *MGWJ* 39 (1895) 1-11, 49-63.

Kreitzer, L. J. "A Numismatic Clue to Acts 19.23-41: The Ephesian Cistophori of Claudius and Agrippina." *JSNT* 30 (1987) 59-70.

Krentz, E. "Roman Hellenism and Paul's Gospel." *BiTod* 26 (1988) 328-37.

————. "Thessalonians: First and Second Epistles to the." *ABD* VI (New York, 1992) 515-23.

Krieger, K. S. "Die Problematik chronologischer Rekonstruktionen zur Amtszeit des Pilatus." *BN* 61 (1992) 27-32.

465

————. "Chronologische Probleme in der Geschichte der ersten fünf Statthalter der Provinz Judäa." *BN* 68 (1993) 18-23.

Krodel, G. A. "Persecution and Toleration of Christianity until Hadrian." In S. Benko and J. J. O'Rourke. *The Catacombs and the Colosseum: The Roman Empire as the Setting of Primitive Christianity* (Valley Forge, 1971) 255-67.

Kroll, G. *Auf den Spuren Jesu* (Leipzig, [10]1988).

Kümmel, W. G. "Das literarische und geschichtliche Problem des ersten Thessalonicher-briefes." *Neotestamentica et Patristica: Festschrift Oscar Cullmann. NTSup* 6 (Leiden, 1962) 213-27 (repr. in *Heilsgeschehen und Geschichte I: Gesammelte Aufsätze 1933-1964* [Marburg, 1965] 406-16).

————. *Jesu Antwort an Johannes den Täufer. Ein Beispiel zum Methodenproblem in der Jesusforschung* (Wiesbaden, 1974).

————. *Introduction to the New Testament* (Eng. trans., Nashville, 1966; rev. ed. 1975).

Kuen, A. *Introduction au Nouveau Testament: Les lettres de Paul* (Saint-Légier, 1982).

Kuhn, H. W., "Die Bedeutung der Qumrantexte für das Verständnis des Ersten Thessalo-nicherbriefes. Vorstellung des Münchner Projekts Qumran und das Neue Testament." In J. Trebolle Barrera and L. Vegas Montaner. *The Madrid Qumran Congress. Proceedings of the International Congress on the Dead Sea Scrolls. Madrid. 19-21 March 1991*, vol. II (Leiden, 1992) 339-54.

Labriolle, P. de. *La réaction païenne. Étude sur la polémique antichrétienne du Ier au VIe siècle* (Paris, 1934).

Lacey, D. R. de. "Paul in Jerusalem." *NTS* 20 (1973/74) 82-86.

Lacroix, B. *Orose et ses idées. PIEM* 18 (Paris, 1965).

Laet, S. J. de. "Le successeur de Ponce Pilate." *AnCl* 8 (1939) 413-19.

Lake, K. "Proselytes and God-Fearers," *BC* V (London, 1933) 74-96.

————. "The Conversion of Paul and the Events Immediately Following It." *Ibid.,* 188-94.

————. "Paul's Route in Asia Minor." *Ibid.,* 224-40.

————. "The Chronology of Acts." *Ibid.,* 445-574.

Lambertz, M. "Zur Ausbreitung des Supernomen oder Signum im römischen Reiche." *Glotta* 4 (1913) 78-143; 5 (1914) 99-170.

Lambrecht, J. "Thanksgivings in 1 Thessalonians 1–3." In R. F. Collins. *The Thessalonian Correspondence. BETL* 87 (Leuven, 1990) 183-205.

Lampe, P. "Paulus — Zeltmacher." *BZ* 31 (1987) 256-61.

————. *Die stadtrömischen Christen in den ersten beiden Jahrhunderten. Untersuchungen zur Sozialgeschichte. WUNT* II/18 (Tübingen, [2]1989).

————. "Acta 19 im Spiegel der ephesinischen Inschriften." *BZ* 36 (1992) 59-76.

Langevin, P. E. "L'intervention de Dieu selon 1 Thes 5,23-24." In R. F. Collins. *The Thessalonian Correspondence. BETL* 87 (Leuven, 1990) 236-56.

La Piana, G. "Foreign Groups in Rome during the First Centuries of the Empire." *HTR* 20 (1927) 183-394.

Larfeld, W. "Die delphische Gallioinschrift und die paulinische Chronologie." *NKZ* 34 (1923) 638-47.

Larsson, E. "Claudius, judarna och den nya pauluskronologin." In P. W. Bøckman and R. E. Kristiansen. *Context: Essays in Honour of Peder Johan Borgen. Relieff* 24 (Trondheim, 1985) 107-20.

LaSor, W. W. "Cyrene." *ISBE* I (Grand Rapids, 1979) 844f.

————. "Lud, Ludim." *ISBE* III (Grand Rapids, 1986) 178.

————. "Put." *Ibid.,* 1059.

Lassus, J. "La ville d'Antioche à l'époque romaine d'après l'archéologie." *ANRW* II 8 (Berlin/New York, 1978) 54-102.

Last, H. "The Study of the 'Persecutions.' " *JRS* 27 (1937) 80-92.

Laub, F. *Eschatologische Verkündigung und Lebensgestaltung bei Paulus. BU* 10 (Regensburg, 1973).

———. "Paulus als Gemeindegründer (1 Thess)." In J. Hainz, *Kirche im Werden. Studien zum Thema Amt und Gemeinde im Neuen Testament* (Munich/Paderborn/Vienna, 1976) 17-38.

Laurentin, R. *The Truth of Christmas beyond the Myths: The Infancy Narratives of Christ: Exegesis and Semiotics — Historicity and Theology* (Eng. trans., Still River, Mass., 1986).

Laverdiere, E. A. "Paul and the Missions from Antioch: The Role of Antioch in the Missionary Journeys of Paul." *BiTod* 82 (1976) 738-52.

Lawlor, H. J. *Eusebiana: Essays on the Ecclesiastical History of Eusebius, Bishop of Caesarea* (Oxford, 1912).

Lawlor, J. I. *The Nabataeans in Historical Perspective* (Grand Rapids, 1974).

Lazaridis, D. Ἀμφίπολις καὶ Ἄργιλος. Ancient Cities 13 (Athens, 1972).

———. "Οἱ ἀνασκάφες στὴν Ἀμφιπόλη." *AncMac* IV (Thessalonica, 1986) 353-64.

Leary, T. J. "Paul's Improper Name." *NTS* 38 (1992) 467-69.

Leclerq, H. "Paul (Saint)." *DACL* XIII (Paris, 1938) 2568-2699.

———. "Salonique." *DACL* XV/1 (Paris, 1950) 624-713.

Lécrivain, C. "Viator." *DAGR* V (Paris, 1912) 817-20.

Lee, C. L. "Social Unrest and Primitive Christianity." In S. Benko and J. J. O'Rourke. *The Catacombs and the Colosseum: The Roman Empire as the Setting of Primitive Christianity* (Valley Forge, 1971) 121-38.

Lee, G. M. "The Census in Luke." *CQR* 167 (1966) 431-36.

———. "Two Linguistic Parallels from Babrius." *NT* 9 (1967) 41f.

———. "The Aorist Participle of Subsequent Action (Acts 16,6)." *Bibl* 51 (1970) 235-37.

———. "The Past Participle of Subsequent Action." *NT* 17 (1975) 199.

Légasse, S. *Stephanos. Histoire et discours d'Étienne dans les Actes des Apôtres. LD* 147 (Paris, 1992).

———. *Paul apôtre. Essai de biographie critique* (Paris, 1991).

———. "Paul's Pre-Christian Career according to Acts." In R. Bauckham. *The Book of Acts in Its Palestinian Setting.* A1CS IV (Grand Rapids and Carlisle, 1995) 365-90.

Le Glay, M. "Rome, ville surpeuplée." *MBib* 51 (1987) 11f.

Legrand, L. *Unity and Plurality: Mission in the Bible* (Maryknoll, 1990).

Lemerle, P. *Philippes et la Macédoine Orientale à l'époque chrétienne et byzantine I: Texte. BEFAR* 58 (Paris, 1945).

Lemonon, J. P. *Pilate et le gouvernement de la Judée. Textes et monuments. ÉBib* (Paris, 1981).

———. "Ponce Pilate: documents profanes, Nouveau Testament et traditions ecclésiales." *ANRW* II 26.1 (Berlin/New York, 1992) 741-78.

Lentz, J. C. *Luke's Portrait of Paul. SNTSMS* 77 (Cambridge, 1993).

Leon, E. F. "The 'Imbecillitas' of the Emperor Claudius." *TAPA* 79 (1948) 79-86.

Leon, H. J. *The Jews of Ancient Rome* (Philadelphia, 1960).

Lerle, E. *Proselytenwerbung und Urchristentum* (East Berlin, 1960).

Levick, B. M. *Roman Colonies in Southern Asia Minor* (Oxford, 1967).

———. "Antiquarian or Revolutionary? Claudius Caesar's Conception of His Principate." *AJP* 99 (1978) 79-105.

———. *Claudius* (London, 1990).

Levinskaya, I. "The Inscription from Aphrodisias and the Problem of God-fearers." *TynBul* 41 (1990) 312-18.

————. *The Book of Acts in Its Diaspora Setting*. A1CS V (Grand Rapids and Carlisle, 1996).

Lewis, R. G. "Suetonius' 'Caesares' and Their Literary Antecedents." *ANRW* II 33.5 (Berlin/New York, 1991) 3623-74.

Lichtenberger, H. "Täufergemeinden und frühchristliche Täuferpolemik im letzten Drittel des 1. Jahrhunderts," *ZTK* 84 (1987) 36-57.

————. "Josephus und Paulus in Rom. Juden und Christen in Rom zur Zeit Neros." In D. A. Koch and H. Lichtenberger. *Begegnungen zwischen Judentum und Christentum in Antike und Mittelalter. Festschrift Heinz Schreckenberg. Schriften des Institutum Judaicum Delitzschianum* 1 (Göttingen, 1993) 245-61.

Liebeschuetz, J. H. W. G. *Antioch: City and Imperial Administration in the Later Roman Empire* (Oxford, 1972).

Liechtenhan, R. *Die urchristliche Mission. Voraussetzungen, Motive und Methoden. ATANT* 9 (Zurich, 1946).

Lightfoot, J. B. *Essays on the Work entitled Supernatural Religion* (London, 1889).

————. "The Chronology of St. Paul's Life and Epistles." *Biblical Essays* (London, 1893) 213-33.

————. "The Churches of Macedonia." *Ibid.,* 235-50.

————. "The Church of Thessalonica." *Ibid.,* 251-69.

Limbeck, M. *Mit Paulus Christ sein. Sachbuch zur Person und Theologie des Apostels* (Stuttgart, 1989).

Linck, K. *De antiquissimis veterum quae ad Iesum Nazarenum spectant testimoniis. RVV* XIV/1 (Gießen, 1913).

Lindblom, J. *Gesichte und Offenbarungen. Vorstellungen von göttlichen Weisungen und übernatürlichen Eingebungen im ältesten Christentum. SHVL* 65 (Lund, 1968).

Lindemann, A. Review of G. Lüdemann, *Paulus, der Heidenapostel I* (Göttingen, 1980). *ZKG* 92 (1981) 344-49.

————. "Christliche Gemeinde und das römische Reich im 1. und 2. Jahrhundert." *WuD* 18 (1985) 105-33.

————. "Paulus und die korinthische Eschatologie. Zur These von einer 'Entwicklung' im paulinischen Denken." *NTS* 37 (1991) 373-99.

Lindner, M. "Die Geschichte der Nabatäer." In M. Lindner, *Petra und das Königreich der Nabatäer. Lebensraum, Geschichte und Kultur eines arabischen Volkes der Antike* (Munich, ³1980) 38-103.

Linton, O. "The Third Aspect: A Neglected Point of View: A Study in Gal. I–II and Acts IX and XV." *ST* 3 (1949) 79-95.

Lintott, A. W. "Provocatio: From the Struggle of the Orders to the Principate." *ANRW* I/1 (Berlin/New York, 1972) 226-67.

Lipsius, R. A. *Die apokryphen Apostelgeschichten und Apostellegenden. Ein Beitrag zur altchristlichen Literaturgeschichte* I (Leipzig, 1883); II/1 (1887); II/2 (1884); Erg. H. (1890).

Llewelyn, S. R. "The Provincial Census and Jesus' Birth in Bethlehem." *NewDoc* VI (Macquarie University, 1992) 119-32.

————. "Claudius Lysias (Acts 22) and the Question of Paul's Roman Citizenship." *Ibid.,* 152-55.

————. "The Official Postal Systems of Antiquity." *NewDoc* I (Sydney, 1994) 1-25.

————. "The Provision of Transport for Persons." *Ibid.,* 58-92.

————. "The Transport of Grain." *Ibid.,* 112-29.

Lodder, W. *Die Schätzung des Quirinius bei Flavius Josephus* (Leipzig, 1930).

Löhr, G. "1 Thess 4,15-17: Das 'Herrenwort'." *ZNW* 71 (1980) 269-73.

Löning, K. "Der Stephanuskreis und seine Mission." In J. Becker. *Die Anfänge des Christentums* (Stuttgart, 1987) 80-101.

Lohse, B. "Das Passafest der Quartadecimaner." *BFCT* II/54 (Gütersloh, 1953).

Lohse, E. *The Formation of the New Testament* (Eng. trans., Nashville, 1981).

―――. *Paulus. Eine Biographie* (München, 1996).

Longenecker, R. N. *The Ministry and Message of Paul* (Grand Rapids, 1971).

―――. *Biblical Exegesis in the Apostolic Period* (Grand Rapids, 1975).

―――. "The Nature of Paul's Early Eschatology." *NTS* 31 (1985) 85-95.

Lüdemann, G. "The Hope of the Early Paul: From the Foundation-Preaching at Thessalonika to I Cor. 15:51-57." *PerspRelSt* 7 (1980) 195-201.

―――. *Paulus der Heidenapostel I: Studien zur Chronologie. FRLANT* 123 (Göttingen, 1980).

―――. *Paulus der Heidenapostel II: Antipaulinismus im frühen Christentum. FRLANT* 130 (Göttingen, 1983). Eng. trans., *Opposition to Paul in Jewish Christianity* (Minneapolis, 1989).

―――. "A Chronology of Paul." In B. C. Corley. *Colloquy on New Testament Studies: A Time for Reappraisal and Fresh Approaches* (Macon, 1983) 289-307.

―――. Review of R. Jewett, *A Chronology of Paul's Life* (Philadelphia, 1979). *JBL* 103 (1984) 118-21.

―――. *Paul: Apostle to the Gentiles: Studies in Chronology* (Eng. trans., Philadelphia, 1984) (revised translation of *Paulus der Heidenapostel I*).

―――. *Early Christianity according to the Traditions in Acts* (Eng. trans., Minneapolis, 1989).

Lührmann, D. "The Beginnings of the Church of Thessalonica." *Greeks, Romans, and Christians: Essays in Honor of Abraham J. Malherbe* (Minneapolis, 1990) 216-36.

Lütgert, W. *Die Vollkommenen in Philippi und die Enthusiasten in Thessalonich. BFCT* 13.6 (Gütersloh, 1909).

Lundgren, S. "Ananias and the Calling of Paul in Acts." *ST* 25 (1971) 117-22.

Luz, U. *Das Geschichtsverständnis des Paulus. BEvT* 49 (Munich, 1968).

Lyonnet, S., "De ministerio romano S. Petri ante adventum S. Pauli." *VD* 33 (1955) 143-54.

Lyons, G. *Pauline Autobiography: Towards a New Understanding. SBLDS* 73 (Atlanta, 1985).

Macadam, H. I. *Studies in the History of the Roman Province of Arabia: The Northern Sector. BAR International Series* 295 (London, 1986).

McCasland, S. V. "Travel and Communication in the N[ew] T[estament]." *IDB* IV (New York/Nashville, 1962) 690-93.

McCullough, W. S. *A Short History of Syriac Christianity to the Rise of Islam. Scholars Press General Series* 4 (Chico, 1982).

McGehee, M. "A Rejoinder to Two Recent Studies Dealing with 1 Thess. 4:4." *CBQ* 51 (1989) 82-89.

McGing, B. C. "Pontius Pilate and the Sources." *CBQ* 53 (1991) 416-38.

MacKay, P. A. "The Route of the Via Egnatia around Lake Ostrovo." *AncMac* II (Thessalonica, 1977) 203-10.

McKnight, S. *A Light among the Gentiles: Jewish Missionary Activity in the Second Temple Period* (Minneapolis, 1991).

McLean, B. H. "Galatians 2.7-9 and the Recognition of Paul's Apostolic Status at the Jerusalem Conference: A Critique of G. Luedemann's Solution." *NTS* 37 (1991) 67-76.

MacLennan, R. S., and Kraabel, A. T. "The God-Fearers — A Literary and Theological Invention." *BARev* 12/5 (1986) 46-53.

MacMullen, R. *Enemies of the Roman Order: Treason, Unrest, and Alienation in the Empire* (Cambridge, Mass., 1966).

―――. *Roman Social Relations* (New Haven, 1974).

McNally, R. E. "Isidoriana." *TS* 20 (1959) 432-42.

―――. "Isidorian Pseudepigrapha in the Early Middle Ages." *Isidoriana. Festschrift Manuel C. Diáz y Diáz* (Leon, 1961) 305-16.

McPherson, I. W. "Roman Roads and Milestones of Galatia." *AnSt* 4 (1954) 111-20.

McRey, J. "Damascus: The Greco-Roman Period." *ABD* II (New York, 1992) 7f.

Macro, A. D. "The Cities of Asia Minor under the Roman Imperium." *ANRW* II 7.2 (Berlin/New York, 1980) 748-830.

Mader, J. "Wandlungen und Wanderungen Pauli bis zum Apostelkonzil." *SchwRd* 1 (1900/01) 301-23.

Madvig, D. H. "Thessalonica." *ISBE* IV (Grand Rapids, 1988) 836-38.

―――. "Beroea." *ISBE* I (Grand Rapids, 1979) 462.

Magass, W. "Theophrast und Paulus exemplarisch für Umstände und Ethos in Korinth und Saloniki." *Kairos* 26 (1984) 154-65.

Magie, D. *Roman Rule in Asia Minor* I: *Text;* II: *Notes* (Princeton, 1950).

Maiberger, P. *Topographische und historische Untersuchungen zum Sinaiproblem. Worauf beruht die Identifizierung des Gabal Musa mit dem Sinai? OBO* 54 (Freiburg [Switzerland]/Göttingen, 1984).

Maiburg, U. " 'Und bis an die Grenzen der Erde. . . .' Die Ausbreitung des Christentums in den Länderlisten und deren Verwendung in Antike und Christentum." *JAC* 26 (1983) 38-53.

Maier, F. W. *Paulus als Kirchengründer und kirchlicher Organisator* (Würzburg, 1961).

Maier, H. *Die christliche Zeitrechnung. Herder Spektrum* 4018 (Freiburg, 1991).

Maier, J. *Jesus von Nazareth in der talmudischen Überlieferung. EdF* 82 (Darmstadt, 1978).

Maier, P. L. "Sejanus, Pilate, and the Date of the Crucifixion." *CH* 37 (1968) 3-13.

―――. "The Date of the Nativity and the Chronology of Jesus' Life." In J. Vardaman and E. M. Yamauchi. *Chronos, Kairos, Christos: Nativity and Chronological Studies Presented to Jack Finegan* (Winona Lake, 1989) 113-30.

Maistrello, I. "Il viaggio di S. Paolo da Cesarea a Roma alla luce della scienza nautica pografia." *Archeologia* (Rome, 1963) 163-92.

Makaronas, C. I. "Ἀνασκάφη παρὰ τὸ Σαραπεῖον," *Mak* 1 (1940) 464f.

―――. "Via Egnatia and Thessalonike," in *Studies Presented to David Moore Robinson* I (Washington, 1951) 380-88.

―――. "Ἀπολλωνία ἡ Μυγδονική." *AncMac* II (Thessalonica, 1977) 189-94.

Malherbe, A. J. "The Beasts at Ephesus." *JBL* 87 (1968) 71-80 (repr. in *Paul and the Popular Philosophers* [Minneapolis, 1989] 79-90).

―――. " 'Gentle as a Nurse': The Cynic Background to I Thess. II." *NT* 12 (1970) 203-17 (repr. in *Paul and the Popular Philosophers,* 35-48).

―――. *Social Aspects of Early Christianity* (Baton Rouge/London, 1977; Philadelphia, ²1983).

―――. "Exhortation in First Thessalonians." *NT* 25 (1983) 238-56 (repr. in *Paul and the Popular Philosophers,* 49-68).

―――. *Paul and the Thessalonians: The Philosophic Tradition of Pastoral Care* (Philadelphia, 1987).

―――. " 'Pastoral Care' in the Thessalonian Church." *NTS* 36 (1990) 375-91.

Mann, C. S. "Saul and Damascus." *ET* 99 (1988) 331-34.

Manni, E. "Dall'avento di Claudio all'acclamazione di Vespasiano." *ANRW* II/2 (Berlin/New York, 1975) 131-48.

Manns, F. "Marc 6,21-29 à la lumière des dernières fouilles du Machéronte." *SBFLA* 21 (1981) 287-90.

Manson, T. W. "St. Paul in Greece: The Letters to the Thessalonians." *BJRL* 35 (1953) 428-47.

Manus, C. U. "Luke's Account of Paul in Thessalonica (Acts 17,1-9)." In R. F. Collins. *The Thessalonian Correspondence. BETL* 87 (Leuven, 1990) 27-38.

Mariani, B. "Il viaggio di S. Paolo da 'Forum Appii' a 'Tres Tabernae.' Atti 28,15." In B. Mariani, *S. Paolo da Cesarea a Roma. Esegesi, Storia, Topografia, Archeologia* (Rome, 1963) 87-140.

Marki, E. "'Η ταφική ζωγραφική τῶν πρώτων Χριστιανικῶν χρόνων στή Θεσσαλονίκη," Χριστιανική Θεσσαλονίκη ἀπό τοῦ Ἀποστόλου Παύλου μέχρι καί τῆς Κωνσταντινείου ἐποχῆς (Thessalonica, 1990) 171-93.

Marshall, I. H. "Pauline Theology in the Thessalonian Correspondence." In M. D. Hooker and S. G. Wilson. *Paul and Paulinism: Essays in Honour of C. K. Barrett* (London, 1982) 173-83.

———. "Election and Calling to Salvation in 1 and 2 Thessalonians." In R. F. Collins. *The Thessalonian Correspondence. BETL* 87 (Leuven, 1990) 259-76.

———. *The Acts of the Apostles. New Testament Guides* (Sheffield, 1992).

Martin, E. L. *The Birth of Jesus Recalculated* (Pasadena/Newcastle, [2]1980).

———. "The Nativity and Herod's Death." In J. Vardaman and E. M. Yamauchi. *Chronos, Kairos, Christos: Nativity and Chronological Studies Presented to Jack Finegan* (Winona Lake, 1989) 85-92.

Martin, R. A. *Studies in the Life and Ministry of the Early Paul and Related Issues* (Lampeter, 1993).

Martin, T. W. "Paulus (Sergius)." *ABD* V (New York, 1992) 205f.

Mason, S. *Josephus and the New Testament* (Peabody, 1992).

Mattingley, H. B. "The Origin of the Name *Christiani.*" *JTS* 9 (1958) 26-37.

May, G. "L'activité juridique de l'empereur Claude," *RHDFE* 15 (1936) 55-97, 213-54.

———. "La politique religieuse de l'empereur Claude." *RHDFE* 17 (1938) 1-46.

Mazar, B. "The Royal Stoa in the Southern Part of the Temple Mount." In H. Shanks, *Recent Archaeology in the Land of Israel* (Washington/Jerusalem, 1985) 141-48.

Mearns, C. L. "Early Eschatological Development in Paul: The Evidence of I and II Thessalonians." *NTS* 27 (1981) 137-57.

———. "Early Eschatological Development in Paul: The Evidence of 1 Corinthians." *JSNT* 22 (1984) 19-35.

Meeks, W. A. Review of H. D. Betz, *Galatians* (Philadelphia, 1979). *JBL* 100 (1981) 304-7.

———. *The First Urban Christians: The Social World of the Apostle Paul* (New Haven/London, 1983).

Meeks, W. A., and Wilken, R. L. *Jews and Christians in Antioch in the First Four Centuries of the Common Era. SBLSBS* 13 (Ann Arbor, 1978).

Mehl, A. "Orosius über die Amnestie des Kaisers Claudius: Ein Quellenproblem." *RMP* 121 (1978) 185-94.

Meinardus, O. F. A. *Die Reisen des Apostels Paulus nachvollzogen im 20. Jahrhundert* (Hamburg/Regensburg, 1981).

———. "The Site of the Apostle Paul's Conversion at Kaukab." *BA* 44 (1981) 57-59.

Meinertz, M. *Einleitung in das Neue Testament* (Paderborn, [5]1950).

Meistermann, B. *Durch's Heilige Land. Führer für Pilger und Reisende.* Edited by E. Huber (Trier/Munich, 1919).

Méleze-Modrzejewski, J. "Les tourments de Paul de Tarse." *Mélanges Jean Imbert* (Paris, 1989) 397-412.

Mellersh, H. E. L. *Chronology of the Ancient World: 10,000 B.C. to A.D. 799* (London, 1976).

Mendels, D. *The Land of Israel as Political Concept in Hasmonean Literature: Recourse to History in Second Century B.C. Claims to the Holy Land. TSAJ* 15 (Tübingen, 1987).

Merk, O. "Paulus-Forschung 1936-1985." *TRu* 53 (1988) 1-81.

———. "Zur Christologie im Ersten Thessalonicherbrief." In C. Breytenbach and H. Paulsen. *Anfänge der Christologie. Festschrift Ferdinand Hahn* (Göttingen, 1991) 97-110.

Merrill, E. T. *Essays in Early Christian History* (London, 1924).

Metzger, B. M. "The Nazareth Inscription Once Again." In E. E. Ellis and E. Grässer. *Jesus und Paulus. Festschrift Werner Georg Kümmel* (Göttingen, [2]1978) 221-38.

Metzger, H. *St. Paul's Journeys in the Greek Orient* (Eng. trans., London, 1955).

Metzger, W. *Die letzte Reise des Apostels Paulus. Beobachtungen und Erwägungen zu seinem Itinerar nach den Pastoralbriefen. ATh* 59 (Stuttgart, 1976).

Meyer, B. F. *The Early Christians: Their World Mission and Self-Discovery. GNS* 16 (Wilmington, 1986).

———. "Did Paul's View of the Resurrection of the Dead Undergo Development?" *TS* 47 (1986) 363-87.

Meyer, E(duard). *Ursprung und Anfänge des Christentums* I: *Die Evangelien;* III: *Die Apostelgeschichte und die Anfänge des Christentums* (Stuttgart/Berlin, [4/5]1924; 1923).

Meyer, E(rnst). *Römischer Staat und Staatsgedanke* (Zurich/Stuttgart, [2]1961).

———. "Epeiros." *KP* II (Stuttgart, 1967) 284-87.

Meyer, R. "Himmelfahrt und Martyrium des Jesaja." *RGG*[3] III (Tübingen, 1959) 336f.

Michaelis, W. *Die Gefangenschaft des Paulus in Ephesus und das Itinerar des Timotheus. Untersuchungen zur Chronologie des Paulus und der Paulusbriefe. NtF* I/3 (Gütersloh, 1925).

———. "Judaistische Heidenchristen." *ZNW* 30 (1931) 83-89.

———. "Teilungshypothesen bei Paulusbriefen. Briefkompositionen und ihr Sitz im Leben." *TZ* 14 (1958) 321-26.

———. *Einleitung in das Neue Testament* (Bern, [3]1961).

Michel, O. *Paulus und seine Bibel* (Darmstadt, [2]1972).

———. "Das Licht des Messias." In E. Bammel, *Donum gentilicium: New Testament Essays in Honor of David Daube* (Oxford, 1978)·40-50.

Millar, F. "The Date of the *Constitutio Antoniniana.*" *JEA* 48 (1962) 124-31.

———. *A Study of Cassius Dio* (Oxford, 1964).

———. "Empire, Community and Culture in the Roman Near East: Greeks, Syrians, Jews and Arabs." *JJS* 38 (1987) 143-64.

———. "Reflections on the Trial of Jesus." In P. R. Davies and R. T. White. *A Tribute to Geza Vermes: Essays on Jewish and Christian Literature and History. JSOTSup* 100 (Sheffield, 1990) 355-81.

———. "Hagar, Ishmael, Josephus and the Origins of Islam." *JJS* 44 (1993) 23-45.

———. *The Roman Near East 31 BC–AD 337* (Cambridge, MA, and London, 1993).

Mills, W. E. *An Index to Periodical Literature on the Apostle Paul. NTTS* 16 (Leiden, 1993).

Minear, P. S. "The Jerusalem Fund and Pauline Chronology." *ATR* 25 (1943) 389-96.

Mitchell, M. M. "New Testament Envoys in the Context of Greco-Roman Diplomatic and

Epistolary Conventions: The Example of Timothy and Titus." *JBL* 111 (1992) 641-62.

Mitchell, S. "Iconium and Ninica: Two Double Communities in Roman Asia Minor." *Hist* 28 (1979) 409-38.

———. "Population and the Land in Roman Galatia." *ANRW* II 7.2 (Berlin/New York, 1980) 1053-81.

———. "Galatia under Tiberius." *Chiron* 16 (1986) 17-33.

———. "Antioch of Pisidia." *ABD* I (New York, 1992) 264f.

———. "Galatia." *ABD* II (New York, 1992) 870-72.

Mitford, T. B. "Roman Cyprus." *ANRW* II 7.2 (Berlin/New York, 1980) 1285-1384.

Mittmann, S. "Handel und Verkehr." *GBL* II (Wuppertal/Gießen, 1988) 515-19.

———. "Reisen." *GBL* III (Wuppertal/Gießen, 1989) 1284-86.

Moberly, R. B. "When Was Revelation Conceived?" *Bibl* 74 (1993) 376-93.

Moda, A. "Per una biografia Paolina. La Lettera di Clemente, il Canone Muratoriano, la letteratura Apocrifa." *Testimonium Christi. Scritti in onore di Jacques Dupont* (Brescia, 1985) 289-315.

———. "Paolo prigionero e martire." *BeO* 34 (1992) 179-88, 193-252; 35 (1993) 21-59, 89-118.

Moehring, H. R. "*The Acta pro Judaeis* in the *Antiquities* of Flavius Josephus: A Study in Hellenistic and Modern Apologetic Historiography." In J. Neusner, *Christianity, Judaism and Other Greco-Roman Cults III: Judaism before 70: Festschrift Morton Smith. SJLA* 12/3 (Leiden, 1975) 124-58.

Möller, C., and Schmitt, G. *Siedlungen Palästinas nach Flavius Josephus. BTAVO B* 14 (Wiesbaden, 1976).

Moffatt, J. *An Introduction to the Literature of the New Testament* (Edinburgh, [2]1912).

Mohrmann, C. "Das Sprachenproblem in der frühchristlichen Mission." *ZMR* 38 (1954) 103-11.

Molland, E. "L'antiquité chrétienne a-t-elle eu un programme et des méthodes missionaires?" *Opuscula Patristica. BTN* 2 (Oslo, 1970) 103-16.

Molthagen, J. "Die ersten Konflikte der Christen in der griechsich-römischen Welt." *Hist* 40 (1991) 42-76.

Momigliano, A. *L'opera dell'imperatore Claudio* (Florence, 1932).

———. *Claudius: The Emperor and His Achievement* (London, 1943; [2]1961).

———. "Was Flavius Josephus nicht sah." *Die Juden in der Antiken Welt. Kleine Kulturwissenschaftliche Bibliothek* 5 (Berlin, 1988) 67-78.

Mommsen, T. "Der Religionsfrevel nach römischem Recht." *HZ* 64 (1890) 387-429.

———. "Die Rechtsverhältnisse des Apostels Paulus." *ZNW* 2 (1901) 81-96.

———. *Römische Geschichte V: Die Provinzen von Caesar bis Diocletian* (Leipzig, [5]1904).

———. *The History of Rome*. Vol. V (Eng. trans., New York, 1898).

Monachino, V. *Le persecuzione e la polemica pagano-cristiana* (Rome, 1974).

Montevecchi, O. "Nomen christianum." In R. Cantalamessa and L. F. Pizzolato. *Paradoxos politeia. Studi patristici in onore di Giuseppe Lazzati* (Milan, 1979) 485-500.

Montgomery, J. A. *Arabia and the Bible* (Philadelphia, 1934).

Moody, D. "A New Chronology for the Life and Letters of Paul." *PerspRelSt* 3 (1976) 248-71.

———. "A New Chronology for the New Testament." *RExp* 78 (1981) 211-31.

———. "A New Chronology for the Life and Letters of Paul." In J. Vardaman and E. M. Yamauchi. *Chronos, Kairos, Christos: Nativity and Chronological Studies Presented to Jack Finegan* (Winona Lake, 1989) 223-40.

Moreau, J. *Les plus anciens témoignages profanes sur Jésus* (Brussels, 1944).
———. "Le nom des Chrétiens." *NC* 1/2 (1949/50) 190-92.
———. "Rome and the New Testament — Another Look." *BR* 10 (1965) 34-43.
———. *Die Christenverfolgung im römischen Reich. AWR* N.S. 2 (Berlin/New York, ²1971).
Morgan-Gillman, F. "Jason of Thessalonica (Acts 17,5-9)." In R. F. Collins. *The Thessalonian Correspondence. BETL* 87 (Leuven, 1990) 39-49.
Morgenstern, J. "The Reckoning of the Day in the Gospels and in Acts." *CrozQ* 26 (1949) 232-40.
Morris, L. "ΚΑΙ ΑΠΑΞ ΚΑΙ ΔΙΣ." *NT* 1 (1956) 205-8.
Mott, S. "The Power of Giving and Receiving: Reciprocity in Hellenistic Benevolence." In G. F. Hawthorne, *Current Issues in Biblical and Patristic Interpretation: Studies in Honor of Merrill C. Tenney* (Grand Rapids, 1975) 60-72.
Müller, G. "Die missionarische Tätigkeit des Apostels Paulus in Thessalonich. Eine Studie über die Thessalonicherbriefe." *Missionswissenschaftliche Studien. Festschrift Gustav Warneck* (Berlin, 1904) 81-102.
Müller, P. G. "Judenbeschimpfung und Selbstverfluchung bei Paulus." *BK* 44 (1989) 58-65.
Müller, W. W. "Araber." In M. Görg and B. Lang, *Neues Bibel-Lexikon* I (Zurich, 1991) 143-45.
Munck, J. *Paul and the Salvation of Mankind* (Eng. trans., Richmond, 1959).
———. "I Thess I.9-10 and the Missionary Preaching of Paul." *NTS* 9 (1962/63) 95-110.
Munro, J. A. R., and Anthony, H. M. "Explorations in Mysia." *GJ* 9 (1897) 150-69, 256-76.
Munro, W. *Authority in Peter and Paul: The Identification of a Pastoral Stratum in the Pauline Corpus and 1 Peter* (Cambridge, 1983).
Murphy-O'Connor, J., ed. *Paul and Qumran: Studies in New Testament Exegesis* (London, 1968).
———. "Pauline Missions before the Jerusalem Conference." *RB* 89 (1982) 71-91.
———. *St. Paul's Corinth: Texts and Archaeology. GNS* 6 (Wilmington, 1983).
———. "Pauline Studies." *RB* 92 (1985) 456-64.
———. Review of N. Hyldahl, *Die paulinische Chronologie* (Leiden, 1986). *RB* 95 (1988) 309f.
———. Review of R. Jewett, *The Thessalonian Correspondence* (Philadelphia, 1986). *RB* 95 (1988) 311.
———. "Corinth." *ABD* I (New York, 1992) 1134-39.
———. "Lots of God-fearers? Theosebeis in the Aphrodisias Inscription." *RB* 99 (1992) 418-24.
———. Review of M. F. Baslez, *Saint Paul* (Paris, 1991); S. Légasse, *Paul apôtre* (Paris, 1991). *RB* 99 (1992) 440-44.
———. "Paul the Letter-writer." *RB* 100 (1993) 151-53.
———. "Paul in Arabia." *CBQ* 55 (1993) 732-37.
———. "Paul and Gallio." *JBL* 112 (1993) 315-17.
———. *Paul the Letter-Writer: His World, His Options, His Skills.* GNS 41 (Collegeville, MN, 1995).
———. *Paul: A Critical Life* (Oxford, 1996).
———. "Paul's Early Life." *RB* 103 (1996) 141-43.
Mussies, G. "Greek in Palestine and the Diaspora." *CRINT* II (Assen, 1976) 1040-64.
———. "Greek as the Vehicle of Early Christianity." *NTS* 29 (1985) 356-69.
Nar, A. Οἱ συναγωγὲς τῆς Θεσσαλονίκης (Thessalonica, 1985).

Nasrallah, J. *Les souvenirs chrétiens de Damas I: Souvenirs de saint Paul* (Harissa, 1944).
———. "Damas." *MBib* 31 (1983) 32-39.
———. "Damas et la Damascène: Leurs églises à l'époque byzantine." *POC* 35 (1985) 37-58, 264-76.
Neesen, L. *Untersuchungen zu den direkten Abgaben der römischen Kaiserzeit (27v.-284n. Chr)* (diss., Tübingen, 1980).
Negev, A. "The Chronology of the Middle Nabataean Period." *PEQ* 101 (1969) 7-14.
———. *Die Nabatäer. AW* 7 (1976) Sonderheft.
———. "The Nabataeans and the Provincia Arabia." *ANRW* II 8 (Berlin/New York, 1978) 520-686.
———. "Numismatics and Nabataean Chronology." *PEQ* 114 (1982) 119-28.
———. "Understanding the Nabataeans." *BARev* 14/6 (1988) 26-45.
Nehama, J. *Histoire des Israelites de Salonique I/II: La Communauté Romaniote — Les Sefaradis et leur dispersion* (Thessalonica, 1935).
Nepper-Christensen, P. "Das verborgene Herrenwort. Eine Untersuchung über 1. Thess 4,13-18." *ST* 19 (1965) 136-54.
Neudorfer, H. W. *Der Stephanuskreis in der Forschungsgeschichte seit F. C. Baur* (Gießen/Basel, 1983).
———. "Mehr Licht über Galatien?" *JET* 5 (1991) 47-62.
Neubauer, A. *La Géographie du Talmud* (Paris, 1868; repr. Amsterdam, 1965).
Neugebauer, F. *Die Entstehung des Johannesevangeliums. Altes und Neues zur Frage seines historischen Ursprungs. ATh* I/36 (Stuttgart, 1969).
Newton, M. *The Concept of Purity in Qumran and in the Letters of Paul. SNTSMS* 53 (Cambridge, 1985).
Nickelsburg, G. W. E. "Enoch, Levi, and Peter: Recipients of Revelation in Upper Galilee." *JBL* 100 (1981) 575-600.
Nickle, K. F. *The Collection: A Study in Paul's Strategy. SBT* 48 (London, 1966).
Nicolet, C. *L'Inventaire du Monde. Géographie et politique aux origines de l'Empire Romain* (n.p. [Paris], 1988).
Niebuhr, K. W. "Einige Tendenzen und Probleme neutestamentlicher Forschung der Gegenwart." *ZdZ* 41 (1987) 293-303.
———. *Heidenapostel aus Israel. WUNT* I/62 (Tübingen, 1992).
Noack, B. "TESTE PAULO: Paulus as the Principal Witness to Jesus and Primitive Christianity." In S. Pedersen, *Die Paulinische Literatur und Theologie. Teologiske Studier* 7 (Aarhus/Göttingen, 1980) 9-28.
Nobbs, A. "Cyprus." In D. W. J. Gill and C. Gempf. *The Book of Acts in Its Graeco-Roman Setting.* A1CS II (Grand Rapids and Carlisle, 1994) 279-90.
Nock, A. D. "Religious Developments from the Close of the Republic to the Death of Nero." *CAH* X (London, 1934) 465-511.
———. *St. Paul* (New York, 1938).
———. "Downey's Antioch: A Review." *GRBS* 4 (1963) 49-54.
Nock, A. D., Roberts, C., and Skeat, T. C. "The Guild of Zeus Hypsistos." *HTR* 29 (1936) 39-88.
Nörr, D. "Origo. Studien zur Orts-, Stadt- und Reichszugehörigkeit in der Antike." *TRG* 31 (1963) 525-600.
Nösgen, C. F. *Geschichte der neutestamentlichen Offenbarung II: Geschichte der Apostolischen Verkündigung* (Munich, 1893).
Norris, F. W. "Antiochien I. Neutestamentlich." *TRE* III (Göttingen, 1978) 99-103.
———. "Antioch on-the-Orontes as a Religious Center I: Paganism before Constantine." *ANRW* II 18.4 (Berlin/New York, 1990) 2322-79.

————. "Antioch of Syria." *ABD* I (New York, 1992) 265-69.

Oberhummer, E. "Thessalonike." *PRE* II 6 (Stuttgart, 1937) 143-63.

O'Brien, P. T. *Introductory Thanksgivings in the Letters of Paul. NTSup* 49 (Leiden, 1977).

Oehler, W. "Wie Paulus Missionar wurde." *EMM* 73 (1929) 225-33, 257-62, 321-30, 356-71.

Oepke, A. *Die Missionspredigt des Apostels Paulus. Eine biblisch-theologische und religionsgeschichtliche Untersuchung. Missionswissenschaftliche Forschungen* II (Leipzig, 1920).

————. "Probleme der vorchristlichen Zeit des Paulus." *TSK* 105 (1933) 387-424 (repr. in K. H. Rengstorf, *Das Paulusbild in der neueren deutschen Forschung. WdF* 24 [Darmstadt, 1969] 410-46).

Ogg, G. *The Chronology of the Public Ministry of Jesus* (Cambridge, 1940).

————. "A New Chronology of Saint Paul's Life." *ET* 64 (1952/53) 120-23.

————. "Derbe." *NTS* 9 (1962/63) 367-70.

————. *The Chronology of the Life of Paul* (London, 1968).

Okeke, G. E. "1 Thess 2:13-16: The Fate of the Unbelieving Jews." *NTS* 27 (1980/81) 127-36.

Oliver, J. H. "The Epistle of Claudius Which Mentions the Proconsul Junius Gallio." *Hesp* 40 (1971) 239f.

Ollrog, W. H. *Paulus und seine Mitarbeiter. Untersuchungen zu Theorie und Praxis der paulinischen Mission. WMANT* 50 (Neukirchen-Vluyn, 1979).

————. "Die Abfassungsverhältnisse von Röm 16." In D. Lührmann and G. Strecker, *Kirche. Festschrift Günther Bornkamm* (Tübingen, 1980) 221-44.

Oost, S. I. "Marcus Antonius Pallas." *AJP* 79 (1958) 113-39.

Orchard, B. "The Problem of Acts and Galatians." *CBQ* 7 (1945) 377-97.

Osborne, R. E. "Did Paul Go to Qumran?" *CJT* 10 (1964) 15-24.

————. "St. Paul's Silent Years." *JBL* 84 (1965) 59-65.

————. "Paul and the Wild Beasts." *JBL* 85 (1966) 225-30.

Oster, R. E. "Acts 19:23-41 and an Ephesian Inscription." *HTR* 77 (1984) 233-37.

————. *A Bibliography of Ancient Ephesus. ATLA Bibliography Series* 19 (Methuen/London, 1987).

————. "Ephesus." *ABD* II (New York, 1992) 542-49.

————. "The Supposed Anachronism in Luke Acts' Use of ΣΥΝΑΓΩΓΗ: A Rejoinder to H. C. Kee." *NTS* 39 (1993) 178-208.

O'Sullivan, F. *The Egnatian Way* (London, 1972).

Otto, W. *Herodes* (Stuttgart, 1913 = *PRESup* 2 [Stuttgart, 1913]).

Overman, J. A. "The God-fearers: Some Neglected Features." *JSNT* 32 (1988) 17-26.

Palmer, D. W. "Acts and the Ancient Historical Monograph." In B. W. Winter and A. D. Clarke. *The Book of Acts in Its Ancient Literary Setting.* A1CS I (Grand Rapids and Carlisle, 1993) 1-30.

Pak, J. Y. *Paul as Missionary: A Comparative Study of Missionary Discourse in Paul's Epistles and Selected Contemporary Jewish Texts. EHS* XXIII/410 (Frankfurt, 1991).

Pallas, D. *Les monuments paléochrétiens de Grèce découverts de 1959 à 1973. SSAC* 5 (Rome, 1977).

Palmer, D. W. "Acts and the Historical Monograph." *TynBul* 43/2 (1992) 373-88.

Pandermalis, D. *Dion: The Sacred City of the Macedonians at the Foothills of Mt. Olympos* (Athens, 1987).

Papazoglou, F. "Quelques aspects de l'historie de la province de Macédoine." *ANRW* II 7.1 (Berlin/New York, 1979) 302-69.

————. "Politarques en Illyrie." *Hist* 35 (1986) 438-48.

————. *Les villes de Macédoine à l'époque Romaine. BCH.S* 16 (Athens/Paris, 1988).

Paribeni, R. "Sull-origine del nome Cristiano." *NBAC* 19 (1913) 37-41.

Parker, P. "Once More, Acts and Galatians." *JBL* 86 (1967) 175-82.

Parker, R. A., and Dubberstein, W. H. *Babylonian Chronology 626 B.C.–A.D. 75. Brown University Studies* 19 (Providence, 1956).

Paschoud, F. *Roma Aeterna. Études sur le patriotisme Romain dans l'occident latin à l'époque des grandes invasions. BHR* 7 (Rome, 1967).

Pasinya, M. "Antioche, berceau de l'église des gentils (Act 11,19-26)." *RATh* 1 (1977) 31-66.

Patsch, H. "Die Prophetie des Agabus." *TZ* 28 (1972) 228-32.

Paulsen, H. Review of R. Jewett, *Paulus-Chronologie. Ein Versuch* (Munich, 1982). *TZ* 40 (1984) 85-87.

Pax, E. "Beobachtungen zur Konvertitensprache des ersten Thessalonicherbriefes." *SBFLA* 21 (1971) 220-61.

————. "Konvertitenprobleme im ersten Thessalonicherbrief." *BibLeb* 13 (1972) 24-37.

————. "Spuren der Nabatäer im Neuen Testament." *BibLeb* 15 (1974) 193-206.

Pazaras, T. "Δύο παλαιοχριστιανικοὶ τάφοι ἀπὸ τὸ δυτικὸ νεκροταφεῖο τῆς Θεσσαλονίκης." *Mak* 21 (1981) 373-89.

Pearson, B. A. "1 Thessalonians 2:13-16: A Deutero-Pauline Interpolation." *HTR* 64 (1971) 79-94.

————. "Earliest Christianity in Egypt: Some Observations." In B. A. Pearson and J. E. Goehring. *The Roots of Egyptian Christianity: Studies in Antiquity and Christianity* (Philadelphia, 1986) 132-59.

Pekary, T. *Untersuchungen zu den römischen Reichsstrassen. Antiquitas 1. R. Abhandlungen zur alten Geschichte* 17 (Bonn, 1968).

————. "Kleinasien unter römischer Herrschaft." *ANRW* II 7.2 (Berlin/New York, 1980) 595-657.

Penna, R. "Les Juifs à Rome au temps de l'apôtre Paul." *NTS* 28 (1982) 321-47.

Perkins, P. "Johannine Traditions in *Ap.Jas.* (NHC I,2)." *JBL* 101 (1982) 403-14.

————. "1 Thessalonians and Hellenistic Religious Practices." In M. P. Horgan and P. J. Kobelski. *To Touch the Text: Biblical and Related Studies in Honor of Joseph A. Fitzmyer S.J.* (New York, 1989) 325-34.

Perowne, S. *The Life and Times of Herod the Great* (London, 1960).

————. *The Journeys of St. Paul* (London/New York, 1973).

Perriman, A. C. "Paul and the Parousia: 1 Corinthians 15.50-57 and 2 Corinthians 5.1-5." *NTS* 35 (1989) 512-21.

Pesch, R. *Simon-Petrus. Geschichte und geschichtliche Bedeutung des ersten Jüngers Jesu Christi. PuP* 15 (Stuttgart, 1980).

————. *Die Entdeckung des ältesten Paulus-Briefes, Paulus — neu gesehen. Die Briefe an die Gemeinde der Thessalonicher. Herder Tb* 1167 (Freiburg, 1984).

————. "Voraussetzungen und Anfänge der urchristlichen Mission." *ThJb(L) 1987* (Leipzig, 1987) 332-73.

Peters, F. W. "City Planning in Greco-Roman Syria: Some New Considerations." *DaM* 1 (1983) 269-77.

Peterson, E. "Christianus." *Frühkirche, Judentum und Gnosis* (Rome/Freiburg/Vienna, 1959) 64-87.

Petsas, P. "Ἡ Ἀγορὰ τῆς Θεσσαλονίκης," *AAA* 1 (1968) 156-61.

Pfleiderer, O. *Paulinism: A Contribution to the History of Primitive Christian Theology.* 2 vols. (Eng. trans., London, 1891).

—————. *Primitive Christianity: Its Writings and Teachings in Their Historical Connections.* 4 vols. (Eng. trans., New York, 1906-1911).

Pherigo, L. P. "Paul's Life after the Close of Acts." *JBL* 70 (1951) 277-84.

Philipp, H. "Tres Tabernae." *PRE* II 4.2 (Stuttgart, 1932) 1875.

Philonenko, M. "Le *Martyre d'Esaïe* et l'Histoire de la secte de Qumrân." *Pseudépigraphes de l'Ancien Testament et les manuscripts de la mer Morte* I (Paris, 1967) 1-10.

Piattelli, D. " 'Missione' e 'proselitismo' in Israele: effetti dell-insurrezione maccabaica nel pensiero di Qumran e nella letteratura rabbinica." In G. Ghiberti. *La missione nel mondo antico e nella Bibbia. Ricerche Storico Bibliche* 1/1990 (Bologna, 1990) 87-100.

Pieper, K. *Paulus. Seine missionarische Persönlichkeit und Wirksamkeit.* NtA XII/1-2 (Münster, ²/³1929).

—————. "Antiochien am Orontes im apostolischen Zeitalter. Ein Kapitel aus der frühesten Geschichte der Katholischen Aktion." *TGl* 22 (1930) 710-28.

Pilhofer, P. *Philippi I: Die erste christliche Gemeinde Europas.* WUNT I/87 (Tübingen, 1995).

Pillinger, R. "Das Grabmal von Ossenovo (Bulgarien) im Rahmen des frühen Christentums der westlichen Schwarzmeerküste." *AÖAW.PH* 120 (1983) 196-215.

Pixner, B. "The History of the 'Essene Gate' Area." *ZDPV* 105 (1989) 96-104.

Pixner, B., and Riesner, R. "Kochaba." *GBL* II (Wuppertal/Gießen, 1988) 801f.

Plassart, A. "L'inscription de Delphes mentionnant le proconsul Gallion." *RÉG* 80 (1967) 372-78.

Plevnik, J., "The Parousia as Implication of Christ's Resurrection: An Exegesis of 1 Thess. 4:13-18." In J. Plevnik. *Word and Spirit: Essays in Honor of David Michael Stanley* (Willowdale, 1975) 199-277.

—————. "1 Thess 5:1-11: Its Authenticity, Intention and Message." *Bibl* 60 (1979) 71-90.

—————. "The Taking Up of the Faithful and the Resurrection of the Dead in 1 Thessalonians 4:13-18." *CBQ* 46 (1984) 242-83.

—————. "Paul's Eschatology." *Toronto Journal of Theology* 6 (1990) 86-99.

—————. "Pauline Presuppositions." In R. F. Collins. *The Thessalonian Correspondence.* BETL 87 (Leuven, 1990) 50-61.

Plooij, D. *De Chronologie van het Leven van Paulus* (Leiden, 1918).

Plümacher, E. *Lukas als hellenistischer Schriftsteller. Studien zur Apostelgeschichte.* SUNT 9 (Göttingen, 1972).

—————. "Wirklichkeitserfahrung und Geschichtsschreibung bei Lukas. Erwägungen zu den Wir-Stücken der Apostelgeschichte." *ZNW* 68 (1977) 2-22.

—————. "Apostelgeschichte." *TRE* III (Berlin/New York, 1978) 483-528.

Pobee, J. S. *Persecution and Martyrdom in the Theology of Paul.* JSNTSup 6 (Sheffield, 1985).

Pölzl, F. X. *Die Mitarbeiter des Weltapostels Paulus* (Regensburg, 1911).

Polomé, E. C. "The Linguistic Situation in the Western Provinces of the Roman Empire." *ANRW* II 29.2 (Berlin/New York, 1983) 509-53.

Pope, R. H. *On Roman Roads with Saint Paul* (London, 1939).

Porter, J. R. "The 'Apostolic Decree' and Paul's Second Visit to Jerusalem." *JTS* 47 (1946) 169-74.

Porter, S. E. "The 'We' Passages." In D. W. J. Gill and C. Gempf. *The Book of Acts in Its Graeco-Roman Setting.* A1CS II (Grand Rapids and Carlisle, 1994) 545-74.

Potter, D. S. "Persecution of the Early Church." *ABD* V (New York, 1992) 231-35.

—————. "Quirinius," *Ibid.,* 588f.

478

Pottier, M. E. "Rapport sur les travaux archéologiques en Syrie et à l'École Français de Jérusalem." *Syr* 4 (1923) 316-23.

Power, E. "John 2,20 and the Date of the Crucifixion." *Bibl* 9 (1928) 257-88.

Praeder, S. M. "The Problem of the First Person Narration in Acts." *NT* 29 (1987) 193-218.

Pratscher, W. *Der Herrenbruder Jakobus und die Jakobustradition. FRLANT* 139 (Göttingen, 1987).

Preisker, H. "Jerusalem und Damaskus — Ein Beitrag zum Verständnis des Urchristentums." *TBl* 8 (1929) 49-54.

Prentice, W. K. "St. Paul's Journey to Damascus." *ZNW* 46 (1955) 250-55.

Preuschen, E. "Todesjahr und Todestag Jesu." *ZNW* 5 (1904) 1-17.

———. "Chresto impulsore." *ZNW* 15 (1914) 96.

Price, J. J. *Jerusalem under Siege: The Collapse of the Jewish State 66-70 C.E. Brill's Series in Jewish Studies* 3 (Leiden, 1992).

Prior, M. *Paul the Letter-Writer (and the Second Letter to Timothy). JSNTSup* 23 (Sheffield, 1989).

Pritz, R. A. *Nazarene Jewish Christianity: From the End of the New Testament Period until Its Disappearance in the Fourth Century. SPB* 37 (Jerusalem/Leiden, 1988).

Probst, H. *Paulus und der Brief. Die Rhetorik des antiken Briefes als Form der paulinischen Korintherkorrespondenz (1 Kor 8–10). WUNT* II/45 (Tübingen, 1991).

Przybylski, B. "The Role of Calendrical Data in Gnostic Literature." *VC* 34 (1980) 56-70.

Puech, É. "Notes sur le manuscrit de 11QMelkîsédeq." *RQ* 12 (1987) 483-513.

Pummer, R. "Samaritan Material Remains and Archaeology." In A. D. Crown. *The Samaritans* (Tübingen, 1989) 135-77.

Purvis, J. D. "The Palaeography of the Samaritan Inscription from Thessalonica." *BASOR* 221 (1976) 121-23.

Questa, C. "Tecnica biografica e tecnica annalistica dei ll. LIII–LXIII di Cassione Dio." *StUrb* 31 (1957) 37-53.

Quinn, J. D. "Paul's Last Captivity." In E. A. Livingstone. *Studia Biblica 1978 III: Papers on Paul and Other New Testament Authors. JSNTSup* 3 (Sheffield, 1980) 289-99.

Radin, M. *The Jews among the Greeks and Romans* (Philadelphia, 1915).

Radke, G. "Viae Publicae Romanae." *PRESup* 13 (Munich, 1973) 1417-1686.

Räisänen, H. *Paul and the Law. WUNT* I/29 (Tübingen, 1983).

Rajak, T. *Josephus: The Historian and His Society* (Philadelphia, 1983).

Ramsay, W. M. *The Church in the Roman Empire before A.D. 170* (London, 1893).

———. *St. Paul the Traveller and the Roman Citizen* (London, 1895; ³1897).

———. "A Fixed Date in the Life of St. Paul." *Exp* V/3 (1896) 336-45.

———. "Cornelius and the Italic Cohort." *Exp* V/4 (1896) 194-201.

———. "On Dr. Schürer's Reply." *Exp* V/5 (1897) 69-72.

———. "Pauline Chronology." *Exp* V/5 (1897) 201-11.

———. "Some Recent Editions of the Acts of the Apostles." *Exp* VI/2 (1900) 321-35.

———. "The Jews in the Graeco-Asiatic Cities." *Exp* VI/5 (1902) 19-33, 92-109.

———. "Travel and Correspondence among the Early Christians." *Exp* VI/8 (1903) 401-22.

———. "Roads and Travel (in N[ew] T[estament])." *HD(B)*. Extra volume (Edinburgh, 1904) 375-403.

———. "Numbers, Hours, Years, and Dates." *Ibid.,* 473-84.

———. "The Statesmanship of Paul." *Pauline and Other Studies in Early Christian History* (London, ²1906) 49-100.

———. "St. Paul's Road from Cilicia to Iconium." *Ibid.,* 273-98.

———. "The Pauline Chronology." *Ibid.,* 345-65.

————. *The Cities of St. Paul* (London, 1907).

————. "Luke's Authorities in the Acts, Chapters I–XII." *Exp* VII/7 (1909) 450-69.

————. "The Family and Religion of L. Sergius Paullus, Proconsul of Cyprus." *ET* 29 (1917/18) 324-28.

————. *The Bearing of Recent Discovery on the Trustworthiness of the New Testament* (London, ⁴1920).

————. "The Speed of the Roman Imperial Post." *JRS* 15 (1925) 60-74.

————. "Studies in the Roman Province of Galatia X: The Romans in Galatia." *JRS* 16 (1926) 201-15.

Ramsay, W. M., and Hemer, C. J. "Galatia; Galatians." *ISBE* II (Grand Rapids, 1982) 377-79.

Ramsey, H. L. *The Place of Galatians in the Career of Paul* (diss., Columbia University, 1960).

Rapsaet-Charlier, M. T. *Prosopographie des femmes de l'ordre sénatorial (Ier-IIe siècles)* (Louvain, 1987).

Rapske, B. *The Book of Acts and Paul in Roman Custody.* A1CS III (Grand Rapids and Carlisle, 1994).

————. "Acts, Travel, and Shipwreck." In D. W. J. Gill and C. Gempf. *The Book of Acts in Its Graeco-Roman Setting.* A1CS II (Grand Rapids and Carlisle, 1994) 1-48.

Rathbonne, D. "The Grain Trade and Grain Shortages in the Hellenistic East." In P. Garnsey and C. R. Whittaker. *Trade and Famine in Classical Antiquity. CPSSV* 8 (1983) 45-55.

Rees, W. "Gallio the Proconsul of Achaia (Acts xviii,12-17)." *Scrip* 4 (1949/51) 11-20.

Reese, B. "The Apostle Paul's Exercise of His Rights as a Roman Citizen as Recorded in the Book of Acts." *EQ* 47 (1975) 138-45.

Refoulé, F. "Date de l'épître aux Galates." *RB* 95 (1988) 161-83.

Refshauge, E. "Literaerkritiske overvejelser: Til de to Thessalonikerbreve." *DTT* 34 (1971) 1-19.

Reicke, B. "Γαλλίων." *EDNT* I (Grand Rapids, 1990) 234.

————. *Neutestamentliche Zeitgeschichte* (³1982).

————. *The New Testament Era: The World of the Bible from 500 B.C. to A.D. 100* (Eng. trans., Philadelphia, 1968).

Reinach, S. "La première allusion au Christianisme dans l'histoire. Sur un passage énigmatique d'une lettre de Claude." *RHR* 90 (1924) 108-22.

Reinach, T. "L'empereur Claude et les Juifs d'après un nouveau document." *RÉJ* 79 (1924) 113-44.

Reinbold, W. *Der älteste Bericht über den Tod Jesu. Literarische Analyse und historische Kritik der Passionsdarstellungen der Evangelien. BZNW* 69 (Berlin/New York, 1994).

Reiser, M. "Hat Paulus Heiden bekehrt?" *BZ* 39 (1995) 76-91.

Rémy, B. *L'évolution administrative de l'Anatolie aux trois premiers siècles de notre ère. Collection du Centre d'Études Romaines et Gallo-Romaines* N.S. 5 (Lyon, 1986).

————. *Les fastes sénatoriaux des provinces romaines d'Anatolie au Haut-Empire (31 av. J.-C.-284 ap. J.-C.: Pont-Bithynie, Galatie, Cappadoce, Lycie-Pamphylie et Cilicie)* (Paris, 1988).

————. *Les carrières sénatoriales dans les provinces romaines d'Anatolie au Haut-Empire (31 av. J.-C.-284 ap. J.-C.)* (Istanbul/Paris, 1989).

————. "L'activité des fonctionnaires sénatoriaux dans la province de Galatie au Haut-Empire d'après les inscriptions." *RÉA* 92 (1990) 85-108.

Rese, M. "Zur Geschichte des frühen Christentums — Ein kritischer Bericht über drei neue Bücher." *TZ* 38 (1982) 98-110.

Reumann, J. "The 'Itinerary' as a Form in Classical Literature and the Acts of the Apostles." In M. P. Horgan and P. J. Kobelski. *To Touch the Text: Biblical and Related Studies in Honor of Joseph A. Fitzmyer S.J.* (New York, 1989) 335-57.

Rey-Coquais, J. P. "Syrie romaine, de Pompée à Dioclétien." *JRS* 68 (1978) 44-73.

Ricard, R. "Navigations de Saint Paul." *Études* 190 (1927) 448-65.

Richard, E. *Jesus, One and Many: Christological Concepts of New Testament Authors* (Wilmington, 1988).

———. "Early Pauline Thought: An Analysis of 1 Thessalonians." In J. M. Bassler. *Pauline Theology* I (Minneapolis, 1991) 39-51.

Richards, E. R. *The Secretary in the Letters of Paul. WUNT* II/42 (Tübingen, 1991).

Richards, J. R. "Romans and I Corinthians: Their Chronological Relationship and Comparative Dates." *NTS* 13 (1966/67) 14-30.

Rickman, G. E. *The Corn Supply of Ancient Rome* (Oxford, 1980).

Riddle, D. W. *Paul, Man of Conflict* (New York/Nashville, 1940).

Riesenfeld, H. "Har vi tva kulturer? Till dateringen av Jesu död." *SEÅ* 51/52 (1986/87) 192-202.

Riesner, R. *Formen gemeinsamen Lebens im Neuen Testament und heute. Theologie und Dienst* 11 (Gießen/Basel, ²1984).

———. "Johannes der Täufer auf Machärus." *BK* 39 (1984) 176.

———. "Essener und Urkirche in Jerusalem." *BK* 40 (1985) 64-76.

———. "Bethany beyond the Jordan (John 1:28). Topography, Theology and History in the Fourth Gospel." *TynBul* 38 (1987) 29-63.

———. "Begräbnis- und Trauersitten." *GBL* I (Wuppertal/Gießen, 1987) 173-78.

———. "Gischala." *Ibid.*, 468.

———. *Jesus als Lehrer. Eine Untersuchung zum Ursprung der Evangelien-Überlieferung. WUNT* II/7 (Tübingen, ³1988).

———. "Adolf Schlatter und die Geschichte der Judenchristen Jerusalems." In K. Bockmühl. *Die Aktualität der Theologie Adolf Schlatters* (Gießen/Basel, 1988) 34-70.

———. "Hermon." *GBL* II (Wuppertal/Gießen, 1988) 562f.

———. "Jerusalem." *Ibid.*, 661-73.

———. "Kenchreä." *Ibid.*, 775.

———. "Korinth." *Ibid.*, 815-19.

———. "Lysanias." *Ibid.*, 904.

———. "Nazareth-Inschrift." *Ibid.*, 1037.

———. "Neapolis." *Ibid.*, 1037f.

———. "Amphipolis. Eine übersehene Paulus-Station." *BK* 44 (1989) 79-81.

———. "Philippi." *GBL* III (Wuppertal/Gießen, 1989) 1196-99.

———. "Sergius Paul(l)us." *Ibid.*, 1435.

———. "Thessalonich." *Ibid.*, 1545-48.

———. *Die Frühzeit des Paulus. Studien zur Chronologie, Missionsstrategie und Theologie des Apostels bis zum Ersten Thessalonicher-Brief* (Habilitationsschrift, Tübingen, 1990).

———. "Essener und Urkirche in Jerusalem." In B. Mayer, *Christen und Christliches in Qumran?* ESt n.s. 32 (Regensburg, 1992) 139-55.

———. Review of D. Trobisch, *Die Entstehung der Paulusbriefsammlung* (Fribourg/Göttingen, 1989). *JET* 6 (1992) 164-68.

———. "Prägung und Herkunft der lukanischen Sonderüberlieferung." *TBei* 24 (1993) 228-48.

———. "Das Jerusalemer Essenerviertel und die Urgemeinde. Josephus, Bellum V 145; 11QMiqdasch 46,13-16; Apostelgeschichte 1–6 und die Archäologie." *ANRW* II 26.2 (forthcoming).

———. "Synagogues in Jerusalem." In R. Bauckham. *The Book of Acts in Its Palestinian Setting.* A1CS IV (Grand Rapids and Carlisle, 1995) 179-212.

———. "Chronologie und Theologie bei Paulus." *JETS* 10 (1996) 110-22.

———. "Paulus und die Jesus-Überlieferung." In J. Ådna and O. Hofius. *Evangelium — Schriftauslegung — Kirche. Festschrift für Peter Stuhlmacher* (Göttingen, 1997) 345-65.

Riesner, R., and Thiede, C. P. "Tres Tabernae." *GBL* III (Wuppertal/Gießen, 1989) 1595.

Rigaux, B. *The Letters of St. Paul: Modern Studies* (Eng. trans., Chicago, 1968).

Rinaldi, G. "Procurator Felix. Note prosopografiche in margine ad una rilettura di at 24." *RBI* 39 (1991) 423-66.

Robbins, V. K. "The We-Passages in Acts and Ancient Sea-Voyages." *BR* 20 (1975) 5-18.

———. "By Land and By Sea: The We-Passages and Ancient Sea Voyages." In C. H. Talbert. *Perspectives on Luke-Acts* (Edinburgh, 1978) 215-42.

Rogert, J., and Rogert, L. "Bulletin épigraphique." *RÉG* 82 (1969) 424-540.

Robert, L. "Les inscriptions de Thessalonique." *RPh* 98 (1974) 180-246.

Roberts, C. H. *Manuscript, Society and Belief in Early Christian Egypt. The Schweich Lectures 1977* (Oxford, 1979).

Robinson, D. F. "A Note on Acts 11,27-30." *JBL* 63 (1944) 169-72.

———. "A Reply." *Ibid.*, 411f.

Robinson, J. A. T. *Redating the New Testament* (Philadelphia, 1976).

———. *The Priority of John.* Edited by J. F. Coakley (London, 1985).

Robinson, T. A. *The Bauer Thesis Examined: The Geography of Heresy in the Early Christian Church* (Lewiston/Queenston, 1988).

Roetzel, C. J. "Theodidaktoi and Handwork in Philo and I Thessalonians." In A. Vanhoye. *L'Apôtre Paul. Personnalité, style et conception du ministère.* BETL 73 (Paris/Leuven, 1986) 324-31.

Roller, O. *Das Formular der paulinischen Briefe. Ein Beitrag zur Lehre vom antiken Briefe.* BWANT IV/6 (Stuttgart, 1933).

Rordorf, W. "Nochmals: Paulusakten und Pastoralbriefe." In G. F. Hawthorne and O. Betz. *Tradition and Interpretation in the New Testament: Essays in Honor of E. Earle Ellis* (Grand Rapids/Tübingen, 1987) 319-27.

Roschinski, H. P. "Geschichte der Nabatäer." In G. Hellenkemper-Salies, *Die Nabatäer: Erträge einer Ausstellung im Rheinischen Landesmuseum Bonn. Kunst und Altertum am Rhein* 106 (1981) 1-26.

Rosner, B. S. "Acts and Biblical History." In B. W. Winter and A. D. Clarke. *The Book of Acts in Its Ancient Literary Setting.* A1CS I (Grand Rapids and Carlisle, 1993) 65-82.

Rossano, P. "Note archeologiche sulla antica Tessalonica." *RBI* 6 (1958) 242-47.

Rossbach, O. "L. Annaeus Novatus." *PRE* 1 (Stuttgart, 1894) 2236f.

Rostovtzeff, M. *Gesellschaft und Wirtschaft im römischen Kaiserreich* I-II (Leipzig, 1931).

———. *A History of the Ancient World* (Eng. trans., Oxford, 1945).

———. *Economic History of the Roman Empire* I-II. Edited by P. M. Fraser (Oxford, ²1957).

Rougé, J. "La navigation hivernale sous l'empire Romain" *RÉA* 54 (1952) 316-25.

———. "Actes 27,1." *VC* 14 (1960) 193-203.

————. *Recherches sur l'organisation du commerce maritime en Méditerranée sous l'empire Romain. École Pratique des Hautes Études (VIe Section: Centre de Recherches Historiques) — Ports, Routes, Trafics* 21 (Paris, 1966).

Rowlingson, D. T. "The Geographical Orientation of Paul's Missionary Interests." *JBL* 59 (1950) 341-44.

————. "The Jerusalem Conference and Jesus' Nazareth Visit." *JBL* 71 (1952) 69-74.

Ruckstuhl, E. *Die Chronologie des Letzten Mahles und des Leidens Jesu." BiBe* 4 (Einsiedeln, 1963).

————. "Zur Chronologie der Leidensgeschichte Jesu." *SNTU* 10 (1985) 27-61; 11 (1986) 97-129 (repr. with addendum in *Jesus im Horizont der Evangelien. SBAB* 3 [Stuttgart, 1988] 101-84).

————. "Zur Frage einer Essenergemeinde in Jerusalem und zum Fundort von 7Q5." In B. Mayer. *Christen und Christliches in Qumran? ESt* 32 (Regensburg, 1992) 131-37.

Rudolph, K. "Gnosis und Gnostizismus, ein Forschungsbericht." *TR* 34 (1969) 121-75.

————. *Gnosis: The Nature and History of Gnosticism* (Eng. trans., San Francisco, 1984).

Ruge, W. "Tarsos." *PRE* II 8 (Stuttgart, 1932) 2413-39.

————. "Perge 2." *PRE* I 37 (Stuttgart, 1937) 694-704.

————. "Troas." *PRE* II 13 (Stuttgart, 1939) 526-84.

Russel, E. A. "Convincing or Merely Curious? A Look at Some Recent Writing on Galatians." *Irish Biblical Studies* 6 (1984) 156-76.

Russell, R. "The Idle in 2 Thess. 3,6-12: An Eschatological or a Social Problem." *NTS* 34 (1988) 105-19.

Russell, W. B. "Rhetorical Analysis of the Book of Galatians, Part 1." *BS* 150 (1993) 341-58.

Sabugal, S. *Análisis exegética sobre la conversión de San Pablo. El problema teológica e histórica* (Barcelona, 1976).

————. "La Mención neotestamentaria de Damasco (Gál 1,17; 2 Cor 11,32; Act 9,2-3.8.10 par. 19.22.27 par) ¿ciudad de Siria o región de Qumrân?" In M. Delcor. *Qumrân. Sa piété, sa théologie et son milieu. BETL* 46 (Paris/Leuven, 1978) 403-13.

Sack, D. "Damaskus — Die antike und islamische Stadt." In *Land des Baal: Syrien — Forum der Völker und Kulturen* (Mainz, 1982) 360-63.

————. "Damaskus, die Stadt *intra muros.* Ein Beitrag zu den Arbeiten der 'Internationalen Kommission zum Schutz der Altstadt von Damaskus'." *DaM* 2 (1985) 207-90.

————. *Damaskus. Entstehung und Struktur einer orientalisch-islamischen Stadt. Damaszener Forschungen* 1 (Mainz, 1989).

Saddington, D. B. "Race Relationships in the Early Roman Empire." *ANRW* II 2 (Berlin/New York, 1975) 131-48.

Saffrey, H. D. *Histoire de l'apôtre Paul ou Faire chrétien le monde* (Paris, 1991).

Saint-Denis, E. de. "La vitesse des navires anciens." *RA* VI/18 (1941) 121-38.

————. "Mare Clausum." *RÉL* 25 (1947) 196-214.

Sampley, J. P. *Pauline Partnership in Christ: Christian Community and Commitment in Light of Roman Law* (Philadelphia, 1980).

Sanchez, Bosch J. "La chronologie de la première aux Thessaloniciens et les relations de Paul avec d'autres églises." *NTS* 37 (1991) 336-47.

Sanders, E. P. *Paul and Palestinian Judaism* (Philadelphia, 1977).

————. *Paul* (Oxford/New York, 1991).

Sanders, J. T. "Paul's 'Autobiographical' Statements in Galatians 1-2." *JBL* 85 (1966) 335-43.

Sandnes, K. O. *"Paul — One of the Prophets"? A Contribution to the Apostle's Self-Understanding. WUNT* I/43 (Tübingen, 1991).

Sarikakis, T. C. "Des soldats Macédoniens dans l'armée Romaine." *AncMac* II (Thessalonica, 1977) 431-38.

———. "Prosopographie des militaires Macédoniens." *Ibid.,* 439-64.

Sartre, M. *Trois études sur l'Arabie romaine et byzantine. Collection Latomus* 175 (Brussels, 1982).

Saulnier, C. "Hérode Antipas et Jean le Baptiste. Quelques remarques sur les confusions chronologiques de Flavius Josèphe." *RB* 92 (1984) 362-76.

———. *Histoire d'Israël III: De la conquête d'Alexandre à la destruction du temple (331 B.C.–135 A.D.)* (Paris, 1985).

———. "Rome et la Bible." *DBS* X (Paris, 1985) 863-1008.

———. "Il les chassa de Rome." *MBib* 51 (1987) 8-10.

———. "Flavius Josèphe et la propagande Flavienne." *RB* 96 (1989) 545-62.

Saumagne, C. "Saint Paul et Félix, procurateur de Judée." In R. Chevallier. *Mélanges d'archéologie et d'histoire offerts à André Piganiol* (Paris, 1966) 1373-86.

Sauvaget, J. *Les monuments historiques de Damas* (Beirut, 1932).

———. "Le plan antique de Damas." *Syr* 26 (1949) 314-58.

Scaliger, J. J. *De emendatione temporum* (Frankfurt, 1598).

Scarpat, G. *Il pensiero religioso di Seneca e l'ambiente ebraico e cristiano* (Brescia, 1977).

Schade, H. H. *Apokalyptische Christologie bei Paulus. Studien zum Zusammenhang von Christologie und Eschatologie in den Paulusbriefen. GTA* 18 (Göttingen, [2]1984).

Schalit, A. *König Herodes. Der Mann und sein Werk. SJ* 4 (Berlin, 1969).

Scharberg, G. B. von. *Die Chronologie des Lebens Jesu* I (Hermannstadt, 1928); II: *Ergänzungen zum historischen Teil* (Hermannstadt, 1929).

Schedl, C. *Talmud — Evangelium — Synagoge* (Innsbruck, 1969).

Schelkle, K. H. *Paulus. Leben — Briefe — Theologie. EdF* 152 (Darmstadt, 1981).

Schenk von Stauffenberg, A. *Die römische Kaisergeschichte bei Malalas. Griechischer Text der Bücher IX-XII und Untersuchungen* (Stuttgart, 1931).

Schenk, W. "Gefangenschaft und Tod des Täufers. Erwägungen zur Chronologie und ihren Konsequenzen." *NTS* 29 (1983) 453-83.

Schenke, H. M., and Fischer, K. M. *Einleitung in die Schriften des Neuen Testaments I. Die Briefe des Paulus und die Schriften des Paulinismus* (East Berlin, 1978).

Schenke, L. *Die Urgemeinde. Geschichtliche und theologische Entwicklung* (Stuttgart, 1990).

Schermann, T. *Propheten- und Apostellegenden nebst Jüngerkatalogen des Dorotheus und verwandter Texte. TU* n.s. 3.1 (Leipzig, 1907).

Scherrer, P. "Augustus, die Mission des Vedius Pollio und die Artemis Ephesia." *JÖAI* 60 (1990) 87-101.

Schiby, B. "Τὰ κηρύγματα τοῦ ἀποστόλου Παύλου εἰς τὴν Θεσσαλονίκην: Ποῦ ἀκριβῶς βρίσκοταν ἡ συναγώγη," Μακεδονικὸν Ἡμερολόγιον (Athens, 1966) 55-58.

Schiby, J. "קהילה שומרונית בסלוניקי" [A Samaritan Community in Thessalonica]." *Zion* 42 (1977) 103-9.

Schille, G. "Die Fragwürdigkeit eines Itinerars der Paulusreisen." *TLZ* 84 (1959) 165-74.

———. *Die urchristliche Kollegialmission. ATANT* 48 (Zurich/Stuttgart, 1967).

———. "Γαλατία κτλ.." *EDNT* I (Grand Rapids, 1990) 232-33.

Schilling, C. "Tarsus." *GBL* III (Wuppertal/Gießen, 1989) 1530-33.

Schilling, F. A. "Why Did Paul Go to Damascus?" *ATR* 16 (1934) 199-205.

Schimanowski, G. " 'Abgrenzung und Identitätsfindung.' Paulinische Paränese im 1. Thes-

salonicherbrief." In R. Feldmeier and U. Heckel. *Die Heiden. Juden, Christen und das Problem des Fremden. WUNT* I/67 (Tübingen, 1993) 297-316.

Schlatter, A. *Der Chronograph aus dem Zehnten Jahre Antonins. TU* 12.1 (Leipzig, 1894).

————. *Die Tage Trajans und Hadrians. BFCT* I/3 (Gütersloh, 1897) (repr. in *Synagoge und Kirche bis zum Barkochba-Aufstand. Vier Studien zur Geschichte des Rabbinats und der jüdischen Christenheit in den ersten zwei Jahrhunderten. Kleinere Schriften* 3 (Stuttgart, 1966) 9-97.

————. *Die Geschichte der ersten Christenheit. BFCT* II/11 (Gütersloh, 1926; repr. ed.). Edited by R. Riesner (Stuttgart, [6]1983).

Schlatter, T. "Gallio und Paulus in Korinth." *NKZ* 36 (1925) 500-513.

Schlunk, M. *Paulus als Missionar. AMS* 23 (Gütersloh, 1937).

Schmauch, W. "Aretas." *RGG* I (Tübingen, [3]1957) 590.

Schmidt, A. "Das historische Datum des Apostelkonzils." *ZNW* 81 (1990) 122-31.

————. "Das Missionsdekret in Galater 2.7-8 als Vereinbarung vom ersten Besuch Pauli in Jerusalem." *NTS* 38 (1992) 149-52.

Schmithals, W. "Die Thessalonicherbriefe als Briefkompositionen." In E. Dinkler. *Zeit und Geschichte. Dankesgabe an Rudolf Bultmann* (Tübingen, 1964) 295-315.

————. "The Historical Situation of the Thessalonian Epistles." *Idem, Paul and the Gnostics* (Eng. trans., Nashville, 1972) 123-218.

————. *Der Römerbrief als historisches Problem. SUNT* 9 (Gütersloh, 1975).

————. *Die Briefe des Paulus in ihrer ursprünglichen Form* (Zurich, 1984).

————. "Paulus als Heidenmissionar und das Problem seiner theologischen Entwicklung." In D. A. Koch. *Jesus Rede von Gott und ihre Nachgeschichte im frühen Christentum. Festschrift Willi Marxsen* (Gütersloh, 1989) 251-68.

Schmitt, G. "Die dritte Mauer Jerusalems." *ZDPV* 97 (1981) 153-70.

Schmitt, J. "Nazareth (Inscription dite de)." *DBS* VII (Paris, 1960) 323-63.

Schmitt, R. "Die Sprachverhältnisse in den östlichen Provinzen des römischen Reiches." *ANRW* II 29.2 (Berlin/New York, 1983) 554-86.

Schmitt-Korte, K. "Daten der nabatäischen Geschichte." In M. Lindner. *Petra und das Königreich der Nabatäer* (Munich, [3]1980) 104-6.

Schnackenburg, R. "Ephesus: Entwicklung einer Gemeinde von Paulus zu Johannes." *BZ* 35 (1991) 41-64.

Schneemelcher, W. *Das Urchristentum* (Stuttgart, 1981).

Schneider, H. C. *Altstrassenforschung. EdF* 170 (Darmstadt, 1982).

Schnelle, U. *Gerechtigkeit und Christusgegenwart. Vorpaulinische und paulinische Tauftheologie. GTA* 24 (Göttingen, [2]1986).

————. "Der erste Thessalonicherbrief und die Entstehung der paulinischen Anthropologie." *NTS* 32 (1986) 207-24.

————. *Wandlungen im paulinischen Denken. SBS* 137 (Stuttgart, 1989).

————. "Die Ethik des 1. Thessalonicherbriefes." In R. F. Collins. *The Thessalonian Correspondence. BETL* 87 (Leuven, 1990) 295-305.

Schober, F. "Nikopolis." *PRE* 17.1 (Stuttgart, 1937) 511-18.

Schöllgen, G. "Was wissen wir über die Sozialstruktur der paulinischen Gemeinden? Kritische Anmerkungen zu einem neuen Buch von W. A. Meeks." *NTS* 34 (1988) 71-82.

Schoenbeck, H. von. "Die Stadtplanung des römischen Thessalonike. Bericht über den VI. Internationalen Kongress für Archäologie (Berlin 21.-26 August 1939) (Berlin, 1940) 478-82 (repr. in Θεσσαλονίκην Φιλίππου Βασιλίσσαν [Thessalonica, 1985] 346-50).

Schonfield, H. J. *The Lost Book of the Nativity of John* (Edinburgh, 1929).

Schreckenberg, H. *Die Flavius-Josephus-Tradition in Antike und Mittelalter. ALGHJ* 5 (Leiden, 1972).

―――. "Neue Beiträge zur Kritik des Josephustextes." *Theok. II. Festgabe Karl Heinrich Rengstorf* (Leiden, 1973) 81-106.

―――. "Josephus in Early Christian Literature and Medieval Christian Art." In H. Schreckenberg and K. Schubert. *Jewish Historiography and Iconography in Early and Medieval Christianity. CRINT* III/2 (Assen/Minneapolis, 1991) 1-138.

Schubert, P. *Form and Function of the Pauline Thanksgivings. BZNW* 20 (Berlin, 1939).

Schuerer, E. *The History of the Jewish People in the Age of Jesus Christ.* A New English Version Revised and Edited by G. Vermes, F. Millar, and M. Black. I (Edinburgh, 1973); II (1979); III/1 (1986 [Co-Editor M. Goodman]); III/2 (1987) (abbrev. Schuerer in notes).

Schürer, E. "Lucas und Josephus." *ZWT* 19 (1876) 574-82.

―――. "Reply to Professor Ramsay." *Exp* V/4 (1896) 469-72.

―――. "Zur Chronologie des Lebens Pauli, zugleich ein Beitrag zur Kritik der Chronik des Eusebius." *ZWT* 41 (1898) 21-42.

―――. "Der Ethnarch des Königs Aretas 2 Kor. 11,32." *TSK* 72 (1899) 95-99.

―――. *Geschichte des jüdischen Volkes im Zeitalter Jesu Christi* I: *Einleitung und politische Geschichte* (Leipzig, [3/4]1901); II: *Die inneren Zustände* ([4]1907); III: *Das Judentum in der Zerstreuung und die jüdische Literatur* ([4]1909).

Schulten, A. "Tartessos." *PRE* II 8 (Stuttgart, 1932) 2446-51.

Schulz, F. "Roman Registers of Births and Birth Certificates II." *JRS* 33 (1943) 55-64.

Schulz, S. "Der frühe und der späte Paulus. Überlegungen zur Entwicklung seiner Theologie und Ethik." *TZ* 41 (1985) 228-36.

―――. *Neutestamentliche Ethik. Zürcher Grundrisse zur Bibel* (Zurich, 1987).

Schwank, B. "Und so kamen wir nach Rom (Apg 28,14). Reisenotizen zu den letzten beiden Kapiteln der Apostelgeschichte." *EA* 36 (1960) 169-92.

―――. " 'Setze über nach Mazedonien und hilf uns!' Reisenotizen zu Apg 16,9–17,15." *EA* 39 (1963) 399-416.

―――. "Der sogenannte Brief an Gallio und die Datierung des 1 Thess." *BZ* 15 (1971) 265f.

Schwartz, D. R. *Agrippa I: The Last King of Judaea. TSAJ* 23 (Tübingen, 1990).

―――. "Joseph ben Illem and the Date of Herod's Death." In *Studies in the Jewish Background of Christianity. WUNT* I/60 (Tübingen, 1992) 157-66.

―――. " 'Caesarea' and Its 'Isactium': Epigraphy, Numismatics and Herodian Chronology." *Ibid.*, 167-81.

―――. "Pontius Pilate's Appointment to Office and the Chronology of Josephus' *Antiquities,* Book 18–20." *Ibid.*, 182-201 (previously Modern Hebrew in *Zion* 48 [1983] 325-45).

―――. "Pontius Pilate's Suspension from Office: Chronology and Sources." *Ibid.*, 202-17 (previously Modern Hebrew in *Tarb* 51 [1982] 383-98).

―――. "Ishmael ben Phiabi and the Chronology of Provincia Judaea." *Ibid.*, 218-42 (previously Modern Hebrew in *Tarb* 52 [1982/83] 177-220).

―――. "Pontius Pilate." *ABD* V (New York, 1990) 395-401.

Schwartz, E. "Cassius Dio Cocceianus." *PRE* 6 (Stuttgart, 1899) 1684-1722.

―――. *Über den Tod der Söhne Zebedäi. AGWG.PH* VII/5 (Göttingen, 1904) (repr. in *Gesammelte Schriften V. Zum Neuen Testament und zum frühen Christentum* [Berlin, 1963] 48-123).

―――. "Die Aeren von Gerasa und Eleutheropolis." *NGWG.PH 1906* (Berlin, 1906) 340-95.

—. "Zur Chronologie des Paulus." *NGWG.PH 1907* (Göttingen, 1907) 262-99) (repr. in *Gesammelte Schriften* V [Berlin, 1963] 124-69).

—. "Noch einmal der Tod der Söhne Zebedaei." *ZNW* 11 (1912) 89-104.

Schwartz, J. "Note sur la famille de Philon d'Alexandrie." *Mélanges Isidore Lévy. AIPh* 13 (1953) (Brussels, 1955) 591-603.

Schwegler, T. *Biblische Zeitrechnung. BBe* 13 (Baden, 1953).

Schweitzer, A. *Paul and His Interpreters: A Critical History* (Eng. trans., London, 1912).

Schwemer, A. M. "Gott als König und seine Königsherrschaft in den Sabbatliedern aus Qumran." In M. Hengel and A. M. Schwemer. *Königsherrschaft Gottes und himmlischer Kult im Judentum, Urchristentum und in der hellenistischen Welt. WUNT* I/55 (Tübingen, 1991) 45-118.

Scobie, C. H. H. "Jesus or Paul? The Origin of the Universal Mission of the Christian Church." In P. Richardson and J. C. Hurd. *From Jesus to Paul: Studies in Honour of Francis Wright Beare* (Waterloo, 1984) 47-60.

Scott, J. M. "Luke's Geographical Horizon." In D. W. J. Gill and C. Gempf. *The Book of Acts in Its Ancient Literary Setting.* A1CS II (Grand Rapids and Carlisle, 1994) 483-544.

—. *Paul and the Nations: The Old Testament and Jewish Background of Paul's Mission to the Nations with Special Reference to the Destination of Galatians.* WUNT I/84 (Tübingen, 1995).

Scramuzza, V. M. "The Policy of the Early Roman Emperors towards Judaism." *BC* V (London, 1933) 277-97.

—. *The Emperor Claudius* (Cambridge, Mass., 1940).

Scullard, H. H. *From the Gracchi to Nero: A History of Rome from 133 B.C. to A.D. 68* (London/New York, [5]1982).

Segal, A. F. *Paul the Convert: The Apostolate and Apostasy of Saul the Pharisee* (New Haven/London, 1990).

Seidensticker, P. *Paulus, der verfolgte Apostel Jesu Christi. SBS* 8 (Stuttgart, 1965).

Seifrid, M. A. *Justification by Faith: The Origin and Development of a Central Pauline Theme.* NTSup. 68 (Leiden, 1992).

Sen, A. *Poverty and Famines: An Essay on Entitlement and Deprivation* (Oxford, 1981).

Seston, W. "L'Empereur Claude et les Chrétiens." *RHPR* 11 (1931) 275-304.

Seyrig, H. "Antiquités Syriennes." *Syr* 27 (1950) 33-56.

Sherk, R. K. "Roman Galatia: The Governors from 25 B.C. to A.D. 114." *ANRW* II 7.2 (Berlin/New York, 1980) 954-1052.

Sherwin-White, A. N. "Procurator Augusti." *PBSR* n.s. 2 (1939) 11-25.

—. *Roman Society and Roman Law in the New Testament* (Oxford, 1963).

—. "The Roman Citizenship. A Survey of Its Development into World Franchise." *ANRW* I/2 (Berlin/New York, 1972) 23-58.

—. *Roman Citizenship* (Oxford, [2]1973).

—. "Pilate, Pontius." *ISBE* III (Grand Rapids, 1986) 847-49.

Siat, J. "L'empire: ses routes au Ier siècle." *MBib* 5 (1978) 16-22.

Sickenberger, J. "Julius Africanus." *PRE* 19 (Stuttgart, 1918) 116-25.

Siegert, F. "Unbeachtete Papiaszitate bei armenischen Schriftstellern." *NTS* 27 (1980/81) 605-14.

Simcox, G. A. "A Point in Pauline Chronology." *JTS* 2 (1901) 586-90.

Simon, M. "Sur les débuts du proselytisme juif." *Hommages à André Dupont-Sommer* (Paris, 1971) 509-20.

—. "Trente ans de recherches sur l'apôtre Paul." *Ktema* 3 (1978) 3-33.

—. "Remarques sur les origines de la Chrétienté romaine." *Religion et culture dans la citée Italienne de l'antiquité à nos jours. Bulletin du CIRI* II (Strasbourg, 1981) 40-50.

Simons, J. *The Geographical and Topographical Texts of the Old Testament: A Concise Commentary in XXXII Chapters* (Leiden, 1959).

Simpson, J. W. "The Problems Posed by 1 Thessalonians 2,15-16 and a Solution." *Horizons in Biblical Theology* 12 (1990) 42-72.

Slingerland, D. "Chrestus: Christus?" In A. J. Avery-Peck. *New Perspectives on Ancient Judaism IV: The Literature of Early Rabbinic Judaism. Issues in Talmudic Redaction and Interpretation* (Lanham, 1989) 133-44.

———. "Suetonius *Claudius* 25.4 and the Account in Dio Cassius." *JQR* 79 (1989) 305-22.

———. "Acts 18:1-17 and Luedemann's Pauline Chronology." *JBL* 109 (1991) 686-90.

———. "Acts 18:1-18, the Gallio Inscription, and Absolute Pauline Chronology." *JBL* 110 (1990) 439-49.

———. "Suetonius Claudius 25.4, Acts 18, and Paulus Orosius' Historiarum Adversum Paganos Libri VII: Dating the Claudian Expulsion(s) of Roman Jews." *JQR* 58 (1993) 127-44.

Smallwood, E. M. "The Date of the Dismissal of Pontius Pilate from Judaea." *JJS* 5 (1954) 12-21.

———. "High Priests and Politics in Roman Palestine." *JTS* 13 (1962) 14-34.

——— "Jews and Romans in the Early Empire." *HT* 15 (1965) 232-39, 313-19.

———. "Consules suffecti of A.D. 55." *Hist* 17 (1968) 384.

———. *The Jews under Roman Rule from Pompey to Diocletian: A Study in Political Relations. SJLA* 20 (Leiden, ²1981).

Smilda, H. *C. Suetonii Vita Divi Claudii* (Groningen, 1896).

Smith, M. *Jesus the Magician* (San Francisco, 1978).

Smith, W. "The Chronology of Acts and Epistles." *LQR* 23 (1954) 270-76.

Snape, H. C. "After the Crucifixion or 'The Great Forty Days'." *Numen* 17 (1970) 188-99.

Soards, M. L. *The Apostle Paul: An Introduction to His Writings and Teaching* (New York, 1987).

Soares, T. G. "Paul's Missionary Method." *BW* 34 (1909) 326-36.

Soden, H. von. "Chronology B. New Testament." *EB(C)* I (London, 1899) 799-819.

Söding, T. "Zur Chronologie der paulinischen Briefe. Ein Diskussionsvorschlag." *BN* 56 (1991) 31-59.

Solin, H. "Juden und Syrer im westlichen Teil der römischen Welt. Eine ethnisch-demographische Studie mit besonderer Berücksichtigung der sprachlichen Zustände." *ANRW* II 29.2 (Berlin/New York, 1983) 587-789, 1222-49.

Songer, H. S. "Acts 20–28: From Ephesus to Rome." *RExp* 87 (1990) 551-63.

Sordi, M. "Sui primi rapporti dell'autorità Romana con il cristianesimo (A proposito della cronologia degli *Atti*)." *StRo* 8 (1960) 393-409.

———. *Il Cristianesimo e Roma* (Bologna, 1965).

———. "Sergia Paullina e il suo collegium." *RIL.L* 113 (1979) 14-20.

———. *The Christians and the Roman Empire* (Eng. trans., Norman/London, 1986).

———. "I rapporti fra cristiani e l'Impero da Tiberio ai Severi." *Humanistica e Teologia* 13 (1992) 59-71.

Sordi, M., and Cavigiolo, M. L. "Un'antica 'chiesa domestica' di Roma? (Il *collegium quod est in Domo Sergiae L. F. Paullinae*)." *RSCI* 25 (1971) 369-74.

Souter, A. "Did St. Paul Speak Latin?" *Exp* VIII/1 (1911) 337-42.

Spadafora, F. "Qua occasione Apostoli profecti sint in universum mundum." *VD* 21 (1941) 281-86, 306-10.

Spicq, C. "Les *ataktoi* sont-ils des parresseux?" *ST* 10 (1956) 1-13.

————. "La charité fraternelle selon I. Th., 4,9." *Mélanges bibliques. Redigés en l'honneur de André Robert. Travaux de l'Institut catholique de Paris* (Paris, 1957) 507-11.

————. "Ce que signifie le titre de chrétien." *ST* 15 (1961) 68-78.

————. "Saint Paul est venu en Espagne." *Helm* 15 (1964) 45-70.

Spieser, J. M. "Note sur la chronologie des remparts de Thessalonique." *BCH* 98 (1974) 507-19.

Spitta, F. "Die chronologischen Notizen und die Hymnen in Lc. 1 u. 2." *ZNW* 7 (1906) 281-317.

Stahl, M. *Imperiale Herrschaft und provinziale Stadt. Strukturprobleme der römischen Reichsorganisation im 1.-3. Jh. der Kaiserzeit. Hyp* 52 (Göttingen, 1978).

Stambaugh, J. E.. "Appian Way," *ABD* I (New York, 1992) 318.

Stambaugh, J. E., and Balch, D. *The Social World of the First Christians* (London, 1986).

Stange, E. *Paulinische Reisepläne. BFCT* II/5 (Gütersloh, 1918).

Starcky, J. "The Nabataeans: A Historical Sketch." *BA* 18 (1955) 84-106.

————. "Pétra et la Nabatène." *DBS* VII (Paris, 1966) 866-1017.

————. "Damas." *MBib* 28 (1983) 26-31.

Stauffer, E. "Zur Münzprägung und Judenpolitik des Pontius Pilatus." *NC* 1/2 (1949/50) 495-514.

Steele, E. S. "Jewish Scriptures in 1 Thessalonians." *BTB* 14 (1984) 12-17.

Stegemann, E. "Aspekte gegenwärtiger Paulusforschung." *EvErz* 37 (1985) 491-502.

Stegemann, E. W., and Stegemann, W. *Urchristliche Sozialgeschichte. Die Anfänge im Judentum und die Christusgemeinden in der mediterranen Welt* (Stuttgart, 1995).

Stegemann, H. "The Qumran Essenes — Local Members of the Main Jewish Union in Late Second Temple Times." In J. Trebolle Barrera and L. Vegas Montaner. *The Madrid Qumran Congress. Proceedings of the International Congress on the Dead Sea Scrolls, Madrid, 18-21 March,* I (Leiden, 1992) 83-166.

Stegemann, W. "Zwei sozialgeschichtliche Anfragen an unser Paulusbild." *EvErz* 37 (1985) 480-90.

————. *Zwischen Synagoge und Obrigkeit. Zur historischen Situation der lukanischen Christen. FRLANT* 152 (Göttingen, 1991).

————. "War der Apostel Paulus ein römischer Bürger?" *ZNW* 78 (1987) 200-229.

Stegmann, A. *Silvanus als Missionar und "Hagiograph." Eine exegetische Studie* (Rottenburg, 1917).

Steidle, W. *Sueton und die antike Biographie. Zet* 1 (Munich, ^{2}1963).

Stein, A. "Some Notes on the Chronology of the Coins of Agrippa I." *Israel Numismatic Journal* 5 (1981) 22-26.

Steinmann, A. *Der Leserkreis des Galaterbriefs. Ein Beitrag zur urchristlichen Missionsgeschichte. NtA* 3/4 (Münster, 1908).

————. *Aretas IV. König der Nabatäer. Eine historisch-exegetische Studie zu 2 Kor 11,32 F.* (Freiburg, 1909).

————. *Die Welt des Paulus im Zeichen des Verkehrs. Verzeichnis der Vorlesungen and der Kgl. Akademie zu Braunsberg im WS 1915/16* (Braunsberg, 1915).

————. *Zum Werdegang des Paulus: Die Jugendzeit in Tarsus* (Braunsberg, 1928).

Steinmetzer, F. X. "Census." *RAC* II (Stuttgart, 1954) 969-72.

Steinwenter, A. "Libertinus." *PRE* II 13 (Stuttgart, 1927) 104-10.

Stengel, P. "Antiocheia 15 (Pisidiae)." *PRE* 1 (Stuttgart, 1894) 2446.

Stenger, W. "Biographisches und Idealbiographisches in Gal 1,11–2,14." In P. G. Müller and W. Stenger. *Kontinuität und Einheit. Festschrift Franz Mussner* (Freiburg, 1981) 123-40.

Sterling, G. E. *Historiography and Self-Definition: Josephos, Luke-Acts and Apologetic Historiography. NT.S* 64 (Leiden, 1992).

Stern, M. "Appendix: Chronology." *CRINT* I/1 (Assen, 1974) 62-77.

———. "The Jewish Diaspora." *Ibid.,* 117-83.

———. "The Province of Judaea." *Ibid.,* 308-76.

———. "גירושי היהודים מרומא בזמן העתיק" (The Expulsions of Jews from Rome in Antiquity)." *Zion* 44 (1979) 1-27.

Stieger, R. "Martyrologien." *LTK* VII (Freiburg, 1962) 138-40.

Stier, H. E. "Die Erfüllung der Zeiten im Lichte moderner Geschichtsforschung." *Paderborner Studien* 3/4 (1983) 75-87.

Stiewe, K. "C. Dio Cocceianus." *KP* I (Munich, 1964) 1076f.

Stoops, R. F. "Riot and Assembly: The Social Context of Acts 19:23-41." *JBL* 108 (1989) 73-91.

Stowers, S. K. *Letter Writing in Greco-Roman Antiquity. Library of Early Christianity* 5 (Philadelphia, 1986).

Strecker, G. "Die sogenannte zweite Jerusalemreise des Paulus (Act 11,27-30)." *ZNW* 53 (1962) 67-77 (repr. in *Eschaton und Historie. Aufsätze* [Göttingen, 1979] 132-41).

———. "Befreiung und Rechtfertigung. Zur Stellung der Rechtfertigungslehre in der Theologie des Paulus." In J. Friedrich, W. G. Pöhlmann, and P. Stuhlmacher, *Rechtfertigung. Festschrift Ernst Käsemann* (Tübingen, 1976) 479-508.

Strelan, R. *Paul, Artemis, and the Jews in Ephesus.* BZNW 80 (Berlin, 1996).

Strickert, F. M. "Damascus Document VII,10-20 and Qumran Messianic Expectation." *RQ* 12 (1986) 327-49.

Strobel, A. "Der Termin des Todes Jesu. Überschau und Lösungsvorschlag unter Einschluß des Qumrankalenders." *ZNW* 51 (1960) 69-101.

———. "Zeitrechnung." *BHH* III (Göttingen, 1966) 2211-28.

———. "Das apokalyptische Terminproblem in der sogen. Antrittspredigt Jesu (Lukas 4,16-30)." *TLZ* 92 (1967) 251-54.

———. "Die Ausrufung des Jobeljahrs in der Nazarethpredigt Jesu." In E. Grässer and W. Eltester, *Jesus in Nazareth.* BZNW 40 (Berlin, 1972) 38-51.

———. *Ursprung und Geschichte des frühchristlichen Osterkalenders. TU* 121 (East Berlin, 1977).

———. *Die Stunde der Wahrheit. Untersuchungen zum Strafverfahren gegen Jesus.* WUNT I/21 (Tübingen, 1980).

———. "Weltenjahr, große Konjunktion und Messiasstern. Ein themageschichtlicher Überblick." *ANRW* II 20.2 (Berlin/New York, 1987) 988-1187.

———. "Plädoyer für Lukas. Zur Stimmigkeit des chronistischen Rahmens von Lk 3.1." *NTS* 41 (1995) 466-69.

Stuhlmacher, P. *Das paulinische Evangelium I. Vorgeschichte. FRLANT* 95 (Göttingen, 1968).

———. "The Theme: The Gospel and the Gospels." In *idem,* ed. *The Gospel and the Gospels* (Eng. trans., Grand Rapids, 1991) 1-25.

———. "The Pauline Gospel." *Ibid.,* 149-72.

———. "Weg, Stil und Konsequenzen urchristlicher Mission." *TBei* 12 (1983) 107-35.

———. "Der Abfassungszweck des Römerbriefs." *ZNW* 77 (1986) 180-93.

———. "Die Stellung Jesu und des Paulus zu Jerusalem. Eine Erinnerung." *ZTK* 86 (1989) 140-56.

———. *Biblische Theologie des Neuen Testaments I: Grundlegung. Von Jesus zu Paulus* (Göttingen, ²1997).

Styger, P. *Juden und Christen im alten Rom. Streiflichter aus der ersten Verfolgungszeit* (Berlin, 1934).

Suggs, M. J. "Concerning the Date of Paul's Macedonian Ministry." *NT* 4 (1960) 60-68.

Suhl, A. *Paulus und seine Briefe. Ein Beitrag zur paulinischen Chronologie. StudNT* 11 (Gütersloh, 1975).

————. Review of R. Jewett, *Paulus-Chronologie* (Munich, 1982). *TLZ* 109 (1984) 813-20.

————. "Der Galaterbrief — Situation und Argumentation." *ANRW* II 25.4 (Berlin/New York, 1987) 3067-3134.

————. Review of N. Hyldahl, *Die paulinische Chronologie* (Leiden, 1986). *TLZ* 113 (1988) 186-91.

————. "Die Galater und der Geist. Kritische Erwägungen zur Situation in Galatien." In D. A. Koch. *Jesu Rede von Gott und ihre Nachgeschichte im frühen Christentum. Festschrift Willi Marxsen* (Gütersloh, 1989) 267-96.

————. "Gestrandet! Bemerkungen zum Streit über die Romfahrt des Paulus." *ZTK* 88 (1991) 1-28.

————. "Der Beginn der selbständigen Mission des Paulus. Ein Beitrag zur Geschichte des Urchristentums." *NTS* 38 (1992) 430-47.

————. "Paulinische Chronologie im Streit der Meinungen." In W. Haase. *ANRW* II 26/2 (Berlin and New York, 1995) 939-1188.

Suhl, A., and Reicke, B. "Thessalonich." *BHH* III (Göttingen, 1966) 1968f.

Swain, J. W. "Gamaliel's Speech and Caligula's Statue." *HTR* 37 (1944) 341-49.

Syme, R. *Tacitus I-II* (Oxford, 1958).

————. "Observations on the Province of Cilicia." *Roman Papers* I. Edited by E. Badian (Oxford, 1979) 120-48.

————. "The Titulus Tiburtinus." *Roman Papers* III. Edited by A. R. Birley (Oxford, 1984) 869-84.

————. "An Eccentric Patrician." *Ibid.,* 1316-36.

————. "The Year 33 in Tacitus and Dio." *Roman Papers* IV. Edited by A. R. Birley (Oxford, 1988) 223-44.

————. "Domitian: The Last Years." *Ibid.,* 252-77.

————. "Correspondents of Pliny." *Roman Papers* V. Edited by A. R. Birley (Oxford, 1988) 440-77.

————. "Hadrian as Philhellene: Neglected Aspects." *Ibid.,* 546-62.

————. "Antonine Government and Governing Class." *Ibid.,* 668-87.

Szilagi, J. "Illyrikum." *KP* II (Munich, 1967) 1367-69.

Taatz, I. *Frühjüdische Briefe. Die paulinischen Briefe im Rahmen der offiziellen religiösen Briefe des Frühjudentums. NTOA* 16 (Freiburg [Switzerland]/Göttingen, 1991).

Tafrali, O. *Topographie de Thessalonique* (Paris, 1913).

Tajra, H. W., *The Trial of St. Paul: A Juridical Exegesis of the Second Half of the Acts of the Apostles.* WUNT II/35 (Tübingen, 1989).

————. *The Martyrdom of St. Paul: Historical and Judicial Context, Traditions, and Legends.* WUNT II/67 (Tübingen, 1994).

Talbert, C. H. "Again: Paul's Visits to Jerusalem." *NT* 9 (1967) 26-40.

Tambyah, T. I. "Θεοδιδακτοί: A Suggestion of an Implication of the Deity of Christ." *ET* 44 (1933) 527f.

Tarn, W. W., and Griffith, A. T. *Hellenistic Civilization* (London, [3]1952).

Taylor, J. "The Ethnarch of King Aretas at Damascus: A Note on 2 Cor. 11,32-33." *RB* 99 (1992) 719-28.

491

————. "Why were the Disciples first called 'Christians' at Antioch?" *RB* 105 (1994) 75-94.

————. "St Paul and the Roman Empire: Acts of the Apostles 13–14." In W. Haase. *ANRW* II 26/2 (Berlin and New York, 1995) 1189-1231.

Taylor, N. H. "The Composition and Chronology of Second Corinthians." *JSNT* 44 (1991) 67-87.

————. *Paul, Antioch and Jerusalem: A Study in Relationships and Authority in Earliest Christianity. JSNTSup* 66 (Sheffield, 1992).

Tcherikover, V. *Hellenistic Civilization and the Jews* (Philadelphia/Jerusalem, ²1961).

Teichmann, E. *Die paulinischen Vorstellungen von Auferstehung und Gericht und ihre Beziehungen zur jüdischen Apokalyptik* (Freiburg/Leipzig, 1896).

Teja, R. "Die römische Provinz Kappadokien in der Prinzipatszeit." *ANRW* II 7.2 (Berlin/New York, 1980) 1083-1124.

Tenney, M. C. *New Testament Times* (Grand Rapids, 1965).

Teuffel, W. S. *Teuffel's History of Roman Literature.* Edited by Ludwig Schwabe, I-II (Eng. trans., London, 1900).

Theissen, G. " 'Wir haben alles verlassen' (Mc. X.28). Nachfolge und soziale Entwurzelung in der jüdisch-palästinischen Gesellschaft des 1. Jahrhunderts n. Ch." *Studien zur Soziologie des Urchristentums. WUNT* I/19 (Tübingen, ²1983) 106-41. Eng. trans., *Social Reality and the Early Christians: Theology, Ethics, and the World of the New Testament* (Minneapolis, 1992).

————. "Soziale Schichtung in der korinthischen Gemeinde. Ein Beitrag zur Soziologie des Hellenistischen Urchristentums." *Ibid.,* 231-71.

————. *The Gospels in Context: Social and Political History in the Synoptic Tradition* (Eng. trans., Minneapolis, 1991).

Thiede, C. P. *Simon Peter: From Galilee to Rome* (Exeter, 1986).

————. "Babylon, der andere Ort: Anmerkungen zu 1 Petr 5,13 und Apg 12,17." In C. P. Thiede, *Das Petrusbild in der neueren Forschung* (Wuppertal, 1987) 221-29.

————. "Kornelius." *GBL* II (Wuppertal/Gießen, 1988) 822f.

————. *Jesus: Life or Legend?* (Oxford, 1990).

Thieme, K. "Le plan des 'Actes des Apôtres' et la chronologie de son contenu." *Dieu Vivant* 26 (1954) 127-33.

Thiessen, W. *Christen in Ephesus. Die historische und theologische Situation in vorpaulinischer und paulinischer Zeit und zur Zeit der Apostelgeschichte und der Pastoralbriefe.* TANZ 12 (Tübingen and Basel, 1995).

Thompson, E. "The Sequence of the Two Epistles to the Thessalonians." *Et* 56 (1944/45) 306f.

Thompson, M. *Clothed with Christ: The Example and Teaching of Jesus in Romans 12.1–15.13. JSNTSup* 59 (Sheffield, 1991).

Thorley, J. "When Was Jesus Born?" *GaR* 28 (1981) 81-89.

Thorne, E. A. "The Early Missionary Journeys in Acts of Apostles." *CQR* 121 (1935/36) 109-17.

Thornton, C. J. *Der Zeuge des Zeugen. Lukas als Historiker der Paulusreisen. WUNT* I/56 (Tübingen, 1993).

Thraede, K. *Grundzüge griechisch-römischer Brieftopik. Zet* 48 (Munich, 1970).

Thurston, R. W. "The Relationship between the Thessalonian Epistles." *ET* 85 (1974) 52-56.

Tornos, A. M. "La fecha del hambre de Jerusalén, aludida por Act 11,28-30." *EstEccl* 33 (1959) 301-16.

Tourazoglou, J. P. "Ἀπὸ τὴν πολιτεία καὶ τὴν κοινωνία τῆς ἀρχαῖας Βεροίας: Ἐπιγράφιχες σημειώσεις." *AncMac* II (Thessalonica, 1977) 481-93.

Toussaint, S. D. "The Chronological Problem of Galatians 2:1-10." *BS* 120 (1963) 334-40.

Tov, E. "Une inscription Grecque d'origine Samaritaine trouvée à Théssalonique." *RB* 81 (1974) 394-99.

Townend, G. B. "The Date of Composition of Suetonius' *Caesares.*" *CQ* 9 (1959) 285-93.

———. "The Post *ab epistulis* in the Second Century." *Hist* 10 (1961) 375-81.

———. "Suetonius and His Influence." In T. A. Dorey. *Latin Biography* (London, 1967) 79-111.

Townsend, J. T. "The Contributions of John Knox to the Study of Acts: Some Further Notations." In M. C. Parsons and J. B. Tyson. *Cadbury, Knox and Talbert: American Contributions to the Study of Acts* (Atlanta, 1992) 81-89.

Trebilco, P. *Jewish Communities in Asia Minor. SNTSMS* 69 (Cambridge, 1991).

———. "Asia." In D. W. J. Gill and C. Gempf. *The Book of Acts in Its Graeco-Roman Setting.* A1CS II (Grand Rapids and Carlisle, 1994) 291-362.

Treidler, H. "Europe." *KP* II (Stuttgart, 1967) 448f.

Trevijano, Etcheverria R. "La mision en Tesalónica (1 Tes 1:1–2:16)." *Salm* 32 (1985) 263-91.

Trilling, W. "Die beiden Briefe des Apostels Paulus an die Thessalonicher. Eine Forschungsübersicht." *ANRW* II 25.4 (Berlin/New York, 1987) 3365-3403.

Trimaille, M. "Tableau chronologique de la vie de saint Paul." *MBib* 81 (1993) 9.

———. "Le troisième voyage: triomphe ou suite des épreuves?" *MBib* 81 (1993) 33-37.

Trobisch, D. *Paul's Letter Collection. Tracing the Origins* (Eng. trans., Minneapolis, 1994).

Troiani, L. "La missione nel mondo greco-romano." In G. Ghiberti. *La missione nel mondo antico e nella Bibbia. Ricerche Storico Bibliche* 1/1990 (Bologna, 1990) 71-85.

Tronskij, I. M. "Chrestiani (Tac. Ann. 15,44,2) i Chrestus (Sueton., Div. Claud. 25,4)." (Russian) *Mel. Petrovskij* (1976) 34-43 (cf. *ANRW* II 33.5 [1991] 3612).

Trummer, P. "Neutestamentliche Zeitgeschichte aus östlicher Perspektive: Die Nabatäer." *Aufsätze zum Neuen Testament. Grazer Theologische Studien* 12 (Graz, 1987) 207-20.

Tuckett, C. M. "Synoptic Traditions in 1 Thessalonians?" In R. F. Collins. *The Thessalonian Correspondence. BETL* 87 (Leuven, 1990) 160-82.

Turlington, H. "Paul's Missionary Practice." *RExp* 51 (1954) 168-86.

Turner, C. H. "Chronology of the New Testament." *DB(H)* I (Edinburgh, 1898) 403-25.

Turner, H. E. W. "The Chronological Framework of the Ministry." In D. E. Nineham, *et al. Historicity and Chronology in the New Testament. TCSPCK* 6 (London, 1965) 59-74.

Twelftree, G. H. "Jesus in Jewish Traditions." In D. Wenham. *Gospel Perspectives V: The Jesus Tradition outside the Gospels* (Sheffield, 1985) 289-341.

Tyson, J. B. "John Knox and the Acts of the Apostles." In M. C. Parsons and J. B. Tyson. *Cadbury, Knox, and Talbert: American Contributions to the Study of Acts* (Atlanta, 1992) 55-80.

Ulonska, H. "Christen und Heiden. Die paulinische Paränese in I Thess 4,3-8." *TZ* 43 (1987) 210-18.

Ulrichs, K. F. "Grave verbum, ut de re magna. Nochmals Gal 1,18: ἱστορῆσαι." *ZNW* 81 (1990) 262-69.

Unger, M. F. *Archaeology and the New Testament: A Companion Volume to Archaeology and the Old Testament* (Grand Rapids, 1962).

———. "Historical Research and the Church at Thessalonica." *BS* 119 (1962) 38-44.

Unnik, W. C. van. "The Origin of the Recently Discovered 'Apocryphon Jacobi'." *VC* 10 (1956) 149-56.

————. "Aramaisms in Paul." *Sparsa Collecta I: Evangelia — Paulina — Acts. NTSup* 29 (Leiden, 1973) 129-43.

————. "Reisepläne und Amen-Sagen. Zusammenhang und Gedankenfolge in 2. Korinther i 15-24." *Ibid.,* 144-59.

————. "Tarsus or Jerusalem, the City of Paul's Youth." *Ibid.,* 259-320.

————. "Once Again: Tarsus or Jerusalem." *Ibid.,* 321-27.

Vacalopoulos, A. E. *A History of Thessaloniki* (Thessalonica, 1972; repr. 1984).

Vanhoye, A. "La composition de 1 Thessaloniciens." In R. F. Collins. *The Thessalonian Correspondence. BETL* 87 (Leuven, 1990) 73-86.

Vardaman, J. "Jesus' Life: A New Chronology." *Biblical Illustrator* 4/1985, 12-18.

————. "Jesus' Life: A New Chronology." In J. Vardaman and E. M. Yamauchi. *Chronos, Kairos, Christos: Nativity and Chronological Studies Presented to Jack Finegan* (Winona Lake, 1989) 55-82.

Vermes, G. "The Jesus Notice of Josephus' Re-Examined." *JJS* 38 (1987) 2-10.

Vickers, M. "The Date of the Walls of Thessalonica." *Istanbul Arkeoloji Müzeleri Yilgi* 15/16 (1969) 313-18.

————. "The Late Roman Walls of Thessalonica." In E. Birley, *et al. Roman Frontier Studies 1969 (8th International Congress of Limesforschung)* (1970) 249-55.

————. "Towards a Reconstruction of the Town Planning of Roman Thessaloniki." *AncMac* I (Thessalonica, 1970) 239-51.

————. "Hellenistic Thessaloniki." *JHS* 92 (1972) 156-70.

————. "Therme and Thessaloniki." *Ancient Macedonian Studies in Honor of Charles F. Edson* (Thessalonica, 1981) 327-33.

Victor, U. "Pax Romana." *BTZ* 4 (1987) 95-106.

Vielhauer, P., *Geschichte der urchristlichen Literatur* (Berlin/New York, 1975).

Villoslada, R. G. "Estrategia misionera del itinerario de San Pablo." *MisEx* 11 (1964) 215-27.

Vincent, L. H. "Découverte de la 'Synagogue des Affranchis' à Jérusalem." *RB* 30 (1921) 247-77.

Vitti, A. M., "L'anno della conversione di S. Paolo." *CivCatt* 88 (1937) I.385-94.

Vogels, H. J. "Die Tempelreinigung und Golgotha (Joh 2,19-22)." *BZ* 6 (1962) 102-7.

Vogelstein, H., and Rieger, P. *Geschichte der Juden in Rom I: 139 v. Chr.-1420 n. Chr.* (Berlin, 1896).

Vogüé, M. de. *Mélanges d'archéologie orientale* (Paris, 1868).

Volkmann, H. "Galatia (Γαλατία) II." *KP* II (Munich, 1962) 666-70.

Voss, B. R. "Orosius." *KP* IV (Munich, 1972) 350f.

Votaw, C. W. "Recent Discussions of the Chronology of the Apostolic Age." *BW* 11 (1898) 112-19, 177-87.

————. "Inductive Studies in the Acts," *BW* 9 (1897) 44-57, 122-34, 204-17, 291-300, 363-74, 385-91.

————, "The Conversion and Early Ministry of Paul." *BW* 33 (1909) 272-78.

Voulgaris, C. S. Χρονολογία τῶν γεγονότων τοῦ βίου τοῦ Ἀποστόλου Παύλου (Athens, 1980).

————. "Χρονολογία τῶν γεγενότων τοῦ βίου τοῦ Ἀποστόλου Παύλου." *Theol(A)* 52 (1981) 75-99; 53 (1982) 129-57, 476-89.

Wacholder, B. Z. "The Calendar of Sabbatical Cycles during the Second Temple and the Early Rabbinic Period." *HUCA* 44 (1973) 153-96 (repr. in *Essays on Jewish Chronology and Chronography* [New York, 1976] 1-44).

———— "Chronomessianism: The Timing of Messianic Movements and the Calendar of Sabbatical Cycles." *HUCA* 46 (1975) 201-18.

————. "The Calendar of Sabbath Years during the Second Temple Era: A Response." *HUCA* 54 (1983) 123-33.

Waele, F. J. de. *Corinth et St. Paul. Les hauts lieux de l'histoire* (Paris, 1961).

Wagenmann, J. *Die Stellung des Apostels Paulus neben den Zwölf in den ersten zwei Jahrhunderten. BZNW* 3 (Gießen, 1926).

Wainwright, A. "Where Did Silas Go? (and What Was His Connection with Galatians?)" *JSNT* 8 (1980) 66-70.

Walaskay, P. W. *"And so we came to Rome." The Political Perspective of St Luke. SNTSMS* 49 (Cambridge, 1983).

Walbank, F. W. "The Via Egnatia: Some Outstanding Problems." *AncMac* IV (Thessalonica, 1986) 673-80.

Walker, W. O. "Why Paul Went to Jerusalem: The Interpretation of Galatians 2:1-5." *CBQ* 54 (1992) 503-10.

Wallace-Hadrill, A. *Suetonius: The Scholar and His Caesars* (London, 1983).

Walton, S. "What Has Aristotle to Do with Paul? Rhetorical Criticism and 1 Thessalonians." *TynBul* 46 (1995) 229-50.

Walton, W. H. M. "St. Paul's Movements between the Writing of 1 and 2 Corinthians." *ET* 56 (1944/45) 136-38.

Wanamaker, C. A. "Apocalypticism at Thessalonica." *Neotestamentica* 21 (1987) 1-10.

Wandel, G. "Zur Chronologie des Lebens Pauli I: Paulus in Damaskus." *ZKWKL* 8 (1887) 433-43, 489-99.

————. "Zur Chronologie des Lebens Pauli II: Paulus in Antiochia und Jerusalem." *ZKWKL* 9 (1888) 127-44, 167-76.

Wander, B. *Trennungsprozesse zwischen frühem Christentum und Judentum im 1. Jh. n. Chr. Datierbare Abfolgen zwischen der Hinrichtung Jesu und der Zerstörung des Jerusalemer Tempels. TANZ* 16 (Tübingen and Basel, ²1997).

Warneck, J. *Paulus im Lichte der heutigen Heidenmission* (Berlin, 1913).

Warnecke, H. *Die tatsächliche Romfahrt des Apostels Paulus. SBS* 127 (Stuttgart, 1987).

Warnecke, H., and Schirrmacher, T. *War Paulus wirklich auf Malta?* (Neuhausen/Stuttgart, 1992).

Watson, F. *Paul, Judaism and the Gentiles: A Sociological Approach. SNTSMS* 56 (Cambridge, 1986).

Watt, J. G. van der. "The Use of ζάω in 1 Thessalonians: A Comparison with ζάω/ζωή in the Gospel of John." In R. F. Collins. *The Thessalonian Correspondence. BETL* 87 (Leuven, 1990) 356-69.

Watzinger, C., and Wulzinger, K. *Damaskus, die antike Stadt. Wissenschaftliche Veröffentlichungen des deutsch-türkischen Denkmalschutz-Kommandos* (Berlin/Leipzig, 1921).

Weatherly, J. A. "The Authenticity of 1 Thessalonians 2,13-16: Additional Evidence." *JSNT* 42 (1991) 79-98.

Weber, E. *Die Beziehungen von Röm. 1–3 zur Missionspraxis des Paulus. BFCT* I/9 (Gütersloh, 1905).

Weber, V. *Die Abfassung des Galaterbriefs vor dem Apostelkonzil. Grundlegende Untersuchungen zur Geschichte des Urchristentums und des Lebens Pauli* (Ravensburg, 1900).

————. *Die antiochenische Kollekte; die übersehene Hauptorientierung der Paulusforschung. Grundlegende Radikalkur zur Geschichte des Urchristentums* (Würzburg, 1917).

495

Weber, W. "Der Census des Quirinius nach Josephus." *ZNW* 10 (1909) 307-19.

Wechsler, A. *Geschichtsbild und Apostelstreit. Eine forschungsgeschichtliche und exegetische Studie über den antiochenischen Zwischenfall (Gal 2,11-14). BZNW* 62 (Berlin/New York, 1991).

Wedderburn, A. J. M. "Keeping Up with Recent Studies VIII: Some Recent Pauline Chronologies." *ET* 92 (1981) 103-8.

——. *Baptism and Resurrection: Studies in Pauline Theology against Its Graeco-Roman Background. WUNT* I/44 (Tübingen, 1987).

Wehnert, J. *Die Wir-Passagen der Apostelgeschichte. Ein lukanisches Stilmittel aus jüdischer Tradition. GTA* 40 (Göttingen, 1989).

——. "Gestrandet. Zu einer neuen These über den Schiffbruch des Apostels Paulus auf dem Wege nach Rom (Apg 27–28)." *ZTK* 87 (1990) 67-99.

——. " '. . . und da erfuhren wir, daß die Insel Kephallenia heißt.' Zur neuesten Auslegung von Apg 27–28 und ihrer Methode." *ZTK* 88 (1991) 169-80.

Weinel, H. *Paulus als kirchlicher Organisator. SgV* 17 (Freiburg, 1899).

Weiss, E. "Manumissio." *PRE* II 14.2 (Stuttgart, 1930) 1366-77.

Weiss, J. "Paulinische Probleme: Die Chronologie der paulinischen Briefe." *TSK* 68 (1895) 252-96.

Weizsäcker, C. *The Apostolic Age of the Christian Church* I-II (Eng. trans., London, [3]1907-1912).

Welles, C. B. "Hellenistic Tarsus." *MUSJ* 38 (1962) 41-75.

Wellhausen, J. *Kritische Analyse der Apostelgeschichte. AAG* 15.2 (Berlin, 1914).

Wells, C. *The Roman Empire* (Stanford, Calif., 1984).

Wengst, K. *PAX ROMANA and the Peace of Jesus Christ* (Eng. trans., Philadelphia, 1987).

Wenham, D. "Paul and the Synoptic Apocalypse." In R. T. France and D. Wenham. *Gospel Perspectives II: Studies of History and Tradition in the Four Gospels* (Sheffield, 1981) 345-75.

——. *The Rediscovery of Jesus' Eschatological Discourse. Gospel Perspectives* IV (Sheffield, 1984).

——. "The Paulinism of Acts Again." *Them* 13 (1988) 53-55.

——. "Acts and the Pauline Corpus II: The Evidence of the Parallels." In B. W. Winter and A. D. Clarke. *The Book of Acts in Its Ancient Literary Setting.* A1CS I (Grand Rapids and Carlisle, 1993) 215-58.

——. *Paul: Follower of Jesus or Founder of Christianity?* (Grand Rapids, 1995).

——. "Piecing Together Paul's Life: A Review Article." *EQ* 68 (1996) 47-58.

Wenham, J. W. "Did Peter Go to Rome in A.D. 42?" *TynBul* 23 (1972) 94-102.

Wenning, R. *Die Nabatäer — Denkmäler und Geschichte. Eine Bestandesaufnahme* [sic!] *des archäologischen Befundes. NTOA* 3 (Freiburg [Switzerland]/Göttingen, 1987).

——. "Die Dekapolis und die Nabatäer." *ZDPV* 110 (1994) 1-35.

Wesenberg, G. "Pro consule (proconsul)." *PRE* I 23.1 (Stuttgart, 1957) 1232-34.

Westberg, F. *Die Biblische Chronologie nach Flavius Josephus und das Todesjahr Jesu* (Leipzig, 1910).

——. *Zur Neutestamentlichen Theologie und Golgathas Ortslage* (Leipzig, 1911).

White, L. J. "New Testament Epistolary Literature in the Framework of Ancient Epistolography." *ANRW* II 25.2 (Berlin/New York, 1984) 1730-56.

——. "Ancient Greek Letters." In D. E. Aune. *Greco-Roman Literature and the New Testament. SBLSBS* 21 (Atlanta, 1988) 85-105.

Whitton, J. "A Neglected Meaning for *SKEUOS* in I Thessalonians 4.4." *NTS* 28 (1982) 142f.

Wieder, N. *The Judean Scrolls and Karaism* (London, 1962).

————. "The 'Land of Damascus' and Messianic Redemption." *JJS* 30 (1969) 86-88.

Wiefel, W. "Vätersprüche und Herrenworte. Ein Beitrag zur Frage der Bewahrung mündlicher Traditionssätze." *NovT* 11 (1969) 105-20.

————. "Die jüdische Gemeinschaft im antiken Rom und die Anfänge des römischen Christentums. Bemerkungen zu Anlaß und Zweck des Römerbriefs." *Jud* 26 (1970) 65-88. Eng. trans., "The Jewish Community in Ancient Rome and the Origins of Roman Christianity." In K. P. Donfried, ed. *The Romans Debate* (Peabody, MA, [2]1991) 85-101.

————. "Die Hauptrichtung des Wandels im eschatologischen Denken des Paulus." *TZ* 30 (1974) 65-81.

————. "Die missionarische Eigenart des Paulus und das Problem des frühchristlichen Synkretismus." *Kairos* 167 (1975) 218-31.

Wieseler, K. *Chronologie des apostolischen Zeitalters bis zum Tode der Apostel Paulus und Petrus. Ein Versuch über die Chronologie und Abfassungszeit der Apostelgeschichte und der paulinischen Briefe* (Göttingen, 1848).

Wikenhauser, A. *Die Apostelgeschichte und ihr Geschichtswert. NtA* VIII/3-5 (Munich, 1921).

————. *New Testament Introduction* (Eng. trans., New York, 1958).

Wilcken, U. "Aretas (IV)." *PRE* I.3 (Stuttgart, 1895) 673-75.

Wilcox, M. "The 'God-Fearers' in Acts: A Reconsideration." *JSNT* 13 (1981) 102-22.

Wild, R. A. Review of G. Lüdemann, *Paulus der Heidenapostel I/II* (Göttingen, 1980). *Bibl* 65 (1984) 423-28.

Will, E., and Orrieux, C. *"Prosélytisme juif"? Histoire d'une erreur* (Paris, 1992).

Willenbücher, H. "Der große Brand in Rom und die neronische Christenverfolgung (Tacitus XV 38ff.)." *Vergangenheit und Gegenwart* 3 (1913) 357-73.

————. "Der Kaiser Claudius. Eine historische Studie." *Jahresbericht des Großherzoglichen Neuen Gymnasiums zu Mainz. Ostern 1914,* Progr. Nr. 917 (Mainz, 1914) 3-14.

Wilson, J. C. "The Problem of the Domitianic Date of Revelation." *NTS* 39 (1993) 587-605.

Windisch, H. "Die Dauer der öffentlichen Wirksamkeit Jesu nach den vier Evangelien." *ZNW* 12 (1911) 141-75.

Winkler, G. "Sergii Paulli." *KP* V (Munich, 1975) 136f.

Winter, B. W. "The Public Honouring of Christian Benefactors. Romans 13,3-4 and 1 Peter 2,14-15." *JSNT* 34 (1988) 87-103.

————. "Secular and Christian Responses to Corinthian Famines." *TynBul* 40 (1989) 86-106.

————. " 'If a Man Does Not Wish to Work'." *TynBul* 40 (1989) 303-15.

————. *Seek the Welfare of the City: Christians as Benefactors and Citizens* (Grand Rapids and Carlisle, 1994).

Wirgin, W. *Herod Agrippa 1: King of the Jews. Leeds University Oriental Society Monograph Series* 10(A) and 10(B) (Leeds, 1968).

Wirth, G. "Einleitung." *Cassius Dio, Römische Geschichte I* (Zurich, 1985) 7-60.

Wiseman, J. *The Land of the Ancient Corinthians. SIMA* 50 (Göteborg, 1978).

————. "Corinth and Rome I: 228 B.C.-A.D. 267." *ANRW* II 7.1 (Berlin/New York, 1979) 438-548.

Wiseman, T. P. " 'There went out a Decree from Caesar Augustus. . . .'" *NTS* 33 (1987) 479f.

Witherington, B. *Jesus, Paul and the End of the World: A Comparative Study in New Testament Eschatology* (Downers Grove, 1992).

———. "Birth of Jesus." *Dictionary of Jesus and the Gospels.* Edited by J. B. Green, S. McKnight, and I. H. Marshall (Downers Grove/Leicester, 1992) 60-74.

Witt, R. E. "The Egyptian Cults in Ancient Macedonia." *AncMac* I (Thessalonica, 1970) 324-33.

———. "The Kabeiroi in Ancient Macedonia." *AncMac* II (Thessalonica, 1977) 67-80.

Wlosok, A.. *Rom und die Christen. Zur Auseinandersetzung zwischen Christen und römischen Staat* (Stuttgart, 1970).

Wohlenberg, G. "Eine Claudius-Inschrift von Delphi in ihrer Bedeutung für die paulinische Chronologie." *NKZ* 23 (1912) 380-96.

———. "Zur Chronologie der Bekehrung des Apostels Paulus." *TLBl* 33 (1912) 505-8.

Wolff, H. "Zum Erkenntniswert von Namensstatistiken für die römische Bürgerrechtspolitik der Kaiserzeit." In W. Eck, H. Galsterer, and H. Wolff. *Studien zur antiken Sozialgeschichte. Festschrift Friedrich Vittinghoff* (Cologne/Vienna, 1980) 229-55.

Woloch, M. "St. Paul's Two Citizenships." *Helikon* 11 (1971/72) 452-54.

Workman, W. P. "A New Date-Indication in Acts." *ET* 11 (1899/1900) 316-19.

Wotke, F. "Orosius." *PRE* II 35 (Stuttgart, 1939) 1185-95.

Wrede, W. "Paulus." *RV* I 5-6 (Halle, 1904).

Wright, N. T. "Putting Paul Together Again: Toward a Synthesis of Pauline Theology (1 and 2 Thessalonians, Philippians, and Philemon)." In J. M. Bassler. *Pauline Theology I: Thessalonians, Philippians, Galatians, Philemon* (Minneapolis, 1991) 183-211.

Wuellner, W. "The Argumentative Structure of 1 Thessalonians as Paradoxical Encomium." In R. F. Collins. *The Thessalonian Correspondence. BETL* 87 (Leuven, 1990) 117-36.

Wurm, A. "Cerinth — Ein Gnostiker oder Judaist?" *TQ* 86 (1904) 20-38.

Xyngopoulos, A. "Ἡ παλαιοχριστιανικὴ τοιχογραφία τῆς ῥωμαϊκῆς ἀγορᾶς Θεσσαλονίκης." Βυζαντινά 9 (1977) 411-46.

Yamauchi, E. M. "Troas." *ABD* VI (New York, 1992) 666f.

Yaure, L. "Elymas — Nehelamite — Pethor." *JBL* 79 (1960) 297-314.

Zahn, T. "Die syrische Statthalterschaft und die Schätzung des Quirinius." *NKZ* 4 (1893) 633-54.

———. "Missionsmethoden im Zeitalter der Apostel." *Skizzen aus dem Leben der Alten Kirche* (Erlangen/Leipzig, 1894) 106-55, 296-301.

———. "Weltverkehr und Kirche während der drei ersten Jahrhunderte." *Ibid.,* 156-95, 302-9.

———. "Brüder und Vettern Jesu." *FGNKAL* VI (Leipzig, 1900) 225-63.

———. *Introduction to the New Testament.* 3 vols. (Eng. trans., Edinburgh, 1909).

———. "Paulus." *RE*³ 15 (Leipzig, 1904) 61-88.

———. "Zur Lebensgeschichte des Apostels Paulus." *NKZ* 15 (1904) 23-41, 189-200.

———. "Ariccia." *Altes und Neues in Vorträgen und kleineren Aufsätzen für weitere Kreise* (Leipzig, 1927) 114-23, 131-36.

———. *Grundriß der Geschichte des Apostolischen Zeitalters* (Leipzig, 1929).

Zeitlin, S. "Paul's Journeys to Jerusalem." *JQR* 57 (1967) 171-78.

Zeller, D. "Theologie der Mission des Paulus." In K. Kertelge. *Mission im Neuen Testament. QD* 93 (Freiburg, 1982) 164-89.

Zielinski, T. "L'empereur Claude et l'idée de la domination mondiale des Juifs." *RUB* 32 (1926/27) 128-48.

Zimmermann, A. F. *Die urchristlichen Lehrer. Studien zum Tradentenkreis der* διδάσκαλοι *im frühen Urchristentum. WUNT* II/12 (Tübingen, ²1988).

Zingg, P. *Das Wachsen der Kirche. Beiträge zur Frage der lukanischen Redaktion und Theologie. OBO* 3 (Freiburg [Switzerland]/Göttingen, 1974).

Zmijewski, J. *Der Stil der paulinischen "Narrendrede." Analyse der Sprachgestaltung in 2 Kor 11,1–12,10 als Beitrag zur Methodik von Stiluntersuchungen neutestamentlicher Texte. BBB* 52 (Cologne/Bonn, 1978).

Zumpt, A. W. *Das Geburtsjahr Christi* (Leipzig, 1869).

Zuntz, G. "Wann wurde das Evangelium Marci geschrieben?" In H. Cancik. *Markus — Philologie. Historische, literargeschichtliche und stilistische Untersuchungen zum zweiten Evangelium. WUNT* I/33 (Tübingen, 1984) 47-71.

Zwaan, J. de. "The Use of the Greek Language in Acts." *BC* II (London, 1933) 30-65.

Index of Authors

Aberbach, M., 221n.64
Alexander, L., 201n.256, 413
Arrington, F. L., 26, 27
Aus, R. D., 245n.55

Bacon, B. W., 4, 5
Bammel, E., 166, 354
Barnikol, Ernst, 13-14, 53
Baronius, C., 3
Barrett, C. K., 290n.56
Baslez, M. F., 26, 27, 303n.131
Basnage, S., 3
Bauer, K., 116
Baumert, N., 375
Baur, F. C., 270
Becker, J., 26, 27, 413
Belser, J. E., 4
Bengel, J. A., 4, 135
Bengtson, H., 93, 95
Benko, S., 164, 165
Betz, H. D., 232
Bietenhard, H., 257
Binder, H., 409, 410
Blinzler, J., 37-38, 328
Böcher, O., 232
Bornkamm, G., 295
Borse, U., 395, 396
Botermann, H., 28n.112, 201n.256,
    352n.89, 358n.124
Bourguet, E., 4, 203
Bowers, W. P., 241, 242, 243, 244, 292,
    304n.136, 305n.139
Brandle, R., 201n.256

Brassac, A., 203
Briggs, C. W., 262n.154
Bringmann, K., 161
Bruce, F. F., 6, 26, 27, 221n.64, 287,
    301n.113, 304, 332, 354, 392n.55
Buck, C. H., 14, 15, 18-19, 25, 26, 30,
    32
Burchard, C., 263

Cadbury, H. J., 167
Caird, G. B., 223
Calvin, John, 8, 262, 320
Carrez, M., 212, 216
Carson, D. A., 27
Cerfaux, L., 236
Cichorius, C., 41n.38
Clemen, Carl, 11-13, 141, 368, 406
Collins, R. F., 406
Conzelmann, H., 263, 366
Corssen, P., 71
Cranfield, C. E. B., 247, 301n.113
Cumont, F., 103

Daniélou, J., 240n.24
Dassmann, E., 27
Dautzenberg, G., 115
Deissmann, A., 203, 204, 204n.18, 213,
    265n.3
Delitzsch, F., 245, 249
Dessau, H., 91, 143
Detlefsen, D., 142
de Vogüé, M., 80
Devreker, J., 143

500

Index of Names and Subjects

Ummidius Quadratus, 220
Usuard of St. Germain, 68

Valentinus, 64
Valerius Asiaticus, 98
Valerius Gratus, 38, 39
Valley of the Cestrus, 275
Vardanes, 133n.54
Varro, 214n.21
Varus, 152
Vespasian, 82, 91
Vetissus, 276

Via Sebaste, 285
Vindex, Julius, 91

wintering, 308-9

Xiphilinus, 175

Year of Release, 43, 45

Zebulun, 237, 238
Zerubbabel, 55
Zonaras, 175

Index of Scripture and Other Ancient Writings

2065   184n.165
2085   184n.165
Commentarium in Isaiam
(PL 24)
125 (ad 9:1)   238, 239
Commentarii in
Epistulam S. Pauli ad
Philemonem
1   143
23   152
De Viris Illustribus
5   119, 121n.86,
        143, 152, 172

Hippolytus of Rome
Commentarium in
Danielem
3.29   212

Hippolytus of Thebes
3.1f.   59
3.3f.   120

Irenaeus
Adversus Haereses
i.3.2   64
i.23.1   189
i.30.14   64
iii.1.1   412

John Chrysostom
Commentarii in
Epistolam S. Pauli ad
Galatas (PG 61)
2.1   7

Julius Africanus
(ed. Dindorf)
I 610   198n.246

Justin Martyr
Apologie
i.14.1f.   198
i.26f.   189
i.35   63

i.48   63
Dialogus cum Tryphone
Judaeo
78.2   239
78.9   239
78.10   239, 257
Epit.
36.2   238n.17

Lactantius
Divinae Institutiones
iv.7.5   165n.47

Malalas
242.8-22   121n.86
244.15–245.20   113
244.15–246.2   135
246.9-19   135
247.5-10   196

Marcus Diaconus
Vita Porphyrii
6   315
27   315
55   315

Nicephoros Kallistos
Historia Ecclesiastica
ii.3   59

Origen
Contra Celsum
i.26   197n.236
i.47   186
i.57   332
iv.52   348n.63
Commentarii in
Epistulam S. Pauli ad
Romanos (PG 14)
(praef.) 836   143
In Mt.
x.17   186

Paulus Orosius
Adversus Paganos
iii.praef.1f.   180
iii.2.9f.   180
vii.6.1f.   172, 183
vii.6.2   184n.165
vii.6.1-5   182
vii.6.9   184n.165
vii.6.12   129, 133,
      184n.165, 187
vii.6.13   184n.165
vii.6.14   184n.165
vii.6.15   157, 181, 182,
         187
vii.6.15f.   181
vii.6.16   184
vii.6.17   129, 184n.165,
         187

Photius
Quaestiones
Amphilochiae
116   152

Pseudo-Hippolytus
167   70n.65

Sozomenos
vii.15   260

Syrian Chronicon ad
846 (CSCO III/4)
137   59

Tertullian
Ad Nationes
1.3   165n.47
Adversus Judaeos
8   51
9   257
Adversus Marcionem
1.15   40n.31
3.13   257

Apologeticum
3.5 165n.47
5.2 63
5.6 267
21.24 63
De Praescriptione
Haereticorum
36 406
45 123n.94

Theodoret von Kyros
Interpretatio Epistulae
ad Romanos (PG 82)
15 293

Zonaras 130
11.10 199

Rabbinic Writings

Mishna
'Abot
1:10 155
Pesachim
8:6 49
Ta'anit
1.3 311

Babylonian Talmud
Pesachim
93b 311
Sanhedrin
43a 49
Yebamot
15b 133
Yoma
9a 225
10a 252

Jerusalem Talmud
Megilla
71b 252
Shabbat
5b 308

Midrashim
Genesis Rabba
6 (12a) 308
Leviticus Rabba
9 (111a) 238
Sifre Deuteronomium
41 (79b) 238

Targumim
Midrash Cant.
1:3 (85b) 241

Greco-Roman Writings

Achilles Tatius
v.15.1 315
v.17.1 315

Antistius Vetus
Anthologia Plantarum
ix.428 339n.9

Appianus
Bella Civilia Romana
iv.105 338
iv.118 339
Illyrica
i.7 243n.42
Mithridates
46f. 376
101 242

Apuleius
Metamorphoses
xi.7ff. 308

Aristotle
Politica
vii.11.2 341

Aurelius Victor
De Caesaribus
iv.3 129

Caesar
De Bello Gallico
iv.36.2 225
v.23.5 225
vii.40f. 311n.25

Cicero
De Provinciis
Consulatoribus
2.4 341
4 339n.8
Epistulae ad Atticum
i.2.10 314
i.13.1 314
ii.12.10 314
ii.13.1 314
v.14.1 311
v.20.2 266
In Flaccum
28-68 275
In Pisonem
17.40 341
36 360

Dio Cassius
Hist.
vii.10.12 170n.80
vii.21.4 170n.80
ix.23.5 170n.80
xxxvii.17 200
xl.46.2 203n.5
xlvi.41.5 170n.80
liii.15.6 36
liii.17.1-9 168n.70
liv.7 46
liv.9.2 278n.81
lvi.25.5f. 356-57
lvii.14.5 206
lvii.15.8 357
lvii.18.5 174, 176, 177
lvii.18.5a 174, 195, 199
lix.8.2 278n.81
lix.12.2 82

530